Socio-Economic Perspectives on Consumer Engagement and Buying Behavior

Hans Ruediger Kaufmann
University of Applied Management Studies Mannheim, Germany & University of Nicosia, Cyprus

Mohammad Fateh Ali Khan Panni
City University, Bangladesh

A volume in the Advances in Marketing, Customer Relationship Management, and E-Services (AMCRMES) Book Series

IGI GLOBAL
DISSEMINATOR OF KNOWLEDGE

www.igi-global.com

Published in the United States of America by
IGI Global
Business Science Reference (an imprint of IGI Global)
701 E. Chocolate Avenue
Hershey PA, USA 17033
Tel: 717-533-8845
Fax: 717-533-8661
E-mail: cust@igi-global.com
Web site: http://www.igi-global.com

Library of Congress Cataloging-in-Publication Data

Names: Kaufmann, Hans Ruediger, 1958- editor. | Panni, Mohammad Fateh Ali Khan, 1981- editor.
Title: Socio-economic perspectives on consumer engagement and buying behavior / Hans Ruediger Kaufmann and Mohammad Fateh Ali Khan Panni, editors.
Description: Hershey : Business Science Reference, [2017]
Identifiers: LCCN 2016054471| ISBN 9781522521396 (hardcover) | ISBN 9781522521402 (ebook)
Subjects: LCSH: Consumer behavior. | Customer relations. | Electronic commerce.
Classification: LCC HF5415.32 .S5966 2017 | DDC 658.8/342--dc23 LC record available at https://lccn.loc.gov/2016054471

This book is published in the IGI Global book series Advances in Marketing, Customer Relationship Management, and E-Services (AMCRMES) (ISSN: 2327-5502; eISSN: 2327-5529)

British Cataloguing in Publication Data
A Cataloguing in Publication record for this book is available from the British Library.

For electronic access to this publication, please contact: eresources@igi-global.com.

Advances in Marketing, Customer Relationship Management, and E-Services (AMCRMES) Book Series

Eldon Y. Li
National Chengchi University, Taiwan & California Polytechnic State University, USA

ISSN:2327-5502
EISSN:2327-5529

Mission

Business processes, services, and communications are important factors in the management of good customer relationship, which is the foundation of any well organized business. Technology continues to play a vital role in the organization and automation of business processes for marketing, sales, and customer service. These features aid in the attraction of new clients and maintaining existing relationships.

The Advances in Marketing, Customer Relationship Management, and E-Services (AMCRMES) Book Series addresses success factors for customer relationship management, marketing, and electronic services and its performance outcomes. This collection of reference source covers aspects of consumer behavior and marketing business strategies aiming towards researchers, scholars, and practitioners in the fields of marketing management.

Coverage

- E-Service Innovation
- B2B marketing
- Relationship marketing
- Ethical Considerations in E-Marketing
- Legal Considerations in E-Marketing
- Social Networking and Marketing
- Electronic Services
- CRM strategies
- Cases on CRM Implementation
- Mobile CRM

IGI Global is currently accepting manuscripts for publication within this series. To submit a proposal for a volume in this series, please contact our Acquisition Editors at Acquisitions@igi-global.com or visit: http://www.igi-global.com/publish/.

The Advances in Marketing, Customer Relationship Management, and E-Services (AMCRMES) Book Series (ISSN 2327-5502) is published by IGI Global, 701 E. Chocolate Avenue, Hershey, PA 17033-1240, USA, www.igi-global.com. This series is composed of titles available for purchase individually; each title is edited to be contextually exclusive from any other title within the series. For pricing and ordering information please visit http://www.igi-global.com/book-series/advances-marketing-customer-relationship-management/37150. Postmaster: Send all address changes to above address.

Titles in this Series

For a list of additional titles in this series, please visit: www.igi-global.com

Strategic Uses of Social Media for Improved Customer Retention
Wafaa Al-Rabayah (Independent Researcher, Jordan) Rawan Khasawneh (Jordan University of Science and Technology, Jordan) Rasha Abu-shamaa (Yarmouk University, Jordan) and Izzat Alsmadi (Boise State University, USA)
Business Science Reference • copyright 2017 • 311pp • H/C (ISBN: 9781522516866) • US $180.00 (our price)

Analyzing Children's Consumption Behavior Ethics, Methodologies, and Future Considerations
Jony Haryanto (President University, Indonesia) and Luiz Moutinho (Dublin City University, Ireland)
Business Science Reference • copyright 2017 • 278pp • H/C (ISBN: 9781522509936) • US $165.00 (our price)

Handbook of Research on Leveraging Consumer Psychology for Effective Customer Engagement
Norazah Mohd Suki (Universiti Malaysia Sabah, Malaysia)
Business Science Reference • copyright 2017 • 374pp • H/C (ISBN: 9781522507468) • US $230.00 (our price)

Handbook of Research on Strategic Retailing of Private Label Products in a Recovering Economy
Mónica Gómez-Suárez (Universidad Autónoma de Madrid, Spain) and María Pilar Martínez-Ruiz (University of Castilla-La Mancha, Spain)
Business Science Reference • copyright 2016 • 625pp • H/C (ISBN: 9781522502203) • US $330.00 (our price)

Handbook of Research on Consumerism and Buying Behavior in Developing Nations
Ayantunji Gbadamosi (University of East London, UK)
Business Science Reference • copyright 2016 • 565pp • H/C (ISBN: 9781522502821) • US $235.00 (our price)

Managing Public Relations and Brand Image through Social Media
Anurag Singh (Banaras Hindu University, India) and Punita Duhan (Meera Bai Institute of Technology, India)
Business Science Reference • copyright 2016 • 353pp • H/C (ISBN: 9781522503323) • US $195.00 (our price)

Handbook of Research on Promotional Strategies and Consumer Influence in the Service Sector
Upendra Singh Panwar (Shri Govindram Seksaria Institute of Technology and Science, India) Raj Kumar (Banaras Hindu University, India) and Nilanjan Ray (Netaji Mahavidyalaya, India)
Business Science Reference • copyright 2016 • 492pp • H/C (ISBN: 9781522501435) • US $335.00 (our price)

Global Marketing Strategies for the Promotion of Luxury Goods
Fabrizio Mosca (University of Turin, Italy) and Rosalia Gallo (Universitat Autònoma de Barcelona, Spain)
Business Science Reference • copyright 2016 • 329pp • H/C (ISBN: 9781466699588) • US $200.00 (our price)

IGI GLOBAL
DISSEMINATOR OF KNOWLEDGE
www.igi-global.com

701 E. Chocolate Ave., Hershey, PA 17033
Order online at www.igi-global.com or call 717-533-8845 x100
To place a standing order for titles released in this series, contact: cust@igi-global.com
Mon-Fri 8:00 am - 5:00 pm (est) or fax 24 hours a day 717-533-8661

List of Reviewers

Abu Zafar Mahmudul Haque, *City University Bangladesh, Bangladesh*
Dursun Yener, *Istanbul Medeniyet University, Turkey*
Sandra Maria Correia Maria Correia Loureiro, *Instituto Universitário de Lisboa (ISCTE-IUL), Portugal & Business Research Unit (BRU/UNIDE), Portugal*
S.M. Riad Shams, *Ural Federal University, Russia*

Table of Contents

Detailed Table of Contents

The chapter defines the concept of 'consumerism' and discusses its different perspectives which emerged during its historical development. The author adopts the second perspective of consumerism which posits that consumerism is a movement aimed at safeguarding the interests and rights of consumers. This view is closely related to the concept of social responsibility (CSR) and subsequently societal marketing. There is evidence in the literature to suggest that in an era of increasing social problems and environmental challenges, there is a need for CSR and sustainable marketing. In fact, the second definition of consumerism is inextricably linked with CSR and societal marketing. The chapter is conceptual in nature and provides a review of some of the latest trends in the field such as boycotting, sustainable consumption, internet activism, anti-branding, Fair trade, green consumerism, and sustainable marketing. The discussion is concluded by providing some suggestions to practitioners and directions for future research.

Consumerism is not a new concept for marketing, but its importance is growing in the recent years. Researchers have studied the phenomenon of consumerism from within different dimensions. However, its relationship with social impact theory and consumer boycotts has not been dealt with accurately. Social impact can be defined as the effect of people on other people. A consumer boycott is a type of consumer behaviour in which consumers collectively prefer not to use their purchasing power towards a product, brand or all products of a country and boycott them. Motivations for participating in boycotts differ in accordance with various factors such as consumers' beliefs, needs or attitudes. Organizing a boycott and calling for people's participation is much easier today than it used to be in the past. Since

organization. The importance of the Marketing Strategy in the current economic conditions provides a practical indication of marketing decision making and if managed carefully and closely monitored it can offer a number of direct competitive benefits to the industries.

The potential influence of music in eliciting organic reactions has been appreciated since ancient times. Knowing that consumers typically receive exposure to many hours of music each day, scientists and marketers have recognized its potential in consumer behaviour and decision making. Literature suggests that customers like hearing music when they shop, and feel that the retailer providing music cares about them. Retailers have to work diligently to keep their stores favourable in the mind of consumers. Both practitioners and researchers supported the argument that music is a beneficial element in the use of atmospherics in business. Based on the empirical research this chapter provides an insight into the role of music as an important element in retail store atmosphere. The chapter explains the complex character of music, its classifications and key variables, and interaction with other atmospheric cues. The chapter concludes that music has a significant influence on consumer behavior, and that retailers must ensure that they are playing music that their target markets like in their stores.

The chapter aims at investigating the effects that the Communication of Corporate Social Responsibility and Sustainability exerts on consumers' perception considering the fast food industry in Italy. the McDonald's case study has been developed through managerial interviews and formal documents analysis in order to report on its strategies for CSR activities implementation and their communication in Italy. Moreover, through surveys conducted in Italy, the case study has been tested on a particular group of young consumers - Generation Z - less influenced by the past McDonald's activity in order to demonstrate how communications of sustainability are better believed and perceived, when a brand has a long tradition of misperceptions.

This case study illustrates the effectiveness of pursuing a customer centric marketing approach in order to achieve long term strategic success and global market leadership in the fashion industry. The case study provides the most significant elements of Zara's history. Then it describes the competitive environment. Next it reveals how Zara has set up a unique, lean, and agile supply chain strategy in order to deliver new products on a very frequent basis and faster than any of its competitors, as fashion customers expect constant changes. Then the case study details the customer centric marketing strategy, with the use of customers as the source of the inspiration for fashion design, the central role of the stores to build a very high level of trust with its customers, which is used by Zara to make a distinctive brand strategy. Finally, the case study discusses the new challenges of Zara to adapt its customer centric marketing strategy to the digital market.

Preface

In this modern new trend of marketing practices marketing dimensions are changing and the new horizons are appearing in consumer behavioral contexts/perspectives. As consumer behavior is the cornerstone of any marketing domain, the strategies, tools, concepts and services of consumer engagement and their buying behavior are now being influenced by a variety of new emerging factors and antecedents. This research oriented book will delineate some new emerging trends relating to consumer buying behavior which are enhanced versions of the previously published IGI Global chapters though there are three new fresh submissions where two chapters are related to consumer behavior and engagement from a macroeconomic context and one on marketing strategy influence on pharmaceutical sector. To this vein, this book is illustrating some interesting new perspectives like: consumer behavior on some basic social perspectives, from macro perspectives, innovative, digital and technological platform in the context of some industry and corporate cases. This book is providing some insights on new dimensions and emerging contexts on the socioeconomic perspectives on the consumer engagement and behavior. The book has mainly a strong international orientation representing about 29 chapter authors from around 13 countries like Canada, Croatia, Cyprus, Finland, Germany, Greece, Italy, New Zealand, Portugal, Romania, Spain, Turkey, and UK.

The book is contributing in the area or discipline by providing some new trendy topics on some very novel and innovative perspectives of consumer engagement and buying behavior which illustrates an overall picture from the socio-economic perspective as well. In this regard, the book demonstrates some interesting contexts like fundamental concepts on consumerism, consumer boycotts or activism, customer satisfaction and consumption of green products. The book also contains some vital chapters in the area consumer behavior and engagement from marketing and technological perspective like marketing 4.0, consumer information system, surveillance in service encounters, e-commerce etc. In addition to this the book reveals about consumer engagement and buying behavior from macroeconomic perspective and finally the book delineates some interesting cases on tourism sector, pharmaceutical sector, retailing sector and technological sector.

TARGET AUDIENCE

The book can be seen as a collection of some conceptual, empirical and case studies on trendy contexts of consumer engagement and buying behavior in the canvas of socio economic context. As a result, the book is expected to serve as a high level reference to the University library, researchers and research students. Since the topic of the book covers some new innovative dimensions on consumer behavioral studies, it will also help to prepare an upper-level course supplement in the marketing discipline like consumer behavior, marketing management, strategic marketing or international/global marketing. Finally, the book reveals these new modern perspectives, tools and concepts on consumer behavior, thus, it will be a useful resource and reference to the marketing practitioners, for example, in the area of Marketing Management, Innovative, Strategic Marketing and Marketing Communications.

OBJECTIVES/PURPOSE OF THIS BOOK

This book contains cutting edge contributions on some new perspectives on dimensions on consumer engagement and buying behavior from both theoretical/conceptual context and corporate and industrial cases. Hence, it will serve as a comprehensive guide and reference to both academics and practitioners since it will expand their understanding on the role of these different cutting edge consumer behavior concepts and studies as learning tools for the academics, marketing students and marketing practitioners.

The book contains 16 chapters critically engaging the reader with new modern dimensions on consumer behavior from socio economic perspective under 4 different sections.

The structure of the book has been designed to achieve the overall objectives of the book as to provide deeper conceptual understanding of Consumer Engagement and Buying Behavior as well as revealing different conceptual/ theoretical frameworks and some interesting industrial and corporate cases.

RATIONALE OF THE SEQUENCE OF THE CHAPTERS WITHIN THE DIFFERENT SECTIONS

Section 1 'Social Perspectives of Consumer Behavior and Engagement' begins with a contribution by Ioanna Papasolomou (Chapter 1) representing the consumer activism. This chapter delineates the concept of consumerism as consumer movement that has a far-reaching effect on consumer behavior which closely stays in socio-economic context. Thc chapter reveals all the necessaries of consumerism integrated part of consumer movement.

Crystallizing the basic importance of consumer activism and consumer movement Chapter 2 of the section by Dursun Yener illustrates consumer boycotts as a specific dominant tool of consumer activism or movement. In this perspective, the chapter has clarified the definition of consumer boycotts as well as the motivational factors for participating in boycotts.

The third chapter by Lisa Watson and Anne M. Lavack of the section illustrates the fuel-efficient vehicles and its roles on the social marketing. This chapter examines the market for fuel efficient vehicles (FEVs) and alternate fuel vehicles (AFVs), including a discussion of consumer willingness to trade personal comfort in order to buy more fuel-efficient vehicles, and consumer price sensitivity with regard to purchasing higher-priced alternative fuel vehicles including hybrid-electric vehicles.

The last chapter of the section (Chapter 4) by Violeta Sima and Ileana Georgiana Gheorghe has explained the customer satisfaction level in consumption of green products, the applied chapters of the previous chapters. In this chapter the authors propose a new approach of the dimensions of the evaluation model for customer satisfaction including a new one, called The Green Dimension. An important goal was identifying the drivers of the consumer purchasing. The authors identified three main specific levels of the green dimension of customer satisfaction. They are related to: Company, Product/service, and Price.

Section 2 'Consumer Behavior and Engagement in the Nexus of Marketing and Technology' starts with a very trendy topic by Ana Isabel Jiménez-Zarco, Asher Rospigliosi, María Pilar Martínez-Ruiz and Alicia Izquierdo-Yusta (Chapter 5) of consumer behavioral study marketing 4.0 in enhancing consumer-brand engagement through the tool of big data analysis. The chapter is particularly discussing the means of understanding marketing 4.0 and how it is growing and how a range of technologies including internet and social media can be used for this innovative marketing strategy and to enhance consumer brand relationship.

Interlinking the previous chapter the second chapter of this section (Chapter 6) by Angelo Bonfanti focuses on significance of effective surveillance in service encounters. The chapter has proposed a theoretical/conceptual framework that has provided a solid ground identifying some significant/important dimensions of service management.

The very next chapter (Chapter 7) by Tuure Tuunanen and Michael D. Myers, has focused on consumer information systems in a particular sector, from more conceptual, to a particular sector, interactive television. In fact, the chapter aims to pursue this agenda by primarily using design science research, supplemented by other research methods as needed. The expected contributions include new insights into effective management processes for service design, a better understanding of issues of integration of information systems development practices used to develop consumer information systems, and the development of methods for requirements discovery for service innovation. These three components aim to contribute to a holistic evaluation of consumer information systems.

The next Chapter of the section (Chapter 8) by Tuure Tuunanen, Lesley Gardner and Martin Bastek has revealed the consumer information system in a particular emerging market in New Zealand. In fact, this chapter is providing a picture regarding consumer information by providing a sort of empirical evidence though initially presents a theoretical framework in the earlier stage. Thus, this chapter can be considered as an immediate application of the conceptual discussions of consumer information system outlined in the previous chapter.

The last chapter of the section (Chapter 9) by Rauno Rusko and Joni Pekkala is an entire comprehensive empirical study of the nexus of marketing and technology. The chapter focuses on the activities of e-commerce from both the part of consumers and entrepreneurs in a Northern Finland. Through a detail empirical investigation, the chapter has also pointed out the challenges that SMEs face while starting e-commerce activities in Northern Finland. Thus, this chapter is a source of detail empirical investigation and data of the conceptual developments of the section made by the earlier chapters of the section.

Section 3 'Consumer Behavior and Engagement from a macroeconomic context' contains two chapters from a broader socio-economic perspective. The first chapter of the section (Chapter 10) by Sadullah Çelik and Emel Baydan assesses the behavior of emerging stock markets during the turmoil using weekly data for Brazil, China, India, Indonesia, Russia, South Africa and Turkey with US as the benchmark for January 2003–March 2014 while the last chapter of this section (Chapter 11) by Özlem Taşseven has portrayed some very important socio economic factors and determinants of capacity utilization particularly from a specific country like Turkey. In this perspective, those well important socio-economic dimension of consumption and consumer behavior perspective like industrial production, gross domestic product growth rate, unemployment rate, consumer expenditures, financial variables such as return on BIST 100 index, exchange rate of currency basket, interest rates, survey variables such as consumer consumption index, business tendency survey and survey of expectations is investigated using data between 2006 and 2015 for Turkey.

Section 4 'Consumer Behavior and Engagement: Industry and Corporate Cases' is a dedicated section on industry and corporate cases which has clearly outlined some dominant case studies both from the total industrial sector and the particular corporate context. The first chapter of the section (Chapter 12) by Sandra Maria Correia Loureiro provides a proposed framework with the state-of-art on consumption, anti-consumption and subjective well-being and a study into rural tourism context. Normally, this chapter contributes to the existing literature giving insights for a better understanding of the problematic of consumers, anti-consumers and subjective well-being as a whole and rural tourism consumption experience industry in particularly. The next chapter of the section (Chapter 13) by Irene Samanta is a comprehensive empirical study which provides a very important insight on the pharmaceutical sector in Greece. As per the chapter the importance of the Marketing Strategy (as outlined in the chapter) in the current economic conditions provides a practical indication of marketing decision making and if managed carefully and closely monitored it can offer a number of direct competitive benefits to the industries.

The next chapter of the section (Chapter 14) by Sanda Renko and Tomislav Gregur provides the atmospherics perspectives of retail setting where based on the empirical research the chapter provides an insight into the role of music as an important element in retail store atmosphere. The chapter concludes that music has a significant influence on consumer behavior, and that retailers must ensure that they are playing music that their target markets like in their stores.

The last two chapters (Chapter 15) by Elena Candelo, Cecilia Casalegno and Chiara Civera and (Chapter 16) by Eric Viardot and Petra A. Nylund are specific industrial cases where Chapter 15 has empirically investigated about the sustainability and CSR (Corporate Social Responsibility) practices in McDonald's Italy while Chapter 16 is a detail case study on Zara regarding the effectiveness of pursuing a customer centric marketing approach to the digital market.

The value of the book can be summarized as follows:

1. Detailed conceptual and philosophical underpinnings on new trendy consumer engagement and buying behavior broadly from the socio-economic perspective.
2. An extensive review of conceptual and empirical studies in this area from new, dynamic innovative and international contexts and perspectives on the consumer engagement and buying behavior.
3. Interesting insights from some industrial cases like on tourism sector, pharmaceutical sector, retail sector and some corporate cases like McDonalds and Zara.
4. Recommendations to guide practitioners to successfully implement the concept in practice.
5. In general, a synthesis on some very new novel and emerging concepts, theories and practices related to modern era of consumer engagement and buying behavior in the socio-economic domain.

Acknowledgment

The journey of publication of an edited reference book is a challenging and very difficult task where a collective and disciplined support is highly required. We would like to gratefully acknowledge the selfless support of people who extended their hands to help us to make this project successful. First of all, we sincerely thank the chapter authors for their valuable contributions to this endeavor. In this regard since the book is mainly a collection of enhanced chapters where the chapters were previously published by prior IGI Global Publication, we would like to express our sincere thanks to the editors of those books from which these chapters have been selected. In addition, many thanks go to the reviewers who reviewed three new/fresh submissions. Furthermore, we would like to acknowledge the friendly and supportive role of the editorial staff of IGI Global, for their relentless help and support in different stages of the manuscript development. Last, but definitely not least, we are very grateful to all our family members for their continuous encouragement and inspiration to make this project a success.

Section 1
Social Perspectives of Consumer Behavior and Engagement

Chapter 1
The Concept of "Consumerism" from a Consumer Activist Perspective

Ioanna Papasolomou
University of Nicosia, Cyprus

ABSTRACT

The chapter defines the concept of 'consumerism' and discusses its different perspectives which emerged during its historical development. The author adopts the second perspective of consumerism which posits that consumerism is a movement aimed at safeguarding the interests and rights of consumers. This view is closely related to the concept of social responsibility (CSR) and subsequently societal marketing. There is evidence in the literature to suggest that in an era of increasing social problems and environmental challenges, there is a need for CSR and sustainable marketing. In fact, the second definition of consumerism is inextricably linked with CSR and societal marketing. The chapter is conceptual in nature and provides a review of some of the latest trends in the field such as boycotting, sustainable consumption, internet activism, anti-branding, Fair trade, green consumerism, and sustainable marketing. The discussion is concluded by providing some suggestions to practitioners and directions for future research.

INTRODUCTION

The concept of consumerism has been explored by several academics (Bloom and Greyser, 1981; Bloom and Smith, 1986; Greyser and Diamond, 1974; Greyser, 1977). The term consumerism is linked to the behavior of organizations and the expectations of the society. Corporations should identify and define their purpose and objectives in a way that align with the expectations of society. If customers lack trust in businesses because they are not meeting the customers' and society's expectations then they may be perceived as unnecessary, they may be heavily criticized, accused and boycotted. In the 21st century consumers have become more caring and socially aware, moving towards a more responsible and responsive attitude to issues which may not directly concern them such as Third World exploitation. The mass media and social media highlight that there is increased consumer and public concern about health

DOI: 10.4018/978-1-5225-2139-6.ch001

issues, animal welfare, environmental protection, child labour and ethical trading. The current trend in Europe, largely due to the current economic crisis and the masses of refugees moving from the Middle East into EU countries, is for consumers to engage in more socially responsible behavior, move away from leading a life of excessive consumption and materialism, towards more enduring values such as respect, compassion, and empathy. Similarly, there is evidence in the press and literature suggesting that the business sector has become more responsive to social and environmental problems and engage more in societal and sustainable marketing. Consumerism has the potential to play a constructive role in building a sustainable business environment by emphasizing for example consumer awareness, fair trading, codes of conduct and ethical business practices. It motivates managers to adopt a new way of thinking beyond the narrow boundaries of generating short-term sales and profits, and more towards adopting a sustainable approach aimed at safeguarding the quality of life of future generations.

EVOLUTION AND FUNDAMENTAL DEFINITIONS OF CONSUMERISM

When the term "Consumerism" first made its appearance in the academic literature it was coined with the over-consumption of goods and services. Veblen (1899) studied the newly emergent middle class at the turn of the twentieth century and wrote a detailed social critique of conspicuous consumption. According to Veblen (1899) the upper social class at the time engaged in practices of conspicuous consumption and conspicuous leisure. However, the term has acquired several meanings over time based on different perspectives. The first perspective of consumerism views the term as:

1. The manipulative business activities to entice consumers to buy products,
2. The second perspective holds the idea that consumerism is the movement that aims as ascertaining consumers' rights, and
3. The third perspective refers to consumption as a way of life or ideology (Yani-de-Soriano and Slater, 2009).

The First Definition: The "Manipulative Perspective"

Vance Packard (1957) stated that consumerism is related to strategies and techniques that aim at encouraging consumers to consume more hence, expanding their needs and desires. According to this view, consumerism is associated with the overuse of promotion, aggressive selling and advertising. Packard (1957) expressed his concern in relation to the overuse of advertising highlighting the risk of manipulating customers into over-consuming. The evolution of the marketing management orientation was characterized by a phase of aggressive selling whereby marketers were mostly concerned with stock levels and as a result businesses focused their efforts on aggressive and promotion. This philosophy, which was identified by Kotler et al. (2008), has been known as the selling orientation. This orientation nourished the "manipulative perspective" whereby businesses focused on aggressive selling rather than customer focus which was at the heart of the marketing orientation and stipulated intense criticism for exploitative and manipulative behavior on the part of businesses.

The Second Definition: Consumers' Movement in the USA

In an effort to eliminate manipulative techniques and aggressive marketing, the US public authorities enacted legislation for the protection of consumers' rights. At the same time consumers joined efforts and formed associations to protect themselves hence, providing the foundation for the second definition of consumerism. This definition is founded on reactions portrayed by the society to the type of marketing used in the first definition. According to this perspective "consumerism is defined as a "social movement seeking to augment the rights and powers of buyers in relation to sellers (Kotler, 1972, p. 49). Later on, Kotler (2000, p. 152) redefined consumerism as follows: "an organized movement of citizens and government to strengthen the rights and powers of buyers in relation to sellers." McIlhenny (1990) describes consumerism as a citizens' movement with demands on suppliers of goods and services with social, ecological and political implications. The consumer movement emerged in the USA with President Kennedy's 1962 call for a "Bill of Consumer Rights" (Lampman, 1988). This specific view of consumerism, known also as consumer activism, is similar to another social movement known as *environmentalism*, which is defined as: "an organized movement of concerned citizens and government agencies to protect and improve people's living environment (Kotler et al., 2005, p. 184). Both movements are closely related to the "societal marketing concept", A philosophy that holds that businesses today should attempt to balance the organizational goals for profitability, customers' needs and society's wellbeing (Kotler and Keller, 2006, p. 22).

The Third Definition: The Consumer Culture

According to Yani-de-Soriano and Slater (2009) the third definition of consumerism refers to consumption as a means for happiness and wellbeing. Murphy (2000, p. 636) defines this type of consumerism as: "the doctrine that the self cannot be complete without a wealth of consumer goods and that goals can be achieved and problems solved through proper consumption." He moves on to suggest that from an economic perspective this consumer culture reflects the emphasis of economies from exchange or production to consumption. From a social perspective, the notion of a consumer culture is founded on the notion of acquiring products as a form of communicating the owner's wealth and using them as "status symbols". Consumers use these products as a form of signaling to others their social standing and power. Slater (1997, p. 31) posits that "it is partially through the use of goods and services that we formulate ourselves as social identities and display these identities." The third definition of consumerism links personal happiness with material consumption. Abela (2006) and Burroughs and Rindfleisch (2002) claim that "consumption as a means of happiness and well-being can have detrimental consequences for consumers and society".

As stated in the abstract, the chapter examines the concept of consumerism in the context of consumer movement/consumer activism. This perspective uses the terms "consumerism" and "consumer protection" or "consumer activism" as synonyms. The movement is undertaken on behalf of consumers to promote and protect consumer rights. It promotes the adoption of practices such as honest packaging and advertising, product guarantees, improved safety standards, environmental protection, and not testing products on animals. In essence, consumer activism is a movement aimed at regulating the products, services, methods, and standards of manufacturers, sellers, and advertisers in the interests of the buyer.

CONSUMER ATTITUDES/CONCERNS ON CONSUMERISM ISSUES

Over the last decade, a number of studies attempted to investigate the consumer attitudes towards marketing and consumerism issues (Keown, 1982; Dubinsky and Hensel, 1984). The majority of these studies were carried out in different national settings.

Barksdale and Darden (1972) showed that 70% of respondents in the USA believed that most manufacturers were not satisfactorily handling complaints associated with the quality of products, reliability and safety. It was widely shared that firms were promoting products that were potentially dangerous for people's health and life. Studies that were carried out in Venezuela and Norway (Arndt et al. 1980), England (French et al., 1982) and in other countries (Barksdale et al. 1982) revealed common problems associated with high prices, lack of product quality, lack of adequate repair and maintenance services, deceptive advertising and ineffective handling of complaints. Wee and Chan (1989) identified that consumers in Hong Kong tend to have more favorable attitudes towards marketing than those in the USA mainly due to better marketing practices in Hong Kong. Studies carried out by Anon (2003); Bhushan (2003); Brunk (1973); Koslow (2000); and Lisa (2004) support that the majority of consumers share the perception that corporations do not practice business ethics and they are not socially responsible.

Darley and Johnson (1993) studied marketing and consumerism issues in multiple countries: Singapore, India, Nigeria and Kenya. They found differences among the countries but some degree of disagreement was identified as well. In a study carried out by Uray and Menguc (1996) it was evident that consumers also had negative perceptions towards the consumerism practices. Varadarajan et al. (1990) showed that consumers were dissatisfied with marketing practices and desired greater government regulation. In general, consumers' degree of awareness towards consumerism issues varies significantly across demographic profiles especially in terms of age, gender, education qualification and income level. This finding was corroborated by Panni (2006) who found that consumers' concerns towards the consumerism issues significantly vary across demographic profiles. Bhuian et al. (2001) revealed that young adults with a business education background in Saudi Arabia had more favourable perceptions towards marketing and consumerism than those with a non-business background. Evidence generated by empirical studies for example Berkowitz and Lutterman (1968); Bourgeois and Barnes (1979); Anderson and Cunningham (1972); found that the individuals who are most likely to express consumerist views toward marketing tend to be younger. Authors like Hustad and Pessemier (1973); Bourgeois and Barnes (1979); Peattie (1992); and Ruiz, Arcas and Cuestas (2001) claimed that the socially conscious consumers are typically female. Anderson and Cunningham (1972); Hustad and Pessemier (1973); Kinnear et al., (1974); and The Roper Organization (1971) found that consumerists tend to have higher socio-economic profiles (Berkowitz and Lutterman1968; Bourgeois and Barnes 1979). Knauer (1971) argued that in general consumerist issues tend to attract the better educated and better informed consumers.

At the micro level, studies have explored consumer dissatisfaction with and complaints about specific products and services. At a macro level, national and cross-national studies have addressed consumer attitudes towards marketing practices, consumerism and government regulations (Barksdale 1982; French et al 1982; Gaski and Etzel 1986). While most studies reported to date are cross-sectional in nature, there have been recent attempts to provide a longitudinal perspective of consumers' attitudes towards marketing. In a study carried out by Lysonski et al. (2003) it was found that consumers appeared to be less negative about marketing and consumerism issues since 1986. This is largely due to the fact that marketers have adopted a more proactive approach towards consumers' complaints and discontents. The study revealed that consumers have relatively more favorable attitudes toward product quality and when compared to the attitudes held 15 years ago, consumers today believe that manufacturers are more customer centered in that they make products that satisfy customers' needs. The results from this study indicate that there has been a significant change in consumer perceptions over the last 15 years (2001 vs 1986) and that manager demonstrated more responsiveness to consumer issues. Nevertheless, this scenario differs from country to country where is some countries it is found that the consumers are still skeptical regarding the firms' engagement and involvement towards consumerism practices (Panni, 2006 and Ismail and Panni, 2008).

CONSUMER ACTIVISM

This section provides a definition for consumer activism based on the context in which it will be discussed in the chapter and explores its influences and limitations. According to Jacobsen and Dulsrud (2007, p.470), consumer activism, is often referred to as "ethical shopping, ethical purchase behavior, ethical consumption, political consumption, political consumerism, and critical consumerism". It is associated with the consumers' buying choices which are influenced by ethical and/or moral factors when making purchase decisions. The consumer attempts to give an ethical and a moral impact through his purchase (ibid.).

There are various theories as to why consumer activism exists and has evolved. One such theory is based on consumer's lack of trust in government's ability to address ethical or moral issues concerning trade (Hertz, 2001). Klein (2000) on the other hand, states that: "Rather than improved human rights flowing from increased trade, 'governments ignore human rights in favour of perceived trade advantages" (p. 338). This statement suggests that the private sector uses consumer activism as a way to compensate for the inability of the public sector to address human rights. The legal structures of the various countries in the world either restrict or encourage consumer activism. For example, the European Union adheres to international treaties and domestic legislation which appear to encourage or protect consumer activism. For example, treaties that contain provisions relating to ethical trade (Art. 34, 35, 36 and 39.1b of the TFEU) and personal freedoms which allow, if not encourage, consumer activism (Art. 19.1, 20.2d, 23 and 24 of the TFEU) in Lohman (2012).

Jacobsen and Dulsrud (2007) describe consumer activism as a means to "supplement and extend 'the arm of law'" (p. 475). In other words, consumer activism supports or better compensates for the inability of the government to take corrective measures to counteract unethical trading, controversial trade or other practice which harms the interests of consumers. For example, consumer activists are credited for the removal of genetically modified foods from the shelves of Marks & Spencer in the United Kingdom in 1999, which was followed by other food producers and retailers.

BOYCOTTING

Hertz (2001) and other authors support that businesses must consider the potential negative impact that consumer activism (e.g. in the form of boycott) could have on the viability of their business. Boycotting, negative publicity and negative press coverage can have a detrimental impact on the reputation of a firm. According to Hertz (2001) 20% of world consumers are considered activists. In the US consumer activists are about 40% of consumers. She refers to a study that showed that three out of five consumers in Britain and as many as 75% of the consumers in the United States had already boycotted a product on the basis of ethical choice (pp. 119-120). A simple definition of boycotting is: "to refuse to buy, use, or participate in (something) as a way of protesting: to stop using the goods or services of (a company, country, etc.) until changes are made" (Boycott, n. d.). The Nestlé boycott of 1977 is an excellent example since it demonstrates how boycotting can bring change. Nestlé hired women who even though were not nurses asked them to wear a nurse uniform and pretend to be ones in order to distribute free samples of baby formula in an effort to generate sales in third world countries. The free samples had the right quantity to dry up the mother's breast milk from lack of use, eventually forcing the mother to purchase the formula. The world-wide boycott against the Nestlé resulted in the The International Code of Marketing of Breastmilk Substitutes by the World Health Organization (WHO) (Breastfeeding, 2011).

Boycotts are very powerful in creating social change and achieving specific campaign goals such withdrawing products from the market or stopping harmful organizational practices. The Ethical Consumer site (Consumer, n.d.) presents several examples to illustrate the power of boycotting some of which are cited in the chapter. Among the early examples of boycotting was the one against Safeway which was aimed at 'forcing' the company to employ African Americans in 1941. Another example was the boycott in England of sugar produced by slaves. In 1791, after Parliament refused to abolish slavery, thousands of pamphlets were printed encouraging the boycott. The result of the boycott was a dramatic sales drop by between a third and a half. In 2012 Johnson & Johnson reformulated all of its baby products to remove a formaldehyde-releasing preservative. This move occurred in response to a report and boycott call from the US Campaign for Safe Cosmetics (CSC) over the company's use of harmful chemicals in its baby shampoo.

In 2010 Fruit of the Loom crumbled in the face of pressure from the largest ever student boycott. In an incredible about-face the company re-opened a Honduran factory it had closed after workers had unionised. Furthermore, it also gave all 1,200 employees their jobs back, awarded them $2.5 million in compensation and restored all union rights. The campaign started in 2009 when United Students Against Sweatshops started a campaign that led to 96 US colleges severing their contracts with the company. Ten British universities followed suit. The campaign was estimated to have cost the company 50million.

SUSTAINABLE CONSUMPTION

The "consumer movement" or "consumer activism" provided an environment that has been conducive to the growth of sustainable consumption. Consumerism has the potential to play a constructive role in building a sustainable business environment by emphasizing for example consumer awareness, fair trading, codes of conduct and ethical business practices. It encourages managers to think beyond the narrow boundaries of generating short-term sales and profits. It motivates them to adopt a sustainable approach to production which is not at the expense of the standard of living of future generations.Several studies in the existent literature like (Biswas, Liecata, Mckee, Pullig and Daughtridge, 2000; Mainieri, Barnett, Unipan and Oskamp, 1997; and Schwepker and Cornwell, 1991) revealed that a growing number of consumers are becoming inclined towards purchasing green and environmentally friendly products. Others, Beach-Larsen (1996); Eagly and Kulesa (1997); and Swenson and Wells (1997) found that there is a growing environmental consciousness among consumers, that leads to a general positive attitude towards brands that are perceived as environmentally sound. As a result, managers and corporations may find it difficult to neglect or avoid this issue in designing their corporate strategy.

Heightened corporate responsibility emerged as a phenomenon in the 1980s and early 1990s when corporations such as Cadbury's, Body Shop, and Ben & Jerry's were increasingly adopting ethical consumerism in their purchasing and supply policies. Food retailers such as Tesco, Sainsbury's and Safeway have played a crucial role in the green consumer revolution. There are also examples of businesses that had to replace components of their products that were found to be dangerous or harmful for use or consumption such as Johnsons and Johnsons that replaced the baby acre oil bottles in the USA market following a legal dispute as well as Sony which replaced the battery of the Dell brand at their own cost. These examples suggest that the business sector has become more responsive to consumerism, societal and sustainable marketing. The increasing acceptance of consumerism by managers and corporations is founded on its positive role on society and the economy. Corporations that have realized this have identified and defined their purpose and objectives in a way that aligns with the expectations of society.

The emphasis on sustainable consumption is also highlighted by several international bodies and associations. The European Commission (2012) stipulates that Europe's environmental footprint is one of the largest on the planet and suggests that if the rest of the world lived like Europeans, it would require the resources of more than two and a half earths to support all humans. The European Environment Agency (2012) claims that 'the consumption of products and services impacts the environment in many different ways' implying that 'the things we buy contribute, directly or indirectly through the product life cycle, to climate change, pollution, biodiversity loss and resource depletion.' According to the agency unsustainable consumption is the main cause of all environmental issues. The World Economic Forum (2012) emphasizes the importance of businesses reshaping demand by making sustainable consumption more personal and relevant to consumers and by investing in redesigning products and services to deliver increased value with fewer resources. According to Jackson (2006), sustainable consumption appears to be a major challenge for corporations as they will have to carry out major improvements in the efficiency with which they turn resources into finished goods whilst from the perspective of consumers, sustainable consumption involves changes in consumer behavior and lifestyles as consumers need to consume more efficiently, responsibly and of course in fewer quantities.

Consumerism and sustainable consumption have also flourished as a result of consumers becoming more caring, environmentally and socially aware and arc demanding a say in the production, processing and resourcing of the products that they regularly purchase. The increasingly well-informed consumers and their heighten expectations and demands have put pressure upon marketers for fairly traded products, for guarantees of the ethical claims marketers make about their products, for safe products, and for the careful disposal of waste. This trend puts pressure on the business sector to respond and adapt but it also creates a market opportunity for companies since those that manage to respond quickly to the shopping public's concern about for example issues such as health, animal welfare and environmental damage have the potential to build a strong reputation, a consumer preference and gain a competitive advantage.

Another trend which nourishes sustainable consumption and consumerism is that an increasing number of consumers move away from leading a life of excessive consumption and materialism towards more enduring values such as respect, compassion, and empathy. Similarly, studies have supported the emergence of environmentally and ethically conscious consumers who have shown increased demand for fairly-traded products. These consumers demonstrate an increased demand for fairly traded products which led to the development of the "Fair Trade Label" introduced by the Fair Trade Foundation, an independent fair trade validating body that is supported by many charities. The consumers of the 21st century are becoming more caring and socially aware, moving towards a more responsible and responsive attitude to issues which do not directly concern them such as Third World exploitation. There is evidence of increased consumer concern about health, animal welfare, environmental protection, and ethical trading. Numerous media reports on sustainable development, fair pay, safety, fair trading, and a steady cash flow for Third World producers are regularly featured in newspapers with a mass circulation such as The Guardian, The Financial Times, Marketing Week, and The Independent (Cowe, 1993; Hargreeves 1994; Matthews 1994). The media often extensively covers stories on exploitation and scandalous corporate behavior. Strong (1996) makes reference to ethical consumerism, a marketing concept which has emerged only recently in the UK but like green consumerism is a source of motivating consumers to become more actively ecologically and ethically aware gaining a competitive advantage for organizations that are socially and ethically conscious. The emergence of ethical consumerism has been supported by a number of features: the evolving caring consumer of the 1990's; pressure group support for Third world countries; fair trade issues endorsed by media interest, heightened corporate responsibility, and supplier power. Strong's study revealed that consumers were not solely interested in price, quality, delivery and environmental issues but were also concerned about the ethical dimension of the marketing exchange. This finding highlights the importance of managers realizing the power of ethical consumerism which drives consumers towards brands with an ethical marketing focus.

INTERNET ACTIVISM

Internet activism is a synonym to online activism, digital campaigning, digital activism, online organizing, electronic advocacy, cyberactivism, e-campaigning, and e-activism). It refers to the use of electronic communication technologies such as social media, especially Twitter, Facebook, YouTube, e-mail, and podcasts to enable faster communication by citizen movements and the delivery of local information to a large audience (Internet activism, n. d.).

The internet has increased the power of consumers over businesses as it enables them to express their views and reach other consumers in geographically dispersed areas in the fight for a common cause. The internet enables activists to voice their concerns and express their dissatisfaction in terms of unethical organizational practices. NGOs supporting environmental and social causes use the internet extensively in their campaigns. For example, Greenpeace has become incredibly adept at online campaigning, with its petitions often gaining millions of signatures. Its latest 'Save the Arctic' petition has over 5 million signatures (Consumer, n. d.)

Another example of an NGO that uses internet campaigning is SumOfUs, a global organisation that runs online petitions for "a better global economy." They often campaign against corporate malpractice, the fair treatment of workers and better environmental standards. WikiLeaks is another important campaigning organisation which has released some classified documents on its site that have helped to shed light onto some of the most unethical behavior exhibited by both governments and corporations (Consumer, n. d.).

Undoubtedly, the use of the internet by consumer activists is expanding as it has the potential to make their fights easier at least in terms of creating awareness for their cause and reaching bigger numbers of supporters. The popularity of the internet has also provided a fertile ground for the creation of anti-brand communities. According to Christodoulides (2009) and Rowley (2004) the new information technology has changed the marketing environment and has created a new reality, one in which the consumers are no longer passive recipients of information and brand value but rather skeptical, critical and sophisticated receivers and senders of information about brands and corporations.

ANTI-BRAND COMMUNITIES: THE NEW FACE OF CONSUMER ACTIVISM

Anti-branding covers different aspects of negativity. Anti-consumption, word of hate, consumer rebellion, boycotts, counter-cultural movements are just few areas which are present as a common purpose in the minds of activists (Cherrier, 2009). Social network sites have given more power to consumer activists in the sense that their "voices" can reach more people on the social web. According to Krishnamurthy and Kucuk (2009, pp. 1119) "anti-brand web sites are spaces that focus negative attention on a specific targeted brand." These sites use negative visual expressions, memorable domain names (often including the brand name itself) and offensive language to damage the brand's identity (Krishnamurthy & Kucuk 2009). According to Krishnamurthy & Kucuk (2009) and Kucuk (2008) anti-brand sites are usually community-oriented and they are often used to exchange negative experiences, organize boycotts and lawsuits. Complaints expressed on these sites are not only focused around transactional dissatisfaction, they usually evolve around everything from ethical to legal matters (Krishnamurthy & Kucuk 2009). According to Petty (2012) the American federal law protects these sites as long as they do not generate profit or can be confused with the original brand website.

Usually, anti-brand communities express their concerns about the corporate unethical practices related to environmental and human right issues. In essence, they unite people with a common moral code of social responsibility, they enable them to share resources and information, to disseminate information to alert other consumers, to criticize corporate actions, to fight for common causes and to try to make a difference in the society. One common view shared by anti-brand activists is that the society is negatively influenced by businesses today (Hollenbeck and Zinkhan, 2006). According to Krishnamurthy and Kucuk (2009, p. 1120), anti-branding is a result of "consumer empowerment as a precondition and consumer dissatisfaction as a trigger". The internet provides the anti-brand communities with a platform to disseminate their message, to share information and create awareness, and to facilitate interaction, to advocate and fight for a common cause. The internet has become one large contributor to consumer empowerment providing a platform for the formation of anti-brand communities which enable dissatisfied customers to 'air' and 'share' their dissatisfaction and concerns regarding "branding strategy, irresponsible business practices, anti-consumer business processes and defective products and technologies"(Krishnamurthy and Kucuk, 2009). One example that demonstrates the power of anti-brand communities and social media is the 2010 Nestlé case of environmental "irresponsibility". In particular, an "anti-social" wave of comments spread on Facebook targeting Nestlé in 2010. Their 'fan page' on Facebook was overwhelmed with negative comments regarding the corporation's unethical use of palm oil, which was destroying the palm tree forests which are a natural habitat of the orangutan species (Guardian.co.uk, 2010). Another example of anti-branding is the Facebook page which is dedicated to ant-branding activity targeting the Apple brand. The page is called Anti Apple (Brand) Company and has more than 3,000 page likes. Its key purpose is to "Protect Earth & Environment and save the consumers' MONEY!" It targets all people who in essence dislike Apple products and more importantly the brand itself. This page acts as an archival domain gathering all articles discussing Apple Inc. failures such as those covering poor production quality and innovation, those questioning the Apple brand's trustworthiness and responsibility against customers', those highlighting undelivered promises for customers as well as negative employee attitudes (Paulikaite, 2015).

FAIR TRADE

There is no doubt that consumer activism emerged through the efforts of individual consumers to ensure that the business sector is acting in a manner that is morally and ethically correct. Undoubtedly consumers have become more sensitive and critical towards organizational practices that either affect them or others in a negative manner. Consumers have also become more concerned towards the impact of trading practices on producers. According to Boonman, Huisman, Sarrucco-Fedorovtsjv and Sarrucco, 2010, p. 4) is:

Fair Trade is responsible production and consumption. It is a social and economical development model for companies and families that gives them the opportunity to fulfil their basic needs and develop themselves. For consumers Fair Trade is a way to consume in a corporate social responsible way that contributes to the wellbeing of themselves and the producers.

Fair Trade enables consumers who live in the developed world to help producers operating in Third World countries by buying Fair Trade products. It enables producers to engage in sustainable development and consumers to practise responsible consumption (Boonman, Huisman, Sarrucco-Fedorovtsjv and Sarrucco, 2010). Fair Trade is in essence a trading partnership, which is founded on dialogue, integrity, transparency and respect between all trading partners. It contributes to sustainable development by offering better trading conditions and securing the rights of producers and workers especially those working in third world countries.

Fair trade began as a way of supporting women in third world countries who created handcrafts as a source of income that were sold internationally. Several countries have embraced and engage in fair trade. The European Fair Trade Association which was founded in 1987 reports that in 1973 the Netherlands was the first country to be importing "fairly traded" coffee that was sourced from cooperative farmers in Guatemala. Ever since fair trade coffee has become one of the most successful fair trade products in the world. Several other products such as tea, cocoa, sugar, wine, fruit juices, nuts, spices, rice, flowers and cotton are distributed worldwide under the FairTrade© brand. Fair trade is the "mission" of the EFTA (European Fair Trade Association) which is an association of ten Fair Trade importers in nine European countries (Austria, Belgium, France, Germany, Italy, The Netherlands, Spain, Switzerland and the United Kingdom). EFTA was established informally in 1987 by some of the oldest and largest Fair Trade importers and it gained formal status in 1990.

A research carried out by Timothy Devinney in 2006, shows that 54 percent of consumers are willing to pay more for Fair Trade or sustainable products (cited in European Fair Trade Association, n. d.). According to TNS NIPO, a Dutch research centre, 55 percent of consumers want to consume in a corporate socially responsible way (cited in European Fair Trade Association, n. d.). Fair Trade encourages consumers to actively engage in supporting producers through selecting and buying fair trade products. According to the official website of the Fair Trade International Organisation: "Not all trade is fair! Farmers and workers at the beginning of the chain don't always get a fair share of the benefits of trade. Fair Trade enables consumers to put this right." (About Fairtrade, n. d.). In essence, Fair Trade offers an alternative approach to traditional trade founded on a partnership between producers and consumers. It gives the power to consumers to reduce poverty and ease the daily struggles of producers through their daily shopping. When a product carries the FAIRTRADE Mark it means the producers and traders have met Fairtrade Standards which are designed in order to compensate for any imbalances and injustices in trading relationships.

GREEN MARKETING

Green marketing, which is also referred to as environmental marketing or ecological marketing, emerged in the late 1980s and early 1990s. The first book entitled "Ecological Marketing" was the outcome of the first workshop on "Ecological Marketing", which was organised by the American Marketing Association (AMA) in 1975. The AMA workshop attempted to bring together academics, practitioners, and public policy makers to examine marketing's impact on the natural environment. At this workshop ecological marketing was defined as:

The study of the positive and negative aspects of marketing activities on pollution, energy depletion and non-energy resource depletion. (Henion and Kinnear, 1976).

According to the American Marketing Association, Green Marketing is: "1. (retailing definition) the marketing of products that are presumed to be environmentally safe. 2. (social marketing definition) the development and marketing of products designed to minimize negative effects on the physical environment or to improve its quality. 3. (environments definition) the efforts by organisation to produce, promote, package and reclaim products in a manner that is sensitive or responsive to ecological concerns." (White, 2011). "Green or Environmental Marketing consists of all activities designed to generate and facilitate any exchanges intended to satisfy human needs or wants, such that the satisfaction of these needs and wants occurs, with minimal detrimental impact on the natural environment." (Polonsky 1994a). McDaniel and Rylander (1993) support that: "Green Marketing is taking shape as one of the key business strategies of the future, and that the increasing environmental consciousness makes it incumbent on consumer marketers not just to respond to it, but to lead the way in environmental programs." Several companies have started marketing themselves as green by engaging in activities that enable them to demonstrate their social responsibility towards the physical environment. The Dell Corporation focuses on producing green IT products under their strategy called "Go Green with Dell". In addition, Dell products are packaged in eco-friendly packaging. The company is also investing in green innovations (Services, n. d.). In their official site, Xerox Corporation claims that it focuses towards: "Making Green Work better" and "Saving energy and protecting our climate is our responsibility and our promise". The company is engaged in a number of actions that are directed towards these aims such as: recycling Xerox Supplies and Xerox Equipment and has launched a number of environmental programs that aim at demonstrating the company's sustainability commitment. There are numerous other examples of firms that have strived to become more environmentally responsible, in an attempt to better satisfy their consumer needs.McDonald's replaced its clam shell packaging with waxed paper because of increased consumer concern relating to polystyrene production and Ozone depletion (Gifford 1991, Hume 1991).Tuna manufacturers modified their fishing techniques because of the increased concern over driftnet fishing, and the resulting death of dolphins (Advertising Age 1991). Shell, Esso, Not all companies promote their environmental activities. Coca-Cola has invested large sums of money in various recycling activities, as well as has modified their packaging to minimize its environmental impact it has not these. While being concerned about the environment, Coca Cola has not promoted these activities and used them as a promotional tool (Polonsky 1985). Thus, many consumers may not realize that Coke is a very environmentally committed organization. Another firm that is very environmentally responsible but does not promote this, at least outside the organization, is Walt Disney World (WDW). WDW has an extensive waste management program and infrastructure in place, yet these facilities are not highlighted in their general tourist promotional activities (Murphy 1985).

The term is closely related to green consumerism. Henion and Kinnear (1976) defined green consumers as environmentally conscious consumers. According to Krishnan (2013) the green consumer is an individual deeply concerned about the environment subsequently someone that only buys products that are environmentally friendly or eco-friendly, products with little packaging or products that are made from natural ingredients. The term refers to recycling, purchasing and using eco-friendly products that minimize the damage to the physical environment (Krishnan, 2013). This orientation results in an environmentally conscious behaviour which influences the purchase choices of consumers so for example, the green consumer will be more likely to buy hybrid cars that emit less carbon dioxide, will be using solar energy to generate electricity and even buying locally grown vegetables and fruits. Antil (1984) described green consumerism as a specific type of socially conscious consumer behavior centered around the protection of the physical environment. Green consumerism was described as a form of "pro-social" consumer behavior (Weiner and Doescher, 1991). The literature reviewed revealed that consumers today prefer environmentally friendly brands which in essence puts pressure on corporations to adopt ethical and green practices in their interactions with customers, suppliers, dealers, and employees (Bhatia and Jain, 2013). Consumers are becoming increasingly conscious about the environment and the detrimental impact of consumption behavior onto it. This has in essence become the ultimate driving force of green marketing.

SUSTAINABLE MARKETING: THE DEMAND FOR MORE CORPORATE SOCIAL RESPONSIBILITY

The growth of consumerism has resulted in consumers being critical of questionable business practices and led to the imposition of increasing regulation on the corporate sector. Corporate behaviour varies when it comes to responding to consumer issues. Some corporations are simply inactive whereas others have adapted to the growing trend of consumerism. Adapting and responding to consumerism has become routine exercise for most businesses operating in the Western part of the world. However, in the developing countries, the level of corporate attitude and action has been rather slow. Consumers in the least developed countries emphasize the satisfaction of their physiological needs. The prevalence of seller's market conditions in the least developing countries has also contributed to the low response of business. Consumers in these markets tend to accept whatever it is offered to them and have very little voice in the marketplace (Reddy and Campell 1994; Kaynak 1985; Kaynak et al. 1992). Another important factor that contributes negatively to the growth of consumerism in the least developed countries is the lack of a supportive macro-economic environment, which is an essential condition for consumerism activity. In these countries, consumerism is concerned with micro issues including product safety, packaging, unit pricing, misleading advertising or labeling and product quality. In the developed countries consumerism focuses on macro issues such as pollution, poverty, welfare system, health care, tax system and anti-nuclear issues (Kaynak 1985). These areas are reflected in the attitudes and actions of corporations in the developed world.

Sustainable marketing is defined by Kotler et al. (2013, p. 11) as: "socially and environmentally responsible marketing that meets the present needs of consumers and businesses while also preserving or enhancing the ability of future generations to meet their needs". Marketers have to re-examine their attitudes and relationships with social values and responsibilities as worldwide consumerism and environmentalism movements gain ground and prevail. Cherrier et al. (2012) claim that managers and senior executives have a critical role to play in corporate environmentalism which is defined as "processes by which firms integrate environmental concerns into their decisions (Banerjee 2002, p. 117). The company's stance towards corporate ethics, environmental concerns and social responsibility has the power to influence customer relationships. Customers are no longer indifferent as to the impact of company actions on the well-being of consumers, the society and the environment. Today's consumers expect companies to deliver value in a socially and environmentally friendly way. Some companies such as Marks & Spencer's, the Body Shop, and others invest in sustainable marketing creating a reputation for being civic minded and responsible. They embed social responsibility in their mission statement and company values. Marks & Spencer's 2003-2004 CSR Report focused on five key issues: sustainable raw materials, responsible use of technology, animal welfare, ethical trading and community programmes. These issues were identified as being important to consumers.

Other companies resist movements such as consumerism and environmentalism and simply follow the legal framework or do the very minimum just to get by. However, it can be suggested that today's consumers who have experienced the impact of the recent global economic crisis, are buying less and look for greater value, as well as demand greater responsibility and accountability from companies as well. They are not willing to ignore, forgive or forget corporate unethical behavior, mistakes and scandals. In order to build competitive and sustainable brands, companies need to understand the mindset and concerns of consumers by engaging in a more proactive way with society and its citizens. They also need to instill trust and loyalty with customers to form the foundations for long lasting customer relationships.

SOLUTIONS AND RECOMMENDATIONS

- Practitioners need to acknowledge that consumers have become more critical and will scrutinize business activities more than ever before. Corporate behavior has a direct impact on the natural environment since the tendency towards materialism leads to environmental destructiveness caused through the increased usage of the earth's natural resources. Subsequently, practitioners have a duty and responsibility to preserve and protect the physical environmental for the current and future generations. They need to adopt practices such as recycling, energy efficiency and renewable sources of energy. Managers can also reshape demand towards sustainable consumption by informing and educating consumers through integrated marketing communications that highlights the importance of practicing ethical and green consumerism.
- Practitioners need to address the concerns, expectations and demands of an ever-growing number of green and ethical consumers. Similarly, they need to respond to the increasing power of pressure groups that campaign for environmental and ethical issues and principles of fair trading. More importantly, they need to develop appropriate marketing management strategies that address these concerns, and develop an organizational philosophy that is embedded and guided by ethical, environmental and social responsibility principles.
- At times where the uncertain economic environment has touched practically most countries in the developed world and in a world where consumers are more demanding, cynical, and fickle, corporations and brands are faced with the task of becoming more responsible and accountable. Corporations cannot afford to ignore the power of consumers and public opinion. They need to

become good corporate citizens and adopt a more proactive approach towards consumerist issues both micro and macro such as fair pricing, advertising ethics, environmentalism, green marketing and sustainability.

- Companies need to provide evidence regarding their sustainability agendas through their websites and annual reports as part of their commitment to corporate social responsibility. The agendas need to encompass environmental and social issues: environmental initiatives that have the potential to reduce waste, energy and resources and social initiatives such as training, health and safety at work to increase employee security and efficiency amongst the workforce as well as morale and productivity.
- As the level of importance and acceptance of consumerism increases in a society, the likelihood of consumer pressure for increased regulation will increase and a favorable commitment of business translated into responsive action is likely to follow. Companies that are guided by consumerist issues, have embedded them into their principles and have turned them into practice are the ones that will see them as an opportunity to gain a competitive advantage, strengthen their corporate reputation and instill customer trust and loyalty at a time which are mostly needed.
- Practitioners cannot ignore the power of social media which enables consumers to share information, perceptions, feelings and experiences with others regarding brands and corporations. There is need for continuous monitoring of the information flow between consumers, customers, other publics and the society in general to ensure that there is no scrutiny, boycotting, cynicism and other unfavorable publicity targeting the business, its products and services.

FUTURE RESEARCH DIRECTIONS

Businesses need to be aware of consumer attitudes towards issues related to consumerism as these have direct implications on customers' perceptions of brands and corporations. Marketers will have to adjust their marketing strategies and practices to accommodate and respond to the issues that are prioritized by consumers. Future research could focus on exploring the adoption of sustainable marketing in the European Business sector and particularly, the nature of activities and business practices pursued. The implementation of a cross-European research study can enable the comparison of data which could reveal similarities and differences between businesses operating in different European countries. There is also a need to investigate how corporations deal with boycotting and anti-brand communities. Another study could focus on exploring whether businesses in Europe are engaging in fair-trade activities and which are these activities, and whether companies have measured consumers' attitudes towards business activities that support fair trade. Finally, future research could also focus on exploring the implementation of green marketing by businesses operating in Europe and internationally.

CONCLUSION

The chapter discusses consumerism from the perspective of safeguarding the interests and rights of consumers, a view which is closely related to the concept of social responsibility (CSR) and subsequently societal marketing. Undoubtedly, the increasing social problems and environmental challenges, highlight the need for CSR and sustainable marketing. In analyzing this relationship in this chapter one cannot ignore the increasing importance of some of the latest trends in the field such as boycotting, sustainable consumption, internet activism, anti-branding, Fair trade, green consumerism, and sustainable marketing. One cannot doubt that corporations and practitioners are faced with many developments, multiple stakeholders, and new challenges but the most important one is perhaps the consumer market. Consumers have been empowered in many ways primarily due to the advancements in the fields of technology and communications. Their perceptions and experiences have the power to either harm or enhance corporate reputation, and this can be done within seconds through the use of social media. So perhaps now more than ever before consumerism should be included in the agenda of top management and addressed through a combination of initiatives and activities that are closely coordinated and managed to ensure success.

REFERENCES

Abela, A. (2006). Marketing and consumerism: a response to O'Shaughnessy and O'Shaughnessy. *European Journal of Marketing*, *40*(1 & 2), 5-16.

Age, A. (1991). Spurts and Starts: Corporate Role in '90s Environmentalism Hardly Consistent. *Advertising Age*, *62*(46), GR14–GR16.

Anderson, W. T., & Cunningham, W. H. (1972). The social conscious consumer. *Journal of Marketing*, *36*(3), 23. doi:10.2307/1251036

Anon. (2003). Adulteration of edible oils. Food safety and Security, May, 14.

Antil, J. H. (1984). Socially Responsible Consumers: Profile and Implications for Public Policy. *Journal of Macromarketing,* 4(2), 18-39.

Arndt, J., Barksdale, H., & Perreault, W. (1980). Comparative study of attitudes toward marketing, consumerism and Government regulation: The United States versus Norway and Venezuela. In R. Day & H. K. Hunt (Eds.), *New Findings in Consumer Satisfaction and Campaigning* (pp. 66–72). Bloomington, IN: Indiana University.

Banerjee, S. B. (2002). Corporate environmentalism: The construct and its measurement. *Journal of Business Research*, *55*(1), 177–191. doi:10.1016/S0148-2963(00)00135-1

Barksdale, H. C., & Darden, W. R. (1972). Consumer attitudes toward marketing and consumerism. *Journal of Marketing*, *36*(4), 28–35. doi:10.2307/1250423

Barksdale, H. C., Perreault, W. D., Arndt, J., Barnhill, J., French, W., Halliday, M., & Zif, J. (1982). A cross national survey of consumer attitudes towards marketing practices, consumerism and Government regulations. *The Columbia Journal of World Business*, *17*, 71–86.

Beach-Larsen, T. (1996). Danish consumers attitudes to the functional and environmental characteristics of food packaging. *Journal of Consumer Policy*, *19*(3), 339–363. doi:10.1007/BF00411413

Beastfeeding.com. (2011). The Nestlé Boycott. Retrieved from http://www.breastfeeding.com/advocacy/advocacy_boycott.html

Berkowitz, L., & Lutterman, K. G. (1968). The traditional socially responsible personality. *Public Opinion Quarterly*, *32*(2), 169. doi:10.1086/267597

Bhatia, M, and Jain, A. (2013). Green Marketing: A Study of Consumer Perception and Preference in India. *Electronic Green Journal*, 1(36).

Bhuian, S. N., Abdul-Muhmin, A. G., & Kim, D. (2001). Business education and its influence on attitudes to business, consumerism, and Government in Saudi Arabia. *Journal of Education for Business*, *76*(4), 226–230. doi:10.1080/08832320109601315

Bhushan, R. (2003, October 2). A Question of Quality. *The Hindu*.

Biswas, A., Licata, J.W., McKee, D., Pullig, C., and Daughtridge, C. (2000). The recycling cycle: An empirical examination of consumer waste recycling and recycling shopping behaviors. *Advertising and Environmental issues, 19*(1), 93-115.

Bloom, P. N., & Greyser, S. A. (1981). The Maturing of Consumerism. *Harvard Business Review*, *59*(November-December), 130–139. PMID:10252236

Bloom, P. N., & Smith, R. B. (1986). *The Future of Consumerism*. Lexington, Mass: Lexington Books.

Boonman, M., Huisman, W., Sarrucco-Fedorovtsjv, E., & Sarrucco, T. (2010). A success story for Producers and Consumers. *Dutch Association of Workshops*.

Bourgeois, J. C., & Barnes, J. G. (1979). Viability and profile of the consumerist segment. *The Journal of Consumer Research*, *5*(March), 217–227. doi:10.1086/208734

Brunk, M. E. (1973). The anatomy of consumerism. *Journal of Advertising*, *2*(1), 9–12. doi:10.1080/00913367.1973.10672477

Burroughs, J. E., & Rindfleisch, A. (2002). Materialism and well-being: A conflicting values perspective. *The Journal of Consumer Research*, *29*(3), 348–370. doi:10.1086/344429

Cherrier, H. (2009). Anti-Consumption Discourses and Consumer Resistant-Identities. *Journal of Business Research*, *62*(2), 181–190. doi:10.1016/j.jbusres.2008.01.025

Cherrier, H., Russell, S. V., & Fielding, K. (2012). Corporate environmentalism and top management identity negotiation. *Journal of Organizational Change Management*, *25*(4), 518–534. doi:10.1108/09534811211239209

Christodoulides, G. (2009). Branding in the post-internet era, *Marketing Theory*, 9(1). Retrieved from http://mtq.sagepub.com/content/9/1/141

EthicalConsumer. (n. d.). Successful Consumer Boycotts: Ethical Consumer. Retrieved from http://www.ethicalconsumer.org/boycotts/successfulboycotts.aspx

Consumer, E. (n. d.). Product Guides. Retrieved from http://www.ethicalconsumer.org/ethicalreports/internetreport/activism.aspx

Cowe, R. (1993). Companies find ethics makes commercial sense. *The Guardian,* 27 April.

Darley, W. K., & Johnson, D. M. (1993). Cross-national comparison of consumer attitudes toward consumerism in four developing countries. *The Journal of Consumer Affairs*, *27*(1), 37–54. doi:10.1111/j.1745-6606.1993.tb00736.x

Dell. (n. d.). DFS home page. Retrieved from http://www.dell.com/learn/us

Devinney, T. (2006). The other CSR, FLO. Retrieved from http://www.fairtrade.net

Dubinsky, A. J., & Hensel, P. J. (1984). Marketing student attitudes toward advertising: Implications for marketing education. *Journal of Marketing Education*, *6*(Summer), 22–26. doi:10.1177/027347538400600206

Eagly, A. H., & Kulesa, P. (1997). Attitudes, attitude structure, the resistance to change. In M.H. Bazermann, D.M. Messick, A.E. Tenbrunsel et al. (Eds.), Environment, Ethics, and Behavior (pp. 122-153). San Francisco, CA: The New Lexington Press.

European Commission. (2012a). Retail Forum. Retrieved from http://ec.europa.eu/environment/industry/retail/indexen.html

Wikipedia. (2012). European Environment Agency. Retrieved from http://en.wikipedia.org/wiki/European_environmnet_agency

European Fair Trade Association. (n. d.). Retrieved from http://www.european-fair-trade-association.org/efta/index.php

Fairtrade Labelling Organizations International. (n. d.). What is FairTrade? Retrieved from http://www.fairtrade.net/about-fairtrade/what-is-fairtrade.html

French, W. A., Barksdale, H. C., & Perreault, W. D. (1982). Consumer attitudes towards marketing in England and the United States. *European Journal of Marketing*, *16*(6), 20–30. doi:10.1108/EUM0000000004853

Gaski, J. F., & Etzel, M. J. (1986, July). The Index of Consumer Sentiment toward Marketing. *Journal of Marketing*, *50*(3), 71–81. doi:10.2307/1251586

Gifford B. (1991, August 19). The Greening of the Golden Arches-McDonald's Teams With Environmental Group to Cut Waste. *The San Diego Union*, C1 & C4.

Greyser, S. A. (1977). Public Attitudes and Consumerism. In Cady, J.F. (Ed.), *Marketing and Public Interest:Proceedings of Symposium*, Cambridge, Mass. (pp. 299-309).

Greyser, S. A., & Diamond, S. L. (1974). Business in Adapting to Consumerism. *Harvard Business Review*, *52*(September-October), 38–58.

Hargreeves, D. (1994). The cost of a fair deal. *Financial Times*, 17 March.

Henion, K. E., & Kinnear, T. C. (1976). *Measuring the Effect of Ecological Information and Social Class on Selected Product Choice Criteria Importance Ratings, Ecological Marketing* (pp. 145–156). Chicago: American Marketing Association.

Hertz, N. (2001). *The Silent Takeover. Global Capitalism and The Death of Democracy*. London: William Heinemann.

Hollenbeck, C. R., & Zinkhan, G. M. (2006). Consumer Activism on the Internet: The Role of Anti-brand Communities. *Advances in Consumer Research*, 33, 479-485. Retrieved from http://www.acrwebsite.org/volumes/v33/v33_10337.pdf

Hume, S. (1991). McDonald's: Case Study. *Advertising Age*, *62*(5), 32.

Hustad, T. P., & Pessemier, E. A. (1973). Will the real consumer activist please stand up: An examination of consumers opinions about marketing practices? *JMR, Journal of Marketing Research*, *10*(Nov), 319–324. Retrieved from http://www.ethicalconsumer.org/boycotts/successfulboycotts.aspx doi:10.2307/3149703

Ismail, H. B., & Panni, M. F. A. K. (2008). Consumer perceptions on the consumerism issues and its influence on their purchasing behavior: A view from Malaysian food industry. *Journal of Legal, Ethical and Regulatory Issues*, *11*(1), 43–64.

Jackson, T. (2006). Prosperity without growth? Sustainability Development Commission. Retrieved from http://www.sd-commission.org.uk/publications/downloads/prosperitywithoutgrowthreport.pdf

Jacobsen, E., & Dulsrud, A. A. (2007). Will consumers save the world? The framing of political consumerism. Journal of Agricultural and Environmental Ethics, 20, 469–482.

Kaynak, E. (1985). Some thoughts on consumerism in developed and less developed countries. *International Marketing Review*, *2*(2), 15–31. doi:10.1108/eb008273

Kaynak, E., Kucukemiroglu, O., & Odabasi, Y. (1992). Consumer complaint handling in an advanced developing economy: An empirical investigation. *Journal of Business Ethics*, *11*(11), 813–829. doi:10.1007/BF00872359

Keown, C. F. (1982). Attitudes of practitioners and students toward marketing. *Journal of Marketing Education*, *4*(Fall), 14–20. doi:10.1177/027347538200400203

Kinnear, T. C., Taylor, J. R., & Ahmed, S. A. (1974). Ecologically concerned consumers: Who are they? *Journal of Marketing*, *38*(April), 20–24. doi:10.2307/1250192

Klein, N. (2000). No Logo (pp. 3-26 and pp. 325-343). London. Flamingo

Knauer, V. (1971, April 21). Special assistant for consumer affairs to the president of the United States, in an address to National Application and Radio- TV Dealers Association, Chicago.

Koslow, S. (2000). Can the truth hurt? How honest and persuasive advertising can unintentionally lead to increased consumer skepticism. *The Journal of Consumer Affairs*, *34*(2), 16–32. doi:10.1111/j.1745-6606.2000.tb00093.x

Kotler, P. (1972). What consumerism means for marketers. *Harvard Business Review*, *3*, 48–57.

Kotler, P. (2000). *Marketing Management*. New York, NY: Prentice Hall.

Kotler, P., Armstrong, G., Harris, L., & Piercy, N. (2013). *Principles of Marketing*. Essex: Pearson Education.

Kotler, P., Armstrong, G., Wong, V., & Saunders, J. (2005). *Principles of Marketing* (4th European Ed.). Essex: Pearson Education.

Kotler, P., Armstrong, G., Wong, V., & Saunders, J. (2008). *Principles of Marketing* (5th European Ed.). Essex: Pearson Education.

Kotler, P., & Keller, K. L. (2006). Marketing Management (12thed.). Upper Saddle River, NJ: Pearson Education.

Krishnamurth, S., & Kucuk, S. U. (2009). Anti-branding on the Internet, *Journal of Business Research,* 62, 1119-1126, Retrieved from http://www.ehl.lu.se/biblioteket

Krishnan, M. S. (2013). Green Consumerism. Retrieved from http://slideshare.net/subudhrakrishnan3/the-green-consumer

Kucuk, S. U. (2008). Negative Double Jeopardy: The role if anti-brand sites on the internet, *Journal of Brand Management*, 15, 209–222. Retrieved from http://www.palgrave-journals.com/bm/journal/v15/n3/abs/2550100a.html

Lampman, R. J. (1988). JFK's four consumer rights: a retrospective view. In E. S. Maynes (Ed.), *The Frontier of Research in the Consumer Interest* (pp. 19–33). Columbia, MO: American Council of Consumer Interests.

Lisa, A. (2004). Is it unfair pricing? *Tire Business*, *22*(14), 15.

Lohman, P. (2012). Consumer Activism: Reinforcing Moral Identity through fair trade coffee. Retrieved from http://www.e-ir.info/2012/05/24/consumer-activism-reinforcing-moral-identity-through-fair-trade-coffee/

Lysonski, S., Durvasula, S. and Watson, J. (2003). Should marketing managers be concerned about attitudes towards marketing and consumerism in New Zealand? A longitudinal study. *European Journal of Marketing*, 37(3 & 4), 385-406.

Mainieri, T., Barnett, E. G., Unipan, J. B., & Oskamp, S. (1997). Green buying: The influence of environmental concern on consumer behavior. *The Journal of Social Psychology*, *137*(2), 189–204. doi:10.1080/00224549709595430

Matthews, V. (1994). Give farmers a coffee break. *Marketing Week*, *13*(May), 26.

McDaniel, S. W., & Rylander, D. H. (1993). Strategic Green Marketing. *Journal of Consumer Marketing*, *10*(3), 4–10. doi:10.1108/07363769310041929

McIllhenny, J.H. (1990). The new consumerism: how will business respond. *At Home with Consumers*, 11(5), 9-10.

Merriam-Webster Dictionary. (n. d.). Boycott. Retrieved from http://www.merriam-webster.com/dictionary/boycott

Murphy, P. (1985). *Tourism: A Community Approach*. New York: Methuen Inc.

Murphy, P. (2000). The commodified self in consumer culture: A cross-cultural perspective. *The Journal of Social Psychology*, *40*(October), 636–647. doi:10.1080/00224540009600504 PMID:11059210

Packard, V. (1957). *The Hidden Persuaders*. London: Longman.

Panni, M. F. A. K. (2006). *The Effect of Consumerism towards customer attitudinal behavior in food insustry in Malaysia* [Unpublished Master's Thesis]. Multimedia University, Melaka, Malaysia.

Paulikaite, M. (2015). Anti-branding: a way to destroy brands? Case of Apple Inc. Oct. http://www.brandba.se/blog/2015 (accessed 17 April 2016).

Peattie, K. (1992). *Green Marketing*. Pitman.

Petty, R. D. (2012). Using the law to protect the brand on social media sites: A three "M"s framework for marketing managers, *Management Research Review*, 35(9), 758 – 769. Retrieved from http://www.emeraldinsight.com/journals.htm?issn=20408269&volume=35&issue=9&articleid=17044169&show=html

Polonsky, M. J. (1994a). A Stakeholder Theory Approach to Designing Environmental Marketing Strategy (Unpublished Working Paper).

Polonsky, M. J. (1994b, November). An introduction to Green Marketing. *Electronic Green Journal, 1*(2).

Reddy, A. C., & Campell, D. P. (1994). *Marketing's role in Economic Development*. London: Quorum Books.

Rowley, J. (2004). Online branding, *Online Information Review*, 28(2), 131–138. Retrieved from http://www.emeraldinsight.com/journals.htm?issn=1468-4527&volume=28&issue=2&articleid=862248&show=html&PHPSESSID=ufafbm4asi1f8kfsedv58qea12 13)

Ruiz, S., Arcas, N., & Cuestas, P. (2001). Consumer attitudes towards ecological agrarian fruits and vegetables in Spain. A Segmentation Approach. *Acta Horticulturae*, *559*(559), 681–686. doi:10.17660/ActaHortic.2001.559.100

Schwepker, C. H., & Cornwell, R. B. (1991). An examination of ecologically concerned consumers and their intention to purchase ecologically packaged products. *Journal of Public Policy & Marketing*, *10*(2), 77–101.

Slater, D. (1997). *Consumer, Culture and Modernity*. Cambridge: Policy Press.

Swenson, M. R., & Wells, W. D. (1997). Useful correlates of per-environmental behavior, Goldberg. In M.E., Fishbein, M. Middlestadt, S.E. (Eds.), Social Marketing: Theoretical and Practical Perspectives (pp. 91-109). Mahwah, NJ: Lawrence Erlbaum.

The Guardian. (2010). Nestlé hit by Facebook "anti-social" media surge. Retrieved from http://www.guardian.co.uk/sustainable-business/nestle-facebook

The Roper Organization. (1971). *The cost of cleaner Air: How much do people want it?* (6th ed.). Ames, IA: Iowa State University Press.

Uray, N., & Menguc, B. (1996). Testing the cross-cultural generalizability of the scale of consumer attitudes toward marketing and consumerism. *Journal of International Consumer Marketing*, *9*(2), 65–93. doi:10.1300/J046v09n02_04

Varadarajan, P., Rajan, P., & Thirunarayana, P. (1990). Consumers attitudes towards marketing practices, consumerism, and government relations: Cross-national perspective. *European Journal of Marketing*, *24*(6), 6–24. doi:10.1108/03090569010137934

Veblen, T. (1899): The Theory of the Leisure Class: an economic study of institutions. Mineola, NY: Dover Publications.

Wee, C. H., & Chan, M. (1989). Consumer sentiment towards marketing in Hong Kong. *Asia Pacific International Journal of Marketing*, *1*(1), 25–29.

Weiner, J. L., & Doescher, T. A. (1991). A Framework for Promoting Cooperation. *Journal of Marketing*, *55*(2), 38–47. doi:10.2307/1252236

White, S. (2011). Defining Green Marketing. Retrieved from http://dstevenwhite.com/2010/08/04/defining-green-marketing

Wikipedia. (n. d.). Internet activism. Retrieved from https://en.wikipedia.org/wiki/Internet_activism

World Economic Forum. (2012). More with less: Scaling Sustainable Consumption and Resource Efficiency. Retrieved from http://www3.weforum.org/docs/IP/CO/WEFCoScalingSustainableConsumpionResourceEfficiencyReport2012.pdf

Yani-de-Soriano, M., & Slater, S. (2009). Revisiting Druckers theory: Has consumerism led to the overuse of marketing. *Journal of Management History*, *15*(4), 452–466. doi:10.1108/17511340910987347

ADDITIONAL READING

Quazi, A.M. (2002). Managerial Views of Consumerism. *European Journal of Marketing*, 36(1 & 2), 36-50.

KEY TERMS AND DEFINITIONS

Boycotting: An act of voluntarily refraining from using, buying, or dealing with a person, organization, or country as an expression of protest for social or political reasons. It is sometimes a form of consumer activism.

Consumerism: An initiative supported by both citizens and government agencies to improve the rights and power of buyers in relation to sellers.

Green Consumerism: The buying habits of consumers influenced by green and other environmental issues.

Green Marketing: The marketing of products that are perceived to be environmentally friendly and preferable to others.

Marketing: An organisational activity and a management philosophy focusing on satisfying customers' needs and building profitable customer relationships by creating value for customers.

Sustainable Consumption: Consumption behaviour shaped by a concern towards the environment and the society.

Sustainable Marketing: Socially and environmentally responsible marketing addresses the needs and concerns of present and future generations.

Chapter 2
Social Impact in Consumer Behaviour–Consumer Boycotts as a Consumerism Activity:

Dursun Yener
Istanbul Medeniyet University, Turkey

ABSTRACT

Consumerism is not a new concept for marketing, but its importance is growing in the recent years. Researchers have studied the phenomenon of consumerism from within different dimensions. However, its relationship with social impact theory and consumer boycotts has not been dealt with accurately. Social impact can be defined as the effect of people on other people. A consumer boycott is a type of consumer behaviour in which consumers collectively prefer not to use their purchasing power towards a product, brand or all products of a country and boycott them. Motivations for participating in boycotts differ in accordance with various factors such as consumers' beliefs, needs or attitudes. Organizing a boycott and calling for people's participation is much easier today than it used to be in the past. Since consumer boycotts is a type of consumer behaviour and consumers are affected various factors including people in their family or friends or members in their reference groups, they can be thought a derivation of social impact.

INTRODUCTION

Consumerism is a concept of growing importance especially for the last decades. Generally, it covers all activities which are aimed to protect consumers from some illegal activities such as fraud or negative concepts such as misperception etc. However, it also refers to the consumer activism against those illegal activities or negative concepts. Social impact theory determines the effect of people on other people. Although this theory is originated in social psychology area, it recently used in many different disciplines. However, its importance and effect did not be handled accurately. Social impact theory analyzes how people affect opinions, attitudes and behaviours of other people and consumers cannot be excluded from the scope of this theory. Today most of marketing activities aims to influence consumers to persuade

DOI: 10.4018/978-1-5225-2139-6.ch002

to buy their products and services. At the same time, some people or groups try to effect consumers to react companies for their unethical activities through some activities such as boycotts. Social impact theory has three important components which are strength, immediacy and number of the source. All these factors determine how much effect people have on other people. One of the most important tools for consumers to protecting themselves is boycotts. Consumer boycotts are used for various reasons such as unethical marketing activities, religious and political reasons. The main goal of boycotts is to lead to the desired change in the policies of the targeted body, thus boycotts can well be described as an effective economic weapon that the consumers have. With developing information technology and proliferation of the Internet related social media, it is nowadays relatively easy and costless to call people to boycott. Individuals and/or organizations share information with people about the reason why the target firms or countries should be boycotted.

CONSUMERISM

Consumerism is a social and economic order that is based on the systematic creation and fostering of a desire to purchase goods or services in even greater amounts. The term "consumerism" is also used to refer to the consumerist movement or consumer activism, which seeks to protect and inform consumers by requiring such practices as honest packaging and advertising, product guarantees, and improved safety standards (Mirchevska and Markova, 2011). Consumerism defines a specific analysis category that studies the phenomenon that came up with mass production development and consumption expansion (Bostan, Burciu and Grosu, 2010). It has been defined for example as "organized group pressure which has become a set of values held not only by the consumers of a company's products but also within the wider society" (Jones et al., 2005, p. 35). Kotler defined consumerism "as a social movement designed to augment the rights and powers of buyers in relation to sellers" (Varadarajan and Thirunarayana, 1990, p. 6). By consumerism, it is understood that assembly of ideologies regarding social activism, pressure groups (consumer associations) and in general that trend that tries to raise the rights and the consumer's power in relation to the entities (Bostan, Burciu and Grosu, 2010).

In the twentieth century capitalism, the focus shifted increasingly from production to consumption, resulting in a parallel shift from the control and exploitation of workers to the control and exploitation of consumers. Capitalism has created a controllable "consuming mass" to complement the control of the "producing mass". The central concern here is to concentrate the means of consumption on the control of consumers in order to get them to spend as much as possible (Assad, 2007).

Protecting the consumer is not an invention of our times, the consumer protection legislation, for example against altered food and scale fraud appears ever since the Old Testament and also in the Hammurabi's Code of Laws (Bostan, Burciu and Grosu, 2010). Various scholars have traced the roots of consumerism back to the 16th century England, with its inspiration seeming to come from the Renaissance Italy (Brunner, 1996). The emergence of consumer-oriented societies has become the central trait of our era. In such societies, sustaining a productive economy demands that consumption should become a way of life, along with the purchase and usage of goods to be converted from a utilitarian exercise to ritualistic excess. The consumerism phenomenon was born in the beginning of the 20th century in the USA, where in the year 1906, the first mass protests were so powerful that they constrained the federal government to approve a very important set of rules to the industry at that time (Bostan, Burciu and Grosu, 2010, p. 20).

The consumer society had already expanded from the USA to Western Europe and Japan by the 1960s (Assad, 2007). In the early 1960's, consumer protection movement started in the United States and then in Europe as a result of consumer dissatisfaction. In response to this movement, Consumer Rights were officially recognized in 1962 by US President J.F. Kennedy and the idea of consumerism has gained importance (Orel and Zeren, 2009) Consumers' four basic rights are (Estes, 1971);

1. The right to safety,
2. The right to be informed,
3. The right to choose,
4. The right to be heard.

It has long been recognized that the aggregate behaviour of consumers can be understood as the result of economic and socio-psychological forces. Consumer behaviour is part of a larger process of interaction among consumers, advertising agencies, mass media, and other institutions, which are all functionally related to one another. Consumption behaviour is also central to understanding the structure and functioning of societies (Assad, 2007).

Consumption may be viewed in two ways. The first is concerned with satisfying the basic needs, and thus in this sense it can be regarded as "natural" and "legitimate"; although it is a mundane matter, not related to other-worldly activity. In the second perspective, consumption may be viewed as a matter of gratifying desires and wants through luxury and unnecessary services and goods, that is, consumerism. The first sense can be accepted within most religious boundaries, but the second form of consumption appears far removed from religion's serious and significant messages (Godazgar, 2007).

Consumerism is a protest of consumers against unfair business practices and business injustices. It aims to remove those injustices, and eliminate unfair marketing practices (Ismail and Panni, 2008). Various authors have addressed the issues of consumerism, consumer dis/satisfaction, and complaining behaviour with varying degrees of generality and orientation. At the micro level, studies have explored consumer dissatisfaction with and complaints about specific products and services. At the macro level, national and cross-national studies have explored consumer attitudes towards marketing practices, consumerism and government regulations (Varadarajan and Thirunarayana, 1990).

SOCIAL IMPACT

People affect each other in many different ways. They are influenced by the behaviour, performances, opinions, attitudes, and feelings of other people. These influences may be positive or negative for us, and are collectively called "social impact" (Lee and Lee, 2014, p. 43). The effects of other people are defined as social impact and this concept are originated in social psychology area. Social impact theory, which was first formulated by Latané (1981) and has been widely used in social science research (Argo, Dahl, & Machanda, 2005; Harton, Green, & Jackson, 1998). The theory was developed as a metatheoretical framework for modelling situations where beliefs, attributes or behaviours of an individual are influenced by those others around him/her (Nettle, 1999, pp. 100-101).

Latané (1981 , p. 343) defines social impact as any of the great variety of changes in psychological states and subjective feelings, values and behaviour, that occur in an individual, human or animal, as a result of the real, implied, or imagined presence or actions of other individuals. Social impact theory is a broad theory, with specific predictions, about the effect, or influence, of social actors on individuals and groups (Latané & Nida, 1980).

The core tenet of the social impact theory is that three "social forces" account for a great variety of changes in a target's physiological states and subjective feelings, emotions and behaviours, as a result of the real, implied, or imagined presence or actions of other individuals (Miao, 2008, p. 12). Latané (1981) states these three forces as the strength (S), immediacy (I), and number (N). Social impact is a function of these factors and the relationship between these three components is expressed accordingly as I = f(SIN), where "I" stands for impact (Colon, 1997, p. 13).

Strength refers to the power or social status of the source of influence (Sedikides & Jackson, 1990). It means the capability, salience, or authority of a given informant in relation to the target. Strength is indicated by the source's economic status, former relationship with the other party, job, or anticipated power, all of which are normally, communicated in person in social impact theory (Latané, 1981). Strength is usually determined by the source's status, age, relationship, or possible future power over the target (Colon, 1997, p. 13).

Immediacy refers to the closeness in space or time and absence of intervening barriers or filters (Latané & Nida, 1980, p.7). Sedikides and Jackson (1990) note that immediacy can be either the physical or psychological distance. There is more social impact when higher status individuals are the source, when the action is more immediate, and when there are a greater number of sources (Zhang, 2011, p. 8). If the source's power increases (Jackson and Latané, 1981), the degree of immediacy to the target person also increases (Basset and Latané, 1976). Social impact theory in the empirical research focuses on the impact of the existence of others on personal reactions and behaviours (Lee and Lee, 2014, p. 43).

Number of the source refers to the number of individuals present who constitute the source of influence (Latané, 1981). According to social impact theory, the first source will have the strongest effect on the target and each subsequent source will increase impact (Sedikides & Jackson, 1990). Each subsequent source should have some impact. Each subsequent individual providing the same information should have diminishing effects, however, as the information is no longer novel and agreement has been established. (Djurdjevic, 2013, p. 34)

Latané (1981 , p. 355) defines social impact theory as a general theory that draws on basic laws, predicts too many domains and encompasses a variety of processes. It is also specific in the sense that it is quantifiable, deals with parametric variations, and makes precise predictions about observable aspects or the real world. The theory is falsifiable and useful which can provide a foundation for the development of many areas of social sciences.

According to Latané (1981, p. 355), social impact theory has also two shortcomings. The model views people as passive recipients of social impact and not so active seekers. Also, the model is static and does not have a needed dynamic aspect. Social impact theory was not intended to explain the underlying mechanisms of social influence (Jackson, 1986). Rather, it predicts the magnitude of influence and is most useful when combined with other theories that explicate the mechanisms underlying social influence (Latané & Nida, 1980).

CONSUMER BOYCOTTS

Opposition behaviour can range from verbal complaints to negative word of mouth or even protest action (Claudy, 2011). Consumer boycotts are the structural form of "a vote in the marketplace" as the weapon of resistance (Penaloza and Price, 1993, p. 124) however they are only minimal forms of opposition compared to a more massive rebellion against the consumer society (Roux, 2007).

"A consumer boycott was defined as an attempt by one or more parties to achieve certain objectives by urging individual consumers to refrain from making selected purchases in the marketplace" (Friedman, 1985, pp. 97-98). A review of past literature provides a variety of definitions of boycotts. Garreth (1987) defines a boycott as "a concerted refusal to do business with a particular person or business to obtain concessions or to express displeasure". John and Klein (2003) define a boycott as "a tactic to influence the behaviour of a firm (or other institution) by withholding purchase of their products." Yüksel and Mryteza (2009, p. 249) define consumer boycotts "as the collective action of foregoing or withholding consumption in response to perceived wrongdoing." What is common across these definitions is the fact that boycotts are a form of anti-consumption behaviour, typically a planned collective action by a consumer community in order to express displeasure or achieve specific objectives (Al-Shebil, Rasheed and Al-Shammari, 2011).

The boycott as a civil disobedience tool is used to protest not only unethical behaviours, but also discourage businesses from marketing to certain populations and from giving employees of that group recognition (Baxter, 2007). They are an extreme case of a broader category of consumer behaviour in which social and ethical issues, such as environmentalism, influence purchase decisions. Sen, Gürhan-Canlı and Morwitz (2001) conceptualize boycotts as social dilemmas, wherein a consumer chooses between the individual benefit of consumption and the wish of a collective to refrain from consumption so that all receive the shared benefits of a successful boycott (Klein, Smith and John, 2004). Boycotting can lead to a loss in sales, and damage to corporate reputation and the brand image.

The history of boycotts comes from political science. Authors in that field have categorized them in the context of nonviolent direct action. The term is derived from an 1880 protest by Irish peasants. When their landlord, Captain Charles Boycott, deprived them of wages and evicted them from their land, the peasants mobilized all the workers in the area to refuse to do any kind of business with him (Gelb, 1995).

There are some similar concepts like boycott such as divestment and embargo. Boycotts and divestment both involve a "concerted refusal to do business." However, a boycott is the refusal to conduct marketing transactions with a target whereas divestment is the cessation of financial investment in a target. Additionally, while an embargo is mandated by a governmental decree that people must refuse to deal with another party, organizers of a boycott may use only social pressure but not any form of legal obligation to encourage the participation.

A boycott involves an organized group effort to force a target to modify its policies. Hence, a boycott may well be defined more specifically as the concerted, but non-mandatory, refusal by a group of actors to conduct marketing transactions with one or more other actors for the purpose of communicating displeasure with certain target policies and attempting to coerce the target to modify those policies (Garrett, 1987).

BOYCOTT TYPES

Boycotts are of two basic types; marketing policy boycotts which aim to change the boycott target's marketing practices such as lowering price, and political boycotts which attempt to coerce their targets toward specific ethical or socially responsible actions (Sen, Gürhan-Canlı and Morwitz, 2001).

Friedman identifies two main purposes for boycotts: instrumental and expressive. An instrumental boycott aims to coerce the target to change a disputed policy. Its goals are precise and quantifiable, such as forcing down the price of a particular product. Expressive boycotts are characterized by a vague statement of goals and may simply vent the frustrations of the protesting group (Ettenson and Klein, 2005). Expressive boycotts are a more generalized form of protests which communicate the consumers' displeasure with the actions of the target. They aimed at protecting consumers from potential health and safety risks or defending minorities (Cisse-Depardon and N'Goala, 2009).

The target of a boycott can be either directly or indirectly related to the offending party. In a direct boycott target, consumers find the policies of a particular firm objectionable. In this case, the firm and its managers have direct control over policies. In an indirect boycott, the targeted firm serves as a surrogate for the party whose actions are objectionable. Consumers in this situation manifest their social activism by rejecting goods from firms that are perceived to be associated with the offending party (Ettenson and Klein, 2005).

International boycotts are described as primary, secondary and tertiary as the function of the remoteness of behaviour sought from the boycotting countries towards the target country. A primary international boycott is the one in which a country forbids its nationals to trade with another country. Under a secondary boycott, firms that trade with the target country are barred from trade with the boycotting country and its nationals, in which a "blacklist" is maintained of firms barred from trade. A tertiary boycott is a variation of the secondary boycott in which firms that are not connected with the target country are blacklisted for dealing with other blacklisted firms. The most aggressive among the Arab boycotting countries is the one which bars trade with firms whose only connection is through a blacklisted component in one of its products (Reingold and Lansing, 1994). The most well-known international boycott is the Arab economic boycott. Following the establishment of Israel, the Arab League banned all commercial and financial transactions between Israel and the Arab states. In 1951, the Arab League set up a central boycott office (CBO) in Damascus, Syria, with branches in member states to administer the boycott (Fershtman and Gandal, 1998). Trade was banned with those foreign companies that had offices or branches in Israel. Three levels of boycott activities were delineated (Reingold and Lansing, 1994):

1. **Primary:** Arab countries are prohibited from doing business with Israel.
2. **Secondary:** Non-Arab businesses anywhere in the world are subject to blacklisting if they trade with Israel.
3. **Tertiary:** Business dealing with blacklisted firms is themselves blacklisted regardless of any economic relationship with Israel.

Persian Gulf countries stopped enforcing the boycott following the Middle East Peace Talks in Madrid in 1991. On October 1, 1994, the Gulf Cooperation Council officially announced that it would no longer enforce the secondary and tertiary boycotts (Fershtman and Gandal, 1998).

Consumer "buycotts" are specific types of boycotts and present the flip side of consumer boycotts. Instead of punishing companies, buycotts are used to reward companies for actions that are consistent with their own goals by inducing consumers to purchase products and services of selected target companies. A buycott call may be direct or indirect. A direct call would take the form of a public announcement requesting consumers to purchase one or more products or services. An indirect call could take several forms such as consisting of published lists or seals of approval that identify available products, services, and/or retail firms being recommended to consumers. Buycotts can also be classified as beneficiary buycotts and conscience buycotts (Friedman, 1996).

Boycott Effectiveness

Effectiveness of a boycott should be measured as the achieved change in the target's disputed policies. Three variables are posited as determinants of the effectiveness of a boycott. These are economic pressure, image pressure and policy commitment (Garrett, 1987).

1. **Economic Pressure:** As marketing exchange partners, including consumers, suppliers, and/or distributors, refuse to interact with a target, the target may suffer from economic loss to some extent, especially if these exchange partners cannot be easily replaced.
2. **Image Pressure:** the announcement of a boycott against an organization may create undesirable publicity for the target, whether or not the agents' charges are justified.
3. **Policy Commitment:** Policy commitment is the level of resistance that the target decides to adopt, at the outset of the boycott, in response to the agents' coercive efforts to modify its policies.

Marketers will benefit from a fuller exploration of the boycott phenomenon for a number of reasons. First, the use of boycotts as a coercive marketplace tactic is already extensive and is expected to increase (Gelb, 1995; Sen, Gürhan-Canlı and Morwitz, 2001). Concurrently, many consumers are seeking products from firms that advocate particular positions on social and political issues. Another motivation for studying consumer boycotts involves the serious threat they pose to the firm's ongoing marketing activities. In addition to a direct negative effect on sales the boycotted firm faces other potentially debilitating consequences. Boycotts severely disrupt the planning, implementation and analysis of the firm's current and routine marketing activities. This disruption often stems from management uncertainty as to how to react when faced with a protest (Ettenson and Klein, 2005). The literature on consumer boycotts consists of three areas of research:

1. The frequency, causes, and goals of boycotts;
2. The consequences of boycotts; and
3. The motivations of participating individuals (Hoffman and Müller, 2009).

Boycotts have become an unavoidable aspect of the business environment especially for international companies due to religious or ideological reasons. Consumer boycotts can turn into potent economic weapons in the hands of political activists. They cause real financial harm to the targeted companies easily and virtually at almost no cost for boycotters (Al-Shebil, Rasheed and Al-Shammari, 2011). In today's marketplace, companies are more and more judged by consumers according to their being environmentally and/or ethically responsible (Bauer et al, 2008).

There are several aspects to boycott intensity such as the size, duration and aggressiveness. Size refers to how many people are boycotting the brand or product. Duration is about how long it would likely to continue. Finally, aggressiveness reflects violent acts or attacks that are likely to be conducted against the outlets or offices of the foreign firm (Al-Shebil, Rasheed and Al-Shammari, 2011).

There are strong relationship between boycott intensity and brand-country association. Some brands are highly associated with its country thus can become a primary target for some boycotts. Although boycotts are targeted against a specific company or companies from a specific country, very often there are spillover effects. It occurs because of misperceptions about the national identity of a product (Al-Shebil, Rasheed and Al-Shammari, 2011).

The substitutes provide an alternative to the customers who still want to satisfy their need for the boycotted brand. Many of these substitutes may have previously had only small market shares. Some may even be completely new, exploiting the window of opportunity created by the boycott. The Ülker group in Turkey launched a product named Cola Turka immediately after the US invasion of Iraq and within a few months, they managed to capture a 10% market share by solely tapping into the general anti-American political sentiment (Al-Shebil, Rasheed and Al-Shammari, 2011). The religious orientations of consumers are not the only factors shaping their decision to boycott; their political inclinations seem to affect their participation decision as well (Farah and Newman, 2009).

BOYCOTT PARTICIPATION

Although there has been an increased interest in consumer boycotts, the factors that motivate individual boycott decisions remain largely unexplored (Hoffmann and Müller, 2009). This lack of research is unfortunate because the number of boycotts and the number of consumers participating in them have been increasing (Sen, Gürhan-Canlı and Morwitz, 2001) from 18% in 1992 to almost 67% in 2005 in the U.S. alone. This increase is partially attributed to the widespread adoption of the Internet which has become an inexpensive and quick way of educating millions of consumers about boycotts and has helped to facilitate the pervasiveness and power of boycotts (Braunsberger and Buckler, 2011).

The success or failure of the protest largely depends on an individual's willingness to participate. Consumers may have different motivations for boycott participation. Also, not all boycotts are organization based. An individual's decision to participate in a boycott may be a form of protest that is independent of any direct affiliation with a formal organization (Ettenson and Klein, 2005). Free riding is a major cause of boycott failures. A crucial issue concerning boycott successes is the lack of coordination. Individual consumers only consider the gain from a boycott success if they participate (Delacote, 2009). However, there are some costs associated with boycotting that impact consumer willingness to participate. The higher a potential boycotter considers these costs to be, the less likely s/he is to participate (Klein, Smith and John, 2004). Consumers seem more likely to participate in a boycott if the targeted product has satisfactory substitutes (Braunsberger and Buckler, 2011).

The actions of a single consumer are generally imperceptible to a firm, and so it is improbable that an individual boycotter truly expects to influence the behaviour of the firm s/he targets. Yet boycotts, which are called on a regular basis, often have a large number of participants, and sometimes succeed in changing the behaviour of firms (John and Klein, 2003). The boycotts usually target a surrogate and not the "real" target that the boycotters are trying to affect and harm. That is, firms from a country represent a softer target than the government itself against whom the boycotters have grievances. Boycotts seem to be an effective tool to attract public attention to an issue. Furthermore, the low cost of activating a consumer boycott combined with its negative economic consequences for the affected firms make it a potent political tool (Al-Shebil, Rasheed and Al-Shammari, 2011).

Consumers might participate in a boycott simply to express their anger about the egregious behaviour. Anger can be a more powerful boycott motivation than the belief that a boycott can coerce the target to change its policies and behaviours (Ettenson and Klein, 2005) as demonstrated by the Muslim boycott of Danish companies (Braunsberger and Buckler, 2011). Consumer activists are motivated to boycott for many reasons, including expressing outrage, to maintain self-esteem, and to enhance their identity and sense of belonging (Farah and Newman, 2009). Foremost among these reasons is the desire to express a collective religious conservative identity (Swimberghe, Flurry and Parker, 2011).

Most of these studies rely on a cost-benefit approach and socio-psychological theories. The free riding effect reduces an individual's motivation to actively take part in a boycott. Consequently, rational cost-benefit calculations cannot fully explain the boycott decision. To overcome this limitation, researchers integrate psychological theories into research in this field. The content analysis of Kozinets and Handelman (1998) reveals that individuals do not boycott merely to achieve a collective effect. Consumers also perceive boycotting as a means of moral self-actualization, or as an attempt to express them emotionally. In the most sophisticated study to date, Klein, Smith and John (2004) combine cost-benefit assumptions with the socio-psychological foundations of boycott participation in order to examine boycotting motives. Klein, Smith and John (2004) also propose an "awareness-egregiousness-boycott" model (AEB). Hence, consumers first need to be aware of a company's controversial behaviour. The perceived egregiousness of the behaviour is the main driver of boycott participation. Several variables moderate the relationship between the perception of the company and the decision to boycott. Two factors tending to decrease motivation are the individual cost of constrained consumption and the concern that a boycott may prompt the company to engage in even more antisocial actions. Variables that promote boycott participation include the individual consumer's desire to make a difference and the expected degree of self-enhancement (Hoffman and Müller, 2009).

Garrett (1987, p. 48) found six factors as the determinants of boycott participation, according to these factors potential participants;

1. Cannot support a boycott if they are unaware of the target of the boycott.
2. With certain values are, in general, more likely to participate in any boycott.
3. Support only those boycotts whose goals are consistent with their attitudes.
4. Will not join a boycott if their personal cost to participate is high.
5. Are more likely to join the boycott, if the social pressure to support a boycott is high.
6. Are more likely to support a boycott that is promoted by a highly credible leader.

Participating in a boycott called for by a group which one identifies with also helps to preserve one's sense of belonging. Research suggests that people's consumption decisions are strongly influenced by their reference groups. It is expected to affect consumers' boycotting decisions (Sen, Gürhan-Canlı and Morwitz, 2001). In addition to perceived social pressure, one's sense of moral obligation can be a significant boycotting motivator (Farah and Newman, 2009). "The urging of a boycott typically comes from a nongovernmental organization (NGO) that is protesting corporate practices (Klein, Smith and John, 2004).

Calls for a boycott can have one of three effects. Consumers can honour the boycott, leading to a decline in sales of the product being boycotted. They can ignore the boycott, leading to no change in sales. Or, expressing opposition to the goals of the boycott, they can increase their purchases, leading to increases in sales (Ashenfelter, Ciccarella and Shatz, 2007). Any commercial group can call for a boycott. Groups have been more successful in calling for and executing boycotts than individuals because there is strength in numbers (Murtagh and Lukehart, 1994).

With the spread of the Internet (forums, buzz marketing, brand communities, etc), calls for boycotts can be organized, broadcast and disseminated more rapidly and easily. As a result, companies can experience a significant deterioration of their image, a loss of marketing efficiency and a decline in their market share (Cisse-Depardon and N'Goala, 2009).

CONCLUSION

Consumerism is defined as protecting the consumers, but some authors describe it as consumer activism, which, then, can be thought of as the self-protection of consumers from unethical activities. Since consumerism includes an activism, we can talk about people and group behaviour. In a group, all members cannot have an equal power to influence others. People have different motivations to be affected by others. The theory of social impact, which is originated from social psychology area, analyzes these effects and has three important factors that determine effects of people on other people's behaviours. Although social impact is a concept that is frequently used in psychology, recently its usage became more common in different disciplines. Unfortunately, marketing area could not take advantage of this theory yet, although it has a sub-discipline which is called consumer behaviour. One of the most important targets of marketing is understand and analyse behaviours of consumers. Sometimes their behaviours can show contradictions to marketing activities of some companies. This anti-buying behaviour of consumers is called as boycotts.

In today's economy, consumers' primary weapon is their purchasing power. If they wish to make a change in any of the activities of a particular company, they resort to this particular weapon and this process is called as boycott. The size of the impact of a particular boycott mostly depends on how well it is organized. Every consumer has different motivation for participating in boycotts provided that they are aware of boycotts. Today, thanks to the Internet and social media, calling for a boycott is relatively easier, faster and almost at no cost. In every country, from time to time, people are called to boycott some firms for a different set of reasons based on political, religious or environmental concerns. Many websites provide information as to why the target company should be boycotted. However, some boycott callings might be based on misinformation; while some of them can be organized mistakenly (i.e. spillover effect), with some of them organized on purpose. Internet is an uncontrollable environment, where it is almost impossible to find out who shared any misleading information in the first place. That is to say, she/he might well be one of the firm's competitors, merely an angry consumer, or just a resentful employee. The important point which is worthy of note here is that, an otherwise protective weapon for consumers may be used beyond its purpose and in return, an economic damage is incurred by a company which is normally not guilty of anything at all.

In this chapter consumer boycotts are analyzed in details. Motivations underlying participation to consumer boycotts and components of social impact theory are closely related. The duration of boycotts and immediacy factor, number of participants and number of the source, and finally power of boycott leaders and strength factor show us the importance of social impact theory in many marketing activities. Consumer boycotts can be categorized as a consumerism activity that aims to protect consumers from illegal or unfair marketing activities. Social impact is a tool that directly affects all consumer activities including consumer boycotts.

REFERENCES

Al-Shebil, S., Rasheed, A., & Al-Shammari, H. (2011). Coping with boycotts: An analysis and framework. *Journal of Management & Organization*, *17*(03), 383–397. doi:10.1017/S183336720000153X

Argo, J. J., Dahl, D. W., & Machanda, R. V. (2005). The influence of a mere social presence in a retail context. *The Journal of Consumer Research*, *32*(2), 207–212. doi:10.1086/432230

Ashenfelter, O., Ciccarella, S., & Shatz, H. J. (2007). French wine and the U.S. boycott of 2003: Does politics really affect commerce? *Journal of Wine Economics*, *2*(1), 55–74. doi:10.1017/S1931436100000298

Assad, S.W. (2007). The rise of consumerism in Saudi Arabian society. *International Journal of Commerce & Management*, 17(1/2), 73-104.

Basset, R. L., & Latane, B. (1976). Social Influences and News Stories. Paper presented at American Psychological Association, Washington DC.

Bauer, H.H., Albrect C.M, Bryant M.D., & Haber T.E. (2008). The consumer strikes back: Assessing antecedents to boycott participation. *American Marketing Association,* Winter, 350-351.

Baxter, S. (2007). Is it worth the cost? Marketing to negatively perceived consumer groups. *Global Journal of Business Research*, *1*(1), 87–96.

Bostan, I., Burciu, A., & Grosu, V. (2010). The consumerism and consumer protection policies in the European Community. *Theoretical and Applied Economics*, *17*(4), 19–34.

Braunsberger, K., & Buckler, B. (2011). What motivates consumers to participate in boycotts: Lessons from the ongoing Canadian seafood boycott. *Journal of Business Research*, *64*(1), 96–102. doi:10.1016/j.jbusres.2009.12.008

Brunner, F. M. (1996). *A Psychological rendering of consumerism* [Unpublished Doctorate Thesis]. Pacifica Graduate Institute.

Cissé-Depardon, K., & NGoala, G. (2009). The effects of satisfaction, trust and brand commitment on consumers decision to boycott[English Edition]. *Recherche et Applications en Marketing*, *24*, 43–66. doi:10.1177/076737010902400103

Claudy, M. (2011). *An empirical investigation of consumer resistance to green product innovation* [Unpublished Doctoral Thesis]. Dublin Institute of Technology.

Colon, R. M. (1997). *Causal Relationships of Familial Influence and Adolescents' Attitude toward Substance Use in the Theory of Planned Behavior: A Social Impact Model* [Unpublished PhD Thesis]. University of Houston.

Delacote, P. (2009). On the sources of consumer boycotts ineffectiveness. *Journal of Environment & Development*, *18*(3), 306–322. doi:10.1177/1070496509338849

Djurdjevic, E. (2013). *The Effects of Social Contextual Factors on Rater Motivation and Performance Ratings* [Unpublished PhD Thesis]. University of Arkansas.

Estes, R. M. (1971). Consumerism & Business. *California Management Review*, *14*(2), 5–11. doi:10.2307/41164327

Ettenson, R., & Klein, J. G. (2005). The fallout from French nuclear testing in the South Pacific: A longitudinal study of consumer boycotts. *International Marketing Review*, *22*(2), 199–224. doi:10.1108/02651330510593278

Farah, M. F., & Newman, A. J. (2009). Exploring consumer boycott intelligence using a socio -cognitive approach. *Journal of Business Research*.

Fershtman, C., & Gandal, N. (1998). The effect of the Arab boycott on Israel: The automobile market. *The Rand Journal of Economics*, *29*(1), 193–214. doi:10.2307/2555822

Friedman, M. (1985). Consumer boycotts in the United States, 1970-1980: Contemporary events in historical perspective. *The Journal of Consumer Affairs*, 19(1), 96-117.

Friedman, M. (1996). A positive approach to organized consumer action: The buycott as an alternative to the boycott. *Journal of Consumer Policy*, *19*(4), 439–451. doi:10.1007/BF00411502

Garrett, D. (1987). The effectiveness of marketing policy boycotts: Environmental opposition to marketing. *Journal of Marketing*, *51*(April), 46–57. doi:10.2307/1251128

Gelb, B. D. (1995). More boycotts ahead? Some implications. *Business Horizons*, *38*(2), 70–77. doi:10.1016/0007-6813(95)90058-6

Godazgar, H. (2007). Islam versus consumerism and postmodernism in the context of Iran. *Social Compass*, *54*(3), 389–418. doi:10.1177/0037768607080835

Harton, H. C., Green, L. R., Jackson, C., & Latane, B. (1998). Demonstrating dynamic social impact: Consolidation, clustering, correlation and (sometimes) the correct answer. *Teaching of Psychology*, *25*(1), 31–35. doi:10.1207/s15328023top2501_9

Hoffman, S., & Müller, S. (2009). Consumer boycotts due to factory relocation. *Journal of Business Research*, *62*(2), 239–247. doi:10.1016/j.jbusres.2008.01.031

Ismail, H. B., & Panni, M. F. A. K. (2008). Consumer perceptions on the consumerism issues and its influence on their purchasing behaviour: A view from Malaysian food industry. *Journal of Legal. Ethical and Regulatory Issues*, *11*(1), 43–64.

Jackson, J. M. (1986). In defense of social impact theory: Comment on Mullen. *Journal of Personality and Social Psychology*, *50*(3), 511–513. doi:10.1037/0022-3514.50.3.511

Jackson, J. M., & Latane, B. (1981). Strength and Number of Solicitors and the Urge Toward Alturism. *Personality and Social Psychology Bulletin*, *7*(3), 414–422. doi:10.1177/014616728173009

John, A., & Klein, J. (2003). The boycott puzzle: Consumer motivations for purchase sacrifice. *Management Science*, *49*(9), 1196–1209. doi:10.1287/mnsc.49.9.1196.16569

Jones, P., Hillier, D., Comfort, D., & Eastwood, I. (2005). Sustainable retailing and consumerism. *Management Research News*, *28*(1), 34–44. doi:10.1108/01409170510784760

Klein, J. G., Smith, N. C., & John, A. (2004). Why we boycott: Consumer motivations for boycott participation. *Journal of Marketing*, *68*(3), 92–109. doi:10.1509/jmkg.68.3.92.34770

Kozinets, R. V., & Handelman, J. (1998). Ensouling consumption: A netnographic exploration of the meaning of boycotting behaviour. Advances in Consumer Research, 25, 475-480.

Latane, B. (1981). The Psychology of Social Impact. *The American Psychologist*, *36*(4), 343–356. doi:10.1037/0003-066X.36.4.343

Latane, B., & Nida, S. (1980). Social impact theory and group influence: A social engineering perspective. In P.B. Paulus (Ed.), Psychology of group influence (pp. 3-34).

Lee, H. S., & Lee, H. J. (2014). Factors Influencing Online Trust. *Academy of Marketing Studies Journal*, *18*(1), 41–50.

Miao, L. (2008). *Consumers' Emotional Responses to Service Encounters: The Influence of Other Consumers* [Unpublished PhD Thesis]. The Pennsylvania State University.

Mirchevska, T. P., & Markova, S. (2011). Emergence of the social consumer – The impact of personalization, localization and social collaboration on consumerism. *Annals of the University of Petrosani Economics*, *11*(3), 229–236.

Murtagh, C., & Lukehart, C. (1994). *Boycott organizer's guide*. Retrieved from http://www.greenamerica.org/PDF/GuideBoycottOrganizers.pdf

Nettle, D. (1999). Using Social Impact Theory to simulate language change. *Lingua*, *108*(2-3), 95–117. doi:10.1016/S0024-3841(98)00046-1

Orel, F. D., & Zeren, D. (2009). Pazarlama ve tüketici yandaşlığı anlayışına yönelik tüketici tutumları: Boylamsal bir çalışma. *Finans Politik & Ekonomik Yorumlar*, *46*(536), 65–78.

Penaloza, L., & Price, L. L. (1993). Consumer resistance: A conceptual overview. *Advances in Consumer Research. Association for Consumer Research (U. S.)*, *20*, 123–128.

Reingold, R. N., & Lansing, P. (1994). An ethical analysis of Japans response to the Arab boycott of Israel. *Business Ethics Quarterly*, *4*(3), 335–353. doi:10.2307/3857451

Roux, D. (2007). Consumer resistance: Proposal for an integrative framework. *Recherche et Applications en Marketing*, *22*(4), 59–79. doi:10.1177/076737010702200403

Sedikides, C., & Jackson, J. M. (1990). Social impact theory: A field test of source strength, source immediacy and number of targets. *Basic and Applied Social Psychology*, *11*(3), 273–281. doi:10.1207/s15324834basp1103_4

Sen, S., Gürhan-Canlı, Z., & Morwitz, V. (2001). Withholding consumption: A social dilemma perspective on consumer boycotts. *The Journal of Consumer Research*, *28*(3), 399–417. doi:10.1086/323729

Swimberghe, K., Flurry, L. A., & Parker, J. M. (2011). Consumer religiosity: Consequences for consumer activism in the United States. *Journal of Business Ethics*, *103*(3), 453–467. doi:10.1007/s10551-011-0873-2

Varadarajan, P. R., & Thirunarayana, P. N. (1990). Consumers attitudes towards marketing practices, consumerism and government regulations: Cross-national perspectives. *European Journal of Marketing*, *24*(6), 6–23. doi:10.1108/03090569010137934

Yüksel, U., & Mryteza, V. (2009). An evaluation of strategic responses to consumer boycotts. *Journal of Business Research*, *62*(2), 248–259. doi:10.1016/j.jbusres.2008.01.032

Zhang, X. (2011). *Essays on Social Influence in Shopper Marketing* [Unpublished PhD Thesis]. Indiana University Kelley School of Business.

KEY TERMS AND DEFINITIONS

Boycott Effectiveness: A measurement about size and duration of consumer boycotts.
Boycotts: Rewarding companies through buying its products, opposite of boycotts.
Consumer Boycotts: Consumers' preferences about not buying a product, brand etc.
Consumerism: Protecting consumers themselves from unethical marketing activities.
Immediacy: The closeness in space or time and absence of intervening barriers or filters.
Social Impact: The effects of people on other people's attitudes and behaviours.
Strength: The power or social status of the source of influence.

Chapter 3
Fuel Efficient Vehicles:
The Role of Social Marketing

Lisa Watson
University of Regina, Canada

Anne M. Lavack
Thompson Rivers University, Canada

ABSTRACT

Consumers have been slow to switch to more fuel efficient vehicles, in spite of the threat of a future global shortage of fossil fuels. To understand consumer reluctance to adopt hybrid automotive technology, this chapter begins by reviewing consumer decision-making with regard to consumer automotive purchases. We examine the market for fuel efficient vehicles (FEVs) and alternate fuel vehicles (AFVs), including a discussion of consumer willingness to trade personal comfort in order to buy more fuel efficient vehicles, and consumer price sensitivity with regard to purchasing higher-priced alternative fuel vehicles including hybrid-electric vehicles. We discuss the tenuous link between environmental attitudes and behavior, and outline the role of social marketing in creating behavior change relating to automotive purchase decisions.

INTRODUCTION

The number of automobiles in the world has increased from approximately 127 million in 1960 to over 1.1 billion in 2013 (Davis, Diegel, & Boundy, 2015). Around the globe, the growing reliance on the automobile as a mode of personal transportation has led to enormous consumption of gasoline, a non-renewable resource. Gasoline consumption could be substantially reduced if more drivers would switch to fuel efficient vehicles (FEVs) or alternate fuel vehicles (AFVs). However, drivers in most countries have been very slow to adopt these technologies. A pattern of worldwide declining gasoline prices in 2015 (Economist, 2016) has only exacerbated the situation, leaving most drivers with less financial incentive to switch to fuel efficient vehicles.

DOI: 10.4018/978-1-5225-2139-6.ch003

In spite of declining gasoline prices in 2015, global sales of hybrid and electric cars rose by 15% in 2015, with the Asia-Pacific region accounting for over 60% of sales (MarketLine, 2015). The number of alternative fuel vehicles in the United States has risen from under 250,000 in 1995 to almost 1.2 million in 2011, an increase of approximately 10% per annum (Davis et al., 2015). While these figures look promising, they equate to less than 1% of all vehicles in the United States, so there is substantial room for growth in the AFV sector. This leads to a key question: How can we encourage consumers to switch from conventional automobiles and instead purchase FEVs and AFVs?

Through a review of the recent literature on how consumers make vehicle purchasing decisions, this chapter will illustrate consumer attitudes and choices related to fuel efficiency. Consumer attitudes and behaviors toward the environment will also be reviewed. Gaining insight into consumer decision processes with regard to selecting their motor vehicles will provide the necessary background for developing effective social marketing campaigns, which can convince consumers to purchase fuel efficient vehicles in the future.

The chapter begins by reviewing consumer decision-making with regard to consumer automotive purchases. We examine the market for FEVs and AFVs. We discuss the tenuous link between environmental attitudes and behavior, and outline the role of social marketing in creating behavior change relating to automotive purchase decisions. The chapter concludes by making recommendations for developing future social marketing campaigns.

AUTOMOTIVE PURCHASE DECISION-MAKING

The research literature indicates that, to date, there has been only a moderate willingness on the part of consumers to purchase vehicles that are more fuel efficient (DEFRA, 2008). In general, consumers do not give a great deal of thought to the issue of fuel efficiency when making a vehicle purchase, or it is not their primary issue of concern. There are several possible reasons for this relative lack of concern about fuel efficiency, including issues relating to convenience, self-identity, and unwillingness to pay higher initial costs for AFVs.

Consumers also seem to have relatively low levels of awareness with regard to the amount of fuel they consume, and what their fuel costs are over time (Turrentine, Kurani, & Heffner, 2007). This suggests that consumers may have little understanding of the potential long-range impact that a more fuel efficient vehicle would have on their fuel costs and energy consumption. As well, consumers seem to consistently underestimate their annual driving mileage by approximately 2,000 miles per year, on average, which would also contribute to an underestimation of the amount of fuel consumed annually (Kavalec, 1999).

There are two basic categories of vehicle that consumers could consider if they were interested in reducing fuel consumption. The first category consists of conventional fuel efficient vehicles (FEVs), which are fuel efficient by virtue of being smaller and lighter, and which use conventional gasoline or diesel fuel. The second category, alternate fuel vehicles (AFVs), is largely comprised of Hybrid Electric Vehicles (HEVs), which do not need to be plugged in, and Electric Vehicles (EVs) and Plug-in Hybrid Electric Vehicles (PHEVs), which do need to be plugged in (Ahmadi et al., 2015). While AFVs could also be thought of as including fuel options such as liquid petroleum gas, propane, and compressed natural gas (CNG), or bio-fuel options such as methanol and ethanol, these types of alternative fuel options in North America are most commonly used for commercial vehicles or fleet vehicles. Therefore our discussion of AFVs in the consumer context will focus only on the three types of electric-based vehicles (HEVs, EVs, and PHEVs). Because the literature suggests that the consumer decision-making processes for conventional vehicles and AFVs differ, these two categories will be addressed separately here.

Conventional Fuel Efficient Vehicles

When consumers are intending to purchase a conventional vehicle, the factors which are a significant influence on vehicle choice are price, size, acceleration, and operating cost, including both maintenance costs and fuel costs (Garcia & Balbaky, 2006). A study by Decima Research (2004) found that 80% believe fuel efficiency is an important attribute when making new vehicle decisions. Consistent with these findings are reports that annual purchasing volume in the U.S. van, SUV, and pick-up truck markets decreased by as much as 20% in total following years where there were significant gas price increases, while sales of more fuel efficient cars rose by 20% (West, 2007). This suggests that fuel efficiency is important to some consumers, but that for many consumers, other factors are more important, including initial vehicle price, comfort, and performance.

Garcia and Balbaky (2006) found that the consumer demographic attributes of gender, age, and income were statistically significant with regard to vehicle choice. Higher levels of age, education level, and income were all positively related to higher purchase price and larger size of vehicle chosen. Women were consistently more likely to choose smaller cars and minivans than men, who were more likely to choose larger vehicles and sport models. Younger consumers were more likely to drive smaller vehicles than their older counterparts; older consumers were more likely to choose larger, more luxurious vehicles. Older, more affluent consumers in an aging population are less concerned about vehicle operating costs than other demographic segments. This relationship between larger vehicles and affluence is also linked to the issue of status and the symbolism of vehicle ownership.

Choo and Mokhtarian (2002; 2004) have provided insight into how consumer attitudes and lifestyles affect vehicle choice, by incorporating both demographic and psychographic variables into their models. They found that some personality traits, along with a variety of psychographics (pro-environmental and pro-high density attitudes, status-seeking, workaholism, dislike of travel, travel distance), are all significant predictors of vehicle choice. In terms of personality traits, calm personalities are more likely to choose small cars, introverts tend to drive small cars or SUVs, and adventurers tend to prefer sports cars. In terms of psychographics, pro-environmental and pro-high density attitudes are more likely to lead to smaller car choice. Conversely, status-seeking and workaholism are positively related to choosing larger cars. Status seekers are more likely to choose luxury vehicles, sports cars, and SUVs. The effect of travel dislike on vehicle choice is moderated by travel distance. For many people, higher travel demands lead to more fuel efficient vehicle choice, but for those who dislike travel, higher travel demands lead to the selection of larger, more comfortable cars.

In general, less affluent consumers who are concerned about fuel efficiency will simply choose smaller conventional automobiles because of the lower upfront cost and low operating costs. More affluent upscale consumers will likely not be interested in these same types of fuel efficient small conventional vehicles, because these types of vehicles will not meet their status-seeking needs. Instead, upscale status-seeking individuals are likely to choose a relatively more expensive alternate fuel vehicle if they are seeking fuel efficiency or wishing to display attributes of environmental concern. These findings help to provide some initial insight into how lifestyle and other internal consumer influences affect the vehicle decision-making process.

Alternate Fuel Vehicles: EV and PHEV

The EV and PHEV categories both require access to plug-in recharging facilities, and generally have less public acceptance to date. This is primarily due to the limited range, time required for battery recharging, and the need for public charging facilities (Bailey, Miele, & Axsen, 2015; Graham-Rowe, et al., 2012; Rezvani, Jansson, & Bodin, 2015). However, it is important to note that the limitations of EV and PHEV ownership are overcome, to some extent, when individuals or households own multiple vehicles (Bilotkach & Mills, 2012). Owning an EV or PHEV as a second vehicle means that issues relating to range, charging time, and public charging infrastructure become less critical, because a conventional vehicle or hybrid vehicle is available as either the primary or back-up mode of transportation. As well, future technology may improve the range and reduce the charging time required for the EV and PHEV categories, which could lead to greater consumer acceptance (Haddadian, Khodayar, & Shahidehpour, 2015).

Government policy has played a significant role in determining the (limited) growth of EV / PHEV technologies, particularly in terms of the extent to which government provides or encourages the provision of public charging facilities (Bohnsack, Kolk, & Pinske, 2015). Bonges and Lusk (2016) have examined the issue of public charging facilities, and have suggested numerous ways that 'EV only' parking spots can be improved to ensure that they are used for short-term charging, rather than for all-day parking.

In understanding the energy efficiency of electric vehicles and plug-in hybrid-electric vehicles, it is important to note that these vehicles use electricity from the grid for all or part of their operation (Al-Alawi & Bradley, 2013a). In North America and other regions where most of the electricity production is hydro-electricity, this is an environmentally sound choice because hydro-electricity represents a renewable resource. However, it should be noted that in regions where coal is used to produce electricity, the resulting amount of CO_2 means that there is no net environmental benefit derived from EVs and PHEVs (Ajanovic, 2014).

Several demographic and behavioral variables are related to electric vehicle ownership, including education, gender, age, and travel distance. Women and those with college degrees were more likely to choose hybrid-electric and electric vehicles than other segments. For women, this choice preference seems to be linked to a lower concern with quick acceleration than men, since there is a common perception that hybrid-electric and electric vehicles do not accelerate as quickly. Older consumers in their 40s and 50s, who tend to have longer commutes and longer overall travel distances, value fuel availability more highly than other age segments, creating less desire for an electric vehicle (Potoglou & Kanaroglou, 2007). This is known as 'range anxiety,' which is a concern about the availability of fuel or recharging facilities for consumers who drive long distances (Daziano, 2013).

Alternate Fuel Vehicles: HEVs

In general, the perceived benefits of buying hybrid-electric vehicles include fuel efficiency and being environmentally friendly (Carley, Krause, Lane, & Graham, 2013; Li, et al., 2013). The main drawback of HEVs is considered to be the higher initial purchase price (Al-Alawi & Bradley, 2013b). Even among those who are environmentally conscious, the much higher initial purchase price is a major issue for many (Barker, et al., 2009; Krupa, et al., 2014; Larson, et al., 2014; Liu, 2014). According to one survey, less than half the population would be willing to pay more than a $2,000 premium for a hybrid-electric vehicle, while 30% of the population would be willing to pay only a $1,000-2,000 premium for a hybrid-electric vehicle, and 22% would not be willing to pay anything more (Decima, 2004). Were the cost and performance of a hybrid vehicle the same as a comparable conventional vehicle, virtually all consumers would be willing to purchase the hybrid vehicle (Choy & Prizzia, 2010).

It is useful to note that while the absolute resale price for a used hybrid-electric vehicle exceeds that of a comparable non-hybrid vehicle by as much as 30% (Gilmore & Lave, 2013), hybrid-electric vehicles in general tend to depreciate more quickly than their conventional vehicle counterparts (Majid & Russell, 2015). Among hybrid vehicles, hybrid models that share a brand name with a conventional model, such as the Toyota Camry, tend to depreciate more quickly than pure green brands, such as the Toyota Prius (Majid & Russell, 2015). However, the overall resale value for hybrid-electric vehicles tends to rise when gas prices are high, and fall when gas prices are lower (Gilmore & Lave, 2013).

The symbolism and social status associated with owning a hybrid-electric vehicle appear to play a major part in consumer motivation, particularly in the case of early adopters. Some of the symbolic meanings associated with hybrid vehicle ownership include ethics, concern for others, intelligence/awareness, and independence (Heffner, Turrentine, & Kurani, 2006). Because of the higher initial hybrid vehicle price, purchasing a hybrid vehicle makes a very public statement about one's personal commitment to environmental beliefs (Barth, Jugert, & Fritsche, 2016). As well, social context and social networks can play an important role in influencing consumer behavior toward choosing green technology (He, Wang, Chen, & Conzelmann, 2014).

In terms of HEV ownership, the Toyota Prius is the acknowledged market leader, accounting for more than half of the hybrid vehicles ever sold in the United States (Champniss, Wilson, & Macdonald, 2015). Sales of the Toyota Prius are seven times higher than its next competitor, a Honda hybrid. Much of Toyota's success can be attributed to the fact that the Prius is only sold as a hybrid model, and the appearance of the Prius is distinctive compared to Toyota's conventional models. For consumers who view themselves as being environmentally responsible, driving a Toyota Prius is a clear signal of their social identity (Champniss, Wilson, & Mcdonald, 2015) and their willingness to comply with peer group norms (Ozaki & Sevastyanova, 2011). Toyota Prius owners signal their environmental consciousness to others through their willingness to pay the higher price required for owning this type of hybrid vehicle (Delgado, Harriger, & Khanna, 2015).

Incentives for AFV Purchase

Consumers often do not understand the lifetime operating costs of HEVs or other types of AFVs (Dumortier, et al., 2015), and as a result they tend to demand an extremely short payback on the initial investment (Turrentine, Kurani, & Heffner, 2007). While this suggests a need for greater consumer education about the total cost of ownership (Hagman, et al., 2016), it also indicates that financial and other incentives for purchasing AFVs and reducing emissions need to be explored (Gallagher & Muehlegger, 2011).

Coninx (2004) estimates that instituting a 7% carbon tax on gasoline in the U.S. would be enough to fully fund the carbon offset of the CO^2 emissions caused by conventional vehicles, while simultaneously providing a financial disincentive to continue driving them. There is clear evidence that a substantially higher gasoline price can act as an incentive to purchase vehicles in the HEV, EV, or PHEV categories (Diamond, 2009). In some countries, higher fuel prices can prove to be more effective than government subsidies in encouraging the purchase of AFVs (Hsu, Li, & Lu, 2013).

Income tax rebates on AFV purchase and ownership have been utilized as incentives for reducing CO^2 emissions (Coninx, 2004; de Haan, et al., 2006). Depending on the size of the income tax rebate, the effective cost of the AFV could be reduced to a level equal to, or closer to, the cost of a conventional vehicle of the same model or size (Chandra, Gulati, & Kandlikar, 2010). However, this method suffers from a lack of proximity between the financial incentive and the purchase date, since purchasers must wait for annual tax filing to receive their rebate.

A more effective strategy is to provide cash discounts or cash rebates at the time of purchase, rather than income tax rebates (Beresteanu & Li, 2011). This puts the purchase incentive into the hands of the consumer immediately, rather than rewarding the consumer at a later date. In Norway, for example, EV owners are exempted from purchase tax and VAT (Bjerkan, Nørbech, & Nordtømme, 2016). In Ireland, those who purchase environmentally friendly cars are rewarded with lower car purchase tax rates, resulting in savings at the time of the vehicle purchase (Caulfield, Farrell, & McMahon, 2010). In general, the amount of the financial incentive must be relatively large in order to motivate purchase; incentives of less than $1,000 are generally insufficient to motivate this behavior (Jenn, Azevedo, & Ferreira, 2013).

California and many other jurisdictions now allow fuel efficient hybrid-electric vehicle owners to obtain special license plates or stickers, which enable them to use the less congested HOV (high occupancy vehicle) lane or bus lane, even when the vehicle has only one occupant (Khan & Kar, 2009; Shewmake & Jarvis, 2014). In Norway, EV owners are exempted from road tolling and provided with bus lane access (Bjerkan, Nørbech, & Nordtømme, 2016). HOV access or bus lane access can be a particularly important purchase incentive for some segments of the public who experience long commutes on congested freeways. The personal time savings gained by using an HOV lane with a hybrid or electric vehicle can be well worth the substantial financial premium paid for AFVs (Hackbarth & Madlener, 2013).

One study has predicted that ownership rates for the EV, HEV, and PHEV categories could increase to more than 30% of vehicles sold in the USA by the year 2050 (Ahmadi, et al., 2015). However, future adoption rates depend on a variety of factors, including gasoline prices, reductions in the costs of these types of vehicles, improvements in technology, and changes in consumer predispositions to adopt new technology (Al-Alawi & Bradley, 2013a).

A recent study divided the car-buying population into five categories, based on an interpretation of their predisposition to prefer EV, HEV, PHEV, or conventional vehicles (Axsen, Bailey, & Castro, 2015). Respondents were educated about the characteristics of EV, HEV, and PHEV, and were then asked to complete a 3-day driving and parking diary, along with measures of environmental concern, in order to gain insight into their readiness to adopt new vehicle technologies. Results indicated that while 23% of the population remained Conventional Vehicle oriented, 28% were HEV-leaning, 16% were HEV oriented, 25% were PHEV oriented, and 8% could be labelled as EV enthusiasts. Given these predispositions, an appropriate set of incentives could be effective in motivating future purchase behavior (Axsen, Bailey, & Castro, 2015).

Environmental Attitudes

The predictors of green consumer behavior include a variety of knowledge-based, attitudinal, value-driven, and behavioral measures (Banerjee & McKeague, 1994; Chan, 1999). However, in a meta-analysis of 128 studies, there was a correlation of only 0.35 between expressed concern for the environment and environmentally conscious behavior (Hines, Hungerford, & Tomera, 1986). There does not seem to be a clear consensus regarding what it is that environmentally concerned consumers want or how much they are willing to do to align their behavior with their environmental attitudes (Kilbourne, Beckman, & Thelen, 2002).

Straughan and Roberts (1999) found that an individual's belief that his or her own actions can have an impact on the environment was a much stronger determinant of environmentally responsible behavior. This is consistent with the finding that among highly environmentally concerned students, intention to act is predicted more strongly by perceived behavioral control than by attitudes or social norms (Bamberg, 2003). Hines, Hungerford, and Tomera (1986) concluded that the following variables predict environmentally responsible behavior: knowledge of the issues and their associated action responses, perceived individual ability and responsibility to make a difference, verbal commitment, and pro-environmental attitude. However, the relationship between pro-environmental attitudes and pro-environmental behavior is relatively weak (Ungar, 1994).

The two most commonly studied attitudes regarding environmentally friendly behavior are perceived inconvenience and perceived importance (Laroche, Bergeron, & Barbaro-Forleo, 2001). Not surprisingly, the perceived level of inconvenience of environmentally responsible behavior has been shown to be negatively related to environmentally responsible actions. In other words, the more inconvenient it is to act responsibly, the less likely that people will do so. For many people, environmentally responsible behavior occurs only when there is a relatively high degree of convenience attached to it (e.g., recycling behavior is increased when curbside recycling is available). However, there is much weaker and mixed evidence to support a positive relationship between beliefs about the importance of acting responsibly toward the environment and actually doing so. These results suggest that inconvenience is weighted more heavily than importance when making environmental behavior choices (Laroche, Bergeron, & Barbaro-Forleo, 2001; McCarty & Shrum, 1994).

The basic self-transcendent or altruistic values of individuals also have a strong influence on their pro-environmental behavioral intentions, both directly and indirectly through their beliefs about environmental conditions (Stern, et al., 1995). Those who maintain collectivist values, placing the needs of society over the needs of the individual, are also likely to place significance on environmental responsibility (McCarty & Shrum, 1994)

Several authors have identified that consumers who are willing to pay more for environmental products make up a sizeable enough portion of the market to be worth actively pursuing (Laroche, Bergeron, & Barbaro-Forleo, 2001; Myburgh-Louw & O'Shaunnessey, 1994; Suchard & Polonsky, 1991). Self-report studies regarding selection of, and willingness to pay for, environmentally conscious products show overwhelming consumer concern about making environmentally sound purchases. An array of studies has indicated consumer willingness to pay anywhere from 5%-40% more for environmentally conscious products (Coddington 1990; Suchard & Polonsky, 1991; Myburgh-Louw & O'Shaunnessey, 1994). However, findings further suggest that we cannot assume that environmentally responsible behavior will transcend product categories (Laroche, Bergeron, & Barbaro-Forleo, 2001; Picket, Grove, & Kangun, 1993; Suchard & Polonsky, 1991). For example, those who recycle may not purchase products made from recycled materials. Further, there is evidence to suggest that the likelihood of actually paying more for an environmentally sound option, after expressing a willingness to do so, is quite low (Rowlands, Parker, & Scott, 2002). As such, these results must be interpreted with care.

Dwyer et al. (1993) demonstrate that social marketing campaigns that try to change attitudes in order to change behavior are generally ineffective. Instead, one should look at the situation from the consumer's point of view to identify what limiting factors are hindering pro-environmental choices. Social marketers should then attempt to address these constraints in a way that is meaningful to consumers and stays within their tolerance for intervention (Stern, 2000).

In the context of vehicle purchasing, the lack of a strong linkage between pro-environmental attitudes and pro-environmental behavior makes it difficult to predict consumer decision-making with regard to the purchase of FEVs or AFVs. Comfort, convenience, and price are often important factors, and may overwhelm pro-environmental attitudes when it comes to making a vehicle purchase decision.

Vehicle Purchasing Market Segments

Several international studies have been identified that segment the vehicle purchasing market using psychographic variables (Environics, 2005; Redmond, 2000; Shell, 2004). In general, market segments can be categorized as being of high-, medium-, or low-relevance. It is important to understand which of these segments will be of most relevance for social marketing campaigns.

The high-relevance market segments consist of consumers who are already very interested in FEVs or AFVs. These high-relevance market segments only need to have resources made available to them in order to help them make fuel efficient vehicle decisions. High-relevance segments are already motivated to act. Thus, simply ensuring that they have the right types of information and infrastructure to suit their needs is all that is required. For example, Toyota identified three possible target segments for the Prius based on personal values and self-concept. One segment valued the new technology Prius offered, meaning that the information of most value to this segment simply explained how the car operates (Andidas, 2003). Another segment valued environmental consciousness, so this segment needed information about how the Prius' fuel efficiency created a reduced impact on the environment. Because the high-relevance market segments are already very interested in FEVs or AFVs, the persuasion task is greatly simplified. Based on this reasoning, those in the high-relevance segments will generally make environmentally sound choices with little to no prompting.

On the other hand, there is little chance of convincing low-relevance consumers that any possible sacrifice in terms of a loss of convenience or product function would be personally rewarding. Therefore, it makes little sense to devote any resources to the low-relevance consumers, since they are not predisposed to choose fuel efficient vehicles.

This leaves the medium-relevance group of consumers. Many consumers in the medium-relevance category tend to be later market entrants who need reassurance that their choices will be rewarded with satisfactory post-purchase outcomes. Thus, it makes the most sense to devote the majority of social marketing resources toward those who need some enticing, which are those in the medium-relevance category.

Social Marketing and Behavior Change

Effectively facilitating change in environmental behavior requires an understanding of consumer motivation, ability, and opportunity (Olander & Thøgersen, 1995). Recommended tools often include information provision, moral argument, and financial incentives. DEFRA (2008) offers strategies for engaging various categories of environmental segments. For those segments that are highly willing and able to act, they recommend providing tools that enable action and actively engaging consumers through two-way communications and community action. For those with moderate willingness and ability to do more, providing encouragement such as financial incentives, leading by example, and providing enabling tools like information and infrastructure to increase ease of action are again recommended. Finally, for low potential segments, encouragement and enabling activities are recommended in the form of regulation and limiting product choices. These strategies can be adapted to suit the vehicle purchasing market.

Social marketing attempts to change consumer behavior by creating exchanges that will both satisfy personal self-interest and benefit the greater good (Rothschild, 1999). The three key tools available to social marketers to achieve behavior change are education, law, and marketing (Rothschild, 1999). Education uses a combination of informative and persuasive messages that tell a consumer how to behave, and why it is in their best interest to do so. This allows the receiver to accept or reject a message, and does not necessarily cause behavior change. Responses may include selective perception in which only parts of the message that are consistent with current views are retained, and counter arguments to message elements that are inconsistent with currently held views. Laws are designed to force behavior change through the coercive use of legitimate power. In this case, unless the punishment is extremely onerous, there is still free choice based on the costs and benefits associated with the available choices (Rothschild, 2002). Marketing, however, is intended to provide incentives or disincentives consistent with consumer self-interest, in order to motivate voluntary behavior change.

Successful social marketing programs begin with an understanding of the consumer. Issues that must be centrally understood and incorporated into the campaign include consumer exchange, relationship power, market competition, and self-interest (Rothschild, 1999). Successful social marketing campaigns also require application of a full range of marketing strategies and tactics, including segmentation, competitive positioning, and a variety of tactics drawn from all 4 Ps (product, price, place, and promotion) of the marketing mix (Andreasen, 2002).

Exchange

Mutually beneficial exchanges are those that provide satisfaction to both parties. This requires that both the social marketer and the consumer see benefit in the exchange. For the marketer, this means that the desired behavioral change is made and maintained. For the consumer, this generally means that the behavioral change, at minimum, either does not reduce his or her current level of personal comfort, or promises to increase long term comfort at the expense of a short term decrease in comfort. If one or both of the parties does not believe that their needs will be successfully met, the exchange will not be successful.

Relationship Power

Equally important to understanding the requirements of a successful exchange are the nuances of power within the exchange relationship (Andreasen, 2002). Mutual benefit does not always mean equal benefit, and it is possible for one party to want an exchange to occur more than the other. In this case, the more powerful party tends to be the more apathetic one. In a social marketing context, the consumer is often apathetic and requires active recruitment to participate in an exchange, despite its mutual benefits, because the value received is usually intangible and long term and comes with a short term cost (Rothschild, 2002).

Self-Interest

Consumers weigh behavior choices based on short term and long term costs and benefits. Not surprisingly, consumers tend to prefer options that have short term benefits and long term costs over those with short term costs and long run benefits, despite the fact that it is usually the latter which is better for us (Rothschild, 2002). Consumers who perceive risk in achieving long term benefit from a choice may want added short term service or other incentive benefits that complement the longer term benefit in order to reduce the perceived risk associated with their choice.

Competitive Positioning

As with commercial firms, social marketing campaigns will be more successful if they are able to identify a differentiating factor that makes them a superior choice than their competitors on some dimension. The chosen dimension should ideally include an attribute that the desired behavior has which competitive behavior does not, and which is also of significant relevance and/or value to the consumer. Toyota, for example, had success in positioning the Prius as trendy by having celebrities drive them to the Academy Awards rather than arriving in limousines. The Smart car drew attention away from limited interior space by focusing on ease of parking instead. These strategies were also matched to appropriate target segments; in both cases, the target was young urban professionals.

The Marketing Mix

The marketing mix is comprised of what is commonly known as the 4 Ps (product, price, place, and promotion). The marketing mix is often tailored to meet the specific needs of each relevant segment of consumers.

Products comprise goods, service, ideas and experiences. Social marketing campaigns are traditionally associated with selling ideas, but this is a very limited and limiting view. Social marketing campaigns can, and should, include within them other forms of product. First, satisfactory goods and services, that include all desired attribute combinations so as to satisfy various target segments, must exist so as to allow consumers to act in the desired fashion. This could include providing hybrid or otherwise fuel efficient automobiles in a range of classes and price points, and providing adequate support services to customers who need further assistance in order to make behavior change feasible.

Branding is also an element of product strategy that should not be under-rated in importance. Any organization with a corporate reputation is nurturing a brand image, and that brand has value. Social marketers should find ways to develop brands for the products they provide in order to encourage behavior change, such as the ecoAuto label, in order to increase the value of such tools in the eyes of consumers over time. As with the product life cycle, brands gain recognition and acceptance over time, thus patience is required before firm associations between brands and desired behaviors will be seen.

It is also important to recall that the product life cycle and innovation adoption start very slowly before exponential growth is reached. Many social marketing campaigns have very short-term timelines and benchmarks for measuring success. While commercial ventures traditionally see results quickly, they usually offer immediate gratification with short term benefits, whereas social marketing campaigns often require not just personal, but cultural, change before acceptance is reached. This sort of long term effect can take decades, not years, to achieve.

Price is usually associated with the exchange of money for goods and services; however, time, barter, hedonic experience, and anything else of value can be thought of as the price paid in an exchange. A price can not only include value that is gained, but also value that is foregone. In the case of social marketing, price is often associated with short term costs in the form of benefits that are foregone in exchange for long term intangible gains. In many cases, these gains are of public benefit, as opposed to personal benefit. The immediate perceived value of an altruistic long term benefit is significantly less than a short term hedonic benefit. Thus, the social marketer's task requires adding short term value for the consumer.

Place or distribution, also thought of as convenience, involves getting the social marketing products and services out to the consumer. Keys to successful distribution include making products and services conveniently available where, when, and how consumer want to have them delivered. Issues such as dealer location, opening hours, staffing, and inventory are critical success factors to both commercial and social marketing efforts.

Promotion involves all tools used in a campaign to communicate with the target audience. Because so many social marketing campaigns are limited to ideas delivered through media, this method is generally understood the most readily. Integrated marketing communication is intended to move the consumer from attention, to information/understanding, to desire, to intention, and finally action (reflective of the cognition – affect - behavior order of decision making), and is most effective when all tools work together to convey a single unified message. Tools include advertising, public relations, direct marketing, sales promotion, and word-of-mouth media. All informational/educational communication should be targeted at the identified consumer segments, since education is foundational to all other campaign elements as a major contributing factor to informed free choice. Other persuasive aspects of the campaign should be tailored to specific segments based on their unique needs.

Advertising and direct marketing both offer ways to deliver messages to target consumers, either directly or through mass media. Direct marketing and print media are able to deliver a high level of information, while broadcast media are better suited to simple messages. When direct marketing achieves response from the consumer and two-way communication ensues, persuasion and behavior change can result. Public relations can also provide information indirectly through third party media sources. Sponsorships and product placements are used primarily as affective tools for making associations between the brand and an event or show that the target consumer likes, in order to elicit positive attitudes toward the product. Short term incentives are provided through sales promotion techniques, through either monetary or non-monetary means. Monetary incentives are most suited to well-known brands that provide functional benefits, while non-monetary incentives are more appropriate for relatively unknown brands or well-known brands that provide more hedonic benefits. Sales promotion techniques are most commonly associated with motivating behavior change through brand switching or increased purchasing volume.

By achieving a better understanding of social marketing techniques, campaign success in terms of behavior change can increase. By putting continued campaigns in place over the course of the entire product life cycle and continually monitoring how the needs of consumers change over time, as commercial marketers do, maintenance of such change is much more likely to occur, adding to overall success for the initiative.

Summary

The above review has provided a review of the literature on fuel efficient vehicles, with a focus on market segments and environmentally conscious attitudes and behavior. We have concluded with a review of social marketing methods as they might apply to the automotive market. The objective has been to provide greater insight into consumer decision-making, in order to be able to convince consumers to make more transportation choices that are more fuel efficient and contribute less to greenhouse gases. This section will summarize some of the key insights.

- **Automotive Purchasing is Not Always Rational:** Although an automotive purchase involves a major investment that should be characterized by high consumer involvement, it is not necessarily a rational purchase. Self-concept, attitudes, and lifestyle can influence automotive choice, allowing emotional factors to take precedence over the practical.
- **Many Consumers are Slow to Adopt New Products:** AFVs represent a relatively new product category, and it will be some time before the majority of consumers feel comfortable enough with this new concept to become product adopters in this new category.
- **Social Influences are Important in Transportation Decisions:** Automotive purchase decisions are often driven by social influences, since cars are often a sign of status and social standing.
- **Consumer Attitudes and Behavior Don't Always Line Up:** What consumers say they will do, and what they actually do, are often two different things. For this reason, measures of purchase intention are often poor predictors of actual purchasing behavior. People may say they believe in being environmentally responsible, but a close examination of their actual behavior often demonstrates relatively poor adherence to their lofty ideals.
- **Research has Shown Only a Moderate Consumer Willingness to Buy More Fuel Efficient Vehicles:**
    - Consumers insist on comfort and convenience, and therefore few are willing to trade down from a van or SUV to a smaller vehicle that would be less comfortable or convenient.
    - Consumers are generally relatively unwilling to pay more for improved fuel efficiency, so few are willing to pay significantly more for an AFV version of their current van or SUV model.
    - Consumers do not understand the lifetime operating costs of operating AFVs, and demand a short payback on their initial investment.
    - Self-identity is a key factor, so few consumers are willing to downsize for greater fuel efficiency, since that would impact their personal image.
    - Consumers who currently switch to a highly fuel efficient or alternate fuel vehicle are likely to see this as part of their environmentally conscious self-identity, or are early adopters who enjoy having novelty products.
- **Demographic Variables can be Predictors of Fuel Efficient Automotive Purchases:**
    - Younger and less affluent consumers are more concerned about fuel costs.
    - Those who drive more miles are more concerned about fuel costs (but would prefer not to sacrifice comfort).
    - Women tend to be more concerned about fuel costs (likely because they also often have lower incomes) and less concerned about power and rapid acceleration.
- **Consumers are More Likely to Conserve when Natural Resource Consumption Levels are Visible and Understood:** Automotive fuel consumption is highly visible. While consumers lack a full understanding of how much fuel they consume on a long term basis, purchase price, fuel costs, and operating costs all consistently work to reduce the likelihood of selecting more expensive vehicle options. Gas price increases have demonstrated a notable impact on the market for larger vehicles.
- **No Clear Consensus has Emerged Regarding Environmentally Concerned Consumers:** This may be due to the large gap between consumer attitudes and behaviors, making it difficult to predict consumer behavior based on what people say they believe. However, the inconvenience associated with environmentally responsible behavior appears to be the greatest barrier.

- **Social Marketing can be Used to Motivate Changes in Consumer Behavior:** Social marketers typically target specific markets and manipulate the 4 Ps (product, price, place, promotion) in order to motivate behavior change.

FUTURE RESEARCH DIRECTIONS

There is substantial need for future research examining the use of social marketing to promote the purchase of fuel efficient vehicles and alternate fuel vehicles. Governments and nonprofit environmental organizations both have a potential role to play in developing future social marketing campaigns to promote FEVs and AFVs. The relative newness of some of the AFV technologies means that consumers will require education, incentives, and persuasion in order to convince them to adopt these vehicles.

Future research should focus on the types of incentives that will be required to ensure a favorable exchange within the context of a social marketing campaign. Research could examine the degree to which monetary incentives are required, such as reduced prices or tax rebates work best. Research could also examine the efficacy of alternative incentives such as green license plates and freeway HOV access.

Future research could also focus on determining which elements are essential for a social marketing campaign to successfully increase the rate of FEV and AFV ownership. The marketing mix elements would be an area for investigation, as well as determining the appropriate consumer segments to target.

Finally, because marketing for FEVs and AFVs will necessarily involve automotive manufacturers, there are issues of competition that will play a role. Research examining the role of competition versus cooperation in the market for FEVs and AFVs will be of particular interest.

CONCLUSION

In order to encourage more consumers to make more environmentally friendly choices, several things will need to be done:

- If gasoline prices are to be increased through taxes in order to make it attractive to switch to more fuel efficient vehicles, such price increases need to be of the significant 50% magnitude of increases seen in North America during 2008, which had an impact on reducing SUV purchases. There is no evidence to suggest that smaller gasoline price increases of 5-15% will have the desired impact. Substantially higher gas prices at a sustained level have the demonstrated effect of changing buying patterns for automobiles by encouraging the purchase of more fuel-efficient vehicles.
- Greater financial incentives should be offered for purchasing FEVs (through income tax incentives, or preferably through immediate cash discounts or cash rebates), in order to make fuel efficient vehicles more attractive. This reduces the risks for consumers, and encourages them to make innovative choices that they would otherwise fear making.
- An alternate model would suggest charging tax penalties on purchases of non-fuel efficient vehicles, directly in proportion to the fuel consumption of the vehicle (Beck, Rose, & Hensher, 2013). This approach penalizes purchase behaviors which are not environmentally friendly.

- Innovative solutions such as green license plates allowing AFVs or FEVs to use the less HOV (high occupancy vehicle) lane may have the ability to persuade commuters to choose these types of fuel efficient vehicles.
- FEVs need to be offered in a wide range of model choices. Consumers want vehicles that fit as many of their purchase criteria as possible, so comfortable and affordable FEVs need to be available in as many product classes as possible. Where options are available, they need to be promoted to overcome awareness barriers.
- FEVs need to be offered in sufficient numbers to avoid delivery delays. Consumers tend to want rapid availability, so FEVs need to be available in sufficient quantities to satisfy consumer demand.
- Manufacturers should be offered incentives for selling more FEVs. Alternatively, manufacturers could face legislated goals for selling FEVs that would include financial penalties for failing to meet the goals. Such legislated goals would force automotive manufacturers to price FEVs at more attractive levels, and would also force automotive manufacturers to heavily promote FEVs.

In addition to the above policy initiatives, social marketing campaigns can be developed to encourage consumers to adopt FEVs. Such a campaign would focus on manipulating the 4 Ps of social marketing, in order to create a persuasive argument for consumers to purchase FEVs:

- **Product:** In the automotive sector, the product needs to be made more desirable, which would include creating an aura of prestige surrounding the ownership of FEVs. The FEV product itself also needs to be perceived as being at least as reliable, if not more reliable, than traditional automobiles. Consumers have little understanding of hybrid vehicles, and may have misperceptions about high maintenance costs.
- **Price:** The price of FEVs needs to be made more attractive, preferably on par with traditional vehicles. Consumers tend to focus on the current price rather than the long-term operating cost, so prices of FEVs need to be on par with traditional vehicles. Alternatively, or as a supplement, if gas prices are increased substantially (50%+) through taxes, this can also have an impact on making the operating costs more salient, and encouraging consumers to look beyond the initial purchase price of FEVs.
- **Place:** Smaller cities or towns tend to not carry or service more exotic types of vehicles such as FEVs. For example, in smaller towns that service rural areas, availability of parts may be an issue for FEVs. Therefore, distribution of FEVs and their parts needs to ensure that they are readily available in smaller centres as well as in major cities. Furthermore, a heavy reliance on traditional trucks and 4-wheel drive vehicles for farming and rural enterprises needs to be overcome by educating the consumer about the comparability, performance, and availability of HFEV choices.
- **Promotion:** Consumers in general need more education about FEVs and the benefits of switching to FEVs. Consumers are generally unaware of the benefits of FEVs, and are unwilling to switch if there is not a significant cost benefit to offset the perceived risk of choosing a novel FEV product. Therefore, promotional materials need to educate the consumer about FEVs, and motivate the consumer to desire FEVs in preference to conventional automotive products.

By combining policy levers and an effective social marketing campaign, it is possible to change consumer purchasing habits away from gas-guzzling vehicles toward more environmentally-friendly choices. However, these are long-term initiatives that require a dedicated effort now, in order to achieve results for the future.

REFERENCES

Ahmadi, L., Croiset, E., Elkamel, A., Douglas, P. L., Entchev, E., Abdul-Wahab, S. A., & Yazdanpanah, P. (2015). Effect of socio-economic factors on EV/HEV/PHEV adoption rate in Ontario. *Technological Forecasting and Social Change*, *98*, 93–104. doi:10.1016/j.techfore.2015.06.012

Ajanovic, A. (2014). Promoting environmentally benign electric vehicles. *Energy Procedia*, *57*, 807–816. doi:10.1016/j.egypro.2014.10.289

Al-Alawi, B. M., & Bradley, T. H. (2013a). Review of hybrid, plug-in hybrid, and electric vehicle market modeling studies. *Renewable & Sustainable Energy Reviews*, *21*, 190–203. doi:10.1016/j.rser.2012.12.048

Al-Alawi, B. M., & Bradley, T. H. (2013b). Total cost of ownership, payback, and consumer preference modeling of plug-in hybrid electric vehicles. *Applied Energy*, *103*, 488–506. doi:10.1016/j.apenergy.2012.10.009

Andidas.com (2003). *Toyota Prius: Marketing Communications Plan.*

Andreasen, A. R. (2002). Commercial marketing and social change. *Social Marketing Quarterly*, *8*(2), 41–45. doi:10.1080/15245000212552

Axsen, J., Bailey, J., & Castro, M. A. (2015). Preference and lifestyle heterogeneity among potential plug-in electric vehicle buyers. *Energy Economics*, *50*, 190–201. doi:10.1016/j.eneco.2015.05.003

Bailey, J., Miele, A., & Axsen, J. (2015). Is awareness of public charging associated with consumer interest in plug-in electric vehicles? *Transportation Research Part D, Transport and Environment*, *36*, 1–9. doi:10.1016/j.trd.2015.02.001

Bamberg, S. (2003). How does environmental concern influence specific environmentally related behaviors? A new answer to an old question. *Journal of Environmental Psychology*, *23*(1), 21–32. doi:10.1016/S0272-4944(02)00078-6

Banerjee, B., & McKeague, K. (1994). How green is my value: Exploring the relationship between environmentalism and materialism. In C. T. Allen & D. R. John (Eds.), *Advances in Consumer Research* (Vol. 21, pp. 147–152). Provo, Utah: Association for Consumer Research.

Barke, R. L., Clouse, R., Stout, T. G., & Stout, G. R. (2009). The Economics of Buying a More Fuel-Efficient Automobile: An Interactive Analysis. *Journal of Financial Planning*, *22*(6), 62–71.

Barth, M., Jugert, P., & Fritsche, I. (2016). Still underdetected–Social norms and collective efficacy predict the acceptance of electric vehicles in Germany. *Transportation Research Part F: Traffic Psychology and Behaviour*, *37*, 64–77. doi:10.1016/j.trf.2015.11.011

Beck, M. J., Rose, J. M., & Hensher, D. A. (2013). Environmental attitudes and emissions charging: An example of policy implications for vehicle choice. *Transportation Research Part A, Policy and Practice*, *50*, 171–182. doi:10.1016/j.tra.2013.01.015

Beresteanu, A., & Li, S. (2011). Gasoline prices, government support, and the demand for hybrid vehicles in the United States. *International Economic Review*, *52*(1), 161–182. doi:10.1111/j.1468-2354.2010.00623.x

Bilotkach, V., & Mills, M. (2012). Simple Economics of Electric Vehicle Adoption. *Procedia: Social and Behavioral Sciences*, *54*, 979–988. doi:10.1016/j.sbspro.2012.09.813

Bjerkan, K. Y., Nørbech, T. E., & Nordtømme, M. E. (2016). Incentives for promoting Battery Electric Vehicle (BEV) adoption in Norway. *Transportation Research Part D, Transport and Environment*, *43*, 169–180. doi:10.1016/j.trd.2015.12.002

Bohnsack, R., Kolk, A., & Pinkse, J. (2015). Catching recurring waves: Low-emission vehicles, international policy developments and firm innovation strategies. *Technological Forecasting and Social Change*, *98*, 71–87. doi:10.1016/j.techfore.2015.06.020

Bonges, H. A. III, & Lusk, A. C. (2016). Addressing electric vehicle (EV) sales and range anxiety through parking layout, policy and regulation. *Transportation Research Part A, Policy and Practice*, *83*, 63–73. doi:10.1016/j.tra.2015.09.011

Carley, S., Krause, R. M., Lane, B. W., & Graham, J. D. (2013). Intent to purchase a plug-in electric vehicle: A survey of early impressions in large US cites. *Transportation Research Part D, Transport and Environment*, *18*, 39–45. doi:10.1016/j.trd.2012.09.007

Caulfield, B., Farrell, S., & McMahon, B. (2010). Examining individuals preferences for hybrid electric and alternatively fuelled vehicles. *Transport Policy*, *17*(6), 381–387. doi:10.1016/j.tranpol.2010.04.005

Champniss, G., Wilson, H. N., & Macdonald, E. K. (2015). Why your customers' social identities matter. *Harvard Business Review*, *93*(1/2), 88–96.

Chandra, A., Gulati, S., & Kandlikar, M. (2010). Green drivers or free riders? An analysis of tax rebates for hybrid vehicles. *Journal of Environmental Economics and Management*, *60*(2), 78–93. doi:10.1016/j.jeem.2010.04.003

Choo, S., & Mokhtarian, P. L. (2002). The relationship of vehicle type choice to personality, lifestyle, attitudinal, and demographic variables (Research Report UCD-ITS-RR-02-060. Institute of Transportation Studies, University of California. Retrieved from its.ucdavis.edu/publications/2002/RR-02-06.pdf

Choo, S., & Mokhtarian, P. L. (2004). What type of vehicle do people drive? The role of attitude and lifestyle in influencing vehicle type choice. *Transportation Research*, *38*(3), 201–222.

Choy, D., & Prizzia, R. (2010). Environmental Consumerism and the Role of the Hybrid Auto in Hawaii. *International Management Review*, *6*(1), 58.

Coddington, W. (1990). It's no fad: Environmentalism is now a fact in corporate life. *Marketing News*, *15*(Oct), 7.

Coninx, P. (2004). Hybrid vehicles - Targeting Incentives for the Next Step Forward. Report by Automobile Consumer Coalition.

Davis, S. C., Diegel, S. W., & Boundy, R. G. (2015). *Transportation Energy Data Book* (34th ed.). Vehicle Technologies Office, Office of Energy Efficiency and Renewable Energy, U.S. Department of Energy.

Daziano, R. A. (2013). Conditional-logit Bayes estimators for consumer valuation of electric vehicle driving range. *Resource and Energy Economics*, *35*(3), 429–450. doi:10.1016/j.reseneeco.2013.05.001

de Haan, P., Duthaler, C., Peters, A., & Smieszek, T. (2006). Characteristics of buyers of hybrid Honda Civic IMA: Preferences, decision process, vehicle ownership, and willingness-to-pay [Bericht zum Schweizer Autokaufverhalten]. ETH Zurich.

Decima Research Inc. (2004). Automotive Purchase Considerations in Canada (Report 23496-052112/001/CY).

DEFRA. (2008, January). A Framework for Pro-Environmental Behaviors Report by Department for Environment, Food and Rural Affairs.

Delgado, M. S., Harriger, J. L., & Khanna, N. (2015). The value of environmental status signaling. *Ecological Economics*, *111*, 1–11. doi:10.1016/j.ecolecon.2014.12.021

Diamond, D. (2009). The impact of government incentives for hybrid-electric vehicles: Evidence from US states. *Energy Policy*, *37*(3), 972–983. doi:10.1016/j.enpol.2008.09.094

Dumortier, J., Siddiki, S., Carley, S., Cisney, J., Krause, R. M., Lane, B. W., & Graham, J. D. et al. (2015). Effects of providing total cost of ownership information on consumers intent to purchase a hybrid or plug-in electric vehicle. *Transportation Research Part A, Policy and Practice*, *72*, 71–86. doi:10.1016/j.tra.2014.12.005

Dwyer, W. O., Leeming, F. C., Cobern, M. K., Porter, B. E., & Jackson, J. M. (1993). Critical review of behavioral interventions to preserve the environment: Research since 1980. *Environment and Behavior*, *25*(5), 275–321. doi:10.1177/0013916593255001

Environics Research Group. (2005). *Development of a New Vehicle Rating System: Psychographic Segmentation and Consumer Consultations*. Report prepared for Natural Resources Canada.

Gallagher, K. S., & Muehlegger, E. (2011). Giving green to get green? Incentives and consumer adoption of hybrid vehicle technology. *Journal of Environmental Economics and Management*, *61*(1), 1–15. doi:10.1016/j.jeem.2010.05.004

Garcia, R., & Balbaky, S. (2006). Vehicle choice decision-making: What are the factors with which consumers choose their automobile purchases? (working paper). Northeastern University.

Gilmore, E. A., & Lave, L. B. (2013). Comparing resale prices and total cost of ownership for gasoline, hybrid and diesel passenger cars and trucks. *Transport Policy*, *27*, 200–208. doi:10.1016/j.tranpol.2012.12.007

Graham-Rowe, E., Gardner, B., Abraham, C., Skippon, S., Dittmar, H., Hutchins, R., & Stannard, J. (2012). Mainstream consumers driving plug-in battery-electric and plug-in hybrid electric cars: A qualitative analysis of responses and evaluations. *Transportation Research Part A, Policy and Practice*, *46*(1), 140–153. doi:10.1016/j.tra.2011.09.008

Hackbarth, A., & Madlener, R. (2013). Consumer preferences for alternative fuel vehicles: A discrete choice analysis. *Transportation Research Part D, Transport and Environment*, *25*, 5–17. doi:10.1016/j.trd.2013.07.002

Haddadian, G., Khodayar, M., & Shahidehpour, M. (2015). Accelerating the Global Adoption of Electric Vehicles: Barriers and Drivers. *The Electricity Journal*, *28*(10), 53–68. doi:10.1016/j.tej.2015.11.011

Hagman, J., Ritzén, S., Stier, J. J., & Susilo, Y. (2016). Total cost of ownership and its potential implications for battery electric vehicle diffusion. *Research in Transportation Business & Management*.

He, L., Wang, M., Chen, W., & Conzelmann, G. (2014). Incorporating social impact on new product adoption in choice modeling: A case study in green vehicles. *Transportation Research Part D, Transport and Environment*, *32*, 421–434. doi:10.1016/j.trd.2014.08.007

Heffner, R., Turrentine, T., & Kurani, K. (2006). *A Primer on Automobile Semiotics.* Institute of Transportation Studies. University of California.

Hines, J. M., Hungerford, H. R., & Tomera, A. N. (1986). Analysis and synthesis of research on responsible pro-environmental behavior: A meta-analysis. *The Journal of Environmental Education*, *18*(2), 1–8. doi:10.1080/00958964.1987.9943482

Hsu, C. I., Li, H. C., & Lu, S. M. (2013). A dynamic marketing model for hybrid electric vehicles: A case study of Taiwan. *Transportation Research Part D, Transport and Environment*, *20*, 21–29. doi:10.1016/j.trd.2013.01.001

Jenn, A., Azevedo, I. L., & Ferreira, P. (2013). The impact of federal incentives on the adoption of hybrid electric vehicles in the United States. *Energy Economics*, *40*, 936–942. doi:10.1016/j.eneco.2013.07.025

Kavalec, C. (1999). Vehicle choice in an aging population: Some insights from a stated preference survey from California. *The Energy Journal (Cambridge, Mass.)*, *20*(3), 123–138. doi:10.5547/ISSN0195-6574-EJ-Vol20-No3-5

Khan, M., & Kar, N. C. (2009). Hybrid electric vehicles for sustainable transportation: A Canadian perspective. *World Electric Vehicle Journal*, *3*, 1–12.

Kilbourne, W. E., Beckman, S. D., & Thelen, E. (2002). The role of the dominant social paradigm in environmental attitudes: A multinational examination. *Journal of Business Research*, *55*(3), 193–204. doi:10.1016/S0148-2963(00)00141-7

Krupa, J. S., Rizzo, D. M., Eppstein, M. J., Lanute, D. B., Gaalema, D. E., Lakkaraju, K., & Warrender, C. E. (2014). Analysis of a consumer survey on plug-in hybrid electric vehicles. *Transportation Research Part A, Policy and Practice*, *64*, 14–31. doi:10.1016/j.tra.2014.02.019

Lane, B. (2005). *Car Buyer Research Report: Consumer Attitudes to Low Carbon and Fuel-efficient Passenger Cars.* Report prepared for the Low Carbon Vehicle Partnership.

Laroche, M., Bergeron, J., & Barbaro-Forleo, G. (2001). Targeting consumers who are willing to pay more for environmentally friendly products. *Journal of Consumer Marketing*, *18*(6), 503–520. doi:10.1108/EUM0000000006155

Larson, P. D., Viáfara, J., Parsons, R. V., & Elias, A. (2014). Consumer attitudes about electric cars: Pricing analysis and policy implications. *Transportation Research Part A, Policy and Practice*, *69*, 299–314. doi:10.1016/j.tra.2014.09.002

Li, X., Clark, C. D., Jensen, K. L., Yen, S. T., & English, B. C. (2013). Consumer purchase intentions for flexible-fuel and hybrid-electric vehicles. *Transportation Research Part D, Transport and Environment*, *18*, 9–15. doi:10.1016/j.trd.2012.08.001

Liu, Y. (2014). Household demand and willingness to pay for hybrid vehicles. *Energy Economics*, *44*, 191–197. doi:10.1016/j.eneco.2014.03.027

Majid, K. A., & Russell, C. A. (2015). Giving green a second thought: Modeling the value retention of green products in the secondary market. *Journal of Business Research*, *68*(5), 994–1002. doi:10.1016/j.jbusres.2014.10.001

McCarty, J. A., & Shrum, L. J. (1994). The recycling of solid wastes: Personal values, value orientations, and attitudes about recycling as antecedents of recycling behavior. *Journal of Business Research*, *30*(1), 53–62. doi:10.1016/0148-2963(94)90068-X

Myburgh-Louw, J., & O'Shaughnessy, N. J. (1994). Consumer perception of misleading and deceptive claims on the packaging of green fast moving consumer goods. In R. Achrol, & A. Mitchell, (Eds.) *American Marketing Association Summer Educators' Conference Proceedings*, Chicago, Ill., USA (Vol. 5, pp. 344-353).

Olander, F., & Thøgersen, J. (1995). Understanding of consumer behavior as a prerequisite for environmental protection. *Journal of Consumer Policy*, *18*, 345–385. doi:10.1007/BF01024160

Ozaki, R., & Sevastyanova, K. (2011). Going hybrid: An analysis of consumer purchase motivations. *Energy Policy*, *39*(5), 2217–2227. doi:10.1016/j.enpol.2010.04.024

Pickett, G. M., Grove, S. J., & Kangun, N. (1993). An analysis of the conserving consumer: A public policy perspective. In C.T. Allen, et al. (Eds.) *American Marketing Association Winter Educator's Conference Proceedings*, Chicago, IL, USA (Vol. 3, pp. 151-153). American Marketing Association.

Potoglou, D., & Kanaroglou, P. S. (2007). Household demand and willingness to pay for clean vehicles. *Transportation Research Part D, Transport and Environment*, *12*(4), 264–274. doi:10.1016/j.trd.2007.03.001

Redmond, L. (2000*). Identifying and Analysing Travel-related Attitudinal, Personality and Lifestyle Clusters in the San Francisco Bay Area* [MSc Thesis]. University of California, Davis.

Rezvani, Z., Jansson, J., & Bodin, J. (2015). Advances in consumer electric vehicle adoption research: A review and research agenda. *Transportation Research Part D, Transport and Environment*, *34*, 122–136. doi:10.1016/j.trd.2014.10.010

Rothschild, M. L. (1999). Carrots, sticks and promises: A conceptual framework for the management of public health and social issues behaviors. *Journal of Marketing*, *63*(4), 24–37. doi:10.2307/1251972

Rothschild, M. L. (2002). Accommodating self-interest. *Social Marketing Quarterly*, *8*(2), 32–35. doi:10.1080/15245000212559

Rowlands, I. H., Parker, P., & Scott, D. (2002). Consumer perceptions of green power. *Journal of Consumer Marketing*, *19*(2), 112–127. doi:10.1108/07363760210420540

Shewmake, S., & Jarvis, L. (2014). Hybrid cars and HOV lanes. *Transportation Research Part A, Policy and Practice*, *67*, 304–319. doi:10.1016/j.tra.2014.07.004

Stern, P. C. (2000). Toward a coherent theory of environmentally significant behavior. *The Journal of Social Issues*, *56*(3), 407–424. doi:10.1111/0022-4537.00175

Stern, P. C., Dietz, T., Kalof, L., & Guagnano, G. A. (1995). Values, beliefs and pro environmental action: Attitude formation toward emergent attitude objects. *Journal of Applied Social Psychology*, *25*(18), 1611–1636. doi:10.1111/j.1559-1816.1995.tb02636.x

Straughan, R. D., & Roberts, J. A. (1999). Environmental segmentation alternatives: A look at green consumer behavior in the new millennium. *Journal of Consumer Marketing*, *16*(6), 558–575. doi:10.1108/07363769910297506

Suchard, H. T., & Polonsky, M. J. (1991). A theory of environmental buyer behavior and its validity: The Environmental Action-Behavior Model. In M.C. Gilly et al. (Eds.), *American Marketing Association Summer Educator's Conference Proceedings*, Chicago, IL., USA (Vol. 2, pp. 187-201). American Marketing Association.

The Economist. (2016, January 23). The oil conundrum.

Turrentine, T., Kurani, K., & Heffner, R. (2007). Fuel economy: What drives consumer choice? *Access*, *31*(Fall), 14–19.

Ungar, S. (1994). Apples and oranges: Probing the attitude behavior relationship for the environment. *The Canadian Review of Sociology and Anthropology. La Revue Canadienne de Sociologie et dAnthropologie*, *31*(3), 288–304. doi:10.1111/j.1755-618X.1994.tb00950.x

West, S. (2007). The effect of gasoline prices on the demand for sport utility vehicles. Working Paper prepared for the "Demand Estimation in Environmental Economics" session, 2007 Midwest Economics Association Meetings.

ADDITIONAL READING

Axsen, J., & Kurani, K. S. (2012). Interpersonal influence within car buyers social networks: Applying five perspectives to plug-in hybrid vehicle drivers. *Environment & Planning A*, *44*(5), 1047–1065. doi:10.1068/a43221x

Bosetti, V., & Longden, T. (2013). Light duty vehicle transportation and global climate policy: The importance of electric drive vehicles. *Energy Policy*, *58*, 209–219. doi:10.1016/j.enpol.2013.03.008

Burgess, M., King, N., Harris, M., & Lewis, E. (2013). Electric vehicle drivers reported interactions with the public: Driving stereotype change? *Transportation Research Part F: Traffic Psychology and Behaviour*, *17*, 33–44. doi:10.1016/j.trf.2012.09.003

Caperello, N. D., & Kurani, K. S. (2012). Households stories of their encounters with a plug-in hybrid electric vehicle. *Environment and Behavior*, *44*(4), 493–508. doi:10.1177/0013916511402057

Chekima, B., Wafa, S. A. W. S. K., Igau, O. A., Chekima, S., & Sondoh, S. L. (2016). Examining green consumerism motivational drivers: Does premium price and demographics matter to green purchasing? *Journal of Cleaner Production*, *112*, 3436–3450. doi:10.1016/j.jclepro.2015.09.102

Cohn, D. Y., & Vaccaro, V. L. (2013). A Consumer Values Analysis of Attitudes Towards Green & Non-Green Vehicle Purchase. *Proceedings of the Northeast Business& Economics Association*, 40-43.

Cooper, L. G. (2000). Strategic marketing planning for radically new products. *Journal of Marketing*, *64*(1), 1–16. doi:10.1509/jmkg.64.1.1.17987

Driscoll, A., Lyons, S., Mariuzzo, F., & Tol, R. S. (2013). Simulating demand for electric vehicles using revealed preference data. *Energy Policy*, *62*, 686–696. doi:10.1016/j.enpol.2013.07.061

Gao, P., Hensley, R., & Zielke, A. (2014). A road map to the future for the auto industry. *The McKinsey Quarterly*, (October), 1–11.

Hahnel, U. J., Ortmann, C., Korcaj, L., & Spada, H. (2014). What is green worth to you? Activating environmental values lowers price sensitivity towards electric vehicles. *Journal of Environmental Psychology*, *40*, 306–319. doi:10.1016/j.jenvp.2014.08.002

He, L., Chen, W., & Conzelmann, G. (2012). Impact of vehicle usage on consumer choice of hybrid electric vehicles. *Transportation Research Part D, Transport and Environment*, *17*(3), 208–214. doi:10.1016/j.trd.2011.11.005

Hur, W. M., Woo, J., & Kim, Y. (2015). The role of consumer values and socio-demographics in green product satisfaction: The case of hybrid cars. *Psychological Reports*, *117*(2), 406–427. doi:10.2466/01.PR0.117c19z1 PMID:26444836

Klöckner, C. A. (2014). The dynamics of purchasing an electric vehicle–A prospective longitudinal study of the decision-making process. *Transportation Research Part F: Traffic Psychology and Behaviour*, *24*, 103–116. doi:10.1016/j.trf.2014.04.015

Lane, B., & Potter, S. (2007). The adoption of cleaner vehicles in the UK: Exploring the consumer attitude-action gap. *Journal of Cleaner Production*, *15*(11-12), 1085–1092. doi:10.1016/j.jclepro.2006.05.026

Lazaros, E. J. (2012). Comparing Cars-Environmental and Cost Concerns. *Tech Directions*, *72*(4), 13.

McGovern, E. (2007). Transport behavior: A role for social marketing. *Journal of Nonprofit & Public Sector Marketing*, *17*(1-2), 121–134. doi:10.1300/J054v17n01_06

Oliver, J. D., & Lee, S. H. (2010). Hybrid car purchase intentions: A cross-cultural analysis. *Journal of Consumer Marketing*, *27*(2), 96–103. doi:10.1108/07363761011027204

Oliver, J. D., & Rosen, D. E. (2010). Applying the environmental propensity framework: A segmented approach to hybrid electric vehicle marketing strategies. *Journal of Marketing Theory and Practice*, *18*(4), 377–393. doi:10.2753/MTP1069-6679180405

Peterson, S. B., & Michalek, J. J. (2013). Cost-effectiveness of plug-in hybrid electric vehicle battery capacity and charging infrastructure investment for reducing US gasoline consumption. *Energy Policy*, *52*, 429–438. doi:10.1016/j.enpol.2012.09.059

Schuitema, G., Anable, J., Skippon, S., & Kinnear, N. (2013). The role of instrumental, hedonic and symbolic attributes in the intention to adopt electric vehicles. *Transportation Research Part A, Policy and Practice*, *48*, 39–49. doi:10.1016/j.tra.2012.10.004

Shin, J., Bhat, C. R., You, D., Garikapati, V. M., & Pendyala, R. M. (2015). Consumer preferences and willingness to pay for advanced vehicle technology options and fuel types. *Transportation Research Part C, Emerging Technologies*, *60*, 511–524. doi:10.1016/j.trc.2015.10.003

Skerlos, S. J., & Winebrake, J. J. (2010). Targeting plug-in hybrid electric vehicle policies to increase social benefits. *Energy Policy*, *38*(2), 705–708. doi:10.1016/j.enpol.2009.11.014

Thomas, C. S. (2012). How green are electric vehicles? *International Journal of Hydrogen Energy*, *37*(7), 6053–6062. doi:10.1016/j.ijhydene.2011.12.118

Tscharaktschiew, S. (2015). How much should gasoline be taxed when electric vehicles conquer the market? An analysis of the mismatch between efficient and existing gasoline taxes under emerging electric mobility. *Transportation Research Part D, Transport and Environment*, *39*, 89–113. doi:10.1016/j.trd.2015.06.007

Tuttle, D. P., & Baldick, R. (2015). Technological, Market and Policy Drivers of Emerging Trends in the Diffusion of Plug-in Electric Vehicles in the US. *The Electricity Journal*, *28*(7), 29–43. doi:10.1016/j.tej.2015.07.008

Whitehead, J., Franklin, J. P., & Washington, S. (2015). Transitioning to energy efficient vehicles: An analysis of the potential rebound effects and subsequent impact upon emissions. *Transportation Research Part A, Policy and Practice*, *74*, 250–267. doi:10.1016/j.tra.2015.02.016

Yuan, X., Liu, X., & Zuo, J. (2015). The development of new energy vehicles for a sustainable future: A review. *Renewable & Sustainable Energy Reviews*, *42*, 298–305. doi:10.1016/j.rser.2014.10.016

Zhang, P., Yan, F., & Du, C. (2015). A comprehensive analysis of energy management strategies for hybrid electric vehicles based on bibliometrics. *Renewable & Sustainable Energy Reviews*, *48*, 88–104. doi:10.1016/j.rser.2015.03.093

KEY TERMS AND DEFINITIONS

Alternate Fuel Vehicle (AFV): A vehicle that runs on a fuel other than gasoline or diesel. This may include vehicles that run on electricity or hybrid technologies, but may also more broadly include vehicles that run on non-traditional fossil-derived fuels such as liquid petroleum gas, propane, and compressed natural gas (CNG), or bio-fuels such as methanol and ethanol.

Discrete Choice Modeling: Statistical procedures used to model choices people make among a set of alternatives, such as different types of automobiles.

Electric Vehicle (EV): A vehicle that runs on electricity and must be plugged in periodically to recharge the battery.

Environmental Concern: Concerned or worried about the protection of the natural environment, including protecting land, sea, and air from pollution.

Fuel Efficient Vehicle (FEV): Any vehicle that achieves a very favorable rate of miles per gallon or kilometres per litre. The reason for its fuel efficiency may be because of its small and light design, efficient engine, specialized fuel, or advanced technology.

Hybrid Electric Vehicle (HEV): A vehicle that uses a combination of a conventional internal combustion engine and an electric propulsion system, enabling it to achieve superior fuel economy.

Market Segmentation: The process of dividing a broad consumer target market into subsets of consumers who have common characteristics, such as age, gender, income, or other relevant variables.

Plug-In Hybrid Electric Vehicle (PHEV): A vehicle that uses a combination of a conventional internal combustion engine and an electric propulsion system, but which must be plugged in periodically to recharge the battery.

Psychographics: The study of personality, values, attitudes, interests, and lifestyles, with a focus on interests, activities, and opinions. Psychographics can be used as a means of market segmentation.

Social Marketing: The application of marketing concepts and techniques in order to change behavior and achieve a positive social outcome.

Chapter 4
Customer Satisfaction in the Consumption of Green Products

Violeta Sima
Petroleum-Gas University of Ploieşti, Romania

Ileana Georgiana Gheorghe
Petroleum-Gas University of Ploieşti, Romania

ABSTRACT

This chapter aimed to identify those factors that determine the green consumer satisfaction, having as the emerging point the consumer behavior definition and the sustainable development concept. The authors propose a new approach of the dimensions of the evaluation model for customer satisfaction including a new one, called The Green Dimension. An important goal was identifying the drivers of the consumer purchasing. The authors identified three main areas of the green dimension of customer satisfaction. They are related to Company, Product/service, and Price. Then some considerations regarding an integrated approach of strategic mix from a 'green' perspective have been presented. According to research from Boston Consulting Group, in order to obtain a Green Advantage, companies should enhance their strategic mix taking into considerations green planning, green processes, green product, and green promotion. The authors added two more elements, namely people and eco-efficiency, resulting "The Green Strategy Mix".

INTRODUCTION

Green Economy involves the use of natural resources, energy, new technologies, and cleaner production methods in order to promote economic growth and create new jobs. To implement this concept, new models for sustainable consumption and production should be developed, which does not force the ecosystem.

In order to operationalize the Green Economy concept, the three aspects of sustainable development (environmental, economic and social) should be incorporated, to obtain a multi-dimensional outcome changing consumption patterns will require a multi-prong strategy focusing on demand, meeting the basic needs of the poor, and reducing wastage and the use of finite resources in the production process.

DOI: 10.4018/978-1-5225-2139-6.ch004

In order to implement the green economy at the national level, it is required close involvement of consumers and producers, along with the implementation of the main measures proposed and adopted at the national and international governing bodies.

The green economy requires changing consumer habits.

In order to assess consumer satisfaction, it is important to know the degree to which they are willing to pay extra for green products and services. This chapter is a theoretical approach to this problem.

The authors identified three main areas of the green dimension of customer satisfaction. They are related to Company, Product/Service, and Price.

The objective of this study is to highlight the links between green satisfaction and the three mentioned elements but also the transformations they bring in consumption patterns.

Background

The concept of satisfaction has been a subject of study for many researchers. However, satisfaction is still difficult to be defined, as Oliver asserted in 1997 in his book, "Satisfaction: A Behavioural Perspective on the Consumer" (p. 13). Thus, although satisfaction seems to be a widely-known concept, when a definition is required it is difficult to obtain.

The subject of this thesis is to reveal multiple senses of customer satisfaction emphasizing the Green Dimension (Sima & Gheorghe, 2009).

Customer satisfaction is subject to study not only for scholars but also for companies. The purpose of this analysis is very pragmatic, namely to determine its maximizing in order to increase customer loyalty. To achieve this, it is essential to identify key factors which determine customer behaviour.

Although in the literature of specialty there is widely accepted the opinion that satisfaction represents a response to consumption related experiences (Yi, 1990; Anderson, Fornell & Lehmann, 1994; Oliver, 1997; Giese, & Cote, 2000), it has a wide range of definitions and assessment ways (Peterson & Wilson1992; Giese, & Cote, 2000).

A customer who has achieved a high level of satisfaction will be tempted to repeat the purchase, thus becoming loyal. The final effect will be the customer retention (Zairi, 2000). Moreover, he will be prompted to provide positive recommendations to other potential customers. On the contrary, a dissatisfied customer will give up in the future buying the product or service or even he will return it. Another possibility to reduce dissonance is also searching for information that confirms the high value of the product or service (Kotler, 2000).

In the research studies for satisfaction more operationalizations of satisfaction were used (Westbrook, & Oliver, 1981; Hausknecht, 1990; Peterson, & Wilson, 1992; Wirtz, & Lee, 2003). Thus, Hausknecht (1990) listed 34 measures, including measures of behaviour (namely, behaviour registrations, such as a number of complaints about the main product) and self-report measures (namely, survey items, such as rating scales).

Also, the marketing studies showed that customer satisfaction depends on the specific psychological construction such as reliability, quality, customer loyalty, commitment, word-of-mouth and image, and customer profitability. It has been shown that quality and reliability are required by satisfaction, which in turn is necessary for customer loyalty and customer profitability (Yi, 1990; Anderson et al., 1994; Oliver 1997; Verhoef, 2001; Hennig-Thurau, Gwinner & Gremler, 2002).

The meaning of the concept is context-specific satisfaction (Giese & Cote, 2000).

As a result of a learning process which can be developed only in the presence of a permanent client, who asks repeatedly for a particular product, brand or company, in order to meet a specific need, as a form of attachment to the benefits provided by the company, static vision of the satisfaction resulted from the client-producer relationship, has been replaced gradually and improved by cumulative satisfaction paradigm.

Satisfaction refers to the fact that a particular feature of a product or the product itself offered a "pleasurable level of consumption-related fulfilment, including levels of under or over fulfillment" (Oliver, 2006).

According to Rust and Oliver, "consumer satisfaction can be seen as the consumer's fulfilment response" (1994).

In 2001 Parker and Matthew referred to the existence of two complementary approaches to the concept of consumer satisfaction, namely satisfaction as a process and respectively satisfaction as a result of consumption experiences.

In 1977 and two years later, in 1979, Olson and Oliver asserted that in terms of process, customer satisfaction can be defined as an assessment of the significance of what was received and what was expected. Vavra, in 1997, emphasized that perceptual, psychological and assessment processes determine consumer satisfaction.

Consumer satisfaction, as a result, can be defined as a final state resulting from the consumption experience. This condition may be the result obtained without comparing expectations (Oliver, 2006) or a cognitive state obtained as a result of comparing the expected and actual performance or cost comparison of rewards and anticipated consequences (1997).

In marketing literature two main groups of models evaluation of consumer satisfaction can be identified:

- Models that put in relation the concept of customer satisfaction with concepts such as quality, value, and loyalty behaviour complaints. These models have an essential role at the level of organizational policy. Thus, they provide the strategic context for designing a marketing research on consumer satisfaction.
- Models based on the constructs of the customer satisfaction concept such as the discrepancy between expectations and actual results, attribution, equity, affect, and regret. These models allow proper operationalization of measurements of customer satisfaction providing appropriate constructs.

In order to measure consumer satisfaction with a broad range of organizations, indexes have been developed. Thus, at the national level, customer satisfaction index (CSI) is used in order to measure how companies and organizations are able to satisfy customer needs. The CSI Model is also used for comparing the services and products within a sector. Most countries have developed their own customer satisfaction indexes. The first such model was the national Swedish customer satisfaction barometer (SCSB), developed in 1989. It has included 31 major industries in Sweden. This model used perceived value as a single measure of customer expectations (Fornell, 1992). In 1992, in Germany, Deutsche Kundenbarometer (DK) was introduced, which in 1994 also included 31 industries.

In USA American Customer Satisfaction Index (ACSI) is being used since 1994. This model takes into account both the field of production as well as the field of public area. Thus, seven economic sectors, nearly 40 industries, 200 private sector companies and two local public services are taken into account.

Customer satisfaction index is calculated by taking into account proportional role of three categories of variables, namely: overall satisfaction, satisfaction expectations and satisfaction with the organization "ideal".

A model used to assess customer satisfaction is European Customer Satisfaction Index (ECSI) Model. This is an econometric model that links customer satisfaction index with a set of causal latent variables (such as customer expectations and customer perceptions about quality and value), being based on the verified theory of consumer behaviour modelling. It aims to determine the perceived quality and the company image to customers and customer loyalty.

Kristensen et al. (2000) described it as "a structural equation model with unobservable latent variables... that link customer satisfaction to its determinants and, in turn, to its consequence, namely 'trust' and 'repurchase intention".

Customer satisfaction study aims at four main aspects, namely:

1. Identifying the means of measuring customer satisfaction;
2. Finding the ratio of the number of satisfied clients and the total number of customers;
3. Identifying key indicators for the satisfaction assessing;
4. Finding the evolution of the level of customer satisfaction.

In order to answer those questions, the relationship between actual performance and desired performance must be considered. The Bender Model (1991) and The Rapp Model (1995), cited by Schneider, emphasized five dimensions to be considered when assessing customer satisfaction:

1. Technical quality of the product;
2. Reputation quality;
3. Service quality;
4. Quality of personal relationships;
5. Price perception.

According to Meyer-Waarden (2004), satisfaction is an essential element for modelling customer purchasing behaviour, based on three categories of variables:

1. Cognitive variable;
2. Affective variables;
3. Co-native variables.

In the beginning, pro-environmental models have started from the premise that between environmental knowledge and concern about this there is a direct linear relationship, leading to pro-environmental actions as a consequence (Kollmuss & Agyeman, 2002).

Ottman (1993) has defined "environmental consumerism" as a reaction of the consumers, who, noting environmental problems, increasingly buy more eco-friendly products, gradually abandoning classic products. The stated purpose was to protect "themselves and the planet".

Thus, marketers should address this category of products similarly to the target market (Ottman, 2006) because consumers look for them, especially (Pickett, 2008).

Consumers claim to be well informed about the benefits of the products they intend to purchase. In doing so, marketers must consider this aspect in establishing the communication strategy and use instruments which best matching with the beliefs and behaviour of consumers, determining thus interest for the product (Kilbourne, 1995).

Ottman (1993) defined green consumers as "those who actively seek and support those products satisfy their needs that are having less impact on the environment". Besides that, Macdonald, S. et al. (2006) said that all consumers are potential green consumers, because when a consumer has the opportunity to choose between two products that satisfy the same need, he will prefer to buy green products.

If gender is taken into account, it was found that there is no a "significant relationship between women and men and green behaviour" (Kreidler & Joseph, 2009). However, there are studies which showed that women are generally more concerned about the environment are more willing to buy green products (Mainieri et al., 1997).

If the geographic region is taken into consideration, it is demonstrated on the basis of consumer surveys that across Europe consumers express concern for the environment. Thus, they look for eco - friendly products and services, being at the same time willing to pay more for environmental features. This obvious serious concern of the European consumers for green products has led to 90% of European multinationals to adopt programs of environmental sustainability (Peattie & Crane, 2005).

People can be induced to adopt green consumption model if additional benefits, cost effective or environmentally friendly solutions are offered (Ottman, 1993).

In marketing literature is shown by research (Pickett, 2008) that product perception is influenced by situational variables and social reference groups. Also, there are studies which showed that many of the consumers perceive organic products having a high price and low quality (Mendleson, 1994; Ginsberg, and Bloom, 2004).

Gupta, S.et. al. (2009) referred to the „green buying behaviour". Thus, he showed that the concern for the environment and about pollution, willingness to recycle, and to pay more for environmentally friendly products form this behaviour. Many studies on this topic have been performed starting from the analysis of the willingness of the consumer to pay more for green energy (Wiser, 1998; Hansla et. al., 2007).

Marketers may contribute to change consumer behaviour by emphasizing benefits and desired features of the products in the messages communicated by the producing companies to their potential customers. In relational marketing „long term benefits" of the product are submitted, leading to attract and retain consumers for long periods (Antonies & Raaij, 1998).

Thus, consumer behaviour can be shaped by emphasizing relative advantages of eco-friendly products in comparison with those products which create environmental damages (Peattie, 2001).

Related to this, Ottman (1993) stated that consumers can be the emotionally motivated to get involved because they want to differentiate themselves from other members of society or in their groups.

Another issue taken into consideration by the American scientist J. Ottman is the period of life when certain purchasing and consumption behaviours are induced. Thus, she stated that "habits are decided early in life" (1993). The conclusion is that consumers will take more favorable to environment decisions if environmental education will start early.

Instead, Peattie (2001) believes that to form such habits, companies should be those that should get involved. Thus, in the early stages of forming purchasing habits, they should use some systems to reward customers.

Mass media is another factor that can contribute decisively to the formation of buying habits. This, as a stakeholder (Ottman, 1993) and opinion promoter, can effectively convey environmental information.

However, in practice consumers tend to become suspicious in some cases when companies put too emphasis on the environment in their communication systems.

The label is another factor to be taken into account in substantiation of the decision to purchase (Chase & Smith, 1992). The label may highlight specific environmental information that can contribute to an attitude of buying an eco-friendly product.

In other words, we can say that a system of an environmentally friendly communicating system can lead to a favorable attitude to green products (Baldwin, 1993).

It follows from the above that the companies need to pay great importance to develop long-term strategies (Darling et al., 2009).

There are a number of studies have shown that environmental issues have become important issues for the population. This, also, led to changes in purchasing and consumption behaviour. Thus, consumers become more aware of environmental issues, giving more time for the prospection stage, seeking, primarily those energy efficient products. These behavioural patterns suggest the intention of engaging in a green consumer behaviour (Roberts, 1996; Kalafatis et al., 1999). However, the explanation may come from increased energy prices.

Factors which consumers take into account in substantiation the purchasing decision, ultimately support marketers when they design the marketing mix. Thus, if environmental factors are considered, sustainability goals can be more easily pursued. In order to achieve these objectives criteria of compatibility of the ecosystems with production systems should be considered. In this respect, Fuller stated that „Customers need to learn to base purchasing decisions not only on how well the products meet the individual needs but also on how these products affect the natural environment" (1999).

Regarding the evaluation of the substantiation of the decision to purchase, Ottman (1993) stated that the products or services are evaluated not only in terms of "performance and price," but also on the "social responsibility of manufacturers."

Consumers tend to repeat purchase in those cases where post-purchasing evaluation gives them satisfaction (Wood & Neal, 2009).

Thus, the concept of customer loyalty is related to environmental concerns and decisions having an impact on them.

IMPLICATIONS OF THE SUSTAINABLE DEVELOPMENT IN CONSUMER BEHAVIOUR

Sustainable Development: Frame for Sustainable Consumption

Sustainable development offers a frame for communities for an efficient use of the resources, in order to create new commercial activities, to protect and improve the life quality, to create new commercial activities which consolidate their economy. It can help to create a healthy community, which can sustain even the actual generation, and the next one. The concept of the environmental degradation unplumbed from the economic growth by eco-efficiency promotion and by interpretation of the high standards of environmental protection as a challenge to innovation, new markets and new business development, if we take into consideration the fact that a healthy environment is essential to ensure the welfare and quality of life.

There are increasingly more voices claiming that production and consumption of goods would become sustainable if consumption of raw materials would be reduced. Consumption should be reported to the ecological potential of the environment. Sustainable non-inflationary growth thus became one of the economic objectives of the European economic model. An economy which would meet these conditions is called "dematerialized." To that context, consumer behavior gets a more important role in this economic model (Beatley, 2000).

Lester R. Brown argued that the economy is part of the environment, showing that considering that the environment is part of economy generated a destructive economic model. He showed that if China would adopt the American lifestyle, demand for oil would increase by 80 million barrels per day, and paper consumption would exceed the global production capacity. Extrapolating this reasoning, he says that this economic model based on fossil fuel consumption is not suitable for any other developing countries, nor for the world. Eco-economy is presented as an optimistic alternative model. Thus, the main concern of the theoreticians in economics consists in integrating the ecological principles. Brown shows that the seeds of this new sustainable economic model can be seen even today, as new wind turbines, solar panels, electric cars or networks of bike trails, which are becoming increasingly visible in the big cities. This new economic model should be integrated into ecosystem so that allowing further economic and social development (Brown, 2001).

Sustainability principle designates the gear of three dimensions – ecology, economy and social sphere. Mixing up the consumer behavior with the ecological dimension of sustainability is very important. Economic development and social welfare are possible in long-term, only in a well-established frame which involves nature as a vital element. The economic and social aspects are important in order to make ecology becoming feasible: ecological manufacturing and consumption are elements that can be realized only if the consumer is able to afford them and if both are realized under acceptable social guidance. 30-40% of the environmental problems are based directly or indirectly on some prevailing consumption models (Using UBA, 1997, p. 1).

In this context, new strategies must propose a way for the sustainable development:

- Quality and preservation of the environment and natural resources essential elements of the sustainable development;
- Management of the manufacturing flow, so that, taking into consideration the finite character of resources, to facilitate and encourage reuse and recycle at an optimum level, in order to avoid loss and depletion of natural resources;
- Modification of the planned society concordant to the confined character of the natural resources, so that their consumption or use to be not made in another's detriment, so that exploitation by a generation of the natural resources to not confine consumption possibilities of the future generations.

The global expansion of environmentalism is ascertained in the current period. The objectives envisaged aim, on the one hand, to improve the efficiency of production processes, using, and recycling of consumer goods and, on the other hand, further progress in global governance policies. This means greening of the corporate codes of conduct, international environmental law increasingly tougher or stronger cultural norms of "appropriate" consumption (Dauvergne, 2008). However, the current pace of implementation of these policies is considered too slow and the real involvement, too sporadic to prevent the negative effects of the excessive consumption.

According to Dauvergne (2008), the expenditures for environmental rehabilitation and human health are increasingly larger and require immediate action. In this regard, measures are required at the legislative level, both on the production and market. These measures have already begun to generate changes in customer behavior and society in general. But for this environment-oriented behavior could be generalized globally improvement of communication is required.

The regulatory policy tools must be chosen so that they outcrop a matched mix of their, adapting them to specific application situations. They include:

- Persuasion policy, which assumes promotion of the ecological technologies and research, awareness and education and use of market mechanisms;
- Information transfer policy encompasses tools for social communication - education, mass-media and public relation – informational systems affordable for the public.

Traditional policies pursuing minimization of the environment harmfulness, policies having as main goals demand satisfaction with a minimum input are added, in manufacturing area, production policies with a minimum output of wasted resources and, also changes in the demand profile.

Nowadays, urban environment became more and more crowded especially by increasing the frequency of the transportation activities. Urbanities specialists are highly concerned with problems of the territorial use. Planning of the territory use needs to be closely correlated with regulatory for activities of the transportation services, which must accurately reflect costs of the needs of environment rehabilitation and social costs of maintaining or development of the transportation infrastructure.

A more deepened knowledge of the premises of consumption structuring for other goods and services, is, also, necessary, as a response to the multitude of needs expresses by different consumers' categories. For instance, option for replacing an old product with a new one can be underlined by many motivations – that the old one can't be mended, that the new one has superior properties, that there is a use for periodic shopping. The emergency of the consumerism era, in occidental countries, was possible just as a complexity of the consumption behavior of modern people and his striving for innovation (Stanciu, 2006).

The paper is a consumer good, which manufacturing depends on, essentially of the exploitation of wooded lands. Paper consumption clearly reflects the level of civilization and economic development for a country. But the industry of cellulose and paper is not only the biggest wood consumer in the world but, also the third industry in the world in respect of the financial results, being, at the same time among the first ten most polluting industries. Therefore, in the next 50 years, the demand for cellulose and paper is expected to increase with a hundred percent, according to The National Institute of Statistics of Romania, 2004. But, on the other hand, there are still over a billion of illiterate people and over 100 millions of children who don't yet benefit of primary school education.

Generally, encouraging of goods and services demand, mass-media and advertising industries play a decisive role. Mainly, advertising industries affect consumers' motivations, having a decisive role for consumption structuring and modelling of the concepts regarding goods and services. Some recent studies of the consumption habits sustain that manufacturing response for some consumption needs can become more sustainable, by encouraging the taking up some services destined to contribute to the raising of sustainability of the goods already purchased, instead to encourage purchasing of new goods. These kinds of practices lead to diminishing pressure of the extractive industries to the environment that can lead to a new conceptualization of the life quality increasing. Also, some recent analyses of companies affirmed that consumers' loyalty for a brand seems to be more encouraged by a bid for services destined to extend the life of the goods in use and less by encouraging of the purchasing new products.

Sustainable consumption and manufacturing models represent important determinants of the environmental problems at every level, from the local level to the global level. For this reason, Changing Consumption Patterns was a main object in Agenda 21 (The World Conference in Rio de Janeiro, 1992). Sustainable consumption represents a very wise area, requesting an interdisciplinary approach. The change of the consumer behavior is a process involving many social groups: ménages, which represent the biggest group of consumers, authorities, economy, educational institutions, NGOs and many others.

In September 2015, the United Nations adopted the Agenda 2030 for Sustainable Development which established a comprehensive framework for eradicating poverty and achieving sustainable development by 2030, based on the Millennium Development Goals (MDGs), adopted in 2000. Thus, the 2030 Agenda includes an ambitious set of 17 Goals for Sustainable Development (SDG). Among them, goal no.12 aims to "ensure sustainable consumption and production patterns". Paragraph 28 of the 2030 Agenda states the clear commitment of signatory countries on the implementation of fundamental changes in the how societies produce and consume goods and services. Thus, the involvement of all categories of stakeholders, namely, international organizations, governments, business sector and other non-state actors and individuals is required. Each of them must be involved in changing the unsustainable patterns of production and consumption. The involvement must target both technical plan, and the financial sectors. Developed countries must assume the role of leading this movement. At the same time, protecting economies in developing countries should be considered. In this regard, new investments must be carried out. They must contribute to "strengthen developing countries' scientific, technological and innovative capacities" of these weaker economies, to enable their evolution towards more sustainable consumption and production patterns. (United Nations, Transforming our world: the 2030 Agenda for Sustainable Development, retrieved on January, the 10th, 2016, from https://sustainabledevelopment.un.org/post2015/transformingourworld)

EU leads the efforts for a sustainable world. The EU has already adopted the leading position in terms of efforts for a sustainable world. In this context, the EU was committed carrying forward this agenda, both internally (e.g. through thc future EU initiatives such as the strategy for circular economy, designed to tackle more sustainable patterns of production and consumption), and through its external policies, by supporting implementation efforts in other countries, especially those with the most urgent needs. The most important EU's Contribution to the Millennium Development Goals for the 2004-2014 period, in terms of ensuring environmental sustainability, consist of:

- Connecting more than 74 million people to improved drinking water;
- Connecting 27.5 million people to sanitation facilities;
- Protecting 1.9 million km2 of forest;
- Continuing conservation of 1.1 million km2 of protected areas.

A change of the consumers' behavior means primarily a fundamental transformation of the values and life style. The change of the thinking and acting kind of the consumers can't be imposed by the authorities. The emergence of new and durable traditions in consumers' behavior requests a wise informing and consulting campaign. As regards of the consumer, goods and transportation ways must become more transparent, the price of the ecological true need to be clearly expressed and those alternatives for the environment protection must be as soon as possible shown.

Ways to Ensure a Sustainable Consumption

- Development by companies of products and services that maximize social value and minimize environmental effects. This requires strengthening the role of research and development function at the micro level.
- Education in this regard and influencing consumer choice of goods and services. Important roles in this regard can play promoting and raising awareness of consumer options. Companies can encourage consumers to choose environmentally friendly products and services and to consider the sustainable way to use them.
- Changing of the demand's characteristics and elements related to the dominant lifestyle, especially in developed countries - decreasing the quantity of purchased goods and services.

Areas of Activity of the Sustainable Consumption

Question about the concrete measures for the implementation of the sustainable behaviour regarding consumption appears only in a second stage. A very important role was allotted for areas as:

- Avoiding of the waste products accumulation;
- Energy and water consumption;
- Mobility;
- Feed;
- Reuse of the objects.

In order to attain a sustainable growth, material consumption of the industrialized countries must be diminished. This is possible because of the fact that in the last period goods having a low content of raw material were introduced in market, for the automobile industry, for the equipment industry and for that of the wrapper. There are motives for which a decrease of the material and energy consumption doesn't necessarily lead to a diminution of the total consumption. Thus, increasing total quantity of the used merchandise cancel savings obtained in technology of their realization. Secondly, motivation for producers to realize ecologic goods is related mainly with economic interest, which operationalizes the new sustainable technologies. The classic case is represented by the fridge with low energy consumption, but more expensive than the conventional one. Another solution for the sustainable consumption consists of realization of goods having long term of working. This is only a part of the new approach, which imposes a new vision to merchandise, according consumers' needs.

There are many problems: it is not clearly how the consumers are prepared to accept prizes of the ecologic goods. A strict legislation in this area imposes serious pressures to the economic agents.

They began to understand that not only attention paid to different goods separately seen. This imposes a new approach, named metabolic, which approach the whole anthropic system.

Also, they began to understand that the attention paid to different goods separately seen is not sufficient.

Some specific studies showed the ecologic impact of the services, building the concept of services efficiency meaning to offer a maximum result for consumers by use a minimum quantity of raw materials and energy. The most important feature of this concept consists of the fact that in our days, satisfaction is generated not only by the products but even by services which they provided. In other words, products offered represent only tools for services obtaining.

The 12th goal of Agenda 2030 aims to "encourage companies, especially large and transnational companies, to adopt sustainable practices and to integrate sustainability information into their reporting cycle". In this context, colleges and universities could become very important actors. Thus, it would be appropriate for them to upgrade their curricular areas by introducing disciplines and developing specializations able to confer appropriate competencies for their graduates, especially in developing countries.

Reducing waste is another issue that has been also taken into account at UN summit in September 2015. In this regard, a proposed measure consists in the rationalization of inefficient fossil fuel subsidies.

Restructuring taxation and gradual reduction of harmful subsidies are expected mentioned as methods for implementing these measures. Each country must take into account the specificities of the national economy. UN document clearly stipulates "minimizing the possible adverse impacts on their development in a manner that protect the poor and the affected communities".

Implications for the Elementary Processes Which Define Consumer Behaviour

All the same, consumer behaviour is influenced by numerous variables acting tightly. Consumers' behaviour is influenced by many factors:

1. Directly observable influences:
   a. Demographic factors
   b. Economic factors
   c. Factors specific for the marketing mix
2. Endogenous influences:
   a. Perception
   b. Information/learning personality
   c. Motivation
   d. Attitude
3. Exogenous influences:
   a. Family
   b. Membership group
   c. Reference group
   d. Social class
   e. Culture
   f. Sub-culture

In the last two decades, social analyses focused on goods and services consumption of the occidental people. These were significantly changed in terms of a general sense of the message, leaving pro-consumerist messages in favour of those anti-consumerist.

Some papers published after 2000, underlined a new criticism current in the area of consumption patterns in the occidental area, highlighting more clear tendencies of some social categories, to engage in activities less oriented to consumption. Some authors, as Zavestoski (2002), Schor and Holt (2000) or Hamilton and Mail (2003) was concerned even to initiate market studies for anti-consumeristic attitude or for return to some extremely simple consumption practices, protective with maintaining the environmental ecologic equilibrium. There are analysts of the consumption patterns like Lunt & Livingstone

(1992) or Humphery (1998), who study a new orientation of the consumers – to limit satisfaction of the consumption needs by different good and services markets, as a consequence of the high critic attitudes.

Perception

The most important feature of perception is the fact that is selectivity, as being complementary to needs, because of the consumers' features.

A useful concept is just a difference indistinguishable, for instance, in cases of price increasing motivated by different factors, such as green tax. If the increasing of price doesn't exceed the difference just indistinguishable, it is possible that demand for a specific good to be not affected.

"An environmentally sustainable economy — an eco-economy — requires that the principles of ecology establish the framework for the formulation of economic policy and that economists and ecologists work together to fashion the new economy. Ecologists understand that all economic activity, indeed all life, depends on the earth's ecosystem — the complex of individual species living together, interacting with each other and their physical habitat." (Brown, 2001)

The Need for Comprehensive Regulations

The ecological manufacturing and sustainability can gain a certain influence on consumers' decisions, but the price still represents the key variable. All researchers agree on this. Nobody will pay, for instance, fourfold for a fridge just for its less energy consumption. Central administrations need to establish specific regulations, to recommend minimal prices for the unfriendly goods for the environment, in order to make certain the fact that they are not cheaper than those being friendly for the environment. These could increase consumers trust.

In the context of the 12th goal of the 2030 Agenda, mentioned above, the implementation of a 10-year framework program on sustainable consumption and production is envisaged. Developed countries are asked to take the lead of these programs.

Currently, the use of renewable energy resources, ecological agriculture and implementation of an intelligent management of urban waste must be major objectives for both environmental policies as well as those relating to the quality of life.

Feelings and Emotions Consideration

There is a real potential in this area, for instance that demonstrated by the success of some brands in the cosmetic industry. Companies should recognize opportunities and gains generated by the sustainable goods and shouldn't only pertain to risks and costs.

Another example in this area is represented by the fact that some studies demonstrated that those advertisings which highlight the fact that the good had in sight don't encompass children' work are irritating for consumers because they assume a priori that manufacturing is correctly from the point of view of the policies. Furthermore, terms like children exploitation have negative connotations and can cause damages to the positive experience of goods or its purchasing, irrespective of context.

In marketing terms, it is vital, the fact that green goods meet their goals, this making consumer fell that he does the right things.

Selection of the consumers' perceptions is much influenced by their attitudes in the moment of their reception.

Consumers' expectations are closely linked to the process of perceptual selection, implying them percept goods and their performances from the point of view of the benefits they expect to obtain. Market researches show that consumers consider first personal benefits and not these for the environment. For instance, in a supermarket consumers don't wonder first: Do I the right thing buying this? But: If I will buy this, it will be good for me? Thus, they are ready to pay more for this kind of goods. And only after that, they consider that the good must be manufactured in ecological conditions.

Reasons can play an essential role, too, in the perceptual selection, being known the fact that people perceive good related their needs and desires. An intense need determines a person to ignore some perceptions and select only those are related to this satisfaction.

Information

Perception is first, related to the awareness/learning process, which represents an ensemble through people know goods.

In awareness process, specialists pay attention to information sources.

Researches upon consumers' behaviour and attitudes in last decades showed a real interest in problems of environmental harmfulness. But there is still a long distance from attitude to their transformation in practices. In real life, consumers almost don't possess information about present and future effects of consumption decisions to environment or to other people.

In the same time, consumers manifest their decisions in a world where merchandise already are in last processing stage a major change being hard to obtain. The observed changes in consumer behaviour can be seen only in tight areas; they must be supported by strong awareness campaigns in order to become dominant market behaviour being significant for producers. But there is another dike: market is already saturated with advertising messages that increase chances that these campaigns be fast forgotten.

Generating important changes will occur only after a radical change of consumers' attitude. This requests a redesigning of prices policies in order that non-harmful for the environment goods to be chosen and opposite policies to be punished. These request other policies for consumers' information. A study performed in 1990 by Winkler and Voller identified a correlation between consumers' attitude and environmental impact of goods. This correlation was revealed related domestic energy consumption which decreased in those countries where ecological attitude increased, Holland, Germany, Denmark and Sweden.

Goal no.12 of the 20130 Agenda refers the issue of "the relevant information and awareness for sustainable development and lifestyles in harmony with nature". These should be available by 2030 for people everywhere.

Attitude

Attitude was accepted more and more as a multidimensional concept, as a syndrome of constant reactions against social objects (WBCSD, 1996).

An interesting fact is that, in fact, consumers are not concerned directly with reducing energy consumption, but in a specific choice about buying daily goods. Consumers take decisions when they use or discard concrete goods. This means that concrete manifestations of these mental attitudes need to be analysed.

Globally, specific studies identified phenomena of take-over consumption models from developed countries by the developing countries; there is a problem regarding this because first habits related goods having most important impact against environment (cars, steel, and electricity), whilst consumption models for less harmful goods are less convincing. Though, solution consists of modelling consumption attitudes.

Care for environment protection is confronted with interest for personal satisfaction obtaining.

There are researches showing that people have familiar attitudes towards environmental consciousness in terms of factors related to awareness and action, environmental friendliness and willingness to act to act environmentally friendly (Mostafa, 2007; Tuna & Özkoçak, 2012).

Awareness of environmental issues grows day by day. This led to an increased demand for green products. Nowadays globalization is a key feature of the business environment. The technology and information boom represent, also current features of its. These elements have contributed to increase awareness of environmental issues and to generate a favourable attitude toward environmentalism, causing consumers' inclination to purchase green products. But, although the environmental concerns play an important role on consumer intention to buy green products, they are not the only determining factor for purchase (Phau & Ong, 2007; Agyeman, 2014). There are many factors which have been identified as influencing this process, namely, company's environmental reputation (Schwepker & Cornwell, 1991), credibility of environmental advertising (Thøgersen, 2000), environmental knowledge (Mostafa, 2006), and perceived product price and quality (D'Souza et al., 2007).

Investments for Sustainability

Transparency and accessibility of goods and producers are essential both for consumers and stakeholders. Many companies accomplish increasingly sustainability criteria. A specific degree of this criteria knowledge can determine consumers of the goods they offer to identify themselves with these companies' values.

In order to achieve its stated objective of ensuring sustainable consumption and production patterns, the Agenda 2030 takes into account, too, supporting countries developing to strengthen scientific and technological capacities to evolve towards more sustainable consumption and production.

Motivation

Motives have a broad multidimensional character, being built between biologic and social, between internal manifestations and knowledge, between subjective necessity and values as a reference system, between objects and their linkages with people. Because of these, they can't be reduced only at a determinant factor. In order to design an efficient marketing policy, it is important to concern that motives are learnt and they have stability in time, being hardly changeable.

Effective Behaviour

Effective behaviour is not an autonomous process though it can be studied relatively independent; it is a specific resultant of a system constituted by the above-mentioned elementary processes.

There are numerous studies on green consumption behaviour. Wu and Chen (2014) have attempted to translate several descriptive variables in such a model. Thus, a positive relationship between attitude and perceived benefit and a negative relationship between perceived risk and attitude were highlighted. This result shows that consumers' evaluation of green consumption is affected by uncertainty; role of perceived benefits is much greater than that of perceived risk, which confirms results of previous research (Rohm & Swaminathan, 2004). Also, positive relationships between normative beliefs and moral obligation and respectively, subjective norm were highlighted. Another significant positive relationship was emphasized on control strength and control belief and behavioural control, supporting the findings of Ajzen's (1991; 2002) that availability of time and financial resources influence the green consumption behaviour, which makes consumers to practice green consumption as they are more confident of their resources. The findings of Cheng, Lam, and Hsu (2006), Baker, Al-Gahtani, and Hubona (2007), and Cronan and Al-Rafee (2008) regarding the significant positive relationship between attitude, subjective norm, and behavioural control and behavioural intention were also supported by Wu and Chen (2104). Also, a significant positive relationship was revealed between behavioural intention and behavioural control, respectively real behaviour, confirming the conclusions of Mostafa (2007) and Norman and Conner (2005).

Avant-Gardist Demand

As consumers become more informed and more educated, increasingly more of them are beginning to realize the impact that their consumption habits have on the environment. On the other hand, green marketing began to gain importance both in theory and in business (Ryan, 2014).

According to Obermiller and Spangenberg (1998) and Marques and Almeida (2013), the consumers' skepticism about the green features is no different compared to general skepticism towards the features usually communicated by marketers.

There are practical demonstrations of the fact that avant-gardist demand establishes trends which involve most of the consumers. In this respect, female consumers play a decisive role as follows they manifest much more responsibility and involvement in buying acts. They stand on utility, longevity and social or ethical standard.

ECOLOGICAL CONSCIOUSNESS

The ecological consciousness has complex character multidimensional. Thus, consumers should be informed about several aspects as follows.

Consumers must know the environmental consequences of their consumption behaviour. At the same time, they must understand the consequences of their behaviour as a result of attitudes towards environmental issues and products. The first effect consists of changing the consumption patterns; behaviour resulting from their ecological attitude will contribute to solving environmental problems and increasing the quality of life.

In the current conditions, the environmental awareness as a form of social consciousness plays an important role. Thus, ecological consciousness must contribute to building the ecological culture of human personality. Ecological culture requires deep knowledge of the laws of nature and society development, of the interdependence between man and the environment, of the awareness of the need to protect nature and to use the natural resources as rationally and efficiently as (Uhl, 2004; Schendler, 2009).

In summary, ecological consciousness can be defined as a form of social consciousness reflecting the correlation between society and nature, the actions of man over nature and consequences of these actions, as well as the substantiation of the ways and means of environmental protection.

Ecological consciousness comprises two distinct components, namely: a theoretical component and another one with practical character. The theoretical part of the ecological consciousness is a system of ideas, concepts and theories about the forms of interaction between society and nature. These ideas and theories expand and deepen the spiritual basis of the ecological design that reflects the character and the purpose of the environmental activity. Ecological consciousness with practical character is formed spontaneously as a result of practical activities of the people. It is the primary form of perception by a man of his place and his role in relation to the environment. These components are reflected in the multidimensional nature of the ecological consciousness (Gray, 1985).

The Dimensions of the Ecological Conscience of Consumers

- Informative Dimension
- Cognitive Dimension
- Operative Dimension

THE GREEN DIMENSION OF THE MODEL OF CUSTOMER SATISFACTION

Drivers of the Green Dimension of the Model of the Assessment of Consumer Satisfaction

Reality has shown that proactive, long-term, visionary strategies, companies bring more benefits for companies than those based on classical management based on traditional resources. The companies concern for the environment represents, from this perspective, an opportunity. Thus, an organization will gain a competitive ecological advantage over the competition ecological if it is "better" than this, in terms of environmental issues, at least in a specific area.

The companies' interest for environment first appeared in campaigns for social responsibility inspired by the multinationals model. The adoption of "green" strategies has been boosted, too, by environmental regulations in certain areas.

In the current context, economic organizations are evaluated not only in terms of economic performance, but also in relation to their contributions to economic and social development of the community. Thus, the concept of social responsibility (SR) emerged. WBCSD World Business Council Sustainable Development) defined corporate social responsibility as "the Continuing Commitment by business to contribute to economic development while improving the quality of life of the workforce and Their Families as well as of the community and society at large" (WBCSD Business Solutions for a sustainable world). Thus, SR aims to help companies to become actively involved in local community life, enabling them to assume roles as global citizens and local neighbours in a fast-changing world. Such programs have become, genuine marketing tools designed to bring image benefits for their proposers. Corporations acquire "human face" is more than just products and services (Sima & Gheorghe, 2007).

Figure 1. A new model of the assessment of customers' satisfaction
Source: Sima, 2010.

"Greener means cheaper." Investment in "green products" is manifested as an eco-trend in business. Some players have already intuited this trend and began to pay attention to this segment.

Companies that make the step to launch organic products want to achieve consumer awareness by associating their image with clean products, but they also look for new customers.

People want an ecological approach to everyday life, but they seek, primarily, personal gain, which can be transposed into incentives and facilities.

On the one hand, green customers and the public generally are more aware of the ecological behaviour of organizations and to their social involvement.

On the other hand, organic products and environmental activities are not easily accepted by a large part of the audience, especially by the one who does not have a strong and clear ecological awareness.

The degree of concern for the environment has increased significantly so that environmental problems have come to represent now an essential factor in making consumer decisions.

The items presented above have led us to take into account a new category, in modeling and evaluation of customer satisfaction, which the authors have called Green Dimension. (Figure 1).

ECSI model was the starting point. In relation to the determinants of ECSI model, green dimension can be justified at least by a few elements namely:

- In terms of image, the green dimension can be expressed in the concept of Corporate Social Responsibility. CSR activities of a company provide benefits at two levels: the social level and the company level. The social benefits are related to the welfare and the public interest. In terms of benefits of the company, at least four issues are to be mentioned, namely:
    - Possibility of differentiation over the competition and achieving brand loyalty. There are studies which have shown that when consumers have to choose between similar products, their preferences are turning to those brands perceived as being "responsible". Thus:
        - 70% of European consumers believe that the responsibility of a company is important in the decision to buy a product or service (MORI 2000);

        - 86% of Americans were inclined to change a brand in favour of another similar, but involved in a social cause (2004 Cone Corporate Citizenship Study).
    - Improving the company reputation.
    - Currently, companies' success depends directly on the trust given them by the authorities, media, partners and the community in which it operates.
    - On the other hand, if a company demonstrates its responsibility to the community, the related to reputation benefits have immediate consequences. Thus:
        - 61% of opinion leaders around the world are willing to recommend the products of a responsible company (The Insightpoll.com Opinion Elite Panel, 2004);
        - 84% of Americans believe that social responsibility is important when they think about the companies they agree to see operating in their community (2004 Cone Corporate Citizenship Study).
    - Increased sales and market share of the company.
    - Attracting and retaining valuable employees.
- In terms of perceived value, The Green Dimension may be considered in many respects. Thus, in Romania, Daedalus Consulting and Green Report conducted the first quantitative Romanian research on environmental issues. The result of the survey was published in February 2008 and showed a high willingness of Romanian people to pay more for green products. Compared to values at international level, almost 90% of Romanian citizens have expressed willingness to pay more for environmentally friendly products. After Romania, according to the TGI survey the highest availability was recorded in Brazil, India and Mexico. Countries that were not subjected to the rigors of environmental discipline are top ranking. This result can be explained by the fact that those countries, not having the costs experience of these measures, have a higher receptivity to them. Thus, a few results are noticeable:
    - Over 73% of respondents are willing to pay more for organic food.
    - Over 49% of respondents are willing to pay more for renewable energy.
    - Over 36% of respondents are willing to pay for products with biodegradable compounds. (Daedalus Consulting, Green Thinking, prepared for Green Report, 2008)
- In terms of customer expectations, The Green Dimension can be primarily expressed by their expectations about the energy efficiency of products, meaning that they seek products operation of which does not require high energy consumption. Also, customers have expectations regarding low emission of pollutants. A good example is the case of passenger cars, for which the level of the paid taxes is inversely proportional to the emissions level. It appears, therefore, that customer expectations related to green product features are primarily determined by the pragmatic attitude of the new consumer.
- Regarding perceived quality of the green products, the green dimension can be recognized in the low polluting level of the eco-friendly products, due to the use of new production technologies.

Specific Issues of the Green Dimension for Customers Satisfaction

People seek personal benefit rather than an ecological approach to the everyday life. Beyond awareness, the ecological approach should be assumed by consumers (Sima, Gheorghe, 2009).

The question arises is: How strong is consumer interest in environmental issues?

Based on the results recorded in The 2009 BBMG Conscious Consumer Report: Redefining Value in a New Economy, Raphael Bemporad, co-founder of BBMG, said that brands would be able "to close the green trust gap" if they would take into account new customer expectations, which evaluates acquisitions "based on both value and value" (BBMG Conscious Consumer Report: Redefining value in a new Economy, June 2009, p.34). Thus, they have to provide performance products that match consumers' goals; with acceptable prices that for them.

According to Sivesan, Achchuthan and Umanakenan (2013) there is a significant positive relationship between green marketing practices are positively and customer satisfaction. The green customer satisfaction is strongly influenced by the quality of the product (Johnson & Ettlie, 2001).

Taking into account the above, we can identify three specific levels of customer satisfaction green dimension, namely (Figure 2):

- Company
- Product/Service
- Price

The Company Level

Consumers reward those brands which are based on the best practices of the company.

In addition to the classical requirements such as economic performance, quality management and communication policies, a modern assessment of a company is also considering specific issues such as the organization's involvement in the social life of the community. Modern organization as a legal entity - has primarily, duties to society.

Customer satisfaction is considered by Scott M. Smith as "a reflection of the expectations and experiences that the customer has with a product or service".

Evaluation of products and services is actually made following customer expectations. They are found in the rules of performance that reflects accepted environmental standards set by the business

Figure 2. Tree of customer satisfaction for the green dimension
Source: Adapted after Sima & Gheorghe, 2009.

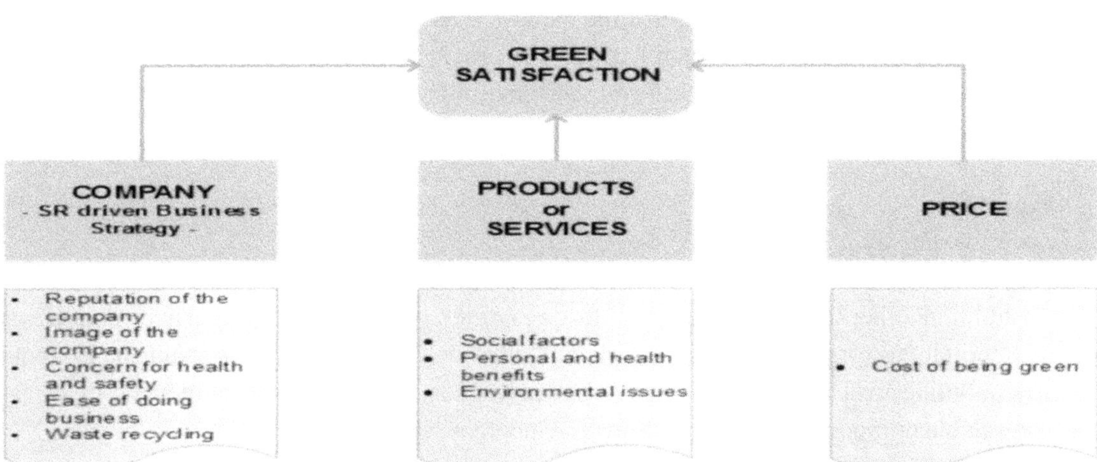

environment, other companies, industries, and even organizational and national culture. The most effective strategic approach seems to belong to those companies that have adopted social responsibility and sustainable development as a business philosophy. Integrating social and sustainability principles in their operation provides long-term value for the shareholders through practices that are, in fact, satisfactory to all stakeholders. Social Responsibility was developed by taking into account environmental and social opportunities as business opportunities. In this respect, the strategic capacity of organizations is adapted in order to efficiently exploit such opportunities.

The new consumer is increasingly more concerned about his image that reflects the image of his suppliers. Therefore, their reputation becomes, in turn, increasingly more important to the consumer. Thus, elements which are subject to social responsibility activities such as concern for health and safety as well as customer requests, ensuring environmental conservation, supporting philanthropy, come to be positioned in the core of companies concern. The result of such strategic approach is to eliminate barriers to communication with the customer, such as mistrust, negative perceptions, lack of information, low availability, leading, ultimately, to increase sales of environmentally sensitive products. The importance of each factor varies by product, industry and geographic area.

The 2009 BBMG Conscious Consumer Report: Redefining Value in a New Economy has found that 77% of American consumers agree that "can make a positive difference by purchasing products from socially or environmentally responsible companies".

There are differences between proactive and reactive companies, in terms of performance. These differences are starting to decrease as the environmental education becomes more important. This highlights the role of governments. They can support cooperation between companies and provide educational programs to help companies in understanding the benefits of involvement in environmental protection. This is especially true in the case of small and medium enterprises in developing countries, which should encourage and reward innovation at all levels (El Dief & Font, 2010).

The Product/Service Level

Consumers are looking for "green" features of the products and services.

Climate changes seem to be those that have drawn attention to environmental issues to the greatest extent. At the same time, rising energy prices is another factor that appears to significantly influence the buying decision. Thus, the consumers are getting more and more interested, firstly, in products of high energy efficiency classes. At the same time the low level of environmental damage may represent an important factor in the decision of purchasing. The conclusion is that, firstly, the personal benefits are tracked and only after that the ones affecting the environment.

The most popular and demanded "green products" are:

- Organic food
- Renewable energy

But in addition, other important ecological features of the products / services may be considered to represent important factors in purchasing decisions: "superior energetic class, low maintenance requirements, low polluting level, biodegradable/recycled compounds, no highly toxic compounds, being easily reused, recyclable or biodegradable etc." (Sima & Gheorghe, 2009).

Figure 3. Green satisfaction sources
Source: Sima & Gheorghe, 2009.

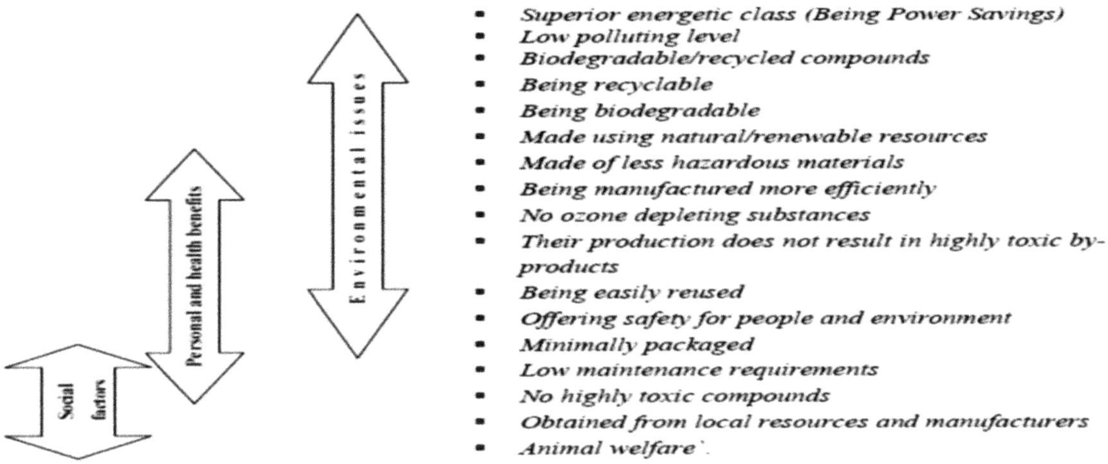

Thus, in terms of involvement in purchasing decisions, environmental issues can be classified into three categories, namely: environmental issues, personal benefits and social factors (Figure no.3).

The Price Level

At this level, the main issue is about consumers' willingness to pay more for "green products/services".

There are numerous studies conducted all over the world that show the green procurement volume is increasing, but the question that arises is: Are the consumers willing to pay more for green?

A McKinsey survey of 1,000 consumers in Europe and the United States performed in 2012, showed that many people would pay more, but only up to a point (Miremadi et. al., 2012). The study took into account acquisitions in the automotive, building, electronics, furniture, and packaging categories. Between 70 and 80 percent of the respondents said they would pay an additional 5 percent for a green product if it is at the same level of performance as a non-green alternative. But as the premium increase first, willingness to pay decreases.

The "historical" reluctance to pay a bonus for ecological products is reduced as consumers associate the responsibility for protecting the environment to their health and other direct benefits.

The core of this internal belief system is ecological value.

Ecological value can be explained by the implicit or explicit philosophy of desired value and it may be placed as a behavioral variable within the system of values.

The Green Strategy Mix: A New Holistic Approach

Two international studies, conducted in 2009 (Sustainability in the 2009 Recession and Green Brands Survey 2009) showed that the recession has not lowered the interest in 'green' products or services, quite the contrary. Worldwide consumers associate ecologic products with the idea of reducing consumption and saving, despite the fact that the main barrier for purchasing of these products is the perception that their price would be higher than that of the classic ones.

In January 2009, the Boston Consulting Group presented the results of a study entitled "Capturing the Green Advantage for Consumer Companies". The aim of this study was to discover if and how consumer attitudes towards green products and services has been affected by the economic crisis. The conclusion was that during the crisis, consumers remained interested in organic products. Determinants of this behavior were represented by the benefits that eco-friendly products have, on the one hand, upon the environment and, on the other hand, at the personal level. As a conclusion, BCG advised companies on how to respond to consumer expectations regarding environmental protection being, at the same time, able to reach, their business targets.

It should be noted that the study was conducted in a gray period, characterized globally by uncertainties, among others, regarding the appropriateness of investing in a new environmental strategy.

As a concrete result of the study a best practice guide for the company was drawn up.

In this guide guidance for companies was offered, divided into four categories, based on which companies can meet consumer requirements on environmental protection and their business objectives. The four categories are Planning, Process, Product, and Promotion.

From our point of view, "the green products and services are designed, manufactured, priced and promoted by people for people" (Sima & Gheorghe, 2009). This approach has led us toward a holistic approach to green satisfaction, according to which people and their double the role of producers and consumers should be in the same time considered.

Some analysts say that for companies, there is only one thing which is more important than environmental initiatives, namely the ability to communicate it to consumers.

Thus, in terms of green strategy, we consider that a fifth element can be added, namely the People.

Another observation we had regard was that the eco-efficiency represent a production principle requested by the green products. It refers to less polluting production systems used to produce goods and services which have a lower environmental impact, which better corresponding with customer needs, being, thus, more competitive.

Starting from this, the authors, also, integrated Eco-Efficiency into a strategy mix that they named "The Green Strategy Mix" (5P+EE) (Figure 4).

- Planning Strategy
- Processes Strategy
- Product Strategy
- Promotion Strategy
- People Strategy
- Eco-Efficiency Strategy (Sima & Gheorghe, 2009)

The first four was highlighted by the Boston Consulting Group into a recent study, aiming to assess green attitudes and shopping behaviors. They call them The Four Ps of Green Advantage.

Being "green" has become a business plan itself. Producers attempt to differentiate the competition and gain a large share of the market. There is a "green" competition, in which each company tries to move forward, aiming to move forward having regarded the continuous growth of the customer preferences for 'green' products.

Nowadays, producers, not just consumers, seem to show a wave of interest in the environmental aspects of the business, because they realized that eco-environmental production methods can be profitable. So we can say that in a comprehensive approach, the strategic mix can be improved.

Figure 4. The 'Green Strategy Mix'
Source: Adapted after Sima & Gheorghe, 2009.

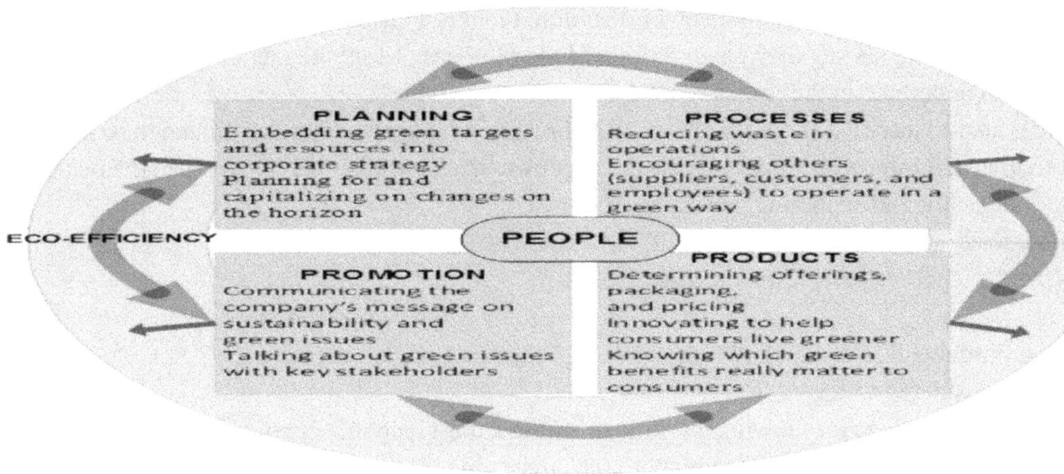

Given the continued growth of customer preferences for 'green' products, the existence of a product having a less impact on the environment, in the company's portfolio, it is often better in terms of quality and marketing.

Being "green" has become a business plan itself.

Solutions and Recommendations

Four main determinants of population's attitude towards the green dimension can be identified:

1. Phenomena with negative environmental effects;
2. Activities to protect environment;
3. Willingness to save and motivation for it;
4. Willingness to pay extra for green products and justification for it.

Phenomena with Environmental Impact

According to the above-mentioned study conducted by Daedalus Consulting in Romania in 2008, atmospheric pollution and deforestation are considered to have the highest environmental impact (Over 84% of respondents placed this issues on the first and second place). Respondents considered that pollution can be greatly influenced by each of us.

These two results seem to be in a relationship of interdependence that can be verified in future research through correlation analysis.

Genetically modified foods are ranked third, nearly of the above mentioned two categories.

Regarding how respondents considered that they might influence each of these phenomena, it can be observed that in all cases the population is considered largely unable to act.

Activities for Environment Protection

As regards activities for the environmental protection, there is a clear correlation between the activities about which respondents say they have performed over the past 12 months and those who declare that they intend to undertake in the next 12 months.

There is also an increase of approximately 10% of those who declare that they intend to be involved in such activities in future, which may suggest a tendency to declare rather act or to reflect the behavioural changes induced by the economic recession.

Willingness to Save and Justification for It

Regarding products that respondents say they save, the most name energy (over 70%). On the second place, they considered water (60%).

Regarding the reasons for showing this kind of attitude, most respondents stated that they try to reduce costs (85%) and only 13% say they care about the environment.

This shows serious problems in society and requires a deep study in order to identify determinants of this behaviour to improve.

"Green Products" and Willingness to Pay More for Them

The products were grouped into three categories:

1. Organic food;
2. Renewable energy;
3. Products with biodegradable compounds.

Organic foods are outlined of these, almost three-quarters of the respondents (73.1%) saying they were willing to pay higher amounts. About a half (49.1%) were willing to pay more for renewable energy and almost a third (36.3%) for products with biodegradable components.

And this result matches to the behavioural pattern mentioned above, showing that for Romanian people care for the environment not prevail, but rather care for them.

A mismatch occurs when respondents are asked to respond if they are willing to pay more for "green products". On this question, nearly two-thirds affirmative answer, and if we add them those who are in partial agreement, we achieve a percentage of over 84%. This response comes, however, contradict the results mentioned above. Thus, this it seems to support, too, the conclusion that the people of Romania are well in words, but less than in facts.

FUTURE RESEARCH DIRECTIONS

All of these above-mentioned elements determine a model of an ecological community, including:

- **Resource Ecology:** Identifying local resources that can be ecologically exploited;

- **Activity Ecology:** Directing investment towards non-polluting activities (ecological agriculture, "clean" technologies, ecological services, ecological tourism, etc.) and writing and implementation of local development projects that take into account ecological constraints;
- **Ecological Behavior:** Building awareness within the local community regarding the serious long-term consequences of non-ecological behavior (development of ecological citizenship);
- **Ecological Culture:** The introduction of ecology information in school curricula, as a support for the formation of ecological culture.

Given the above, we believe that an investigation should be conducted in order to help us to shape and measure the consumer green behavior. The ultimate goal is to develop a system of indicators which may be used to measure the green satisfaction of the consumers, namely, Green Dimension Index.

The starting point of this research will be the model shown in figure no. 5.

CONCLUSION

Operationalizing studying of the needs, values, behaviours, psychology or aspirations of goods and services consumers is a laborious and complex process because every chapter of people consumption as well as market dynamic of every good or service follow specific laws and there are necessary separate investigations for every good or consumption chapter, in order to explain or forecast general or sequential behaviour of the consumers.

Nowadays, there is no exhaustively understood of consumption components or of real motivations for adopting specific consumption practices, even in this area there already are accumulated many studies, observations and methodical researches.

But it was never possible an investigation totally satisfying in respect of the rationality of the consumers, so much the less in respect of the unconsciousness impulses lying the effective consumption

Figure 5. Model for green dimension index evaluation
Source: Enhanced after Sima & Gheorghe, 2015.

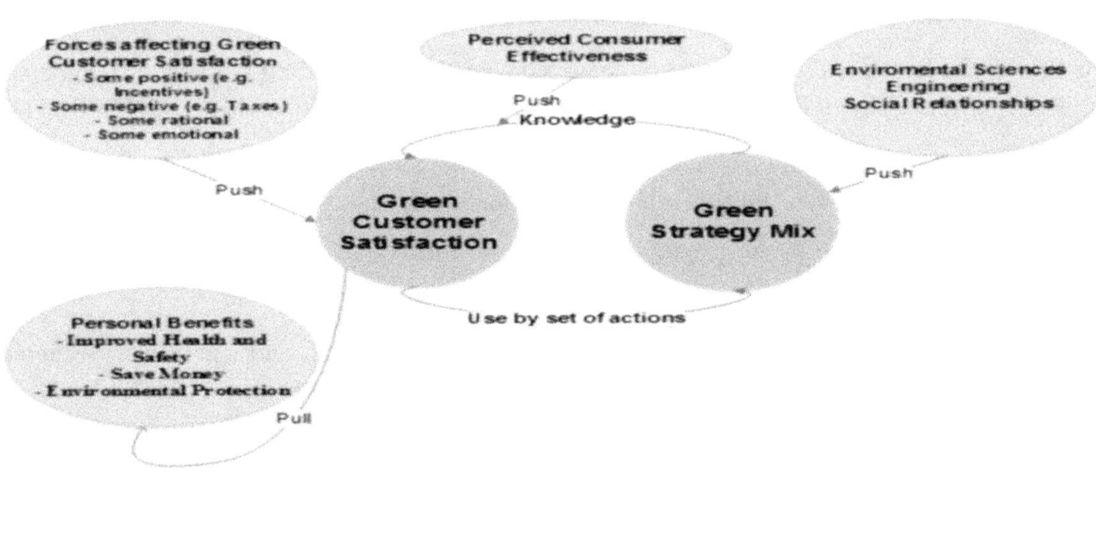

behaviour. Anyway, the social and economic theory of consumption made important steps in respect of the delimitation between rational and emotional motivations of goods and services purchasing.

Changes dynamic in goods and services markets was very high in the last two decades. In those countries having market economies, where profile if demand rapidly changed, these lead to a rapidly change of the offer parameters and default changes of some elements of the research methods and techniques of the consumption patterns.

Adoption of some sustainable practices of consumption involves the use of correlated goods and services which answer to the satisfaction of basic needs, under conditions of minimization of the natural resources exploitation, avoiding resources waste and polluting emissions, along an entire life-cycle, so that these don't affect life chances of future generations.

Desirable changes of some features of the consumption patterns as follow as new exigency imposed to manufacturing processes involve:

- Promotion of the examination of those consumption patterns which block sustainable development, as well as of the modalities of changing this behaviour, at the global level, endorsing especially those people having a consumerist life style.
- Identification of the most efficient policies and tools for break-up the unsustainable consumption/manufacturing patterns, including by information dissemination and ecological alert.
- Performing a more equitable distribution of developing resources inside and between countries.

REFERENCES

Agyeman, C. M. (2014). Consumers' buying behavior towards green products: An exploratory study. *International Journal of Management Research and Business Strategy*, *3*(1), 189.

Ahmad, A. & Thyagaraj, K. S. (2015). Consumer's Intention to Purchase Green Brands: The Roles of Environmental Concern, Environmental Knowledge and Self Expressive Benefits. *Current World Environment*, 10(3), 879-889.

Ajzen, I. (1991). The theory of planned behavior. *Organizational Behavior and Human Decision Processes*, *50*(2), 179–211. doi:10.1016/0749-5978(91)90020-T

Ajzen, I. (2002). Residual effects of past on later behavior: Habituation and reasoned action perspectives. *Personality and Social Psychology Review*, *6*(2), 107–122. doi:10.1207/S15327957PSPR0602_02

Anderson, E.W., Fornell, C., & Lehmann, D.R. (1994). Customer satisfaction, market share and profitability: Findings from Sweden. *Journal of Marketing*, *58*, 53-66.

Antonies, G., & Raaij, V. W. (1998). *Consumer Behavior: A European Perspective*. West Sussex, England: John Wiley & Sons Ltd.

Baker, E., Al-Gahtani, S., & Hubona, G. (2007). The effects of gender and age on new technology implementation in a developing country: Testing the theory of planned behavior (TPB). *Information Technology & People*, *20*(4), 352–375. doi:10.1108/09593840710839798

BBMG. (n. d.). The 2009 BBMG Conscious Consumer Report: Redefining Value in a New Economy. Retrieved from http://bbmg.com/

BCG.com. (2008). Creating People Advantage Summary. Retrieved from http://www.bcg.com/impact_expertise/publications/files/Creating_People_Advantage_Summary_May_2008.pdf

Beatley, T. (2000). *Green Urbanism: Learning from European Cities* (p. 17). Washington: Island Press.

Bemporad, R. & Baranowski, M. (2010). *Marketing to Conscious Consumers: Identify, Engage and Leverage Your Most Passionate Customers*. John Wiley & Sons.

Brown, L. R. (2001). *Eco-Economy* (1st ed.). W. W. Norton & Company.

Chase, D., & Smith, T. K. (1992). Consumers keen on green but marketers don't deliver. *Advertising Age*, *63*(29), 2–4.

Cheng, S., Lam, T., & Hsu, C. H. C. (2006). Negative Word-of-Mouth Communication Intention: An Application of the Theory of Planned Behavior. *Journal of Hospitality & Tourism Research (Washington, D.C.)*, *30*(1), 95–116. doi:10.1177/1096348005284269

Conner, M., & Norman, P. (Eds.), (2005). *Predicting Health Behaviour: Research and Practice with Social Cognition Models* (2nd ed., pp. 170–222). Maidenhead: Open University Press.

Consulting, D. (2008). Green Thinking, prepared for Green Report. Retrieved from http://www.green-report.ro/dynamic/studii/sondaje/daedalus-consulting-green-thinking-sondaj-pe-teme-de-mediu-printre-romani---9288.htm

Cronan, T. P., & Al-Rafee, S. (2008). *Factors that influence the intention to pirate software and media. Journal of Business Ethics*, *78*(4), 527–545. doi:10.1007/s10551-007-9366-8

Darling, R. J., Heller, V. L., & Tablada, D. M. (2009). Positioning a firms initial market offering: A strategic application of a consumer-oriented model. *European Business Review*, *21*(6), 516–530. doi:10.1108/09555340910998814

Dauvergne, P. (2008). *The Shadows of Consumption: Consequences for the Global Environment*. Cambridge, MA: The MIT Press.

DSouza, C., Taghian, M., & Khosla, R. (2007). Examination of Environmental Beliefs an its Impact on the Influence of Price, Quality and Demographic Characteristics with respect to Green Purchase Intention. *Journal of Targeting. Measurement and Analysis for Marketing*, *15*(2), 69–78. doi:10.1057/palgrave.jt.5750039

El Dief, M., & Font, X. (2010). The determinants of hotels marketing managers green marketing behaviour. *Journal of Sustainable Tourism*, *18*(2), 157–174. doi:10.1080/09669580903464232

Fornell, C. (1992, January). A national customer satisfaction barometer: The Swedish experience. *Journal of Marketing*, *56*(1), 6–21. doi:10.2307/1252129

Giese, J. L., & Cote, J. A. (2000). *Defining customer satisfaction*. Academy of Marketing Science Review. Retrieved from www.amsreview.org/articles/giese01-2000.pdf

Ginsberg, J. M., & Bloom, P. N. (2004). Choosing the right green marketing strategy. *MIT Sloan Management Review*, *46*(1), 79–84.

Gray, J. (1985). *Ecological Beliefs and Behaviour*. London: Greenwood Press.

Gupta, S., & Ogden, D. T. (2009). To buy or not to buy? A social dilemma perspective on green buying. *Journal of Consumer Marketing*, *26*(6), 376–391. doi:10.1108/07363760910988201

Hamilton, C., & Mail, E. (2003). *Downshifting in Australia: A Sea-Change in the Pursuit of Happiness*. Australia Institute, Canberra.

Hausknecht, D. R. (1990). *Measurement scales in consumer satisfaction/dissatisfaction*. Journal of Consumer Satisfaction. *Dissatisfaction and Complaining Behavior*, *3*, 1–11.

Hennig-Thurau, T., Gwinner, K. P., & Gremler, D. D. (2002). *Understanding relationship marketing outcomes: An integration of relational benefits and relationship quality. Journal of Service Research*, *4*(3), 230–247. doi:10.1177/1094670502004003006

Humphery, K. (1998). *Shelf Life: Supermarkets and the Changing Cultures of Consumption*. Melbourne: Cambridge University Press.

Johnson, M. D., & Ettlie, J. E. (2001). Technology, customization, and reliability. *Journal of Quality Management*, *6*(2), 193–210. doi:10.1016/S1084-8568(01)00037-2

Kalafatis, S. P., Pollard, M., East, R., & Tsogas, M. H. (1999). Green marketing and Ajzens theory of planned behavior: A cross-market examination. *Journal of Consumer Marketing*, *16*(5), 441–460. doi:10.1108/07363769910289550

Kilbourne, W. E. (1995). Green Advertising: Salvation or Oxymoron? *Journal of Advertising*, *24*(2), 7–19. doi:10.1080/00913367.1995.10673472

Kollmuss, A., & Agyeman, J. (2002). Mind the Gap: Why do people act environmentally and what are the barriers to pro-environmental behavior? *Environmental Education Research*, *8*(3), 239–260. doi:10.1080/13504620220145401

Kotler, P. (2000). *Marketing Management* (10th ed.). New Jersey: Prentice-Hall.

Kreidler, N. B., & Joseph, M. S. (2009). *How green should you go? Understanding the role of green atmospherics in service environment evaluations*. International Journal of Culture. *Tourism and Hospitality Research*, *3*(3), 228–245.

Kristensen, K., Martensen, A., & Grønholdt, L. (2000). Customer satisfaction measurement at post Denmark: Results of application of the European Customer Satisfaction Index methodology. *Total Quality Management*, *11*(7), 1007–1015. doi:10.1080/09544120050135533

Lunt, P. K., & Livingstone, S. M. (1992). *Mass Consumption and Personal Identity: Everyday economic experience*. Buckingham, U.K.: Open University Press.

Mainieri, T., Barnett, E. G., Valdero, T. R., Unipan, J. B., & Oskamp, S. (1997). Green buying: The influence of environmental concern on consumer behavior. *The Journal of Social Psychology*, *137*(2), 189–204. doi:10.1080/00224549709595430

Marques, C. P., & Almeida, D. (2013). A Path Model of Attitudinal Antecedents of Green Purchase Behaviour. *Economia e Sociologia (Evora, Portugal)*, *6*(2), 135–144.

McDonald, S., & Oates, C.J. (2006). Sustainability: Consumer Perceptions and Marketing Strategies. Business Strategy and the Environment, 15, 157-170.

Mendleson, N. (1994). Environmental marketing business partnering at AFC developing strategic, Environmental Marketing: Critical Success Strategies for Reaching the Green Consumer. *Proceedings of The 1994 Conference* (pp. 87-103).

Meyer-Waarden, L. (2004, October 27-28). in Brătianu, C., Lixăndroiu D., Pop Nicolae Al. (Eds.), (2006). Business Excellence. *Proceedings of the International Conference on Business Excellence ICBE*, Braşov, România.

Miremadi, M. (2012). How much will consumers pay to go green. Retrieved from http://www.mckinsey.com/insights/manufacturing/how_much_will_consumers_pay_to_go_green

Mostafa, M. M. (2007). A hierarchical analysis of the green consciousness of the Egyptian consumer. *Psychology and Marketing*, *24*(5), 445–473. doi:10.1002/mar.20168

Mostafa, M. M. (2007). Antecedents of Egyptian Consumers Green Purchase Intentions. *Journal of International Consumer Marketing*, *19*(2), 97–126. doi:10.1300/J046v19n02_06

Obermiller, C., & Spangenberg, E. R. (1998). Development of a Scale to Measure Consumer Skepticism Toward Advertising. *Journal of Consumer Psychology*, *7*(2), 159–186. doi:10.1207/s15327663jcp0702_03

Oliver, R. L. (1997). *Satisfaction: A behavioral perspective on the consumer*. New York: McGraw Hill.

Oliver, R. L. (2006). *Customer satisfaction research. The handbook of marketing research*. California: Sage.

Ottman, J. A. (1993). *Green Marketing: Challenges & Opportunities for the New Marketing Age*. Chicago: NTC Publishing Group.

Ottman, J. A. et al.. (2006). *Avoiding GreenMarketing Myopia. Issue of Environment*, *48*(5), 22–36.

Peattie, K. (2001). Golden Goose or Wild Goose? The Hunt for the Green Consumer. *Business Strategy and the Environment*, *10*(4), 187–199. doi:10.1002/bse.292

Peattie, K., & Crane, A. (2005). Green Marketing: Legend, myth, farce or prophesy. *Qualitative Market Research*, *8*(4), 357–370. doi:10.1108/13522750510619733

Peterson, R. A., & Wilson, W. R. (1992). Measuring customer satisfaction: Fact and artefact. *Journal of the Academy of Marketing Science*, *20*(1), 61–71. doi:10.1007/BF02723476

Phau, I., & Ong, D. (2007). An Investigation of the Effects of Environmental Claims in Promotional Messages for Clothing Brands. *Marketing Intelligence & Planning*, *25*(7), 772–788. doi:10.1108/02634500710834214

Pickett, B. J. (2008). Pro-environmental products: Marketing influence on consumer purchase decision. *Journal of Consumer Marketing*, *25*(5), 281–293. doi:10.1108/07363760810890516

PSBresearch. (2009). Retrieved from http://www.psbresearch.com/green_2009.htm#top

PSBresearch. (n. d.). Retrieved from http://www.psbresearch.com/green_JWT.htm

Roberts, J. (1996). Green consumers in the1990s: Profile and implications for advertising. *Journal of Business Research*, *36*(3), 217–232. doi:10.1016/0148-2963(95)00150-6

Rohm, A., & Swaminathan, V. (2004). A typology of online shoppers based on shopping motivations. *Journal of Business Research*, *57*(7), 748–757. doi:10.1016/S0148-2963(02)00351-X

Rust, R. T., & Oliver, R. L. (1994). Service quality: insights and managerial implications from the frontier. In R. T. Rust & R. L. Oliver (Eds.), *Service Quality: New Directions in Theory and Practice* (pp. 1–19). London: Sage. doi:10.4135/9781452229102.n1

Ryan, T. (2014). Green Intentions: An Exploratory Study on Advertising and the Environmental Movement. *Journal of Research for Consumers*, 26, 13.

Schendler, A. (2009). *Getting green done: Hard truths from the front lines of the sustainability revolution*. New York, NY: Public Affairs.

Schor, J. B., & Holt, D. B. (Eds.). (2000). *The Consumer Society Reader*. New Press.

Schwepker-Jr, C. H., & Cornwell, T. B. (1991). An Examination of Ecologically Concerned Consumers and their Intention to Purchase Ecologically Packaged Products. *Journal of Public Policy & Marketing*, *10*(2), 77–101.

Scott, M. S. (2007). How to Measure Customer Satisfaction: Satisfaction Measurement and Theory. Retrieved from http://www.aboutsurveys.com/how-to-measure-customer-satisfaction-satisfaction-measurement-and-theory/

Sima, V. (2010). Motivations for a Systemic Approach of the Innovative Strategies for a "Green" Product. *Petroleum-Gas University of Ploieşti Bulletin*, *12*(3), 104–111.

Sima, V., & Gheorghe, I. (2009). Eco-Efficiency – A Romanian Perspective. *Proceedings of the 11th IBIMA Conference, Creating Global Economies through Innovation and Knowledge Management* (pp. 1642-1650).

Sima, V., & Gheorghe, I. (2009). The Green Strategy Mix – A New Marketing Approach, *Proceedings of the 13th IBIMA Conference on Knowledge Management and Innovation in Advancing Economies, Analyses & Solutions* (pp. 1344-1347).

Sima, V., & Gheorghe, I. G. (2007). The Corporate Social Responsibility – a Modern Marketing Concept. *Annals Of The Oradea University, Fascicle of Management and Technological Engineering*, *6*(14), 2592–2596.

Sima, V., & Gheorghe, I. G. (2009). The Opportunity for a Reconsideration of the Dimensions of the Assessment Model of the Customers Satisfaction. *Communications of the IBIMA*, *9*, 64–68.

Sima, V., & Gheorghe, I. G. (2009). The 'Green Dimension' of Customer satisfaction. *Proceedings of the 11th IBIMA Conference, Creating Global Economies through Innovation and Knowledge Management* (pp. 1638-1641).

Stanciu, M. (2006). Metode de cercetare a modelelor de consum. Studii şi Cercetări Economice, 42.

TGI surveys. (n. d.). Retrieved from http://www.tgisurveys.com/knowledgehub/reports/KMR_TGI_Green_Values.pdf

Hansla, A., Gamble, A., Juliusson, A., & Gärling, T. (2007). The relationships between awareness of consequences, environmental concern, and value orientations. *Journal of Environmental Psychology*, *28*(10), 1–9.

Thøgersen, J. (2000). Psychological Determinants of Paying Attention to Ecolabels in Purchase Decisions: Model Development and Multinational Validation. *Journal of Consumer Policy*, *23*(3), 285–313. doi:10.1023/A:1007122319675

Tuna, Y., & Özkoçak, L. (2012). The First Step to Communication with Environmentally Responsible Consumer: Measuring Environmental Consciousness of Turkish Consumers. *Online Journal of Communication and Media Technologies*, *2*(3), 145.

Uhl, Ch. (2004). *Developing Ecological Consciousness: Path to a Sustainable World*. Rowman & Littlefield Publisher, Inc.

United Nations. (n. d.). Transforming our world: the 2030 Agenda for Sustainable Development. Retrieved from https://sustainabledevelopment.un.org/post2015/transformingourworld

Unpublished doctoral dissertation or master's theses:

Vavra, T. G. (1997). *Improving Your Measurement of Customer Satisfaction: A Guide to Creating, Conducting, Analyzing, and Reporting Customer Satisfaction Measurement Programs*. ASQ Quality Press.

Verhoef, P. C. (2001). *Analysing customer relationships: Linking relational constructs and marketing instruments to customer behavior* [Unpublished doctoral dissertation]. Erasmus University, Rotterdam.

WBCSD. (1996). A Changing Future for Paper. Retrieved from http://pubs.iied.org/pdfs/X136IIED.pdf

WBCSD. (n. d.). Corporate social responsibility. Retrieved from http://www.wbcsd.org/work-program/business-role/previous-work/corporatc-social-responsibility.aspx

Westbrook, R. A., & Oliver, R. L. (1981). Developing better measures of consumer satisfaction: Some preliminary results. In K. B. Monroe (Ed.), *Advances in consumer research* (8th ed., pp. 94–99). MI: Association for Consumer Research.

Wirtz, J., & Lee, M.C. (2003). An examination of the quality and context-specific applicability of commonly customer satisfaction measures. *Journal of Service Research*, *5*, 345–355. doi:10.1177/1094670503005004006

Wiser, R. H. (1998). Green power marketing: Increasing customer demand for renewable energy. *Utilities Policy*, *7*(2), 107–119. doi:10.1016/S0957-1787(98)00005-8

Wood, W., & Neal, D. T. (2009). The habitual consumer. *Journal of Consumer Psychology*, *19*(4), 579–592. doi:10.1016/j.jcps.2009.08.003

Wu, S.-I. & Chen, J.-Y. (2014). A Model of Green Consumption Behavior Constructed by the Theory of Planned Behavior. *International Journal of Marketing Studies*, *6*(5), 128.

Yi, Y. (1990). A critical review of consumer satisfaction. In V. A. Zeithaml (Ed.), *Review of marketing Chicago* (pp. 68–123). American Marketing Association.

Zairi, M. (2000). Managing customer satisfaction: A best practice perspective. *The TQM Magazine*, *12*(6), 389–494. doi:10.1108/09544780010351670

Zavestoski, S. (Ed.). (2002). *Anti-Consumption Attitudes: Psychology & Marketing, Special Issue*. New York: Wiley.

ADDITIONAL READING

Belk, R. W. (1995). Studies in the New Consumer Behavior. In D. Miller (Ed.), *Acknowledging Consumption: A Review of New Studies* (pp. 58–95). London: Routledge.

Belk, R. W., Devinney, T., & Eckhardt, G. (2005). Consumer Ethics Across cultures. *Consumption Markets & Culture*, *8*(3), 275–289. doi:10.1080/10253860500160411

Berry, L., Carbone, L. P., & Haeckel, St. H. (2002). Managing the Total Customer Experience. *Sloan Management Review*, (Spring): 85–89.

Burkart, K. (2012). *How to define the "green economy*, retrieved at 2013-23-11 from http://www.mnn.com/green-tech/research-innovations/blogs/how-do-you-define-the-green-economy

Cato, M. S. (2009). *Green Economics: An Introduction to Theory, Policy and Practice*. London: Earthscan.

Graedel, T. E., & Allenby, B. R. (2003). Industrial Ecology (2nd ed.). Upper Saddle River, NJ: Prentice Hall.

Grant, J. (2007). *The Green Marketing Manifesto*. John Wiley & Sons.

Gustafasson, A., Johnson, M. D., & Roos, I. (2005). The effects of customer satisfaction, relationship commitment dimensions and triggers on customer retention. *Journal of Marketing*, *69*(October), 210–218. doi:10.1509/jmkg.2005.69.4.210

Kennet, M., & Courea, E. P. (2011). *Handbook of Green Economics*. The Green Economics Institute.

King, A., & Lenox, M. (2002). Does it really pay to be green? *Journal of Industrial Ecology*, *5*(1), 105–117. doi:10.1162/108819801753358526

Kotler, Ph. (1969). Behavioral models for analyzing buyers, in Dimensions of consumer beahviour, New York: Meredith Corporation.

Lanktree, C., & Briere, J. (1991, January). Early data on the Trauma Symptom Checklist for Children (TSC-C). *Paper presented at themeeting of the American Professional Society on the Abuse of Children*, San Diego, CA, USA.

Milani, B. (2005). *What is green economics?* Retrieved from www.greeneconomics.net

Mintzer, M. (1992). Confronting Climate Change, Risks, Implications and Responses. Cambridge: Cambridge University Press.

Moisander, J. (2007). Motivational complexity of green consumerism. *International Journal of Consumer Studies*, *31*(4), 404–409. doi:10.1111/j.1470-6431.2007.00586.x

National Institute of Statistics of Romania. (2004). Tendinţe Sociale.

Neff, J. (2009). Green-marketing revolution defies economic downturn. *Advertising Age*, *80*(14). Retrieved from http://ecoamerica.typepad.com/blog/2009/04/greenmarketing-revolution-defieseconomic downturn.html

Peattie, K., & Charter, M. (2003). Green Marketing. In M.J. Baker (Ed.), The Marketing Book (5th ed., pp. 726-756). Butterworth-Heinemann.

Peattie, K., & Crane, A. (2005). Green marketing: Legend, myth, farce or prophesy? *Qualitative Market Research*, *8*(4), 357–370. doi:10.1108/13522750510619733

Porter, M. E., & Van der Linde, C. (1995). Toward a New Conception of the Environment-Competitiveness Relationship. *The Journal of Economic Perspectives*, *9*(4), 97–118. doi:10.1257/jep.9.4.97

Porter, M. E., & van der Linde, C. (1995). Green and competitive. *Harvard Business Review*, *73*(5), 120–134.

Salzman, M., & O'Reilly, A. (2010), *10 Trends in Mindful Consumption*. Retrieved from http://www.thenewconsumer.com/2010/10/29/10-trends-in-mindful-consumption/

Sima, V., & Gheorghe, I. (2008). Eco-Efficiency – A Romanian Perspective. *Proceedings of The 11th IBIMA Conference, "Creating Global Economies through Innovation and Knowledge Management"* (pp. 1642-1650).

Sima, V. & Gheorghe, I. G. (2014, May 20). Analyze of environmental performance in Romania based on Environmental Performance Index. *Proceedings of International Conference "Sustainable Energy Use and Management,"* Targu-Jiu, Romania (pp. 16-19).

Tse, D. K., & Wilton, P. C. (1988). Models of consumer satisfaction: An extension. *JMR, Journal of Marketing Research*, *25*(2), 204–212. doi:10.2307/3172652

Umweltbundesamt. (1997). *Nachhaltige Konsummuster und postmaterielle Lebensstile*, Berlin

Voigt, K. (2006). Business Sees Green in Going Green. CNN Report.

Wier, M., & Anderson, L. M. (2003). Demand for Organic foods-Attitudes, Values and Purchasing Behaviors. *Newsletter from Danish Research Center Farming.*, *2*, 1–3.

KEY TERMS AND DEFINITIONS

Green Behavior: A pro-environmental behaviour, people being good administrator of natural resources.

Green Customer Satisfaction: A state which results from the green consumption experience, including: green product satisfaction, companies reputation and image satisfaction, and less harmfulness satisfaction.

Green Dimension: A new category proposed in order to model the customers' satisfaction. The main elements need to be had in sight are: superior energetic class, renewable energy, low polluting level, products with biodegradable compounds, organic food.

Green Product: An ecological product. It's manufacturing process and its use does not generate negative environmental effects.

Green Strategy Mix: A strategic system which integrates Planning Strategy, Processes Strategy, Product Strategy, Promotion Strategy, People Strategy, and Eco-Efficiency Strategy.

Sustainable Consumption: A consumption model which seeks to preserve resources for future generations to be able to satisfy their needs.

Sustainable Development: A concept 'that meets the needs of the present without compromising the ability of future generations to meet their own needs' (Brundtland Commission, 1987, Report of the World Commission on Environment and Development, United Nations). It includes economic development, social development and environmental protection.

Section 2

Consumer Behavior and Engagement in the Nexus of Marketing and Technology

Chapter 5
Marketing 4.0:
Enhancing Consumer-Brand Engagement through Big Data Analysis

Ana Isabel Jiménez-Zarco
Open University of Catalonia, Spain

María Pilar Martínez-Ruiz
University of Castilla la Mancha, Spain

Asher Rospigliosi
Brighton University, UK

Alicia Izquierdo-Yusta
University of Burgos, Spain

ABSTRACT

Marketing evolves in parallel with technology. During the last five years, Marketing 3.0 has become the most innovative marketing approach, but of growing, is research focusing on Marketing 4.0: the marketing of big data. Much has been speculated, but academic journals have published little about Marketing 4.0. Maybe, because the total understanding of Marketing 4.0 requires: firstly, a depth knowledge about the evolution of marketing, especially about Marketing 3.0, and secondly, an analysis of how a range of technology –not only the Internet and social media- can be used to design marketing strategies that enhance the brand-consumer relationship. Taking into account how consumers' behavior has been changing since the beginning of this century, this chapter seeks to review Marketing 4.0 concepts, analyzing how big data can be used to enhance the consumer-brand relationship.

INTRODUCTION

Companies in both the public and private sector continue to explore not only new ways to influence the decisions of individual consumers but also to look to gain the hearts and minds of the consumers. Ten years ago, a new context became apparent, where the increasingly visible emerging social and economic trends highlighted the need for alternative, more sustainable forms of living, creating and consuming. In this last decade, this need has become more widely recognised, and technologies at the consumers service make it increasingly possible.

DOI: 10.4018/978-1-5225-2139-6.ch005

The new consumer exhibits a socially responsible buying and consumption behavior. As this is a demanding and informed consumer, he/she has more power with respect of the company, sometimes being able to participate actively in the development of certain business processes. In this context, companies must reconsider how they appeal to their clients. Developing new formulae to achieve their total and active participation, as well as their emotional engagement, which is essential for a companies' survival. The key might be in the new Marketing approach: Marketing 4.0. This shift is especially crucial for retail companies, which once they have moved online, have increased the understanding of their consumers (Corstjens and Lal, 2012). Online retailers can track not only what customers bought, but also what else they looked at; how they navigated through the site; how much they were influenced by promotions, reviews, and page layouts; and similarities across individuals and groups (McAfee et al., 2012). All this flow of information increases the power of the company, if it has the right tools and also knows how to use them.

In line with these changes, this chapter seeks to offer evidence regarding the ways that companies use to enhance their relationship with consumers, using big data marketing as a way to measure, know and understand the new consumers' needs and behaviours. With these ideas in mind, we revise the marketing concept evolution from Marketing 1.0 to Marketing 3.0. Then, we will present the concept of Marketing 4.0, as the evolution of Marketing 3.0 when used intensively with technology. Finally, once defined as Marketing 4.0: big data marketing, we analyse the philosophy and strategic changes exhibited by retail companies to better serve their consumers. This chapter concludes with some key conclusions and managerial recommendations for retail companies. For example, companies must know how the use of big data marketing has the potential to transform traditional businesses as well was retail, offering them even greater opportunities for competitive advantage. Managers can measure and therefore manage more precisely than ever before. Also, they can make better predictions and smarter decisions, as well as target more-effective interventions, in areas that so far have been dominated by gut and intuition rather than by data and rigor. But as with any other major change in business, the challenges of becoming a big data– enabled organization can be enormous and requires a correct design and leadership.

BACKGROUND: THE ETHICAL CONSUMER AND A NEW MARKETING APPROACH

During the last decade, the world has gone through a period of rapid and unexpected turbulence. The financial meltdown has increased the level of poverty and unemployment, thus reducing the rate of growth of developed countries. Meanwhile, economic power has shifted to countries in the East, which are experiencing higher rates of growth. Moreover, climate change and rising pollution are forcing countries to limit the emission of carbon dioxide into the atmosphere, which is also imposing a higher burden on business. These changes had a profound impact on the economic and social context. But it is the case that their effect had been enhanced by two other factors which are: new technological developments and the globalization process.

Technological advances have brought about huge changes in consumers, markets and society in general. Since the end of the last century, many new information technologies have been introduced into marketing and further developed into what it is considered as a new-wave of marketing technology.

Technology

As technology evolves, consumers and especially businesses and other organizations adopt it in order to enhance their activities. Initially this application of technologies to commercial activities in the network were known as electronic-marketing or e-marketing, based on the use of ICT in the field of marketing. But this use has gone beyond just marketing, revolutionizing the way that information is obtained and used during the business decision making process.

Traditionally, companies implant complex technological applications, which collect, analyze, store and distribute information, which is used in decision-making processes: systems, which ultimately constitute the heart of the intelligence system of the organization (Barry et al., 2016). But the sources and size of the data available is changing, Increasingly companies are able to quickly analyze a large and varied amount of data that they and their consumers generate. As an example, take into account that in 2012, about 2.5 exabytes of data was created each day, and that number was doubling every 40 months or so. More data travels across the Internet every second than was stored in the entire Internet just 20 years ago. This gives companies an opportunity to work with many petabyes of data in a single data set—and not just from the Internet.

To a large extent these changes are caused by connectivity, interactivity, and information processing capacity, thus enabling the use of technology. The first two characteristics are more typical of Information Technology and communication, and particularly the Internet, and the third is more suitable for certain types of software designed for the collection, processing, and analysis of data.

Connectivity and Interactivity: The Growth of Web 2.0 and Social Media

People and organizations are more inter-connected than ever. This allows them to share a virtual space with global reach in order to obtain information, to communicate, interact and exchange information, knowledge or any other product, thus overcoming time and space barriers (Fortis, 2015; Tuban et al., 2015). On the other hand, the high degree of interactivity which is possible by means of the communications with these technologies allows the different actors involved in the value creation process - in particular the consumers – to develop a more active role in their relationship with the company (McAfee, 2009). In this line, Copeland and Malik (2005) show that new technology enables connectivity and interactivity of individuals and groups, as well as facilitating the spread of word-of-mouth information sharing.

New wave technology enables people to change from being consumers to prosumers. Technology, -especially web 2.0 and social media- has become a tool that allows individuals to express themselves and collaborate with others. In this situation, people can create new ideas, entertain themselves and consume them. At this point, we consider it necessary to consider the difference between the two main terns used to describe these new wave technologies: social media and web 2.0. Social media is a broad term and covers the many different online social communication platforms. Social media communication platforms include social network sites (e.g. Myspace, Facebook, LinkedIn etc.), Wikis (e.g. Wikipedia), Multimedia sharing sites (e.g. YouTube and Flickr), Bookmarking sites (e.g., Del.icio.us and Digg), Virtual worlds (e.g., Second Life), and Ratingsites (e.g. Yelp) (Kaplan and Haenlein, 2010). These famous social media platforms which are used for generating, sharing and refining information are collectively labelled as Web 2.0 (McAfee, 2006).

Social media and Web 2.0 are often used interchangeably. In fact, social media and web 2.0 are two distinct terms and concepts. Web 2.0 is related to the online software applications; it is the Internet based technology that enables none-technical users across the world to participate in information generation and dissemination. Whereas, social media refers to the social aspects of using web 2.0 applications. These social uses are participation, openness, interaction, conversation, community and connectedness (SpannerWorks, 2007). These social aspects are based on four "principles of openness (of standards and external involvement), peer production, sharing, and acting globally". (Tapscott and Williams, 2007). Social media tools provide a common platform to people across nations and cultures to generate and share knowledge, information, media, ideas, experiences, opinions and so on. The unique characteristics of social media which differentiate it from traditional and online media are: (1) Social media is generated by users and they have more control over its content generation and utilization. Social media tools not only allow users to generate, publish, and share the content but also enable them to criticize and rank the online content (Dickey and Lewis, 2011). In addition, social media is ubiquitous in nature. It provides the opportunities to many people across the world and across cultures to interact with each other and form a global community based on shared experiences and common interests (Edwards, 2011).

Accessing Information: The First Steps to Big Data

Technology allows organizations to access and manage quickly a large amount of information that is key to their decision-making processes (McAfee, 2006). In this regard, there are many companies, which have installed information systems to capture orders, processes and communicate information effectively and efficiently. Some systems, such as CRM, allow the company to monitor and measure contact with their customers. CRM systems store customers' data and therewith automates connection, according to the information it holds. This value is added to the offer made by the company, to differentiate the brand from its competitors and improve the quality of care dispensed to the customer.

Other systems such as ERP (Enterprise Resource Planning) provide integral information, facilitating the flow of information between departments or activities of the company. ERP is a defined as a business management software, a suite of integrated applications, that are used to collect, store, manage and interpret data from many different business activities. These include: product planning, and materials purchase; manufacturing or service delivery; marketing and sales; inventory management; and shipping and payment. This system provides an integrated view of core business processes, often in real-time, using common databases maintained by a database management system. The applications that make up the system share data across various departments (manufacturing, purchasing, sales, accounting, etc.) that provide the data. ERP facilitates information flow between all business functions, and manages connections to outside stakeholders. However, as we see in the next sections, for online companies the main technological advance in the marketing area, is the emergence of software tools that in real-time enable the capture and analysis of information generated by online consumers' behaviour (Shankar et al., 2016).

In summary, we can see that technology makes it possible to deal directly with clients, as well as suppliers and partners. Companies can even use technology to establish direct and collaborative client relationships. But, as we shall see, technology also implies the loss of power of the company with respect to consumers. Thus, the consumers' role is changing due to the intensive use of new technologies. Consumers are no longer isolated individuals: rather, they are connected with one another. In making decisions, they are no longer unaware but informed. They are no longer passive but active in giving useful feedback to companies (Prahalad & Ramaswamy, 2004).

The Globalization Process

Globalization is the second element that drives the new social and economic age. Advances in transportation, and in telecommunications are major factors in driving globalization. But also, infrastructures, such as the Internet, and mobile phones, have been important in globalization, generating further interdependence of economic and cultural activities. These changes foster international integration arising from the interchange of world views, products, ideas and other aspects of culture. Thus, without doubts we can say that globalization is significantly influenced by technology, as information technology enables the exchange of information between nations, corporations and individuals throughout the world (Beck, 2015)

Like technology, globalization reaches everyone around the world and creates an interlinked economy. But unlike technology, globalization is a force that stimulates economic and social imbalance and creates paradoxes that have a direct impact on firms' and individuals' behaviour. Globalization has made the world a different place. This is important for today's marketers to recognize because they face the necessity of designing an effective strategy that will promote their products and services in foreign markets, in addition to their home countries. It is important to understand consumer needs within target countries to create a global marketing mix where product, price, place and promotion are geared toward specific country's needs.

Globalization has also increased market competition. Companies have to recognise that there are new competitors appearing all the time- some of which may be international. One benefit of this globalization has been an increase in product variety for consumers. The Internet has opened new opportunities for browsing from home, office or train, with products available worldwide (Dunn, 2015). Today, consumers have more purchasing choices than ever before due to globalization. The natural barriers of time have been reduced, and the cost of moving information, people, goods and capital across the globe has been dramatically reduced. Markets are now global in scope and encompass an expanding range of goods and services. Consumers use technology to reach out to the world on the Internet gathering and sending information, and purchasing goods and services.

Globalization has also profoundly changed the way people think, and companies have to take this into account. Thus, people search for a sense of continuity in their lives, instead of being anxious and bearing conflicting, intertwined values in their minds. People search for connection with others and begin to blend into their local community and society. Yet a sense of direction is also essential in times of paradox as people start to unite in support of social causes or begin to have a greater awareness and concern about poverty, injustice, environmental sustainability, community responsibility and social purpose. Finally, another globalization effect is that companies are now competing to be seen as providing continuity, connection and direction. According to Holt (2004), companies, and especially their brands, seek to address social, economic and environmental issues in as a way of engaging with society.

The New Consumer Profile: Why Companies Need a New Marketing Concept

During the last decade, the aforementioned changes, particularly evident in Western societies, have favored a change in individuals' purchasing and consumption trends. In countries like China, India and Brazil, high GDP growth rates have allowed the development of a strong middle class, characterized by a markedly consumer behavior while in Europe and the U.S. this consumption model has been strongly questioned (Majfud, 2009). Consumerism involves accumulation, purchase or consumption of goods and services considered nonessential. The same is considered a direct consequence of a social and economic model that promotes the acquisition of wealth as a sign of social status and prestige. In recent years, consumerism has been seen as one of the causes of the economic, social and environmental crisis that we are experiencing. This indicates that the mass consumption that has characterized firms since the 1950s has severely compromised the natural resources and ecological balance, while favoring social and economic imbalance between the north and south.

In response, there are new social and cultural trends emerging that advocate sustainable development, as well as environmental and responsible consumption. In the markets, their impact is evidenced by:

1. The development of new business models in companies;
2. A strong concern for society regarding the responsibility of organizations as social agents, and
3. The emergence of a new consumer model.

The new consumer, also called ethical consumers or green consumer, is characterized by being responsible: that is to say, they are concerned about consuming what they need in a sustainable, responsible manner (Boztepe, 2016). For such a consumer, buying also involves a range of economic, social and environmental processes. This is a type of individual who, at the time of purchasing, questions what is expendable and what is not whilst judging their own financial ability to purchase (Polonsky et al., 2016). Moreover, in relation to the product or service, these consumers take the decision to buy based not only on price or quality (Bostman, 2010), they also try to protect and respect the environment and care about the fact that manufacturing companies or service providers respect human rights and principles of social justice. For example, Biwas and Roy (2015) show that green consumers will try to protect the environment in a range of different ways (e.g. recycling, checking that a package is made of recycled material, purchasing green products, saving energy, etc.). According to Laroche et al., (2001), these kinds of behaviors are expected in these ethical consumers. But consumers do not always base their buying decisions on their attitudes towards the environment, even though these attitudes may have a fairly strong influence. In this sense, Strandvik et al., (2013) note that ethical consumers reject some brands, especially those which focus their image on the positive aspect of consumption. Brand avoidance has been defined as a deliberate rejection or abandonment of a brand (Lee et al., 2009), that can result in a range of different responses, according to the strength of feelings and behaviors that consumers express (Hogg et al. 2009).

Access to technology has supported the emergence of such consumers. ICT, especially the Internet, allow them to provide a means for seeking information, but also to communicate and disseminate their opinions and experiences. This demanding and informed consumer is not limited to searching for information online about products and the companies that sell them. They also have enough capacity and power to be heard and to demand certain a kind of behavior from firms (Mourali and Yang, 2013). In fact, the report prepared by Insider in 2012 noted that, the consumer has more power than ever and is extremely important for businesses. "We live in a world where everything is just a click away. The Internet has conditioned us to expect information and services on demand at anytime, anywhere — and often free. It has also given us the power to share our experiences immediately, at the touch of a button. The consumer, rather than the brand, controls the interaction. As consumers, we do not need advertisers to speak directly to us anymore; through social media and our mobiles, we can instantly share recommendations and content with our friends. We can also turn to the opinions of strangers via the ratings and reviews of social commerce to help us determine which products and services we buy. Brands need to work harder to make themselves heard."

As well as reframing the individual's identity (e.g., by interacting with others, role-playing, learning and testing of one's social skills), technology can enhance empowerment of the individual through increasing self-efficiency and skills (Amichai-Hamburger et al. 2008). This latter form of empowering is especially relevant for the new consumers, because it offers a new ability to play a more important role in the process of companies' value creation.

This behavior is determined by the desire which the individual demonstrates to know whether the products are produced efficiently, or if the company is sustainable in terms of economic, social and environmental terms. This process is referred to as co-creation and can occur in a variety of contexts (Bolton and Saxena-Iyer, 2009). In general, co-creation involves the joint creation of value by the firm and its network of various entities (such as customers, suppliers and distributors) termed here actors (Perjs et al., 2012). This concept has been extensively studied in the field of marketing. In marketing co-creation refers to the involvement of consumers in the various value creating activities through which products and services are made. These activities include the production and distribution processes which are usually performed in the course of manufacturing a product or creating a service for a given target group of consumers.

According to Ranjan and Read (2016), co-creation is a bi-dimensional concept. The first dimension is co-production, which involves customer participation and engagement of the customer base. The second co-creation dimension involves collaborative value-in-use activities that enhance customer lifetime value. Co-production involves customers taking an active role during key steps of the production of goods and services. For example, they might design their own newspapers and magazines by using Really Simple Syndication (RSS), to download particular types of news items or they might self assemble their own furniture that they have purchased from IKEA. This trend towards greater consumer involvement has been facilitated by the substantial changes in technology, consumer sophistication, and regulatory environments. In particular, the development of Internet technologies which allow consumers to have instant access to stored information and to create and disseminate text, pictures and voice messages at minimal cost. Thus technology is generally viewed as a key enabler of co-creation with the term referring to customer participation in the development of the core offering (Vargo et al., 2008). On the other hand, consumers have evolved from 'passive audiences' to 'active players'. With this evolution, the role of customer-to-customer and customer-to-enterprise interactions has become increasingly important in generating new co-created customer value. The rise of social media has further augmented the role of customer and brand communities (Hakanen and Jaakkola, 2012) with customers and firms collaborating in personalized co-created value.

One context in particular where consumer co-creation is increasingly vital is the area of new product development (NPD). In this regard, it is important to take into account the fact that, independently of the loss of control over certain activities which it can represent, the company finds important benefits in the development of co-creation processes. Cost-efficient and interaction opportunities offered have made co-creation a suitable means of creating value and improving the overall success of new products. In that case, consumers are able and willing to provide ideas for new goods or services that may fulfil needs that have not yet been met by the market or might improve on existing offerings (Ernst et al., 2010). Hauser et al., (2006) show that successful NPD depends on in-depth understanding of consumer needs and product development efforts that meet those needs (Hauser et al., 2006) and, in particular, ideas generated through co-creation that will more closely mirror consumer needs.

Many businesses positively regard this kind of behavior by the consumer. Some companies even consider that the participation of the customer should take place in all phases of product innovation (Ernst et al.2010). However, as pointed out by Etgar (2008), consumers often vary greatly in their interest and ability to participate usefully in co-creation tasks. Thus, there are only some segments of consumers who might be especially willing and able to participate in co-creation activities. These include innovators (the lead users) emergent consumers and market mavens.

At a strategic level, companies establish two types of objectives:

1. That the number of consumers with which they have a close relationship is high.
2. That the relation established, aside from having a behavioral dimension (a collaborative behavior) also has an affective dimension.

Currently, reaching the hearts and minds of a large number of consumers is critical for businesses and especially in the field of marketing, it is a key factor. However, the values and motivations that characterize the new consumer are different from a decade ago: this raises the need for a new marketing concept best suited to the reality of the current situation.

MARKETING EVOLUTION: FROM MARKETING 1.0 TO MARKETING 3.0

During the last five decades, marketing has evolved through three stages that we call Marketing 1.0, 2.0, and 3.0. In the last decade, a significant proportion of companies have adopted Marketing 3.0, especially through the use of Social Corporate Responsibility (SCR) strategies, as that they provide a great opportunity to adapt the company to the new social and economic environment.

As we can see in the next section, the evolution of marketing is based around three major disciplines: product management, customer management and brand management. This continuous change responds to the marketing discipline's need to adapt to different aspects of human lives. Thus, in the 1950s and 1960s it was focussed on product management and in the 1970s and the 1980s it evolved towards consumer management. The discipline of brand management was added at the end of the 1990s, and at the beginning of the 2000s.

The First Marketing Steps of Marketing: Marketing 1.0 and Marketing 2.0

In the early 1950s, the manufacturing sector was the centre of the developed economies. In such an environment, marketing was viewed as just one of several important functions supporting production, along with finance and human resources.

The marketing function is the sole responsibility of specialists who comprise the marketing department. They are responsible for guiding the company towards customer satisfaction. The treatment given to clients is carried out by means of the actions contained in the marketing mix program. The basic objective is that customers choose the products of the company (Sánchez et al., 2000). Ultimately, this approach focuses on the product itself and is aimed at winning new customers, while not worrying too much about their further treatment. The marketing mix is the cornerstone on which the transactional marketing approach is based. Thus, the idea is that the marketer uses four basic tools in order to act on its mass market (Grönroos, 1994)

The 1970s and 1980s were a turbulent time. Western economies were in crisis. For companies generating demand was harder, and required more than four Ps. The increased offer, the maturity and fragmentation of the markets, the intensification and globalization of competition and the rapid pace of technological development substantially altered the competitive landscape of enterprises.

The new reality forced a change in companies' strategy and their conception of the environment, so a new marketing approach to understanding and providing solutions to the challenges arose (Grönroos, 2000). Marketing professionals were forced to think harder and create better marketing concepts in order to give a response to new consumer profiles. Also, during this time, consumers became smarter buyers. In consumers' minds, many products had a distinct positioning due to the fact that they were viewed as different and superior from the rest of the products in the market. Other variables, such as people, processes, physical evidence, public opinion or political power had to be considered in marketing strategy (Boom and Bitner, 1981).

To stimulate product demand, marketing needed to evolve from purely tactical – Marketing 1.0 - to a more strategic level: Marketing 2.0, also known as relational marketing. Relationship marketing not only promotes a new way of understanding the markets, it also provides a new way to deal with and act with regard to the agents that form them. In its new understanding of reality:

1. The market passes from being analyzed from the traditional and simple dyadic perspective between two parties or agents, to a different one in which every relationship is considered a network.
2. The consumer is seen as an increasingly sophisticated agent who refuses to be anonymous and requires a personalized treatment.
3. Relationship-marketing technology is considered to go beyond the stage of simple automation for cost savings.
4. Customer loyalty has become a priority.

The concept of value is of great importance as the center of the design of the corporate competitive strategy. Offering customers more value than the competition becomes the only way to attract and keep their loyalty. In this sense, the existence of an in-depth knowledge and personal attention to customers becomes a priority. This is only possible if the organization as a whole and all its resources are managed towards the market and to customer satisfaction (Raval and Grönroos, 1996). Competitive strategies based on the use of company resources outperforming competitors in service levels, prices, adaptation, and/or creating and delivering other benefits of a psychological and social nature (security, confidence, etc...) are sought (Grönroos, 1994). The way to do that is by creating a superior value for the customer and to keep it linked to the organization.

The actions most commonly developed for these purposes are: on the one hand, permanently enriching the content of the commercial offer through the joint delivery of products and customer services (Grönroos, 2000); on the other hand, to jointly develop a long-term behavior that is conducive to maintaining a relationship with the customer, where in addition to the above, benefits of a psychological and social nature are delivered, at the same time reducing sacrifices associated with the process of exchange and relationship for the consumer.

For the company, these actions have serious implications that go beyond the development of a new product concept, or a change in the way of understanding the act of consumption developed by the subject. The concept of marketing is altered by modifying their processes and management.

To adopt a relationship-oriented marketing implies a profound process of change for the company which goes beyond the goal of setting objectives focused on client development or the development of marketing practices which seek their loyalty. The focus on relationships is a new way of thinking about marketing activity, as well as to understanding the market and the activities which the agents who comprise it develop. The main implications of adopting such an orientation lead to relations for the organization, including those listed and discussed below:

1. The active participation of consumers in the business.
2. The importance of the concept of value, which is at the center of business strategy.
3. The change in the concept of supply and the act of consumption.
4. Consideration of long-term relationships as a means to creating and conveying value.
5. The concept of marketing as a process that affects and involves the whole enterprise.

Marketing 2.0 initiates the consumer oriented era. Companies need to know their consumers, in order to offer them a set of products and services totally adapted to their requirements. But, this approach implicitly assumes the view that consumers are passive targets of marketing campaigns. Companies know the market through market research, but do not have a direct and continuous contact with them. Fortunately, nowadays people are not passive and wish to be treated as simple consumers. They are playing an active role in their social and economic context, and their concerns regarding human, social environmental problems leads them to look for solutions to their worries with respect to how to make the globalized world a better place.

This leads to the next marketing era: Marketing 3.0 the values-driven era, where people are not treated simply as consumers, and marketers approach them as whole human beings with minds, hearts, and spirits. Meanwhile, companies have to address their deepest needs for social, economic and environmental justice in their mission, vision, and values. Their aim is to provide solutions in order to address problems in society. Table 1 shows the main differences between Marketing 1.0, 2.0 and 3.0

Table 1. The main differences between Marketing 1.0, 2.0 and 3.0

	Marketing 1.0: Product-Centric	Marketing 2.0: Consumer-Centric	Marketing 3.0: Value-Centric
Objective	Sell products to the masses	Satisfy customers & brand loyalty	Meet emotional and rational needs of consumers
Enabling forces	Industrial revolution	Information technology	Connectedness of consumers (new wave technology)
How marketers see the market	Product driven market	Smarter consumers & mass market	People instead of segments
Key marketing concept	Product development	Differentiation	Values
Value propositions	Functional	Functional & emotional	Functional, emotional & rational
Company marketing guidelines	Product specification	Corporate and product positioning	Corporate mission, vision, and values
Interaction with consumers	Mass communication (one-to-many transactions)	Micro segmentation	Consumers collaborate with each other
Power of branding	Marketers/companies	Marketers/companies	Consumers

Source: Kotler et al., (2010).

Marketing 3.0

As we can appreciate from Table 1, Marketing 3.0 places the concept of marketing in the area of human aspirations, values and spirit. It proposes that consumers are complete human beings whose other needs and hopes should never be neglected (.Kotler et al., 2010). This new marketing view complements emotional marketing with human spirit marketing. Thus, marketing practices are very much influenced by changes in consumer behaviour and attitude. Also, it is a more sophisticated form of the consumer-centric orientation where the consumer demands more collaborative, cultural and spiritual marketing approaches.

According to Kotler (2011), to reach success, new marketing must:

1. Be holistic;
2. Build strong brands;
3. Dispose of information and communication system that enhance the brand building performance through some marketing actions based on promotion and electronic leadership.

The axes of Marketing 3.0 are thus defined by the three principal changes which – as we previously saw – characterize the new social and economic context: new technology development, globalization and a new consumer profile. It is a marketing where companies:

1. Understand community issues that relate to their business;
2. Have defined perfectly what they are, why they are in business and what they want to become: in other words, what is the corporate mission, objectives and vision; and have to invite consumers to participate in the development of the product and communication of the company.

As Figure 1 shows, Marketing 3.0 is a collaborative, cultural and spiritual marketing.

Figure 1. Three changes that lead to marketing 3.0
Source: Kotler et al. (2010).

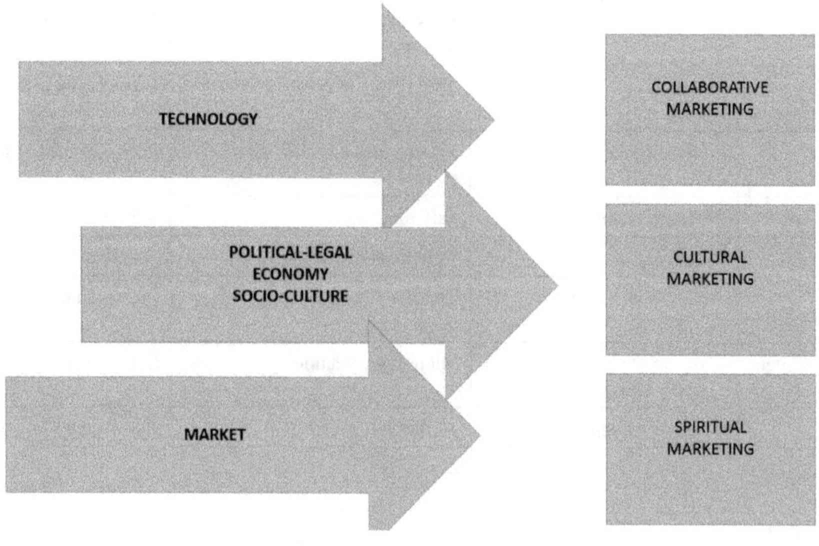

Collaborative marketing is the first building block of Marketing 3.0. Companies practising Marketing 3.0 aim to change the world. They cannot do it alone. In the interlinked economy, they must collaborate with one another, with their shareholders, with their channel partners, with their employees, and with their consumers. As we have previously shown, co-creation is one of the principal trends in the new marketing area, but, collaboration must be started with partners who share similar sets of values and desires. On the other hand, cultural marketing is the second building block of Marketing 3.0. It is an approach that addresses the concerns and desires of global citizens. Companies practising Marketing 3.0 should understand community issues that relate to their business and puts them at the heart of company's business model. Marketing 3.0 demonstrates its concern for the communities around it: communities of consumers, employees, channel partners, and shareholders.

Finally, the spiritual or human spirit marketing, from the company's point of view, is the third building block of marketing. Thus, like creative people, companies should think about their self-actualization beyond their material objectives. They should know what they want to become and give expression to their corporate mission, vision and values. Only in this way will the business performance be the result of the consumer's appreciation of these companies' contributions to human well-being.

According to Kotler and Keller (2013), to reach success, new marketing must be holistic and build stronger brands through performance rather than simply via promotion. They need to lead electronically as well, through building superior systems of information and communication.

Brands become the mainstay of this new marketing approach. They offer products an integral value connecting them with the human spirit of their customers who desire that the brands assume their fair share of social responsibility for issues that concerns everyone (e.g. environment, hunger, poverty, human rights, health and well-being, etc). Brands that behave and conduct themselves properly with regards to the environment and the general community at large and that create real meaningful demonstrable value that align with the social good will be welcomed and respected.

The media will promote caring companies which will influence buying behaviours. Companies can enhance brand building performance through a superior use of information and communication systems. Customers must not be treated just as consumers, but as complex, multi-dimensional human beings – customers with complex human spirits who are active, engaged, anxious, informed, creative and have the ability to easily connect with others. And Marketing 3.0 can address the complexity of the human spirit with the help of brands that create products, services, and company cultures that lead, inspire, reflect, communicate and share the values of their customers. Table 2 shows the value-based matrix model for Marketing 3.0

Table 2. The value-based matrix model for Marketing 3.0

		Consumer		
		Mind	**Heart**	**Spirit**
Company	**Mission (Why)**	Deliver Satisfaction	Realize Aspiration	Practice Compassion
	Vision (What)	Profitability	Returnability	Sustainability
	Values (How)	Be Better	Differentiate	Make a difference

Source: Kotler et al., (2010).

MARKETING 4.0: THE NEXT STEP IN MARKETING EVOLUTION

Marketing 3.0 is the values-driven marketing approach where the customers are treated as human beings who are active, anxious, and creative. That involves an important challenge to consumer-brand relationships, because consumers have their own voice, opinion and experience (Kotler et al., 2010). They demand that brands satisfy their deepest anxieties and desires, and request more participation in value creation. Therefore, it is just not only focused on the customers traditional needs and wants. Brands, create personal conversations with their customers, encouraging them to feel free to talk about their feelings and experiences. Social media becomes the interaction space in which customers share opinions and experiences and it offers to business a useful medium where consumers validate, confirm and check other consumers' experiences with the brands.

According to Choo et al., (2013), the first solutions for superior systems of information and communication implemented offered companies limited benefits. They were:

1. Based on online platforms to which the access of some consumers are restricted;
2. Focused on very specific users and sectors, and
3. Based on consumers' information which does not integrate the offer point of view –such as the opinion and justification from the vendors. Companies needed a new marketing approach, such as Marketing 4.0 that integrates with consumer-technology and also provides solutions based on the analysis of the consumer information about their preferences, opinions, and needs.

Jara et al (2012) show that Marketing 4.0 as a simple evolution of Marketing 3.0. The authors show that the value-driven approach evolves to strong consumer-brand integration thanks to the intensive use of technologies. But Yeh et al., (2016), highlight that Marketing 4.0 is more than that, this new marketing approach transforms the business rules by changing the interaction with customers in time and space. Thus:

1. Marketing goals are described in terms of brand engagement, loyalty, retention, and recommendation, while consumer quality perception, satisfaction, and experience are the tools used to obtain them (Sashi, 2012).
2. Online sales are consolidated, so that marketing strategies start to be designed according to the two-dimensional stores of the web browser (instead of the three-dimensions of physical stores). In the electronic marketing environment of the last decade, the discontinuous connections points (home phone, work phone, e-mail) have been replaced by the single, always reachable mobile phone. The implications are great as the new marketing is characterized by network ubiquity, universality, uniqueness and unison (Kurkovsky and Harihar, 2006).
3. Technology evolution goes beyond human-computer interaction. For example, the Internet of things (IoT) is a system of interrelated computing devices, mechanical and digital machines, objects, animals, plants or people that are provided with unique identifiers and the ability to transfer data over a network without requiring human-to-human or human-to-computer interaction.
4. Companies can access vast amounts of information about the consumer-brand relationships across a multitude of channels that influence their decision making process.

In this situation, companies need to sort all these pieces in order to design successful marketing strategies Accessing all of these pieces is key to achieving a successful market position and performance. But, to identify and analyse the information is only the first step to assembling this puzzle, in the following sections we address the steps companies need to take to gain the benefits of Marketing 4.0 and big data.

The First Step: Big Data

In 2013, Forbes published an article entitled Big Data, Analytics and the Future of Marketing and Sales. It stated that: "Big Data is the biggest game-changing opportunity for marketing and sales since the Internet went mainstream almost 20 years ago. That statement often prompts vigorous head nodding from executives, but is quickly followed by head scratching. "How can we make this happen" (Gordon, 2013).

In the following years the revolution that is Big Data has reshaped much business practice. Companies generate vast quantities of information about consumer-brand relationships across a multitude of channels that influence their decision making process. This constant stream of information on consumer audiences and their interactions is vital to design new marketing practices, such as programmatic media buying, granular audience segmentation and targeted, real-time trigger marketing.

Big Data, in short, has gone mainstream. But that raises an important question: If everyone is "data-driven" in both theory and action, how can companies get meaningful competitive differentiation through their use of information? It is obvious that this matter raises some doubts and questions about the drivers, challenge and consequences of how the use of information can directly influence a companies marketing strategy approach. How can companies obtain data?, How can data be part of the business marketing approach? Or, how can data analysis help to develop marketing applications? All these questions are relevant to the new marketing approach, Marketing 4.0, also called big data marketing.

What Is Big Data?

Big data describes the information, both structured and unstructured, that companies can access, analyse and use in the decision making processes. For companies, the volume of data is important but, data analysis requires them to consider five dimensions of data:

- **Volume:** Organizations collect data from a variety of sources, including business transactions, social media and information from sensor or machine-to-machine data.
- **Velocity:** Data streams in at an unprecedented speed and must be dealt with in a timely manner. RFID tags, sensors, and smart metering are driving the need to deal with torrents of data in near-real time.
- **Variety:** Data comes in all types of formats – from structured, numeric data in traditional databases to unstructured text documents, email, video, audio, stock ticker data and financial transactions.
- **Variability:** In addition to the increasing velocities and varieties of data, data flows can be highly inconsistent with periodic peaks. Is something trending in social media? Daily, seasonal and event-triggered peak data loads can be challenging to manage. Even more so with unstructured data.
- **Complexity:** Today's data comes from multiple sources, which makes it difficult to link, match, cleanse and transform data across systems. However, it's necessary to connect and correlate relationships, hierarchies, and multiple data linkages or the data can quickly spiral out of control.

The Data Sources: The Internet of Things

The World Wide Web characterized the early years of Internet use, but gradually it has evolved into Web 2.0, a two-way communication system that enables users' participation, collaboration and interaction. While web 2.0 dominates the Internet architecture, engineers and scholars are working in order to achieve another goal: to allow machines and engines to behave more intelligently, as if they can understand web content.

Referred to as the Semantic Web, or Web 3.0, Wortmann and Flüchter, (2015) show that the use of standardized formats to mark up web content, would allow machines to process and share data on their own, without the need for human mediation. The direct machine-to-machine communication over the Internet has produced a paradigm being referred to as the Internet of Things (IoT).

According to Parahasar et al (2016) the Internet of Things is: "a paradigm where everyday objects can be equipped with identifying, sensing, networking and processing capabilities that will allow them to communicate with one another and with other devices and services over the Internet to accomplish some objective." The main goal is that IoT devices will be ubiquitous, context-aware and will enable ambient intelligence via embedded systems which will lead to a highly distributed network of devices communicating with human beings as well as other devices (Wan et al., 2015).

IoT is opening new opportunities for consumers and business. A large number of novel applications that promise to improve the quality of consumers' lives are been developed. For instance, in Britain the government has encouraged energy companies to roll out smart meters that have clever functions that let people turns on their home heating remotely, turn down the temperature if it is a sunny day, or even turn off when there is no-one at home (The Guardian, 2014). But IoT is more than smart homes and connected appliances; it is scaling up to include smart cities. Those are, cities where connected traffic signals monitor utility use, or smart bins that signal when they need to be emptied. IoT can facilitate smart industries, with connected sensors for everything from tracking parts to monitoring crops. According to a report from Cisco Systems, 2050 will be the ideal time for such technology, since more than 60% of the world's population will live in smart cities (Helmy, 2015). Currently, the earlier adopters of smart city technologies include the European cities of Barcelona and Amsterdam, although, the concept has quickly spread into other countries, where cities such as San Francisco, Copenhagen, New York, Dubai, Singapore, Hamburg, and Nice, are following suit.

IoT could offer business opportunities to different companies such as Cisco, IBM, Intel, Silver Spring Networks, Build.io, GE Lighting and Siemens who are among those providing smart city solutions worldwide. For instance, banks and financial institutions are looking to exploit the trends in the Internet of Things by using data streams from devices and cloud computing to develop new financial products. For example, American Banker states

... some banks are piloting a 'healthy savings account.' Customers who opt in for this account would allow the bank to track their fitness levels via a wearable device, such as how often they go jogging or go to the gym. They could then get higher rates on their savings depending on how many calories they burn per week or month. Also, the bank is exploring partnering with sporting goods retailers, who would provide offers to these customers on running shoes or other sporting equipment (Yurcan, 2016).

IoT offers opportunities to companies. As mobile devices and wearables proliferate, companies have the ability to collect enormous amounts of data. This ability means companies can offer a much greater degree of convenience. This could help deepen the relationship between companies and their customers, as well as provide a personalized experience to their customers.

Other Data Sources: Internet and Databases

As companies and organizations go about their business and interact with individuals; they are generating a tremendous amount of digital data. Social media sites, smartphones, and other consumer devices have allowed billions of individuals around the world to contribute to the amount of big data available. And the growing volume of multimedia content has played a major role in the exponential growth in the amount of big data (Donnelly et al, 2015).

Big data refers to datasets whose size is beyond the ability of typical database software tools to capture, store, manage, and analyse. In this definition, we assume that as technology advances over time, the size of datasets -that qualify as big data- will also increase. We also note that the definition can vary by sector, depending on what kinds of software tools are commonly available and what sizes of datasets are common in a particular industry.

There is strong evidence that big data can play a significant economic role to the benefit of large and small companies. For instance, Donally et al (2015) show how the marketing power of big data is recognised by small firms, where the use of a loyalty card as a source of big data can present significant challenges. In the case of a large retailer such as Tesco, the loyalty card data from its Clubcard represents the buying behaviour of 17m shoppers (approximately 40% of UK households). Managed by the market research firm, Dunnhumby, Clubcard data has acted as a platform for Tesco's rise as a dominant force in the retail sector.

But, across many firms, large and small, the means to extract insight from data are improving rapidly as software available to apply increasingly sophisticated techniques combines with growing computing horsepower. The use of cloud hosted applications even gives SMEs access to these tools (Rospigliosi and Greener, 2015). So, as Chen et al (2012) note, the difference between the success or failure depends on the company's ability to store, aggregate, and combine data, and then use the results to perform deep analyses and take informed market decisions.

Companies have access to big data using many different sources of information. For instance, business intelligence and analytics system, defined as the analysis techniques, technologies, systems, practices, methodologies, and applications that analyse critical business data which can help a company better understand its business and market and make timely business decisions. But also, since the early 2000s, the Internet and the Web provide access to unique data for collection and analytical research, allowing organizations not only to present their businesses online and interact with their customers directly, but to analyse the data that results from these interactions.

It is worth emphasising that big data analysis can be used to address many different purposes, such as:

1. **Enhanced 360º View of the Customer:** With the onset of the digital revolution, the touch points between an organization and its customers have increased many times over; organizations can now use specialized solutions to effectively manage these connections. An enhanced 360-degree view of the customer is a holistic approach that takes into account all available and meaningful information about the customer to drive better engagement, more revenue and long-term loyalty. It combines data exploration, data governance, data access, data integration and analytics in a solution that harnesses the volume, velocity and variety of big data

2. **Security Intelligence Extension:** The growing number of high-tech crimes - cyber-based terrorism, espionage, computer intrusions, and major cyber fraud - poses a real threat to every individual and organization. To meet the security challenge, businesses need to augment and enhance cyber security and intelligence analysis platforms with big data technologies to process and analyse new data types (e.g. social media, emails and sensors) and sources of under-leveraged data. Analysing data in-motion and at rest can help find new associations or uncover patterns and facts to significantly improve intelligence, security and law enforcement insight.
3. **Operation Analysis:** Focuses on analysing machine data (IoT), which can include anything from IT machines to sensors, meters, and GPS devices. It's growing at exponential rates and comes in large volumes and a variety of formats, including in-motion, or streaming data. Leveraging machine data requires complex analysis and correlation across different types of data sets. By using big data for operations analysis, organizations can gain real-time visibility into operations, customer experience, transactions, and behavior.
4. **Data Warehouse Modernization:** Also known as Data Warehouse Augmentation, it is about building on an existing data warehouse infrastructure, to leverage big data technologies to 'augment' its capabilities.

Companies can obtain and analyses big data. While having it doesn't automatically lead to better marketing, the potential is there. It's not the data itself that's so important. Rather, it's the insights derived from big data, the decisions that have been made and the actions that have been taken which make all the difference. In this sense, the real challenge for companies is to find the correct way to combine data with marketing strategy, and as we can see in the next section this is what Marketing 4.0 can help with.

MARKETING 4.0: BIG DATA AND U-MARKETING

Big data is very helpful in marketing strategy, but there are a few things every marketer should keep in mind to help ensure that big data will lead to big success. The range of possible uses for big data can seem overwhelming, so start out by focusing on a few key objectives. Once marketers have decided to do, then identify what data it would be need to support their related analysis. Also, note that the use of big data offers a deep, informed exploration of a measured reality. Big data affords the opportunity to dig deeper and deeper into the data, peeling back layers to reveal richer insights.

The insights gained from the initial analysis can be explored further, with richer, deeper insights emerging each time. These can be helpful to develop some specific strategies and actions to drive growth. But also companies need the knowledge and experience that managers have in order to start the design of a correct marketing strategy. Big data supports and enhances the Marketing 4.0 model. Using the data acquired from customers' shopping and purchasing behavior makes marketers understand how to personalize a customer's shopping experience and undertake a more personalization approach to the company's marketing leading to better customer engagement, retention and loyalty, and marketing optimization and performance.

Watson et al (2002), and more recently, Allen (2012), show that marketing boundaries such as the temporal and spatial separation of buyers and sellers, as well as the sequential stage in marketing planning operations, have changed. These are being extended and blurred as the globalized network era changes the time-space paradigm. According to these authors, new marketing models allows for the design of strategies based on the amount of information that companies have, and according to the new virtual context where companies act.

In 2011, Kotler highlighted that Marketing 3.0 must:

1. Be holistic and
2. Build strong brands.

But now, in the new competitive business context being described, big data use makes it possible to redefine the meaning of both concepts. Thus, in an interconnected world, holistic marketing means to be ubiquitous, universal, unique, and therefore branding must be addressed to improve consumers' experience and engagement.

Big data helps Marketing 4.0 to be holistic and build strong relationships in different ways. Big data can help enrich a company's brand marketing model and customer engagement. Branding can be improved by using the data acquired from customers' shopping and purchasing behavior. This can help marketers understand how to personalize a customer's shopping experience and undertake a more personalization approach to the company's marketing model for better customer engagement. Also, big data can be used in a feedback loop. With the big data analysis process, digital marketers can know whether a particular brand marketing approach is working and is able to engage customers. They use this feedback to transition from one marketing approach to another until they find one that yields better customer response and product interaction. Finally, big data analysis provides newer insights to Marketing 4.0 approaches that were never available before, that will make the brand ever more responsive to market demands.

CONCLUSION

Marketing 4.0 is more than a simple evolution of Marketing 3.0. Marketing 3.0 has come about as a response to several factors: new technological developments, problems caused by globalization and the interest of people to express their creativity, values, and spirituality. While Marketing 4.0 is the response in a new business context transformed by the ubiquitous integration of technology in peoples' lives.

Marketing 3.0 focused on the person, not as a contradiction of the previous marketing vision, but as a refinement of it. Companies as active agents in the environment must demonstrate social responsibility through the development of actions in favour of the community, all with the aim of positioning themselves as companies whose brands earn respect and admiration. It is the evolution from Marketing 1.0, based on the product and which appealed to the "reason" of the customer via rational arguments and passed to Marketing 2.0 which focused on customers, and aimed to get to the heart of the customers (marketing oriented relations). Marketing 3.0 aimed to know their customers an to be concerned about them (their emotions, their feelings, their concerns) and co-create products with them.

Now, companies are moving from Marketing 3.0 to Marketing 4.0. Those Companies which currently correctly apply Marketing 3.0 are those which have been good at Marketing 1.0 and 2.0. The marketing of the future means that companies are no longer freelance fighters, but must become an organization that acts as part of a loyal network of partners, where people are not just consumers, but "whole persons" with "human spirit" who want to make the world a better place.

In Marketing 4.0 we see how technology can press companies in many different ways. On the one hand, to use large volumes of data; on the other to change their marketing point of view. Marketing 4.0

encourages companies to search for goals based on consumers, engagement, loyalty, and retention. The new marketing approach is ubiquitous, universal, unique and in unison. It fosters the building of strong brand-consumer relationships. Big data use can help marketing to achieve a companies, goals as it makes it easier to understand consumers' behaviors and thus to design marketing actions to personalize a customer's shopping experience. Thus, Marketing 4.0 can facilitate a more personalised approach to the company's marketing model for better customer engagement.

ACKNOWLEDGMENT

This work was funded by Research Project ECO2014-59688-R, Planificacion e Implementacion de Estrategias de Gestion Optimas del Pdv Fisico, Online y Movil a Partir de las TIC y la Innovacion, Ministerio de Economía y Competitividad (Spain).

REFERENCES

Aaker, D. A. (1996). *Building Strong Brands*. N.Y.: Free Press.

Allen, M. (2012). What was Web 2.0? Versions as the dominant mode of internet history. *New Media & Society*, *15*(2), 260–275. doi:10.1177/1461444812451567

Barry, D., Helstrom, B., and Potter, J. (2016). and Related Technology. *Asset Management Excellence: Optimizing Equipment Life-Cycle Decisions*, 89.

Beck, U. (2015). *What is globalization?* John Wiley & Sons.

Biswas, A., & Roy, M. (2015). Green products: An exploratory study on the consumer behaviour in emerging economies of the East. *Journal of Cleaner Production*, *87*, 463–468. doi:10.1016/j.jclepro.2014.09.075

Bolton, R. N., & Saxena-Iyer, S. (2009). Interactive Services: A Framework, Synthesis and Research Directions. *Journal of Interactive Marketing*, *23*(1), 91–104. doi:10.1016/j.intmar.2008.11.002

Botsman, R., & Rogers, R. (2010). *What's mine is yours: How collaborative consumption is changing the way we live*. N.Y.: Harper Collins Publisher.

Boztepe, A. (2016). Green marketing and its impact on consumer buying behavior. *European Journal of Economic and Political Studies*, *5*(1), 5–21.

Brown, C., & Vessey, I. (2003). Managing the next wave of enterprise systems: Leveraging lessons from ERP. *MIS Quarterly Executive*, *2*(1), 45–57.

Choo, C. W., Detlor, B., & Turnbull, D. (2013). *Web work: Information seeking and knowledge work on the World Wide Web* (Vol. 1). Springer Science & Business Media.

Coe, N.M. and Wrigley, N. (2009). The Globalization of Retailing (Vol. I and II). Cheltenham, MA: Edward Elgar Publishing Ltd.

Copeland, M.V & Malik, O. (2005). How to Ride the Fifth Wave. *Business 2.0*, July.

Corstjens, M. and Lal, R. (2012). Retail Doesn't Cross Borders: Here's Why and What to Do About It. *Harvard Business Review*, *90*(4), 104-111.

Donnelly, C., Simmons, G., Armstrong, G., & Fearne, A. (2015). Digital loyalty card 'big data and small business marketing: Formal versus informal or complementary? *International Small Business Journal*, *33*(4), 422–442. doi:10.1177/0266242613502691

Dunn, K. (2015). Globalization and consumer: What marketer needs to know. *The Neumann Business Review*, 2015, 16-30.

Edwards, S. M. (2011). A social media mindset. *Journal of Interactive Advertising*, *12*(1), 1–3. doi:10.1080/15252019.2011.10722186

Ernst, H., Hoyer, W. D., Krafft, M., & Soll, J.-H. (2010). Consumer Idea Generation (working paper). WHU, Vallendar.

Etgar, M. (2008). A Descriptive Model of the Consumer Co-Production Process. *Journal of the Academy of Marketing Science*, *36*(Spring), 97–108. doi:10.1007/s11747-007-0061-1

Feick, L., & Price, L. (1987). The Market Maven: A Dif-fuser of Marketplace Information. *Journal of Marketing*, *51*(1), 83–97. doi:10.2307/1251146

Forbes, (2011). 3 Steps to More Honest Business. Retrieved from http://www.forbes.com/sites/thebigenoughcompany/2011/09/21/3-steps-to-a-more-honest-business/

Fotis, J. N. (2015). *The Use of social media and its impacts on consumer behaviour: the context of holiday travel* [Doctoral dissertation]. Bournemouth University.

Ghemawat, P. (2007). Managing Differences: The Central Challenge of Global Strategy. *Harvard Business Review*, 85(3), 58-68.

Gordon, J. (2013). Big Data, Analytics and The Future Of Marketing And Sales. *Forbes*. Retrieved from http://www.forbes.com/sites/mckinsey/2013/07/22/big-data-analytics-and-the-future-of-marketing-sales/#1a9591ae344d

Hakanen, T., & Jaakkola, E. (2012). Co-creating customer-focused solutions within business networks: A service perspective. *Journal of Service Management*, *23*(4), 593–611. doi:10.1108/09564231211260431

Hauser, J., Tellis, G. J., & Griffin, A. (2006). Research on Innovation: A Review and Agenda for Marketing Science. *Marketing Science*, *25*(6), 686–717. doi:10.1287/mksc.1050.0144

Hoffman, D. L., Kopalle, P. K., & Novak, T. P. (2010). The "Right" Consumers for Better Concepts: Identifying and Using Consumers High in Emergent Nature to Further Develop New Product Concepts. Journal of Marketing Research Insider. Retrieved from http://www.mediacom.com/media/2088012/mediacom%20the%20insider_the%20empowered%20consumer_whitepaper.pdf

Hogg, M. K., Banister, E. N., & Stephenson, C. A. (2009). Mapping symbolic (anti-) consumption. *Journal of Business Research*, *62*(2), 148–159. doi:10.1016/j.jbusres.2008.01.022

Holt, D. B. (2004). *How Brands Become Icons: The Principles of Cultural Branding*. Boston: Harvard Business School Press.

Hoyer, W. D., Chandy, R., Dorotic, M., Kraff, M., & Singh, S. S. (2010). Consumer Cocreation in New Product Development. *Journal of Service Research*, *13*(3), 283–296. doi:10.1177/1094670510375604

Kacker, M. (1986). Coming to Terms with Global Retailing. *International Marketing Review*, *3*(1), 7.

Kaplan, A. M., & Haenlein, M. (2010). Users of the world, unite! The challenges and opportunities of Social Media. *Business Horizons*, *53*(1), 59–68. doi:10.1016/j.bushor.2009.09.003

Kotler, P. (2011). Reinventing marketing to manage the environmental imperative. *Journal of Marketing*, *75*(4), 132–135. doi:10.1509/jmkg.75.4.132

Kotler, P., Kartajaya, H., & Setiawan, I. (2010). *Marketing 3.0: From Products To Customers To The Human Spirit*. New York: John Wiley & Sons Inc. doi:10.1002/9781118257883

Kurkovsky, S., & Harihar, K. (2006). Using ubiquitous computing in interactive mobile marketing. *Personal and Ubiquitous Computing*, *10*(4), 227–240. doi:10.1007/s00779-005-0044-5

Lee, M. S. W., Motion, J., & Conroy, D. (2009a). Anti-consumption and brand avoidance. *Journal of Business Research*, *62*(2), 169–180. doi:10.1016/j.jbusres.2008.01.024

Magnusson, P. R., Matthing, J., & Kristensson, P. (2003). Managing user involvement in service innovation: Experiments with innovating end users. *Journal of Service Research*, *6*(2), 111–124. doi:10.1177/1094670503257028

Majfud, J. (2009). The pandemic of consumerism. *UN chronicle*. Retrieved from http://institucional.us.es/araucaria/otras_res/2009_11/resegna_1109_6.htm#_ftn1

McAfee, A. (2006). Enterprise 2.0: The Dawn of Emergence Collaboration. Reprint 47306. *MIT Sloan Management Review*, *47*(3), 21–28.

McAfee, A. (2009). Enterprise 2.0: New Collaborative Tools for Your Organization's Toughest Challenges. Boston (Massachussetts): Harvard Business Press.

McAfee, A., Brynjolfsson, E., Davenport, T. H., Patil, D. J., & Barton, D. (2012). Big data. *The management revolution. Harvard Business Review*, *90*(10), 61–67. PMID:23074865

Moore, G. (1991). *Crossing the Chasm: Marketing and Selling High-Tech Products to Mainstream Customers*. New York, NY: Harper Business Essentials.

Mourali, M., & Yang, Z. (2013). The Dual Role Of Power In Resisting Social Influence. *The Journal of Consumer Research*, *40*(3), 539–554. doi:10.1086/671139

Nambisan, S., & Baron, R. A. (2009). Virtual Customer Environments: Testing a Model of Voluntary Participation in Value Co-creation Activities. *Journal of Product Innovation Management*, *26*(4), 388–406. doi:10.1111/j.1540-5885.2009.00667.x

O'Hern. M.S., & Rindfleisch, A. (2009). Customer Co-Creation: A Typology and Research Agenda. Review of Marketing Research, 6, 84-106.

Ogawa, S., & Piller, F. T. (2006). Reducing the Risks of New Product Development. *Sloan Management Review*, *47*, 65–72.

Perks, H., Gruber, T., & Edvardsson, B. (2012). Co-creation in radical service innovation: A systematic analysis of microlevel processes. *Journal of Product Innovation Management, 29*(6), 935–951. doi:10.1111/j.1540-5885.2012.00971.x

Polonsky, M. J., Vocino, A., Grimmer, M., & Miles, M. (2016). Past and Future Orientation, Environmental Attitudes and Green Consumer Behaviour. In Looking Forward, Looking Back: Drawing on the Past to Shape the Future of Marketing (pp. 654-654). Springer International Publishing.

Prahalad, C. K., & Ramaswamy, V. (2004). *The Future of Competition: Co-creating Unique Value with Consumers*. Boston: Harvard Business School Press.

Ranjan, K. R., & Read, S. (2016). Value co-creation: Concept and measurement. *Journal of the Academy of Marketing Science, 44*(3), 290–315. doi:10.1007/s11747-014-0397-2

Ravald, A., & Grönroos, C. (1996). The value concept and relationship marketing. *European Journal of Marketing, 30*(2), 19–30. doi:10.1108/03090569610106626

Rospigliosi, A., & Greener, S. (2015) (Ed.), Leading Issues in Social Media Research. Academic Publishing Ltd.

Sashi, C. M. (2012). Customer engagement, buyer-seller relationships, and social media. *Management Decision, 50*(2), 253–272. doi:10.1108/00251741211203551

SpannerWorks. (2007). *What is social media*. Retrieved from www.spannerworks.com/ebooks

Strandvik, T., Rindell, A., & Wilen, K. (2013). Ethical consumers brand avoidance. *Journal of Product and Brand Management, 22*(7), 484–490. doi:10.1108/JPBM-09-2013-0392

Tapscott, D., Williams, A. D., and Herman, D. (2007). Government 2.0: Transforming government and governance for the twenty-first century. *New Paradigm*.

The Guardian. (21014) Smart meters: everything you need to know. Retrieved from https://www.theguardian.com/british-gas-smart-meter-challenge/2014/aug/26/smart-meters-everything-you-need-to-know

Turban, E., King, D., Lee, J. K., Liang, T. P., & Turban, D. C. (2015). Overview of Electronic Commerce. In *Electronic Commerce* (pp. 3–49). Springer International Publishing. doi:10.1007/978-3-319-10091-3_1

Vargo, S. L., Maglio, P. P., & Akaka, M. A. (2008). On value and value co-creation: A service systems and service logic perspective. *European Management Journal, 26*(3), 145–152. doi:10.1016/j.emj.2008.04.003

von Hippel, E. (1986). Lead Users: A Source of Novel Product Concepts. *Management Science, 32*(July), 791–805. doi:10.1287/mnsc.32.7.791

Want, R., Schilit, B. N., & Jenson, S. (2015). Enabling the Internet of Things. *IEEE Computer, 48*(1), 28–35. doi:10.1109/MC.2015.12

Watson, R. T., Pitt, L. F., Berthon, P., & Zinkhan, G. M. (2002). U-commerce: Expanding the universe of marketing. *Journal of the Academy of Marketing Science, 30*(4), 333–347. doi:10.1177/009207002236909

Wortmann, F., & Flüchter, K. (2015). Internet of things. *Business & Information Systems Engineering, 57*(3), 221–224. doi:10.1007/s12599-015-0383-3

Yurcan, B. (2016, June 24). Banking on the internet of things: More than restocking fridges. American Banker. Retrieved from http://www.americanbanker.com/news/bank-technology/banking-on-the-internet-of-things-more-than-restocking-fridges-1081676-1.html

Zohar, D. (1990). *The Quantum Self: Human Nature and Consciousness Defined by the New Physics*. New York: Quill.

ADDITIONAL READING

Bagozzi, R. P. (1995). Reflections on Relationship Marketing in Consumer Markets. *Journal of the Academy of Marketing Science*, *23*(4), 272–277. doi:10.1177/009207039502300406

Baran, R., Zerres, C., & Zerres, M. (2008). Customer Relationship Management (CRM). Disponible en web: http://bookboon.com/es/customer-relationship-management-ebook

Cook, N. (2008). *Enterprise 2.0: How Social Software Will Change the Future of Work*. Hampshire, England: Gower Publishing.

Dyche, J., & Levy, A. (2006). *Customer Data Integration: Reaching a Single Version of the Truth (SAS Institute Inc.)*. Hoboken, New Jersey: John Wiley & Sons, Inc.

Gartner Research Inc. (2003). *Building Business Benefits From CMR. Executive Report*. Stamford, CT: Gartner, Inc.

Grönroos, C. (1989). Defining Marketing: A Market-oriented Approach. *European Journal of Marketing*, *23*(1), 54–58. doi:10.1108/EUM0000000000541

Grönroos, C. (1994a). Quo Vadis, Marketing? Toward a Relationship Marketing Paradigm. *Journal of Marketing Management*, *10*(5), 347–360. doi:10.1080/0267257X.1994.9964283

Grönroos, C. (1994b). From Marketing Mix to the Relationship Marketing Toward a Paradigm Shift in Marketing. *Asia-Australian Marketing Journal*, *2*(1), 1.

Gummesson, E. (1987). Marketing- A long term interactive relationship. *Long Range Planning*, *20*(4), 10–20. doi:10.1016/0024-6301(87)90151-8

Huang, Z., & Benyoucef, M. (2013). From e-commerce to social commerce: A close look at design features. *Electronic Commerce Research and Applications*, *12*(4), 246–259. doi:10.1016/j.elerap.2012.12.003

Spekman, R. E. (1988). Strategic Supplier Selection: Understanding Long-Tern Buyer Relationships. *Business Horizons*, *31*(July/August), 75–81. doi:10.1016/0007-6813(88)90072-9

Zhou, L., Zhang, P., & Zimmermann, H.-S. (2013). Social Commerce Research: An integrated view. *Electronic Commerce Research and Application*. Retrieved from http://melody.syr.edu/pzhang/publications/ECRA_13_Zhou_etal_Social_Commerce.pdf

KEY TERMS AND DEFINITIONS

Big Data: Big data describes the large, varied volume of data -structured and unstructured – that companies can access, analyze and apply in decision making processes.

Co-Creation: A business strategy focus on consumer experience and interactive relationships. Co-creation allows and encourages a more active involvement from the consumer to create a value-rich experience.

Collaborative Consumption: A global concept that involves sharing, bartering, lending, trading, renting, gifting, and swapping goods instead of buying them. This concept has been in communities for thousands of years, but has recently gained popularity in the United States and Europe.

Collaborative Social Media: Term used to refer to digital media that enables broad-range participation where the distinctions between production, consumption and design are dissolved.

Consumer Empowerment: It is a mental state usually accompanied by a physical act which enables a consumer or a group of consumers to put into effect their own choices through demonstrating their needs, wants and demands in their decision-making with other individuals or organisational bodies in the marketplace.

Ethical Consumer: Socially conscious consumers. Their choices are informed by ethical concerns about the well-being of society, humans, animals and the environment.

Expressive Social Media: Term used to refer to digital media that allows people to freely express their ideas, tastes, preferences, opinions, etc.

Globalization: The worldwide movement toward economic, financial, trade and communication integration. Globalization implies the opening of local and nationalistic perspectives to a broader outlook of an interconnected and interdependent world with free transfer of capital, goods, and services across national frontiers.

Internet of Things: It is everyday objects equipped with identifying, sensing, networking and processing capabilities that will allow them to communicate with one another and with other devices and services over the Internet to accomplish some objective.

Perceived Value: An assessment of the worth of a good or service. The product value assessed by a business when setting a price for a particular product can depend on its production costs, its overall market value and the value of the product as perceived by a targeted group of consumers.

Ubiquity: It is the state or capacity of being everywhere, especially at the same time; omnipresence. When applied to technology it may imply it that the IoT is widely available.

Unique: Something is unique when it's the only one around. In marketing in may mean there is customization, or personal adaptation of the product or service to personal requirements of the consumer.

Unison: Something that is synchronized or simultaneous, in marketing unison means that consumers have complete agreement between the characteristics of a product.

Universal: Something is universal when it has the same characteristics, it is the same, wherever it is used.

Chapter 6
Effective Surveillance Management during Service Encounters:
A Conceptual Framework

Angelo Bonfanti
University of Verona, Italy

ABSTRACT

This chapter aims to theoretically examine effective surveillance management (ESM) during service encounters within the servicescape and provide a conceptual framework for the study of this topic in a service management perspective. It analyses antecedents, dimensions and effects of ESM. This study especially proposes as antecedents both improving customer service experience along with meeting customers' need for security and implementing a surveillance service-oriented strategy that includes secure and safe servicescape design, deterrent communication, and trained and motivated security staff. This chapter suggests also that the dimensions of ESM (customer-physical service environment encounters, customer-technological surveillance systems encounters, and customer-security staff encounters) contribute to enhancing service quality, experience quality, and staff productivity. The integration of these dimensions, antecedents, and effects create a theoretically grounded framework that can serve as a starting point for future studies about this topic in the field of service management.

INTRODUCTION

Customers participate to the service delivery process as prosumers/prousers that is as both producers and consumers/users of the service (Toffler, 1980; Baccarani and Golinelli, 2009). Their active participation (e.g., Bettencourt et al., 2002; Bendapudi and Leone, 2003) is relevant for the success of any service encounter (or moment of truth) within the service environment called servicescape (Bitner, 1992). However, a few customers, instead of collaborating in the service delivery process, may create problems or lead to service failure because of their bad manners or misbehaviours that deliberately violate the generally accepted norms of conduct such as disturbance, verbal and physical aggression, vandalism, shoplifting,

DOI: 10.4018/978-1-5225-2139-6.ch006

robberies, and crime (e.g., Fullerton and Punj, 1997; Harris and Reynolds, 2003; Reynolds and Harris, 2009; Harris and Daunt, 2011; Daunt and Harris, 2012b).

Service organizations have to invest in security measures to monitor their customers' intentions and acting reactively (e.g., Perlman and Ozinci, 2014). In this way, they can create a secure and safe service environment for customers and employees. Meeting the need for protection against customers who behave badly should not negatively affect customers' service experience (e.g., Helkkula, 2011; Jüttner et al., 2013).

Although service organizations have to ensure a high level of surveillance within the servicescape without interfering with the customer service experience, little research is still carried out to examine in theoretical and practical terms how to create a safe and, at the same time, pleasant service environment (Bonfanti, 2014; Kajalo and Lindblom, 2015). Given that consumers have several different preferences towards surveillance practices (Kajalo and Lindblom, 2016), neglecting or ignoring the experiential component during the surveillance management will create a negative quality judgement by customers, even if the core service is delivered effectively (Bonfanti, 2016).

The aim of this chapter is to examine the concept of effective surveillance management (ESM) during the service encounters within the servicescape and provide a conceptual framework for the study of this topic in service management perspective. In more detail, it analyses antecedents, dimensions and effects of ESM. The integration of the dimensions, antecedents, and effects of ESM allows the presentation and discussion of a theoretically grounded framework that could serve as a starting point for future studies about this topic in the field of service management. The originality of this conceptual framework is that it is created by taking into account many service settings, i.e. it is not focused on a specific service environment. Therefore, it can be adapted to more service industries.

This is a conceptual research work whose analytical approach draws heavily on theoretical evidence published in service marketing and management, and retailing literature. Identifying the studies that provide significant insights into surveillance management proved to be a laborious task because little and fragmented attention has been given to this issue in service management perspective. Further conceptual aspects are based on experiences acquired during daily service encounters with a number of service organizations such as stores, hotels, airports, and hospitals. This chapter methodologically follows the gap-spotting approach by especially adopting the neglect spotting, that allows to "identify a topic or an area where no (good) research has been carried out" (Sandberg and Alvesson, 2011, p. 30).

The chapter is structured as follows. The next section proposes a literature review about security and surveillance management in service management perspective. The main focus of the chapter includes the conceptual framework for surveillance management by examining its dimensions, antecedents and effects. Finally, this study presents some managerial implications and directions for further research.

Background

Customers who behave badly are not the exception but the norm during the service encounters (Harris and Reynolds, 2004). Several forms and profiles have been examined under the different labels. Table 1 and Table 2 summarise the terms most frequently used in marketing and service marketing literature. Several scholars have also examined the effects of customers who behave badly by leading to service failure with more or less grave consequences for employees, other customers, service organizations (Bitner, 1992; Fullerton and Punj, 1993, 1997; Rose and Neidermeyer, 1999; Huefner and Hunt, 2000;

Table 1. Customers behaving badly: terms most frequently used in marketing literature

Terms Used	Definition	Author/s (Year)
Deviant consumer behavior	Behaviour that "society considers inappropriate or in conflict with a previously accepted societal norm"	Mills and Bonoma (1979, p. 347); Mills (1981); Moschis and Cox (1989); Rose and Neidermeyer (1999); Harris and Daunt (2011)
Aberrant consumer behavior	"Behavior in exchange settings which violates the generally accepted norms of conduct in such situations and which is therefore held in disrepute by marketers and by most consumers"	Fullerton and Punj (1993, p. 570)
Consumer misbehavior	"Behavioral acts by consumers which violate the generally accepted norms of conduct in consumption situations, and disrupt the order expected in such situations"	Fullerton and Punj (1997, p. 336); Tonglet (2002); Fullerton and Punj (2004); Harris and Daunt (2011); Echeverri et al. (2012)

Table 2. Customers behaving badly: terms most frequently used in service marketing literature

Terms Used	Definition	Author/s (Year)
Customers from hell or uncooperative customers	Behaviour including the following customers' profiles: a) "egocentric Edgar" places his or her needs above those of all other customers and service employees; b) "bad-mouth Betty" becomes loud, crude, and abusive to service employees and other customers alike; c) "hysterical Harold" reverts to screaming and tantrums to make his point; "dictatorial Dick" assumes superiority over all personnel and management; and d) "freeloading Freeda" uses tricks or verbal abuse to acquire services without paying	Zemke and Anderson (1990); Hoffman and Bateson (1997)
Problem customer behavior	Actions of customers who are "basically uncooperative, that is, unwilling to cooperate with the service provider, other customers, industry regulations, and/or laws"	Bitner et al. (1994, p. 98)
Wrong customers	Customer "who complains frequently or is never satisfied with recovery efforts"	Tax and Brown (1998, p. 85); Woo and Fock (2004)
Jaycustomer behaviors	Customer "who acts in a thoughtless or abusive way, causing problems for the firm, its employees, and other customers"	Lovelock (1994 and 2001, p. 73); Harris and Reynolds (2004)
Dysfunctional customer behavior	"Actions by customers who intentionally or unintentionally, overtly or covertly, act in a manner that, in some way, disrupts otherwise functional service encounters"	Harris and Reynolds (2003, p. 145); Reynolds and Harris (2009); Fisk et al. (2010); Daunt and Harris (2012a, 2012b)
Badness behavior	Customer who "causes problems for the service company, its employees, and other customers in a thoughtless or abusive manner"	Yi and Gong (2006, p. 150)
Unfair customer	Customer who "behaves in a manner that is devoid of common decency, reasonableness, and respect for the rights of others, creating inequity and causing harm for a company and, in some cases, its employees and other customers"	Berry and Seiders (2008, p. 30)
Customers' bad manners	"Conduct that is neither particularly serious nor that is carried out with the actual intention to cause damage," but is behaviour "characterised by lack of respect for or thoughtfulness towards other customers and others in general"	Baccarani and Brunetti (2011, p. 119)
Customer misbehaviors	Same definition proposed by Fullerton and Punj (1997)	Harris and Daunt (2013, p. 282)

Harris and Reynold, 2003; Fullerton and Punj, 2004; Grandey et al., 2004; Harris and Reynold, 2004; Yi and Gong, 2006; Fisk et al., 2010), and society as a whole (Baccarani and Brunetti, 2011).

Service managers have to monitor by means of security measures customers who behave badly in order to limit possible unwanted effects. In service marketing and management literature is more often examined the security issue rather than the surveillance management. Parasuraman et al.'s (1985) pioneering article on the gap analysis model, subsequently called the SERVQUAL scale for measuring service quality (Berry et al., 1988), identified 10 criteria used by customers in assessing service quality. Among these factors, security is understood as the freedom from danger, risk, or doubt. It includes three aspects:

1. Physical security,
2. Financial security, and
3. Confidentiality.

Gummesson (1994) revealed that security can be sought from the following four sources:

1. Relationships,
2. Business culture and ethics,
3. Knowledge, and
4. Laws and regulations.

Such sources are not mutually exclusive given that a strong relationship and a high level of knowledge may require a dose of law. According to Kajalo and Lindblom (2015), surveillance is a key component of crime prevention that includes formal (e.g., guard patrols, closed-circuit television [CCTV] systems, motion-detector devices and other surveillance systems) and informal surveillance (e.g., physical features, activities and people) (Lindblom and Kajalo, 2011). Daunt and Harris (2012b) have argued that the physical provision of security in the form of electronic surveillance and visible personnel is useful in order to manipulate the social facets of the servicescape, such as fellow customers, perceptions of service employees, and customers' perceptions of outlet vulnerability.

Although both the volume and the sophistication of customers who behave badly and especially commit a crime are increasing, little theoretical and empirical research has evaluated and investigated the surveillance management in a service setting. The retail store is the setting analysed more often in literature, mostly from the shoplifting and crime prevention point of view (e.g., Fullerton and Punj, 2004; Hayes and Blackwood, 2006; Kajalo and Lindblom, 2010a; Hayes and Downs, 2011; Hayes et al. 2011). A few studies (e.g., Pretious et al., 1995; Peek-Asa et al., 2006) have highlighted that especially formal security systems such as uniformed guards are perceived by retail managers as an effective deterrent in order to reduce casual thieves and crime. Others studies have analysed the link between security guards and the incidence of crime (Cozens et al., 2005) as well as the use and effectiveness of formal surveillance compared to informal surveillance in reducing store-based crime (Lindblom and Kajalo, 2011). Soars (2009) has also pointed out the importance of using electronic surveillance advances (e.g., radio-frequency identification [RFId] tags) to improve customers' purchasing intentions.

Very little attention is paid to study how service organizations can protect the servicescape through security solutions without adversely compromising customers' service experience. This is a very recent topic. Bonfanti (2014) highlighted that the store surveillance system can allow customers to have direct contacts with the store, its articles and staff. Kajalo and Lindblom (2015) outlined how security problems have a positive impact on investments in formal surveillance but no impact on investments in informal surveillance. Furthermore, retailers perceive that formal surveillance investments have a negative impact on the sense of security felt among customers and employees, whereas informal surveillance investments have a positive impact. Always Kajalo and Lindblom (2016) argued that customer experience of safe retail environments reflects the distinction between informal and formal surveillance and consumers can be grouped according to their preferences for security and surveillance methods into the following groups: "Sense of security based on formal surveillance", "Sense of security based on architectural design", "Sense of security based on well-designed parking" and "Sense of security based on personnel and hard crime protection". Bonfanti (2016) identified customers' needs and expectations regarding servicescape surveillance management in order to suggest to service managers how they can carefully design a service environment to ensure a high level of security and, at the same time, enhance their customer service experience.

EFFECTIVE SURVEILLANCE MANAGEMENT (ESM)

The effectiveness of surveillance management depends on whether service organizations ensure a high level of surveillance during the service encounters without interfering with customers' service experience in terms of interactions between customers and the supervised servicescape. In order to examine the dimensions of ESM, this study takes into account the results of a previous research (Bonfanti, 2014) that identifies how retailers' investments in store design, technological systems and staff training can give stores adequate security levels without compromising their customers' shopping experience. It is therefore possible to identify the three following dimensions of ESM: 1) customer-physical service environment encounters, 2) customer-technological surveillance systems encounters, and 3) customer-security staff encounters. They are elaborated in greater detail in the following subsections.

Customer-Physical Service Environment Encounters

The customer-physical service environment encounters dimension of ESM refers to the design of the physical environment in which service is delivered in such a way that customers perceive a positive service experience and, at the same time, a sense of security. As service encounters positively affect customers' emotional perceptions of aesthetics and peacefulness, and all dimensions of customer experiential value positively affect customer behavioural intentions (Foxall and Greenley, 1999, 2000; Keng et al., 2007), any servicescape element should be designed in such a way that customers have the opportunity both to perceive the physical environment through their senses (Soars, 2009) and to move freely and peacefully by not feeling they are constantly being watched (Jones, 1999). For example, most banks have eliminated all possible obstacles (physical, visual, and auditory) within the servicescape by developing interior design projects, restructuring or modernising old offices, and creating open space structures where banking windows have almost totally disappeared to leave space in front of counters without bulletproof glass in order to facilitate a more direct contact with the customer. Also, points of sale are more pleasant and comfortable: store managers prefer to install security antennas in checkout areas in such a way that they merge with the sale environment. In a number of stores such antennas are integrated into advertising panels in such a way that they avoid intimidating customers while simultaneously informing them about products, promotions, and other marketing initiatives as soon as they enter the store.

Developing this dimension of ESM means that service managers have to design a physical environment in which customer perceives a secure and positive service delivery. As such, the variables in the customer-physical service environment encounters dimension of ESM include the pleasantness, comfort, freedom, and safety of the servicescape.

Customer-Technological Surveillance Systems Encounters

The customer-technological surveillance systems encounters dimension of ESM embodies the interactions between customers and CCTV systems, motion detectors, high-tech scanners, electronic article surveillance (EAS) devices, and RFId tags, antennas, software, and accessories. All of these solutions are capable of storing data in special electronic devices and answering remote queries from fixed or portable radio-frequency readers which communicate information, including warning notices of shoplifting by malicious customers (Jones et al., 2004). The presence in the servicescape of such technological surveillance systems can create a sense of security and positively affect customer service experience if they are professionally used. If in a store (or library) security tags applied on a purchased product (or borrowed book) not are deactivated at a checkout counter (or loan desk) because of technical problems or unprofessional staff, the alarm system is activated even when an innocent customer passes by, and can give rise to feelings of discomfort and embarrassment. When an alarm sounds, customers are required to show their purchases or personal belongings to security personnel, answer probing questions, and, above all, are likely to be viewed as thieves by other customers. Too few or too many technological solutions, as well as security staff, can negatively affect customer experiences (Jones, 1999): if such surveillance systems are reduced, customers may perceive a sense of insecurity, while if they are excessive in quantity, customers' service experience could be impaired by infringements on their right to privacy (Liu and Chen, 2011) and by a sense of intimidation (Tonglet, 2000; Kajalo and Lindblom, 2010b), distrust (Friend et al., 2010), discomfort, embarrassment, and frustration (Citrin et al., 2003; Peck and Childers, 2003).

To develop customer-technological surveillance systems encounters, service organizations have to pay attention to all technological solutions implemented in servicescape without creating adverse emotions to customers. The variables in this dimension of ESM include the reliability, level of invasion of right to privacy, correct functioning, and ease of use provided by technological surveillance solutions.

Customer-Security Staff Encounters

Customer-security staff encounters are the third dimension of ESM. This dimension includes the interactions between customers and security/sworn guards, rangers, or other uniformed staff. Security staff is a useful means of preventing the action of thieves and delinquents, vandals and criminals (Cozens et al., 2005), primarily by acting as human deterrents and guaranteeing that the situation in the servicescape is being monitored. Such practices satisfy customers by creating a sensation of safety. As service personnel play a crucial role in anticipating customer expectations, creating customer-oriented value and building emotional bonds for lifetime relationships (Bitner, 1992), security staff is an important physical and relational reference point for customers in case of unpleasant incidents (Pretious et al., 1995). During service encounters, customer-staff interactions are crucial in creating customer satisfaction and service quality (e.g., Grönroos, 2000; Baker et al., 2002; Gummesson, 2002): for example, knowledgeable staff capable of solving problems and handling claims plays a critical role in delivering a higher quality experience.

Making available into servicescape trained staff in terms of both security and service experience delivery allows service organizations to develop positive customer-security staff encounters. The variables in this dimension of ESM include security personnel's skills of monitoring, its empathy, problem solving, early action, and professionalism.

A CONCEPTUAL FRAMEWORK

In this section, a conceptual framework of the antecedents and effects of ESM is developed, as shown in the Figure 1. First, potential antecedents of ESM are discussed, and corresponding and testable research propositions (RPs) are presented. A focus on variables that service organizations can control in ESM is provided. Second, the main effects of ESM are examined, and corresponding propositions are proposed.

Antecedents of Effective Surveillance Management

All that customers consciously or unconsciously perceive in the servicescape in terms of presence and absence contributes to creating the service experience (e.g., Helkkula, 2011; Klaus and Maklan, 2012; Jüttner et al., 2013; Klaus and Maklan, 2013). Elements of the physical environment, technological sur-

Figure 1.

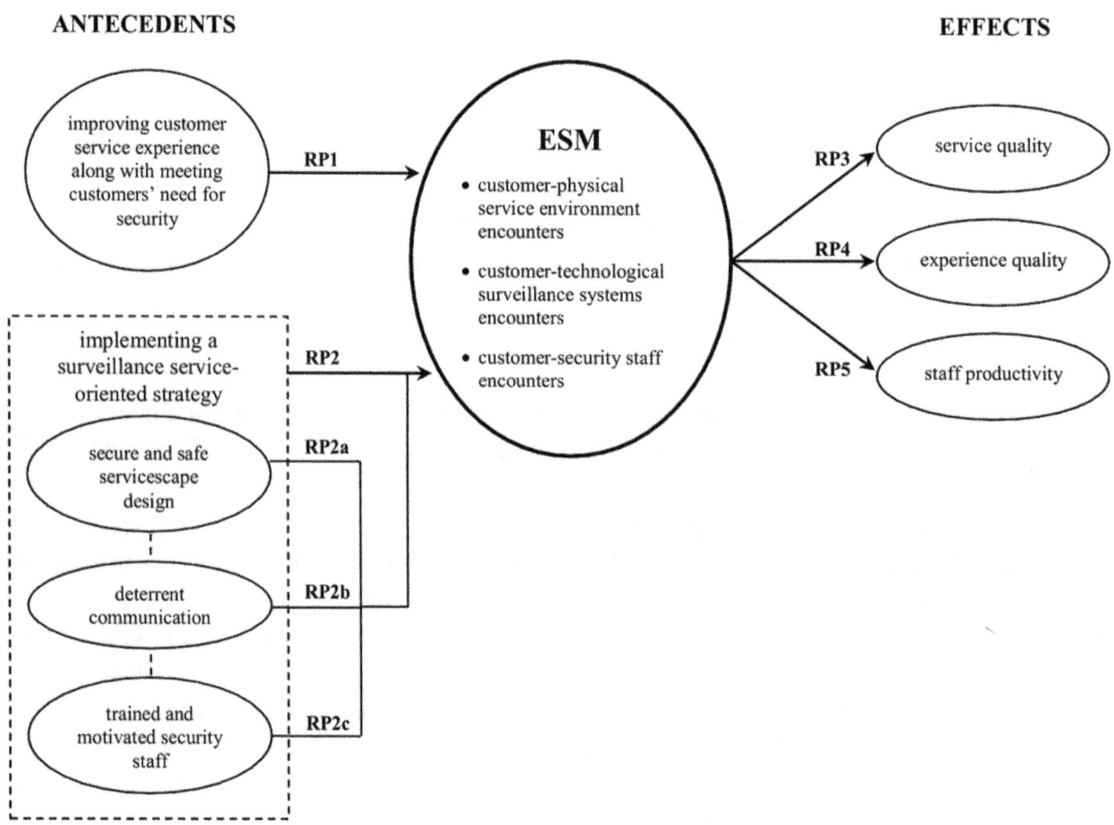

veillance systems, and front-line personnel, including security staff, communicate several signals that customers combine to generate a service experience. The formation processes of customers' experience embrace their cognitive and emotional responses to stimuli provided by service organizations (Meyer and Schwager, 2007). While service quality is closely related to the cognitive evaluation of functional aspects of service delivery, customer service experience is the sum of cognition and emotion (e.g., Liljander and Strandvik, 1997; Berry et al., 2002; Edvardsson, 2005; Schembri, 2006; Jüttner et al., 2013). Implementing security solutions in the servicescape in order to protect employees, customers, and equipment from customers who behave badly allows the creation of a feeling of security: customers positively perceive a servicescape that both offers them a sense of security (Cowper, 1992; Coleman, 2006) and is not associated with concerns about safety (Overstreet and Clodfelter, 1995). Service organizations have to ensure a high level of surveillance within the servicescape without interfering with the customer service experience. Therefore, the following proposition is offered:

RP1: There is a positive relationship between improving customers service experience by meeting their need for security and the ESM dimensions.

Service organizations should develop a service orientation (Homburg et al., 2002; Teng and Barrows, 2009) that includes surveillance management. In general, service orientation is conceptualised at an individual level in relation to the personal traits of the service provider (Hogan et al., 1984; Cran, 1994), and from the organizational point of view (e.g., Lytle and Timmerman, 2006) in relation to the characteristics of the external and internal service environment (Wu et al., 2008), corporate structure, climate, and culture (Bowen et al., 1989). Unlike the concept of customer orientation, service orientation not only focuses on satisfying customer needs during service delivery, but also requires personnel and organizations to take the initiative in providing services (Charles and Schwepker, 2003) in such a way as to meet the needs and expectations of customers in terms of service experience. Implementing a surveillance service orientation-based strategy means not managing single criminal episodes rather than designing the servicescape according to the three following actions:

1. Technological security measures,
2. Communicating the presence of surveillance systems, warnings, and possible sanctions, and
3. Training and motivating security staff.

In particular, security in the servicescape embodies a number of surveillance elements. Floor security personnel, sophisticated CCTV surveillance systems, high-tech scanners, motion detectors, EAS devices, and RFId tags, antennas, software and accessories are the most frequent surveillance solutions used by service organizations. Lindblom and Kajalo (2011) distinguish formal and informal surveillance by highlighting that formal surveillance adversely affects the feeling of security experienced by customers and employees, whereas informal surveillance has a positive impact (Kajalo and Lindblom, 2012). Any security solution has to be implemented in the servicescape to function according to the rational choice perspective (Cornish and Clarke, 1986): this approach suggests that crime can be prevented when service organizations succeed in reducing opportunities for committing crime, and when dishonest customers perceive an increased risk of apprehension. In other words, potential offenders calculate the costs and benefits of the crime and choose the option with the highest utility. Essentially, they are most often led to steal if they believe it is easy to do so and if the possibility of being discovered is low (Tonglet, 2002; Kulas et al., 2007). For example, the introduction of self-service in retail stores has created an environment that favours shoplifting because of a low risk of apprehension. In this sense, stores can be organised in such a way as to create suitable interior lighting (Burns et al., 2010), reduce crowding, especially at checkout counters (Fullerton and Punj, 1993), generate larger interior spaces, eliminate dark zones, and give greater visibility by adjusting the layout of equipment (Wellhoff and Masson, 2005).

In order to increase both the risk of apprehension and a sense of transparency, deterrent communication is useful: the presence of surveillance systems, warnings, and possible sanctions in case of breach have to be exhibited within the servicescape by means of notices, posters, and graphic signals (Liu and Chen, 2011). On the one hand, such communication warns criminals about the consequences of committing wrong actions in the servicescape; on the other hand, it provides customers with the idea and the feeling of being in a safe and secure environment. As the purpose of any security system should be to dissuade people from stealing rather than to catch and punish them, the communication role within the servicescape is crucial.

While organizations once sought to employ people with no training whatsoever, today more and more companies are turning to the contract security industry or sending employees to in-house staff training courses (Mann, 1992) because personnel training is fundamental for the success of a prevention plan (Cozens et al., 2005; Bamfield, 2012) against any customer who behaves badly. Trained security staff is able to identify the customer's misbehaviour, be informed and aware of both the many and constantly renewed criminal methods and the best ways to interact with disturbers of service delivery and potential criminals (e.g., vandals, thieves, and robbers). For example, during a service encounter, a customer who adopts more suspects behaviors such as walking with extreme nervousness, continuing to look left and right, repeatedly entering and exiting the servicescape, and conspicuously sweating, as well as a customer who manipulates a product, especially if he or she throws it on the floor, and refuses the help of staff are telltale signs of potential shoplifters. When a cashier (or usher) suspects that a paying customer has something hidden and asks if he or she has something else to declare when paying (or exiting), often the thief, receiving a simple question, thinks he or she has been unmasked. An employee can achieve the same effect by asking a customer, who has just furtively put an object in his pocket, if he or she can be of help in looking for the product. In addition, motivated security staff by means of incentive programmes allow service organizations to discover thieves and delinquents in the servicescape, employees to be content in their job and, consequently, customers to be satisfied.

Thus, the following propositions capture these observations:

RP2: There is a positive relationship between implementing a surveillance service orientation-based strategy and the ESM dimensions.

RP2a: There is a positive relationship between designing a secure and safe servicescape and the ESM dimensions.

RP2b: There is a positive relationship between adopting a deterrent communication and the ESM dimensions.

RP2c: There is a positive relationship between training and motivating security staff and the ESM dimensions.

Effects of Effective Surveillance Management

Any service encounter between customers and a supervised servicescape (physical service environment, technological surveillance systems, and security staff) affects the customer service experience and also its service quality evaluation in terms of reliability, responsiveness, assurance, empathy, and tangibility. As customers expect service delivery to take place in a comfortable and pleasant as well as a safe and secure physical environment (Cowper, 1992; Coleman, 2006; Bonfanti, 2016), they understand and agree with the use of surveillance systems in the servicescape as long as they do not feel they are constantly being watched (Jones, 1999) or under threat from such security measures. For example, CCTV systems communicated by means of moderately worded notices in the servicescape (i.e., "Please smile, the CCTV is running!" is preferred to "Taping now! All your behaviour here is monitored by the CCTV system!") tend not to infringe on customers' right to privacy (Liu and Chen, 2011) and increase the perceived level of service quality in terms of reliability, empathy, and tangibility. During service encounters, the prompt action of security personnel in case of unpleasant incidents (Pretious et al., 1995) strengthens service quality in terms of responsiveness. The professionalism of security staff and the presence of surveillance systems are symbols of assurance for customers because a perceived sense of security increases the level of trust related to a lived service experience. Investments aimed at enhancing service encounters between customers and the supervised servicescape ensure adequate security levels without compromising customers' service experience as long as formal surveillance in the form of uniformed guards, technological surveillance systems, and motion detectors is used as discreetly as possible within the servicescape (Coleman, 2006; Kajalo and Lindblom, 2011). In this way, customers positively perceive a servicescape that offers a sense of security (Cowper, 1992) because they like to feel safe during service encounters, just as they do when shopping (Coleman, 2006) or carrying out financial transactions in a bank (Liu and Chen, 2011), and do not want concerns about safety keeping them away from a store (Overstreet and Clodfelter, 1995). Thus, the following proposition is suggested:

RP3: The ESM dimensions will have an effect on the service quality in terms of reliability, responsiveness, assurance, empathy, and tangibility.

By responding to security needs expressed by customers, ESM also enhances experience quality understood as customers' perception of the excellence or superiority of the holistic encounters (Lemke et al., 2010). As customer service experience is driven by personal values which are situational in nature, ESM allows the emotional value of security and safety to be integrated into the experience by means of the visual and tactile senses. For example, motion detectors placed at the exit of the service structure can be integrated into informative, advertising, or promotional panels in such a way that customers visually perceive a positive message of assurance that the security exists, but it is not visible at first glance. The use of EAS devices and RFId tags and antennas allows customers to enter a welcoming and reassuringly open service environment in which the articles (on sale) are freely available in accessible displays. ESM allows consumers to take the articles directly from the display, examine them, test them, and then carry them to the checkout counter/loan desk. As customers perceive physical environments through their senses (Soars, 2009; Hultén, 2012; Ugolini et al., 2014), seeing, touching, feeling, and perceiving an article are necessary conditions underlying a quality experience. Therefore:

RP4: The ESM dimensions will have an effect on the experience quality lived by customers during service encounter.

The presence of ESM in terms of the design of the physical environment, technological surveillance systems, and trained and motivated security staff offers a greater sense of security not only to customers but also to all front-line and back-office personnel. In addition, it allows front-line personnel who deliver service to dedicate more time to customer assistance and provide customers with better service because they are not closely engaged in monitoring any bad-mannered behaviour and criminal activity. The same security staff can work effectively by means of the support provided by the technological surveillance systems implemented in the servicescape. For example, CCTV systems allow security staff to detect various forms of bad customer behaviour and possible training errors among employees. Hence:

RP5: The ESM dimensions will have an effect on the staff productivity.

MANAGERIAL IMPLICATIONS

Although conceptual in nature, this study offers some practical implications for managers who want to manage surveillance effectively during the service encounters without interfering with the customer service experience.

Service managers can eliminate, or at least reduce, any opportunity for customers to commit misbehaviours by using a few precautions increasing the risk of apprehension within the servicescape: they can design the layout of the service environment in such a way that customers are forced to pass by a desk or checkout area in order to exit the service structure; they can choose not to expose articles for sale close to the exit of the service structure while using regular CCTV systems or security staff monitoring in that area; they can keep the servicescape clean and organised in such a way that front-line personnel can see at a glance if something is stolen; they can maintain adequate lighting in the service environment; and they can use mirrors to eliminate the blind spots in corners where customers could hide themselves and commit vandalism or criminal actions. In addition, service managers can take advantage of every possible technological innovation. For example, it can occur in stores that customers are able to elude the main controlling system performed primarily by weight scales associated with the products. There are sophisticated technologies using video analytics designed to help prevent false alarms and immediately warn security personnel when customers do not scan all the products they are buying. This logic can be extended to all service settings such as libraries, airports, museums, hotels, stations, hospitals, buses, amusement parks, cinemas, beauty farms, and gyms.

ESM requires service managers to invest in and implement a surveillance service orientation-based strategy combining all security measures discussed above as useful for providing a safe and reliable high-level protection of the servicescape, increasing customers' sense of security, and limiting criminal action while meeting the customer's need to have a positive service experience during service encounters. Among the possible practical actions, service managers can use security solutions wisely and as discreetly as possible (Coleman, 2006; Kajalo and Lindblom, 2011), and encourage customers to move freely and peacefully within the servicescape by not feeling they are constantly being watched (Jones, 1999). They can essentially implement surveillance solutions in such a way as to meet the implicit, expected, and latent needs of customers (Kano et al., 1984), needs that a customer considers to be respectively obvious, expected and not expected. Satisfaction of an implicit need, that is a minimum acceptable level of satisfaction, may include the moment in which the front-line personnel remove an anti-shoplifting tag: the article obviously must not be ruined or damaged, but customers also expect that it will be effectively deactivated at the loan desk or checkout counter, so that that they will not be embarrassed by false alarms. In order to meet expected needs, service managers can try to adopt minimally invasive anti-shoplifting solutions such as small or transparent labels that can be placed over the bar code. These are largely invisible to customers, do not impede the reading of product information, and avoid ruining the visual branding of the product. When labels must necessarily be visible, it is important that they do not disturb the customer's experience quality. Customers do not expect product protection to increase the cost of, prevent direct contact with, or compromise the appearance of the products they wish to buy. Service managers can also meet some latent customer needs by incorporating multimedia technology within servicescape: a customer lifting a product protected by the free to touch system activates a product-specific video containing relevant operating/functional information, without having to waste time searching for front-line personnel. It is also possible to eliminate metal detector barriers from servicescape entryways/exits by connecting special anti-shoplifting tags to detectors hanging from the ceiling or totally concealed inside the servicescape. For example, some stores have created observation booths overlooking sales areas: rooms occupied by one or more employees that are often positioned behind mirrors and that give a good overall view of the entire store. The booths are also often equipped with CCTV screens.

Despite the fact that technological surveillance systems have become most useful for detecting customers' behaving badly, their successful use depends not only on their quality and effectiveness but also on how they are managed. The role of security staff is fundamental for monitoring and actively dealing with all kinds of unwanted behaviour (Kajalo and Lindblom, 2010a) and, at the same time, continuing to create a positive customer service experience during service encounters. The skill of interaction with customers, which is usually disliked by thieves, is difficult to imitate because of the relational element involved, which, unlike the impersonal aspects of service, is very personal in nature (Grönroos, 2000; Baccarani et al., 2010). For this reason, substituting security personnel with increased electronic surveillance is not practical, economic, or helpful: in the case of a technological malfunction of the surveillance systems, effective service recovery occurs by means of face-to-face interactions between staff and customers. To this end, it is important to identify organizational rules and establish service quality specifications which security personnel can follow as guidelines when interacting with customers.

Service managers should therefore ensure that front-line service employees are both skilled and motivated in their roles (Daunt and Harris, 2012b). Continuous training is necessary because security skills are perishable (Walsh, 1994) due to both the erosion of security staff's knowledge of procedures and the personnel turnover. Corporate climate and culture can support and reward those who provide services in an excellent way (Lytle et al., 1998): implementing incentive programmes for security employees who discover thieves and delinquents in the servicescape increases staff motivation. It is important in these strategies to determine the award to be given: if the reward is too small, the programme will not work; if it is too large, the strategy may be too expensive. Employees who are content in their job are more motivated to satisfy their customers than ones who are not content (Yoon et al., 2007).

FUTURE RESEARCH DIRECTIONS

The proposed conceptual framework can be considered a first step toward compensating for the lack of studies of surveillance management during service encounters in a service management perspective because, although it does not claim to be thorough in any way, it should encourage future researchers to explore this topic in greater depth. To further this end, the following suggestions are added.

All of the ideas in this chapter have been conceptually developed on the basis of theoretical evidence contained in service management and marketing literature, but none of them has been empirically validated: that is, the propositions and relationships are theoretically grounded but require empirical verification in order to accelerate future research in this promising area. Interested researchers could develop appropriate scales of measurement and use them as starting points. In order to start the quantitative analysis of ESM evaluation, it is possible to use a multi-informant (users/customers, guard patrols, and surveillance managers) research design. Another possible research method for testing and validating this conceptual framework is the critical incident technique (Bitner et al., 1994): by means of interviews and analysis of human behaviour, this technique allows the researcher to gather relevant observations on service encounters and classify them in such a way as to identify main factors that positively or negatively affect the customer's evaluation.

It would be interesting to analyse how service managers could accurately design and manage service delivery processes in such a way as to educate customers in correct service use. Customers need rules to orient themselves in the servicescape, especially if they have little familiarity with and knowledge of the service delivery process. A few customers behave incorrectly because they misunderstand the conduct rules that they must follow. Communication about security in the servicescape plays a critical role: programmes on customer orientation, written documents provided to customers, moderately worded notices (Liu and Chen, 2011), and information appropriately placed in the physical environment are useful tools that have not been investigated enough from an ESM perspective.

Another promising area for further studies regards the analysis of possible connections between different service settings in such a way as to notice other relevant dimensions and variables of ESM. Research has mainly focused on the retail context but effective surveillance management is increasingly important in all service organizations that want to provide customers with a comfortable servicescape and, at the same time, a sense of security. In addition, significant differences could emerge by comparing servicescapes with high and low customer involvement: for example, the presence of many customers during the service encounter may be a source of grave consequences and problems for security staff, other customers, and service organizations. Furthermore, the racial component of surveillance can be discussed. Not only in the United States buy also in Europe because of many immigrants from North African countries such as Libya and Tunisia, some racial groups feel that they are watched more closely than people of other racial groups.

Although shoplifting is a rational choice (Cornish and Clarke, 1986), dishonesty behaviors of some customers can be examined in terms of moral dimension that is not discussed voluntarily in this study. Some hotels do use the moral dimension when they appeal to customers not to walk away with certain items since that increases the cost of operation.

CONCLUSION

This chapter has proposed to improve customer service experience along with meeting customers' need for security and to implement a surveillance service orientation-based strategy as antecedents of ESM. It also suggests that the dimensions of ESM (customer-physical service environment encounters, customer-technological surveillance system encounters, and customer-security staff encounters) contribute to enhancing service quality in terms of reliability, responsiveness, assurance, empathy, and tangibility, as well as improving both experience quality and staff productivity. The integration of the dimensions, antecedents, and consequences of ESM has allowed the presentation and discussion of a theoretically grounded framework that could serve as a starting point for future studies in the service management field.

In particular, it can contribute to extending knowledge of surveillance management in a service management perspective along four paths. First, it draws the attention of service management scholars to the hitherto under-researched concept of ESM. Second, it clarifies the concept of ESM by discussing its dimensions and its importance during service encounters. Third, it proposes a conceptual framework which offers a foundation for future research. Finally, it presents the influence of antecedents and effects that can influence ESM. The ESM approach is understood in this chapter as a means of enhancing the customer service experience during service encounters.

Ensuring a high level of surveillance during service encounters without interfering with customers' service experience allows service organizations to achieve the following objectives: preventing the action of customers who behave badly in the servicescape by means of the design of the physical environment, making effective use of technological surveillance systems, employing trained and motivated service and security staff, and delivering an effective service by attracting customers who want to perceive a sense of security without feeling they are closely monitored. In other words, by adopting security measures that generate positive effects for security staff, crime prevention teams, and customers, service organizations follow a proactive strategic approach rather than merely a reactive one (Mitchell and Chan, 2002) by performing effectively in today's competitive environment. An ESM-oriented business strategy can therefore become a key factor at the strategic differentiation level for any service organization.

REFERENCES

Baccarani, C., & Brunetti, F. (2011). The Need for Customer Education in High People-Density Services: A New Role for Service Providers? *Proceedings of the14th Toulon-Verona Conference* (pp. 115-131). Alicante, Spain: University of Alicante.

Baccarani, C., & Golinelli, G. M. (2009). *Leadership for Excellence in Services. Sinergie, 78(Gennaio-Maggio).* VII-XVI.

Baccarani, C., Ugolini, M., & Bonfanti, A. (2010). A Conceptual Service Quality Map: The Value of a Wide Opened Perspective. *Proceedings of the13th Toulon-Verona Conference* (pp. 873-892). Coimbra, Portugal: University of Coimbra.

Baker, J. A., Parasuraman, A., Grewal, D., & Voss, G. B. (2002). The Influence of Multiple Store Environment Cues on Perceived Merchandise Value and Patronage Intentions. *Journal of Marketing*, *66*(2), 120–141. doi:10.1509/jmkg.66.2.120.18470

Bamfield, J. A. N. (2012). *Shopping and Crime*. New York: Palgrave Macmillan. doi:10.1057/9780230393554

Bendapudi, N., & Leone, R. P. (2003). Psychological Implications of Customer Participation in Coproduction. *Journal of Marketing*, *67*(1), 14–28. doi:10.1509/jmkg.67.1.14.18592

Berry, L., Carbone, L., & Haeckel, S. (2002). Managing the Total Customer Experience. *MIT Sloan Management Review*, *43*(3), 85–89.

Berry, L. L., Parasuraman, A., & Zeithaml, V. A. (1988). The Service Quality-Puzzle. *Business Horizons*, *31*(5), 35–43. doi:10.1016/0007-6813(88)90053-5

Berry, L. L., & Seiders, K. (2008). Serving Unfair Customers. *Business Horizons*, *51*(1), 29–37. doi:10.1016/j.bushor.2007.09.002

Bettencourt, L., Ostrom, A. L., Brown, S. W., & Roundtree, R. I. (2002). Client Co-Production in Knowledge-Intensive Business Services. *California Management Review*, *44*(4), 100–128. doi:10.2307/41166145

Bitner, M. J. (1992). Servicescapes: The Impact of Physical Surroundings on Customers and Employees. *Journal of Marketing*, *56*(2), 57–71. doi:10.2307/1252042

Bitner, M. J., Booms, B. H., & Mohr, L. A. (1994). Critical Service Encounters: The Employees Viewpoint. *Journal of Marketing*, *58*(4), 95–106. doi:10.2307/1251919

Bonfanti, A. (2014). A Dilemma for Retailers: How to Make Store Surveillance Secure and Appealing to Shoppers? In F. Musso & E. Druica (Eds.), *Handbook of Research on Retailer-Consumer Relationship Development* (pp. 297–317). Hershey, PA, USA: IGI Global. doi:10.4018/978-1-4666-6074-8.ch016

Bonfanti, A. (2016). Customers Needs and Expectations on Servicescape Surveillance Management. *The TQM Journal*, *28*(6), 887–906. doi:10.1108/TQM-05-2015-0067

Bowen, D. E., Siehl, C., & Schneider, B. (1989). A Framework for Analyzing Customer Service Orientations in Manufacturing. *Academy of Management Review*, *14*(1), 75–95.

Burns, D. J., Manolis, C., & Keep, W. W. (2010). Fear of Crime on Shopping Intentions: An Examination. *International Journal of Retail & Distribution Management*, *38*(1), 45–56. doi:10.1108/09590551011016322

Charles, H., & Schwepker, C. H. Jr. (2003). Customer-Orientated Selling: A Review, Extension, and Directions for Future Research. *Journal of Personal Selling & Sales Management*, *23*(2), 151–171.

Citrin, A. V., Stern, D. E., Spangenberg, E. R., & Clark, M. J. (2003). Consumer Need for Tactile Input: An Internet Retailing Challenge. *Journal of Business Research*, *56*(11), 915–922. doi:10.1016/S0148-2963(01)00278-8

Coleman, P. (2006). *Shopping Environments: Evolution, Planning and Design*. Oxford: *Elsevier*.

Cornish, D., & Clarke, R. (1986). *The Reasoning Criminal: Rational Choice Perspectives on Offending*. New York: Springer-Verlag. doi:10.1007/978-1-4613-8625-4

Cowper, R. J. (1992). Shopping Centre Management for the Nineties. *Property Management*, *10*(4), 329–337. doi:10.1108/02637479210030466

Cozens, P., Saville, G., & Hillier, D. (2005). Crime Prevention through Environmental Design (CPTED): Are View and Modern Bibliography. *Journal of Property Management*, *23*(5), 328–356. doi:10.1108/02637470510631483

Cran, D. J. (1994). Towards Validation of the Service Orientation Construct. *Service Industries Journal*, *14*(1), 34–44. doi:10.1080/02642069400000003

Daunt, K., & Harris, L. C. (2012a). Motives of Dysfunctional Customer Behavior: An Empirical Study. *Journal of Services Marketing*, *26*(4), 293–308. doi:10.1108/08876041211237587

Daunt, K. L., & Harris, L. C. (2012b). Exploring the Forms of Dysfunctional Customer Behaviour: A Study of Differences in Servicescape and Customer Disaffection with Service. *Journal of Marketing Management*, *28*(1/2), 129–153. doi:10.1080/0267257X.2011.619149

Echeverri, P., Salomonson, N., & Åberg, A. (2012). Dealing with Customer Misbehaviour: Employees Tactics, Practical Judgement and Implicit Knowledge. *Marketing Theory*, *12*(4), 427–449. doi:10.1177/1470593112457741

Edvardsson, B. (2005). Service Quality: Beyond Cognitive Assessment. *Managing Service Quality*, *15*(2), 127–131. doi:10.1108/09604520510585316

Fisk, R., Grove, S., Harris, L. C., Keeffe, D., Daunt, K. L., Russell-Bennett, R., & Wirtz, J. (2010). Customers Behaving Badly: A State of the Art Review, Research Agenda and Implications for Practitioners. *Journal of Services Marketing*, *24*(6), 417–429. doi:10.1108/08876041011072537

Foxall, G. R., & Greenley, G. E. (1999). Consumers Emotional Responses to Service Environments. *Journal of Business Research*, *46*(2), 149–158. doi:10.1016/S0148-2963(98)00018-6

Foxall, G. R., & Greenley, G. E. (2000). Predicting and Explaining Responses to Consumer Environments: An Empirical Test and Theoretical Extension of the Behavioural Perspective Model. *Service Industries Journal*, *20*(2), 39–63. doi:10.1080/02642060000000019

Friend, L. A., Costley, C. L., & Brown, C. (2010). Spirals of Distrust vs Spirals of Trust in Retail Customer Service: Consumers as Victims or Allies. *Journal of Services Marketing*, *24*(6), 458–467. doi:10.1108/08876041011072573

Fullerton, R. A., & Punj, G. (1993). Choosing to Misbehave: A Structural Model of Aberrant Consumer Behavior. *Advances in Consumer Research. Association for Consumer Research (U. S.)*, *20*, 570–574.

Fullerton, R. A., & Punj, G. (1997). What is Consumer Misbehavior? *Advances in Consumer Research. Association for Consumer Research (U. S.)*, *24*, 336–339.

Fullerton, R. A., & Punj, G. (2004). Repercussions of Promoting an Ideology of Consumption: Consumer Misbehavior. *Journal of Business Research*, *57*(11), 1239–1249. doi:10.1016/S0148-2963(02)00455-1

Grandey, A. A., Dickter, D. N., & Sin, H. (2004). The Customer is not Always Right: Customer Aggression and Emotion Regulation of Service Employees. *Journal of Organizational Behavior*, *25*(3), 397–418. doi:10.1002/job.252

Grönroos, C. (2000). *Service Management and Marketing. A Consumer Relationship Management Approach.* Chichester: John Wiley & Sons.

Gummesson, E. (1994). *Relationship Marketing: From 4Ps to 30Rs.* Stockholm, Sweden: Stockholm University.

Gummesson, E. (2002). *Total Relationship Marketing.* Oxford: Butterworth-Heinemann.

Harris, L. C., & Daunt, K. (2013). Managing Customer Misbehavior: Challenges and Strategies. *Journal of Services Marketing, 27*(4), 281–293. doi:10.1108/08876041311330762

Harris, L. C., & Daunt, K. L. (2011). Deviant Customer Behaviour: A Study of Techniques of Neutralization. *Journal of Marketing Management, 27*(7-8), 834–853. doi:10.1080/0267257X.2010.498149

Harris, L. C., & Reynolds, K. (2003). The Consequences of Dysfunctional Consumer Behavior. *Journal of Service Research, 6*(2), 144–161. doi:10.1177/1094670503257044

Harris, L. C., & Reynolds, K. L. (2004). Jaycustomer Behavior: An Exploration into the Types and Motives in the Hospitality Industry. *Journal of Services Marketing, 18*(5), 339–357. doi:10.1108/08876040410548276

Hayes, R., & Blackwood, R. (2006). Evaluating the Effects of EAS on Product Sales and Loss: Results of a Large-Scale Field Experiment. *Security Journal, 19*(4), 262–276. doi:10.1057/palgrave.sj.8350025

Hayes, R., & Downs, D. M. (2011). Controlling Retail Theft with CCTV Domes, CCTV Public View Monitors, and Protective Containers: A Randomized Controlled Trial. *Security Journal, 24*(3), 237–250. doi:10.1057/sj.2011.12

Hayes, R., Johns, T., Scicchitano, M., Downs, D., & Pietrawska, B. (2011). Evaluating the Effects of Protective Keeper Boxes on Hot Product Loss and Sales: A Randomized Controlled Trial. *Security Journal, 24*(3), 357–369. doi:10.1057/sj.2011.2

Helkkula, A. (2011). Characterising the Concept of Service Experience. *Journal of Service Management, 22*(3), 367–389. doi:10.1108/09564231111136872

Hoffman, K. D., & Bateson, J. E. G. (1997). *Essentials of Services Marketing.* Fort Worth: Dryden Press.

Hogan, J., Hogan, R., & Busch, C. M. (1984). How to Measure Service Orientation. *The Journal of Applied Psychology, 69*(1), 167–173. doi:10.1037/0021-9010.69.1.167 PMID:6698916

Homburg, C., Hoyer, W. D., & Fassnacht, M. (2002). Service Orientation of a Retailers Business Strategy: Dimensions, Antecedents, and Performance Outcomes. *Journal of Marketing, 66*(4), 86–101. doi:10.1509/jmkg.66.4.86.18511

Huefner, J. C., & Hunt, H. K. (2000). Consumer Retaliation as a Response to Dissatisfaction. *Journal of Consumer Satisfaction. Dissatisfaction and Complaining Behavior, 13*, 61–82.

Hultén, B. (2012). Sensory Cues and Shoppers Touching Behaviour: The Case of IKEA. *International Journal of Retail & Distribution Management, 40*(4), 273–289. doi:10.1108/09590551211211774

Jones, M. A. (1999). Entertaining Shopping Experiences: An Exploratory Investigation. *Journal of Retailing and Consumer Services, 6*(3), 129–139. doi:10.1016/S0969-6989(98)00028-9

Jones, P., Clarke-Hill, C., Shears, P., Comfort, D., & Hillier, D. (2004). Radio Frequency Identification in the UK: Opportunities and Challenges. *International Journal of Retail & Distribution Management*, *32*(3), 164–171. doi:10.1108/09590550410524957

Jüttner, U., Schaffner, D., Windler, K., & Maklan, S. (2013). Customer Service Experiences. Developing and Applying a Sequential Incident Laddering Technique. *European Journal of Marketing*, *47*(5/6), 738–768. doi:10.1108/03090561311306769

Kajalo, S., & Lindblom, A. (2010a). The Perceived Effectiveness of Surveillance in Reducing Crime at Shopping Centers in Finland. *Property Management*, *28*(1), 47–59. doi:10.1108/02637471011017172

Kajalo, S., & Lindblom, A. (2010b). Surveillance Investments in Store Environment and Sense of Security. *Facilities*, *28*(9/10), 465–474. doi:10.1108/02632771011057198

Kajalo, S., & Lindblom, A. (2011). Effectiveness of Formal and Informal Surveillance in Reducing Crime at Grocery Stores. *Journal of Small Business and Enterprise Development*, *18*(1), 157–169. doi:10.1108/14626001111106488

Kajalo, S., & Lindblom, A. (2012). Evaluating the Effects of Formal and Informal Surveillance: A Retailer's View.*Proceedings of ASBBS Annual Conference* (Vol. 19, pp. 461-471). Las Vegas.

Kajalo, S., & Lindblom, A. (2015). Creating a Safe and Pleasant Shopping Environment: A Retailers View. *Property Management*, *33*(3), 275–286. doi:10.1108/PM-10-2014-0042

Kajalo, S., & Lindblom, A. (2016). The Role of Formal and Informal Surveillance in Creating a Safe and Entertaining Retail Environment. *Facilities*, *34*(3/4), 219–232. doi:10.1108/F-06-2014-0055

Kano, N., Seraku, N., Takahashi, F., & Tsuji, S. (1984). Attractive Quality and Must-Be Quality. *Journal of Japanese Society for Quality Control*, *14*(2), 39–48.

Keng, C.-J., Huang, T.-L., Zheng, L.-J., & Hsu, M. K. (2007). Modeling Service Encounters and Customer Experiential Value in Retailing. An Empirical Investigation of Shopping Mall Customers in Taiwan. *International Journal of Service Industry Management*, *18*(4), 349–367. doi:10.1108/09564230710778137

Klaus, P., & Maklan, S. (2012). EXQ: A Multiple-Scale for Assessing Service Experience. *Journal of Service Management*, *23*(1), 5–33. doi:10.1108/09564231211208952

Klaus, P., & Maklan, S. (2013). Towards a Better Measure of Customer Experience. *International Journal of Market Research*, *55*(2), 227–246. doi:10.2501/IJMR-2013-021

Kulas, J. T., Mcinnerney, J. E., Demuth, R. F., & Jadwinski, V. (2007). Employee Satisfaction and Theft: Testing Climate Perceptions as a Mediator. *The Journal of Psychology*, *141*(4), 389–402. doi:10.3200/JRLP.141.4.389-402 PMID:17725072

Lemke, F., Clark, M., & Wilson, H. (2010). Customer Experience Quality: An Exploration in Business and Consumer Contexts Using Repertory Grid Technique. *Journal of the Academy of Marketing Science*, *39*(6), 846–869. doi:10.1007/s11747-010-0219-0

Liljander, V., & Strandvik, T. (1997). Emotions in Service Satisfaction. *International Journal of Service Industry Management*, *8*(2), 148–169. doi:10.1108/09564239710166272

Lindblom, A., & Kajalo, S. (2011). The Use and Effectiveness of Formal and Informal Surveillance in Reducing Shoplifting: A Survey in Sweden, Norway, and Finland. *International Review of Retail, Distribution and Consumer Research, 21*(2), 111–128. doi:10.1080/09593969.2011.562677

Liu, T.-C., & Chen, C.-F. (2011). Please Smile, the CCTV Is Running! *Service Industries Journal, 31*(7), 1075–1092. doi:10.1080/02642060903108342

Lovelock, C. (1994). *Product Plus: How Product + Service = Competitive Advantage*. New York: McGraw-Hill.

Lovelock, C. (2001). *Services Marketing: People, Technology, Strategy* (4th ed.). Upper Saddle River, NJ: Prentice Hall.

Lytle, R., Hom, P., & Mokwa, M. (1998). SERV OR: A Managerial Measure of Organizational Service Orientation. *Journal of Retailing, 74*(4), 455–475. doi:10.1016/S0022-4359(99)80104-3

Lytle, R. S., & Timmerman, J. E. (2006). Service Orientation and Performance: An Organizational Perspective. *Journal of Services Marketing, 20*(2), 136–147. doi:10.1108/08876040610657066

Mann, T. (1992). Security Services Under Fire. *Management Services, 36*(1), 28–30.

Meyer, C., & Schwager, A. (2007). Understanding Customer Experience. *Harvard Business Review, 85*(2), 116–126. PMID:17345685

Mills, M. K. (1981). Deviance and Dissatisfaction: An Exploration Study. *Advances in Consumer Research. Association for Consumer Research (U. S.), 8*, 682–686.

Mills, M. K., & Bonoma, T. V. (1979). Deviant Consumer Behavior: New Challenge for Marketing Research. *Proceedings of the Educators'Conference* (pp. 445-449). Chicago, IL: American Marketing Association.

Mitchell, V.-W., & Chan, J. K. L. (2002). Investigating UK Consumers Unethical Attitudes and Behaviours. *Journal of Marketing Management, 18*(1/2), 5–26. doi:10.1362/0267257022775873

Moschis, G. P., & Cox, D. (1989). Deviant Consumer Behavior. *Advances in Consumer Research. Association for Consumer Research (U. S.), 16*(1), 732–737.

Overstreet, J., & Clodfelter, R. (1995). Safety and Security Concerns of Shopping Center Consumers and the Effect of these Concerns on Shopping Behavior. *Journal of Shopping Center Research, 2*(1), 91–109.

Parasuraman, A., Zeithaml, V. A., & Berry, L. L. (1985). A Conceptual Model of Service Quality and Its Implications for Future Research. *Journal of Marketing, 49*(4), 41–50. doi:10.2307/1251430

Peck, J., & Childers, T. L. (2003). To Have and to Hold: The Influence of Haptic Information on Product Judgements. *Journal of Marketing, 67*(April), 35–48. doi:10.1509/jmkg.67.2.35.18612

Peek-Asa, C., Casteel, C., Kraus, J. F., & Whitten, P. (2006). Employee and Customer Injury during Violent Crimes in Retail and Service Businesses. *American Journal of Public Health, 96*(10), 1867–1872. doi:10.2105/AJPH.2005.071365 PMID:17008585

Perlman, Y., & Ozinci, Y. (2014). Reducing Shoplifting by Investment in Security. *The Journal of the Operational Research Society*, *65*(5), 685–693. doi:10.1057/jors.2013.37

Pretious, M., Stewart, R., & Logan, D. (1995). Retail Security: A Survey of Methods and Management in Dundee. *International Journal of Retail & Distribution Management*, *23*(9), 28–35. doi:10.1108/09590559510098681

Reynolds, K. L., & Harris, L. C. (2009). Dysfunctional Customer Behavior Severity: An Empirical Examination. *Journal of Retailing*, *85*(3), 321–355. doi:10.1016/j.jretai.2009.05.005

Rose, R. L., & Neidermeyer, M. (1999). From Rudeness to Roadrage: The Antecedents and Consequences of Consumer Aggression. *Advances in Consumer Research. Association for Consumer Research (U. S.)*, *26*, 12–17.

Sandberg, J., & Alvesson, M. (2011). Ways of Constructing Research Questions: Gap-Spotting or Problematization? *Organization*, *18*(1), 23–44. doi:10.1177/1350508410372151

Schembri, S. (2006). Rationalizing Service Logic, or Understanding Services as Experience? *Marketing Theory*, *6*(3), 381–392. doi:10.1177/1470593106066798

Soars, B. (2009). Driving Sales through Shoppers Sense of Sound, Sight, Smell and Touch. *International Journal of Retail & Distribution Management*, *37*(3), 286–298. doi:10.1108/09590550910941535

Tax, S. S., & Brown, S. W. (1998). Recovering and Learning from Service Failure. *Sloan Management Review*, (Fall): 75–88.

Teng, C.-C., & Barrows, C. W. (2009). Service Orientation: Antecedents, Outcomes, and Implications for Hospitality Research and Practice. *Service Industries Journal*, *29*(10), 1413–1435. doi:10.1080/02642060903026247

Toffler, A. (1980). *The Third Wave*. New York: William Morrow and Co.

Tonglet, M. (2000). Consumer Misbehaviour: Consumers Perceptions of Shoplifting and Retail Security. *Security Journal*, *13*(4), 107–122. doi:10.1057/palgrave.sj.8340063

Tonglet, M. (2002). Consumer Misbehaviour: An Exploratory Study of Shoplifting. *Journal of Consumer Behaviour*, *1*(4), 336–354. doi:10.1002/cb.79

Ugolini, M. M., Rossato, C., & Baccarani, C. (2014). A Five-Senses Perspective to Quality in Hospitals. *The TQM Journal*, *26*(3), 284–299. doi:10.1108/TQM-01-2014-0010

Walsh, P. D. (1994). Training Security Personnel. *Journal of Property Management*, *59*(2), 60–62.

Wellhoff, A., & Masson, J. E. (2005). *Le Merchandising: Bases, Techniques, Nouvelles Tendances*. Paris: Dunod.

Woo, K., & Fock, H. K. Y. (2004). Retaining and Divesting Customers: An Exploratory Study of Right Customers, At-Risk Right Customer, and Wrong Customers. *Journal of Services Marketing*, *18*(3), 187–197. doi:10.1108/08876040410536495

Wu, C. H.-J., Liang, R.-D., Tung, W., & Chang, C.-S. (2008). Structural Relationships among Organisation Service Orientation, Employee Service Performance, and Consumer Identification. *Service Industries Journal*, *28*(9), 1247–1263. doi:10.1080/02642060802230189

Yi, Y., & Gong, T. (2006). The Antecedents and Consequences of Service Customer Citizenship and Badness Behavior. *Seoul Journal of Business*, *12*(2), 145–176.

Yoon, S.-J., Choi, D.-C., & Park, J.-W. (2007). Service Orientation: Its Impact on Business Performance in the Medical Service Industry. *Service Industries Journal*, *27*(4), 371–388. doi:10.1080/02642060701346375

Zemke, R., & Anderson, K. (1990). Customers from Hell. *Training (New York, N.Y.)*, *27*(2), 25–33.

ADDITIONAL READING

Alstete, J. (2006). Inside Advice on Educating Managers for Preventing Employee Theft. *International Journal of Retail & Distribution Management*, *34*(11), 833–844. doi:10.1108/09590550610710237

Beck, A., & Palmer, W. (2011). The Importance of Visual Situational Cues and Difficulty of Removal in Creating Deterrence: The Limitations of Electronic Article Surveillance Source Tagging in the Retail Environment. *Journal of Applied Security Research*, *6*(1), 110–123. doi:10.1080/19361610.2011.529412

Bonfanti, A., & Brunetti, F. (2015). Effects of Customer Education in Terms of Customer Perceived Value: The Role of Customer Evaluation Skills. *Sinergie Italian Journal of Management*, 97, 219-238.

Cardone, C., & Hayes, R. (2012). Shoplifter Perceptions of Store Environments: An Analysis of how Physical Cues in the Retail Interior Shape Shoplifter Behavior. *Journal of Applied Security Research*, *7*(1), 22–58. doi:10.1080/19361610.2012.631178

Choi, S. H., Yang, Y. X., Yang, B., & Cheung, H. H. (2015). Item-Level RFID for Enhancement of Customer Shopping Experience in Apparel Retail. *Computers in Industry*, *71*(August), 10–23. doi:10.1016/j.compind.2015.03.003

Cozens, P., Saville, G., & Hillier, D. (2005). Crime Prevention through Environmental Design (CPTED): Are View and Modern Bibliography. *Journal of Property Management*, *23*(5), 328–356. doi:10.1108/02637470510631483

Mishra, B. K., & Prasad, A. (2006). Minimizing Retail Shrinkage due to Employee Theft. *International Journal of Retail & Distribution Management*, *34*(11), 817–832. doi:10.1108/09590550610710228

Ngai, E.W.T., Moon, K.K.L., Liu, J.N.K., Tsang, K.F., Law, R., Suk, F.F.C., & Wong, I.C.L. (2008). Extending CRM in the Retail Industry: An RFID-Based Personal Shopping Assistant System. *Communications of the Association for Information Systems*, *23*(16), 277–294.

Oliphant, B. J., & Oliphant, G. C. (2001). Using a Behavior-Based Method to Identify and Reduce Employee Theft. *International Journal of Retail & Distribution Management*, *29*(10), 442–451. doi:10.1108/09590550110405321

Xiaoling, Z., Shibo, L., Burke, R. R., & Leykin, A. (2014). An Examination of Social Influence on Shopper Behavior Using Video Tracking Data. *Journal of Marketing*, *78*(5), 24–41. doi:10.1509/jm.12.0106

KEY TERMS AND DEFINITIONS

Customer Service Experience: Service organizations are able of meeting customers' needs into service settings.

Customer-Physical Service Environment Encounters: Interaction time between customer and all elements of physical service environment (servicescape) in which service is delivered.

Customers' Need for Security: Customers expect that servicescape are designed in terms of protection of people from potential injury, danger or death caused by accidents, fire, hazardous materials and natural disasters, as well as from unlawful acts of groups or individuals, or from the occurrence of harmful acts and events due to negligence, neglect and careless behaviour, such as theft, shoplifting and violent crime.

Customer-Security Staff Encounters: Interaction time between customer and security personnel including sworn guards, rangers or other uniformed staff trained to monitor the service environment and make it safe, as well as to deter casual thieves.

Customer-Technological Surveillance Systems Encounters: Interaction time between customer and technological solutions implemented into the servicescape such as closed-circuit television (CCTV) systems, motion-detector devices, high-tech scanners, electronic article surveillance (EAS) devices, and RFId tags, antennas, software, and accessories.

Deterrent Communication: Some communication tools such as notices, posters, and graphic signals are exhibited within the servicescape to alert people of the presence of surveillance systems, warnings, and possible sanctions in case of breach.

Security Measures: Protection solutions and techniques adopted by service organizations in order to create a secure and safe service environment and protect against theft, shoplifting, vandalism, and organised crime.

Servicescape Design: The set of functional or aesthetic elements planned by service organizations in order to attract customers in the service environment.

Surveillance Service Orientation-Based Strategy: Designing the service environment to provide a safe and reliable high-level protection of the servicescape, increase customers' sense of security, limit criminal action and, at the same time, meet the customer's need to have a positive service experience during service encounters.

Chapter 7
Consumer Information Systems Research Agenda:
Meeting Challenges for Interactive Television Service Development

Tuure Tuunanen
University of Jyväskylä, Finland

Michael David Myers
University of Auckland, New Zealand

ABSTRACT

We suggest that a new type of information system appears to be increasing in importance, that of consumer information systems. Compared with traditional information systems development approaches, where the focus is on improving the efficiency and effectiveness of organizational processes, design for consumer information systems focuses more on the enjoyment, pleasure and purchases of the consumer. We argue that the shift in focus from users to consumers in consumer information systems calls for a significant re-appraisal of our current information systems development methods. Hence, this chapter proposes a new research agenda for IS researchers focusing on the development of consumer information systems. The expected contributions include new insights into effective management processes for service design, a better understanding of issues of integration of information systems development practices used to develop consumer information systems, and the development of methods for requirements discovery for service innovation.

INTRODUCTION

We are more and more entering a new era of Consumer Information Systems (CIS). Until now most information systems have been developed to improve the efficiency and effectiveness of organizations. However, the rationale for the development of CIS is different: it is to facilitate the enjoyment and pleasure of the consumer. A consumer is defined by the Concise Oxford English Dictionary as:

DOI: 10.4018/978-1-5225-2139-6.ch007

1. A person or thing that eats or uses something.
2. A person who buys goods and services for personal use (Soanes & Stevenson, 2004).

As can be seen from this definition, the primary meaning of a consumer is of a person who "eats or uses something." The secondary meaning is of person who purchases a service or product. Hence, it is possible for someone to enjoy watching a TV program (consume it) without having to pay for it. In this case, the TV program may actually be "paid for" (indirectly) by advertising. An alternative, of course, is for consumers to purchase TV programs directly (e.g. via a subscription service or pay per view).

It seems to us that the design and development of consumer information systems requires a change in the way we have traditionally thought about users (Lamb & Kling, 2003). Users have been conceptualized as mostly concerned about the effectiveness and efficiency of work processes. Consumers, on the other hand, are mostly interested in the enjoyment or pleasure associated with "consuming" a product or service (cf. Valkonen, Lindström, Natunen, Isoviita & Tuunanen 2015). Users have been thought of as passive "users" of the system (as compared with "developers"). Consumers, by contrast, can be much more active in their use of a product or system. This is especially the case with the emergence of social networks and new internet-enabled multimedia services where consumers can become participants and co-creators of the television experience or "service". Another difference between users and consumers is that of scale: the number of consumers potentially involved in the development process is very large. Finally, the concept of services (Grönroos, 2007; Menor, Takikonda, & Sampson, 2002) takes centre stage (as opposed to the idea of creating a distinct IS artifact product). The focus shifts to innovating, designing and developing internet-enabled services.

This feature of co-creation of the service is facilitated by the social interaction between consumers and producers of services via different feedback mechanisms (such as Facebook-type services). The IP-Television concept, e.g. Netflix or Hulu, is a way to use the Internet to distribute on-demand digital programming in this fashion. Another example is Social Television that merges social media with Television broadcasts and rapid feedback mechanisms, like texting, tweeting, or chatting. These technological changes are driving the market toward real Interactive Television Services (ITS), which will enable consumers not only to participate, but also to create content and be part of the programming i.e. co-creators of CIS (Tuunanen, Myers & Cassab 2010).

In this chapter, then, we propose a research agenda to investigate the challenges academics and practitioners are likely to face when developing consumer information systems. Our targeted case domain area will be Interactive Television Services. We review requirements discovery, information systems development, and service design literature, in order to develop a preliminary framework to drive the proposed research agenda. Finally, we discuss the potential contributions of this chapter to IS research and practice.

Consumer Information Systems: Challenges for Research

An information system is often defined as the interplay of technology, software and people with the purpose of storing, distributing and communicating information. Others have described an information system as a system of communication used by members of some human group (Beynon-Davies, 2002). Consumer Information Systems have been defined as

Systems that enable consumer value co-creation through the development and implementation of information technology enabled processes that integrate system value propositions with customer value drivers. (Tuunanen et al., 2010).

Our chapter seeks to understand more about CIS: how consumer requirements can be determined; the possible changes required to information systems development processes; and finally, design of consumer targeted services. We review relevant literature and raise a few research challenges below.

Requirements Discovery

Various disciplines have been dealing with the issues surrounding the problem of recognizing the needs of end-users of services and products. In Information Systems the usual way of trying to solve these problems has been to determine the needs of the organizational end-user and then to analyze the data in order to achieve requirements specification of feasible quality (Byrd, Cossick, & Zmud, 1992; Davis, 1982; Keil & Carmel, 1995). More recently, however, it has been suggested that users should be reconceptualized as "actors" (Lamb & Kling, 2003). In marketing, a specific discussion has emerged regarding the issues of developing new products. In this field, the problems have been approached more from a consumers' point of view, and the new product development discipline has been strongly arguing for involving them in the development process (Thomke & von Hippel, 2002).

Within the software engineering discipline, requirements engineering has been focusing on the issues surrounding the problems in eliciting, analyzing, validating, and managing end-users' requirements (Dubois & Pohl, 2003; Jarke & Pohl, 1994). The requirements phase has traditionally been regarded as a phase to "capture" end-user requirements. However, this view has started to change. Jirotka and Goguen (1994) have recommended using the term "elicitation" instead of "capture" so as to avoid the suggestion that requirements are out there to be collected simply by asking the right questions. Bergman et al. (2002) suggest that requirements are defined in a political process between the stakeholders.

Building on this recent work, some IS researchers have suggested that requirements elicitation is a voyage to discovering end-users' needs (Mathiassen, Saarinen, Tuunanen, & Rossi, 2007), modeling them using suitable techniques, and finally finding consensus among stakeholders in their prioritization. They have further characterized specific risks associated with CIS kinds of development projects, such as the availability of requirements. If we consider developing consumer information systems for global markets or even for regional markets, how we can reach these end-users efficiently? Tuunanen et al (2004) have proposed specific features to be considered for requirements discovery methods. Among others they raise context and reach as important features for such methods. Context of the developed systems always affects the user experience. The question remains, according to Tuunanen et al (2004), how we can understand the user context of consumers. Similarly, they point out that the techniques used should be able to reach multitudes of users outside of the developing organization cost-efficiently. This leads us to propose our first research question (RQ):

RQ1: How is it possible to elicit requirements of ITS users effectively?

Information Systems Development

The history of Information Systems development can be characterized as a venture to find solutions for raising the productivity of developers, making systems less defective, or developing systems by techniques that pay more attention to the end-users and their needs (Brooks, 1975). Hirschheim et al. (1995) define information systems development as an "organized collection of concepts, methods, beliefs, values and normative principles supported by material resources". They summarize this as a methodology for Information Systems development. Hence we focus on information systems development (ISD) methods in relation to CIS.

Methods for ISD began with the 'code-and-fix' approach (Boehm, 1988). This method was blamed for many problems, starting with poorly understood requirements and problematical structure of coding and resulting in great expenses when fixes are needed later on (Boehm, 1988). The more structured 'waterfall model' emerged as a systematic, sequential solution to software development problems (Brooks, 1975; Hirschheim, Klein, & Lyytinen, 2003). With this method, the IS artifact was not delivered until the whole linear sequence had been completed. With the waterfall method, researchers also became more focused on requirements. Determining requirements was considered to be essential and it was suggested to collect them at the start of the development process.

As projects became larger and more complex, such problems as stagnant requirements and badly structured programming started to emerge. Through an overlapping of the development phases (Sommerville, 2001) and through the introduction of the more incremental spiral model (Boehm, 1988; Iivari, 1990a, 1990b) it was possible to tackle many of the difficulties mentioned above. Recently, different agile methods (Merisalo-Rantanen, Tuunanen, & Rossi, 2005) have gained recognition. Agile methods return to the idea of focusing on working on the code and minimizing documentation, but at the same time trying to maximize customer satisfaction by involving end-users.

However, there is no agreement in the literature with respect to how users of CIS should be involved in the development process. Participatory design (Clemont & Besselaar, 1993; Smart & Whiting, 2001; Vredenburg, Mao, Smith, & Carey, 2002) and the Scandinavian IS development approach (Iivari & Lyytinen, 1999; Kautz, 2001) have been suggested as answers, but exact ways of connecting these approaches with the required development methods for CIS are not present in the literature (Tuunanen, 2003). Thus we present our second research question:

RQ2: How is it possible to modify contemporary information systems development methods for ITS?

Service Design

What is a service? Various definitions exist, but usually the IS research literature concentrates on the difference between physical products and services (Penttinen, 2007). The characteristics of services are often addressed by providing sets of attributes inherent to services as contrasted with products (Bastek et al., 2008). Lovelock and Wirtz (2004) capture the essence of services with the notion that a service is any act, performance, or experience that one party can offer to another and that is essentially intangible and does not result in ownership. Traditionally, services have been considered to have the unique characteristics of intangibility, heterogeneity, inseparability of production and consumption, and perishability. Recently, the generalizability of these characteristics has been challenged (Lovelock and Gummeson, 2004), driving the need for contemporary perspectives in service research.

Clearly, it is important to understand consumer requirements in order to deliver a service that meets consumers' needs. Hill et al (2002) suggest that the flow of the service experience and time of flow of the delivered service is important to consumers, as is the emotional responses of consumers to the service. They present a needs-based approach to understand the consumer, which offers a way of conceptualizing consumer evaluations of a service that is different from the usual "met expectations" model (Zeithmal, Parasuraman, and Berry, 1985).

The consumer-based approach thus raises questions about how the service design process should be conducted (Hill et al., 2002; Menor et al., 2002). Stuart and Tax (2004) have called for an integrative, holistic service design approach, which would tie together all the areas needed for designing a successful service. Menor et al (2002), however, remain uncertain about the actual method needed for new service design. Thus we present our third and final research question:

RQ3: How is it possible for CIS development and requirements discovery methods to take account of the service nature of ITS?

Research Agenda for ITS Development

We see fascinating possibilities in terms of understanding how to develop consumer information systems and ITS in particular. We have proposed three specific research questions drawn from the literature to set the basis for our research agenda (see Table 1). The focus of study will be to understand consumers' requirements and development methods to support the development of a service. The theoretical framework connecting these is presented in Figure 1 below. We see that the interaction between requirements discovery, information systems development, and service design will drive towards a need for a more holistic approach to consumer information systems development. Thus, our main research objective (RO) will be

RO: The design of a holistic approach to consumer information systems development.

We will use Interactive Television Services (ITS) as the domain of the study. Interactive Television Services will see the convergence of current IP-TV, mobile and web based services to one distinct service targeted to mainstream consumers of global markets. We define the concept of *interactivity* as anything that lets the consumer engage in a dialogue with the provider of the given service enabling him or her to make choices and take actions to influence the content of the provided service (Bastek et al., 2008; Gawlinski, 2003). An example ITS scenario could a situation where a television viewer could actively participate to real time programming by terms of voting (Tuunanen, 2009). The voting results would

Table 1. Research questions

Research questions
RQ1: How is it possible to elicit requirements of ITS users effectively?
RQ2: How is it possible to modify contemporary information systems development methods for ITS?
RQ3: How is it possible for CIS development and requirements discovery methods to take account of the service nature of ITS?

Figure 1. Challenges of consumer information systems development

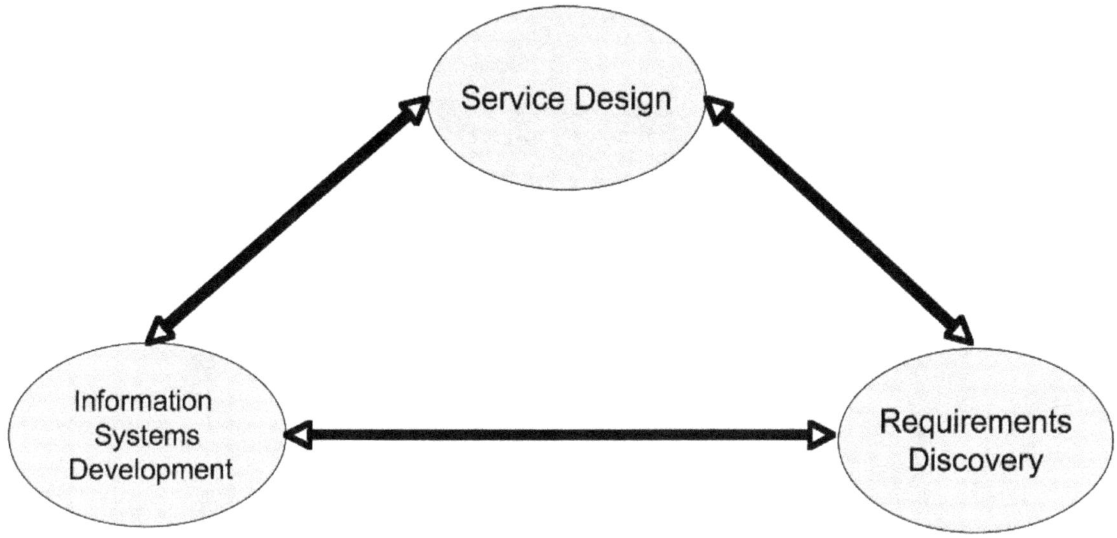

tally up real time as the results come in and then in turn affect the television program real time. Hence, viewer would actually make mental transition from user to actor (Lamb & Kling, 2003) who co-produces the interactive television service.

Currently, the contemporary technology platforms do not support development of such services, although platforms for broadcasting high quality video streams do exist (Netflix and Hulu etc.) One of the pioneering system developers in the area, Redlynx, says that their "participation TV" engages the viewer to program with interaction with the various service formats, such as, game shows, live television chats etc. Figures 2 and 3 provide examples of such ITS. Participation TV engages viewers to participate in games, chats and shows, or send comments to live hosts and animated characters, who will speak them aloud on TV (Redlynx, 2009). Their participation television formats were sold to over 20 countries by leading TV channels, such as SuperRTL (Germany), VTM (Belgium) and Nelonen (Finland). RedLynx is located in Helsinki Finland (head office), China (Beijing), Hong Kong and London UK.

Figure 2 demonstrates one of Redlynx's participation television formats. Viewers can send a text message to throw water balloons towards the live host. Hosts are instructed to comment on the "game play" and interact with the viewers' text messages. It is notable that each of these messages typically cost more than one Euro, or $1.4. Another similar service is "Singing Elves" presented in Figure 3. It is more season-oriented service providing the viewers to possibility to choose Christmas carols song by the animated elves. Redlynx has dozens of such services in their service portfolio with the main features being real time live interaction with the viewers and live hosting of the programs. Remarkably, these shows have been commercially very successful. In Figure 4, we show an infrastructure example provided by Mirial Ltd., which demonstrates how consumers could participate to live television program via their third generation mobile handsets or PCs. The ITS enables, e.g., game show participation for home viewers. The system uses standard serial digital interface (SDI) and telecom interface, namely integrated services digital network (ISDN) and a dedicated server (PSE Broadcaster Genie) to facilitate the service.

All of the above industry examples demonstrate why it is important to consider how to effectively do requirements discovery for such services. For example, Netlix's ITS is simultaneously offered to In-

Figure 2. Interactive television services example: splash produced by Redlynx, Finland

Figure 3. Interactive television services example: singing elves produced by Redlynx, Finland

ternet users around the world. The geographical and cultural differences between potential viewers are enormous. This in turn brings up requirements availability related problems (Mathiassen et al., 2007; Tuunanen & Kuo 2015; Tuunanen, 2003), such as how can we reach consumers in different parts of the markets. This is very challenging question even without considering how the interactive service offering changes its nature when provided through smart phones, such as in the case of making video calls to live television shows (Figure 5). Redlynx's ITS offerings are, at least currently, only provided through

Figure 4. Interactive television services example: making live video calls to television program by Mirial, USA

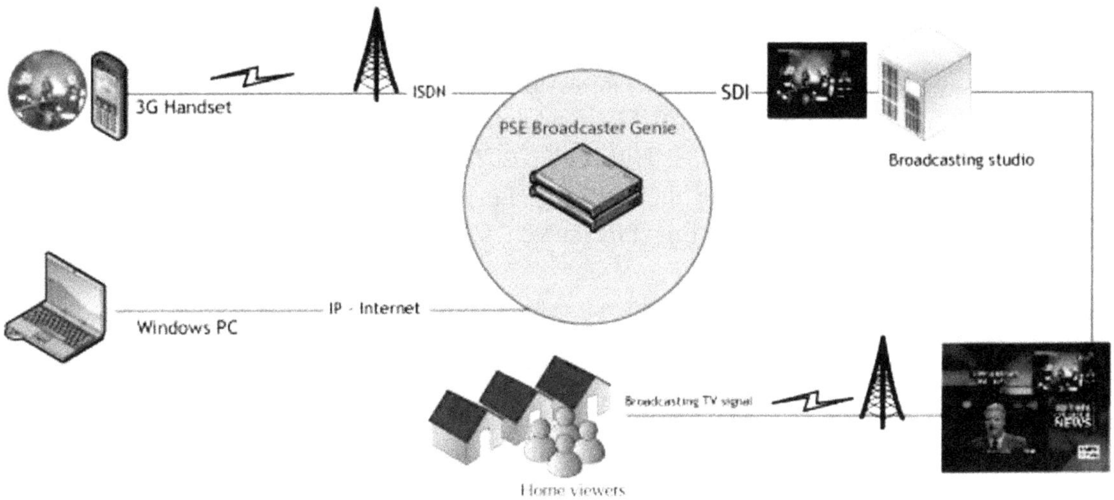

terrestrial and cable television networks. This limits the reach of the service offering and cultural differences among the spectators, or participants as Redlynx characterizes its viewers. This is still a very wide audience of end-users (Tuunanen et al., 2004) with diverse needs and therefore a challenging environment for firms operating in this space. Therefore, the question remains how we can assist elicit consumers' requirements effectively.

Even though the ITS offered by Redlynx were rather simple in their service offering's complexity, they do show what kind of complexities we can expect to face when developing ITS and CIS development in general. Contrary to Netflix's more traditional on-demand video streaming service, the key in participative television formats is real-time interactivity with the spectator, like Mirial's which provisions its service offering through Telecom, Internet and Broadcasting networks. Actually the Mirial example also demonstrates how the information systems development life cycle has to conform to assisting television production in a live show. It is not only systems that were are dealing with but television production. The contemporary ISD methods do not consider this aspect and the closest examples can, perhaps, be found in web service development, which often have strong media components. User participation is said to be essential for CIS development (Iivari & Lyytinen, 1999; Kautz, 2001). This is, however, another challenge, which current ISD methods do not address very well if we think about consumers as users of our systems. In what interval, if any, consumers should take part in the development life cycle? Or should we perhaps take an agile development approach (see e.g., Merisalo-Rantanen et al., 2005) and involve consumers throughout the development process? We need consider how best to modify information systems development methods so that the emerging industry can have better success-ratio with the developed CIS.

Finally, we want to emphasize the need of understanding the service nature of consumer information systems. This reflects two of the previous challenges; requirements elicitation and ISD method related challenges. Services by nature are perishable; they exist in a time and place that the consumer chooses to consume the service. The digital nature of CIS further enhances this problem. For example, Redlynx can easily assume that their text message enabled CIS is consumed from home, or at least from a fixed location where there is a digital television set. Typically, this would be the lounge or living room of a family home. This is not the case with Netflix or Hulu as they also offer a smart phone application for the iPhone. Therefore, it is argued that CIS become a ubiquitous consumer information service (McKenna, Tuunanen and Gardner 2013), which is affected by the use context, difference device user interfaces, network connectivity etc. Furthermore, we can assume that CIS are hedonic in the way consumers want to experience them (Pihlström, 2007; Valkonen et al. 2015). The concept of flow (Agarwal & Karahanna, 2000; Csikszentmihaly, 1991; Hill et al., 2002; Tuunanen & Govindji 2016) might be one way to resolve service design issues, i.e. the service design should be driven by providing the consumer uninterrupted service experience. This might be the goal for a holistic service design to enable hedonic service experience for consumers.

We will use Design Science Research (Hevner, March, & Park, 2004; March & Smith, 1995; Walls, Widmeyer, & El Sawy, 1992) to drive the proposed research agenda. Design Science Research complements both qualitative and quantitative research methodologies by using the development and design of artifacts to assist formulating theories. According to Hevner et al. (2004), the artifacts can be constructs, models, methods, and instantiations. Peffers et al. (2008) reflect on the thoughts of van Aken (2004), and add that artifacts could also include social innovations or, as Järvinen (2007) states, new properties of technical, social, and/or informational resources. Peffers et al. (2008) conclude by defining the artifact as "any designed object with an embedded solution to an understood research problem".

More specifically, we plan to use the Design Science Research Methodology (DRSM) of Peffers et al. (2008) to guide our research. The framework is summarized in Figure 5. The nominal research process is divided into:

1. Problem identification,
2. Objectives,
3. Creation of artifact (in this case Interactive TV platform and Services and a holistic approach to Consumer Information Systems development),
4. Demonstration,
5. Evaluation,
6. Communication of the findings to industry and academia.

The framework also provides different entry points for the research. Our research agenda takes the traditional approach of problem-centered initiation.

CONCLUSION

The chapter has proposed a research agenda for investigating challenges of developing Consumer Information Systems and ITS in particular. More specifically, we have focused on understanding how the change in concept of "end-user" in traditional information systems development methods to "consumer" potentially affects the overall design of the more service-oriented aspects of CIS. We see the intersection of requirements discovery (Mathiassen et al., 2007; Tuunanen, 2003), information systems development, and service design (Grönroos, 2007; Menor et al., 2002; Stuart & Tax, 2004) as an intriguing area of future research. We have suggested a set of research questions in order to understand how to best manage the CIS development process.

Figure 5. Design science research methodology
Source: Adapted from Peffers et al., 2008.

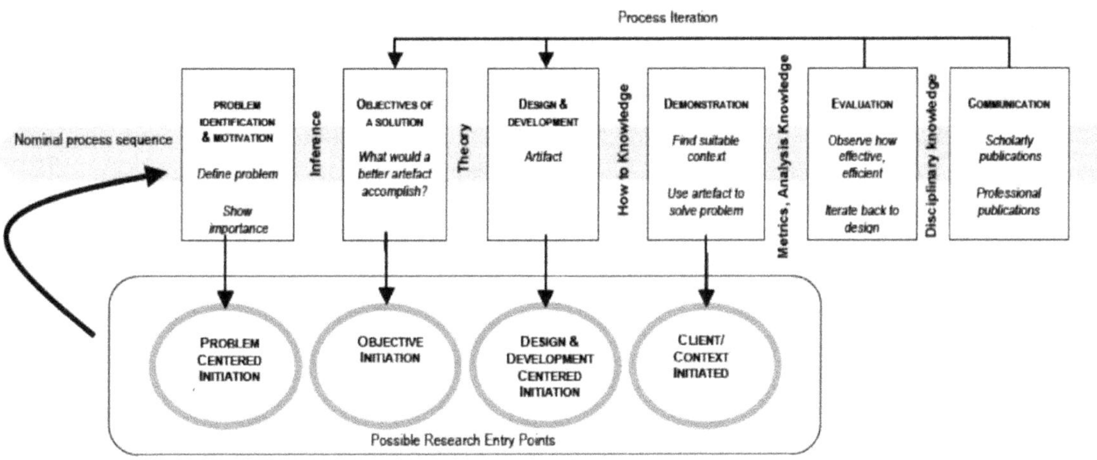

The main academic contribution of our proposed research agenda lies in its contribution to the development of Consumer Information Systems. The study will provide insights of CIS design and development. With the planned studies, we aim to conceptualize how different aspects of CIS impact design and development of CPSS. These findings will provide pathways for future research to investigate, e.g., how IS and service design and developments methods can take account of CIS specific challenges. We plan integrate the earlier findings from multiple case studies (Hänninen, Tuunanen, & Vartiainen, 2015; Vartiainen & Tuunanen, 2016) that has focused on identifying the factors for value co-creation and more specifically to develop a theoretical framework for CIS users' value co-creation behavior. This framework more specifically will seek to explore what system value propositions and users' value drivers impact users' co-value creation behavior. Such value co-creation is thought to occur through interaction between the service provider and the service user. This process is also linked to the service experience of the user and the intangibility of the services, i.e., the service happens at a certain time, in a designated place, and cannot be stored: *in situ*. As such, value co-creation is related to arguments in the literature on participatory design and the Scandinavian school of information systems. These arguments relate to the inclusion and engagement of users in design and development. However, a novel aspect of value co-creation is that the interaction between the service provider and the user is not solely limited to design and development but also to the actual service experience enjoyed by individual users.

Finally, the proposed study will also regenerate service research. Recently, the premier research outlet of the field, *Journal of Service Research*, published a roadmap for service research priorities (Ostrom et al., 2015). The article puts forward twelve research priorities. Our study directly addresses several of these, namely:

1. Developing service networks and systems, and
2. Service infusion, and solutions, and
3. Leveraging service design.

Furthermore, our study seeks to answer the call for a service-dominant logic perspective in IS research (Lusch & Nambisan, 2015) published in the leading IS research outlet *MIS Quarterly*. More specifically, Lusch and Nambisan call for more research in:

1. Understanding mechanisms that facilitate interactions among diverse users (and other actors),
2. Adapting internal processes to accommodate different users (and other actors), and
3. Enhancing the transparency of resource integration activities in the service ecosystem.

We argue that the proposed approach of studying service discovery, design, development would enable us to provide at least initial answers to these challenges highlighted in the call.

REFERENCES

Agarwal, R., & Karahanna, E. (2000). Time flies when youre having fun: Cognitive absorption and beliefs about information technology usage. *Management Information Systems Quarterly*, *24*(4), 665–694. doi:10.2307/3250951

Bastek, M., Tuunanen, T., & Gardner, L. (2008). *Consumer Information Systems Service Families*. The University of Auckland Business School.

Bergman, M., King, J. L., & Lyytinen, K. (2002). Large scale requirements analysis revisited: The need for understanding the political ecology of requirements engineering. *Requirements Engineering*, *7*(3), 152–171. doi:10.1007/s007660200011

Beynon-Davies, P. (2002). *Information systems - an introduction to informatics in organizations*. Houndmills: Palgrave.

Boehm, B. (1988). A Spiral model of software development and enhancement. *IEEE Computer*, *21*(5), 61–72. doi:10.1109/2.59

Brooks, F. (1975). *The Mythical Man Month: Essays on Software Engineering*. Reading, Mass, USA: Addison-Wesley. doi:10.1145/800027.808439

Byrd, T. A., Cossick, K. L., & Zmud, R. W. (1992). A synthesis of research on requirements analysis and knowledge acquisition techniques. *Management Information Systems Quarterly*, *16*(1), 117–138. doi:10.2307/249704

Clemont, A., & Besselaar, O. (1993). A retrospective look at PD projects. *Communications of the ACM*, *36*(4), 29–39. doi:10.1145/153571.163264

Csikszentmihaly, M. (1991). *Flow: the psychology of optimal experience*. New York, USA: Harper Collins.

Davis, G. (1982). Strategies for information requirements determination. *IBM Systems Journal*, *21*(1), 4–31. doi:10.1147/sj.211.0004

Dubois, E., & Pohl, K. (2003). RE 02: A major step toward a mature requirements engineering community. *IEEE Software*, *20*(1), 14–15. doi:10.1109/MS.2003.1159024

Gawlinski, M. (2003). *Interactive television production*. Oxford: Focal Press.

Grönroos, C. (2007). *Service management and marketing - customer management in service competition*. Chichester: Wiley.

Hänninen, J., Tuunanen, T., & Vartiainen, T. (2015, August 13-15). Value Co-Creation for Cyber-Physical Systems in Mining and Construction Industry. *Paper presented at theAmericas Conference on Information Systems (AMCIS)*, Puerto Rico.

Hevner, A. R., March, S. T., & Park, J. (2004). Design Research in Information Systems Research. *Management Information Systems Quarterly*, *28*(1), 75–105.

Hill, A. V., Collier, D. A., Froehle, C. M., Goodale, J. C., Metters, R. D., & Verma, R. (2002). Research opportunities in service process design. *Journal of Operations Management*, *20*(2), 189–202. doi:10.1016/S0272-6963(01)00092-4

Hirschheim, R., Heinzl, K. K., & Lyytinen, K. (1995). *Information Systems Development and Data Modelling*. Cambridge University Press. doi:10.1017/CBO9780511895425

Hirschheim, R., Klein, H. K., & Lyytinen, K. (2003). *Information Systems Development and Data Modeling: Conceptual and Philosophical Foundations*. Cambridge University Press.

Iivari, J. (1990a). Hierarchical Spiral Model for Information-System and Software- Development. 1. Theoretical Background. *Information and Software Technology*, *32*(6), 386–399. doi:10.1016/0950-5849(90)90125-B

Iivari, J. (1990b). Hierarchical Spiral Model for Information-System and Software- Development. 2. Design Process. *Information and Software Technology*, *32*(7), 450–458. doi:10.1016/0950-5849(90)90160-S

Iivari, J., & Lyytinen, K. (1999). Research on Information Systems Development in Scandinavia- Unity in Plurality. *Scandinavian Journal of Information Systems*, *10*(1-2), 135–185.

Jarke, M., & Pohl, K. (1994). Requirements Engineering in 2001 - (Virtually) Managing a Changing Reality. *Software Engineering Journal*, *9*(6), 257–266. doi:10.1049/sej.1994.0035

Järvinen, P. (2007). Action research is similar to design science. *Quality & Quantity*, *41*(1), 37–54. doi:10.1007/s11135-005-5427-1

Jirotka, M., & Goguen, J. (Eds.). (1994). *Requirements Engineering: Social and Technical Issues*. Academic Press.

Kautz, K. (2001). Trends in the research on software process improvement in Scandinavia. *Scandinavian Journal of Information Systems*, *13*, 3–6.

Keil, M., & Carmel, E. (1995). Customer developer links in software-development. *Communications of the ACM*, *38*(5), 33–44. doi:10.1145/203356.203363

Lamb, R., & Kling, R. (2003). Reconceptualizing users as social actors in information systems research. *Management Information Systems Quarterly*, *27*(2), 197–235.

Lusch, R. F., & Nambisan, S. (2015). Service innovation: a service-dominant logic perspective. *Management Information Systems Quarterly*, *39*(1), 155–175.

March, S., & Smith, G. (1995). Design and natural science research on information technology. *Decision Support Systems*, *15*(4), 251–266. doi:10.1016/0167-9236(94)00041-2

Mathiassen, L., Saarinen, T., Tuunanen, T., & Rossi, M. (2007). A Contingency Model for Requirements Development. *Journal of the Association for Information Systems*, *8*(11), 569–597.

McKenna, B., Tuunanen, T., & Gardner, L. (2013). Consumers adoption of information services. *Information & Management*, *50*(5), 248–257. doi:10.1016/j.im.2013.04.004

Menor, L. J., Takikonda, M. V., & Sampson, S. E. (2002). New service development: Areas for exploitation and exploration. *Journal of Operations Management*, *20*(2), 135–157. doi:10.1016/S0272-6963(01)00091-2

Merisalo-Rantanen, H., Tuunanen, T., & Rossi, M. (2005). Is extreme programming just old wine in new bottles: A comparison of two cases. *Journal of Database Management*, *16*(4), 41–61. doi:10.4018/jdm.2005100103

Ostrom, A. L., Parasuraman, A., Bowen, D. E., Patricio, L., Voss, C. A., & Lemon, K. (2015). Service research priorities in a rapidly changing context. *Journal of Service Research*, *18*(2), 127–159. doi:10.1177/1094670515576315

Peffers, K., Tuunanen, T., Rothenberger, M., & Chatterjee, S. (2008). A design science research methodology for information systems research. *Journal of Management Information Systems*, *24*(3), 45–78. doi:10.2753/MIS0742-1222240302

Penttinen, E. (2007). *Transition from products to services within the manufacturing business* [Unpublished Doctoral dissertation]. Helsinki School of Economics, Helsinki.

Pihlström, M. (2007). Committed to content provider or mobile channel? determinants of continuous mobile multimedia service use. *Journal of Information Technology Theory and Application*, *9*(1), 1–23.

Rapoport, R. N. (1970). Three dilemmas of action research. *Human Relations*, *23*(6), 499–513. doi:10.1177/001872677002300601

Redlynx. (2009). TV-centered Cross-Media Games and Entertainment. Retrieved from http://www.redlynx.com

Smart, K. L., & Whiting, M. E. (2001). Designing Systems that support learning and use: A Customer-centered approach. *Information & Management*, *39*(3), 177–190. doi:10.1016/S0378-7206(01)00089-1

Soanes, C., & Stevenson, A. (Eds.). (2004). *Concise Oxford English Dictionary* (11th ed.). Oxford: Oxford University Press.

Sommerville, I. (2001). *Software Engineering* (6th ed.). Addison-Wesley.

Stuart, F. I., & Tax, S. (2004). Toward an integrative approach to designing service experiences Lessons learned from theatre. *Journal of Operations Management*, *22*(6), 690–627.

Thomke, S., & von Hippel, E. (2002). Customers as innovators - A new way to create value. *Harvard Business Review*, *80*(4), 74. PMID:12024760

Tuunanen, T. (2003). A New Perspective on Requirements Elicitation Methods. *Journal of Information Technology Theory and Application*, *5*(3), 45–62.

Tuunanen, T. (2009). The Future of Services is Changing (Video). Retrieved from http://www.tuunanen.fi

Tuunanen, T., & Govindji, H. (2016). Understanding flow experience from users requirements. *Behaviour & Information Technology*, *35*(2), 134–150. doi:10.1080/0144929X.2015.1015167

Tuunanen, T., & Kuo, I. T. (2015). The effect of culture on requirements: A value-based view of prioritization. *European Journal of Information Systems*, *24*(3), 295–313. doi:10.1057/ejis.2014.29

Tuunanen, T., Myers, M., & Cassab, H. (2010). A conceptual framework for consumer information systems development. *Pacific Asia Journal of the Association for Information Systems*, *2*(1), 5.

Tuunanen, T., Peffers, K., & Gengler, C. (2004). Wide audience requirements engineering (WARE): a practical method and case study. Helsinki School of Economics.

Valkonen, K., Lindström, N., Natunen, L., Isoviita, R., & Tuunanen, T. (2015, August). Balance of Hedonic and Utilitarian Values in Information Systems Use. *Proceedings of theScandinavian Conference on Information Systems* (pp. 165-176). Springer International Publishing. doi:10.1007/978-3-319-21783-3_12

van Aken, J. E. (2004). Management research based on the paradigm of the design sciences: The quest for field-tested and grounded technological rules. *Journal of Management Studies*, *41*(2), 219–246. doi:10.1111/j.1467-6486.2004.00430.x

Vartiainen, T., & Tuunanen, T. (2016). Value Co-Creation and Co-Destruction in an IS Artifact: Contradictions of Geocaching. *Paper presented at theHawaii International Conference on System Sciences*, Hawaii. doi:10.1109/HICSS.2016.160

Vredenburg, K., Mao, J., Smith, P. W., & Carey, T. (2002). A survey of user-centered design practise. *CHI Letters, 12*(2).

Walls, J., Widmeyer, G., & El Sawy, O. (1992). Building an Information System Design Theory for Vigilant EIS. *Information Systems Research*, *3*(1), 36–59. doi:10.1287/isre.3.1.36

Chapter 8
Consumer Information Systems as Services:
Study of Emerging IPTV Market in New Zealand

Tuure Tuunanen
University of Jyväskylä, Finland

Lesley Gardner
University of Auckland, Australia

Martin Bastek
DEVK, Germany

ABSTRACT

Consumer Information Systems (CIS) are a type of information systems that provides services to consumers instead of addressing users in traditional organizational settings, such as Internet based television. Services typically involve a trade-off between achieving high service productivity and quality. The use of service mass customization to successfully address these issues of both productivity and quality in a service context is proposed. We suggest that the development of Consumer Information Systems as Services (CISaS) may achieve such service mass customization. This paper presents a conceptual framework and investigates how it applies to a set of Internet Protocol Television (IPTV) offerings as an emerging market in New Zealand.

INTRODUCTION

The era of Consumer Information Systems is upon us. Typically, information systems (IS) have been developed for organisations and their associated users. Today, however, we observe that this traditional view is frequently challenged by the advent of systems that target a new kind of user, the consumer. These users may not reside within organisational reach any longer. As such, they are accustomed to seek entertainment or even pleasure through different kinds of information technology enabled services such

DOI: 10.4018/978-1-5225-2139-6.ch008

as television programming via broadcasting or cable networks (Tuunainen & Tuunanen, 2011; Tuunainen, Tuunanen, & Bastek, 2009). We, therefore, propose that users are becoming discerning consumers and behave as such.

The Concise Oxford English Dictionary (Soanes & Stevenson, 2004) defines a consumer as:

1. A person or thing that eats or uses something.
2. A person who buys goods and services for personal use.

A consumer can enjoy watching a TV program (consume it) without having to pay for it. In this case, the TV program may actually be "paid for" (indirectly) by advertising. An alternative is for consumers to purchase TV programs directly (e.g. via a subscription service or pay per view), this is an increasing trend and is influencing the rapid takeoff of IPTV in all markets in the developed world as well as the developing (Atiq, Srinivasan, & Gardner, 2013; Tuunainen & Tuunanen, 2011; Tuunainen et al., 2009). Decades of research into consumer, behavioral psychology and marketing indicate that consumption is motivated by the predicted utility of the good or service. Consumers use rational and emotional-based assessments of utility in their predictions (Baba & Fedorikhin, 1999). Thus, the object of consumption will have utilitarian and/or hedonic value from the consumer perspective (Valkonen, Lindström, Natunen, Isoviita, & Tuunanen, 2015).

An information system, in turn, is often defined as the interplay of technology, software and people with the purpose of storing, distributing and communicating information. Traditional information systems research has assumed that users derive utilitarian value from the offering. Recently, some researchers have described an information system as a system of communication used by members of some human group or social actors (Beynon-Davies, 2002; Lamb & Kling, 2003). The social nature of modern information systems requires a refocus of thinking about the utility that users derive from the system.

We therefore define Consumer Information Systems as,

Systems that enable consumer value co-creation through the development and implementation of information technology enabled processes that integrate system value propositions with customer value drivers (Tuunanen, Myers, & Cassab, 2010).

This CIS definition covers both the service nature of CIS and the information technology basis for such services, which facilitates the provision of hedonic utility. This point highlights a divergence from the traditional view of systems development and opens interesting avenues for research on the service nature of CIS. This recognition of consumers as users is especially the case with the emergence of new internet-enabled multimedia services where consumers can become participants and co-creators of the television experience or "service encounter". Another difference is that the concept of services (Grönroos, 2007b; Menor, Takikonda, & Sampson, 2002) takes centre stage (as opposed to the idea of creating a distinct IS software product). The focus therefore shifts to innovating, designing and developing Internet-enabled, or similar, services.

To characterize CIS further, we need to define the term service in this context. We suggest that a service provides various kind(s) of value to its receiver and it is an intangible artefact. Current market changes in the mobile services field could be a good way to visualize this. Looking at Apple Inc and Samsung inc, they repeatedly developed ranges of consumer devices, associated software and Internet services to support their machines, Apples iPhone, iPad, Apple Watch, iTunes, and AppStore is a classic and highly successful example of this behaviour (Tuunainen & Tuunanen, 2011; Tuunainen et al., 2009; Tuunainen, Tuunanen, & Piispanen, 2011). Let's consider how Apple Inc has changed the mobile phone market. This has not been the end-result of their innovative touch user interface. Moreover, the change in their business model has been deeper. Apple is actually trying to change the mobile phone to a service platform, which they can manage through their AppStore distribution service. In other words, Apple is providing entertainment, social and educational content as a service offering (Grönroos, 2007a, p. 6), 2012, 2013 to consumers as well as technology.

Hence, we take a broader view as to what is a service in relation to CIS. We see that a service is something that takes place between a service provider and a consumer. It is more specifically an event in time and space where a service encounter (Bitner, Brown, & Meuter, 2000) materializes and the service is consumed mediated through technology. Such a transaction will occur when the consumer's perceived view of utility, hedonic pleasure, ease-of-use and simplicity have been satisfied. An example of CIS can be found within the recently popularised domain of Internet Protocol Television (IPTV) and Internet TV, e.g. Netflix, Hulu etc. These technological changes are driving the market towards enabling consumers not only to participate, but also to be part of the production, or creation, of CIS. Such participation encourages CIS to be used interactively by consumers by providing procedures to enable the access, process, and manipulation of data over a network. This feature of value co-creation is facilitated by the social interaction between consumers and producers of services via different feedback mechanisms (such as Facebook and other social networking services (Edvardsson, Tronvoll, & Gruber, 2011; Kohler, Fueller, Matzler, & Stieger, 2011)).

When looking at CIS we are very mindful that service provision is particularly aimed at consumers. Since CIS are tools for service provision, CIS development needs to pay particular attention to the specific characteristics of services. Service's quality is determined by how a consumer perceives the service (Bleuel & Patton, 1994) by constantly improving the productivity or efficiency of services (Harker, 1995). Thus, this aspect of quality is closely linked with productivity of services (Normann, 2000). However, typically a trade-off between achieving high service quality and high productivity creates challenges to service development (Lovelock, 1983). This is a similar dilemma that software engineers have faced when shifting from project-oriented development to product-oriented development.

Software engineers have adapted product platforms (Robertson & Ulrich, 1998), which constitute the basis for leveraging the development work over multitude of products based on similar features. More specifically research into family-based product development (Du, Jiao, & Tseng, 2001) is proposed as an approach to the mass customisation of software products. One such approach has been Software Product Families (Pohl, Böckle, & van der Linden, 2005), where software products are developed by using a common platform where product families can be 'harvested'. This concept goes beyond of just developing product lines as it sees the 'family ties' between product families. Thus, the software family concept can be said to take the reuse of code further versus product line thinking. Where product lines are based on the core product extension within a single area, such as variations of operating system's versions, which Microsoft has successfully used, product family thinking expands the domain. One such example is how Apple has managed to do this with their operating systems. They have created new product families based on the same code family. Current Apple computers and their portable music players, iPods, share the similar operating system. Similarly, iPhone uses a variation of the same operating system. However, all these are separate product lines from the consumer's perspective.

The area of service mass customisation (Silveira, Borenstein, & Fogliatto, 2001) has not been well researched in comparison to the product and software product development sector. If we consider quality and productivity as key issues in CIS development, service mass customisation becomes interesting. By applying a service mass customisation approach to CIS development both quality and productivity aspects of service could be perhaps addressed. Drawing on insights into family-based software development, the question arises, can we use similar concepts to overcome quality and productivity challenges when developing strongly service oriented information systems, such as CIS? Thus we present our research question, which is "what elements constitute a CIS as Services".

In this chapter, we seek to answer this question through a literature review and a case study. The next sections review literature on service management and software product families to understand these concepts more fully. Subsequently, insights from this literature review are used to construct a framework to describe the elements constituting CIS as Services and present results of our explorative case study. Finally, we present the findings and discuss them before concluding the paper.

MANAGING A SERVICE OFFERING

Grönroos (2007a) presents an interesting view of managing a company's service offering. Here we are addressing how to manage the overarching service offering. It consists of four steps: managing image and communication; developing the service concept; developing a basic service package; developing an augmented service offering. Image and communication are integral parts of developing the service offering (Antioco, Moenaert, Feinberg, & Wetzels, 2008). Hence, the service concept in Grönroos' thinking acts as a foundation for the basic service package and for the subsequent augmentation of this package, which consists of four parts: core solution, enabling service, enhancing services, and the user interface (UI). The subsequent deployment of these packages is supported by Chong and Carraro's, (2006) discussions about their 'software as a service maturity' model. It is a good foundation for managing service offerings from a software product development perspective. The basic four levels of the model were developed to indicate increasing levels of sophistication of software configuration and deployment. The maturity model therefore provides increasing levels of deployment efficiency on behalf of the vendor while the users' individualized experience remains unchanged (Chong & Carraro, 2006). We note here, however, that Grönroos (2007) extends this view of service provision to include enabling services - these are discussed next.

In order for customers to use the core solution, often some additional service components are required. Such services, Grönroos (2007a; 2000) calls enabling services. These services allow the use of the core solution and it is not possible to consume or use the core solution without them. Enhancing services do not facilitate the consumption or use of the core solution. Instead, they are used to increase the value of the core solution and/or to differentiate the core solution from those of competitors. Finally, the UI is responsible for the communication between the user and the system, that is, for every aspect of computerised interaction. Figure 1 presents the NetOffer model (Grönroos et al., 2000), which the above is based on. It shows that the process of developing the service offering is highly integrated. Information is a vital part of all NetOffer elements, and, thus, of any Internet offering. On first inspection, such a service development approach may reflect similar marketing models already in existence, such as Satellite or Cable TV or telecommunication. The main issue to notice here is the effective method of control of these offerings. The end-user must directly interact with the service provider to purchase and adjust the available services, in doing this they must negotiate and enter into a static agreement. Such static agreements may last from a day to several months, but at that point in time the agreement is fixed. Here, however, through the use of CIS a dynamic arrangement may be facilitated where consumers purchase or subscribe on demand for the services required.

The concept of service augmentation, which Grönroos presents, indicates an ever changing environment that is flexible enough to be adapted to fit the requirements of any service development organisation. The general nature of service augmentation allows its constituent aspects to be examined in as much or as little detail as necessary. The basic service package determines what customers receive from the company, that is, it covers outcome-related features. However, it does not cover how customers perceive the service process, that is, no process-related features are taken into account from the service development aspects. Both what customers receive and how they perceive the service process are integral parts of the total service offering (Bitner et al., 2000; Grönroos, 2007a).

Communication (Zeithaml, Berry, & Parasuraman, 1988) and customer participation (see, e.g., Dong, Evans, & Zou, 2008) are the two elements that augment the service. The communication element refers to the dialogue that occurs between the customer and the service provider. Whereas customer participation relates to the amount that customers are able to impact the service delivery. It denotes the skills, knowledge, and interest of consumers in terms of operating the UI. Customers can either improve or depreciate the quality of the service with their willingness to participate in the process. For instance, a customer may: make purchases, ask questions, receive responses, and participate in group discussions with other customers. Customer participation therefore involves two aspects. Firstly, customer participation has a co-production aspect (see, e.g., Anderson, 2006) since the customer is involved in the service delivery process. Secondly, customer participation has a co-creation aspect (Tuunanen et al., 2010; Vartiainen & Tuunanen, 2016). By providing information, a customer can co-create a solution for either his or other customers' value-creating process. Elements of communication and customer participation can be argued to enhance the functional quality of the service offering as they influence how customers perceive the total service offering. The "how" dimension allows the customers to appreciate the technical quality of the basic service package, namely the 'what' dimension.

As mentioned, one of the main challenges in service development has been the optimisation of service offerings (Harker, 1995). The quality of developed services is clearly one of the main focus areas of such optimization efforts. For a product, it is possible to determine its quality objectively by measuring it against the specifications created up-front. In the case of services, however, this is often not possible due to a lack of definite specifications. Moreover, different customers have different expectations of what constitutes a high-quality service. That is, specifications take the form of expectations held by every consumer (Bleuel & Patton, 1994). Customers often hold three types of expectations when it comes to services. Firstly, the service needs to have as few or as many features as requested. Secondly, each of these elements has to meet the customer's standards which implies that a certain threshold of service deficiencies should not be crossed (Normann, 2000). Thirdly, the service needs to be delivered in a timely manner since a customer is only willing to wait for a limited amount of time (Duclos, Siha, & Lummus, 1995). Thus, the quality aspect of services refers to value perceived by the consumer.

Service development often struggles between achieving high service quality through customisation and achieving high productivity by reducing costs through standardisation (Lovelock, 1983). Usually, the introduction of more cost-effective, standardised production resources and processes leads to a decrease in service quality as perceived by the customer (Grönroos, 2007a). Applying a mass customisation approach makes it possible to produce customised services in a cost-effective manner (Normann, 2000). Besides cost-effectiveness and customisation, mass customisation also provides the means of achieving a consistently low level of deficiencies in the service process (MacCarthy, Brabazon, & Bramham, 2002).

This will enable the company to improve time to market for its services (Jiao, Ma, & Tseng, 2003). Thus, mass customisation has the potential to address all aspects of service productivity and quality as previously discussed.

In order to achieve these benefits, service modularity has been seen as a key concept (Dörbecker & Böhmann, 2013). Hence, services in integrated solutions should be designed as modular units and developed by mixing and matching these units to provide different combinations to meet specific customer and market needs (Baines, Lightfoot, Benedettini, & Kay, 2009). A modular service offering of an organization thus consists of standardized base services, customized services, and their combinations. Service process modularity allows reuse of process steps that can be combined in service implementation, which in turn allows flexibility and customization (Bask, Lipponen, Rajahonka, & Tinnilä, 2010). Commonly mentioned benefits of modularization include larger product variety, improved flexibility, simplification of complex systems, enhanced quality, and cost savings (Jose & Tollenaere, 2005; van Liere, Hagdorn, Hoogeweegen, & Vervest, 2004). Thus, the application of modularity has been acknowledged as potentially beneficial in the service context (Bask et al., 2010; Tuunanen & Cassab, 2011). Furthermore, Tuunanen and Cassab (2011) have argued that service process modularization enables the firm to generate market impact efficiently through service extensions characterized by reuse and variation of existing service processes.

Modularity aims to decompose a system into independent module types, where a module type is a grouping of components that share some characteristics. Commonality describes the grouping of similar module variants under a particular module type. That is, modularity, with its decomposed module types, describes a class of possible services (Tuunanen, Bask, & Merisalo-Rantanen, 2012). Specific services are created using the concept of variation (Tuunanen & Cassab, 2011). Service variants share the same

Figure 1. The NetOffer
Source: Based on Grönroos (2000).

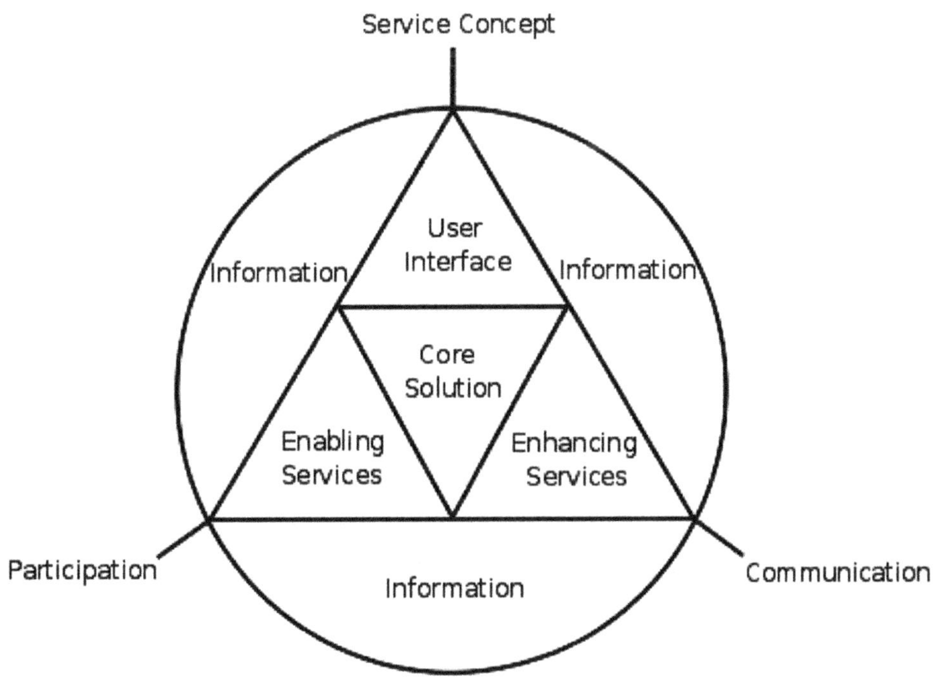

module types but take on different instances of every module type. Thus, service variants differentiate according to the commonality between module variants. With service provision in CIS being realised by IT, a promising step is to turn to mass customisation approaches for software. One such approach is that of Software Product Families (Pohl et al., 2005), which is reviewed below.

SOFTWARE PRODUCT FAMILIES

The concept of a product family can be defined as ``a group of related products that share common features, components or sub-systems and satisfy a variety of markets." (Ramesh, Tiwana, & Mohan, 2002, p. 355). We note that companies such as Nokia have been very successful in the production of a family of products (Bennett et al., 2000), all of which have the same basic features but also have a wide range of product differentiation and configurability, so that all sectors of the consumer and business market are served with satisfactory telecommunication products and services for the task (McDonagh, Olariu, Hava, & Thorpe, 2013; Van der Linden, 2002).

A close concept to this is a product line refers to "a group of related systems that address a market niche or mission." (Brownsword & Clements, 1996, p. 1). The family and line concepts differ in two dimensions: product development and market role. While aspects of product development are not addressed in the line concept, products in a family are developed using shared features, components, or sub-systems. That is, the basis of a product family approach is systematic reuse (Brownsword & Clements, 1996; Mohan & Ramesh, 2003). Software Product Families are an example of a family-based development approach (Pohl et al., 2005). Van der Linden (2002) indicates the European consortium, including Nokia, which defines development of product families, populations and has developed a process for developing such lines. According to Pohl (2005) there are three main drivers for applying a software product family approach:

1. To lower development costs,
2. To raise system quality, and
3. Shorten development times (Pohl et al., 2005).

As a consequence of three an additional benefit is often the higher degree of customer orientation (McDonagh et al., 2013; van Ommering & Bosch, 2002). In order to provide these benefits, the software product family approach relies on two concepts:

1. Reuse
2. Variation (Mohan & Ramesh, 2003).

Building systems with reusable assets inevitably leads to the problem of reusability versus usefulness (van Ommering & Bosch, 2002). If an asset is extremely useful for a particular product it may be less reusable for implementing other products. Conversely, an asset, which is extremely reusable, may, in fact, be useless for production since it does not offer much to be included in the process. Therefore, it is necessary to strive for a sensible balance between reusability and usefulness. How can we then archive customisation? The variation concept may help with this.

When utilising a reuse concept, a trade-off exists between the aspects of commonality and distinctiveness (Robertson & Ulrich, 1998). Products are only customisable to a certain degree without violating the reuse-focused core of the development approach and implementing diversity seems possible with reusable assets alone (van Ommering & Bosch, 2002). Therefore, the solution for addressing the products' distinctiveness is to introduce a sufficient number of variation points to the assets (Mohan & Ramesh, 2003). Variation points can be used to fine-tune assets when instantiating them into a product. They typically control an asset's internals, the presence or absence of certain assets, or the binding between assets (van Ommering & Bosch, 2002). By following a family approach and its concept of variation points, the creation of new products now becomes a matter of generation or modification (Brownsword & Clements, 1996). In the following section, we use these concepts to develop a framework for consumer information systems services.

CONSUMER INFORMATION SYSTEMS AS SERVICES

From the literature review, we see that the demands of service offerings often match those of software products. In the case of services, mass customisation was, in general, found capable of satisfying these demands. Software product family literature in turn shows how to satisfy these demands in a software context. That is, by using a software product family approach we are able to provide better efficiency, higher customer orientation, a lower level of deficiencies, and a speed-up of the delivery process. Service mass customisation and software product family approaches are based on the same concepts, namely reuse and variation. By applying these to service mass customization we might be able to achieve the desired mass customisation of CIS as Services.

Therefore, we suggest framing CISaS by applying the use of the NetOffer model and the two concepts underlying any service family effort: reuse and variation. The elements of NetOffer provide the necessary understanding of the service as such. That is, NetOffer comprises all elements that need attention to provide a service offering. Firstly, the service concept and the basic service package act as a general foundation of a CISaS. Here we explore the aspects of core services, their components and usability. Furthermore, the service augmentation narrows the service scope down to those elements, which are provided by CIS. Because an offering's success is determined by the phase of service augmentation, the add-on services may need to be managed as a service family. That is, the service family concepts of reuse and variation are utilised to successfully augment services in the NetOffer model. This is synthesized in Table 1 where we present the conceptual framework for Consumer Information Systems as Services.

The CISaS framework is a synthesis of the NetOffer service management approach (Grönroos, 2007a; Grönroos et al., 2000) and software product family thinking (Ramesh et al., 2002, p. 355) where reuse and variation can provide the means of service mass customization. However, it should be noted that it only frames the constituting elements of a CISaS and not the actual process of putting these elements into action. This framework does not address how a CISaS can be managed or developed. In the following section, we use the framework as a lens to interpret how service offerings in IPTV domain are represented.

Table 1. The Consumer Information Systems as Services

Foundation	Elements
Service concept	Service concept
Service package	Core solution
	Enabling services
	Enhancing services
	User interface
Service augmentation	Communication
	Customer participation
Service Families	Reuse
	Variation

RESEARCH METHODOLOGY

We have used an explorative approach and case study methodology to capture the knowledge of practitioners (Benbasat, Goldstein, & Mead, 1987). We explore how companies working in IPTV/Internet TV address elements of CISaS. The unit of analysis for the study is the department of an organization developing and/or managing IPTV/Internet TV based consumer information systems. We use a case study design with interviews conducted with key personnel of each case organization. Furthermore, we used theoretical sampling to select the case organizations. More specifically, the cases were selected based on the observability of the processes of interest (Eisenhardt, 1989). The case organizations operate in New Zealand and offer, or plan to offer, consumer-oriented IPTV/Internet TV services. Potential candidates for the case study were all companies in New Zealand working on or already delivering IPTV/Internet TV services.

Three organizations were selected because of their IPTV/Internet TV offerings, their size, and their market power. Data was gathered through semi-structured interviews. The semi-structured interview protocol is provided in Appendix 1. These were supported by secondary sources provided by the organizations, such as service offering documentation. Two interviews were conducted in each company, resulting in a total of six interviews. All but one interview were face-to-face interviews. The remaining interview was done by telephone. One interview was conducted with two interviewees, resulting in a total of seven people interviewed. The interviews took place in the period from August to October 2007 and all were fully transcribed for analysis purposes.

The large telephone company (in the following: LT) is both a fixed line and mobile operator in New Zealand. Telecommunication services are provided to residential and business customers throughout the country. The first interviewee was the manager of the company's video services department. The interviewee provided the interviewer with an additional data source in the form of a document outlining the company's IPTV strategy. The second interviewee was in charge of the operational side of the video department.

The medium-sized telephone company (in the following: MT) initially started out as a wholesale Internet Service Provider (ISP) and moved over the years to being a telephone company (telco). MT now offers a full range of services to both residential and business customers throughout New Zealand.

The first interviewee was managing the company's marketing efforts. The second interviewee was the company's manager.

The large media company (in the following: LM) is primarily involved in the television business. At the moment, the company mostly offers linear video products over its free-to-air TV stations. The advertising on the company's TV channels mainly generates the income. The interviewee of the first interview was the manager of the company's technology department. The second interviewee was conducted with two employees. One of them was in charge of the company's online development efforts. The second interviewee was one of the company's lead developers.

We used thematic analysis to analyse the collected data[1]. Thematic analysis is a way of analysing qualitative information, which allows the researcher to make sense out of seemingly unrelated material. When applying thematic analysis, the researcher examines occurrences of themes in text. Themes can be described as patterns that can be found in the information (Boyatzis, 1998). By using themes for labelling, it is possible to assign meaning to the information compiled during a study (Miles & Huberman, 1994). In this study, we took a semi-predefined approach to thematic analysis which involves the creation of themes prior to the stage of data collection (Miles & Huberman, 1994). The themes of the CISaS framework were used for analysis although we did keep an open mind for theoretical flexibility and avoided forcing any data to the conceptual framework. Moreover, by looking for occurrences of these themes in the data, meaning is assigned to the information gathered. Based on this sense-making process, it is possible to analyse a particular service offering in terms of how this offering addresses each aspect of the CISaS framework.

FINDINGS

In this section, we describe our findings and relate them to our framework, summarised in Table 1, to provide insights into the status of each company service provisions. All case companies had at least some of the core service present. The uncertainties surrounding IPTV/Internet TV offerings currently prevent the companies from addressing all aspects of the service concept. The companies are unsure about what they can deliver that has value to their customers. Lacking a clear focus, they are not able to provide detailed information about the service provision and the kinds of resources needed. The two telcos plan to tie their offering to Freeview[2], the digital TV broadcast system in New Zealand. Generally, the service concepts for all three companies are subject to change once the companies gain a better understanding of the IPTV/Internet TV market.

In terms of the core solution, the two telcos are still evaluating and trialing off-the-shelf streaming server solutions for their IPTV offerings. So far, at the time of interview, neither of the companies has rolled out their service. In case of LM, the core solution of delivering Internet TV is available to customers and the service has been successful.

Quality of Service (QoS) was an important issue to the two telcos who were experiencing problems enabling delivery of service content. Both companies are struggling with slow network speeds and QoS issues, which are critical to their IPTV offering. As telcos, both companies were able to improve the current situation by investing in the network infrastructure. This was, in a matter of fact, one of their main concerns at the moment, which seemed to override everything else. LM was also suffering from low bandwidth availability of Internet, which is a major challenge in general in New Zealand[3]. Only one third of the Internet users had a broadband connection at the time of the study and in New Zealand broadband connection was defined as 256Kbits, which severely limits streaming of video. Furthermore, LM's Internet TV offering did not rely on a managed network with a guaranteed QoS. Thus, LM was already able to deliver its content to consumers although the QoS varied according to the network infrastructure of a geographical location. Although its enabling service is in place, LM was still working on improving its provision by evaluating a common approach to content delivery together with other media companies.

Two of the case organizations have acknowledged the importance of enhancing its service by offering attractive content to consumers. LM is in negotiations with content providers to gain access to additional material on top of that available on Freeview channels. MT, in turn, regards content as one of the main drivers for consumer adoption of its Internet TV offering. Therefore, the company was also in negotiations with content providers to be able to offer additional content besides the Freeview channel content, but it was also convinced that content is a powerful means of differentiation. Actually, for its Internet TV offering, LM considered focusing on local content from New Zealand producers. New Zealand has been very successful in leveraging its success with Peter Jackson's Lord of the Rings trilogy and this has created a relatively large number of film and media production companies in the country[4]. Some of this content comes from the company's archive, which LM currently tries to make available as widely as possible. LM was also the only case organization to produce exclusive content for its Internet TV service offering.

All three companies were aware of the UI's importance for a successful service offering. For the two telcos, the UI is dependent on the IPTV solution selected, i.e. software vendor's streaming server. Since the commercial server software provides the UI, there had been a little need for the companies to put any additional resources into this aspect. In case of LM, however, the UI was partly developed in-house by their information technology department. It had a customized UI built on top of the commercial streaming server solution. This UI is functional and already in use by consumers.

At the time of the study, all three companies were still working on their core solutions for IPTV services. The companies all had adopted the strategy of offering an initially rather limited set of services which are constantly adjusted and extended according to customer demand. The two telcos relied on the service capabilities of their IPTV solutions whereas LM developed its communication services, i.e. customized streaming server, in-house and was at the time concerned with prioritising its future service development efforts and building a development road map. A follow-up of the three organizations showed that only LM has been successful in their IPTV service offering. Furthermore, LT did not have customer participation elements in its IPTV service offering. However, participatory elements were considered to be included in future releases of the service, as the vendor will upgrade its streaming server solution. In the case of MT, participatory elements were not under consideration and disregarded in importance to the service offering. LM, in turn, regarded customer participation as a very important element of its Internet TV offering and the company already had some participatory elements in place in its Internet TV offering and had plans to extend these in future releases. More details about this particular CIS is available from (Tuunainen & Tuunanen, 2011; Tuunainen et al., 2009).

The reuse concept was not applicable to the two telcos. Utilising reuse in the service delivery would require the companies to actually develop services on their own and this was not considered a feasible option in the market situation; two telcos were piloting technical solutions and researching business model possibilities. Moreover, both companies made the use of the services provided by the selected IPTV streaming server solution and did not undertake any development efforts themselves. For LM, reuse was a very important concept. The company, in fact, relied on reuse heavily in its service development efforts in order to leverage its resource to launch new services in a fast tempo (Tuunainen & Tuunanen,

2011; Tuunainen et al., 2009). This was emphasized by the history of the Internet TV solution developed, which was done with a tight budget and delivered in a matter of months.

The concept of varying the service delivery is currently considered by neither LT nor MT. Options to customise the service offering are not seen as a subject of current consumer demand in IPTV. LM considered variation as an important aspect of its Internet TV offering. Making customisation options available to consumers was regarded as a way to differentiate the offering. While the company was not offering any means of customisation at the moment, it planned to automate the customisation process as much as possible so that service differentiation can be introduced without adding a lot of cost. Later, in 2009, they re-launched their Internet TV offering which enabled the company to change and add new content with Web 2.0 technologies.

Table 2 summarises the findings of the analysis. For each element and company, an indicator is given on how this theme is addressed at the particular company. These indicators are: all aspects of the element are in place; some aspects of the theme are in place; company is currently in the planning stage of putting some aspects in place; aspects are currently not considered; element is not applicable to the company. The term "in place" indicates that the facility to provide the service is available to the customer on demand. "Partly in place" suggests that the organisation has some capability but is still experimenting with the final roll out of the service. Some organisations are still in the process of evaluating options in terms of machinery, software and roll out and these are determined as "under consideration". Some elements of services are currently not being considered for release to the consumer for various reasons: stability, market share etc. and these are noted as "not considered".

The analysis of these three organizations shows that all case companies had a rudimentary service concept in place. The uncertainties surrounding IPTV/Internet TV offerings currently prevent the companies from addressing all aspects of the service concept. The companies are unsure about what they can deliver that has value to their customers. Lacking a clear focus, they are not able to provide detailed information about the service provision and the kinds of resources needed. Thus, the service concepts for all three companies are subject to change once the companies gain a better understanding of the IPTV/Internet TV market. In terms of the core solution, the two telcos are still evaluating and trialling off-the-shelf solutions for their IPTV offerings. So far, neither of the companies has rolled out their service and

Table 2. Findings

Foundation	Theme	LT	MT	LM
Service concept	Service concept	Partly in place	Partly in place	Partly in place
Service package	Core solution	Partly in place	Partly in place	In place
	Enabling services	Partly in place	Partly in place	In place
	Enhancing services	Partly in place	Partly in place	Partly in place
	User interface	In place	In place	In place
Service augmentation	Communication	Partly in place	Partly in place	Partly in place
	Customer participation	Under consideration	Not considered	Partly in place
Service Families	Reuse	n/a	n/a	Partly in place
	Variation	Not considered	Not considered	Under consideration

they have downplayed or discontinued their IPTV services. In case of LM, the core solution of delivering Internet TV is available, the service is working and accessible by consumers is proving to be successful.

The evaluation of the case companies shows that the two telcos are basically at the same stage in terms of applying the elements of the CISaS framework. All elements are, at least partly, visible except those of enhancing services, customer participation, and variation. The reuse theme was found applicable to neither of the two companies. The similarities in the evaluation are reflective of the facts that both companies focus on an IPTV offering, were heavily in the planning stage for rolling out their offerings, and also operated in the same geographical market. The LM company was found to, at least partly, address all elements except that of variation where the company were still in the planning stage. Thus, the LM's service offering can be considered to be more advanced than those of the two telcos.

DISCUSSION

We concur with Grönroos et al (2000) and see that the NetOffer service concept can potentially be used as the basis for investigating CIS as Services and that our findings provide preliminary support for the conceptual framework presented by the paper - Consumer Information Systems as Services. All three main elements (i.e. core solution, enabling service, and UI) were in place in the case organizations. However, we also found that the fourth element of enhancing services may not be necessary when first rolling out the CIS. However, we propose that enhancing services should not be neglected especially when a company wants its service offering to have more value for consumers and encourage brand loyalty. Furthermore, the importance of service augmentation was supported by our findings. We found that service augmentation needs a basic set of services to build upon. That is, in case of an insufficient basic service package, it may not be sensible to extensively address the step of service augmentation.

The findings also gave some initial support for the applicability of the reuse and variation concepts derived from software product literature (Brownsword & Clements, 1996; Böckle et al., 2002; Clements & Northrop, 2002; Du et al., 2001; Pohl et al., 2005; Robertson & Ulrich, 1998; Van der Linden, 2002; van Ommering & Bosch, 2002). However, in our case organizations reuse and variation were treated as separate concepts. For the telcos, this separation was due to the fact that the reuse concept did not lie in the companies' sphere of influence, whereas variation of the service does. For LM, reuse was already actively applied but variation was only to be considered for future stages of the service offering. In fact, all remedies identified by the companies to address uncertainty in their CISaS offerings are based on the two concepts of reuse and variation (Tuunanen et al., 2012; Tuunanen & Cassab, 2011). This opens an interesting avenue for repurposing concepts originating from service marketing (Grönroos, 2007a; Grönroos et al., 2000) and how they might apply in other CISaS offerings, such as Apple's AppStore for iPhone, virtual gaming environments etc.

Finally, modularity research has a tradition in product, manufacturing, and organizational contexts, but modularity of services is still an emerging research area services (Dörbecker & Böhmann, 2013; Tuunanen et al., 2012). Modularity can provide benefits to service design (Tuunanen et al., 2012); make complexity manageable (Baldwin & Clark, 2000), help deal uncertainty, improve service quality, and provide cost efficiency. In service design, it is extremely important to understand the nature of service architecture and the related modularity (Voss & Hsuan, 2009). We argue that service augmentation for CISaS needs to be done constantly – as a company needs to adjust their service offering to market demand. One way to address this is to adjust the service delivery and modularize the service development. This concurs with (Lim, 1994) who has argued that the reuse concept could also be used to speed up the development process of new service offerings, which in turn enables a more timely satisfaction of consumer demands (Tuunanen & Cassab, 2011). In addition, a constant adjustment of the available customization options would be needed in order to address development uncertainties. By utilising variation in the service delivery, it might be possible to provide on demand customised services to consumers as proposed by (Jiao et al., 2003).

CONCLUSION

In conclusion we have reviewed the current literature examining the trade-off between quality and productivity in a service context (Lovelock, 1983). In doing so we have explored elements of service mass customisation, (Normann, 2000), and developed the Consumer Information Systems as Services (CISaS) framework. We suggest that this framework can potentially provide the foundations for the first steps towards a mass customisation of CIS based digital services (Tuunanen et al., 2010). In doing so, we recognise that our framework is built upon the NetOffer model (Grönroos et al., 2000) and the concepts of reuse and variation (Tuunanen et al., 2012; Tuunanen & Cassab, 2011) and that it derives some of the elements from the existing literature on services and mass customisation.

From this theorisation we have applied our framework in a case study environment. Within this study we explored how companies working in IPTV/Internet TV address the elements of CISaS. We conducted an explorative case study of three organizations that visualize how the framework's elements are applied within one particular industrial setting. We applied thematic analysis to examine occurrences of the framework's elements in the semi-structured interview data. The case study provides preliminary support for the proposed framework's elements, but it also showed that our case organizations only partly address these elements at present.

This chapter contributes to knowledge by proposing a *Consumer Information Systems as Services* framework. By presenting the CISaS framework, this study takes the one of the first steps towards an actual mass customisation approach to consumer information systems. Besides guiding the efforts towards possible CISaS management approaches, the framework can also potentially be useful for evaluating CISaS offerings from business model perspective (Tuunainen & Tuunanen, 2011; Tuunainen et al., 2009; Tuunainen et al., 2011). Furthermore, our study employed the CISaS framework in a case study with companies working in IPTV/Internet TV in New Zealand. Therefore, our study can potentially provide insights into current practices and issues in the IPTV/Internet TV field, especially in the case of smaller developed countries. The practical contribution of this research lies in setting the stage for the development of a mass customisation approach to CIS as Services. With a CISaS approach in place, companies might be able to address the current trade-off between achieving high service quality and high service productivity. Hence, it can potentially provide a conceptual roadmap for service development in the area.

Our study has two main limitations that should be recognized. Firstly, two out of three case companies had not yet rolled out their CIS service offerings during the time of study and did not undertake any service in-house development efforts, but instead relied on off-the-shelf solutions for their service offerings. Secondly, we faced a limited set of suitable organizations for case study selection and the team sizes in these organizations were as well limited, which in turn is reflected in the number of interviews conducted. However, we were able to interview the key players in each of the organizations and these organizations were selected as they were considered to be the leaders in the IPTV/Internet TV development activities in New Zealand. Therefore, we feel that these limitations do not cast a shadow on our preliminary findings because of the explorative nature of our study. Moreover, we see that our framework can be used in other more established fields of CIS; such as mobile services or self-service technologies. Furthermore, more careful investigation of CISaS elements should be completed to understand viability of the proposed framework in other industry settings.

Finally, in the literature there is an assumption is that there is a value chain type approach of adding value for the user and for the organization a service. The service literature argued that value co-creation is a process that involves both the user of an artifact and the firm providing or developing it (Tuunanen et al., 2010). Furthermore, the service literature also highlights the network nature of this value co-creation process, i.e., there are different stakeholders participating in the process of value co-creation (Lusch & Nambisan, 2015; Tuunanen et al., 2010; Vargo & Lusch, 2004). However, there has been little research done in terms of the negative consequences of design and the possible effects of destruction of value by users and other stakeholders of the value creation process (Vartiainen & Tuunanen, 2016). We see that studying the modularization of services, would benefit if would also link this to the value co-creation and co-destruction literature. This offers great opportunities for researchers and the outcomes of such studies would likely impact how we design consumer information services such as IPTV. Similarly, we see that the emerging type of cyber-physical services (Hänninen, Tuunanen, & Vartiainen, 2015; Peters et al., 2016) that combine Internet-of-Things, artificial intelligence, and analytics of sensor based data, would be a highly interesting application of not only modularization, but also how the modularization impacts the value perceived and received by the consumers of such services.

REFERENCES

Anderson, C. (2006). *The Long Tail: Why the Future of Business Is Selling Less of More*. Hyperion.

Antioco, M., Moenaert, R. K., Feinberg, R. A., & Wetzels, M. G. M. (2008). Integrating service and design: The influences of organizational and communication factors on relative product and service characteristics. *Journal of the Academy of Marketing Science*, *36*(4), 501–521. doi:10.1007/s11747-008-0097-x

Atiq, A., Srinivasan, A., & Gardner, L. (2013). Service System Design (SSD) Innovation through Consumer Participation.

Baba, S., & Fedorikhin, A. (1999). Heart and Mind in Conflict: The Interplay of Affect and Cognition in Consumer Decision Making. *The Journal of Consumer Research*, *26*(3), 278–292. doi:10.1086/209563

Baines, T. S., Lightfoot, H. W., Benedettini, O., & Kay, J. M. (2009). The Servitization of Manufacturing A Review of Literature and Reflection on Future Challenges. *Journal of Manufacturing Technology Management*, *20*(5), 547–567. doi:10.1108/17410380910960984

Baldwin, C. Y., & Clark, K. B. (2000). *Design Rules: The Power of Modularity*. MIT Press.

Bask, A., Lipponen, M., Rajahonka, M., & Tinnilä, M. (2010). The Concept of Modularity: Diffusion from Manufacturing to Service Production. *Journal of Manufacturing Technology Management*, *21*(3), 355–375. doi:10.1108/17410381011024331

Benbasat, I., Goldstein, D. K., & Mead, M. (1987). The Case Research Strategy in Studies of Information Systems. *Management Information Systems Quarterly, 11*(3), 369–386. doi:10.2307/248684

Bennett, K., Layzell, P., Budgen, D., Brereton, P., Macaulay, L., & Munro, M. (2000, 5-8 December). Service-based software: the future for flexible software. *Paper presented at the7th Asia-Pacific Software Engineering Conference.* doi:10.1109/APSEC.2000.896702

Beynon-Davies, P. (2002). *Information systems - an introduction to informatics in organizations.* Houndmills: Palgrave.

Bitner, M. J., Brown, S., & Meuter, M. L. (2000). Technology Infusion in Service Encounters. *Journal of the Academy of Marketing Science, 28*(1), 138–149. doi:10.1177/0092070300281013

Bleuel, W. H., & Patton, J. D. Jr. (1994). *Service Management: Principles and Practices.* North Carolina: ISA Press.

Böckle, G., Munoz, J.B., Knauber, P., Krueger, C.W., do Prado Leite, J.C.S., van der Linden, F., … Weiss, D. (2002, August 19-22). Adopting and Institutionalizing a Product Line Culture. *Proceedings of the Second International Conference on Software Product Lines SPLC 2*, San Diego, CA, USA (pp. 49-59).

Boyatzis, R. E. (1998). *Transforming Qualitative Information - Thematic Analysis and Code Development.* Thousand Oaks, CA: Sage.

Brownsword, L., & Clements, P. (1996). A Case Study in Successful Product Line Development.

Chong, F., & Carraro, G. (2006). Architecture Strategies for Catching the Long Tail.

Clements, P., & Northrop, L. (2002). *Software Product Lines - Practices and Patterns.* Boston: Addison-Wesley.

Dong, B., Evans, K. R., & Zou, S. (2008). The effects of customer participation in co-created service recovery. *Journal of the Academy of Marketing Science, 36*(1), 123–137. doi:10.1007/s11747-007-0059-8

Dörbecker, R., & Böhmann, T. (2013). The Concept and Effects of Service Modularity--A Literature Review. *Paper presented at the 2013 46th Hawaii International Conference on System Sciences (HICSS).*

Du, X., Jiao, J., & Tseng, M. M. (2001). Architecture of Product Family: Fundamentals and Methodology. *Concurrent Engineering, 9*(4), 309–325. doi:10.1177/1063293X0100900407

Duclos, L. K., Siha, S. M., & Lummus, R. R. (1995). JIT in Services: A Review of Current Practices and Future Directions for Research. *International Journal of Service Industry Management, 6*(5), 36–52. doi:10.1108/09564239510101518

Eisenhardt, K. M. (1989). Building Theories from Case Study Research. *Academy of Management Review, 14*(4), 532–550.

Grönroos, C. (2007a). *Service Management and Marketing - Customer Management in Service Competition.* Chichester: Wiley.

Grönroos, C. (2007b). *Service management and marketing - customer management in service competition.* Chichester: Wiley.

Grönroos, C., Heinonen, F., Isoniemi, K., & Lindholm, M. (2000). The NetOffer Model: A Case Example from the Virtual Marketspace. *Management Decision*, *38*(4), 243–252. doi:10.1108/00251740010326252

Hänninen, J., Tuunanen, T., & Vartiainen, T. (2015). Value Co-Creation for Cyber-Physical Systems in Mining and Construction Industry.

Harker, P. T. (1995). *Introduction* (pp. 1–10). The Service Productivity and Quality Challenge.

Jiao, J., Ma, Q., & Tseng, M. M. (2003). Towards High Value-Added Products and Services: Mass Customization and Beyond. *Technovation*, *23*(10), 809–821. doi:10.1016/S0166-4972(02)00023-8

Jose, A., & Tollenaere, M. (2005). Modular and platform methods for product family design: Literature analysis. *Journal of Intelligent Manufacturing*, *16*(3), 371–390. doi:10.1007/s10845-005-7030-7

Lamb, R., & Kling, R. (2003). Reconceptualizing Users as Social Actors in Information Systems Research. *Management Information Systems Quarterly*, *27*(2), 197–235.

Lim, W. C. (1994). Effects of Reuse on Quality, Productivity, and Economics. *Software, 11*(5), 23–30. doi:10.1109/52.311048

Lovelock, C. H. (1983). Classifying Services to Gain Strategic Marketing Insights. *Journal of Marketing*, *47*(3), 9–20. doi:10.2307/1251193

Lusch, R. F., & Nambisan, S. (2015). Service Innovation: A Service-Dominant Logic Perspective. *Management Information Systems Quarterly*, *39*(1), 155–175.

MacCarthy, B. L., Brabazon, P. G., & Bramham, J. (2002). *Key Value Attributes in Mass Customization.* In *Moving into Mass Customization - Information Systems and Management Principles*(pp. 71–87).

McDonagh, P., Olariu, C., Hava, A., & Thorpe, C. (2013). Enabling IPTV service assurance using openflow. *Paper presented at the 2013 27th International Conference on Advanced Information Networking and Applications Workshops (WAINA).* doi:10.1109/WAINA.2013.91

Menor, L. J., Takikonda, M. V., & Sampson, S. E. (2002). New service development: Areas for exploitation and exploration. *Journal of Operations Management*, *20*(2), 135–157. doi:10.1016/S0272-6963(01)00091-2

Miles, M. B., & Huberman, A. M. (1994). *Qualitative Data Analysis: An Expanded Sourcebook.* Thousand Oaks, CA: Sage.

Mohan, K., & Ramesh, B. (2003). Ontology-Based Support for Variability Management in Product and Service Families.*Proceedings of the 36th Annual Hawaii International Conference on System Sciences (HICSS'03).*

Normann, R. (2000). *Service Management - Strategy and Leadership in Service Business.* Chichester: Wiley.

Peters, C., Maglio, P., Badinelli, R., Harmon, R. R., Maull, R., Spohrer, J. C., & Demirkan, H. et al. (2016). Emerging Digital Frontiers for Service Innovation. *Communications of the Association for Information Systems*, *39*(1).

Pohl, K., Böckle, G., & van der Linden, F. (2005). *Software Product Line Engineering - Foundations, Principles, and Techniques*. Berlin: Springer. doi:10.1007/3-540-28901-1

Ramesh, B., Tiwana, A., & Mohan, K. (2002, October 3-5). Supporting Information Product and Service Families with Traceability. *Proceedings of the 4th International Workshop on Software Product-Family Engineering PFE '01*, Bilbao, Spain (pp. 353-363).

Robertson, D., & Ulrich, K. (1998). Planning for Product Platforms. *MIT Sloan Management Review*, *39*(4), 19–31.

Silveira, G. D., Borenstein, D., & Fogliatto, F. S. (2001). Mass Customization: Literature Review and Research Directions. *International Journal of Production Economics*, *72*(1), 1–13. doi:10.1016/S0925-5273(00)00079-7

Soanes, C., & Stevenson, A. (Eds.). (2004). *Concise Oxford English Dictionary* (11th ed.). Oxford: Oxford University Press.

Tuunainen, V. K., & Tuunanen, T. (2011). IISIn-A model for analyzing ICT Intensive Service Innovations in n-sided Markets. *Paper presented at the 2011 44th Hawaii International Conference on System Sciences (HICSS)*. doi:10.1109/HICSS.2011.234

Tuunainen, V. K., Tuunanen, T., & Bastek, M. (2009). A Model for ICT Intensive Service Innovations in two-sided markets–Case Study of IPTV in a National TV Broadcasting Company. *Paper presented at the International Conference on New Trends in Information and Service Science NISS'09*. doi:10.1109/NISS.2009.161

Tuunainen, V. K., Tuunanen, T., & Piispanen, J. (2011). Mobile service platforms: Comparing nokia ovi and apple app store with the iisin model. *Paper presented at the 2011 10th International Conference on Mobile Business*. doi:10.1109/ICMB.2011.42

Tuunanen, T., Bask, A., & Merisalo-Rantanen, H. (2012). Typology for modular service design: Review of literature. *International Journal of Service Science, Management, Engineering, and Technology*, *3*(3), 99–112. doi:10.4018/jssmet.2012070107

Tuunanen, T., & Cassab, H. (2011). Service process modularization: Reuse versus variation in service extensions. *Journal of Service Research*, *14*(3), 340–354. doi:10.1177/1094670511413912

Tuunanen, T., Myers, M., & Cassab, H. (2010). A Conceptual Framework for Consumer Information Systems Development. *Pacific Asia Journal of the Association for Information Systems*, *2*(1), 5.

Valkonen, K., Lindström, N., Natunen, L., Isoviita, R., & Tuunanen, T. (2015). *Balance of Hedonic and Utilitarian Values in Information Systems Use Nordic Contributions in IS Research* (pp. 165–176). Springer.

Van der Linden, F. (2002). Software product families in Europe: The Esaps & Cafe projects. *IEEE Software*, *19*(4), 41–49. doi:10.1109/MS.2002.1020286

van Liere, D. W., Hagdorn, L., Hoogeweegen, M. R., & Vervest, P. H. (2004). Embedded coordination in a business network. *Journal of Information Technology*, *19*(4), 261–269. doi:10.1057/palgrave.jit.2000026 van Ommering, R., & Bosch, J. (2002, August 19-22). Widening the Scope of Software Product Lines - From Variation to Composition. *Proceedings of the Second International Conference on Software Product Lines SPLC 2*, San Diego, CA, USA (pp. 328-3470.

Vargo, S. L., & Lusch, R. F. (2004). Evolving to a new dominant logic for marketing. *Journal of Marketing*, *68*(1), 1–17. doi:10.1509/jmkg.68.1.1.24036

Vartiainen, T., & Tuunanen, T. (2016). Value Co-Creation and Co-Destruction in an IS Artifact: Contradictions of Geocaching. *Paper presented at theHawaii International Conference on System Sciences*, Hawaii. doi:10.1109/HICSS.2016.160

Voss, C. A., & Hsuan, J. (2009). Service architecture and modularity. *Decision Sciences*, *40*(3), 541–569. doi:10.1111/j.1540-5915.2009.00241.x

Zeithaml, V. A., Berry, L. L., & Parasuraman, A. (1988). Communication and Control Processes in the Delivery of Service Quality. *Journal of Marketing*, *52*(2), 35–48. doi:10.2307/1251263

ENDNOTES

1 An example of the thematic analysis process is provided in Appendix 2

2 Please see http://www.freeviewnz.tv/

3 For further details please see http://www.internetnz.net.nz/

4 Please see http://newzealandfilmtv.co.nz/

APPENDIX 1

Semi-Structured Interview Protocol

Questions on the Company:

- What kind of business is your company engaged in?
- What products and services does your company offer in general?
- How many people are working in your company?

Questions on the IPTV/Internet TV Offering:

- What is your company's understanding of IPTV/Internet TV?
- What is your company's strategy in terms of IPTV/Internet TV?
- Did your company develop the solution needed for offering IPTV/Internet TV services in-house, or did your company outsource the development, or does your company rely on an off the shelf solution?
- How does your company tailor the solution to their needs?
- How does your company deliver the IPTV/Internet TV service offering?
- What kind of IPTV/Internet TV content is your company offering or planning to offer?
- What role plays usability in your company's IPTV/Internet TV service offering?
- What is special about offering IPTV/Internet TV services in NZ compared to elsewhere in the world?

Questions on IPTV/Internet TV Services:

- What are the IPTV/Internet TV services your company is offering or planning to offer?
- What is your company's strategy in terms of offering participatory IPTV/Internet TV services?
- How does your company utilise reuse in its IPTV/Internet TV service development process?
- What is your company's strategy in terms of customising the IPTV/Internet TV service offering?

Other Aspects:

- Are there any other topics you would like to discuss in the context of IPTV/Internet TV offerings and services?

APPENDIX 2

Analysis Example for the Theme "Core Solution"

Table 3 summarizes how LT's core solution decision was based on an off-the-shelf IPTV solution. The company considers all current IPTV solutions as rather immature. At the moment, the LT works on integrating the solution with its internal systems.

Table 3. Theme "Core Solution" from LT

Theme Code	Interviewee(s)
Off-the-shelf IPTV solution	LT1, LT2
Immature technology	LT2
Focus on integration	LT1

For the LT, the core solution can be described as delivering IPTV to a set-top box connected to a customer's TV set. The LT opted for an off-the-shelf IPTV solution from a large vendor. This solution is not modified in anyway which the LT regards as the most sensible approach to IPTV delivery at the moment.

And we see that as a way of de-risking the launch and delivery of quite a complicated product and service. (LT1)

All set-top box solutions currently available on the market are thought to be rather immature products.

So the whole kind of ecosystem about what choices there are, is 1.0 sort of products. Not mature, they're not reliable, they have bugs, they're missing features which are fairly obvious. And it's really early days. (LT2)

Thus, the choice of set-top box was basically determined by the question if a given solution works or not. The LT found that currently only one working hybrid IPTV solution is available on the market and chose this solution eventually. This choice, however, is not regarded as the most important decision to make.

Yeah, it's a really easy choice because it's not much money, it's not the defining choice anyway. (LT2)

The LT is currently focusing on the integration of the IPTV solution with their internal systems, like customer records and billing.

And that's actually one of the delay points, there's always a queue of things, everytime you introduce a new ... service you have to go and integrate it. (LT1)

Chapter 9
About the E-commerce Activities in Finnish Lapland – Perspectives of Consumers and Entrepreneurs:
E-Commerce in Lapland

Rauno Rusko
University of Lapland, Finland

Joni Pekkala
University of Lapland, Finland

ABSTRACT

This chapter introduces E-commerce activities of consumers and entrepreneurs in Finnish Lapland. This chapter introduces in addition to the challenges, which SMEs face while starting E-commerce activity in the Northern Finland context, also the state of the E-commerce among consumers. Basing on the results, six interviews and the outcomes of two questionnaires, both entrepreneurs and consumers meet the first steps of E-commerce challenging. The most important question is what is the attainable incremental value for the firms and consumers via E-commerce activities? Entrepreneurs meet both pushing and pulling reasons for the first steps of E-commerce. Consumers have also noticed the incremental value of E-commerce. Mostly the experiences of consumers are encouraging. E-commerce enlarges the available services of sparsely populated areas of Lapland.

INTRODUCTION

This chapter introduces the role of E-commerce among consumers and suppliers of Finnish Lapland. Finnish Lapland is sparsely populated area (density of population 1.95/km2). So low density of population is challenging for the business and consumption. Thus, Finnish Lapland provides an excellent

DOI: 10.4018/978-1-5225-2139-6.ch009

platform to study challenges and possibilities of E-commerce. The standing point of Lapland without E-commerce was difficult: in many areas of Lapland the local services are missing. Whether E-commerce is a robust substitute for missing local services? Furthermore, sparsely populated areas are also challenging for business: the lack in critical mass of local consumers, in which E-commerce might be solution for producers and suppliers (Gallaugher, 2002). The most important question in this chapter is, what is the attainable incremental value for the firms and consumers via E-commerce activities? How does the context, sparsely populated area of Lapland, effect on the role of E-commerce?

Entrepreneurs meet both pushing and pulling reasons for the first steps of E-commerce. Consumers have also noticed the incremental value of E-commerce. Mostly the experiences of consumers are encouraging. Especially in the branches of migration, tourism and entrepreneurship the Push-Pull effects are typical research subjects (Tata, 1977; Edgar et al., 2004; Singer, 2009; Buhalis & Main, 1998; Qian et al., 2011). In tourism, the studies are emphasizing, in addition to challenges faced while starting advanced information technology (Buhalis & Main, 1998), Push-Pull perspective in the context of tourists and destination: what are the reasons for a tourist to travel away from his/her home in order to meet new destinations? or what are those factors of tourism destination, which will attract tourists to that destination? (Murillo, et al., 2008). In entrepreneurship, there are also Push-Pull factors: what kinds of reasons in the current situation of life are pushing individuals towards to establish a new firm? and on the contrary: which factors and opportunities are tempting individuals for entrepreneurship? One forms of push effect in entrepreneurship is business incubator (Qian et al., 2011; Rusko, 2011).

Similarly, associated with push- and pull effects, this chapter considers E-commerce via these two perspectives: What kinds of reasons there are in the current business of brick-and-mortar shop, which requires the enlargement of business activities towards E- commerce? (push effect), and What are the factors for business, which are tempting to establish an E-commerce unit? (pull effect). We consider these two perspectives and other research questions using quantitative and qualitative materials by emphasizing customer experiences, strategies and business practices in the analysis. Altogether, analysis is based on two enquiries focused on Lappish consumers and entrepreneurs, and interviews of entrepreneurs.

This study is based on the combination of literature review about E-commerce emphasizing especially the noticed challenges faced while starting E-commerce activity and its multi-channel marketing possibilities (see, e.g. Bhile et al., 2002; Yang, et al., 2012; Neslin et al., 2006; Zhang, et al., 2010), associated especially with Push-Pull dichotomy. These practical perspectives are based on interviews of six Finnish SME entrepreneurs, which have established E-commerce activities.

This chapter has the following structure: after this introduction follows literature review about E-commerce and especially its features emphasizing first steps towards E-commerce. Then we introduce research design of this chapter. The empirical outcomes of the research have been presented after that. Discussion –part of chapter combines the outcomes of literature review, questionnaire and interviews. Finally, we have concluding remarks with recommendation for further study subjects.

LITERATURE REVIEW

This part of the chapter is basing on two parts. At first, it is focused on the literature introducing the different forms of E-commerce adaptation of consumers. At second, this chapter considers the first steps of E-commerce and then literature emphasizing the reasons for E-commerce. We are interested these themes generally and in the context of Small and Medium Enterprises (SME) especially.

E-Commerce Adaptation of Consumers

Several studies, which focus on E-commerce adaptation of consumers, emphasize the role of trust (See, e.g. Gefen & Straub, 2004; Kim et al., 2008; Ha & Stoel, 2009). According to Kim, Ferrin, and Rao (2008), internet consumers' trust and perceived risk have strong impacts on their purchasing decisions. Furthermore, privacy concerns, security concerns, the information quality of the Website, and the company's reputation, have strong effects on consumers' trust in the Website (Kim, et al., 2008). Routines and practices seem to important factors of consumption: Kim et al. (2008) noticed that familiarity had a strong direct influence on consumers' purchase intentions. Gefen and Straub (2004) emphasize the role of central motivating forces of human behavior, such as social uncertainty with understanding, predicting, and controlling the behavior of other people, in the context of E-commerce adaptation of consumers. According to them, the relative paucity of regulations and customs on the Internet makes consumer familiarity and trust especially important in the case of E-commerce. However, E-commerce action lacks an interpersonal exchange and the one-time nature of the typical business transaction on the Internet makes this kind of consumer trust unique. (Gefen & Straub, 2004) Ha and Stoel (2009) notice that consumer perceptions of usefulness and attitude toward e-shopping have effects on E-commerce adaptation. Also, shopping enjoyment and trust play significant roles. However, they see that perceived ease of use does not influence attitude toward e-shopping. (Ha & Stoel, 2009)

Also, Bakos (2001) emphasizes the importance of easiness/familiarity in E-commerce activities of consumers especially in the form of decreased searching costs. Bakos (2001) notices that buying via will decrease searching costs of consumers. He particularly emphasizes the role of search engines in E-commerce purchasing. Similarly, internet-based transactions will decrease the searching costs of suppliers (Bakos, 2001). Furthermore, lower search costs in digital markets will make it easier for buyers to find low-cost sellers, and thus will promote price competition among sellers (Bakos, 2001). Generally, online marketplaces seem to lower the cost of market transactions because of decreasing number of intermediaries (Bakos, 2001). This may decrease the prices and generally simplify the supply chain of the products.

This chapter studies in the empirical part the same features in the E-commerce adaptation of consumers: experiences, trust, familiarity and usefulness. The analysis is focused on E-commerce experiences of consumers in Finnish Lapland.

The Models about the First Steps of E-Commerce

ICT literature contains several alternative ways to categorize the development of E-commerce (See, e.g. Aranyossy, 2011; Daniel et al., 2002; Levy and Powell, 2003; Mendo and Fitzgerald, 2005; Rao et al., 2003). At first, we consider a very popular stage model for E-commerce, introduced by Rao, Metts and Monge (2003). According to them, there are four stages in E-commerce development:

1. Presence
2. Portals
3. Transactions integration
4. Enterprises integration

Each of these stages has own facilitators and barriers. Their perspective covers possible long-term development of an enterprise associated with E-commerce, although Rao and colleagues do not suppose that all firms will follow all these stages in their E-commerce development. This development contains, for example, high level collaboration between customers and suppliers (Enterprises integration). This stage is somewhat of an ideal concept for the "e-world" environment (ibid., 20-21). However, for the study here the first two stages, Presence and Portals, are the most interesting ones.

Presence –stage contains initial steps that organizations do to get involved in digital environment, that is, they have a window to the Web (Rao et al., 2003, 16). At this stage, web-pages contain one-way information about the organization. Rao and colleagues name the commitment of the most important facilitator, which means the commitment of strategy towards internet as a tool for achieving strategic aims, such as increasing sales, better services for customers, more available information and cost savings. Except cost savings, which is a push factor, the other variables, such as increasing sales, better services for customers, more available information are pull factors of commerce. Of course, the distinction between push or pull factors depends also on the current stage of the business in the firm (internal factors): if the economic or financial situation of the firm is challenging, then it is possible that the current situation pushes towards E-commerce in order to achieve all of these: more sales and savings and more customers via improved business strategy. If the financial situation is stable without E-commerce, then there is not any necessity for E-commerce. In this case, however, an entrepreneur might find tempting to start first steps towards E-commerce because of the possibilities which it provides, such as better services for customers and therefore, perhaps, higher turnover, that is mainly external potential factors.

According to Rao and colleagues (2003), the second stage, portal –stage, has following facilitators: internal organizational changes, investment and usability. Portal –stage contains introduction to two-way communication: customer or supplier order placing, the use of profiles and cookies. It also enables developed customizing activities (Rao et al., 2003, 17). Although the Portal stage is the second stage of development path introduced by Rao and colleagues (2003), its features of E-commerce could also be as an impulse to start E-commerce activities. Again, it might be firm-specific whether these features are associated push- or pull-effects of E-commerce.

Rao and colleagues (2003) also list several barriers to different stages of E-commerce development. In the Presence –stage there might be several organizational reasons not to introduce E-commerce functions, such as technological resistance, acceptance of growth strategy, financial investments and development of telecommunication infrastructure. In the Portals -stage there are following barriers: the development of B2B interfaces and cultural and/or language issues. Of course the power of these barriers has an essential role while an entrepreneur and/or managers of the firms are deciding whether or not to take E-commerce in use and in what form in the enterprise. The strategic decisions are often based on some kinds of cost-benefit analysis (see, e.g. Schwenk, 1984; Shrivastava & Grant, 1985; Klingebiel & Meyer, 2013). In this case, the strategists are deliberating the attractions and barriers associated with E-commerce activities.

One alternative way to consider the stages of SMEs in E-commerce is to use questionnaire and its results in cluster analysis and cluster SMES in groups basing on these results (Daniel et al., 2002). Daniel and colleagues (2002) found following groups: developers, communicators, web presence and transactors.

Developers are at the start of their E-commerce adoption developing their services, such as email communication with customers and suppliers, providing (web) information about company, its products and services and using web for advertising and brand building. "Communicators" also use email for communication for between employees and electronically exchanging documents and designs with customers and suppliers. At this stage the most important development activity is focused on websites in order to provide company, product and service information. (Daniel et al., 2002, 260). After these steps is following "presence" phase, which one is already the first step in the typology of Rao and colleagues (2003). However, these two studies define the contents of these steps differently. According to Daniel and colleagues (2003), in this phase the two-way orders are possible, but Rao and colleagues (2003) see for "presence" step essential the one-way information about the organization and two-way orders are typical for the "portal" stage.

Furthermore, there are some other studies considering the first steps of the E-commerce. For example, also Aranyossy (2011) introduce the first steps of e-commerce development in her working paper. According to her, these steps are building information capabilities, using the company web-site as a marketing tool – affecting the firm performance through the sales volume. In addition, transactional e-commerce function works as a new sales channel having effects on the sales revenue and the cost of administration and sales or inventory turnovers as well. Furthermore, E-commerce has a connection with the building activities of a loyal customer base. In addition, Aranyossy see that these features "are more like future options or intangible assets, their effect on the company performance is more strategic, future-centric and elusive". (Aranyossy, 2011, 11).

Generally, the perspectives of Rao and colleagues (2003), Daniel and colleagues (2003) and Aranyossy (2011) about the first steps of E-commerce development are nearly similar: these studies emphasize the possibilities of E-commerce as a tool of information and a source for the enlargement of turnover. Generally, E-commerce studies consider the following aims of enterprises while studying the first steps of E-commerce: relatively simple technologies, such as e-mail, to dispense and gather information. Then, there is next the own static homepage containing basic information. After that, there are wider range of information and attempts to market products and after-support. (Mendo & Fitzgerald, 2005, 679). According to Mendo and Fitzgerald (2005), traditionally in the most mature E-commerce stages of the E-commerce development models, the web site is claimed to be totally integrated with several backoffice systems, such as ERP, CRM and SCM applications. Also, Rao and colleagues (2003) mention customer relationship management (CRM) and supply chain management (SCM) in their enterprises integration –the stage of E-commerce development model.

Levy and Powell (2003) introduce four roles for web technologies in SMEs: brochureware, support, opportunity and development. They emphasize the role of different business, entrepreneur and his/her attitudes related to E-commerce in the context of this role selection. Furthermore, their model is not associated any growth model with the particular order of phases and it is in that way resembles the model of Rao and colleagues (2003). However, in some models the stages of E-commerce are sequential and activities in them cumulative, that is each stage or cluster is undertaking all of the activities of the previous cluster (see, e.g. Daniel and colleagues, 2003, 260).

Reasons for E-Commerce Adoption of Firms According to Some Literature

According to Grandon and Pearson (2004), there are in the literature of E-commerce three factors affecting the strategic value of information technologies: operational support, managerial productivity and strategic decision aids. In addition, they identified four factors that influence electronic commerce adoption: organizational readiness, external pressure, perceived ease of use and perceived usefulness. Grandon and Pearson (2004) also studied the linkages between the strategic value of E-commerce and adoption of E-commerce. As a result, they noticed that those top managers who perceived E-commerce as adding strategic value to the firm are adopting more easily E-commerce for use.

Among these factors, which Grandon and Pearson (2004) mention, "external pressure" is possible to categorize among the push factors and some of them among the pull factors of E-commerce: operational support, managerial productivity and strategic decision aids. Some of these factors are generally easing the adoption of E-commerce, such as perceived usefulness, organizational readiness and perceived ease of use, but them are difficult to divide into push or pull factors.

Stephen Drew (2003) has also noticed the strategic importance of E-commerce in his study about eastern England. E-commerce is both threat and opportunity for SME business strategies. E-commerce is at the centre of technology and corporate strategies, and associated with transformational change. (Drew, 2003). Drew (2004) find four key management issues of E-commerce: opening new markets, improving the quality of products and services, reducing costs and improving efficiencies and growing the volume of the business. Furthermore, Drew lists relevant driving forces for the adaption of E-commerce:

1. Pressures from suppliers of other business partners,
2. Customers demanding the deal on the internet,
3. Need to increase the value of the business,
4. Orders of top management,
5. Industry changes and trends,
6. Opportunity to expand and grow,
7. Threat of competitors taking the business,
8. Need to keep up with existing competitors.

Only point 6) "opportunity expand and grow" is a pull factor and the rest of the factor are push factors. Among the key management issues push factor is only "reducing costs and improving efficiencies" and pull factors are opening new markets, improving the quality of products and services and growing the volume of the business.

Actually, these two studies differentiate with each other: Drew (2003) emphasizes pull factors of E-commerce and Grandon and Pearson (2004) push factors of E-commerce. On Table 1 is the list of the pull and push factors basing on the literature review. Furthermore, there are some general factors promoting E-commerce, which are difficult to divide between these two categories.

Table 1. Push and pull factors of e-commerce

Push Factors	General Promoting Factors	Pull Factors
• Pressures from suppliers or other business partners • Customers demanding the deal on the internet • Need to increase the value of the business • Orders of top management • Industry changes and trends • Threat of competitors taking the business • Need to keep up with existing competitors • Reducing costs and improving efficiencies • External pressure • Cost savings.	• Perceived usefulness; usability • Organizational readiness • Perceived ease of use • internal organizational changes, • Investment • Marketing tool	• Opportunity to expand and grow • Opening new markets • Improving the quality of products and services • Growing the volume of the business. • Operational support • Managerial productivity • Strategic decision aids • Increasing sales • Better services for customers • More available information and cost savings.

Source: Aranyossy 2011; Drew, 2003; Grandon & Pearson, 2004; Rao et al., 2003.

RESEARCH DESIGN

The research method of this chapter is based on case study strategy. Case study strategy covers several methods and materials in order to achieve the research objectives (See, e.g. Yin, 2003; Eriksson & Kovalainen, 2008). The research material is based on the results of two projects. The first one focused on the themes of sales management and the second one focused on the services of the customers. Material covers both qualitative and quantitative sources: six interviews, implemented in 2012, and two questionnaires. The first questionnaire, which was implemented in 2012, focused on entrepreneurship in E-commerce having 132 respondents of managers or owners. Questionnaire was transmitted via the regional organization of Federation of Finnish Enterprises to about 1800 firms. Thus, the response rate is 7.3 per cent. Practically all of the respondents are SMEs from the Northern Finland. The second questionnaire, which was implemented during autumn 2014, focused on consumption and E-commerce. This questionnaire was sent to 938 email addresses of consumers living (or acting) in the area of Lapland. 45 email addresses were outdated. 61 respondents answered to questionnaire. Thus, response rate was slightly under 7 per cent. Average age of the consumers was nearly 48 years and 54 per cent of the respondents are women.

The target group of *interviews* was chosen carefully: all interviewed six enterprises have E-commerce functions in their business model. The qualitative material of the case study consists of six recorded face to face interviews of entrepreneurs and six enterprises. These interviews implemented during spring 2013 by one of the authors of this chapter. On average, these interviews lasted between 0.5 hours to one hour. The number of the transcribed words of interviews varies between 1850 words to 4300 words. The basic structure of these interviews was the same for all interviews, but the interviewer adapted the nuances and content of the questions during each interview basing on the answers and emphasis of interviewees.

We decided to study the forms of E-commerce of SMEs in addition to the questionnaire by using interviews, because they provide more specific material for research questions compared with the questionnaire. An interviewer is able to react to the answers of the interviewee in order to find more information about the appearing interesting themes during the process of interviews. Furthermore, the structured questionnaire restricts the form of the information coming from the respondents. The interviewees are all entrepreneurs and representing various branches of business in Northern Finland. Although all enterprises have their main office in Northern Finland, their clientele is in some cases even very international. Furthermore, the role of web and the E-commerce is very advanced in all of these firms making them the ideal research object for this study. This was the main criterion for the selection of research population.

Thus, the interviews have been recorded, transcribed, read carefully and encoded manually by the authors of this chapter in order to find the most important underlying themes of E-commerce which these interviewees have met. The analysis is based on qualitative interview material containing micro-stories of these companies and especially content analysis, which is focused on the first steps of E-commerce of the respondents. The respondents are owners or co-owners of the companies. The aim of the content analysis is to investigate the most essential features associated with push- and pull-effects of E-commerce among the research population.

In addition to the questionnaire, interviews and content analysis are typical tools and methods of studying the features of E-commerce in SMEs (see, e.g. McGowan et al., 2001; Koh & Kim, 2004; AlGhamdi et al., 2012; Mavlanova, et al., 2012). In the study of McGowan and colleagues (2001) the firms come from different sectors including manufacturing, services and retail. Also the study here in this chapter covers all these sectors in the questionnaire, but emphasis on the interviews is in the branch of retail and services.

The analysis emphasized the areas of Northern Finland, and especially Lapland, because of two underlying projects, which focused on sales and customer services in Northern Finland. Because of this background, analysis resembles case study method or case study strategy (Yin, 2003; Eriksson & Kovalainen, 2008) with several methods and restricted geographic area, Northern Finland.

THE RESULTS OF THE QUESTIONNAIRES

The Results of the Questionnaire: Entrepreneurs

This study exploits the preliminary outcomes of the questionnaire, which is a part of the results of the project, which focused on the sales management in Northern Finland. The questionnaire contained, for example, the battery of questions about promoting the factors of E-commerce. Among 132 respondents, between 111-116 of them, answered these questions. The most important promoting factors of E-commerce are (in this particular order): Better service to customer (Pull effect)

1. New customers (Pull effect),
2. Customers want to use E-commerce (Push effect),
3. Higher sales (Pull effect),
4. More appearance and new customers to brick-and-mortar (Pull effect),
5. Competitors have E-commerce (Push effect),
6. Higher productivity (Pull effect),
7. Entry to new markets (Pull effect),
8. Achievement of competitive advantage (Pull effect),
9. Synergy effect (Pull effect),
10. Rationalizing via E-commerce (Push effect),
11. Passing intermediary (Pull effect).

The most of the promoting factors of E-commerce is possible to locate in the category of pull effect, only three variables "Customers want to use E-commerce", "Competitors have E-commerce" and "Rationalizing via E-commerce" presents clearly push effects. (Table 2)

The Results of the Questionnaire: Consumers

According to enquiry, most of the customers (76%) in Lapland buy products from webshops occasionally or repeatedly. However, only one fifth of them are active users of E-commerce purchasing products from webshops repeatedly. Only 16 per cent of the respondents do not use webshops at all. Thus, 84 per cent of respondents have bought at least once or more often products from the webshops. This outcome confirms that inhabitants of Lapland are relatively familiarized with E-commerce purchasing. (Figure 1)

However, the share of very active webshop customers among population of Lapland is not so large. These results imply that consumers in Lapland are prepared to purchase products from the webshops, but the volume of the purchases was on the relatively low level in autumn 2014.

The other questions in the enquiry seem to confirm these interpretations. According to the respondents, it is relatively easy to order products from the Web (mean 3.82 in the scale between 1 and 5) and

Table 2. Promoting factors of e-commerce in SMES according to the results of the questionnaire (scale 1-5)

Do You Have Now E-Commerce?		Entry to New Markets	New Customers	More Appearance and New Customers to Brick-and-Mortar	Customers Want Use E-Commerce	Better Service to Customer	Customer Data via E-Commerce	Wider Product Range	Possibility to Sell Totally New Products	Incremental Value for Current Products	Competitors have E-Commerce	Achievement of Competitive Advantage	Passing Intermediary	Higher Productivity	Rationalization via E-Commerce	Synergy Effect	Higher Sales
No E-commerce	Mean	3,15	3,49	3,48	3,46	3,57	2,72	2,27	2,35	2,76	3,40	3,05	2,77	3,46	2,87	3,04	3,44
	N	84	84	83	83	84	80	81	79	80	82	81	79	81	82	80	82
	Std. Dev.	1,468	1,427	1,476	1,262	1,235	1,312	1,379	1,396	1,407	1,404	1,457	1,458	1,415	1,447	1,409	1,297
E-commerce	Mean	4,03	4,16	4,06	4,19	4,00	3,47	3,41	3,34	3,50	4,19	4,16	3,78	4,00	3,56	3,69	4,23
	N	32	32	32	32	32	32	32	32	32	32	32	32	32	32	32	31
	Std. Dev.	,999	1,019	1,190	1,120	1,191	1,077	1,266	1,405	1,320	,998	1,081	1,362	1,164	1,268	1,230	,990
Total	Mean	3,40	3,67	3,64	3,66	3,69	2,94	2,59	2,64	2,97	3,62	3,36	3,06	3,61	3,06	3,22	3,65
	N	116	116	115	115	116	112	113	111	112	114	113	111	113	114	112	113
	Std. Dev.	1,407	1,356	1,422	1,263	1,233	1,289	1,437	1,463	1,417	1,346	1,446	1,497	1,366	1,428	1,387	1,266

Table 3. What do you think about the following questions linked with subscription from the Web? (Scale 1-5)

	N	Mean
It is easy to order products from the Web	61	3,82
It is easy to surf in the Web and to move on while preparing your order	60	3,53
Typically, the appearance of the web pages is robust.	60	3,42
The information provided in the Web page has encouraged me to purchase more than initially planned	59	2,22
Before subscribing I have familiarized with the opinions of the other customers about the product	60	2,6
I have got answers quickly to the questions, which I have asked using the web pages of firm.	58	2,76
Together		3,06

Figure 1. Which one of the following statements best describes your purchasing behavior? (N=61)

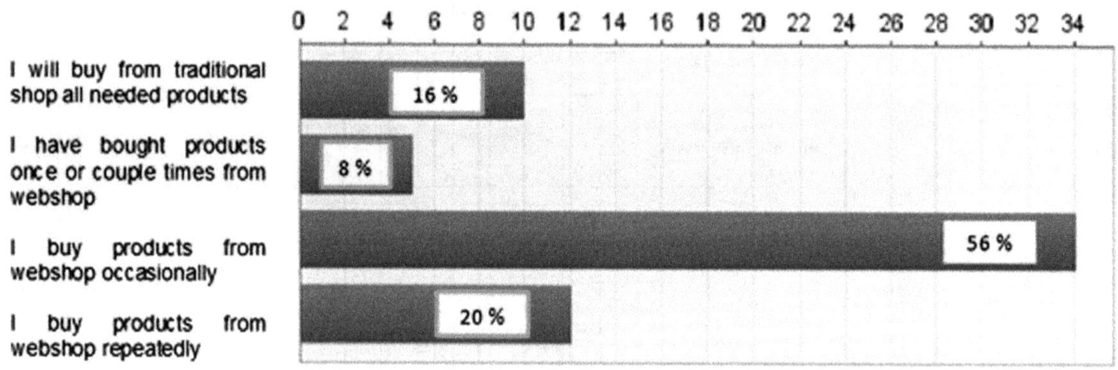

surf in the Web while preparing the order (mean 3.53). Furthermore, most of the respondents see the appearance of the web pages to be robust (3.42). However, the information provided in the Web page has not encouraged the respondents to purchase more than initially planned (mean only 2.22) and they are not interested in the customer feedback in the Web before purchasing (2.6). In addition, the respondents meet the web feedback of the firm to the questions of the consumers not to be so rapid (2.76). (Table 3)

Actually, these results show the some kind of individualism among the E-commerce consumers in Lapland. They are not so interesting the earlier customer feedback of the products, neither the web pages do not encourage them to purchase something more as expected. However, respondents see the appearance of the web pages robust. According to these results, E-commerce purchasing is a private activity without any remarkable social dimension (cf. Ha & Stoel, 2009)

THE RESULTS OF THE INTERVIEWS

In order to achieve in-depth –case study perspective, quantitative results are completed with the interviews of entrepreneurs, which currently have E-commerce activities in their business. Quantitative analysis revealed that there is, among the SMEs of Northern Finland, both push- and pull-effects during the first steps of E-commerce. The aim of the qualitative part of this chapter is to find more descriptive details associated with Push-Pull effects in E-commerce start.

General Underlying Information about the Case Study Enterprises

In order to ensure the anonymity of the respondents we call these firms as A, B, C, D, E and F. All these firms are relatively small: several of them have only a couple of workers, including entrepreneur(s), the largest ones have about 20 workers. The age of the firms fluctuates between 2-40 years. All of these firms have E-commerce activities, which was the main criterion for research population and some of them have even the pioneering role in E-commerce in their branches. Table 4 summarizes some basic details about these firms.

The First Steps of E-Commerce

The reasons to start E-commerce activities fluctuate remarkably among the case study enterprises. Furthermore, some interviewees express these reasons more completely than the other ones. Often this theme has been passed quickly, but during the interviews also these underlying reasons to take to use E-commerce as a part of their business model have usually appeared.

Better Services to the Customers

One of the discourses among the case study material directed towards the better services to customers via E-commerce activities. On Table 1 this feature is located in the pull –site of E-commerce. This fac-

Table 4. The cases of the chapter

Firm	Firm A	Firm B	Firm C	Firm D	Firm E	Firm F
Industry	Tourism/services/ Retail	Retail	Retail, B2B	Content provider, retail	Retail	Retail (and manufacturing)
Age of firm	About 40 years	5 years	Nearly 20 years	About 30 years	2 years	About 30 years
Establishment of E-commerce (First domain)	2005	2009	Over 10 years (At first pages of chain)	About 20 years	2 years (Chain)	About 20 years
The forms of E-commerce	Several sales channels in web including several international portals	Own web pages and web store (with the help of ICT provider)	Most of the sales via traditional shop; web store is e.g. marketing channel	Most of the sales via own international web store. Free partial content in web store (marketing)	Finnish web bases and web store upkeeping by international chain.	Several web shops
Number of domains	Over five	Under five	Under five	Under five	Under five	Over five
Brick-and-mortar shop and Web shop?	Brick-and-mortar shop and Web shop	Brick-and-mortar shop and Web shop	Brick-and-mortar shop and Web shop	Brick-and-mortar shop and Web shop	Brick-and-mortar shop and Web shop	Web shop (initially mail-shop with manufacturing)

tor was the most important pull factor of E-commerce in the questionnaire. Also, interviews showed the importance to achieve better services to customers via E-commerce. Among both qualitative and quantitative case material, one important detail is that many of these SMEs are located in the areas which are nearly unoccupied, which fact might have general effects on the contents of the answers of the interviewees and questionnaire.

The difference is mostly there that in our brick-and-mortar shop visit both local and tourists and travelers and then E-commerce, what we have looked, that it is let's say, that almost 100% it is only in the use of Finnish. (E)

And then we have those... in web is a lot of already in the beginning of 21st century and before the blogs have been invented, that there is discussion groups and hobby groups and ... and we have had a politics in which we take care of this magazine and then we have updated those own web pages. And then we support these kinds of hobby groups and discussion groups and so on in a way, that we will answer their questions, they will other ways do their own business. (D)

For our own web pages, we have constructed online reservation which as if ... customer is able to direct from there to reserving and then so... there as producing gradually then more services which means we will not satisfy only for that, that the customer reserve accommodation from here. Now there is build such a package, that you can ... it is basic price package and then the customer can reserve special package/product, in which belongs in addition to accommodation also meal and... [taken away because of anonymity] ... And in the future meaning to produce also different packages in order to provide option what it can... wants to buy ready while being in home... planning the trip. (A)

E-commerce has bring that kind of ... Let's say that we are able to jump to the so called present time which means, we can achieve different clientele more efficiently and we get customers also to the brick-and-mortar shop. It is actually bipartite there is (1) direct delivery, direct deal in which we have not any contact with customer in spite of via E-commerce, but then we have those (2) consumers, who use it (E-commerce) as a tool in order to become acquainted with products and visit then in the brick-and-mortar shops. E-commerce is absolutely necessity today in retail business. Especially, because of the service, that we are able to service to the customers and being active where, however, all customers, are using most of their media time. (C)

Most of these comments above show the possible synergy effect about having both brick-and-mortar shop and web shop at the same time in Northern Finland. This kind of multi-channel feature seems to increase, according to interviewees, the total quality of services for the contemporary customers by providing several service combinations between the brick-and-mortar shop and E-commerce. Especially, the feature of E-commerce will reduce the costs of customers in the sparsely inhabited areas such as Northern Finland.

Wider Product Selection

It is also possible that the selection of products is wider in the E-commerce compared with the selection of products in brick-and-mortar shop. This feature is associated with pull factor "growing the volume of the business" on Table 1.

Perhaps in that, that we have wider selection of products there (in E-commerce) because we do not those e.g. … products will not keep in the front of brick-and-mortar shop, because of the miscellaneous clientele of this center… (B)

However, also in this case (B) above some of the selection, which is not in the front of the brick-and-mortar shop is possible to find for customers in the warehouse of the same shop building for the visitors of the shop. However, separated service and product selection between and brick-and-mortar shop and E-commerce might generally cause confusion for customers, but this feature did not come up among the case study material. It is noteworthy that in questionnaire wider product selection was not very important factor during the first steps of E-commerce.

Tool of Marketing and Sales

In interviews, the entrepreneurs of SMEs see that E-commerce in its different forms is a necessary tool for marketing and for the growth of sales. "Tool for marketing" generally promotes E-commerce, but growth of sales is pull -factor "Growing the volume of the business" on Table 1. Furthermore, "Higher sales" was important reason for E-commerce also in the questionnaire. The E-commerce strategies and business models of the SMES deviate among the population of the interviewees. Some of them already have long history in marketing via web pages and the other ones have just started their path with E-commerce. For example, the attitudes of respondents about Facebook deviate:

Facebook, I will not see that it is as a marketing channel any excellent or something like that when thinking about sales. It more like parade tool and of course one of them… but it is true that in the side of E-commerce Google has autocrat at least I see so. Google is totally incomparable. (C)

Well, it (Facebook pages) has been constructed lately. And generally we are involved with as if in relatively small effort and other ways we start with so… in practice… We have Facebook –pages, I think that they are constructed during last year. If we think about what our enterprise has, so we has basic web pages, where we introduce our [products] and from where you can order … and also other products. Then we have… Specific blog and it's this kind of official blog of editor, which we will not update so often. About once a two week, or three times a week. Generally we launch new [products] or inform some kinds of changes. But it is such an official as if noticeboard, information channel. Then we have those of Facebook pages, where there is practically plenty of same content as in the blog. D

The importance of E-commerce as a part of the firms' strategy varies among firms according to the interviewees from very first small steps to advanced level, where the firm has several separated shops in Web. In the case of (E) the presence in Web is the most important character of E-commerce. In the case of F the firms have several web shops for different product selection. Actually, they have the whole family of products in Web.

I would encourage (entrepreneur) so that it should be start from concrete and deep in that way that when the entrepreneurs might be afraid of technology and ICT… it will fallen when we start to think about that it is nevertheless so complicated all in all for them who do not know about these (technology) in that way. It should be possible to provide … to entrepreneurs that: "sign this paper and we will provide for you an E-commerce". In other words it is important to make the threshold as low as possible to start (C)

- If the decision is based on about the minds of the 50 years old persons, them it is a big threshold to start the E-commerce. (C)
- And it is really big matter, to choose these systems it is really big matter from the point of view of E-commerce development in the future. It gains to investigate very carefully when you are establishing and planning the web shop. So good to familiarize, that what is the suitable technical platform and solution for my needs and whether we need the co-integration of ERP and E-commerce or not. If we do not need today, what is the situation in the future after five years. Whether it is good to establish ERP, which is integrated with web shop at same time. These are the details which I will chose now afterward differently, if possibly. (C)

The latter comment shows the importance of integrated technology associated with E-commerce: Enterprise Resource Planning (ERP) might be integrated with E-commerce as soon as possible, then the need for re-engineering the systems of enterprise will be smaller in the future.

Location

E-commerce provides several advantages which are based on the fact that it is mostly location-free activity. This question is very important in scarcely populated Northern Finland. Location is an important reason to establish web-store among the case study material. Mostly it is possible to interpret as a push –factor, because it is basing on the current "weak" conditions of business. The decision is based on the aim to service customers carefully in scarcely-populated area of Northern Finland. Thus, this discourse is also possible to include in pull-factor "better service for customers" on Table 1, but only partly. In the questionnaire, this factor was missing in the battery of questions.

Well, web shop is similar to whatever other shop. For example, there is no difference whether you establish a new shop for example in the corner of the municipality of Utsjoki shop, some kinds of special retail shop. It needs placement, production machinery and it needs warehouse. It needs in other words money. (F)

And generally electronic commerce, it enables… At least I think that it is in one form of customer service, I think it is good to have, that those people who like the product, that they have possibility to get them also in other ways as they start to drive it from here. I think that it as a service as more to customer. That if they want, if they like some of the products, so they need not to stop to use it. And it will not mean that you must to drive 500 kilometers and come here to get new but that then you can order it via web, and easily order. I think that it is as if such an added value for customer. That it has not any disadvantages, either. If you have the energy to update them. Or well, have the energy and have the energy, but I mean that you feel like it. It has nothing else. (E)

DISCUSSION

The general aim of this chapter is to find out the state and attitudes of the entrepreneurs and consumers about E-commerce. In more detail, the reasons why the small and medium enterprises (SME), especially in Northern Finland, will start E-commerce, that is, why they will enlarge their activities from brick-and-mortar shops towards E-commerce. Furthermore, we focus our consideration on two types of reasons to start E-commerce: push and pull factors: the current conditions of business in brick-and-mortar shops which are not satisfactory without any remarkable changes and, on the other hand, the attracting possibilities which multi-channel sales and marketing (brick-and-mortar and E-commerce) might provide compared with one-channel sales. In addition, the relationships of consumers with E-commerce possibilities were also analyzed.

The results of the questionnaire about promoting the factors of E-commerce are mainly parallel with the outcomes of literature review. This chapter completes the outcomes with the interviews of the owners of SMEs from Northern Finland. According to the interviews, literature review and questionnaire, a brick-and-mortal shop, completed with different forms of E-commerce, provides better services for customers. It is even so that entrepreneurs in interviews see the business without web pages and E-commerce to be incomplete. The business is not credible without E-commerce, which fact is especially one of the push factors of E-commerce. At the same time, E-commerce is tempting because of its several possibilities for services, such as better option with buying channels, after-sales support and service via web, familiarize with products before buying them from brick-and-mortar shop and possibility to save transportation costs by ordering the product via web. All of these sub-factors is possible to describe with synergy effect basing on the opportunities of multi-channel strategy. Furthermore, some enterprises

Table 5. Push and pull factors of e-commerce basing on literature review (L), questionnaire (Q) and interviews (I)

Push Factors	L	Q	I	Pull Factors	L	Q	I
Pressures from suppliers or other business partners	L			Opportunity to expand and grow	L		
Customers demanding (the deal on the internet)	L	Q	I	Opening new markets	L	Q	I
Need to increase the value of the business	L			Improving the quality of products and services	L		I
Orders of top management	L			Growing the volume of the business	L		
Industry changes and trends	L		I	Operational support	L		
Threat of competitors taking the business	L	Q		Managerial productivity (ERP, CRM, etc.)	L		I
Need to keep up with existing competitors	L			Strategic decision aids	L		
Reducing costs and improving efficiencies	L		I	Increasing sales	L	Q	I
External pressure	L			Better services for customers	L	Q	I
Cost savings/Rationalizing	L	Q		More available information and cost savings	L		
Location			I	More appearance and new customers to brick-and mortal		Q	I
The business is not credible without E-commerce			I	Higher productivity		Q	
Demand is coming abroad			I	After-sale participation and services (Social media)			I
				Synergy effect (multi-channel marketing)		Q	I
				Passing intermediary		Q	
				Achievement of competitive advantage		Q	

among the interviewees notice after-sale participation and services, e.g. in the forms and platforms of social media, the important features of E-commerce (Table 5).

One important pull factor for E-commerce, basing on literature and sample cases, is the possibility to enlarge markets nationally and even internationally. For example according to interviews, most of the enterprises and entrepreneurs emphasize the opportunities to enlarge their markets via internet pages and E-commerce.

There were also enterprises, which have tight connection with tourism in their business. For them, the branch and its surrounding conditions create a situation, where they have to focus their marketing via internet pages and to have multi-channel marketing strategy. In other words, that fact that demand is coming from outside the local area is one of the push factors for E-commerce.

One of the push factors of E-commerce, according to the interviews, is the fact that the firms have electric systems in order to coordinate their business, such as ERP, SCM and CRM. These systems are possible to integrate in the flows of products and information coming from E-commerce. Thus, at its best, E-commerce provides synergy effect with these existing systems of enterprise. Furthermore, for example warehouse activities are possible to combine efficiently between E-commerce and brick-and-mortar shops by using these systems, such as ERP and CRM, which have effects on the managerial productivity. However, typically this kind of robust outcome needs several years and long multiform paths for enterprises. Obviously, it is challenging to establish system which is already initially suitable for the multifaceted needs of the firm with its multi-channels sales. This possibility is potentially a pull factor, but practically this is not so obvious.

The empirical material of this study has several connection points with the theoretical discussions introduced in the literature review as Table 4 shows. However, empirical analysis reveals some factors which were not so evident in the literature review, such as the importance of location and the general fact that business is not so credible without E-commerce. Both of them are push factors for E-commerce. Furthermore, empirical analysis emphasizes some pull factors, which are not so typical in the literature of E-commerce: possibility to shorten distribution channels by passing intermediaries via E-commerce and the high importance of after-sale participation and services.

The outcomes of the consumer questionnaire revealed the preparedness of consumers to use webshops as an important channel of purchases. In spite of large distances of Lapland, the role of brick-and-mortar is essential in the daily purchases. However, inhabitants of the Lapland have noticed the possibilities of E-commerce and most of them have purchased products from the webshops. In autumn 2014, the volume of the purchases seemed to be relatively small, or at least the share of very active E-commerce consumers relatively small (20 per cent).

The circumstances, that is to say the local sparsely populated area, has effects on the activities of firms. The interviews showed the relatively developed positions of some firms in the steps of E-commerce. Some of the firms have already long history with E-commerce activities. They are even some kinds of pioneering firms in the branch of E-commerce. This fact implies that circumstances of the local market have effects on the E-commerce activities of the firms. This seems to be one of the push factors of E-commerce to the firms.

CONCLUSION

As a result, this study provides new viewpoints for E-commerce, which fact is based on several reasons: It provides:

- Completed Push-Pull perspective for E-commerce,
- New pieces of knowledge about SMES and E-commerce,
- Perspectives of SMEs in Northern Finland about E-commerce,
- Customer attitudes and adaptation of E-commerce.

In addition, this chapter emphasizes the importance and incremental value of E-commerce in sparsely populated area, both to the entrepreneurs and consumers. Entrepreneurs have to find enlarged markets via E-commerce and consumers are willing to enlarge their consumption possibilities via E-commerce.

Our study shows that it is possible to divide the first steps of E-commerce into two categories:

1. **Pull Factors:** The reasons for E-commerce coming from the current conditions of the business, that is: why is the firm not satisfied the current state of business, which forces to seek new channels, such as E-commerce
2. **Push Factors:** The features of E-commerce, which are so tempting that it attracts enterprises to start E-commerce.

The processes of the firms associated with E-commerce are multifaceted. Some firms have established their web pages and E-commerce via national or international business chain. This is a relatively easy way to come in E-commerce business. Another example to create E-commerce business is based on long-term learning. This kind of path of E-commerce is long and challenging, but the firms have independent strategy generally and in the context of E-commerce. The latter case suits well in the ideas of learning school and emergent strategy (Mintzberg et al., 1998), which perspective has reflections also in strategy as practice perspective. (See, e.g. Rusko, 2011).

Furthermore, results show the preparedness of inhabitants of Lapland to use E-commerce. Already now one fifth of habitants use the supply of E-commerce repeatedly and most of the consumers have ordered products from internet once or more times. However, the social dimension in E-commerce is not important to the consumers in Finnish Lapland.

This chapter contains several restrictions and possibilities for further studies. The empirical part of this study is based on questionnaire and six interviews of entrepreneurs in Northern Finland. Although the themes were rather universal associated with E-commerce, this geographical background has effects on the empirical results: for example the role of location proved to be especially important for the respondents both in the population of enterprises and consumers. This study revealed the possibility to consider the first steps of E-commerce of firms via division between push- and pull factors. This chapter is only the experiment for this perspective. This theme, focused on this division, provides several possibilities for further studies in the future. Similarly, the practical actions of entrepreneurs and personnel have effects on the E-commerce strategies of the firm. Also, this kind of "strategy-as-practice" perspective provides possibilities for further studies in the field of E-commerce.

REFERENCES

AlGhamdi, R., Nguyen, J., Nguyen, A., & Drew, S. (2012). Factors Influencing e-commerce Adoption by Retailers in Saudi Arabia: A quantitative analysis. *International Journal of Electronic Commerce Studies*, *3*(1), 83–100.

Aranyossy, M. (2011). Resource-based Analysis of E-commerce Business Value (Working paper).

Bakos, Y. (2001). The emerging landscape for retail e-commerce. *The Journal of Economic Perspectives*, *15*(1), 69–80. doi:10.1257/jep.15.1.69

Bhide, M., Deolasee, P., Katkar, A., Panchbudhe, A., Ramamritham, K., & Shenoy, P. (2002). Adaptive Push-Pull: Disseminating dynamic web data. *IEEE Transactions on* Computers, *51*(6), 652–668.

Buhalis, D., & Main, H. (1998). Information technology in peripheral small and medium hospitality enterprises: Strategic analysis and critical factors. *International Journal of Contemporary Hospitality Management*, *10*(5), 198–202. doi:10.1108/09596119810227811

Drew, S. (2003). Strategic uses of e-commerce by SMEs in the east of England. *European Management Journal*, *21*(1), 79–88. doi:10.1016/S0263-2373(02)00148-2

Edgar, B., Doherty, J., & Meert, H. (2004). *Immigration and homelessness in Europe*. Policy Pr.

Eriksson, P., & Kovalainen, A. (2008). Qualitative methods in business research. *Sage.*

Gallaugher, J. M. (2002). E-commerce and the undulating distribution channel. *Communications of the ACM*, *45*(7), 89–95. doi:10.1145/514236.514240

Gefen, D., & Straub, D. W. (2004). Consumer trust in B2C e-Commerce and the importance of social presence: Experiments in e-Products and e-Services. *Omega*, *32*(6), 407–424. doi:10.1016/j.omega.2004.01.006

Grandon, E. E., & Pearson, J. M. (2004). Electronic commerce adoption: An empirical study of small and medium US businesses. *Information & Management*, *42*(1), 197–216. doi:10.1016/j.im.2003.12.010

Ha, S., & Stoel, L. (2009). Consumer e-shopping acceptance: Antecedents in a technology acceptance model. *Journal of Business Research*, *62*(5), 565–571. doi:10.1016/j.jbusres.2008.06.016

Kim, D. J., Ferrin, D. L., & Rao, H. R. (2008). A trust-based consumer decision-making model in electronic commerce: The role of trust, perceived risk, and their antecedents. *Decision Support Systems*, *44*(2), 544–564. doi:10.1016/j.dss.2007.07.001

Klingebiel, R., & De Meyer, A. (2013). Becoming aware of the unknown: Decision making during the implementation of a strategic initiative. *Organization Science*, *24*(1), 133–153. doi:10.1287/orsc.1110.0726

Koh, J., & Kim, Y. G. (2004). Knowledge sharing in virtual communities: An e-business perspective. *Expert Systems with Applications*, *26*(2), 155–166. doi:10.1016/S0957-4174(03)00116-7

Levy, M., & Powell, P. (2003). Exploring SME internet adoption: Towards a contingent model. *Electronic Markets*, *13*(2), 173–181. doi:10.1080/1019678032000067163

Mavlanova, T., Benbunan-Fich, R., & Koufaris, M. (2012). Signaling theory and information asymmetry in online commerce. *Information & Management*, *49*(5), 240–247. doi:10.1016/j.im.2012.05.004

McGowan, P., Durkin, M. G., Allen, L., Dougan, C., & Nixon, S. (2001). Developing competencies in the entrepreneurial small firm for use of the internet in the management of customer relationships. *Journal of European Industrial Training*, 25(2/3/4), 126-136.

Mendo, F. A., & Fitzgerald, G. (2005). A multidimensional framework for SME e-business progression. *Journal of Enterprise Information Management*, *18*(6), 678–696. doi:10.1108/17410390510628382

Mintzberg, H., Ahlstrand, B. W., & Lampel, J. (1998). *Strategy Safari: the Complete Guide Trough the Wilds of Strategic Management*. London: Financial Times Prentice Hall.

Murillo Viu, J., Romani Fernandez, J., & Surinach Caralt, J. (2008). The impact of heritage tourism on an urban economy: The case of Granada and the Alhambra. *Tourism Economics*, *14*(2), 361–376. doi:10.5367/000000008784460481

Neslin, S. A., Grewal, D., Leghorn, R., Shankar, V., Teerling, M. L., Thomas, J. S., & Verhoef, P. C. (2006). Challenges and opportunities in multichannel customer management. *Journal of Service Research*, *9*(2), 95–112. doi:10.1177/1094670506293559

Qian, H., Haynes, K. E., & Riggle, J. D. (2011). Incubation push or business pull? Investigating the geography of US business incubators. *Economic Development Quarterly*, *25*(1), 79–90. doi:10.1177/0891242410383275

Rao, S. S., Metts, G., & Monge, C. A. M. (2003). Electronic commerce development in small and medium sized enterprises: A stage model and its implications. *Business Process Management Journal*, *9*(1), 11–32. doi:10.1108/14637150310461378

Rusko, R. (2011). Virtual Business Incubations: An Alternative Way to Develop and Service Peripheral Areas.[IJIDE]. *International Journal of Innovation in the Digital Economy*, *2*(3), 48–64. doi:10.4018/jide.2011070104

Rusko, R. (2012). Strategic Processes and Turning Points in ICT Business: Case Nokia. *International Journal of Innovation in the Digital Economy*, *3*(3), 25–34. doi:10.4018/jide.2012070103

Schwenk, C. R. (1984). Cognitive simplification processes in strategic decision-making. *Strategic Management Journal*, *5*(2), 111–128. doi:10.1002/smj.4250050203

Shrivastava, P., & Grant, J. H. (1985). Empirically derived models of strategic decision-making processes. *Strategic Management Journal*, *6*(2), 97–113. doi:10.1002/smj.4250060202

Singer, A., Hardwick, S. W., & Brettell, C. B. (2009). *Twenty-first century gateways: Immigrant incorporation in suburban America*. Brookings Institution Press.

Tata, R. J. (1977). Uruguay: Population geography of a troubled welfare state. *The Journal of Geography*, *76*(2), 46–51. doi:10.1080/00221347708980880

Yang, D.-J., Chou, D.-H., & Liu, J. (2012). A Study of Key Success Factors when Applying E-commerce to the Travel Industry. *International Journal of Business and Social Science*, *3*(8), 114–119.

Yin, R. K. (2003). *Case study research: Design and methods* (Vol. 5). Sage.

Zhang, J., Farris, P. W., Irvin, J. W., Kushwaha, T., Steenburgh, T. J., & Weitz, B. A. (2010). Crafting integrated multichannel retailing strategies. *Journal of Interactive Marketing*, *24*(2), 168–180. doi:10.1016/j.intmar.2010.02.002

ADDITIONAL READING

Arduini, D., Denni, M., Lucchese, M., Nurra, A., & Zanfei, A. (2013). The role of technology, organization and contextual factors in the development of e-Government services: An empirical analysis on Italian Local Public Administrations. *Structural Change and Economic Dynamics*, *27*, 177–189. doi:10.1016/j.strueco.2013.06.007

Chen, T. Y., & Shen, H. C. (2016). A network behavior evaluation method for improving interactive security in virtual network worlds. *Information Security Journal: A Global Perspective*, 1-17.

Home, N. (2002). Rural consumers patronage behaviour in Finland. *International Review of Retail, Distribution and Consumer Research*, *12*(2), 149–164. doi:10.1080/09593960210127709

Lennon, S. J., Ha, Y., Johnson, K. K., Jasper, C. R., Damhorst, M. L., & Lyons, N. (2009). Rural consumers online shopping for food and fiber products as a form of outshopping. *Clothing & Textiles Research Journal*, *27*(1), 3–30. doi:10.1177/0887302X07313625

Price, L., White, D., Atherton, A., & Noke, H. (2007, November). Understanding take-up of broadband by small and micro-enterprises: a case study. *Proceedings of the Institute for Small Business and Entrepreneurship Conference*. ISBE.

Richards, C. (2004). Information technology and rural development. *Progress in Development Studies*, *4*(3), 230–244. doi:10.1191/1464993404ps087oa

Taylor, W., & Jewell, R. E. (2003). Progress Toward Establishing Community Networks in Regional Queensland. In S. Marshall & X. Yu. Huo (Eds.), *Closing the Digital Divide: Transforming Regional Economies and Communities with Information Technology, (* (p. 195).

Ulbrich, F. (2000). A decision-support framework for electronic commerce in small and medium-sized enterprises. *Proceedings of theInnovation Through Electronic Commerce Conference* (pp. 14-16).

KEY TERMS AND DEFINITIONS

Brick-and-Mortar Shop: Traditional shop where the customers have possibility to buy products and services.

E-Commerce: Commercial activities associated with internet or web-based platforms in different forms.

Emergent Strategy: Strategy, which is not actually planned. Emergent strategy is part of the "learning school" among the strategy schools.

ERP: Enterprise resource planning.

Push-Pull Effect: Factors which push from the initial state towards better opportunities and factors which pull because of their attractive characteristics towards the future state of business.

SCM: Supply chain management.

SMEs: Small and medium sized enterprises.

Webshop: A shop which supplies goods or services over the Internet.

Section 3

Consumer Behavior and Engagement from a Macro Economic Context

Chapter 10
Do Stock Markets Comove in Emerging Economies?

Sadullah Çelik
Marmara University, Turkey

Emel Baydan
Marmara University, Turkey

ABSTRACT

Great Recession has brought the need to model and assess the financial markets with unconventional approaches. The nature of consumer behavior in financial markets has become crucial as real and financial sector comoving overtime was a dream of no rationality. The union of consumers looking for higher wealth and speculative stock market participants was not a sustainable case. But, what happened to the consumers/investors in emerging economies? This chapter assesses the behavior of emerging stock markets during the turmoil using weekly data for Brazil, China, India, Indonesia, Russia, South Africa and Turkey with US as the benchmark for January 2003–March 2014. Two unconventional methods are used for checking asymmetric contagion; the wavelet comovement and frequency domain causality. The findings show that markets with rather high concentration of foreign investors are highly affected but consumers were not due to smaller participation. The asymmetric contagion argument is verified for some emerging markets as consumers/investors suffered as much as any other market participant.

INTRODUCTION

The recent technological developments, the facilities of communication, the liberalization activities in terms of economies, the augmentation of international trade, the commited free trade agreements and trading blocks, concisely the fact of globalization, have made economies more integrated among countries. Certainly, some advantages and disadvantages occur with financial integration. For instance, emerging economies have become more attractive places for portfolio investors and portfolio capital. Besides all of these above factors, low transaction costs are also one of the other benefits of this integration. Likewise, the presence of strong economic ties between countries can affect stock markets' action

DOI: 10.4018/978-1-5225-2139-6.ch010

by time. However, this integration might be more fragile in terms of economies and its' influences might be contagious. Undoubtly, these are the disadventages of the global integration.

On the other hand, it is not possible to argue that stock markets are destined to wipe away the savings of small investors. There are so many financial institutions which have expertise on stock markets and offer portfolio services at very low costs to their customers (that is consumers who are able to save and are willing to invest in stock markets). Most of these institutions try to pick up a balanced portfolio that could only be achieved through diversification depending on the wealth of their customers. It is well known that the value of the customer's portfolio rises as well as the institution's earnings through brokerage fees and the increase in the number of new customers. This obviously leads to a bigger portfolio to be managed for the institution, a spiral that could lead to enormous benefits for both sides in the longer term. Hence, the increase in wealth for the consumer is expected to increase his/her purchasing power and the living standards. In a stable economic environment with a healthy growth rate, participating in the financial markets-especially the stock market if speculation is not the dominant factor-should definitely lower the cost of living for those consumers (long-term portfolio owners) as production rises and interest rates and inflation are low and stable. Therefore, the study of stock markets are rather different than other asset markets due to the inherent nature of speculation in the market that needs to be minimized through effective and larger participation of small investors who can save some portion of their income but think about the longer term gains rather than being rich during the day and waking up to be broke the next morning. So, the notion of investing in stock markets especially in emerging economies where savings are relatively very low is a bigger challenge than the high volume stock markets of the advanced economies. But, these markets are an important source of wealth creation for the consumers and also reflect whether consumers who could save have some kind of confidence in the stock markets, which also means trusting the major domestic companies that are open to public. If the consumers believe that the risks outweigh the benefits or they have already been affected in an adverse manner from the stock market fluctuations in the past economic history, they would tend to prefer alternative assets which usually are foreign exchange and gold. Reflecting on this issue, Rua and Nunes (2009) argue that:

...the study of the comovement of stock market is crucial for risk assessment of portfolios. A higher comovement among the assets of a given portfolio implies lower gains, in terms of risk management, stemming from portfolio diversification. Hence, the evaluation of the comovement is of striking importance to the investor so that he can best assess the risk of a portfolio.

Besides, movements in stock markets are crucial in effecting the financial policies of corporations and the monetary authorities given that the former should focus on future investment decision and the latter should prefer a stable financial market and lower volatility in the economy. Focusing on this point, Ali et al. (2011) point out that:

... to study comovements among stock markets would be useful for policy makers in a sense if stock markets are found to be closely linked then there is a danger that shocks in one market may spill over to other markets thus require closer cooperation among the authorities of these countries, whose equity markets are closely linked.

This study examines the comovement of US stock market indices with the selected markets of Brazil, China, Indonesia, India, Russia, South Africa and Turkey. We use the US stock market as the anchor and employ causality and wavelet comovement analysis. Our data covers the period 2003 to 2014. We use time domain and frequency domain Granger causality analysis so we can complement the results of these two different methodologies.

The main aim is to check whether the stock markets of emerging economies have experienced similar paths before, during and after the Great Recession vis-à-vis the US stock market. This would mean to check how the stock market participants in the emerging economies reacted to the turmoil in the world economy. Due to unavailability of data, we are not able to differentiate between any types of investor as small-large and/or domestic-foreign.

Our study is also motivated by using new econometric methodology to analyze the dynamic nature of the stock markets that we assess. In this respect, we try to find the similarities and differences of the emerging stock markets versus the US so that we could figure out whether the domestic stock market investors have been capable of increasing their wealth or suffered through the adverse consequences of the Great Recession. This paper is not testing the argument of coupling (or decoupling) directly but it is possible to argue that our results show some direction in terms of the globalization of the stock markets as we examine the relationships for different sub-periods.

LITERATURE REVIEW

The previous empirical studies of comovement of stock markets have not revealed consistent results because of several factors such as being time dependent (daily, weekly or monthly), usig linear estimation techniques or comparing the advanced economies that observe typically boom-bust cycles rather than continuous fluctuations as in emerging markets.

Among many others, Korajczyk (1996) investigates a measure of the financial integration between equity markets by using multifactor equilibrium arbitrage to define risk and to measure deviations by applying the integration measure to equities traded in 24 countries (four developed and twenty emerging) using monthly data. The results show that the measure of market segmentation tends to be much larger for emerging markets than the developed markets. This finding is consistent with larger barriers to capital flows into or out of emerging markets. The measurements often tend to decrease by time which is supporting the growing levels of integration. Large values of adjusted mispricing also occur around the periods of economic turbulences and the periods in which capital controls change significantly. On the other hand, Elyasiani et al. (1998) assess the interdependence and dynamic linkages between the emerging capital markets of Sri Lanka and the markets of its major trading partners (Tawian, Singapore, Japan, South Korea, Hong Kong, India and the US) by using the vector autoregression (VAR) analysis. Their results demonstrate that there is no significant interdependence between Sri Lankan market and the equity markets of the US and the Asian markets.

Husain and Saidi (2000) examine the integration of the equity market in Pakistan with those in some developed countries (USA, UK, Japan, Germany, Hong Kong, and Singapore) through well-known cointegration methodology by employing weekly data from January 1998 to December 1993. They detect a long run relationship of the Pakistani market with the markets of UK and Japan (Morck et al., 2000). Accordingly, Ng (2002) examines the linkages between the South East Asian stock markets over the period 1988-1997. The results of the correlation analysis indicate that the South East Asian stock markets are becoming more integrated than ever. Moreover, the results from the time-varying parameter model display that the stock market returns of Indonesia, the Philippines and Thailand have all become more closely linked with Singapore. Likewise, Chen et al. (2003) examine dynamic interdependece of the major stock markets in Latin America by using data between 1995 and 2000. They employ the stock market indices of Argentina, Brazil, Chile, Colombia, Mexico and Venezuela and use cointegration and error correction vector autoregressions (VAR) techniques. Their findings show that there is one cointegrating vector that explains the dependence in prices and suggests that the potentials for diversifying risk by investing in different Latin American markets are limited.

Worthington et al. (2003) examine price linkages among Asian equity markets during the Asian crisis. Three developed markets (Hong Kong, Japan and Singapore) and the six emerging markets (Indonesia, Korea, Malaysia, the Philippines, Taiwan and Thailand) are included in the data set and they use multivariate cointegration and VAR analysis to examine the causal relationships among these markets. Their results show stationary relationships and significant causal linkages are determined between the Asian equity markets. Furthermore, Wong et al. (2004) use weekly stock indices of the major stock exchanges in US, UK, Japan, Malaysia, Thailand, Korea, Taiwan, Singapore and Hong Kong. They find that Singapore and Taiwan are cointegrated with Japan while Hong Kong is cointegrated with US and UK. There are no long run equilibirum relationship between Malaysia, Thailand and Korea and the advanced markets of US, UK and Japan.

Gallegati (2006) revisits the issue of integration of emerging markets and of the developed markets with each other over different time horizons by using weekly stock indices data from June 1997 till March 2005 for the five major MENA equity markets (Egypt, Israel, Jordan, Morocco and Turkey). By applying the discrete wavelet decomposition analysis, he finds that wavelet variance of MENA stock markets tends to decrease and wavelet correlation among MENA stock markets tends to increase as the wavelet time scale increases. Comparison of MENA stock markets with the S&P 500 and the Eurostoxx indices results in the finding that these indices are neither regionally nor internationally integrated with the exception of Israel and Turkey. Morana and Beltratti (2008) employ monthly data from stock market indices of US, UK, Germany and Japan to assess the linkages for 1973-2004. Their findings show that the linkages have in general grown stronger over time particularly in US and Europe and there is a progressive integration among those stock markets.

Rua and Nunes (2009) focus on the wavelet comovement analysis both for the aggregate and sectoral levels of the markets of Germany, Japan, US and UK. In terms of the aggregate index, the US and UK stock markets seem to present the highest comovement across time and frequencies while the Japanese market shows a low degree of comovement with the other markets. At sectoral level, the weak comovement of Japan with other countries is present while Germany, UK and the US show a significant comovement at lower frequencies. On the other hand, Karim and Majid (2009) assess the stock market integration among the emerging stock markets of Indonesia and its major trading partners (Japan, US, Singapore and China). They use autoregressive distributed lag (ARDL) approach and cointegration analysis by employing weekly stock market data from 1998 to 2007. Their results demonstrate that the Indonesian stock market is cointegrated with the all of its major trading partners' stock markets.

Aktan et al. (2009) study the emerging market indices of Brazil, Russia, China, India and Argentina (henceforth, BRICA) by investigating the linkages among these markets and their respective relations with the US market. They use the vector autoregression (VAR) methodology and Granger causality tests employing daily data from January 2002 to February 2009. Their results display that the most integrated markets are Russia and Brazil whereas the least integrated ones are China and Argentina.

In an interesting study, Caporale and Spagnolo (2010) demonstrate a tri-variate VAR-GARCH (1,1)-in mean-model to assess the relationship between the stock markets of three Central and Eastern European

Countries (CEECs), namely the Czech Republic, Hungary and Poland with the UK and Russia. They find that there is a significant comovement of these CEEC markets with both the Russia and the UK. Similarly, Modi et al. (2010) study with various alternative techniques the comovement among selected developed and emerging stock markets of the world by using daily index data for the time period July 1997 to June 2008. Through cointegration analysis for the market pairs, they examine stock market indices of India (SENSEX), Hong Kong (HANSENG), Mexico (MXX), Russia (RTS), Brazil (BVSP), UK (FTSE-100) and US (DJIA and NASDAQ). They find that MXX, DOWJONES and NASDAQ are the least dependent on other markets, whereas DOWJONES is the most influential one. Likewise, Taş and Tokmakçioglu (2010) check for cointegration focusing on the market efficiency perspective using 11 emerging stock market and weekly data for the period January 1998-December 2008 and for the sub-period of January 2002-December 2008. Their results show that in the long-term, Czech and Indian markets affect Turkish stock market in a positive manner whereas changes in Argentinian, Indonesian and Hungarian markets affect Turkey in an adverse manner. Furthermore, Brasilian stock market has a positive (negative) relationship with Mexican, Israel and Indian (Korean, Indonesian and Hungarian) stock markets.

Another study by Ali et al. (2011) display the comovement of Pakistan's equity market with the markets of China, India, Indonesia, Japan, Malaysia, Singapore, Taiwan, UK and US. Their data set is monthly and cointegration analysis is used for the period of July 1998 - June 2008. They find that there is no comovement of Pakistan's equity market with the markets of the UK, US, Taiwan, Malaysia and Singapore. However, the Pakistanian equity market moves together with the stock prices of India, China, Japan and Indonesia.

On the other hand, Panpura et al. (2011) examine the short-run causal link among equity markets in order to beter understand how shocks in one market are transmitted to the others. They study the comovement of Indian stock market (BSE Sensex) index with 10 developed and developing countries stock market indices employing daily index prices for the period of July 1997 to December 2009. Their results show that SENSEX has highest correlation with BVSP (% 98) among all the pairs. Furthermore, SENSEX is affected by HANGSENG, STI, DJIA, FTSE and DAX. Besides, SENSEX causes SCI, BVSP, NIKKEI, KOSPI and AORD. Recently, Gallegati (2012) uses a wavelet based approach to test the presence of contagion during the Great Recession. His findings show that all stock markets have been affected by the US subprime crisis whereas Brazil and Japan are the only countries where contagion is observed at all frequencies. Similarly, Madaleno and Pinho (2012) assess the time varying pattern of price shock transmission through stock market linkages by using continuous wavelet methodology and wavelet coherence. Their findings indicate that the relationship among indices is strong but not homogenous across the time period. On the other hand, results favor that the markets, which are closer geographically and economically, exhibit higher correlation and short-run comovements which is mostly confined to the paradigm that long-run fluctuations favor contagion. In a general prespective, Blackburn and Chidambaran (2013) examine the world stock market comovement of 23 developed and 10 emerging countries over a 31 year span of 1980-2010 by employing correlation. Their main finding is to underline that the stock return comovement has increased substantially from the mid-1990s to 2010 in both developed and emerging markets.

Finally, the most recent paper by Ftiti et al. (2015) analyzes the comovement dynamics between OECD countries with the US and Europe by applying evolutionary co-spectral and wavelet analysis. Their findings demonstrate that there is a long-run comovement between Greece, Netherlands, Norway,

Portugal, Spain, Sweden, Italy and the US stock market indices and also this long-run comovement had specifically increased during the begining of 1990s and the subprime crisis in 2007.

These studies all point towards a detailed analysis of the emerging stock markets vis-à-vis US, especially after the Great Recession for a better understanding of the dynamics that are inherent in the linkages of these stock markets.

DATA AND METHODOLOGY

This part consists of two sections:

1. The data,
2. The methodology.

It aims to find the stock market comovements in emerging countries by using frequency domain Granger causality and wavelet comovement methods.

The Data

The data is the weekly closing stock market index value for the period of January 2003-March 2014. The sample consists of 585 observations for each country's stock market acquired from the websites of Yahoo Finance and Bloomberg. Weekly data, which is used due to avoid nonsynchronous trading problems arising from different operating hours and time zones, is more useful then daily or monthly data (Husain and Saidi, 2000). The stock markets used are US, Brazil, China, India, Indonesia, Russia, South Africa and Turkey, respectively. Their abbrevations are SPX, IBOVESPA, SCHOMP, SENSEX, JCI, INDEXCF, JALSH and XU100 index.

Methodologhy

Wavelet Analysis

The measurement of comovement among economic variables attains a special role in several applications in the fields of economics and finance, namely in business cycle analysis, in asset allocations, in risk management and assessing non-linear consumer behavior. Wavelet is a designation of the finite-energy functions with localization properties used very efficiently to represent transient signals. Chui (1992) points out that efficiency means only a small finite number of coefficients are needed to represent a complicated signal. In contrast with the sinusoidal functions of infinite extent (big waves), 'wavelet' implies a 'small wave'. The wavelet transform is a tool that cuts up data or functions or operators into different frequency components, and then studies each component with a resolution matched to its scale Daubechies (1992).

Wavelet analysis merges two approaches as both time and frequency domains are taken into account. Through wavelet analysis it is possible to assess simultaneously how variables are related at different frequencies and how such relationship has evolved over time, by capturing the non-stationary features. This is a distinct and noteworthy aspect as both time and frequency varying behaviour cannot be captured using conventional approaches that are build on mainly linear frameworks (Gençay et. al, 2001; Rua, 2010; Barunik et. al, 2011; Ftiti et. al, 2015).

Mathematically, the wavelet transform decomposes a time series in terms of some elementary functions, $\varphi s,\tau\left(t\right)$, which are derived from a time-localized mother wavelet $\varphi\left(t\right)$ by translation and dilation Percival and Walden (2000). Wavelets grow and decay in a limited time period and are defined as $\varphi_{\tau,s}(t)=\frac{1}{\sqrt{s}}\varphi\left(\frac{t-\tau}{s}\right)$, where τ is the time position (translation parameter), s is the scale (dilation parameter), which is related with the ferqunecy, and $\frac{1}{\sqrt{s}}$ is a normalization factor to ensure that wavelet transforms are comparable across scales and time series. To be a mother wavelet, $\varphi\left(t\right)$, must fulfil certain criteria: it must have zero mean, $\int_{-\infty}^{+\infty}\varphi\left(t\right)dt=0$; its square integrates to unity, $\int_{-\infty}^{+\infty}\varphi^{2}_{(t)}dt=1$, which means that $\varphi\left(t\right)$ is limited to an interval of time; and it should also satisfy the so-called admissibility condition, $0<C_{\varphi}=\int_{0}^{+\infty}\frac{\left|\varphi\left(\omega\right)\right|^{2}}{\omega}d\omega<+\infty$ where $\varphi\left(t\right)$ ^ is the Fourier transform of $\varphi\left(t\right)$.

The continuous wavelet transform of a time series x(t) with respect to is given by the following convolution:

$$W_{x}\left(\tau,s\right)=\int_{-\infty}^{+\infty}x\left(t\right)\varphi^{*}_{\tau,s}\left(t\right)dt=\frac{1}{\sqrt{s}}\int_{-\infty}^{+\infty}x\left(t\right)\varphi\left(\frac{t-\tau}{s}\right)^{*}dt \tag{1}$$

where * denotes the complex conjugate. As with its Fourier counterpart, there is an inverse wavelet transform, defined as:

$$X\left(t\right)=\frac{1}{C_{\varphi}}\int_{-\infty}^{+\infty}\int_{-\infty}^{+\infty}\varphi_{\tau,s}\left(t\right)W_{x}\left(\tau,s\right)\frac{d\tau ds}{s^{2}} \tag{2}$$

This allows to recover the original series, x(t), from the wavelet transform by integrating over all scales and time positions. Likewise in Fourier analysis, several interesting quantities can be defined in the wavelet domain. For instance, one can define the wavelet power spectrum as $\left|W_{x}\left(\tau,s\right)\right|^{2}$. It measures the relative contribution at each time and at each scale to the time series' variance. In fact, the wavelet power spectrum can be integrated across τ and s to recover the total variance of the series as follows:

$$\sigma^{2}_{x}=\frac{1}{C_{\varphi}}\int_{-\infty}^{+\infty}\int_{-\infty}^{+\infty}\left|W_{x}\left(\tau,s\right)\right|^{2}\frac{d\tau ds}{s^{2}} \tag{3}$$

Another quantity of interest is the cross-wavelet spectrum which captures the covariance between two series in the time-frequency space. Given two time series x(t) and y(t), with wavelet transforms $W_{x}\left(\tau,s\right)$ and $W_{y}\left(\tau,s\right)$, one can define the cross-wavelet spectrum as $W_{xy}\left(\tau,s\right)=W_{x}\left(\tau,s\right)W_{y}^{*}\left(\tau,s\right)$. The wavelet-based measure can be calculated as:

$$\rho_{xy}\left(\tau,s\right)=\frac{\mathcal{R}\left(W_{x}\left(\tau,s\right)\right)}{\sqrt{\left|W_{x}\left(\tau,s\right)\right|^{2}\left|W_{y}\left(\tau,s\right)\right|^{2}}} \tag{4}$$

This term allows one to quantify the comovement in the time-frequency space and also helps to assess over which periods of time and frequency, the comovement is at its highest levels (Rua, 2010, 2012).

Frequency Domain Granger Causality

The Granger causality test indicates whether the past changes in x(y) have an impact on current changes in y(x) over a specified time period. Nevertheless, these test results can provide the results on causality over all frequencies. Furthermore, Geweke's linear measure of feedback from one variable to another at a given frequency can provide detailed information about feedback relationships between stock market indices over different frequency bands.

By using a Fourier transformation method in order to apply VAR model for x and y series, the Geweke's measure of linear feedback from y to x at frequency ω is defined as:

$$M_{x\rightarrow y}(\omega)=\log\left[\frac{2\pi f_{x}(\omega)}{\left|\varphi_{11}\left(e^{-\omega i}\right)\right|^{2}}\right]=\log\left[1+\frac{\left|\varphi_{12}\left(e^{-\omega i}\right)\right|^{2}}{\left|\varphi_{11}\left(e^{-\omega i}\right)\right|^{2}}\right] \tag{5}$$

If $\left|\varphi_{12}\left(e^{-\omega i}\right)\right|^{2}=0$, then Geweke's measure will be zero, then y will not Granger cause x at the frequency, ω. Breitung and Candelon (2006) mention that the relationship between x and y in VAR equation:

$$x_{t=\alpha_{1}}x_{t-1+\ldots+\alpha_{p}}x_{t-p+\beta_{1}y_{t-1}}+\ldots+\beta_{p}y_{t-p}+\varepsilon_{1t} \tag{6}$$

The null hypothesis tested by Geweke, $M_{y\rightarrow x}\left(\omega\right)=0$ corresponds to the null hypothesis of $H_{0}:R\left(\omega\right)\beta=0$ where β is the vector of the coefficients of y and R(ω) is the matrix of sines and cosines. Breitung and Candelon (2006) simplify Geweke's null hypothesis so that a usual F-statistics can be obtained to test for causality in the frequency domain. Therefore, due to its' obvious superiority to the conventional Granger causality, this study uses Breitung and Candelon (2006) version of Geweke (1982) as the frequency domain Granger causality analysis (Çelik & Haug, 2012).

EMPIRICAL FINDINGS

This section includes the results of the two superior methods compared to the previous empirical studies that have tried to find a properly defined relationship between the stock exchange markets of the world by being constrained to conventional methodologies that had its roots in linearity based assumptions. First, we introduce the findings and the interpretation of the wavelet comovement analysis which is arguably the superior method in non-linear terms for measuring the consumer (investor) behavior in the stock exchange markets compared to the conventional cointegration methodology. Second, we employ the frequency domain Granger causality analysis which is arguably superior to the conventional Granger causality technique that demands stationary variables and provides only one point result whereas the frequency domain analysis presents the causality results for all the frequencies that exist (from left to right, long-run, medium term and short-run).

Wavelet Comovement Analysis Results

This method enables us to check the power of the movements of the variables in short, medium and long run. Thus, the interpretations become easier between the variables as the oscillation signals are derived for the given time and frequency. In essence, the wavelet comovement analysis is presented through a contour plot. The horizontal axis refers to time while the vertical one refers to frequency. For simplifying the interpretations of the figures, frequency is converted to time units (years). The dark colored areas represent the high degree oscillations whereas the light-colored ones correspond to low degrees in a surface plot. Moreover, darker ones denote the strong comovement while lighter ones denote weak comovement between the two variables. Also, each layers of the color bar, located in the right-hand side of the figure, gives the degree of those signals form the light colors to dark colors. Hence, the series can be checked if they move together or not, and if the strength of the comovement changes across frequencies over time (Rua & Nunes, 2009). Figure 1 displays the wavelet comovement analysis with respective correlation coefficients for US and our selected countries.

Figure 1a, which is at the top left part of Figure 1, gives the wavelet results of the US and Brazil. One can conclude that the stock market activity of the US and Brazil seem to present weak but significant comovement at lower frequencies in the beginning of the sample period and then the degree of the comovement seems to spread to all frequencies after 2006. Furthermore, considering the pre-2008 and post-2008 results show that there is a statistically significant and high comovement. However, during the Great Recession the comovement is in an adverse manner. In the whole period, there is generally a highly positive comovement between the US and Brazil stock markets. One of the striking results is in Figure 1b which shows a weak comovement at long term whereas this is reversed at high frequencies for the US-China pair. During the global crisis, even though US and China have both been affected negatively, Chinese stock market seemingly moves in opposite direction compared to the US. This is probably signalling the cash outflow from US to China.

Figures 1c, 1d, 1e and 1f demonstrate similar outcomes and leads us to believe that the comovement relationship between US and India, Indonesia, Russia and South Africa could be summarized as a strong comovement at high level frequencies around the middle parts of the sample period, but then, there is an increasing level of comovement at long term fluctuations which extends to all degrees of frequencies after 2009 for all country pairs. This result especially peaks after 2012 and we find evidence of a strong comovement at all degrees of frequencies. During the Great Recession, our findings are again similar to the case of China but with an adverse relationship in effect. Moreover, it is important to realize that the US and Russia relationship which is in figure 1e shows high and statistically significant wavelet comovement at all frequencies since 2012. This is remarkable when one considers the economic and political differences that have been observed between Russia and the advanced economies since the start of the Great Recession. In addition, Russia's role as a key partner with US is rather difficult to model in economic terms given that China and India are the two main trading partners of the US after Canada.

Figure 1. Wavelet comovement results

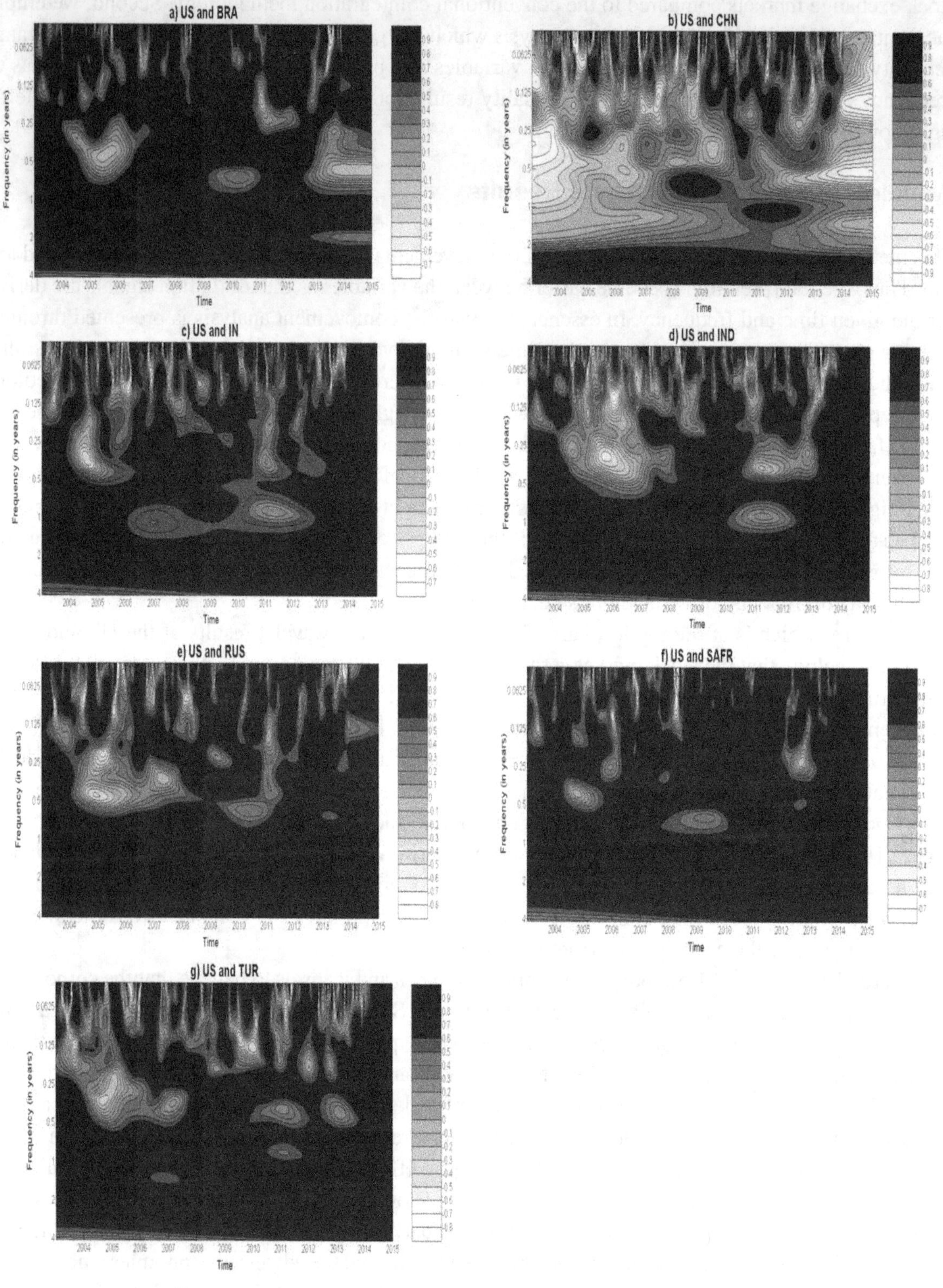

In Figure 1g, the US and Turkish stock markets seem to execise a high degree of comovement across time at almost all frequencies. Especially after the start of the Great Recession, this significant comovement can notably be observed for all the frequencies with a positive degree. There are some local points that display a negative degree of comovement but these are only a few and short instances. Hence, the comovement of the US and Turkish stock markets are statistically significant over almost the entire sample period whereas this result is not observed for other country pairs with the US. Therefore, the capital flows out of Turkish stock exchange market follow a similar pattern with the US market although Turkish stock market is rather shallow and has less global attention compared to the US market. However, the high level of foreign ownership in Turkish stock market is seemingly leading to a similar behavior in the Turkish market compared with the advanced economies. It is also possible that the market participants form expectations in similar manners although their portfolio structure, maturity and magnitude are not even close to each other.

Frequency Domain Causality Test Results

Frequency domain causality analysis is vital because it offers a bigger and presumably better picture than the Granger causality analysis as it is derived to provide the causality test results as F-statistics between any two variables at all frequencies in a given time period. In a typical figure, the results are reported for the F-test statictics with % 5 and % 10 critical values for all frequencies in a continuous manner. High frequencies correspond to short-run periods and low frequencies represent the long term on the vertical axis. Hence, the part on the x-axis close to the origin shows the long-term findings and the right side of the x-axis stands for the short run. By comparing the results that usually are in curves and the lines for the critical values of % 5 and % 10, it is easy to interprete the nature of the causality relationship between any two variables in a frequency domain figure. Only the values above the critical value lines support statistical significance and prove the existence of causality from one variable to the other. Hence, it is possible to observe any type of causality uni-, bi- or none. Figure 2 includes all the vis-à-vis comparison of the US stock market and the emerging markets, starting from 2a and ending with 2g.

Figures 2a, 2b, 2c, 2d demonstrate that the test results of frequency domain Granger causality are not statistically significant for most of the frequency levels, especially for the long run. When we consider the individual results starting with Brazil and US stock markets in Figure 2a, the null hypothesis of IBOVESPA→SPX is rejected at % 5 significance level for high frequencies whereas this finding is not relevant for the entire frequency interval. In particular, the rejection of the null hypothesis takes place for high frequencies that is for the short run, while SPX→IBOVESPA is only rejected in the range around 0.3 corresponding to the long run. At % 10 significance level, there is persistent significance from IBOVESPA to SPX at high frequencies.

Rather contrary findings are in Figure 2b. The null hypothesis of no causality is rejected almost during the entire frequency range [0, 3] except for about 1, which stands for short to medium term as SHCOMP causes SPX at % 5 and % 10 significance levels.

In Figure 2c, the null hypothesis of no conjecturable link between US and India is rejected almost for all frequencies, except for the value of 0.5 (that corresponds to a long-term) at a significance level of % 5. In Figure 2e, the causal relations obtained in the bivariate model for US and Russia is statistically significant from INDEXCF to SPX in the range interval [0.5, 3] whereas in the Figures 2d, and 2f, there is no causality observed between US and Indonesia and US and South Africa, except in Figure 2d for the value of 0.5 (which stands for the long-term) is significant, meaning a causality from JCI to SPX.

Figure 2. Frequency domain granger causality results

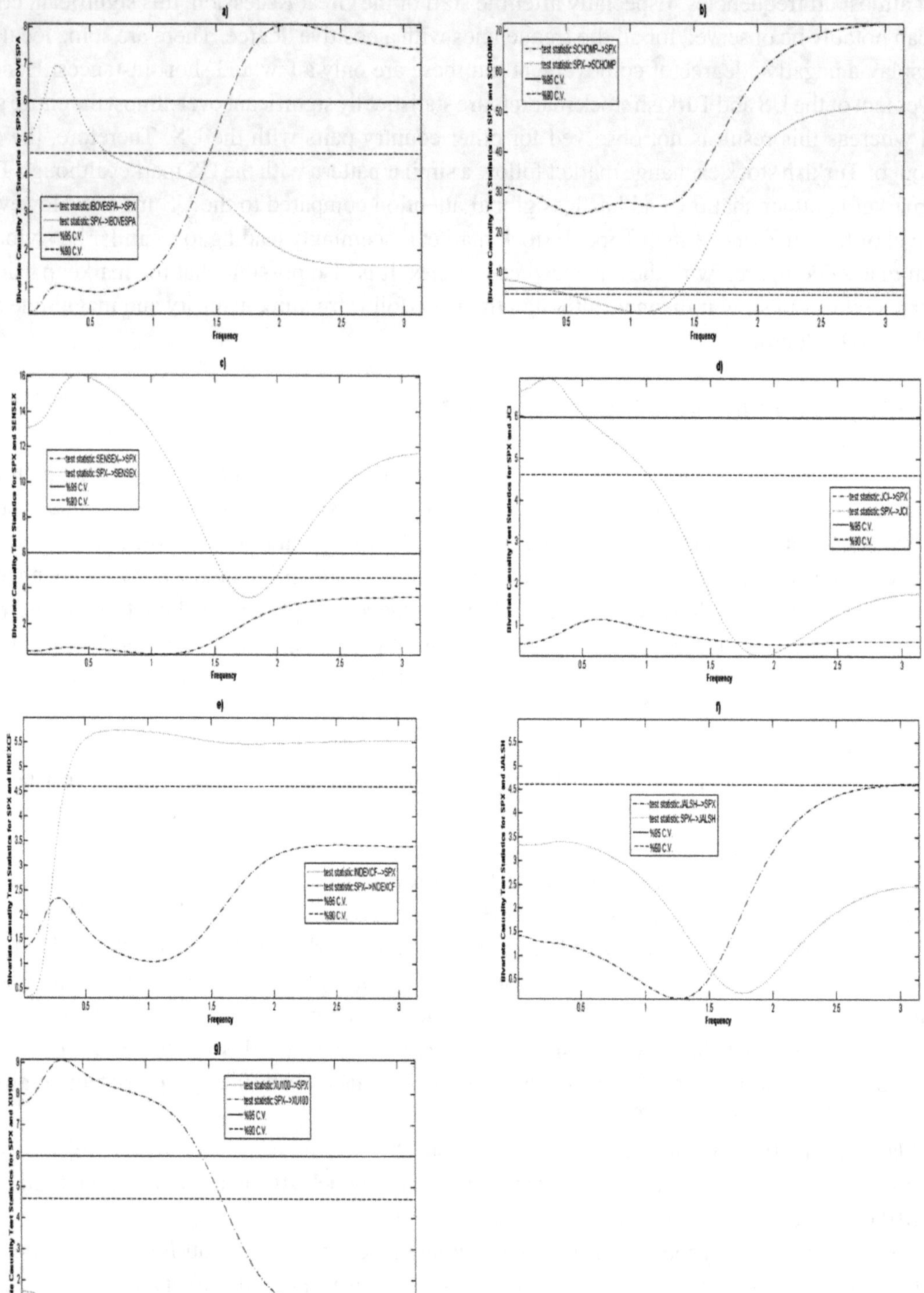

In Figure 2g, we observe that at frequencies less than 1.5 (medium to long run) the causality from SPX to XU100 is significant at % 5 level. Hence, US stock market changes causes Turkish stock market changes in the medium and long term with no response back from the Turkish market.

CONCLUSION

This paper revisits a much studied but still controversial topic of the comovements of stock market indices by empirically testing the relationship between emerging markets of Brazil, China, India, Indonesia, Russia, South Africa and Turkey (the stock market abbreviations as IBOVESPA, SCHOMP, SENSEX, JCI, INDEXCF, JALSH and XU100) and the benchmark US (with the stock mark abbreviation of SPX). The main aim is to assess whether the US stock market and the emerging markets observe any degree of comovement (in the wavelet sense-a recent non-linear method which is superior in observing the consumer/investor behavior in stock markets compared to conventional linear methodologies) and causality in the frequency domain (another recent non-linear method which is capable of measuring the direction and magnitude-possible significance-of causality better than the conventional Granger causality analysis).

In general, the comovement between stock markets is significant and strong at high frequencies. Therefore, short term or long term should be taken into account to address the international portfolio diversification issues. We also observe that the strength of the comovement in the time-frequency band varies across countries. All these results highlight the importance of taking into consideration the comovements of stock markets in designing economic policies while considering the role of financial markets in a capitalist system. Although, financial markets provide valuable data in high frequency and much earlier than many economic variables, we should not disregard the importance of real economy and the data that is announced with a certain lag. In summary, the wavelet comovements of stock markets in India, Indonesia, China, and Turkey are stronger with the US stock market whereas this is hardly the case for the stock markets of Russia, South Africa and Brazil.

Causality tests in frequency domain are also conducted in order to check the possible existence and direction of causality in the time frequency space. The results show that US stock market causes Turkish, Indonesian, Indian and Brasilian stock markets at low frequencies (that is long term) while South African, Brasilian and Russian stock markets cause the US stock market at high frequencies (that is the short run). However, Chinese stock market causes US stock market at all frequencies and so does the US stock market. Hence, the only bi-directional causality in the frequency domain is between US stock market and the Chinese stock market.

Hence, the empirical results show the superiority of the US market in terms of both frequency domain causality and wavelet comovement with China being the only exception as the major trading partner of the US. These findings mean that the consumers who have low levels of wealth in the emerging markets are unable to reap the benefits of the domestic stock exchange markets as these markets are either under the influence of the US stock market and/or too shallow and risky for small investors. In emerging economies, most of the consumers depend on their low levels of income to make a living and hardly have any sources left for saving so that they could start building some level of wealth for their future. Domestic stock markets should provide favorable opportunities to consumers who have small amounts of savings but still want to keep these in stocks rather than converting their savings into foreign currency with the expectation of a future depreciation and/or invest in commodities that are difficult to trade at a faster pace. Therefore, it is very important for policy makers to assess the needs of the consumers that could save in the emerging markets as well as reforming the labor market to provide jobs for those who would be able to save once they start to obtain permanent levels of income. Consumer purchasing power increases leads to healthy levels of consumption and savings, some of which end up in the domestic stock exchange market. These funds further enhance the competition in the economy and the creation of large firms that are capable of employing more workers that presumably would also raise their standards of living once they enter the labor market.

Moreover, there should be attempts to bridge the gap between the financial markets and the real economy rather than just letting the crisis take its' course and cause damage to the system which is hardly recoverable over a long period of time. Hence, the stock market indices should be followed carefully as well as their influence on the real economy. This paper argues that further research is needed to find a way to examine the linkages between high frequency financial market data and low frequency real economic variable data.

REFERENCES

Aktan, B., Mandacı, P. E., Kopurlu, B. S., & Ersener, B. (2009). Behaviour of emerging stock markets in the global financial meltdown: Evidence from bric-a. *African Journal of Business Management*, *3*, 396–404.

Ali, S., Butt, B. Z., & Rehman, K. (2011). Comovement between emerging and developed stock markets: An investigation through cointegration analysis. *World Applied Sciences Journal*, *12*, 395–403.

Barunik, J., Vacha, L., & Kristoufek, L. (2011). Comovement of Central European stock markets using wavelet coherence: evidence from high-frequency data (Working paper). Charles University Prague, Faculty of Social Sciences.

Blackburn, W. D., & Chidambaran, N. K. (2013). Is the world stock market comovement changing? (Working paper). University of Massachusetts.

Breitung, J., & Candelon, B. (2006). Testing for short and long-run causality: A frequency domain approach. *Journal of Econometrics*, *132*(2), 363–378. doi:10.1016/j.jeconom.2005.02.004

Caporale, M. G., & Spagnolo, N. (2010). Stock market integration between three CEECs, Russia and the UK (working paper). CESIFO.

Çelik, S., & Haug, K. (2012, September). Revisiting the link between consumers sentiment and economic activity. *Paper presented at the 31st CIRET Conference*, Vienna.

Chen, G., Firth, M., & Rui, O. M. (2002). Stock market linkages: Evidence from Latin America. *Journal of Banking & Finance*, *26*(6), 113–1141. doi:10.1016/S0378-4266(01)00160-1

Chui, K. C. (1992). *An introduction to wavelets: Wavelet analysis and its applications*. San Diego: Academic Press.

Daubechies, I. (1992). *Ten lectures on wavelet. CBMS-NSF Regional Conference Series in Applied Mathematics* (Vol. 61). Philadelphia: Society for Industrial and Applied Mathematics.

Elyasiani, E., Priyal, P., & Puri, T. N. (1998). Interdependence and dynamic linkages between stock markets of Sri Lanka and its trading partners. *Journal of Multinational Finance Management*, *8*(1), 89–101. doi:10.1016/S1042-444X(98)00020-6

Ftiti, Z., Tiwari, A., Belanes, A., & Guesmi, K. (2015). Tests of financial market contagion: Evolutionary cospectral analysis vs. wavelet analysis. *Computational Economics*, *46*(4), 575–611. doi:10.1007/s10614-014-9461-8

Gallegati, M. (2005). A wavelet analysis of MENA stock markets.

Gallegati, M. (2012). A wavelet-based approach to test for financial market contagion. *Computational Statistics & Data Analysis*, *56*(11), 3491–3497. doi:10.1016/j.csda.2010.11.003

Gelos, G., & Sahay, R. (2000). Financial market spillovers in transition economies. *IMF Working Paper*, *2000*(71).

Gençay, R., Selçuk, F., & Witcher, B. (2001). Differentiating intraday seasonalities through wavelet multi-scaling. *Physica A*, *289*(3-4), 543–556. doi:10.1016/S0378-4371(00)00463-5

Husain, F., & Saidi, R. (2000). The integration of the Pakistani equity market with internatioanl equity markets: An investigation. *Journal of International Development*, *12*(2), 207–218. doi:10.1002/(SICI)1099-1328(200003)12:2<207::AID-JID636>3.0.CO;2-Z

Karim, A. B., Majid, M. S. A. & Karim, S. A. A. (2009). Financial integration between Indonesia and its major trading partners. MPRA.

Korajczyk, A. R. (1996). A measure of stock market integration for developed and emerging markets. *The World Bank Economic Review*, *10*(2), 267–289. doi:10.1093/wber/10.2.267

Madaleno, M., & Pinho, C. (2012). International stock market indices comovements: A new look. *International Journal of Finance & Economics*, *17*(1), 89–102. doi:10.1002/ijfe.448

Markowitz, H. (1952). Portfolio selection. *The Journal of Finance*, *7*, 77–91.

Modi, A. G., Patel, B. K., & Patel, N. R. (2010). The study on co-movement of selected stock markets. *International Research Journal of Finance and Economics*, *47*, 170–185.

Morana, C., & Beltratti, A. (2008). Comovements in international stock markets. *International Financial Markets. Institutions and Money*, *18*(1), 31–45. doi:10.1016/j.intfin.2006.05.001

Morck, R., Yeung, B., & Yu, W. (2000). The information content of stock markets: Why do emerging markets have synchronous stock price movements? *Journal of Financial Economics*, *58*(1-2), 215–238. doi:10.1016/S0304-405X(00)00071-4

Ng, H. T. (2002). Stock market linkages in South-East Asia. *Asian Economic Journal*, *16*(4), 353–377. doi:10.1111/1467-8381.00157

Panpura, D., Patel, B. K., & Patel, N. (2011). Study of comovement and interdependence of Indian stock market with selected foreign stock markets. *Asian Journal of Research in Banking and Finance*, *1*, 74–92.

Percival, B. D., & Walden, A. T. (2000). *Wavelet methods for time series analysis*. Cambridge University Press. doi:10.1017/CBO9780511841040

Rua, A. (2010). Measuring comovement in the time-frequency space. *Journal of Macroeconomics*, *32*(2), 685–691. doi:10.1016/j.jmacro.2009.12.005

Rua, A. (2012). Wavelets in economics. *Banco De Portugal Economic Bulletin, Summer,* 71-79.

Rua, A., & Nunes, L. C. (2009). International comovement of stock market returns: A wavelet analysis. *Journal of Empirical Finance*, *16*(4), 632–639. doi:10.1016/j.jempfin.2009.02.002

Taş, O., & Tokmakçıoğlu, K. (2010). Efficient market hypothesis and comovement among emerging markets. *Dogus University Journal*, *11*, 286–301.

Wong, W., Penm, J., Terrell, R. D., & Lim, K. Y. C. (2004). The relationship between stock markets of major developed countries and Asian emerging markets. *Journal of Applied Mathematics and Decision Sciences*, *8*(4), 201–218. doi:10.1155/S1173912604000136

Worthington, C. A., Katsuura, M., & Higg, H. (2003). Price linkages in Asian equity markets: Evidence bordering the Asian economic, currency and financial crises. *Asia-Pacific Financial Markets*, *10*(1), 29–44. doi:10.1023/B:FEJM.0000039873.53973.3c

ADDITIONAL READING

Christiansen, B., & Erdoğdu, M. M. (Eds.). (2016). Comparative Economics and Regional Development in Turkey. Hershey, PA, USA: IGI Global. doi:10.4018/978-1-4666-8729-5

Das, R. C. (Ed.). (2016). Handbook of Research on Global Indicators of Economic and Political Convergence. Hershey, PA, USA: IGI Global. doi:10.4018/978-1-5225-0215-9

Diehl, M., Alexandrova-Kabadjova, B., Heuver, R., & Martínez-Jaramillo, S. (Eds.). (2016). Analyzing the Economics of Financial Market Infrastructures. Hershey, PA, USA: IGI Global. doi:10.4018/978-1-4666-8745-5

Ianole, R. (Ed.). (2017). Applied Behavioral Economics Research and Trends. Hershey, PA, USA: IGI Global. Doi: doi:10.4018/978-1-5225-1826-6

Munir, Q. (Ed.). (2016). Handbook of Research on Financial and Banking Crisis Prediction through Early Warning Systems. Hershey, PA, USA: IGI Global. doi:10.4018/978-1-4666-9484-2

KEY TERMS AND DEFINITIONS

Emerging Economies: Emerging markets are those economies that are similar in their potential for future growth and market expansion through different forms of economic stimulus such as attracting new technologies, foreign investment, or external participation in their commercial affairs.

Frequency Domain Causality: Breitung and Candelon (2006) propose a test that is able to control for equilibrium relationships and at the same time to distinguish between the short-run and the long-run predictive power. The innovativeness of the frequency domain non-causality test lies on two basic attributes that are usually neglected from the standard causality tests routinely implemented in the literature (e.g. Toda and Yamamoto, 1995; Hsiao, 1981). First, the frequency domain approach can identify non-linear causal relationships and, second, the testing of causality is carried out in a dynamic manner since it is implemented over several alternative frequencies, providing this way a more structured understanding about the true nature of the investigated causal relationship.

Great Recession: The global financial crisis between the years 2007 and 2009 has cast its long shadow on the economic fortunes of many countries, resulting in what has often been called the 'Great Recession'.

Stock Market: The stock market is the market that shares of publicly held companies are issued and traded either through exchanges. Also, known as the equity market, the stock market is one of the most vital components of a free-market economy, as it provides companies with access to capital in exchange for giving investors a slice of ownership in the company. The stock market makes it possible to grow small initial sums of money into large ones, and to become wealthy without taking the risk of starting a business.

Wavelet Comovement: An econometric method developed by Rua (2010) for time series data which uses the wavelet analysis to depict the cross-correlation between two variables over a specified interval so as to determine whether the variables in question have common paths.

Chapter 11
Nowcasting Capacity Utilization in Turkey: A Continuous Wavelet Analysis

Özlem Taşseven
Doğuş University, Turkey

ABSTRACT

Capacity utilization in macroeconomics is always related to inflation rate and unemployment level. However, the Great Recession has taught us that there might have been other factors considered in determining and/or be determined by capacity utilization. In order to further enhance Phillips Curve relationship unconventional variables such as financial and survey variables are considered. The relationship between capacity utilization rates and several real variables such as industrial production, gross domestic product growth rate, unemployment rate, consumer expenditures, financial variables such as return on BIST 100 index, exchange rate of currency basket, interest rates, survey variables such as consumer consumption index, business tendency survey and survey of expectations is investigated using data between 2006 and 2015 for Turkey. All of the above-mentioned variables indicate the production capacity and their repercussions on other macro variables except the level of standard of living. We also highlight the repercussions of production capacity concerning welfare state.

INTRODUCTION

Starting in 1980s Turkish industrial sector has improved its competitive situation as a result of neoliberal policy, technical advances in manufacturing and globalization. Especially, at the macro and micro level real progress is based on technical advances. Supply chain management and technical advances in information systems caused an increase in the productivity of production factors, marketing and distribution channels in horizontal and vertical expansion. Essentially, decrease in production costs improved the competitive power of industrial sector.

One of the important causes of increase in industrial sector is the change in the path of industrial production methods. The primary cause of this change is the transfer of industrial production to devel-

DOI: 10.4018/978-1-5225-2139-6.ch011

oping countries from developed countries. Factors like legal, political and environmental arrangements have caused significant improvements in industrial development of countries like Turkey. Developments in industrial sector have caused significant improvements in the growth of the economy as a result of exchange of information, innovation and spillover effects. The replacement of low value added items with high value added items was encouraged by government authorities.

Although neoliberal policies have added positive contributions to the development of industrial sector, the changes in industrial structure is far away from the desired level of development. The targets were determined as a result of selective policies and fluctuating situations. Therefore, the production is still based in labor intensive technologies. There's very little progress on market research and research & development. In addition to this, the sector has become more dependent on imports instead of domestic production.

There is no doubt the productivity of industrial sector is positively related to capacity utilization. In final analysis, the utilization rate in productive capacity is related to the usage of existing industrial capacity. Capacity utilization ratio is found by comparing existing industrial capacity with the real productive capability. Especially, in economy boom periods this ratio goes up and decreases during economic crises. The capacity utilization rate is never hundred percent. However, the trends in capacity utilization rate give useful information about the direction of the economy. If this rate goes up, we get the sign of an increase in industrial sector output. This ratio becomes more meaningful when it's combined with industrial production index. Capacity utilization helps to explain investment behavior, productivity measurements, inflation and used as an indicator of aggregate demand (Schultze, 1963).

Besides these above effects of capacity utilization we should also focus on the reflection of the changing level of living standard. It is interesting to observe that while the per capita gross domestic product of Turkey had increased from $ 7627 in 2006 to $ 9364 in 2015, the capacity utilization rate in manufacturing between 2006 and 2015 remained constant. This incompatibility between the capacity utilization rate and level of living standard moved in negative direction, because the increase in the standard of living has germinated from the increase in agricultural and services sectors. Additionally, as an indicator of an improvement in living standard of Turkish consumers, human development index could be used. In this context, human development index considering the social and cultural development can be used in order to compare the status of Turkey based on human development and its performance between 2006 and 2015. Turkey has moved from 84th place in 2006 to 72th place in 2015 according to human development index.

As to the relationship between capacity utilization rate and inflation rate, Phillips curve approach is investigated in the literature. The shape of the short-run Phillips curve is a mostly investigated issue. Phillips curve describes a positive short-run relationship between the level of economic activity and inflation. It is observed that the demand fluctuations have a positive effect on price inflation and a negative effect on growth of output. Since the aggregate demand fluctuations are high, this makes aggregate demand unpredictable. Because of aggregate demand uncertainty the output growth would decrease related to these concerns. If the aggregate demand in the economy exceeds the level of aggregate supply, then price pressures and inflation rate increase (Kandil, 1998).

The objective of this chapter is to investigate the relationship between capacity utilization rates and several real variables such as industrial production, gross domestic product growth rate, unemployment rate, consumer expenditures, financial variables such as return on BIST 100 index, exchange rate of currency basket, interest rates, survey variables such as consumer consumption index, business tendency index and survey of expectations using data between 2006 and 2015. Section two reviews the literature on capacity utilization. Section three presents the data and explains the methodology. Section four presents the empirical findings and finally section five provides the summary.

BACKGROUND

Within Keynesian framework aggregate supply curve could be investigated in three different sections. In the first section the changes in demand doesn't affect prices. In the second section the changes in demand affect price and quantity. In the third section, there are only price changes; which mean an excess capacity in the first section. In the third section, there is an excessive usage of resources. The second section is somewhere in between the two alternatives. Kim (1999) argues that deficient product demand leads to lower capacity utilization, whereas expansionary aggregate demand policies could lead to higher capacity utilization rate.

If the level of aggregate demand exceeds the level of aggregate supply, there would be upward pressure on consumer prices which increase inflation. Because of the capacity constraint the supply level can't exceed a certain level. If the demand exceeds that level of output because of the inflation pressure the interest rates would increase. In this case, Central Bank should use monetary policy in short term to achieve price stability.

The basic assumption behind the economic literature in this field is the increase in employment and economic growth as a result of increase in capacity utilization rate. Capacity utilization rate is an important indicator for resource utilization and other macroeconomic variables. Corrado and Mattey (1997) calculate capacity utilization rate by looking at the growth of capital and output.

One of the well- known topics in the literature is the estimation of Phillips curve, which is mostly used in estimating inflation. Phillips Curve theory mentions that capacity utilization rates may be a crucial determinant of inflation. McElhattan (1985), Gordon (1997), Garner (1994), Corrado and Mattey (1997), Belton and Cebula (2000) and Alvarez Lois (2000) state that capacity utilization rates could be considered as forecast of future inflation. When the input level gets closer to its maximum levels, marginal costs of production will increase in the short run. Belton and Cebula state that in the case of low resource usage, capacity utilization rates can be used instead of the unemployment rate. When resource usage reaches its upper limit, changes in prices could be related with capacity constraints (Finn, 1995; Emery and Chang, 1997, Dave, 2006). However, it is claimed that some factors such as greater open economy, technological advances, the level of investment and competitiveness have lowered the relationship between capacity utilization and the inflation.

Arabacı and Arabacı (2008), Finn (1995), Garner (1994) and Fictenbaum (2003) investigate the causal effects of capacity utilization on inflationary trends. External economic developments and changes in exchange rate are also found to affect inflation via import prices. Monetary policy can change inflationary expectations.

Arabacı and Arabacı (2008) investigate the relationship between inflation and capacity utilization rates between 1991 and 2008 using quarterly data for Turkish economy. They determine optimal capacity utilization rate that does not increase the inflation. The analysis period is divided into two phases, covering the period before and after 2002. After 2002 as a result inflation targeting policy of the Central Bank, the inflation rate was lowered to around 10 percent. Arabacı and Arabacı state that optimal capacity utilization rate has increased after 2002. Capacity utilization rate over 82 percent causes inflation to rise in Turkey. The capacity utilization rate is found to be 76 percent for the 1991-2001 period, and 80.65 percent for 2002-2008 period. The difference in the rates could be as a result of structural reforms undertaken after 2002 in the Turkish economy. These reforms include the relatively more opening of the economy after 2002, the increase in the capital inflows, the increase in the productivity as a result of technological progress, the increase in foreign capital investments and research & development expenses.

Arabacı and Eryiğit (2012) estimate an extended Phillips curve relationship using the threshold regression model for Turkish economy. The variables used are the inflation rate, capacity utilization rate, output gap, industrial production, import shocks and monetary shocks. Arabacı and Eryiğit estimate the capacity utilization rate as 75 percent. It is shown that there exists a nonlinear relationship between the real economic activity and inflation.

Finn (1995) argues capacity utilization and inflation are positively related according to Keynesian theory. However, the relationship is the same whether utilization is high or low. The theory indicates that capacity utilization rate can be used as an indicator for future inflation and gross domestic product forecasts inflation better than capacity utilization. Finn states that capacity utilization rate over 82 percent causes inflation to increase for United States economy.

Fictenbaum (2003) states that studies on capacity utilization have estimated the natural rate of capacity utilization (NAIRCU) to be 82 percent. Fictenbaum questions the existence of a vertical long run Phillips curve. It is found that Federal Reserve Bank od United States was careful in raising interest rates to slow down the economy while the policy aims to pursue full employment. It is argued that if capacity utilization was higher than the NAIRCU, inflation would accelerate.

Kim (1999) investigates the optimal capacity utilization rate and its determinants, finds that for Unites States manufacturing sector capital expansion is not supported by demand growth. Higher material and capital prices have led to low capacity utilization. Kim argues that the price of capital is negatively related to capacity utilization rate. Capacity utilization could be seen as a summary index of determinants of investment.

Eres (2011) analyzes the relationship between capacity utilization rate and output for Turkish economy using co-integration methodology and compares with other studies on capacity utilization rate. According to Eres there are various measurements of capacity utilization rate. These are Wharton method, output - capital ratio method, survey method, estimate of production function and co-integration method. Capacity utilization rate which are established by using different methods were compared by manufacturing industry.

Shapiro (1989) analyzes the determinants of capacity utilization rate such as capital stock and time trend using regression method. Assuming ceteris paribus it is found that an increase in capacity utilization rate causes an increase in gross domestic product.

Demiroğlu and Sarıkaya (2013) argue that although gross domestic product, industrial production and unemployment rate are normalized by reaching pre-2008 crises levels, capacity utilization rate couldn't adapt to this trend. As Demiroğlu and Sarıkaya state one percent increase of capital accumulation decreases the capacity utilization by one percent. If the effect of global capital movements is abandoned, a significant recovery is seen on capacity utilization. Another finding of Demiroğlu and Sarıkaya is that investments of machinery and equipment affect production capacity nearly three times more. Because of depreciation effect, spending on machinery and equipment creates marginal capacity.

In the literature some studies argue that there is a strong relationship between capacity utilization and inflation. Eres (2011) considers capacity utilization rate as a leading indicator for inflation. Arabacı

& Arabacı (2008) and Finn (1995) find that there is positive relationship between them. On the other hand Garner (1994), Yamak & Küçükkale (2000) and Yamak & Ceylan (2006) couldn't find significant relationship between capacity utilization and inflation.

Garner (1994) points out the similarity between analyses using both the nonaccelerating inflation rate of capacity utilization (NAIRCU) and the capacity utilization rate. The unemployment rate is replaced with the capacity utilization rate in Phillips curve model. Phillips curve identifies a negative relationship between inflation and unemployment rates. The nonaccelerating inflation rate of capacity utilization is the rate at which inflation equals expected inflation. Garner finds the nonaccelerating inflation rate of capacity utilization (NAIRCU) is around 82 percent for United States. On the other hand, McElhattan (1985) finds a stable-inflation capacity utilization rate of 81.7% for United States between 1959 and1983. Garner states the relationship between capacity utilization and inflation has weakened since there has been an increase in technological advances or strong business investment.

Increase in real production would provide production possibilities to increase, which would decrease unemployment rate. More intense usage of production factors would increase the expenses on production, causing the cost of production upwards. The increasing cost would lead to an increase in inflation. According to another approach there won't be any inflationary pressures since capacity deficit would be completed by imports.

Yamak and Ceylan (2006) investigate the relationship between inflation and capacity utilization rate during the period of 1987 and 2004 for Turkey. They use capacity utilization rate and its square as explanatory variables in the inflation equation. Yamak and Ceylan claim that when the capacity utilization rate exceeds optimal level, there will be inflationary pressures. Optimal capacity utilization rate which provides the price stability has been determined in Turkish case. This rate has been found to be 76% on average. Yamak and Küçükkale (2000) found the optimal capacity utilization rate as 76% as well. It has been found that the degree of the effects of rate of capacity utilization below and above the optimal capacity utilization rate which provides the price stability is different. So, the relationship between the rates of inflation and capacity utilization is found to be asymmetric. Another variable to be considered with capacity utilization is the unemployment rate. Expanding production network of companies with new investment expenditures creates the labor force that would operate at the marginal capacity. If factors are ignored, the unemployment rate is expected to decrease also.

On the other hand, the shape of the Phillips curve has several effects for the conduct of monetary policy. The negative effects of inflation in the long run necessitate the monetary policy to focus on price stability. However, the short-run relationship between economic activity and the raise of inflation has an important role in the conduct of monetary policy.

Clark et al., (1995) analyze the implications of alternative monetary policy reaction functions using a model of output and inflation in United States. Emery & Chang (1997) argue that Federal Reserve Bank of Unites States investigates not only macroeconomic indicators but also some other sub-indicators. One of them is the capacity utilization rate showing the real sector activity in the economy. The forecast of Federal Reserve Bank of Unites States for capacity utilization is used as a leading indicator for inflation rate. In general, a capacity utilization rate above % 82 signals an increase in inflation rate. Global labor and capital markets decrease the importance of capacity utilization for United States. The increase in unmeasurable productivity caused an increase in growth potential of United States economy. Till 1983 the relationship between capacity utilization and inflation was strong, whereas the relationship has weakened because of global capital flows after 1983.

Clark et al., (1995) explore the links between excess demand, inflation and monetary policy. Their model includes two equations which are Phillips curve and aggregate demand equation. The response of monetary policy actions on the economy would have lags. The difference between potential and actual output would have deviations. If the deviations are positive there will be inflationary effects; otherwise there will be disinflationary effects. The costs of running into capacity constraints can be high, as the periods of excess supply needed to reverse the inflationary effects are sharper and longer than the periods of excess demand. The implication for monetary policy is to avoid the effects of overshooting of inflation.

The role of capacity utilization is important in observed business cycle fluctuations. Lucas (1975), Cho and Cooley (1992) and Ireland (1994) state that both technology and money supply shocks have a crucial role in cyclical output fluctuations. They argue that the relationship is positive on average, due to some opposite movements. Finn (1995) argues that the shocks to aggregate demand also affect aggregate supply. Finn states that supply shocks could explain why inflation and real economic activity sometimes move in opposite directions. Boileau and Normandin (1999) employ cross-correlations between capacity utilization and a measure of the business cycle. These correlations summarize the dynamics of the business cycle and capacity utilization. They show whether capacity utilization represents a lagging, coincident, or leading indicator of the business cycle.

Hansen and Prescott (2005) state that when all the plants in the economy operate, there would be a restriction on the capacity utilization. They find that business cycles in their model are asymmetric—troughs are deeper on average and peaks are tall. The share of labor is found to be counter-cyclical.

MAIN FOCUS OF THE CHAPTER

Issues, Controversies, Problems

In the previous literature in the analysis on capacity utilization methodologies such as correlation, regression, co-integration and threshold regression methods are used, however time series data are used and time series dimension was considered only. In this chapter, we use continuous wavelet analysis which concentrates on both time and frequency dimensions.

Empirical Analysis

The Model and the Data Used in the Analyses

In this section, we present the model used in order to estimate capacity utilization, describe the data set used in the analysis, and introduce the basic methodology of continuous wavelet analysis.

The capacity utilization rate equation of our interest in this chapter can be indicated as in equation 1 below using a functional representation:

$$\text{CAPUT} = f(\text{INDPRO, GROWTH, UNEMP, PCE, BIST, EXC, INT, CCI, BTS, CPIEXP}) \quad (1)$$

The determinants of capacity utilization rate are selected as several real variables such as gross growth in industrial production (INDPRO), gross domestic product growth rate (GROWTH), unemployment rate (UNEMP), private consumer expenditures (PCE), financial variables such as return on BIST 100 index (BIST), exchange rate of currency basket (EXC), one week repurchasing agreement interest rates (INT) and survey variables such as consumer consumption index (CCI), business tendency survey (BTS) and consumer price index as a survey of expectations variable (CPIEXP) using data between 2006 and 2015. All data are derived from Central Bank of Turkey database.

The twelve month end consumer price index median is used as survey of expectation variable in the analysis. The return on BIST 100 index is calculated as the change in the value of the index at period t and t-1.

Methodology

The wavelet transform decomposes a time series in terms of some elementary functions, $\psi_{\tau,s}(t)$, which are composed from a time-localized mother wavelet $\psi(t)$ by translation (Percival and Walden (2000)). Wavelets are defined as

$$\psi_{\tau,s}\left(t\right)=\frac{1}{\sqrt{s}}\psi\left(\frac{t-\tau}{s}\right) \tag{2}$$

where τ is the time position (translation parameter), s is the scale (dilation parameter), which is related with the frequency, and $\frac{1}{\sqrt{s}}$ is a normalization so that wavelet transforms are comparable across different scales and time series variables.

Torrence and Compo (1998) developed the approaches to estimating the cross-wavelet power, the cross wavelet coherence, and the phase difference which can be considered as local variance, covariance and the time lag in the time-frequency space. This chapter uses continuous wavelet transform which is suitable for orthogonal wavelet bases. The continuous wavelet transform (CWT), cross wavelet transform (XWT) and wavelet coherence (WTC) is taken from Grinsted et al. (2004).

Continuous Wavelet Analysis

The continuous wavelet transform of a time series $x(t)$ with respect to $\psi(t)$ is given by the following:

$$W_x\left(\tau,s\right)=\int_{-\infty}^{+\infty}x\left(t\right)\psi_{\tau,s}^{*}\left(t\right)dt=\frac{1}{\sqrt{s}}\int_{-\infty}^{+\infty}x\left(t\right)\psi^{*}\left(\frac{t-\tau}{s}\right)dt \tag{3}$$

where * denotes the complex conjugate.

Wavelet transforms a time-frequency analysis of signals as a function of time. Moreover, not only the time-varying power spectrum but also the phase spectrum could be utilized in this respect. A wavelet is a function with zero mean and that is localized in both frequency and time. We can observe a wavelet by how localized it is in time (Δt) and frequency (ΔW or the bandwidth).

In continuous wavelet transform, due to border distortions, the values at the beginning and at the end of the series are incorrectly computed. The Cone of Influence (COI) is considered as the area in which the wavelet power caused by discontinuity.

Cross Wavelet Transform (XWT)

Given the wavelet transforms W^x and W^y of x and y, the cross wavelet transform (XWT) is considered as $W^{XY} = W^X W^Y$. The cross wavelet power is defined as $\left|W^{XY}\right|$. For the cross wavelet power spectra of two time series, the distribution developed by Torrence and Compo (1998) can be used

$$D\left(\frac{W^X_{n(s)} W^Y_{n(s)}}{\sigma_X \sigma_Y} < p\right) = \frac{Z_p\left(p\right)}{v}\sqrt{P^X_k P^Y_k} \tag{4}$$

where $Z_v\left(p\right)$ indicates the confidence level with probability p.

Wavelet Coherence (WTC)

Coherence is very crucial when dealing with volatile variables, showing how closely X and Y are related. It takes place if and only if their degree of coherence is close to its maximum value of unity. In time-series analysis, the degree of coherence of two time series x(t) and y(t) is the magnitude of their temporal correlation coefficient. Coherence shows how strongly the two variables are related at business cycle frequencies. It takes values from 0 (no correlation) to 1 (perfect correlation). The correlations may not be contemporaneous, therefore could contain a lead or a lag.

The wavelet coherence is normalized by the power spectrum of the two time-series. Given two time-series x(t) and y(t) their wavelet coherence can be defined as:

$$R_{xy}\left(\tau, s\right) = \frac{\left|S\left(W_{xy}\left(\tau, s\right)\right)\right|}{\sqrt{S\left(\left|W_{xx}\left(\tau, s\right)\right| S\left(\left|W_{yy}\left(\tau, s\right)\right|\right)\right)}} \tag{5}$$

where S denotes a smoothing operator in both time and scale (Conraria & Soares, 2011).

Wavelet Analysis

The wavelet power spectrum indicates the scale specific variance associated with any macroeconomic time series. The wavelet power spectrum shows the co-movement of the two series, represented in a contour plot with three dimensions: time, frequency (period) and color code (Tiwari et al., 2013). The thick black contour designates the % 5 significance level. The cone of influence (COI), which shows the region affected by edge effects, is shown with a lighter shade black line. The color code for power ranges from blue (low power) to red (high power). Y-axis shows frequencies or scale (measured in years) and X-axis shows the time period.

The cross wavelet transform (XWT) tests the relationship between two variables. The cross wavelet transform is synonymous with the covariance and shows the measure of co-movement between two variables. The cross-wavelet transform exposes the common power of the series and the relative phase in time-frequency space (Tiwari et al., 2013). The thick black contour designates the % 5 significance level. The color code for power ranges from blue (low power) to red (high power). The phase difference between the two series is indicated by arrows. Arrows pointing to the right mean that the variables are in phase (positively related). To the right and up, determinants of capacity utilization (industrial production, growth of gross domestic product and unemployment) are leading. To the right and down, determinants of capacity utilization are lagging. Arrows pointing to the left mean that the variables are out of phase (negatively related). To the left and up, the capacity utilization indicators are lagging. To the left and down, the capacity utilization indicators are leading. In phase indicates that variables will be having cyclical effect on each other and out of phase shows that variables will be having anti-cyclical effect on each other. The wavelet coherence shows the frequency bands and time interval within which the two variables are correlated.

CAPUT and INDPRO

In Figure 1, the wavelet power spectrum of CAPUT shows highly significant power event in the period from 2008 to 2011, in 0.5~2 month scale. Whereas, the WPS (wavelet power spectrum) of INDPRO shows highly significant power event from post 2008 to mid-2012, at around 2 month scale.

In Figure 2, it is very clear from the XWT results that the relationship between CAPUT and INDPRO is significant and high in the time scales of 0.5~2 bands from 2008 – 2012, however, it is clear that there is one significant and low power area in the 1 month scale of between 2009 and 2010. The phase difference between two series indicated by arrows pointing that between 2008-2009 years and 05~1 scale, the arrows right-upward which means CAPUT is lagging INDPRO. Surprisingly, before 2010 the arrows direction is right that is in-phase (the series are positively correlated), but at 2010 the arrows pointing down indicates that the INDPRO leads CAPUT by 90°, whereas post 2010 it is left which means the variables out of phase (negatively correlated) in 1 month scale. Moreover, in the scale of 1~6, the arrows are pointing right-downward that is CAPUT is leading INDPRO. In the scale of around 2 the arrows are pointing right that is in phase. However, after the scale of 2, the direction is right and upward, which means CAPUT is lagging INDPRO.

In Figure 3, the results from the WTC, the arrows point left-downward in the 0.25 month scale at 2008 indicating an anti-phase relationship with INDPRO leading, whereas during 2009, in the 0.5 month scale, the arrows point right indicating an in phase relationship between the series. During 2008-2013, in the 1.5~2 month scale, the arrows point right which means the series are positively correlated, however after the scale of 2, the arrows point right and upward, indicates that CAPUT is lagging INDPRO.

Figure 1.
For a more accurate representation of this figure, please see the electronic version.

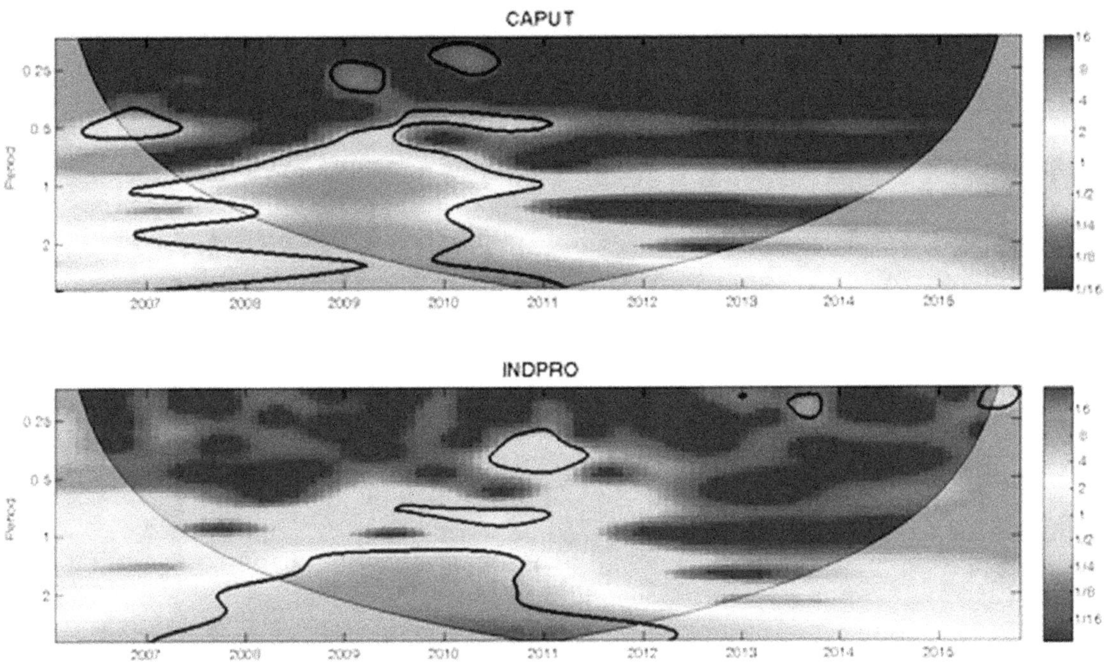

Figure 2.
For a more accurate representation of this figure, please see the electronic version.

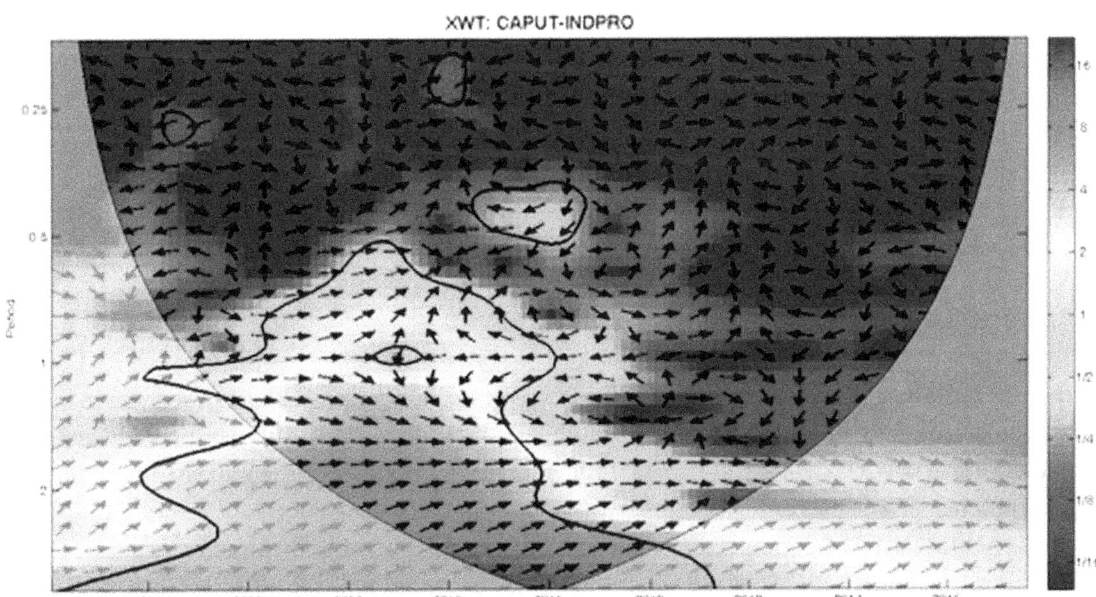

Figure 3.
For a more accurate representation of this figure, please see the electronic version.

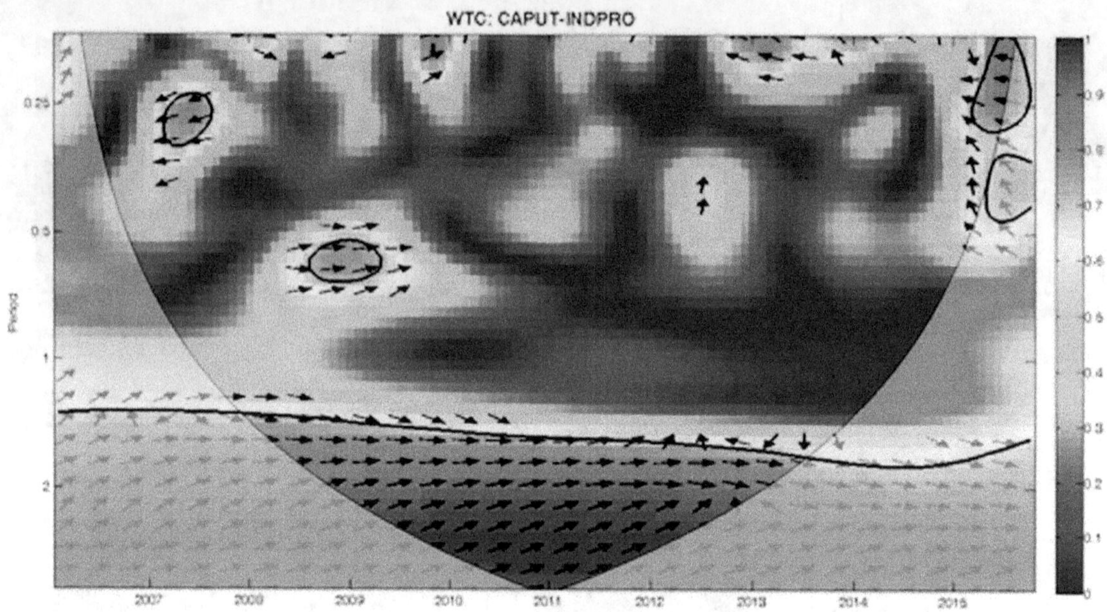

CAPUT and GROWTH

In the Figure 4, wavelet power spectrum of CAPUT shows significant power event around 1 month scale during 2008-2011, also around 2 month scale during the mid 2008-2009 with low power. Whereas, GROWTH has highly significant power event in the time scale of 1~2 at early 2008-2012. In the Figure 5, the results indicate that up to 2 month time scale, the relationship between the two series which are CAPUT and GROWTH is significant and the arrows point right which means in-phase, however, after 2 month time scale the relationship between the two series is highly significant, also the arrows point right and upward that is CAPUT leading GROWTH. In the Figure 6, according to wavelet coherence, there is high statistically significant relationship between CAPUT and GROWTH up to 2 month scale during 2009-2010, and the both series are strongly correlated and in-phase, also after 2 month time scale during 2009-2013 the arrows point right and upward that is CAPUT lagging GROWTH.

CAPUT and UNEMP

In the Figure 7, the wavelet power spectrum of CAPUT shows highly significant power event in the 0.5~2 month scale during 2008-2011. Nevertheless, UNEMP shows low and significant power event around 0.5 scale during 2009-2011 and 2013-2014, while at around 1 scale during 2007-2014 it demonstrates highly significant power event. In the Figure 8, the relationship between the two series CAPUT and UNEMP is significant 0.5~2 month scale, especially 1~2 scale it is highly significant between 2000-2014. Moreover, up to 1 scale the arrows point left and downward indicates CAPUT lagging UNEMP, at 1 month scale it is left that means the series are out of phase, whereas, after around 1.5 scale the arrows point left and upward indicates CAPUT leading UNEMP. In the Figure 9, CAPUT is strongly

Figure 4.
For a more accurate representation of this figure, please see the electronic version.

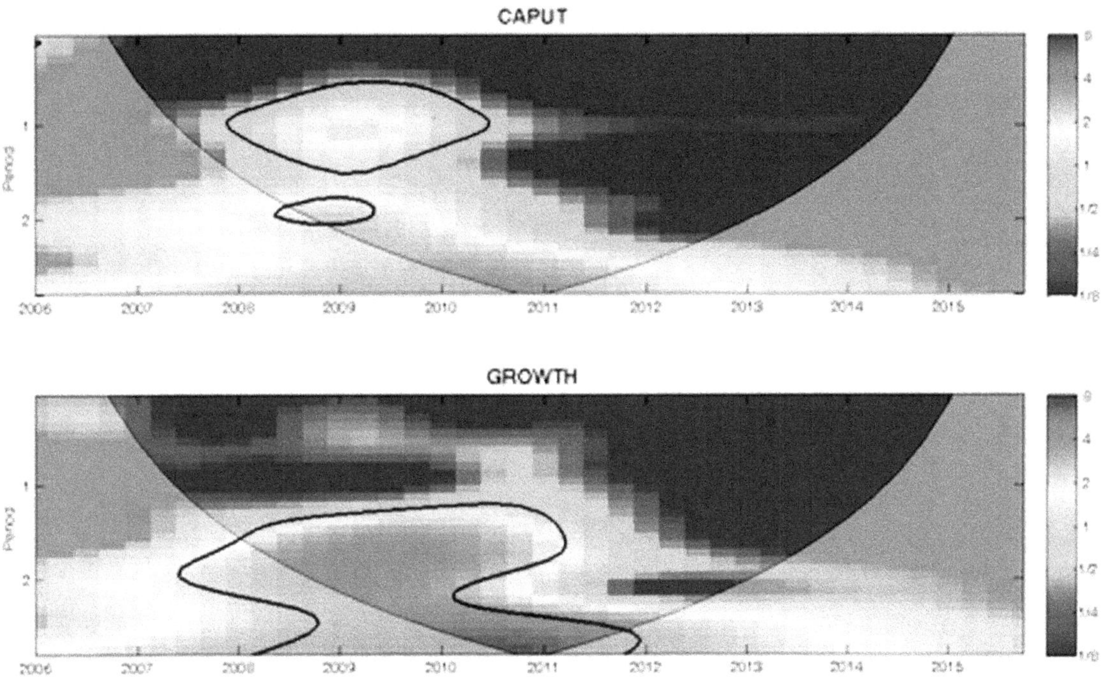

Figure 5.
For a more accurate representation of this figure, please see the electronic version.

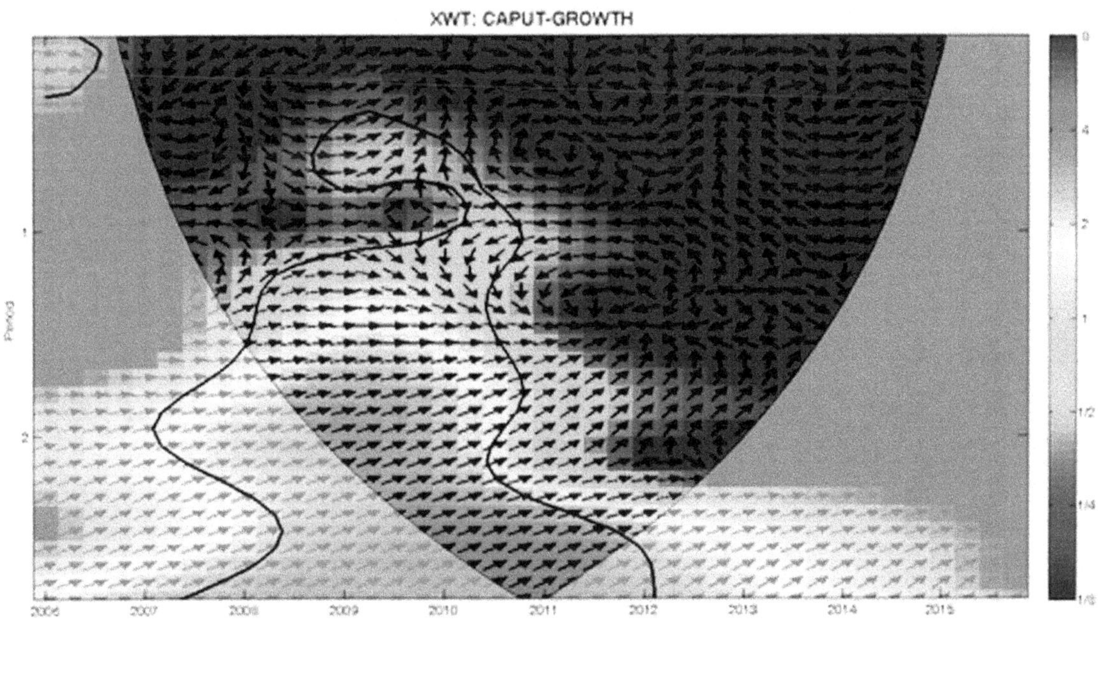

Figure 6.
For a more accurate representation of this figure, please see the electronic version.

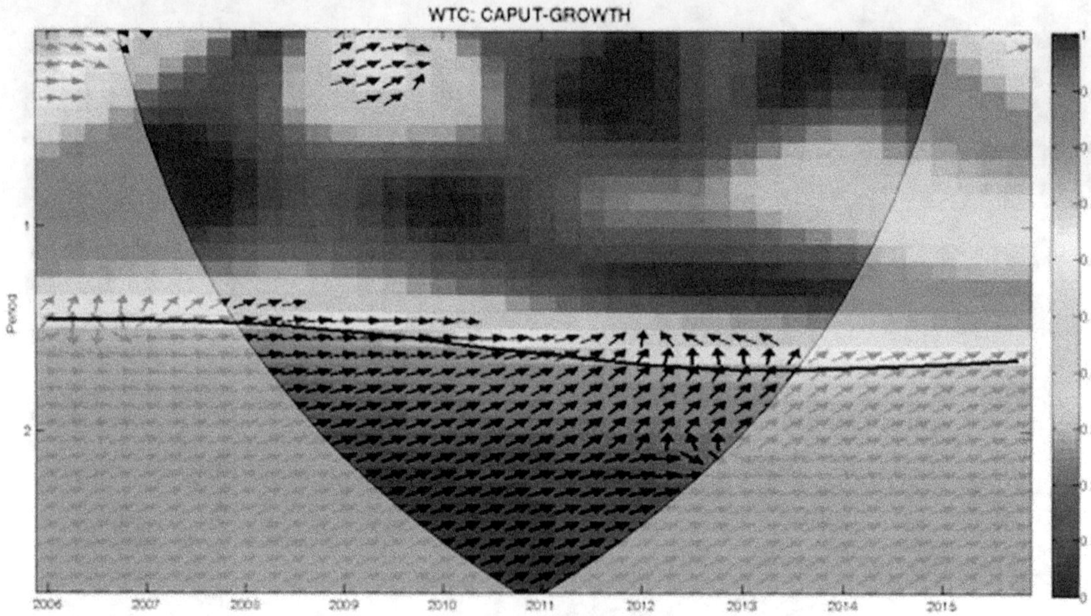

Figure 7.
For a more accurate representation of this figure, please see the electronic version.

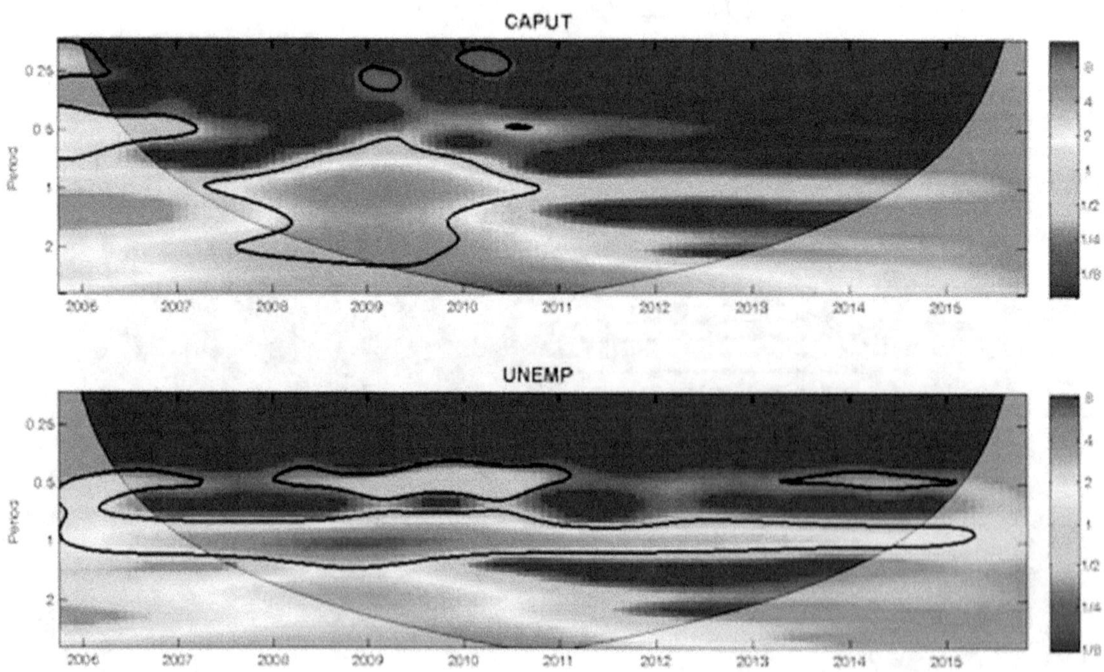

Figure 8.
For a more accurate representation of this figure, please see the electronic version.

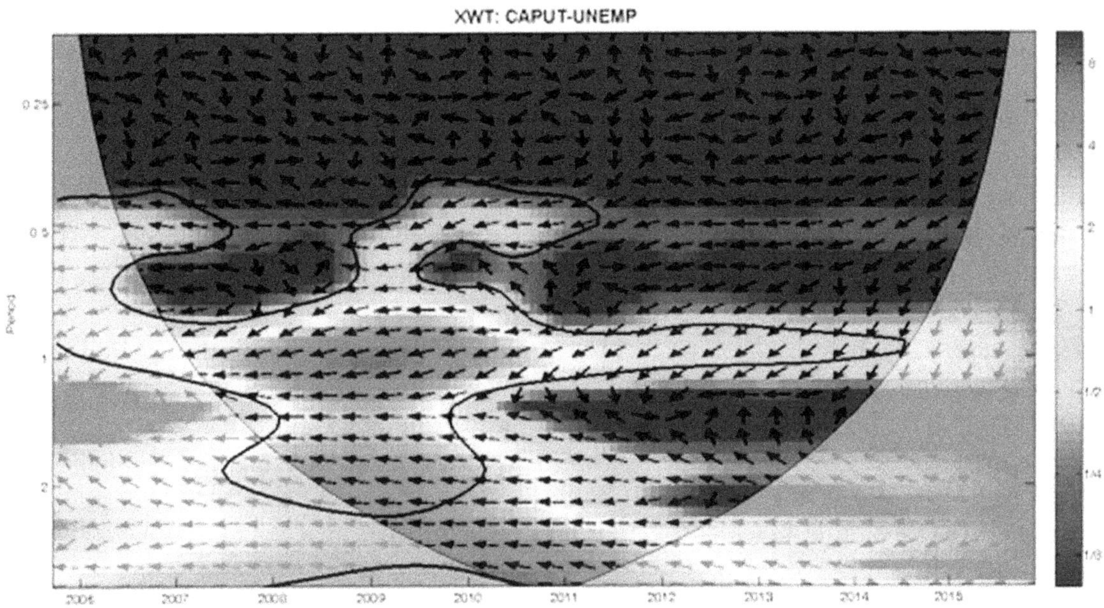

Figure 9.
For a more accurate representation of this figure, please see the electronic version.

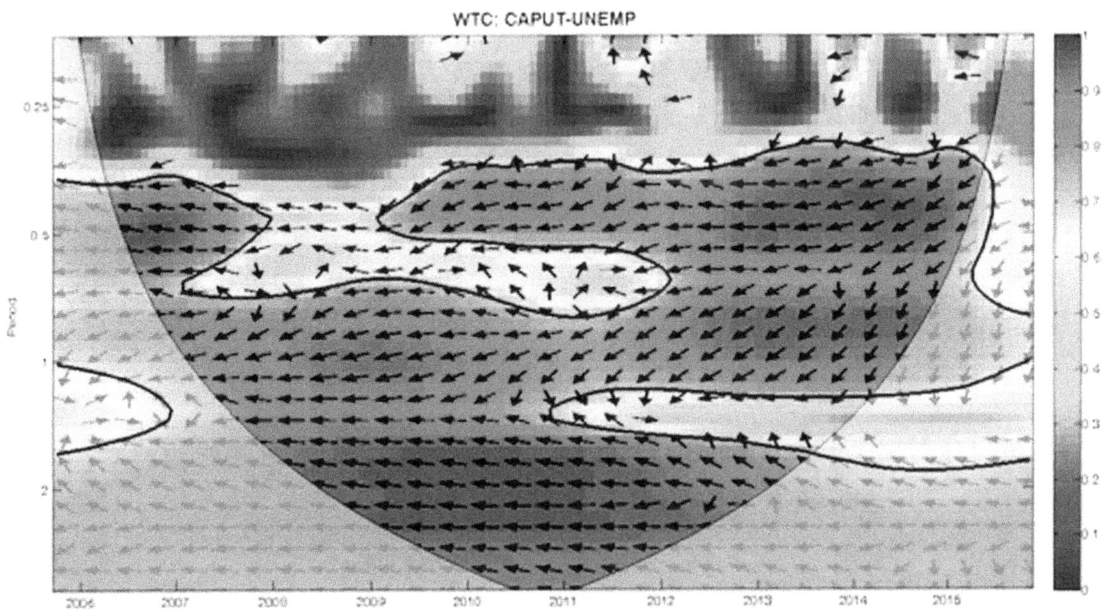

related to UNEMP except around 0.25 month scale, the significant interval from 2007 to 2014. Phases represented by arrows point left mostly at 2007-2014 indicates that the series are out of phase, however one exception at around 1 month scale during 2011-2014, the arrows point left and downward which means CAPUT lagging UNEMP.

CAPUT and PCE

In the Figure 10, wavelet power spectrum of CAPUT shows significant power event around 1 month scale during 2008-2011, also around 2 month scale during the mid 2008-2009 with low power However, wavelet power spectrum of PCE shows highly significant power event at 2 month scale during the mid-2008 to 2009 and mid-2009 to 2012.

In the Figure 11, in the scale of 1~2 and between 2008-2012 years XWT show that CAPUT and PCE are in phase with significant common power. Up to 2 month scale, in general, the arrows point right and upward which means CAPUT is lagging PCE. However, although after 2 month scale the arrows point right that indicates the two of the series, which are CAPUT and PCE, are in phase. In the Figure of 12, the coherency is quite high at around 1.5~2 month scale during 2009-2012. The phase information between 1-5~2 month scale with CAPUT is lagging PCE. Also, after 2 month scale WTC reveals that the series are in phase.

Figure 10.
For a more accurate representation of this figure, please see the electronic version.

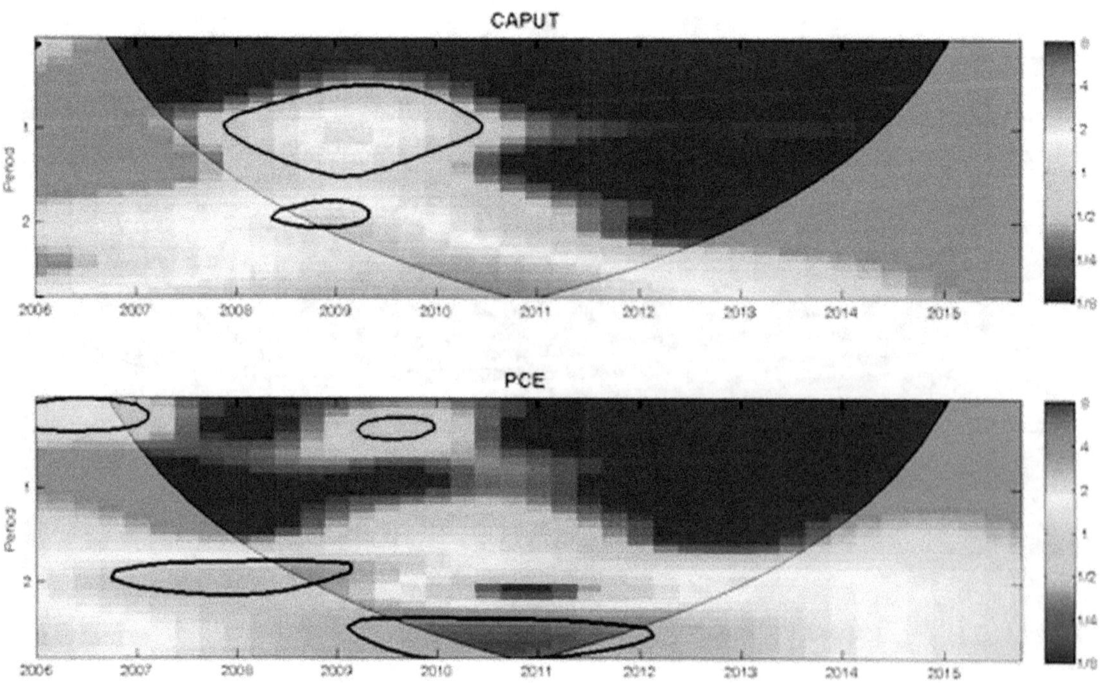

Figure 11.
For a more accurate representation of this figure, please see the electronic version.

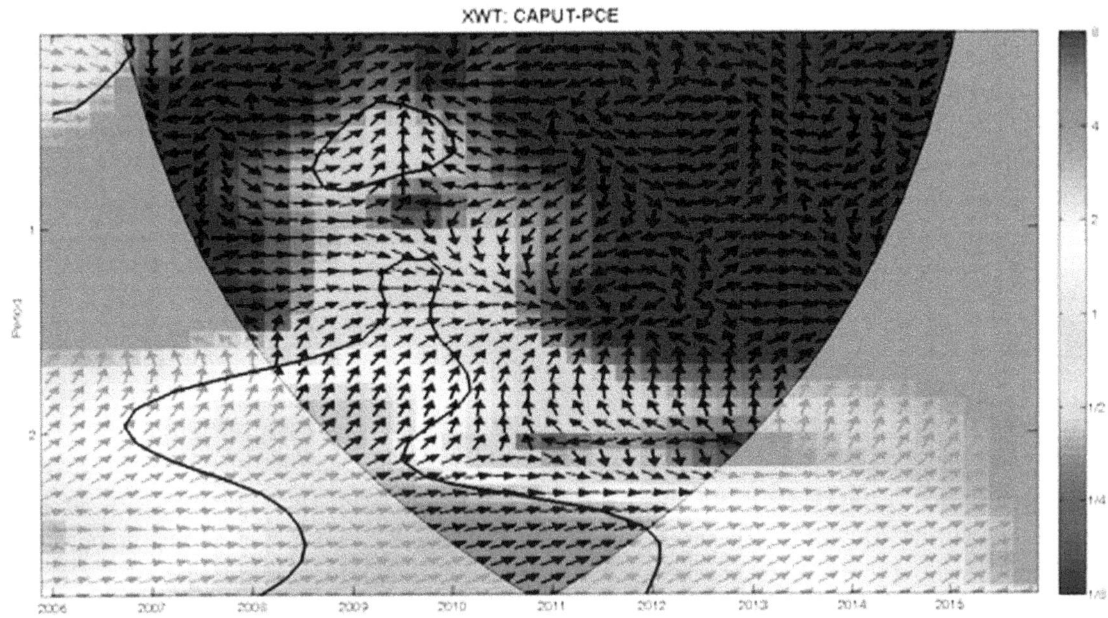

Figure 12.
For a more accurate representation of this figure, please see the electronic version.

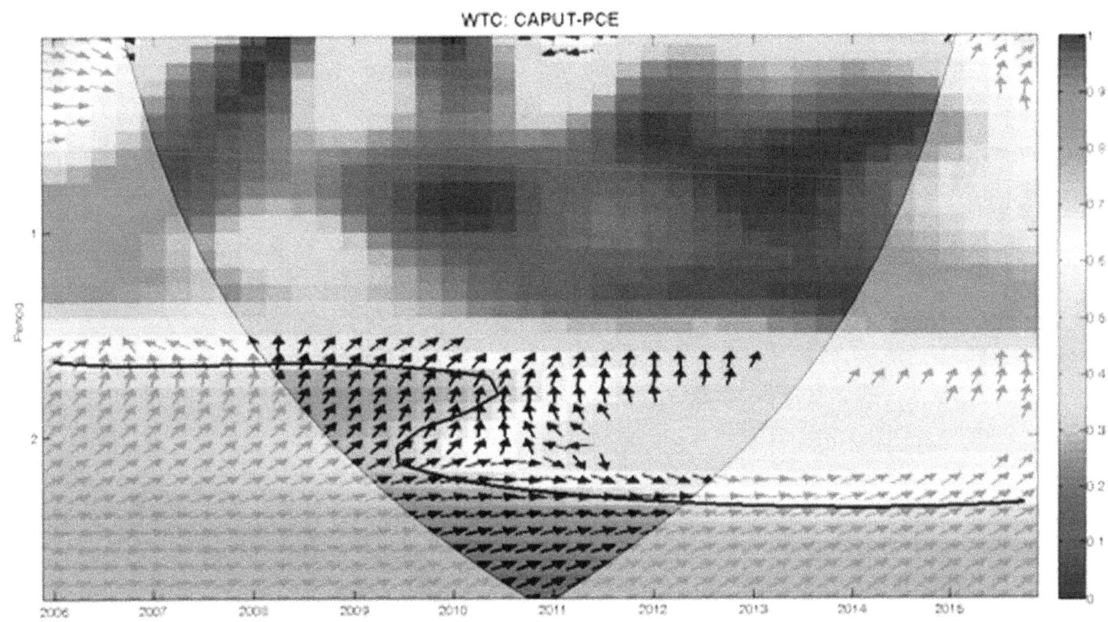

CAPUT and BIST

In the Figure 13, the wavelet power spectrum of CAPUT shows highly significant power event in the 0.5~2 month scale during 2008-2011. Whereas, after 2 month scale and during mid 2008 – 2012 the wavelet power spectrum of BIST is highly significant. In the Figure 14, observed that CAPUT and BIST have highly significant relationship in the scale of between 0.7~2 during 2008-2011. According to phase information, for the scale of 0.7~1 the series are in phase, while for the scale of 1~2 CAPUT is lagging BIST. In the Figure 15, observed that almost all frequencies and almost all years, coherence is highly significant, especially between the scale of 0.5~1 during 2009-2011 and it is in phase. Also, interestingly at around 2 scale during 2009-2012 CAPUT is lagging BIST.

CAPUT and EXC

In the Figure 16, the wavelet power spectrum of CAPUT shows highly significant power event in the 0.5~2 month scale during 2008-2011. Whereas, the wavelet power spectrum of EXC is observed that there is not any significant power event all frequencies and all the years. In the Figure 17, at the around 1 month scale during 2009-mid 2010 cross wavelet has significant common power and the phase gives the information about the relationship there is out of phase. While at the around 2 month scale during 2008-mid 2009 the arrows point left that is the series are out of phase means negatively correlated. In the Figure 18, coherence is significant at around 0.5 month scale between 2013 and 2014 and the phase information indicates that CAPUT is lagging EXC, while at around 1 month scale during 2009-mid 2010 and the arrows point left that is the variables are out of phase.

Figure 13.
For a more accurate representation of this figure, please see the electronic version.

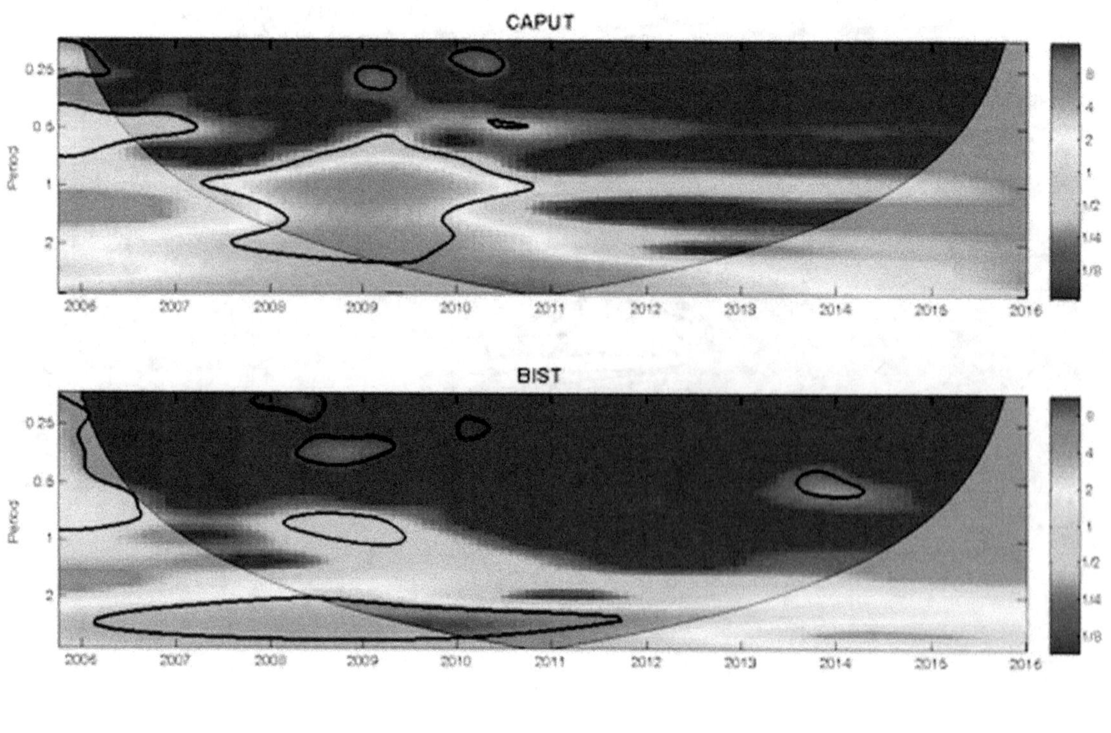

Figure 14.
For a more accurate representation of this figure, please see the electronic version.

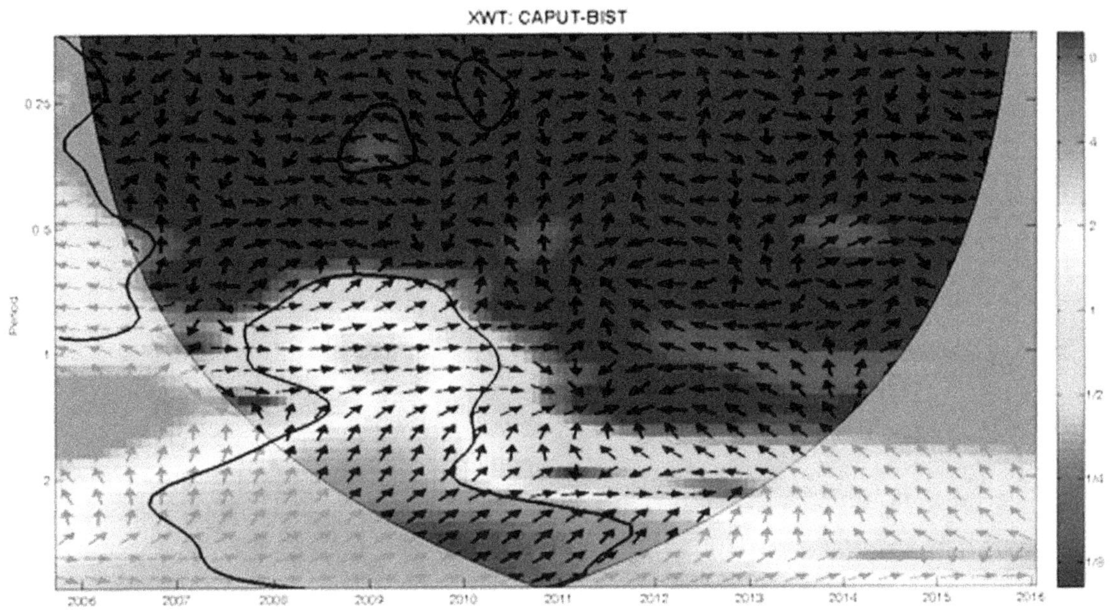

Figure 15.
For a more accurate representation of this figure, please see the electronic version.

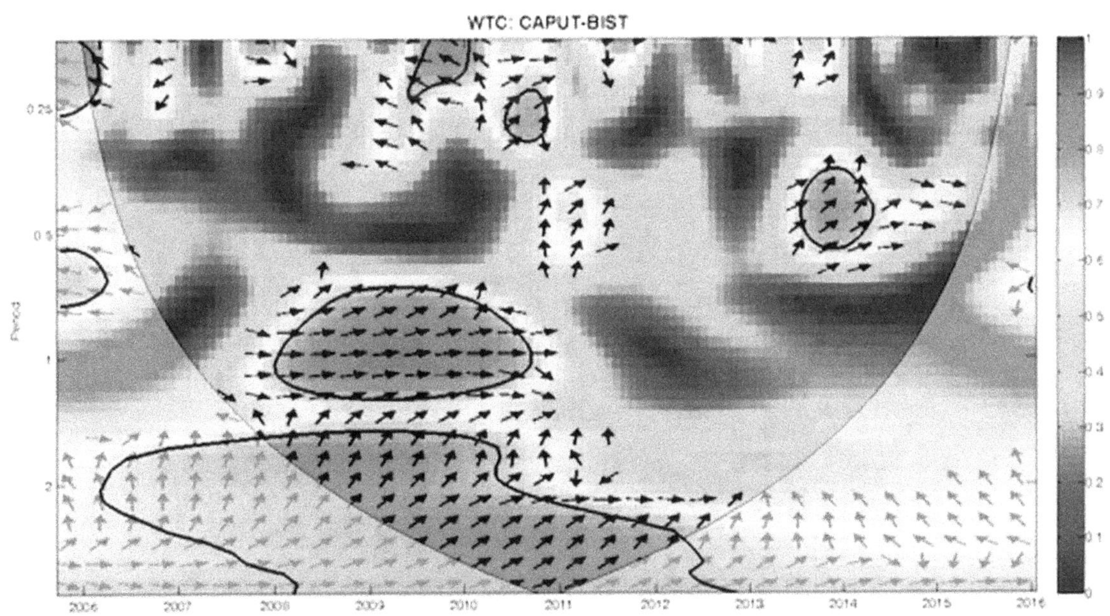

Figure 16.
For a more accurate representation of this figure, please see the electronic version.

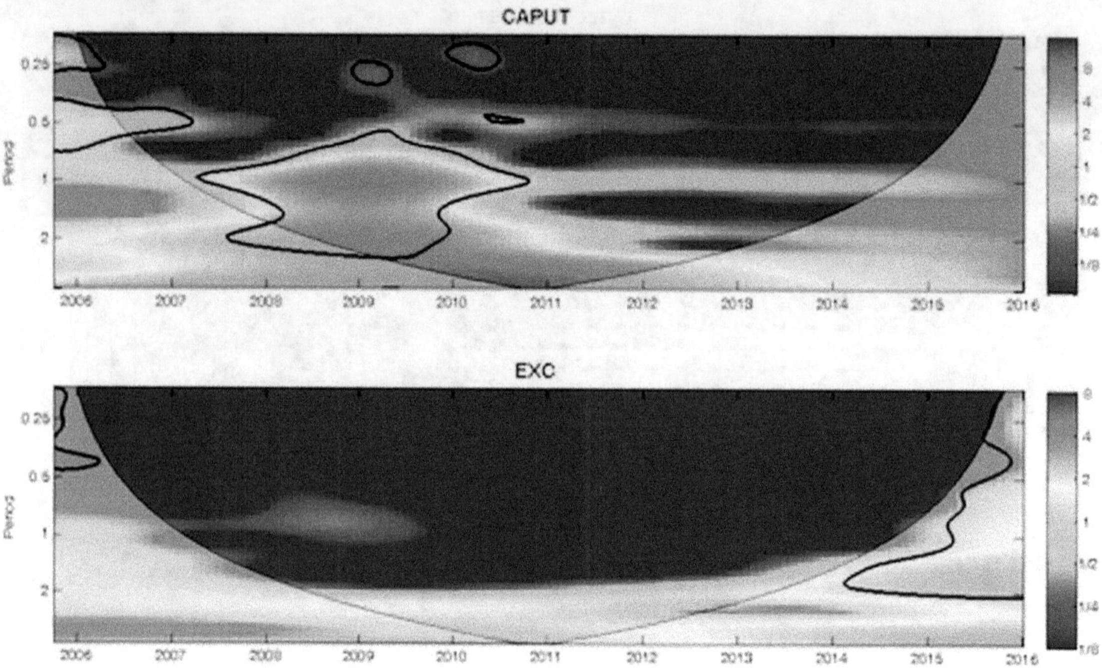

Figure 17.
For a more accurate representation of this figure, please see the electronic version.

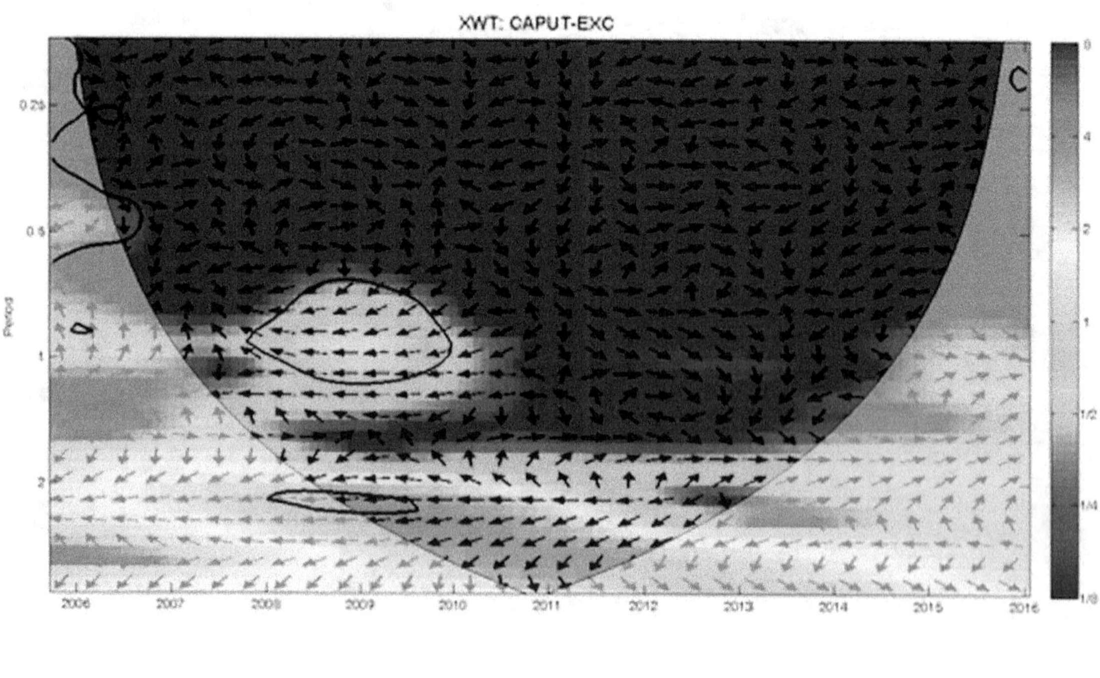

Figure 18.
For a more accurate representation of this figure, please see the electronic version.

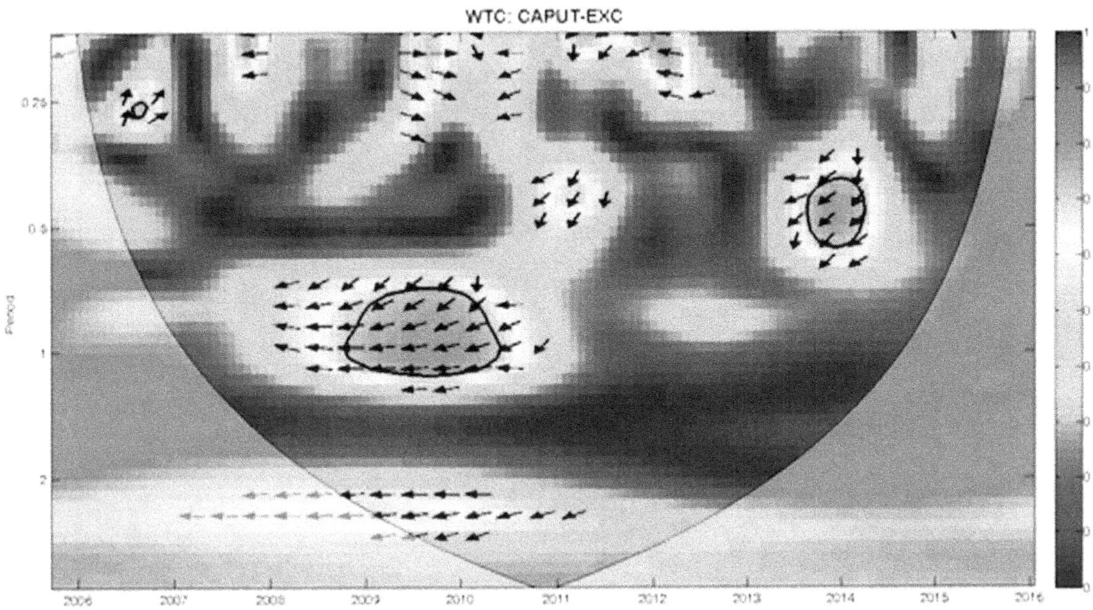

CAPUT and INT

In the Figure 19, the wavelet power spectrum of CAPUT shows significant power event around 0.5 month scale between 2011-2012.5, while it shows highly significant power event around 1 scale between 2011.5 and 2014.5. However, the wavelet power spectrum of INT shows high and significant power event with all frequencies during early 2013-mid 2014.5, except low power up to 1 month scale. In the Figure 20, the relationship between CAPUT and INT is low but significant around 0.5 month scale mid 2013-mid 2014, while around 1 month scale during 2013-2015 it is highly significant. Also, the phase information indicates that the variables are out of phase all significant era. We present the results of cross wavelet coherency in Figure 21. Some short lived relationships, though exist at high and medium frequencies, coherence is significant in the 0.25~0.5 month scale between 2013-2014. Near 0.25 month scale the phase information indicates that CAPUT is lagging INT, however near 0.5 month scale the arrows point that the series are out of phase. Nevertheless, for rest of the frequencies, we do not find any consistent relationship.

CAPUT and CCI

In the Figure 22, the wavelet power spectrum of CAPUT shows highly significant power event in the 0.5~2 month scale during 2008-2011. The wavelet power spectrum of CCI shows significant and low power event in the scale of 0.25~1 between 2008-2010 and approximately around 1.8 month scale during 2008-2009 it shows significant and high power event. In the Figure 23, the relationship among CAPUT and CCI is significant during 2008-2010. The arrows point that in the scale of 0.5~1 CAPUT is lagging CCI, while in the scale of 1.7~2 CAPUT is leading CCI because of the direction of the arrows is left and

Figure 19.
For a more accurate representation of this figure, please see the electronic version.

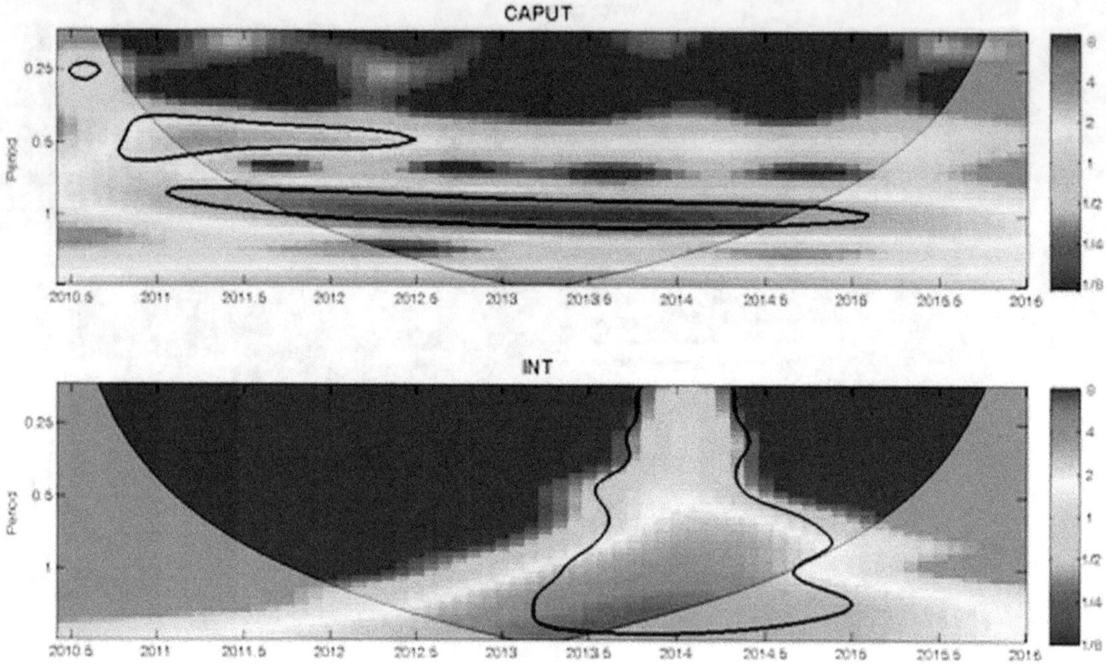

Figure 20.
For a more accurate representation of this figure, please see the electronic version.

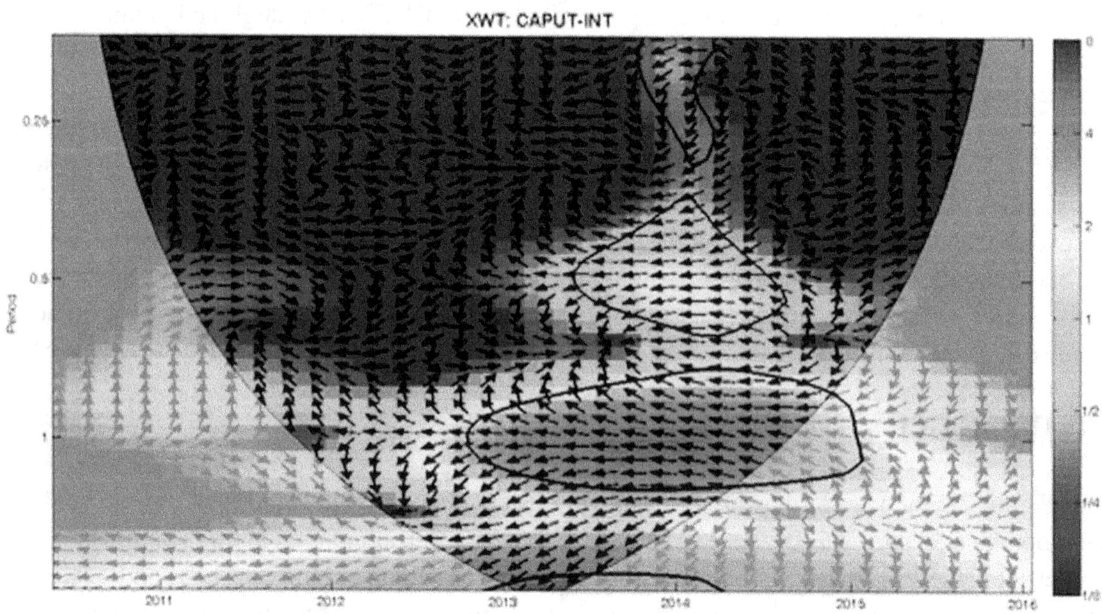

Figure 21.
For a more accurate representation of this figure, please see the electronic version.

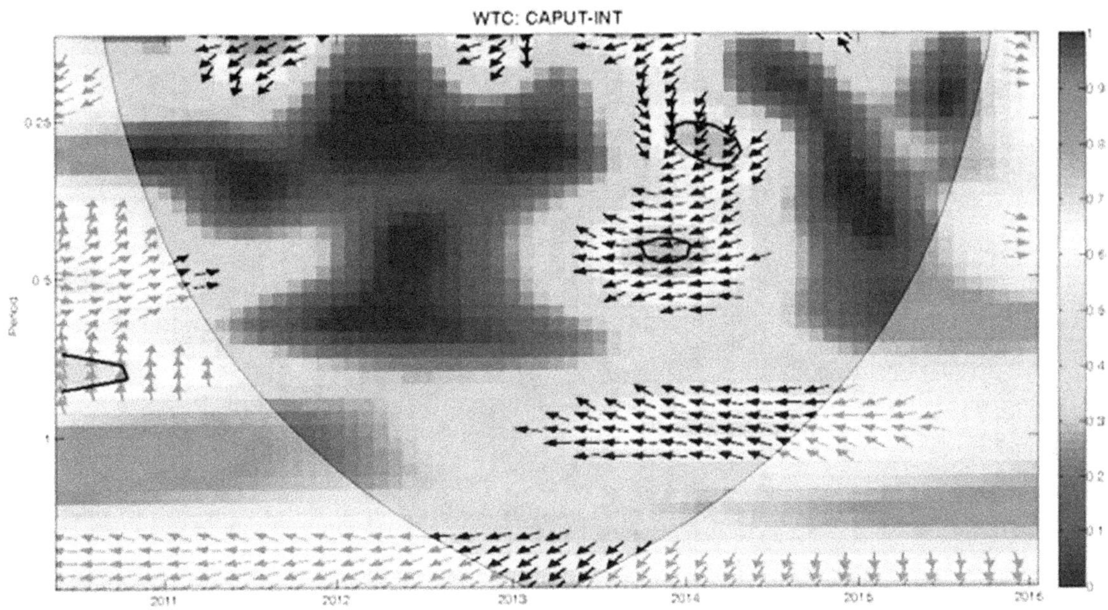

upward. In the Figure 24, the results based on the wavelet coherence tests show that there is a statistically significant and high relationship between CAPUT and CCI at different time scales with CAPUT is lagging CCI (around 0.5 month time scale at 2007 due to point right and upward arrows, also due to left and downward arrows at 2012). At around 1 month time scale during 2009-2011 CAPUT is lagging CCI, while at 2012 CAPUT is leading CCI. Besides, at around 2 month time scale during 2009- mid 2011 the arrows point left and upward indicate that CAPUT is leading CCI.

CAPUT and BTS

In the Figure 25, the wavelet power spectrum of CAPUT and BTS show highly significant and almost the same power event in the scale of 0.5~2 during 2008-mid 2011. In the Figure 26, the cross wavelet results indicate that the relationship between CAPUT-BTS is significant in the 0.5~2 month time scale during 2008-2012 with the phase results that CAPUT is lagging BTS. In the Figure 27, results show that there is highly significant coherence almost all frequencies and almost among all the years with the phase result is CAPUT lagging BTS in general, especially at the scale of 0.5~2.

CAPUT and CPIEXP

In the Figure 28, the wavelet power spectrum of CAPUT shows highly significant power event in the 0.5~2 month scale during 2008-2011. According to the result of wavelet power spectrum of CPIEXP shows significant power event at 0.25~2 month time scale during mid 2006-2012 but especially low power up to 1 month time scale. In the Figure 29, the cross wavelet transform result indicates significant correlation in the scale of 0.5~2 and between 2007- post 2010. However at the 0.5~1 month time scale

Figure 23.
For a more accurate representation of this figure, please see the electronic version.

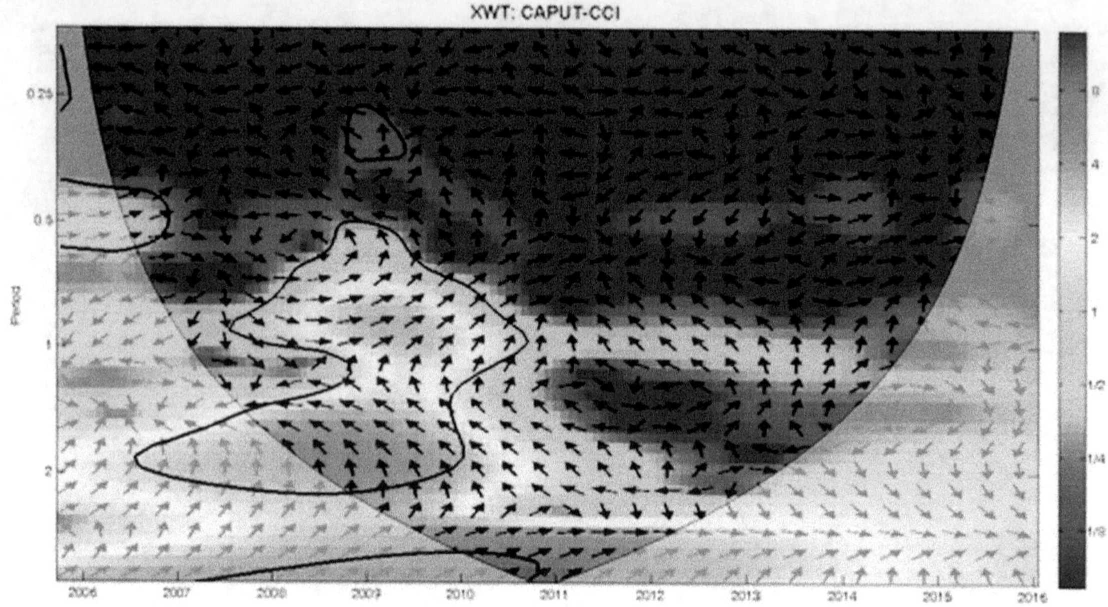

Figure 22.
For a more accurate representation of this figure, please see the electronic version.

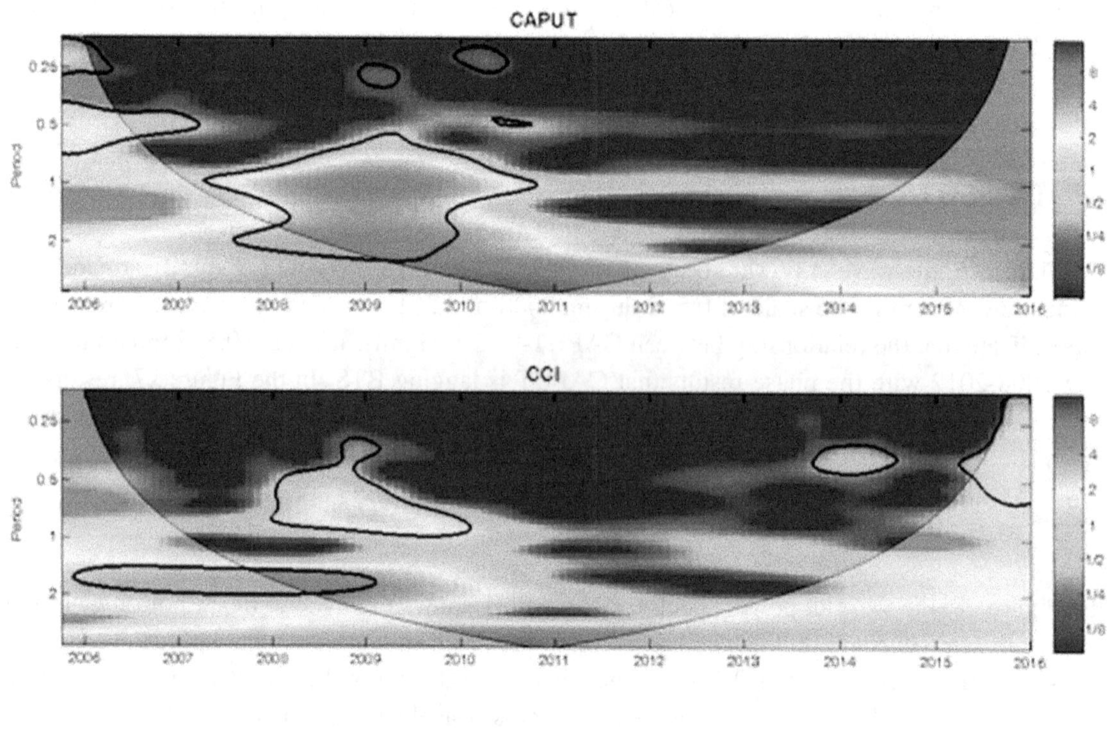

Figure 24.
For a more accurate representation of this figure, please see the electronic version.

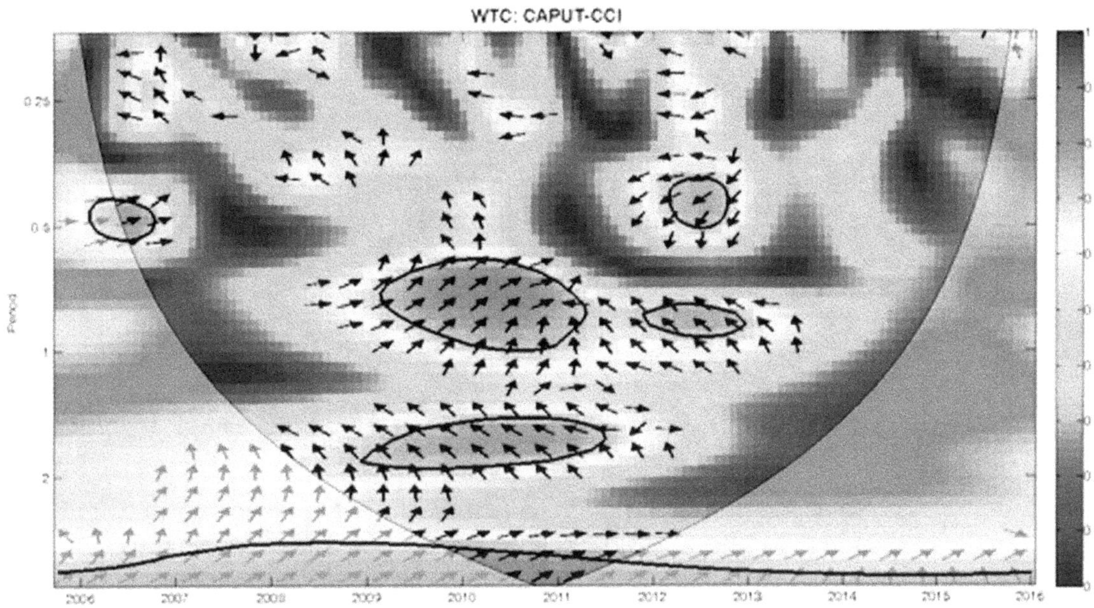

Figure 25.
For a more accurate representation of this figure, please see the electronic version.

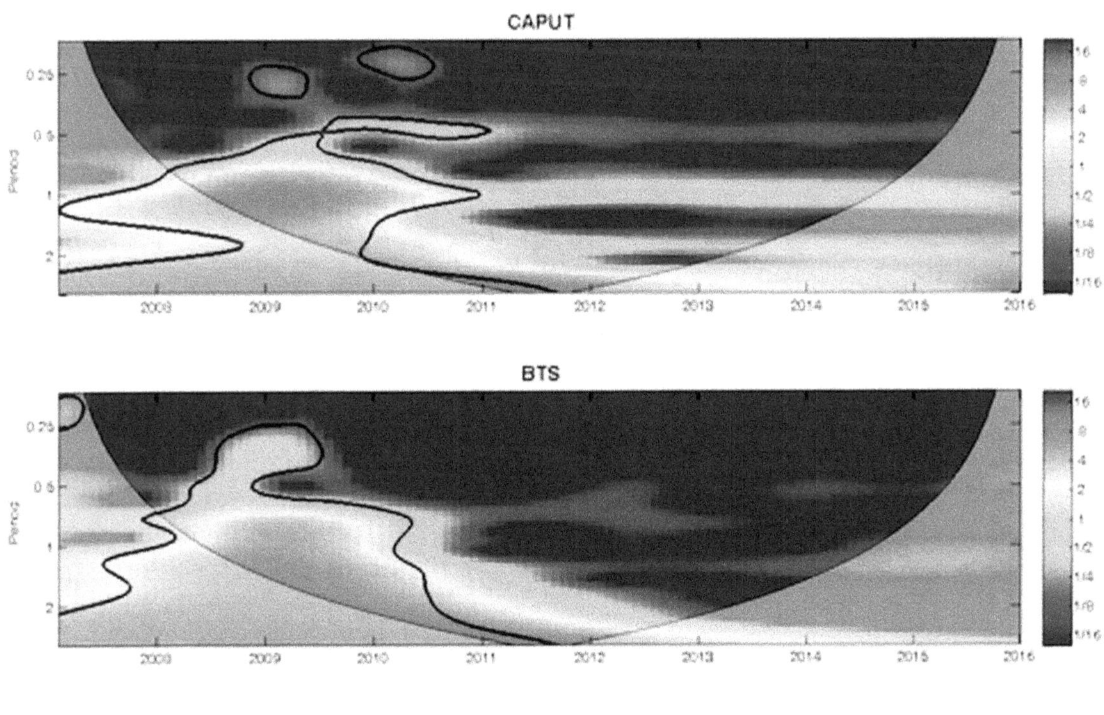

Figure 26.
For a more accurate representation of this figure, please see the electronic version.

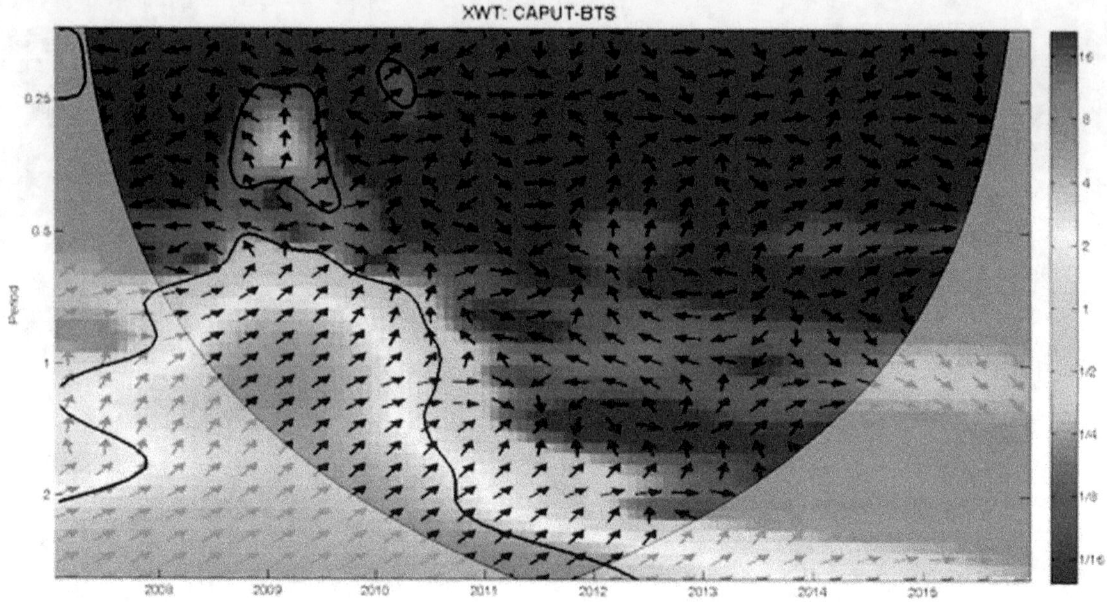

Figure 27.
For a more accurate representation of this figure, please see the electronic version.

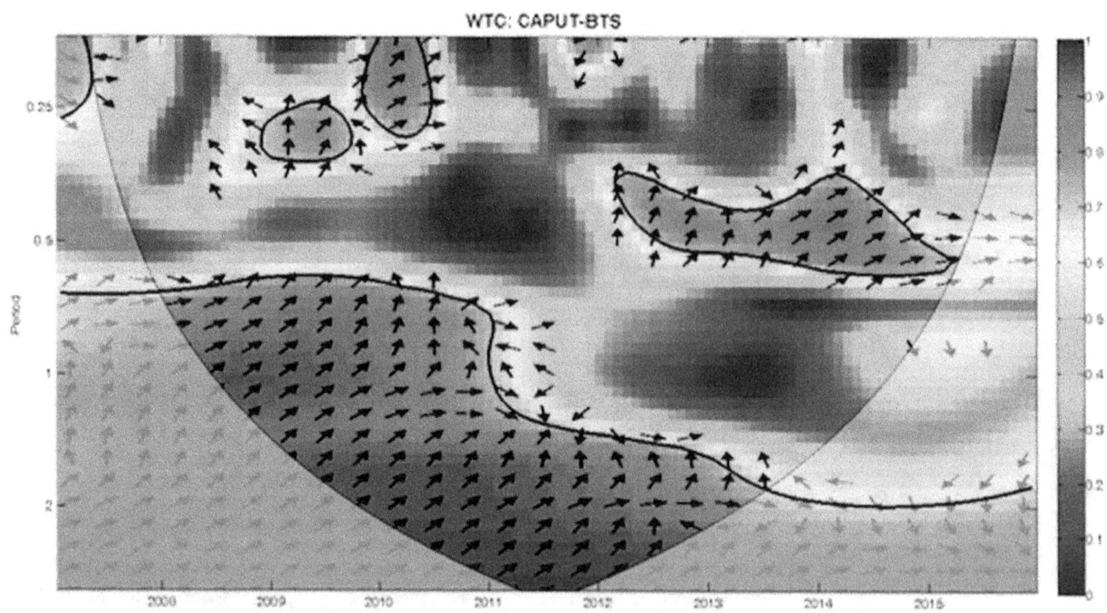

there is low common power with CAPUT and CPIEXP are in phase based on the arrows direction which implies right. However, in the scale of 1~2 observed that high common power event with CAPUT is leading CPIEXP based on the arrow direction is right and downward. In the Figure 30, the results indicate that at around 1 month time scale between mid 2009-mid 2010 and the arrows point right direction which means in phase. However, although at around approximately 1.8~2.2 month time scale between 2008 and 2013 coherence is significant with the arrows point right and downward indicate that CAPUT leading CPIEXP, while after at the scale of 2.2 coherence is highly significant and the arrows point down that indicates CPIEXP is leading CAPUT by 90°.

CONCLUSION

The analysis of Phillips curve has gained importance lately, since the relationship between inflation and economic activity is examined by Phillips curve. The capacity utilization rates are used as future inflation indicators. It is known that there are Keynesian aggregate demand and aggregate supply interactions in the Phillips curve. Finn (1995) has found that the price level is associated with resource utilization and shifts in aggregate demand. The difference in the growth rates of aggregate demand and supply eliminates unused capacity. As a result the decrease in the inventory will cause inflationary pressure. The shortages in resource utilization can be substituted by unemployment rate in the Phillips curve. The reason for this is the association between unemployment rate and capacity utilization rate. The increase in capacity has no one to one correspondence with production.

Figure 28.
For a more accurate representation of this figure, please see the electronic version.

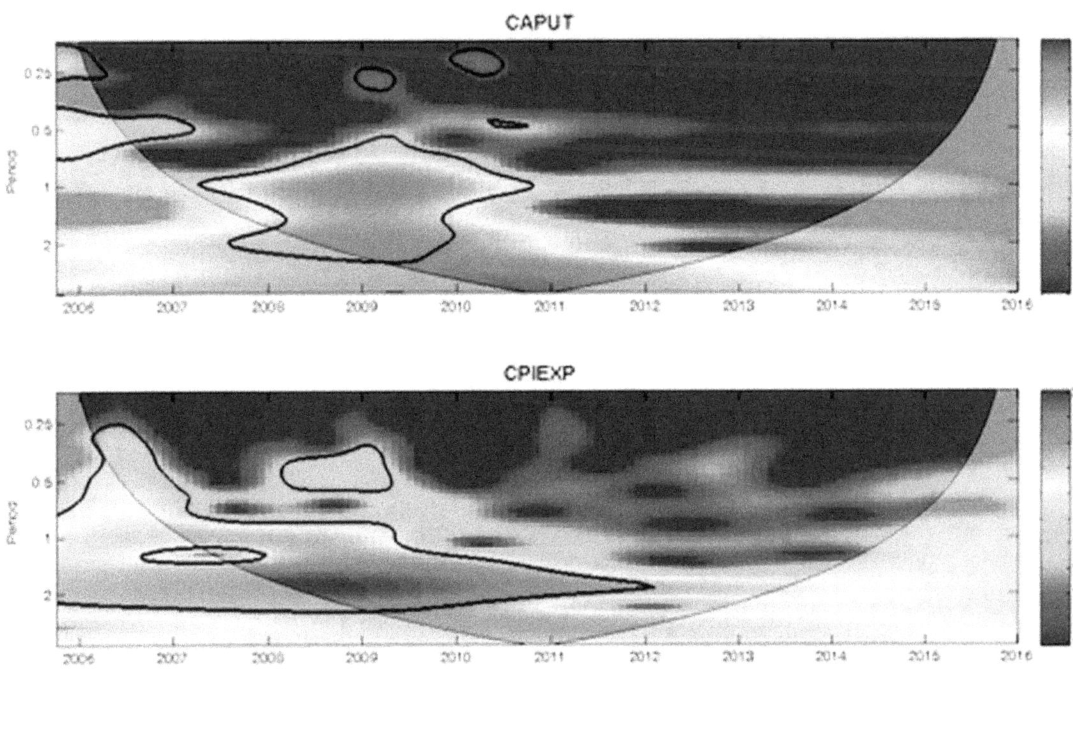

Figure 29.
For a more accurate representation of this figure, please see the electronic version.

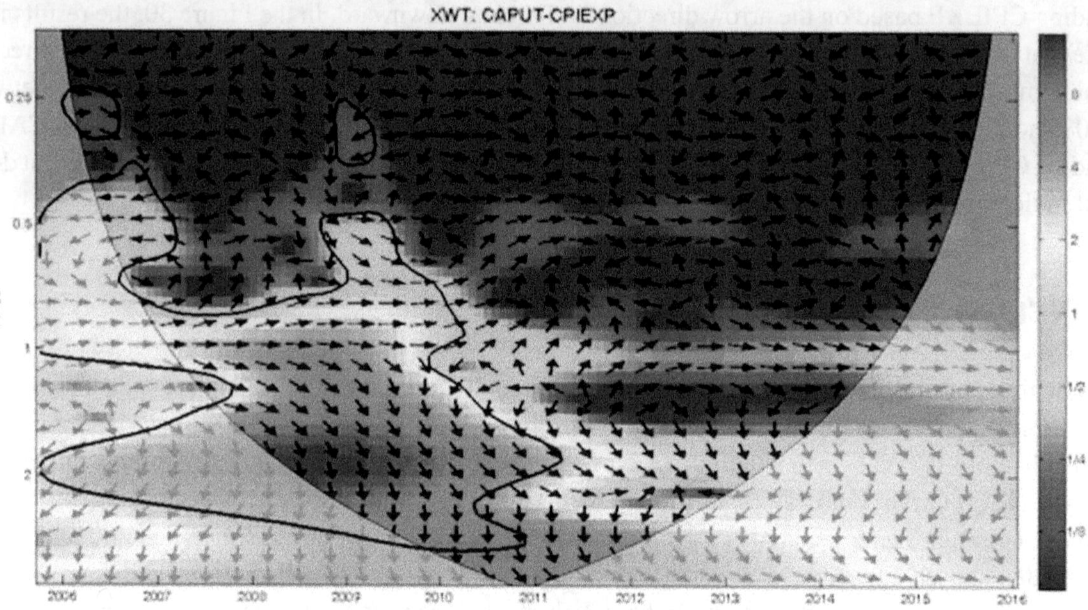

Figure 30.
For a more accurate representation of this figure, please see the electronic version.

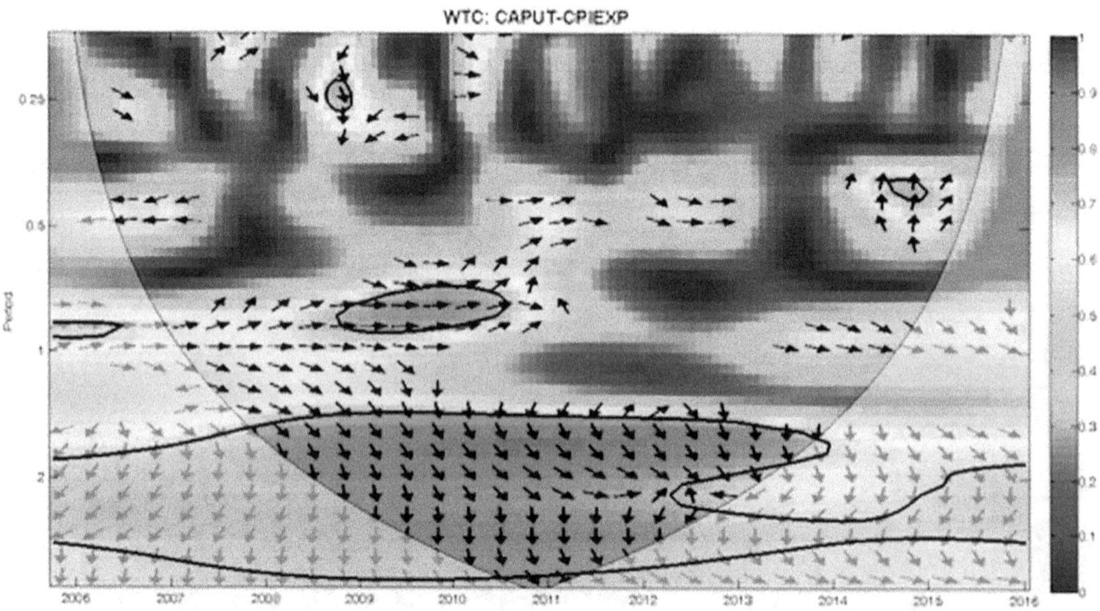

A contrasting point has been observed between the capacity utilization rate in manufacturing and the general level of living standard in Turkey. It is noted that the capacity utilization rate during the period under study hasn't changed substantially, while the general level of living standard (welfare status) has increased, this contrasting point has emerged not owing to the change in manufacturing capacity but to the improvements in other sectors as agriculture and services in Turkey.

This chapter analyzes the relationship between capacity utilization rate and its determinants for Turkey by using monthly data covering 2006 and 2015 period. In order to investigate the relationships, the time-frequency relationship between capacity utilization and its determinants is decomposed by using continuous wavelet approach.

Wavelet analysis can distinguish between different relationships that occur at the same time but at different frequencies. A wavelet representation of a signal constitutes an orthogonal projection, like a shadow of the signal on a space of wavelets (Nievergelt, 1999). The advantage of using continuous wavelet approach is that it is possible to construct a time-frequency representation of a signal that offers very good time and frequency localization for different sets of time-data comparisons on different phases of the variables. The wavelet power spectrum, cross wavelet analysis and wavelet coherence tests are used in wavelet analysis in this chapter. The wavelet power spectrum shows the scale specific variance associated with any macroeconomic time series.

We found from the continuous wavelet power spectrum figures, in general, the wavelet power is high and significant at low frequencies with one exception which is EXC. The Figure 1 highlights that CAPUT and INDPRO show highly significant power event at low frequencies. However, according to Figure 4, while CAPUT is significant at high frequency, GROWTH is highly significant at low frequency. Although, in terms of the Figure 7, CAPUT is highly significant at medium frequency especially at about 2009 year.

It is observed that UNEMP is highly significant at 1 month time scale among all sample years. The Figure 10 indicates that CAPUT is significant at high frequency during 2008-2010. Within the PCE result, the figure shows that it is highly significant at low frequency especially at during 2009-2012 years. In the Figure 13, CAPUT shows significant and high power event at medium and low frequency between 2008-2010 years. However, BIST is highly significant at low frequency during 2009-mid 2011. In the Figure 16 CAPUT is the same as the figure 13. However, it is interesting that the EXC does not show any significance among all frequencies and all years. We found that there isn't any power for exchange rates; therefore they are insignificant in our model.

For the figure 19, observed that CAPUT is quite highly significant at 1 month time scale during all years. Whereas, INT is significant at all frequencies and especially at high frequency it shows high power event between early 2013 and 2014.5. For the CAPUT, the figure 22 is the same as the figure 7. And CCI is highly significant at low frequency between 2008 and 2009. According to the figure 25, CAPUT and BTS show highly significant power event at medium frequency between 2009-2010 years. The figure 28 highlights that CAPUT shows significant power event except high frequency. And CPIEXP shows significant power event almost all frequencies however, it is highly significant at low frequency during 2008-2012 years. Within observed all the wavelet power spectrum results, we attribute the high power at different time scales to the seasonal fluctuations and active cycle at 1~2 month time scales. The growth of industrial production, the growth of gross domestic product, expected consumer price index and unemployment as the determinants of capacity utilization, have the same variance with capacity utilization. This means that the growth of gross domestic product, the growth of industrial production, expected consumer price index and unemployment are effective on the capacity utilization, which signals the deep turmoil in financial markets during the Great Recession.

Cross wavelet transform represents the local covariance between time series at each scale. It shows the common power of the time series considered. The direction of the arrows in the cross wavelet transform figure helps us to interpret the causality between the variables of interest with the phase relationship.

CAPUT and INDPRO indicate a common power event with in phase relationship at low frequency. Similarly, the variables have a common power which is highly significant and the relationship indicates that CAPUT is lagging GROWTH at low frequency. The series which are CAPUT and UNEMP show highly significant common power. And the phase relationship denotes that CAPUT is lagging UNEMP between the years 2008-2010 at medium frequency.

At low frequency (after 2 month time scale) the common power is quite high and the arrows point in a positive relationship with CAPUT is lagging PCE during 2009-mid 2011. The same results observed that between CAPUT and BIST. According the figure B6, there is a common power between capacity utilization and exchange rates with the direction of relationship negative throughout 2009-2011. The increase in exchange rate increases the cost of production, which causes inflationary pressures on the economy. Because of higher cost of production, producing one unit of output would be much more expensive.

At the scale of around 1 month, the series show highly significant common power, however the relationship is out of phase between CAPUT and INT during 2013-2015. Interest rates seem to fail to be successful to lead capacity utilization. At medium frequency, observed that CAPUT and CCI show significant common power and CAPUT is lagging CCI or we can say CCI is leading CAPUT, however at low frequency CAPUT is leading CCI between the years 2008-mid 2011.

At almost all frequencies, CAPUT and BTS show significant common power, whereas it is highly significant 0.5~2 month scale and according the phase relationship CAPUT is lagging BTS between 2009-2012 means BTS predicts capacity of utilization. The series which are CAPUT and CPIEXP show a common power throughout almost all frequencies, however, the relationship is not homogenous across scales, since the arrows point right, left and down constantly. We take consideration only at low frequency because of showing the highest power and at there the phase relationship indicate that CAPUT is leading CPIEXP. Expected consumer price index is lagging capacity utilization, showing that capacity utilization causes expected consumer price index positively between 2007 and 2011. In summary, expected consumer price index seems to fail to lead capacity utilization rates given the results of our cross wavelet analysis.

The gross domestic product, private consumer expenditures, consumer consumption index, Istanbul stock Exchange 100 and business tendency survey are leading capacity utilization rates, that means causes capacity utilization but positively. Also, unemployment rate leads capacity utilization however negatively it is. Besides the growth of industrial production is positively correlated with capacity utilization rates, while exchange rates and interest rates are negatively correlated with capacity utilization rates.

The final method we employ is the wavelet coherence tests which are used to identify both frequency bands and time interval within which two variables are correlated. In addition, wavelet coherence identifies whether there is a comovement between variables. Moreover, the phase differences which are denoted by arrows give lead-lag relation that is causal relation. According to wavelet coherence analysis, we find that CAPUT and INDPRO have strong correlation at low frequency throughout all sample years with the phase relationship is in phase. We found that capacity utilization (CAPUT) and the growth of gross domestic product (GROWTH) are positively correlated between 2008 and 2014 with the growth of gross domestic product leading capacity utilization. Both the growth of industrial production and the growth of gross domestic product have effects on capacity utilization. Normally we expect capacity utilization rate to lead the growth of industrial production and the growth of gross domestic product. However, during the financial crises period the way of relationship has changed.

Between the relationship of CAPUT and UNEMP is highly significant almost throughout all years except high frequency, in general look the phase relationship, the arrows point out of phase. Moreover, unemployment is quite effective on capacity utilization. Our findings are in line with the previous studies. For example, Fichtenbaum (2003) estimates the relationship between capacity utilization and unemployment rate using maximum likelihood estimation method. It is found that for each 1 percent increase in the unemployment rate, capacity utilization rate decreases by 3.5 percent, which justifies our finding.

We found that the relationship between capacity utilization (CAPUT) and private consumer expenditures (PCE) are positively correlated. Private consumer expenditures lead capacity utilization especially between 2009 and 2012. Private consumer expenditures could be regarded as an indicator of aggregate demand. Also, private consumer expenditures could be considered as an indicator of inflation. In Phillips curve the relationship between economic activity and inflation is estimated. Instead of unemployment rate, capacity utilization rate is utilized so that there is a tradeoff between capacity utilization and inflation. Similarly, our findings justify this tradeoff. This shows that the decline in private consumption expenditures had a significant effect on capacity utilization in Turkey, causing high levels of decrease in the capacity utilization rate. Therefore, sharp falls in capacity utilization during the crisis period could be explained in part due to the decreases in private consumption expenditures between 2009 and 2012.

Furthermore, our outcomes point that the relationship between capacity utilization (CAPUT) and İstanbul Stock Exchange 100 index (BIST) is also positively correlated. İstanbul Stock Exchange 100 leads capacity utilization and this is especially clear between 2009 and 2012. This means that the decline in BIST had a significant impact on CAPUT in Turkey, causing high levels of decrease in the capacity utilization rate. Therefore, our findings imply that the sharp falls in CAPUT during the crisis period could be explained in part due to the decreases in BIST in Turkey. A decline in BIST causes concerns or uncertainties over producers, as a result of this production decrease, therefore capacity utilization rate decreases as well. Wavelet coherency results show that capacity utilization and exchange rates are negatively correlated with EXC leads CAPUT especially between 2009 and 2011.

We found that capacity utilization and interest rates are negatively correlated and interest rates (INT) are leading capacity utilization (CAPUT) in 2014 at medium frequency. However, there is not a remarkable correlation (INT-CAPUT) when checked all picture of the figure with detail. Considering financial indicator, high exchange rates and interest rates increase the cost of production; therefore, we expect capacity utilization to decline. There is some lead-lag relationship observed between CCI-CAPUT. We found that capacity utilization and consumer confidence index are correlated especially between 2009-mid 2012 and consumer confidence index is leading capacity utilization at medium frequency, showing that CCI causes CAPUT. Uncertainties in the economy causes consumer confidence to decline therefore, we expect a decrease in capacity utilization rate. We found that capacity utilization and business tendency survey (BTS) are positively correlated between 2008 and 2013 and business tendency survey is leading capacity utilization, showing that business tendency survey causes capacity utilization. If the business confidence increases, the production increases also, therefore capacity utilization rate increase. The results of wavelet coherence test show that capacity utilization and expected inflation are positively correlated between 2008 and 2014 and expected inflation is lagging capacity utilization rate. If capacity utilization rate increases, the production in the economy increases, therefore the confidence in the economy increase. So, that aggregate demand increases, leading to an increase in expected inflation.

Overall, taking into account the arrow direction and the high-power regions, we consider that a link exists between the series of CAPUT and its determinants, as implied by the wavelet coherence analysis. Our results show that the growth of industrial production, the growth of gross domestic product, private consumer expenditures, Istanbul Stock Exchange 100 index, Consumer consume index and business tendency survey cause capacity utilization rates positively, whereas unemployment rate, exchange rates and interest rates causes capacity utilization rates negatively. The last conspicuous result is that the wavelet coherence is high at low frequencies.

After 2008 financial crises the capacity utilization rate has decreased to 70 percent from 80 percent. The primary reason for this is the increase in equipment and machinery. Increase in machinery and equipment has outpaced the growth of production. When the effects of investments are taken away from capacity utilization, it can be seen that other macroeconomic variables are in line with expectations. Fluctuations in the capital flows affect economic growth as well. The quantitative expansion policy of Federal Reserve Bank of America has increased the flow of capital to developing countries. This caused economic growth in developing countries including Turkey.

REFERENCES

Alvarez-Lois, P. (2000). Capacity utilization and monetary policy (Working Paper). Banco de Espana Documento de Trabajo No: 0306.

Arabacı, Ö., & Arabacı, R. Y. (2008). Kapasite kullanım oranları ve enflasyon ilişkisi: Türkiye örneği. *Uludağ Üniversitesi İktisadi ve İdari Bilimler Fakülte Dergisi*, *27*(2), 93–109.

Arabacı, Ö., & Eryiğit, K. Y. (2012). A threshold regression estimation of philips curve: Turkey Case. *Eskişehir Osmangazi Üniversitesi İİBF Dergisi*, *7*, 29–47.

Belton, W. J. Jr, & Cebula, R. J. (2000). Capacity utilization rates and unemployment rates: Are they complements or substitutes in warning about future inflation? *Applied Economics*, *32*(14), 1853–1864. doi:10.1080/000368400425071

Boileau and Normandin. (1999). Capacity utilization and the dynamics of business cycle fluctuations (working paper). University of Colorado at Boulder.

Cecchetti, S.G. (1995). Inflation indicators and inflation policy. In *NBER Macroeconomics Annual* (pp. 189–219).

Cho, J. O., & Cooley, T. F. (1992). *The business cycle with nominal contracts. Manuscript*. University of Rochester.

Corrado, C., & Mattey, J. (1997). Capacity utilization. *The Journal of Economic Perspectives*, *11*(1), 151–167. doi:10.1257/jep.11.1.151

Dave, C. (2006). Why is high capacity utilization no longer inflationary in Canada? (Working Paper). Department of Finance, Canada.

Demiroglu, U., & Sarıkaya, C. (2013). *The capacity buildup over the past decade and the capacity utilization rate in Turkey. CBT Research Notes in Economics 1312*. Research and Monetary Policy Department, Central Bank of the Republic of Turkey.

Emery, K. M., & Chang, C. P. (1997). *Is there a stable relationship between capacity utilization and inflation?* Federal Reserve Bank of Dallas Economic Review First Quarter.

Eres, B. (2011). Alternative measures of rate of capacity utilization for the Turkish economy: A Comparative Analysis in Means of Adequacy for Empirical Investigation and Growth Models. *Sosyoekonomi, 2011-12*, 110211.

Fichtenbaum, R. (2003). Is there a natural level of capacity utilization? *Forum for Social Economics, 33*(1), 45–62. doi:10.1007/BF02778965

Finn, M. G. (1995). Is 'high' capacity utilization inflationary? *Economic Quarterly, Federal Reserve Bank of Richmond.*

Garner, A.C. (1994). Capacity utilization and U.S. inflation. *Federal Reserve Bank of Kansas City Economic Review*, Fourth Quarter, 1–21.

Greenwood, J., Hercowitz, Z., & Huffman, W. (1988). Investment, capacity utilization and the real business cycle. *American Economic Association, 78*(3), 402–417.

Hansen, G. D., & Prescott, E. C. (2005). Capacity constraints, asymmetries, and the business cycle. *Review of Economic Dynamics, 8*(4), 850–865. doi:10.1016/j.red.2005.08.001

Ireland, P. N. (1994). *Monetary policy with nominal price rigidity. Manuscript*. Federal Reserve Bank of Richmond.

Kandil (1998). Supply-side asymmetry and the non-neutrality of demand fluctuations. *Journal of Macroeconomics, 20*(4), 785-809.

Kim (1999). Economic capacity utilization and its determinants: theory and evidence. *Review of Industrial Organization, 15*, 321-229.

Lucas, R. E. Jr. (1975). An equilibrium model of the business cycle. *Journal of Political Economy, 83*(6), 1113–1144. doi:10.1086/260386

McElhattan, R. (1985). Inflation, supply shocks and the stable inflation rate of capacity utilization, Economic Review. Federal Reserve Bank of San Francisco.

Phelps, E. S. (1967). Phillips curves, expectations of inflation and optimal unemployment over time. *Economica, 34*(135), 254–281. doi:10.2307/2552025

Planas, C., Roeger, W., & Rossi, A. (2013). The information content of capacity utilization for detrending total factor productivity. *Journal of Economic Dynamics & Control, 37*(3), 577–590. doi:10.1016/j.jedc.2012.09.005

Schultze, C. L. (1963). Uses of capacity measures for short-run economic analysis. *The American Economic Review, 53*, 76–85.

Shapiro, M. D., Gordon, R. J., & Summers, L. H. (1989). Assessing the federal reserve measure of capacity and utilization. *Brookings Papers on Economic Activity*, *1*(1), 181–241. doi:10.2307/2534498

Yamak R. ve Küçükkale Y. (2000). Kapasite kullanım oranı ve enflasyon. In *Ekonomi ve Yönetim Bilimleri Dergisi* (pp. 101-111).

Yamak ve Ceylan (2006). Kapasite kullanım oranı ve enflasyon ilişkisinde asimetri. *C.Ü. İktisadi ve İdari Bilimler Dergisi*, *7*(2),1-18.

KEY TERMS AND DEFINITIONS

Capacity Utilization Rate: Capacity utilization ratio is found by comparing existing industrial capacity with the real productive capability of the economy.

Continuous Wavelet Analysis: The analysis which decomposes a time series into time–frequency space.

Nonaccelerating Inflation Rate of Capacity Utilization: It is the capacity utilization rate at which inflation equals expected inflation.

Phillips Curve: Phillips curve describes a positive short-run relationship between the level of economic activity and inflation.

The Color Code for Power: The thick black contour showing the 5% significance level in the wavelet power spectrum.

Wavelet Coherence: It gives a quantity between 0 and 1, and measures the cross-correlation between two-time series as a function of frequency.

Wavelet Power Spectrum: By looking at the wavelet power spectrum, it is possible to identify which features of the signal are important and which features can be ignored.

Wavelet Transform: formulates a time-frequency representation of a signal that offers very good time and frequency localization.

Section 4

Consumer Behavior and Engagement:

Industry and Corporate Cases

Chapter 12
Consumption and Well-Being:
Collecting Experiences Rather Than Material Possessions

Sandra Maria Correia Loureiro
Instituto Universitário de Lisboa (ISCTE-IUL), Business Research Unit (BRU/UNIDE) and SOCIUS, Portugal

ABSTRACT

Consumerism can be regarded as a system of beliefs and values in which emerge the idea that happiness is best achieved through possessions. In literature, several terms related to this topic are employed, such as: consumerism, consumption, anti-consumption and consumption communities and subjective well-being. Therefore, the purposes of this chapter are to (i) present an overview of the research concepts, models and main theories of this topic and (ii) discuss and inter-relate consumption and subjective well-being. The chapter provides a proposed framework with the state-of-art on consumption, anti-consumption and subjective well-being and a study into rural tourism context. Finally, the chapter also presents suggestions for further research and managerial implications. In this vein, this chapter contributes to the existing literature giving insights for a better understanding the problematic of consumers, anti-consumers and subjective well-being as a whole and rural tourism consumption experience industry in particularly.

INTRODUCTION

Postmodernism, understood as the movement against assumptions and values of the modern period of the Western exercises its influence on consumption. As Firat and Dholakia (1982) noted, the postmodern consumer imbued of the spirit of cultural relativism is the consumer and the consumed. The postmodern consumer is involved in consumption experiences (Holbrook and Hirschman, 1982; Holbrook, 1987; Schmitt, 1999), materialism (e.g., Belk & Pollay, 1985), meanings of possessions (Belk, 1988; Wallendorf & Arnould, 1988), semiotics (McCracken, 1988; Mick, 1988; Sherry, 1989), and consumption patterns (e.g., Firat & Dholakia, 1982). Consumers seek to self and social express themselves through the products they buy; they do not hesitate to demonstrate feelings through products and brands (such as love and hate) (Batra et al., 2012); and consumer self-image is dependent on the symbolic meanings

DOI: 10.4018/978-1-5225-2139-6.ch012

attached to products and the relationships established through them. Thereby, postmodern consumers have a large number of possibilities to choose from even in a simple everyday purchase. This selection process influences the identity and consumption becomes a 'looming threat of personal meaningless' (Giddens, 1991, p. 201).

Postmodernism is also connected with subjective well-being (SWB), defined as a person's cognitive (what one thinks about his/her life as a whole) and in specific areas, such as work, relationships) and affective (emotions, moods and feelings) evaluations of his or her life' (Diener, Lucas, & Oshi, 2002, p. 63). Well-being conceptualization may lie within the hedonic perspective, where the motto is maximize pleasure and avoid pain, or on the eudiamonic perspective, which means live in accordance with one's diamon, or 'true self' (Waterman, 1993). SWB is a complex concept that some relate with materialist possession or high incomes and other associate to healthcare or social protection.

Following this line of thoughts, the postmodern era becomes the tipping point for a new and more diverse vision of consumerism. Consumption versus anti-consumption or alternative consumptions arises as a discussion topic, which will be addressed throughout this chapter. Therefore, the purposes of this chapter are twofold: (i) present an overview of the research concepts, models and main theories of this topic and (ii) discuss and inter-relate consumption and subjective well-being.

The remainder of this chapter is organised as follows. First, a literature review on consumerism, consumption and subjective well-being (SWB) is presented. This is followed by the theoretical arguments about consumption and anti-consumption concepts, typology of anti-consumption, anti-consumption movements, conceptualization of subjective well-being (SWB) and happiness and, finally, framework on consumption, SWB and happiness. The chapter also provides a set of future research directions and conclusions and managerial implications.

BACKGROUND ON CONSUMERISM, CONSUMPTION, AND SWB

An automated search through the B-On System, containing electronic databases, such as Elsevier, Emerald, Science Direct, EBSCO, Springer, and ISI Web of Knowledge was employed to collect scientific information about consumerism, consumption and subjective well-being (SWB), The search strategy for the identification and inclusion of the relevant research papers included the following three steps:

- A broad screen of the titles of the citations retrieved from the literature search and extraction of the studies irrelevant to the present study.
- A broad screen of the abstracts of the citations passed from stage one and selection of the most relevant to the present research topic.
- A strict screen of the remaining studies that passed the previous two stages and selection of the most appropriate and relevant ones to the present research topic.

Quality Assessment

A quality checklist was developed in order to assess the quality of the selected studies, which includes four basic components: Validity, Reliability, Credibility and Integrity, each one graded with three marks. An explanation of these elements of quality measurement is provided below:

- Validity refers to how successful and accurate the study measurement is in relation to its research question. In other words, it concentrates on the study's successfulness when measuring what the researcher intents to investigate and measure (Caldwell et al., 2010).
- Reliability refers to the consistency and the degree of replication of the results and how generalisable they are (Caldwell et al., 2010).
- Credibility reflects the researchers' appropriate academic qualifications in order to be able to undertake the research project along with the writing style of the paper (Caldwell et al., 2010). In addition, this study measures the credibility of the research papers according to the ranking of the journal in which they were published. The selected studies will pass the quality assessment only if they were published in journals that are included in the Harzing quality list of journals. The reason for selecting the Harzing quality list of journals rests on the fact that is based on the analysis and ranking of 19 business and management official journal rankings (Mingers and Harzing, 2007). By applying the Harzing quality list of journals as a credibility measure, the quality of this paper will be increased because it will include studies published in the best journals worldwide.
- Integrity is translated on how robust the research study is and if there is a strict adoption of the chosen research process. It can be measured by evaluating if the methodology adopted by the researcher of the study is identified and justified (Caldwell et al., 2010).

Data Extraction

In this systematic review, a developed data extraction form was used in order to extract the data from the selected studies and to document the data extraction process. Regarding the elements that have been extracted, we present a table providing a visualization of the general publications scenario about the developed theme. This process is done through a data extraction form that reduces human error and documented this process (Magarey, 2001; Tranfield et al., 2003; White & Schmidt, 2005). Table 1 shows the developed data extraction form along with the data extracted from each of the selected studies.

CONSUMPTION, CONSUMERISM, AND ANTI-CONSUMPTION

A group of the most relevant definitions of consumerism, consumption and anti-consumption is shown in Table 2 based on literature review. Consumerism or better the culture-ideology of consumerism (Arnould & Thompson, 2005) is a set of believes and values which ensure that happiness is best achieved through consumption, possessions, materialism (Sklair, 2010). Consumers tend to consider that things, objects or material possessions will give them success and accomplishment and God is not part of the equation (Setmeyer, 2010). Campbell (1995, 2004) notes that the pleasures of consumerism lie in the endless deferral of the pleasure of fulfilment (Campbell, 1995, 2004).

Consumption is the use of goods and services to somehow represent the understanding of ourselves in the world (Miller, 1995). Borgmann (2000), in turn, considers consumption as an everyday process. Thus, ethical consumption emerges as a postmodern idea. Ethical consumption requires making adaptations in consumer lifestyle in order to reduce the negative effects on the environment, people and animals (Clark, 2006). Ethical consumption has been associated to terms such as fair-trade (e.g., Clarke et al., 2007; Dolan, 2008), local (Pratt, 2008; Seyfang, 2006), organic (Clarke et al., 2008; Dombos, 2008),

Table 1. Data extracted from the selected files

Authors	Journal	Key Concept	Key Findings
Kozlowski, Bardecki, and Searcy (2012)	Journal of Corporate Citizenship	Fashion Industry; Apparel; Environmental impacts; Life-cycle assessment; Stakeholder analysis; Corporate social responsibility; Supply chain management	This paper provides a conceptual and analytical framework by conflating Life-cycle assessment and stakeholder analysis to incorporate these considerations into the design process of fashion products, allowing for a systematic and holistic response. The paper illustrates that the identification of stakeholders and their interests, responsibilities and accountability provides a basis for the development and implementation of appropriate policies and programs.
Krishnamurthy and Kucuk (2009)	Journal of Business Research	Internet; Branding; Anti-consumption; Online consumption; Hate sites	Study 1 investigates the brand value's impact on the likelihood of the presence of anti-brand sites. Strong brands are more likely to have anti-brand sites. Study 2 is a content analysis of a representative sample of anti-brand sites that assesses the nature of the language used by such sites. Anti-brand sites use three types of language - market, ideological and transactional speech.
Sussan, Hall, and Meamber (2012)	Journal of Business Research	Brand divorce; Brand relationship; Introspection meditation; Spirituality; Self-transformation	In this paper brand divorce is viewed as a benefit transformational experience from the perspective of the introspecting author. This view stands in contrast to literature which considers brand divorce, from the perspective of the firm as negative.
Wiedmann, Hennigs, Pankalla, Kassubek, and Seegebarth (2011)	Journal of Business Research	Alternative fuels; Natural gas vehicles (NGV); Perceived risk; Innovation resistance	The results of the paper strongly suggest the presence of four clusters: The Status-Oriented Sceptics, The Ecology-Minded Non-Drivers, The Performance-Oriented Traditionalists, The Risk-Averse Drivers.
Cherrier (2009)	Journal of Business Research	Consumer resistance; Identity; Voluntary simplicity; Culture jamming	By stressing the importance of hero resistant identities and project resistant identities, this article offers the concept of identity formation as central rather than peripheral to the development of consumer resistance.
Ahuvia (2008)	Journal of Economic Psychology	Happiness; Income; Life satisfaction; Motivation; Evolutionary theory	This essay has suggested that subjective well-being is not our only goal in life, that people are overly attracted to near-term rewards, and that our actions often are driven by evolved desires that can be inconsistent with personal subjective well-being.
Mady (2011)	Journal of Consumer Behaviour	Alienation from the marketplace; Readiness to embrace new technologies; Consumer sentiment towards marketing	Alienation from the marketplace is found to be negatively associated with sentiment towards marketing and the drivers of technology readiness, but positively associated with the inhibitors of technology readiness. More significantly, readiness to embrace technology is found to exhibit a strong and consistent relationship with sentiment towards marketing.
Portwood-Stacer (2012)	Journal of Consumer Culture	Activism; Anti-consumption; Consumption; Ethics; Identity; Politics; Subculture	Analytically, they can identify at least five motivations for anti-consumption behaviour: individuals may be motivated by personal, moral, activist, identificatory, and/or social concerns. In any given instance, multiple concerns may be at play and at different degrees of consciousness or acknowledgement on the part of the anti-consumers themselves. It is useful to tease out the various types of motivations, not only because this gives a fuller picture of why people behave the way they do, but also because this can help us to assess the potential effects achieved by anti-consumption practices and lifestyles.

continued on following page

Table 1. Continued

Authors	Journal	Key Concept	Key Findings
Lee, Motion, and Conroy (2009)	Journal of Business Research	Brand avoidance; Anti-consumption; Undesired self; Consumer resistance; Negative symbolic consumption	This study reveals three types of brand avoidance: experiential, identity and moral brand avoidance. Experiential brand avoidance occurs because of negative first hand consumption experiences that lead to unfulfilled expectations. Identity avoidance develops when the brand image is symbolically incongruent with the individual's identity. Moral avoidance arises when the consumer's ideological beliefs clash with certain brand values or associations, particularly when the consumer is concerned about the negative impact of a brand on society.
Black and Cherrier (2010)	Journal of Consumer Behaviour	Anti-consumption practices; motivations and values	Overall, the authors find that anti-consumption is an integral part of trying to live a more sustainable life and, in particular, the acts of rejecting, reducing and reusing consumption are key elements to sustainable consumption. Indeed, we found that green consumption, while practiced, is not an essential part of sustainable living.
Iyer and Muncy (2009)	Journal of Business Research	Anti-consumption; Self-actualization; Assertiveness; Self-consciousness; Global impact consumers; Simplifiers	This research presents an initial attempt to develop scales that differentiate between people who engage in general anti-consumption for societal concerns and those who do so for more personal reasons. The results were promising, as a set of "We" anti-consumption statements and a set of "I" anti-consumption statements emerged from the factor analysis.
Ozanne and Ballantine (2010)	Journal of Consumer Behaviour	Sharing; Anti-consumption	The study reveals four groups – Socialites, Market Avoiders, Quiet Anti-Consumers and Passive Members. Socialites enjoy the social benefits of active participation in their library. Market Avoiders also perceive social and community benefits, are interested in sharing and are the least materialistic of the groups. Quiet Anti-Consumers feel a sense of belonging to their toy library and hold strong anti-consumption, frugality and sharing values. Passive Members are not socially involved, nor do they hold strong anti-consumption values. Thus, the authors found evidence that sharing may be one possible alternative market structure that may be adopted by anti-consumption consumers.
Moraes, Szmigin, and Carrigan (2010)	Consumption Markets & Culture	Anti-consumption; Consumer culture; Community; Ethnography	Reported findings are part of a three-year ethnographic research project and suggest that such communities have been overly perceived as presenting radical resistance to prevailing ideologies of consumer society. Collectively, they are more interested in entrepreneurial positive discourses, practices and choices, than in acting against consumer culture or markets. This view is buttressed by their varied production-engaged practices, which in turn are problematized in relation to (perhaps outdated) notions of consumers, producers and their interrelationships.
Sharp, Høj, and Wheeler (2010)	Journal of Consumer Behaviour	Proscription; Anti-consumption; Ban's announcement; Plastic bags;	Shoppers grouped according to their level of voluntary anti-consumption of plastic bags before the ban; the analysis finds that shoppers who voluntarily showed anti-consumption behaviour were the only group showing any voluntary shift in anti-consumption behaviours during the phasing-out period. These shoppers are supportive of forcing others to show anti-consumption, while the level of behavioural and attitudinal resistance from shoppers that showed little or no voluntary anti-consumption is low. These findings support the use of proscription to achieve anti-consumption behaviours; however, proscription does not necessarily engender full anti-consumption attitudes.
Albinsson and Yasanthi Perera (2012)	Journal of Consumer Behaviour	Alternative marketplaces; Collaborative consumption; Sharing; Un-consumption; Sense of community	The findings indicate that a sense of community is both a driver of participation and an outcome of these events. Organisers and participants utilise these venues to share knowledge and possessions for various ideological and practical reasons. Our findings also indicate that these events challenge the entrenched notions of exchange and reciprocity. Our research contributes to the literature by highlighting the importance of community, collaboration, and changing consumer mindsets to the success of such sharing efforts.

continued on following page

Table 1. Continued

Authors	Journal	Key Concept	Key Findings
Banbury, Stinerock, and Subrahmanyan (2012)	Journal of Business Research	Subjective personal introspection; Sustainable consumption; Ecology; Self-fashioning	The authors uncover several dimensions that, taken together, form a more comprehensive explanation of why individuals may or may not succeed in their effort to consume in a more sustainable way. Several of the dimensions revealed included the presence or absence of public infrastructures of one's place of residence, family composition, and the educational awareness of consumers.
Phipps et al. (2013)	Journal of Business Research	Social cognitive theory; Sustainable consumption; Reciprocal determinism; Sharing; Conservation	What is new in this article is the depiction of the interdependency of the three general factors – personal, environmental and behavioural – using an established theoretical framework, Bandura's social cognitive theory. Rather than offer a contrary view, what this article proposes is a logical next step on how researchers conceive sustainable consumption and how researchers define the problems that they address.
Cromie and Ewing (2009)	Journal of Business Research	Anti-consumption; Brand hegemony; Open source; Brand dominance	Findings elucidate the necessary conditions for the rejection of brand hegemony to occur, revealing valuable lessons for vendors. These conditions comprise environment, positive motivation and negative motivation factors. The first two conditions are relatively constant, regardless of the vendor's actions, while the last is largely of the vendor's creation.
Peattie and Peattie (2009)	Journal of Business Research	Consumption reduction; Sustainability; Social Marketing	This article considers the potential of the discipline of marketing to contribute to consumption reduction from a social marketing perspective. The authors review the difficulties of applying conventional marketing theory and practice in pursuit of more sustainable consumption, and the logic of applying an adapted form of social marketing to promote more sustainable lifestyles and reductions in consumption. This study also uses a health-oriented social marketing campaign to demonstrate the potential of a social marketing approach to address ingrained forms of consumer behaviour and to successfully 'de-market' products.
McGinnis and Gentry (2009)	Journal of Business Research	Anti-consumption; Creolization; Counter-conformity; Globalization; Identification; Underdogs	Findings suggest that underdog consumers support underdogs out of empathy, as a way to ensure the maintenance of equal opportunity in competition, and as a way to provide personal inspiration. Some motives for underdog support can be interpreted to be anti-consumption (or, at least, anti-corporate) in nature. On the other hand, many underdog consumers support and identify with underdogs not necessarily as a way to keep the top dog down, but as a means to keep the little guy competing.
Wheeler (2012)	Cultural Studies	Citizen-consumers; Consumer movements; Fair-trade consumption; Globalization; Mobilization; Reflexivity	The citizen-consumer has many faces depending upon the audience, from compassionate Christian/Oxfam supporter, to supermarket retailer, campaigning activist, caring government department, free-market champion and Western/middle-class supermarket shopper. This paper has shown how the Fair-trade movement can offer some consumers, retailers and organisations the opportunity to act as citizens both within the market and as political campaigners to improve the livelihoods of some producers in the developing world.
Youngberg (2009)	The Explicator	Edward Albee; Superficiality; American Dream	In our push to satisfy our own vain pleasures, in our vain attempts to "get satisfaction", Americans just might end up spawning monsters and killing our own better selves in the process.
Varman and Belk (2009)	Journal of Consumer Research	Nationalist ideology; Anti-consumption; Coca-Cola; Globalization	The research shows that the creation of national space is a reflexive local response to the historical perceptions about the displacements caused by globalization in the region. They identified the role of a nationalist ideology that, apart from the images of the economic exploitation of the local, involves invocations of tradition, patriotism, and an alternate local identity to create deeper challenges to authenticity. Their findings show that authenticity is being created around a particularized notion of nationhood. In the national space, consumers are reflexively taught to become like themselves. Temporal heterogeneity is a reflexive dimension of postcolonial anti-consumption that remains elided in extant theory.

continued on following page

Table 1. Continued

Authors	Journal	Key Concept	Key Findings
Setmeyer (2010)	Dialog: A Journal of Theology	Consumerism, Theology of the Cross, Douglas John Hall, Stephen B. Bevans, Anthropology	Their message is anthropological and eschatological, not technical, though also practical. The message to North America, like is that there is "More!" and they will help you find it, set it free from within, and discover it in the humanity of others.
Penny (2012)	New Statesman	Capitalism; Consumerism; Teenagers; Shopping	The violence and frenzy of consumerism is terrifying – but that does not mean that shopping is inherently evil.
Hall (2011)	Geoforum	Ethics; Consumption; Ethnography; Ethical consumption; Family	By exploring the everyday ethics of money, waste and health choices in family consumption practices, this paper makes the case for recognising the ethical nature of everyday practices and choices of consumption. It is argued that rather than consumers subscribing to a given set of ethics in consumption, there are multiple ways of recognising consumption as an ethically-embedded process.
Tiwsakul and Hackley (2012)	Journal of Business Research	Asian; Identity; Thai; Consumption; Cultural; Autoethnography	This study supports the suggestion that consumption is a primary site for the negotiation of the deep identity conflicts and postmodern paradoxes generated by the Asian encounter with the West and its values. It also contributes to a more nuanced understanding of 'Asianness' as a complex, conflict and variable concept in Western consumer and marketing research, rather than an unproblematic unity.
Soper (2008)	Cultural Studies	Consumerism; Sustainable consumption; Alternative hedonism; Needs and desires; Aesthetics of consumption	In pressing the case for the development of a new 'hedonist imaginary' with which to subvert current perceptions of the attractions of a consumerist material culture, the article also considers the possible contribution of cultural and artistic activities to the formation of an anti-consumerist aesthetic.
Sklair (2010)	Theory, Culture & Society	Consumerism; globalization; Iconic architecture; Shopping; Transnational; Capitalist class	In this article the author has tried to show that most iconic architecture of the global era is also best analysed as a form of hegemonic architecture, serving the interests of the transnational capitalist class through the creation of consumerist space or, more accurately, through the attempt to turn more or less all public spaces into consumerist space.
Hosany (2012)	Journal of Travel Research	Cognitive appraisal theories; Goal-congruence; Self-concept	Results indicate that appraisals of pleasantness, goal congruence, and internal self-compatibility are the main determinants of joy, love, and positive surprise. Overall, the findings offer strategic marketing implications for tourist destinations.
Oishi et al. (2013)	Personality and Social Psychology Bulletin	Happiness; Subjective well-being	Across cultures and time, happiness was most frequently defined as good luck and favorable external conditions. However, in American English, this definition was replaced by definitions focused on favorable internal feeling states. Our findings highlight the value of a historical perspective in the study of psychological concepts.
Nawijn (2011a)	Journal of Travel Research	Affect; Emotions; Happiness; Subjective well-being	During a holiday, holiday stress and attitude toward the travel party are the most important determinants of daily affect balance. These findings imply that on the whole, the tourism industry is doing a good job. The industry could probably do better with more research on experiences during the holiday.
Theodorakis et al. (2015)	Leisure Sciences: An Interdisciplinary Journal	Happiness equation; Easterlin paradox; Subjective well-being; Life satisfaction	The overall expectations on the quality of the event experience can be a focus for event managers aiming to achieve social marketing goals related to positive psychology from the event participation.
Ram et al. (2013)	Journal of Sustainable Tourism	Behavioral change; Leisure mobility; Happiness	The paper shows that happiness is integral to all stages of the tourist experience. Understanding happiness enhances the understanding of tourist behavior, and how it drives, via the speed–distance–demand loop, the three-stage model presented here.

continued on following page

Table 1. Continued

Authors	Journal	Key Concept	Key Findings
Bimonte and Faralla (2014)	Annals of Tourism Research	Happiness	These results confirm that aspects other than money may influence individuals' happiness, and factors such as individuals' values and ideology may impact the connection between aspects of life and happiness in different ways. In this study the way in which people relate to the environment emerges as a distinguishing factor. It seems that proximity to nature can boost personal emotional and physical well-being.
Nawijn (2011b)	Journal Happiness Studies	Affect, Subjective well-being	Happiness did not predict vacationing. The effect of holiday trips on vacationers' happiness is mostly short-lived; among vacationers, happiness was unrelated to the number of trips and days spent on vacation. A separate analysis of vacationers, who value vacationing most, yielded the same results.
Verme (2009)	Journal of Economic Behavior & Organization	Happiness; Utility; Freedom of choice; Locus of control	Freedom of choice and the locus of control is found to predict life satisfaction better than *any* other known factor such as health, employment, income, marriage or religion, across countries and within countries.
Kesebir and Diener (2009)	Perspectives on psychological science	Happiness	This article provides an overview of what various philosophers throughout the ages have claimed about the nature of happiness, and discusses to what extent psychological science has been able to substantiate or refute their claims
Wang and Wong (2014)	Journal Happiness Studies	Happiness; Leisure	Family income and individual demographic variables such as age and health condition are significantly associated with happiness. National unemployment and political stability also have robustly significant effects on happiness.
Bosnjak et al. (2014)	Journal of Travel Research	Eudaimonia; Happiness, Subjective well-being; Self-expressiveness, Hedonic enjoyment	Self-expressiveness in a sport activity experienced by a tourist depends on the activity's perceived difficulty, perceived effort, perceived importance, and potential for self-realization. In turn, a tourist's self-expressiveness in a sport activity exerts a positive influence on the tourist's experience of personal happiness (subjective well-being)
O'Brien (2006)	Canadian Psychology	Sustainable happiness; Liveable communities; Infrastructures of well-being	Sustainable happiness is the pursuit of happiness that does not exploit other people, the environment, or future generations. Bringing sustainability and happiness together within the concept of sustainable happiness holds significant possibilities for individual, community, and global well-being. Sustainable happiness is discussed with respect to liveable communities, child-friendly planning, and education.
McCabe and Johnson (2013)	Annals of Tourism Research	subjective well-being; Quality of life; Happiness	The findings indicate that tourism contributes to social tourist's well-being. There are greater effects in some areas including psychological resources, leisure and family life domains contributing to social well-being. Social tourists have lower levels of SWB than the general population.
Bimonte and Faralla (2012)	Annals of Tourism Research	Happiness; Economic growth; Nature-based tourist; Self or others-oriented motivation.	The authors study whether a relationship exists between self-reported happiness and the type of tourist one belongs to.
Nawijn and Peeters (2010)	Current Issues in Tourism	Climate change; Sustainability; Happiness; Subjective well-being	This article examines the extent to which the average tourist's happiness is affected by 'involuntary green travel.

continued on following page

sustainability (Seyfang, 2004), environmental responsibility (Hobson, 2006), and community (Thompson & Coskuner-Balli, 2007).

Lee et al. (2009) regard anti-consumption as against consumption. Zavestoski (2002) considers anti-consumption, in a postmodern area, as a resistance to, distaste of, or even resentment or rejection of consumption. Research in anti-consumption tends to focus on the reasons behind product/brand avoidance and sustainable lifestyles. Anti-consumption is to try to live a more sustainable life. For instance, green consumers refuse to purchase products that are averse to the environment (Moisander, 2007); ethical consumers reject products from enterprises which are not socially responsible (Ozcaglar-Toulouse et al., 2006); and consumers with strong political ideology do not purchase products/brands that do not correspond to their political ideology (Sandıkcı & Ekici, 2009; Black & Cherrier, 2010).

The alternative consumptions are motivated by alternative intrinsic pleasures, the alternative hedonics. For example, alternative hedonics could be the pleasure of walking and cycling instead of driving a car, to cut down on packaging and plastic, to spend time cooking rather than consuming fast food (Soper, 2008).

Motivations for Anti-Consumption

According to Lang and Gabriel (2005), Hilton (2003) and Moraes, Szmigin and Carrigan (2010), the Western consumption movements' cycles evolved over four main waves beginning in the late 1800s, (1) consumer cooperatives (late 1800s to early 1900s), (2) consumer information (1930s), (3) mass consumption (1960s), (4) green to ethical consumption (late 1980s):

1. The consumer cooperatives wave is marked by a strong desire for social change (in this period the first consumer cooperatives were organised).
2. The consumer information wave was the "first time that consumer activism saw itself as enabling consumers to take best advantage of the market, rather than trying to undermine the market through cooperative action or political agitation" (Lang & Gabriel, 2005, p. 44).
3. The mass consumption wave accepts capitalism and the market.
4. The green to ethical consumption wave emerged because of the rapid growth in consumer organisations and coalitions and proliferation of internet access. Groups of consumers are more aware of ethical issues and their purchase process takes into consideration societal, environmental and animal welfare concerns (Harrison, Newholm, & Shaw, 2005).

Table 2. Conceptualization of consumerism, consumption and anti-consumption

Consumerism	Consumption	Anti-Consumption
The culture-ideology of consumerism refers to a set of beliefs and values integral, but not exclusive, to the system of capitalist globalization, intended to make people believe that human worth is best ensured and happiness is best achieved in terms of our consumption and possessions (Sklair, 2010, p. 135)	Use of goods and services in which the object or activity becomes simultaneously a practice in the world and a form in which we construct our understandings of ourselves in the world. (Miller, 1995, p. 30).	Anti-consumption is 'a resistance to, distaste of, or even resentment or rejection of consumption more generally.' (it is not merely a behavioural phenomenon but also an attitudinal one) Zavestoski (2002, p. 121) in (Cherrier, 2008).
It is the phenomenon produced by the misdirected desire to find fulfilment in things outside of God, particularly in the consumption of material possessions (Setmeyer, 2010, p. 306)	Consumption is an essential everyday process; 'to live is to consume' (Borgmann, 2000, p. 418).	

The green to ethical consumption wave is the birthplace of the new consumption communities, innovative, creative and collaborative through the diffusion of networking technologies. Consumption in online environments is indivisible from production. Consumers act as double agents, entrepreneurs and buyers in a market evolving into experience service. Therefore, social networking sites, websites, blogs and other online sites become the new marketplace.

Portwood-Stacer (2012) considers and explains five motivations for anti-consumption behaviour, that is, (1) personal, (2) moral, (3) activist, (4) identificatory, and/or (5) social concerns:

1. Personal motivations relate to immediate personal benefit achieved through alternative consumption experiences.
2. Moral describes the practices motivated by judgments about right and wrong.
3. Activist. Activist consumers act to put pressure on a system or larger entity to alter a pattern of immoral practice. As Kozinets and Handelman (2004, p. 693) pointed out, activists "repeatedly emphasized that they were also trying to elevate consumers' collective awareness and, through it, change consumer culture and ideology".
4. Identificatory. Norms, rituals can establish "practices which an individual embraces, not only because such practices fulfil utilitarian needs, but because they give material form to a particular narrative of self-identity" (Giddens, 1991, p. 81). Anti-consumers who wish to be identified as anarchists would be motivated to orient their behaviours towards those ideas and habits that are most commonly accepted by their peers (the anarchist group they belong to) and perceive themselves as authentically anarchist.
5. Social. Social anti-consumption is a means of achieving solidarity among participants in the anarchist movement. The anarchist anti-consumers reject the mainstream consumption (Veblen, 1994). Therefore, they unite around their symbolic rejection of mainstream consumption.

Typology of Anti-Consumption

Cromie and Ewing (2009) propose that anti-consumption emerge from at least two distinct phenomena and four distinct sub-groups (see Figure 1). The two phenomena are:

1. The consumers who seek to reduce consumption and
2. Consumers who have no such intention.

The first group of consumers refers to the social movements intending to reduce society's acceptance of consumption as a way of life (Kozinets, 2004; Zavestoski, 2002) and those who are conservative and motivated by personal values.

The second group does not have a direct intention to reduce consumption, but is intentionally selective in its consumption, selection of product/brand based on political, values or lifestyle conviction, or rejects brand hegemony; the people in this group tend to avoid dominant brands in the market.

Iyer and Muncy (2009) suggested a similar typology of anti-consumers regarding four groups:

1. Global impact consumers, interested in reducing the general level of consumption for the benefit of society;

2. Simplifiers, who wish to adopt a less consumer-oriented lifestyle (Zavestoski, 2002), they believe that it is morally wrong to focus so much energy on self-serving consumption activities (Shaw & Newholm, 2002);
3. Market activists are those who avoid using a product/brand because it could cause a specific societal problem;
4. Anti-loyalists are consumers not committed to repurchasing a brand and avoid purchasing a product because of perceived inferiority or because of a negative experience associated with it (Lee et al., 2009) (see Figure 2).

The first group, global impact consumers, is designated by Cromie and Ewing (2009) as the anti-consumption society. The second group, simplifiers, is similar to what Cromie and Ewing (2009) mentioned as conservative. The third group of market activists is known by Cromie and Ewing (2009) as the selective consumption. Finally, anti-loyalists are connected, in part, to selective consumption, but also to rejection of brand hegemony.

SUBJECTIVE WELL-BEING IN POSTMODERN SOCIETY

Subjective well-being (SWB) measures how people think and feel about their lives. Life satisfaction, positive affect and negative affect are three independent components of SWB that should be studied separately (Andrews, & Withey, 1976, Lucas, & Dyrenforth (2006). In this vein, positive affect and negative affect may coexist and be measured using PANAS [positive affect negative affect schedule] (Watson, Clark & Tellegan, 1988). Life satisfaction can be measured using an instrument with 5 items (Diener, Emmons, Larsen & Griffin, 1985; Pavot & Diener, 1993). Yet, not self-reposted measures may be more accurate because do not depend on factors such as situational factors, the type of scales that are used, the order in which the items are presented in the scales, and the mood of the participant at the time when the measurement was taken. This is the case of the Experience Sampling Method (ESM), which is taken over a period of time such as a month or six. Whenever possible a 'multi-method method will be the most appropriated.

Personality traits have been regarded as drivers SWB. For instance, neuroticism is correlated with negative affect and extroversion with positive affect (e.g., Watson & Clark, 1984; Diener & Lucas, 1999). Other personality traits are also correlated to SWB, such as: optimism or the theory of dispositional optimism (Scheier & Carver, 1985) and self-esteem. The way people relate with others and the network

Figure 1. Typology of anti-consumption

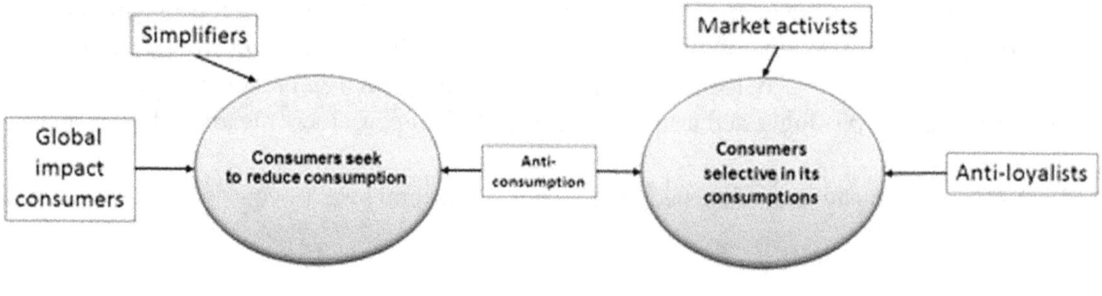

of close social support (family and friends) is being strongly correlated with SWB. Researchers such as Csikszentmihalyi (1975) suggest that people are happier when they are involved in activities that fit in their abilities and have meaning. Leisure and recreation (tourism, see shows or engage in physical exercise) improve mood states in the short term and, in the long term, leads to increased SWB (Argyle, 2001).

The theories of adaptation alluding to the capacity or ability to change behaviors depending on circumstances have been pointed out as explaining SWB from genetic point of view: the dynamic equilibrium model (Headey & Waring, 1992) or the hedonic treadmill theory (Brickman & Campbell, 1971).

Although it is recognized connected to SWB conceptualization (see Figure 2), happiness is not easy to define. In ancient Greece Aristotle highlights the importance of achieving Eudaimonia, which is living life in a fulfilling and meaningful way. Happiness involves the pursuit of pleasure (hedonism) and meaning in one's life (Eudaimonism) (Wang & Wong, 2014), which may overlap with one another. While hedonism is associated with relaxation and escape, Eudaimonism is correlated with activities involving developmental growth.

Hedonic consumption has a subjective nature because Individuals interpret their own meanings of what is pleasurable. Emotions play a crucial role as a source of hedonic value and its role in motivating and reinforcing ethical choices (Malone et al., 2014). Cognitive appraisal theories define emotions as mental states that result from processing, or appraising, personally relevant information (Roseman, Spindel, & Jose 1990). Therefore, individual´s subjective evaluate a situation or event, where emotions play a key role.

Consumption is also related to memories (see Figure 2). People are more likely to remember positive events (compared to bad events) to enhance their self-esteem and well-being (Walker, Skowronski, & Thomson, 1996). Thus, their whole information process is based on selective attention and selective recall, which biased the decision process. Given that people feel much better on vacations compared to their everyday lives (Nawijn, 2011a), their happy memories are reference points, triggering new trips. But going shopping (clothes, gadgets, or other pleasurable objects or even other material possessions) can also activate similar emotions and biased the decision process. This kind of happiness through material possessions is short-term benefit and need to be continuously re-fed.

Flow theory has also been employed to explain the engagement process associated to an experience which can conducted to a higher level of achievement and happiness. When a person is in flow, everything comes together for him/her and the person is totally involved in the activity at hand. The experience is highly rewarding in itself (Csikszentmihalyi, 1990).

The question here is the broadly notion of experience. The seminal work of Pine and Gilmore (1998) leverage the idea of consumption in different economic activities to a stage experience (see Figure 2). Therefore, we cannot talk anymore about a purchase process to acquire material possessions but a purchase process to get a tangible and intangible set of meanings, feeling and sensations.

Pine and Gilmore (1998) argue that after a shift from selling products to selling services there would be another shift to selling experiences. They highlight that consumers desire unique experiences, and businesses should respond to these desires by delivering memorable experiences to consumers. Consumers may either actively and passively participate in experiences. Consumers actively participate in experience when they contribute to affect the experience itself. Yet, consumers may also be more or less connected to the experience. In terms of connectedness, consumers can either absorb experience or immerse themselves in it. Absorb experience means that they have a certain distance between them and the experience (e.g. watching television in a non-interactive way; observing rural activities). Consumers immerse themselves in an experience when there is no distance between them and the experience (e.g.

Figure 2. Framework on consumption and subjective well-being

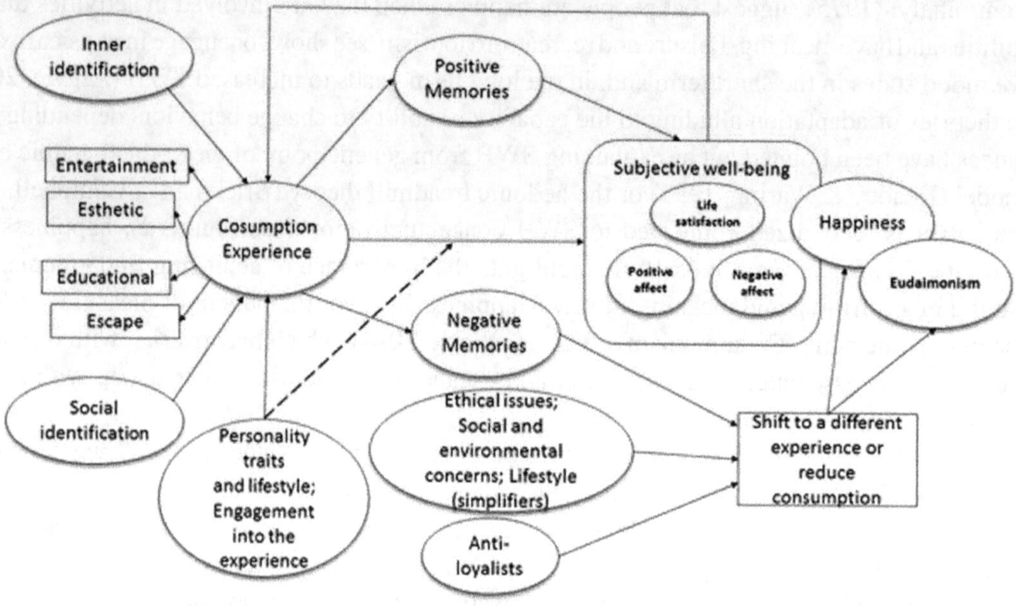

inclusion in the rural live; attending and directly enjoying the live concert). Here emerge the four realms depending on the form of consumer involvement in the experience: entertainment, educational, esthetic, and escape. Figure 2 illustrate the concepts and discussion presented above.

RURAL TOURISM CONSUMPTION EXPERIENCE AND HAPPINESS

Rural tourism is tourism in the countryside that embraces the rural environment as pivotal to the product offered (Loureiro & Kastenholz, 2011). The OECD (1994) defines rural tourism as any "tourism taking place in the countryside". In this context, rural is the "central and unique selling point in the rural tourism package" (OECD, 1994, p. 15). Thus, rural tourism is a niche tourism associated with a set of diversified tourism products in rural areas aiming to preserve, restore and value the regions' architectural, historical, natural and landscape heritage.

The tourism experience is very important for rural areas, which need to develop appealing and distinctive offerings for a demanding and heterogeneous tourism market. Rural tourism comprises a set of possible activities besides the accommodation itself, depending on the region, such as appreciating the landscape, visiting heritage sites or regional fairs and participation in rural activities (e.g., making wine, picking fruit or tasting wine, cheese, stuffed pork or even learning how to make handicrafts) (Loureiro & Kastenholz, 2011; Loureiro, 2014).

As mentioned above in this chapter, experiences are associated with strong emotions and individuals tend to recall positive experiences more easily than negative ones. Loureiro (2014) tests the influence of experience on pleasant arousal and memory in rural tourism context but the influence of rural experience on happiness is not yet properly analyzed, However, positive experiences tend to bring happiness (see figure 2). Thus:

H1: The dimensions of the rural tourism economy experience, Entertainment (H1a), Esthetics (H1b), Educational (H1c), and Escape (H1d) positively influence rural tourists' happiness.

The literature has been highlighting that personality traits, lifestyle or be more or less engaged in the experience may differentiate the way individuals live an experience and feel well and happy or unhappy (see figure 2). In this vein, high engaged rural tourists will have higher involvement and motivation in the rural tourism experience and may feel happier than less engaged rural tourists and so the following hypothesis is proposed:

H2: Engagement moderates the effects of the dimensions of the rural tourism experience and rural tourists' happiness.

The empirical part of this chapter focuses on a block of the whole framework (Figure 2) and so the proposed model is shown in Figure 3.

Data Collection

The survey was conducted during 2014 in Alentejo (Portugal): The goals of this study were explained to the owners and/or managers of the rural lodging units and only guests that were going to leave the lodging were invited to complete the questionnaire. From the 120 rural tourists who were eligible to

Figure 3. Proposed model: effect of rural experience on happiness

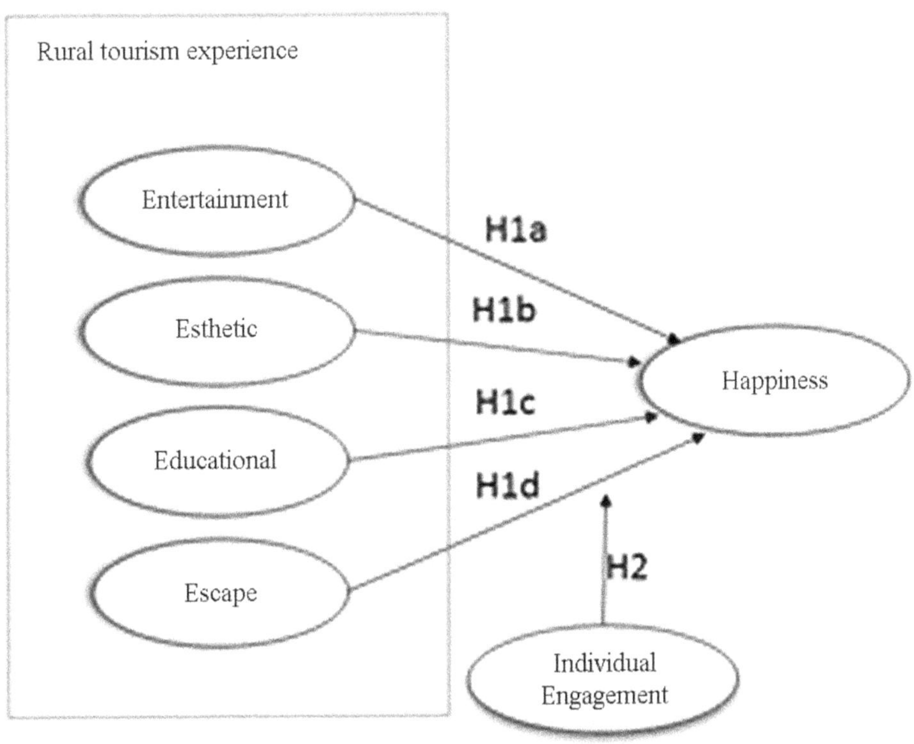

answer the questionnaire, a convenience sample, 10 did not wish to answer, 8 did not respond to the full extent, and 102 questionnaires were usable for validating the model, corresponding to a response rate of 85%. For all participants, this was their first time in Alentejo.

The questionnaire was elaborated in two languages, Croatian and English, with the help of language teachers. Back translation was used to ensure that both questionnaires communicated the same information (Sekaran, 1983). A pilot sample with five rural tourists was used to ensure that the wording of the questionnaire was clear and only a few adjustments were made. Rural tourism experience was measured using 16 items based on Loureiro (2014) and Oh et al. (2007). In order to measure individual engagement, the engagement dimension of the Langer Mindfulness Scale (LMS) (Langer, 2004) was employed. Finally, happiness was adapted from Van Boven and Gilovich (2003). All the items were rated using a 5-point Likert type scale (1 – strongly disagree to 5 – strongly agree).

Findings

The sample was balanced between male and female and most of the respondents were between 21 and 60 years old (88%). The tourists had different professions, such as journalist, professor, doctor, nurse or bank clerk. Table 3 shows the descriptive statistics for each variables.

Multiple regression analysis is employed to test H1. All the assumptions necessary to use regression analysis are confirmed. As we observe in Figure 4, H1 is supported. Even so, the strength of the direct relationship between Esthetic and happiness and between Educational and Happiness are higher than the two other relationships.

The hierarchical linear regression is employed to test H2, the interaction effect. Results in Table 4 reveal that only in the case of educational the interaction effect (Educational x Engagement) is statistically significant. Thus, the individual engagement changes the direction and the magnitude of the relationship between educational experience and happiness.

In order to better understand the moderating effect, the sample is split into high and low individual engagement considering the median of the variable. Figure 5 shows the linear regressions for each dimension of rural experience split in two groups: low engagement and high engagement.

Figure 5 shows that only in the cases of educational and esthetic we may consider differences in variation of happiness moderated by the level of individual engagement. Therefore, H2 is only partially supported.

Table 3. Descriptive statistics

Variable	Mean	Standard Deviation	Cronbach Alpha
Entertainment	3.5	0.908	0.83
Esthetic	3.9	0.896	0.80
Educational	3.7	0.759	0.75
Escape	3.4	0.936	0.74
Happiness	3.7	0.830	0.74
Individual Engagement	3.9	0.729	0.70

Figure 4. Regression results for effect of rural experience on happiness

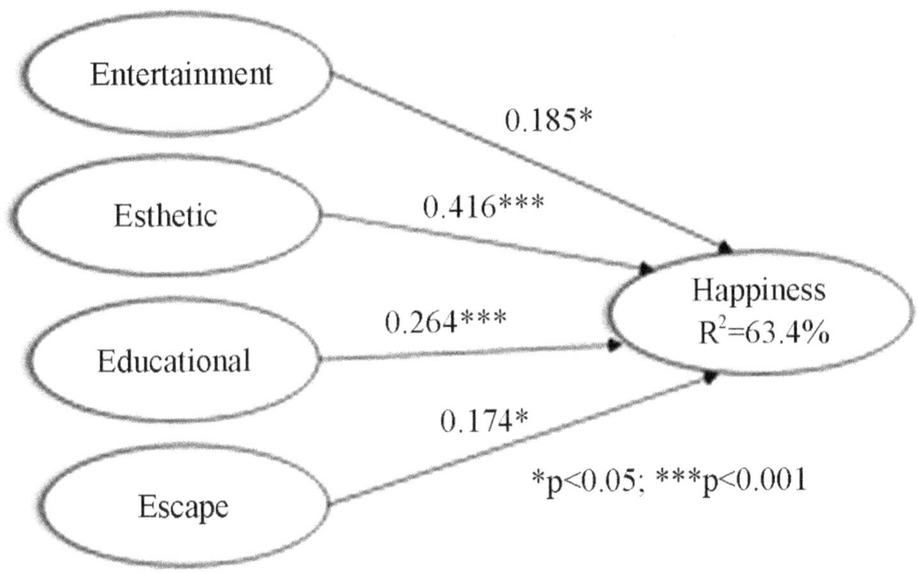

Table 4. Interaction effects of dimensions of rural experience and happiness

Model		Unstandardized Coefficients		Standardized Coefficients	t	Sig.
		B	Std. Error	Beta		
1	(Constant)	3.735	0.064		58.651	0.000
	Engagement_centered	0.458	0.089	0.403	5.179	0.000
	Entcrtainment_centered	0.410	0.072	0.449	5.711	0.000
	Entret x eng_centered (interaction effect)	-0.156	0.102	-0.115	-1.530	0.129
2	(Constant)	3.798	0.060		62.777	0.000
	Engagement_centered	0.263	0.089	0.231	2.947	0.004
	Educational_centered	0.644	0.083	0.589	7.752	0.000
	Edu x eng_centered (interaction effect)	-0.216	0.095	-0.157	-2.269	0.025
3	(Constant)	3.752	0.071		52.916	0.000
	Engagement_centered	0.265	0.109	0.233	2.437	0.017
	Esthetic_centered	0.589	0.111	0.486	5.280	0.000
	Esthe x eng_centered (interaction effect)	-0.123	0.118	-0.082	-1.037	0.303
4	(Constant)	3.762	0.062		61.011	0.000
	Engagement_centered	0.423	0.090	0.371	4.713	0.000
	Escapism_centered	0.422	0.066	0.476	6.398	0.000
	Escapism x eng_centered (interaction effect)	-0.133	0.092	-0.108	-1.442	0.152

Dependent Variable: Happiness.

Figure 5. Moderating effect of individual engagement

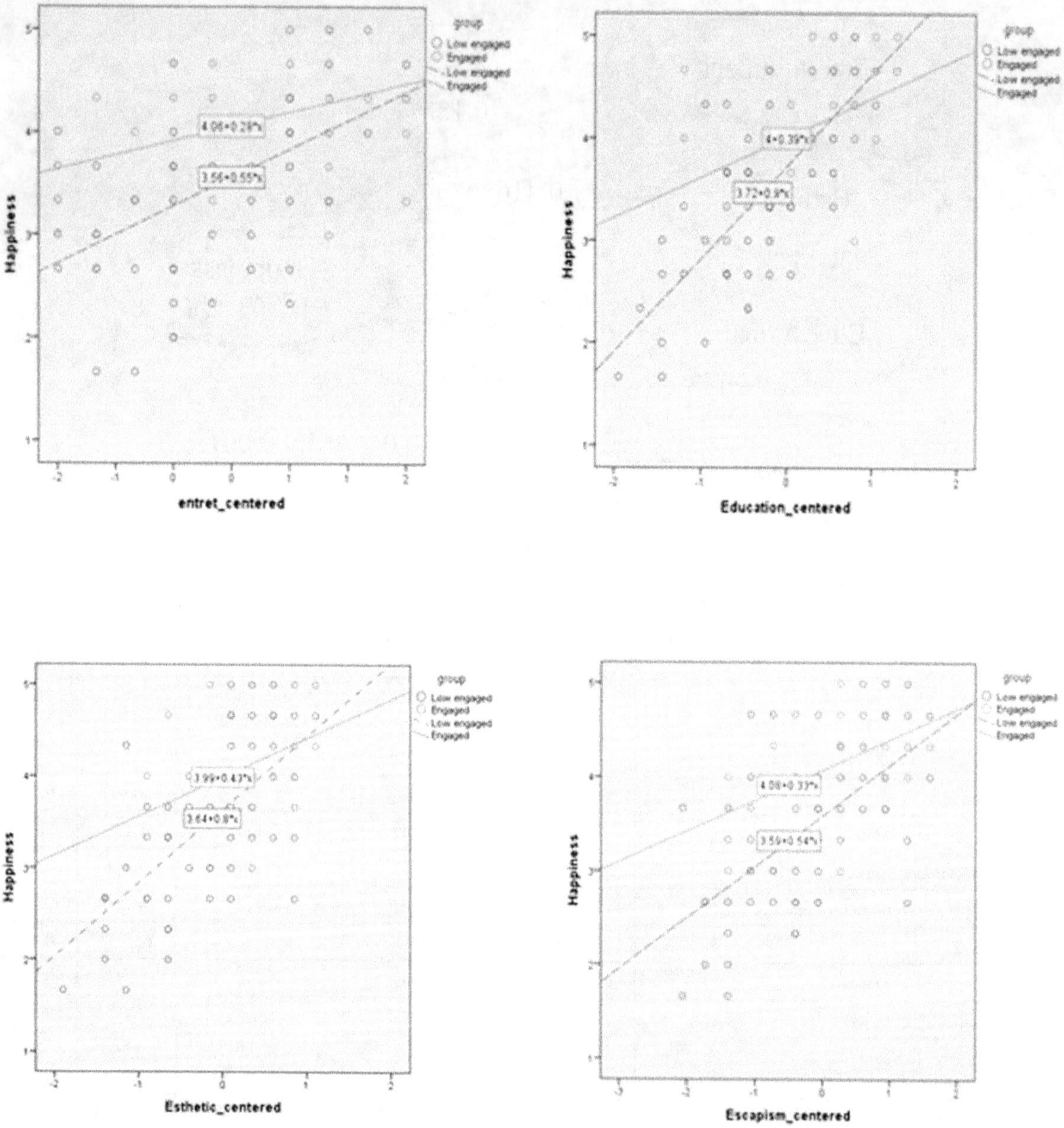

Insights from the Study

Aligned with Loureiro (2014), which proved the influence of rural experience on positive emotions (pleasant arousal) and creating of memories, the current study highlights that a favorable rural tourism experience may indeed generate a feeling of happiness in tourists. The educational and aesthetic dimensions of the experience emerge as the most relevant in inducing happiness with rural experience. Aesthetic (passive participation) means that the rural tourists enjoy the atmospheric cues inside the rural lodging and also contemplation of the landscape Educational (active participation in activities and occupies an individual's attention by bringing the experience into mind) may be viewed as the participation in theme fairs or learning how to make handicrafts and/or performing agricultural activities. Following these dimensions, entertainment (occurs when the rural tourist passively observes the activities of others) and escapism (the rural tourist embraces the rural place's lifestyle and forgets her/his everyday life) emerge. Passive and active participation and immersion experience can be very meaningful and contribute to happiness in life.

Regarding the moderate effect of individual engagement on the relationship between rural tourism experience dimensions and happiness, this study does not prove that tourists who like to investigate things and engaged in the experiences are more willing to feel more happy with the full rural experience than tourists less engaged. Nevertheless, when analyzing the moderate effect considering only educational and esthetic as the dimensions of experience, it seems to reveal that less engaged rural tourists, that is, tourists who do not actively focused on the experience seem to live an intensification of their happiness.

Although more studies on this topic are needed and being aware that this study should be regarded with caution since it is a first step, the current study contributes to bring to light the influence of individual engagement into the context of rural tourism. In the future, this study may be replicated using data gathered in different types of experiences (rural experience or not).

FUTURE RESEARCH DIRECTIONS

Regarding future empirical research, some suggestions may be made:

1. Develop research to further understand how anti-consumption social activists behave in consumption experiences drawn according to their convictions, lifestyle and social and ethical issues.
2. Investigate the drivers to anti-branding attitude, who are the initiators, the leaders and the organisers of the bloggers or other viral mechanisms of anti-branding movements; what are the new attitudes and behaviours.
3. A new group of constructs should be developed and the relationship among them explored: spirituality, brand divorce, and consumption choices.
4. Integrating the research in an international context with several possible economic (e.g., fuel price ratio), ecologic (e.g., directly human life affecting climate change effects), social–cultural (e.g., different perceptions of eco-friendly behaviour), political (e.g., public regulations dictate to the automotive industry), and technological factors (e.g., development of zero-emission vehicles).
5. Understanding if the postmodern activist consumers are motivated and mobilized for projects of social change.
6. Analysing the meaning and the relationship between post-material values, anti-consumption and frugality; to understand if green consumers are truly interested in environmental and sustainable issues or if it is more about self-interested issues.
7. Differentiating between global impact consumers and simplifiers, the new constructs and scales developed may change from "I" to "we".
8. Studying consumer behaviour concerning sharing behaviour, such as, car sharing, home sharing through co-housing, free cycling or clothes swapping, to determine whether other groups of sharers also hold anti-consumption attitudes. Moreover, future research could examine permanent facilities

and programs that foster sharing and their effect on the communities. For example, North Carolina's Warren Wilson College's Free Store, a storefront stocked with goods donated by university members that are, in turn, available to the campus community, and sharing programs such as university sponsored ride and car sharing programs. How to engage consumers, with individualistic-oriented self-enhancement values (i.e., power and achievement), in collaborative consumption efforts is fodder for future research.

9. Understanding the political process to drive sustainability (civic engagement), for instance, a change in behaviour can influence personal motivations, which, in turn, can reinforce behaviours.
10. Differentiating more effectively underdogs from loser consumers. Study is needed to determine just how much of underdog preference is due to resentment towards "corporate" entities, and how much is due to strong attractions to the underdog itself. To the extent that the latter is more important than the former, pro-active positioning of the underdog may be far more effective than any anti-corporate style of positioning, even if done in a subtle fashion
11. Exploring how ethics in consumption is translated from narrative and experience into practice, and to recognise ethics as something that is integral to consumption choices, as the 'ethical everyday'.
12. Understanding how Asian traditions and practices, in a globalized economy, can influence Western marketing and consumers.
13. Go further in understanding the effect of iconic architecture and space on postmodern consumer behaviour, as well as in understanding how sport culture and spirit influence postmodern consumers.
14. Go further in understanding the effect of hedonic adaptations (consumers know the experience due to the past experience) and demotivation on consumers.

CONCLUSION

This chapter starts with a literature review on consumption, anti-consumption and SWB and provides researchers, managers and marketers with a glimpse of social changes and consumers' behaviour in a postmodern era. The chapter presents a discussion of definitions and typologies on consumption, consumerism, anti-consumption and subjective well-being. The chapter also deals with the controversial discussion between SWB and happiness and attempts to illustrate the inter-relations among the terms and concepts.

The issues around the terms consumption, anti-consumption, SWB and inter-relations are not yet completely understood. Therefore, as suggestions for future research, a set of 14 lines for future research directions are pointed out. Thereby, the chapter provides readers with the most up-to-date knowledge about new trends in consumption and new consumers' attitudes, behaviours, values and ethics.

Considering managerial implications, managers should be aware of the new communities of consumers who reject brand hegemony or are selective or even simplifiers. The knowledge about these new consumers, their profile and behaviour help managers to design appropriate products/brands. However, marketing is not only about products/brands, it is also about establishing and maintaining relations. Marketing can operate in such communities, for instance, as a facilitator for new types of productive-consumptive relations and an integral part of the cultural structure of enduring communities of production-engaged consumption. Marketers and managers should follow and listen to how anti-consumption movements operate and inform consumers and change their view and the way they communicate products/brands.

The more intangible components of an experience may be more effective in creating positive memories, which, in turn, contribute to consumer subjective well-being. The close relationship and continuous engagement between an organization and their consumers allow to c-create and improve the consumption experiences and retain consumers.

Managers of rural lodgings and places should be aware that the groups of more conservative tourists, tourists who do not actively seek to learn new things and do not want to challenge their core beliefs, seem to live an intensification and who do not intend to actively search for novelty are more willing to get more happiness from the rural experience where they passively watch others doing rural activities, but at the same time experience living in a different time or place. On the other hand, if owners of rural lodging and places want to capture open minded and creative tourists, they should be able to prepare activities that boost creativity and curiosity. The organization and the planning of the activities should be done in co-creation with tourist.

REFERENCES

Ahuvia, A. (2008). If money doesnt make us happy, why do we act as if it does? *Journal of Economic Psychology*, *29*(4), 491–507. doi:10.1016/j.joep.2007.11.005

Albinsson, P. A., & Yasanthi Perera, B. (2012). Alternative marketplaces in the 21st century: Building community through sharing events. *Journal of Consumer Behaviour*, *11*(4), 303–315. doi:10.1002/cb.1389

Andreasen, A. R. (1995). *Marketing social change*. San Francisco: Jossey Bass.

Andrews, F. M., & Withey, S. B. (1976). *Social indicators of well-being: America 's perception of life quality*. New York: Plenum Press. doi:10.1007/978-1-4684-2253-5

Argyle, M. (1987). *The Philosophy of Happiness*. New York: Methuen.

Arnould, E. J., & Thompson, C. J. (2005). Consumer Culture Theory (CCT): Twenty Years of Research. *The Journal of Consumer Research*, *31*(4), 868–882. doi:10.1086/426626

Banbury, C., Stinerock, R., & Subrahmanyan, S. (2012). Sustainable consumption: Introspecting across multiple lived cultures. *Journal of Business Research*, *65*(4), 497–503. doi:10.1016/j.jbusres.2011.02.028

Bandura, A. (1986). *Social foundations of thought and actions: a social cognitive theory*. Englewood Cliffs, NJ: Prentice–Hall.

Banister, E. N., & Hogg, M. K. (2004). Negative symbolic consumption and consumers drive for self-esteem: The case of the fashion industry. *European Journal of Marketing*, *38*(7), 850–868. doi:10.1108/03090560410539285

Barnett, C., Cloke, P., Clarke, N., & Malpass, A. (2005). Consuming Ethics: Articulating the Subjects and Spaces of Ethical Consumption. *Antipode*, *37*(1), 23–45. doi:10.1111/j.0066-4812.2005.00472.x

Batra, R., Ahuvia, A., & Bagozzi, R. P. (2012). Brand love. *Journal of Marketing*, *76*(2), 1–16. doi:10.1509/jm.09.0339

Belk, R. W. (1988). Possessions and the Extended Self. *The Journal of Consumer Research*, *15*(2), 139–168. Retrieved from http://www.jstor.org/stable/2489522 doi:10.1086/209154

Belk, R. W., & Pollay, R. W. (1985). Images of Ourselves: The Good Life in Twentieth Century Advertising. *The Journal of Consumer Research*, *11*(4), 887–897. doi:10.1086/209024

Bimonte, S., & Faralla, V. (2012). Tourist Types and Happiness a Comparative Study in Maremma, Italy. *Annals of Tourism Research*, *39*(4), 1929–1950. doi:10.1016/j.annals.2012.05.026

Bimonte, S., & Faralla, V. (2014). Happiness and nature-based vacations. *Annals of Tourism Research*, *46*, 163–184. doi:10.1016/j.annals.2014.02.002

Black, I. R., & Cherrier, H. (2010). Anti-consumption as part of living a sustainable lifestyle: Daily practices, contextual motivations and subjective values. *Journal of Consumer Behaviour*, *9*(6), 437–453. doi:10.1002/cb.337

Borgmann, A. (2000). Reflections and Reviews: The moral complexion of consumption. *The Journal of Consumer Research*, *26*(4), 418–422. doi:10.1086/209572

Bosnjak, M., Brown, C. A., Lee, D. J., Yu, G. B., & Sirgy, M. J. (2014). Self-Expressiveness in Sport Tourism: Determinants and Consequences. *Journal of Travel Research*, *19*, 1–10. doi:10.1177/0047287514535845

Botsman, R., & Rogers, R. (2010). *What's Mine Is Yours: The Rise of Collaborative Consumption*. New York: HarperCollins.

Brickman, P., & Campbell, D. T. (1971). Hedonic relativism and planning the good society. In M.H. Appley (Ed.), *Adaptation Level Theory: A Symposium* (pp. 287-304). New York: Academic Press.

Caldwell, K., Henshaw, L., & Taylor, G. (2011). Developing a framework for critiquing health research: An early evaluation. *Nurse Education Today*, *31*(8), e1–e7. doi:10.1016/j.nedt.2010.11.025 PMID:21185111

Campbell, C. (1995). The sociology of consumption. In D. Miller (Ed.), *Acknowledging Consumption* (pp. 96–126). London: Routledge.

Campbell, C. (2004). I shop therefore I know that I am: the metaphysical basis of modern consumerism. In K. M. Ekstrom & H. Brembeck (Eds.), *Elusive Consumption* (pp. 27–43). Oxford: Berg.

Campbell, C. (2005a). The Craft Consumer: Culture, craft and consumption in a postmodern society. *Journal of Consumer Culture*, *5*(1), 23–42. doi:10.1177/1469540505049843

Campbell, C. (2005b). *The romantic ethic and the spirit of modern consumerism.* UK: WritersPrintShop.

Chakrabarti, R., & Berthon, P. (2012). Gift giving and social emotions: Experience as content. *Journal of Public Affairs*, *12*(2), 154–161. doi:10.1002/pa.1417

Cherrier, H. (2009). Anti-consumption discourses and consumer-resistant identities. *Journal of Business Research*, *62*(2), 181–190. doi:10.1016/j.jbusres.2008.01.025

Clark, D. (2006). *The Rough Guide to Ethical Living*. London: Rough Guides.

Clarke, N., Barnett, C., Cloke, P., & Malpass, A. (2007). Globalising the consumer: Doing politics in an ethical register. *Political Geography*, *26*(3), 231–249. doi:10.1016/j.polgeo.2006.10.009

Clarke, N., Cloke, P., Barnett, C., & Malpass, A. (2008). The spaces and ethics of organic food. *Journal of Rural Studies*, *24*(3), 219–230. doi:10.1016/j.jrurstud.2007.12.008

Claussen, D. (2006). On foolishness in football. *Análise Social*, *179*(41), 583–592. Retrieved from http://analisesocial.ics.ul.pt/?page_id=16

Craig-Lees, M., & Hill, C. (2006, June 20-21). Anti-consumption: concept clarification and changing consumption behaviour. *Proceedings of the International Centre for Anti-Consumption Research (ICAR) Symposium*, Auckland, New Zealand.

Crocker, D. A., & Linden, T. (Eds.). (1998). *Ethics of consumption: The good life, justice and global stewardship*. Lanham, MD: Rowman and Littlefield.

Cromie, J. G., & Ewing, M. T. (2009). The rejection of brand hegemony. *Journal of Business Research*, *62*(2), 218–230. doi:10.1016/j.jbusres.2008.01.029

Csikszentmihalyi, M. (1990). *Flow: The psychology of optimal experience*. New York: Harper and Row.

Davies, H. (2011). Why I like my pleasures one at a time. *New Statesman*. Retrieved from http://www.newstatesman.com/sport/2011/03/cup-final-football-madrid

Diener, E., Emmons, R. A., Larson, R. J., & Griffin, S. (1985). The satisfaction with life scale. *Journal of Personality Assessment*, *49*(1), 71–75. doi:10.1207/s15327752jpa4901_13 PMID:16367493

Diener, E., & Lucas, R. (1999). Personality and Subjective Well-being. In D. Kahneman, E. Diener, & N. Schwarz (Eds.), *Well-being: The Foundations of Hedonic Psychology*. New York: Russell Sage Foundation.

Diener, E., Oishi, S., & Lucas, R. E. (2002). Subjective well-being: The science of happiness and life satisfaction. In C. R. Snyder & S. J. Lopez (Eds.), *Handbook of Positive Psychology*. Oxford, New York: Oxford University Press.

Dolan, C. S. (2008). Arbitrating risk through moral values: The case of Kenyan Fairtrade. *Research in Economic Anthropology*, *28*, 271–296. doi:10.1016/S0190-1281(08)28012-1

Dombos, T. (2008). Longing for the West: The geo-symbolics of the ethical consumption discourse in Hungary. *Research in Economic Anthropology*, *28*, 123–141. doi:10.1016/S0190-1281(08)28006-6

Elliott, R. (1997). Existential consumption and irrational desire. *European Journal of Marketing*, *31*(3/4), 285–296. doi:10.1108/03090569710162371

Etzioni, A. (1998). Voluntary simplicity characterization, select psychological implications, and social consequences. *Journal of Economic Psychology*, *19*(5), 619–643.

Firat, A. F., & Dholakia, N. (1982). Consumption Choices at the Macro Level. *Journal of Macromarketing*, *2*(2), 6–15. doi:10.1177/027614678200200202

Frank, B. (2012). How can customer-based brand equity be increased through sports sponsorship? Master of International Business in Strategic Marketing. Netherlands: Maastricht University. Retrieved from http://pt.scribd.com/doc/86734653/How-Can-Customer-Based-Brand-Equity-Be-Increased-Throug-Sports-Sponsorship

Frey, B. S., & Stutzer, A. (2002). *Happiness and Economics: How the Economy and Institutions Effect Human Well Being*. Princeton, NJ: Princeton University Press.

Funk, D. C., & James, J. D. (2004). The Fan Attitude Network (FAN) Model: Exploring attitude formation and change among sport consumers. *Sport Management Review*, *7*(1), 1–26. doi:10.1016/S1441-3523(04)70043-1

Giddens, A. (1991). *Modernity and Self-identity*. Stanford, CA: Stanford University Press.

Halkier, B. (2010). *Consumption Challenged*. Surrey: Ashgate.

Hall, S. M. (2011). Exploring the ethical everyday: An ethnography of the ethics of family consumption. *Geoforum*, *42*(6), 627–637. doi:10.1016/j.geoforum.2011.06.009

Harrison, R., Newholm, T., & Shaw, D. (2005). *The ethical consumer*. London: Sage.

Headey, B., & Wearing, A. (1992). *Understanding Happiness*. Melbourne, Australia: Longman Chesire.

Heaven, P. C. L., & Ciarrochi, J. (2012). When IQ is not everything: Intelligence, personality and academic performance at school. *Personality and Individual Differences*, *53*(4), 518–522. doi:10.1016/j.paid.2012.04.024

Hilton, M. (2003). *Consumerism in twentieth-century Britain: The search for a historical movement*. Cambridge: Cambridge University Press. doi:10.1017/CBO9780511610097

Hobson, K. (2006). Environmental responsibility and the possibilities of pragmatist orientated research. *Social & Cultural Geography*, *7*(2), 283–298. doi:10.1080/14649360600600734

Holbrook, M. B. (1987). O, Consumer, How You've Changed: Some Radical Reflections on the Roots of Consumption. In A. F. Firat, N. Dholakia, & R. P. Bagozzi (Eds.), *Philosophical and Radical Thought in Marketing* (pp. 156–177). Lexington, MA: Lexington Books.

Holbrook, M. B., & Hirschman, E. C. (1982). The Experiential Aspects of Consumption: Consumer Fantasies, Feelings and Fun. *The Journal of Consumer Research*, *9*(2), 132–140. Retrieved from http://www.jstor.org/stable/2489122 doi:10.1086/208906

Hopwood, M. (2007). It's football but not as you know it: Using public relations to promote the world game in Australia. *Humanities & Social Sciences Papers*. Retrieved from http://epublications.bond.edu.au/hss_pubs/164

Hosany, S. (2012). Appraisal Determinants of Tourist Emotional Responses. *Journal of Travel Research*, *51*(3), 303–314. doi:10.1177/0047287511410320

Iyer, R., & Muncy, J. A. (2009). Purpose and object of anti-consumption. *Journal of Business Research*, *62*(2), 160–168. doi:10.1016/j.jbusres.2008.01.023

Kesebir, B., & Diener, E. (2008). In Pursuit of Happiness Empirical Answers to Philosophical Questions. *Perspectives on Psychological Science*, *3*(2), 117–125. doi:10.1111/j.1745-6916.2008.00069.x PMID:26158878

Khan, S. (2012). Enlightenment through play. *New Statesman (London, England)*, *141*(5087), 13–20.

Kotler, P., Roberto, N., & Lee, N. R. (2002). *Social marketing: Improving the quality of life*. London: Sage.

Kozinets, R. V. (2002). Can consumers escape the market? Emancipatory illuminations from burning man. *The Journal of Consumer Research*, *29*(1), 20–38. doi:10.1086/339919

Kozinets, R. V., & Handelman, J. M. (2004). Adversaries of consumption: Consumer movements, activism, and ideology. *The Journal of Consumer Research*, *31*(3), 691–704. doi:10.1086/425104

Kozlowski, A., Bardecki, M., & Searcy, C. (2012). Environmental Impacts in the Fashion Industry: A Life-cycle and Stakeholder Framework. *Journal of Corporate Citizenship*, *45*, 17–37. Retrieved from http://connection.ebscohost.com/c/articles/79191008/environmental-impacts-fashion-industry-life-cycle-stakeholder-framework

Krishnamurthy, S., & Kucuk, S. U. (2009). Anti-branding on the internet. *Journal of Business Research*, *62*(11), 1119–1126. doi:10.1016/j.jbusres.2008.09.003

Lang, T., & Yiannis, G. (2005). A brief history of consumer activism. In R. Harrison, T. Newholm, & D. Shaw (Eds.), *The ethical consumer* (pp. 39–53). London: Sage. doi:10.4135/9781446211991.n4

Langer, E. J. (2004). *Langer Mindfulness Scale User Guide and Technical Manual*. Worthington, OH: IDS Publishing Corporation.

Layard, R. (2005). *Happiness: Lessons from a New Science*. London: Allen Lane.

Lee, M. S. W., Motion, J., & Conroy, D. (2009). Anti-consumption and brand avoidance. *Journal of Business Research*, *62*(2), 169–180. doi:10.1016/j.jbusres.2008.01.024

LEtang, J., & Hopwood, M. (2008). Sports public relations. *Public Relations Review*, *34*(2), 87–89. doi:10.1016/j.pubrev.2008.05.001

Loureiro, S. M. C. (2014). The role of the rural tourism experience economy in place attachment and behavioral intentions. *International Journal of Hospitality Management*, *40*, 1–9. doi:10.1016/j.ijhm.2014.02.010

Loureiro, S. M. C., & Kastenholz, E. (2011). Corporate reputation, satisfaction, delight, and loyalty towards rural lodging units. *International Journal of Hospitality Management*, *30*(3), 575–583. doi:10.1016/j.ijhm.2010.10.007

Lucas, R. E., & Dyrenforth, P. S. (2006). Does the existence of social relationships matter for subjective well-being? In K. D. Vohs & E. J. Finkel (Eds.), *Self and Relationships: Connecting Intrapersonal and Interpersonal Processes* (pp. 254–273). New York: Guildford Press.

Madrigal, R. (1995). Cognitive and Affective Determinants of Fan Satisfaction with Sporting Event Attendance. *Journal of Leisure Research*, *27*(3), 205–227. Retrieved from http://js.sagamorepub.com/jlr/article/view/857

Mady, T. T. (2011). Sentiment toward marketing: Should we care about consumer alienation and readiness to use technology? *Journal of Consumer Behaviour*, *10*(4), 192–204. doi:10.1002/cb.329

Magarey, M. J. (2001). Elements of a systematic review. *The Journal for Nurse Practitioners*, *7*(6), 376–382. doi:10.1046/j.1440-172X.2001.00295.x PMID:11785440

Mahony, D. F., Madrigal, R., & Howard, D. R. (2000). Using the Psychological Commitment to Team (PCT) Scale to Segment Sport Consumers Based on Loyalty. *Sport Marketing Quarterly, 9*(1), 15-25. Retrieved from http://epay.wvsto.com/WVU/WVFITSportBooks/Using-the-Psychological-Commitment-to-Team-PCT-Scale-to-Segment-Sport-Consumers-Based-on-Loyalty-P10550.aspx

McCabe, S., & Johnson, S. (2013). The happiness factor in tourism: Subjective well-being and social tourism. *Annals of Tourism Research, 41*, 42–65. doi:10.1016/j.annals.2012.12.001

McCracken, G. (1988). *Culture and Consumption: New Approaches to the Symbolic Character of Consumer Goods and Advertising*. Bloomington, IN: Indiana University Press.

McCracken, G. (1989). Who is the Celebrity Endorser? Cultural Foundations of the Endorsement Process. *The Journal of Consumer Research, 16*(3), 310–321. doi:10.1086/209217

McCracken, G. (1990). *Culture and Consumption: New Approaches to the Symbolic Character of Consumer Goods and Activities*. Bloomington: Indiana University Press.

McGinnis, L. P., & Gentry, J. W. (2009). Underdog consumption: An exploration into meanings and motives. *Journal of Business Research, 62*(2), 191–199. doi:10.1016/j.jbusres.2008.01.026

Mick, D. G. (1988). Contributions to the Semiotics of Marketing and Consumer Behavior. In T. Sebeok & J. Umiker-Sebeok (Eds.), *The Semiotic Web: A Yearbook of Semiotics*. Berlin: Mouton de Gruyter.

Mick, D. G. (2006). Presidential Address: Meaning and Mattering Through Transformative Consumer Research. In C. Pechmann & L. Price (Eds.), *NA - Advances in Consumer Research* (Vol. 33, pp. 1–4). Duluth, MN: Association for Consumer Research.

Miller, D. (1995). Consumption as the vanguard of history. In D. Miller (Ed.), *Acknowledging Consumption: A Review of New Studies* (pp. 1–57). London: Routledge.

Miller, D. (1998). *A Theory of Shopping. Cambridge*. Cambridge: Polity Press.

Mingers, J., & Harzing, W. A. (2007). Ranking Journals in Business and Management: A Statistical Analysis of the Harzing Data Set. *European Journal of Information Systems, 16*(4), 303–316. doi:10.1057/palgrave.ejis.3000696

Moisander, J. (2007). Motivational complexity of green consumerism. *International Journal of Consumer Studies, 31*(4), 404–409. doi:10.1111/j.1470-6431.2007.00586.x

Moraes, C., Szmigin, I., & Carrigan, M. (2010). Living production-engaged alternatives: An examination of new consumption communities. *Consumption Markets & Culture, 13*(3), 273–298. doi:10.1080/10253861003787015

Morrison, S., & Crane, F. G. (2007). Building the service brand by creating and managing an emotional brand experience. *Journal of Brand Management, 14*(5), 410–421. doi:10.1057/palgrave.bm.2550080

Muniz, A. M. Jr, & OGuinn, T. C. (2001). Brand Community. *The Journal of Consumer Research, 27*(4), 412–433. doi:10.1086/319618

Nawijn, J. (2011a). Determinants of daily happiness on vacation. *Journal of Travel Research, 50*(5), 559–566. doi:10.1177/0047287510379164

Nawijn, J. (2011b). Happiness Through Vacationing: Just a Temporary Boost or Long-Term Benefits? *Journal of Happiness Studies*, *12*(4), 651–665. doi:10.1007/s10902-010-9221-y

Nawijn, J., & Peeters, P. M. (2010). Travelling green: Is tourists happiness at stake? *Current Issues in Tourism*, *13*(4), 381–392. doi:10.1080/13683500903215016

Nenycz-Thiel, M., Beal, V., Ludwichowska, G., & Romaniuk, J. (2013). Investigating the accuracy of self-reports of brand usage behavior. *Journal of Business Research*, *66*(2), 224–232. doi:10.1016/j.jbusres.2012.07.016

OBrien, C. (2008). Sustainable Happiness: How Happiness Studies Can Contribute to a More Sustainable Future. *Canadian Psychology*, *49*(4), 289–295. doi:10.1037/a0013235

(1994). OECD Tourism Policy and International Tourism. InOECD (Ed.), *Countries: 1991–1992*. Organization for Economic Co-Operation and Development.

Oh, H., Fiore, A. M., & Jeoung, M. (2007). Measuring experience economy concepts: Tourism applications. *Journal of Travel Research*, *46*(2), 119–132. doi:10.1177/0047287507304039

Oishi, Sh., Graham, J., Kesebir, S., & Galinha, I. C. (2013). Concepts of Happiness Across Time and Cultures. *Personality and Social Psychology Bulletin*, *39*(5), 559–577. doi:10.1177/0146167213480042 PMID:23599280

Ozanne, L. K., & Ballantine, P. W. (2010). Sharing as a form of anti-consumption? An examination of toy library users. *Journal of Consumer Behaviour*, *9*(6), 485–498. doi:10.1002/cb.334

Ozcaglar-Toulouse, N., Shiu, E., & Shaw, D. (2006). In search of fair trade: Ethical consumer decision making in France. *International Journal of Consumer Studies*, *30*(5), 502–514. doi:10.1111/j.1470-6431.2006.00532.x

Pavot, W., & Diener, E. (1993). Review of the Satisfaction with Life Scale. *Psychological Assessment*, *5*(2), 164–172. doi:10.1037/1040-3590.5.2.164

Peattie, K., & Peattie, S. (2009). Social marketing: A pathway to consumption reduction? *Journal of Business Research*, *62*(2), 260–268. doi:10.1016/j.jbusres.2008.01.033

Penny, L. (2012). Hate capitalism, love shopping. *New Statesman (London, England)*, *141*(5087), 13–13.

Phipps, M., Ozanne, L. K., Luchs, M. G., Subrahmanyan, S., Kapitan, S., Catlin, J. R., & Weaver, T. et al. (2013). Understanding the inherent complexity of sustainable consumption: A social cognitive framework. *Journal of Business Research*, *66*(8), 1227–1234. doi:10.1016/j.jbusres.2012.08.016

Piven, I., Davis, R., & Lim, M. (2012). Conceptualising the Brand Relationship in Social Media Consumption. *Paper presented at the ANZMAC '12*, Adelaide, Australia.

Portwood-Stacer, L. (2012). Anti-consumption as tactical resistance: Anarchists, subculture, and activist strategy. *Journal of Consumer Culture*, *12*(1), 87–105. doi:10.1177/1469540512442029

Pratt, J. (2008). Food values: The local and the authentic. In G. De Neve, L. Peter, J. Pratt, D. C. Wood (Eds.), Hidden Hands in the Market: Ethnographies of Fair Trade, Ethical Consumption, and Corporate Social Responsibility, Research in Economic Anthropology (Vol. 28, pp. 53-70). Emerald Group Publishing Limited. doi:10.1016/S0190-1281(08)28003-0

Ram, Y., Nawijn, J., & Peeters, P. (2013). Happiness and limits to sustainable tourism mobility: A new conceptual model. *Journal of Sustainable Tourism*, *21*(7), 1017–1035. doi:10.1080/09669582.2013.826233

Roseman, I. J., Spindel, M. S., & Jose, P. E. (1990). Appraisals of Emotion-Eliciting Events: Testing a Theory of Discrete Emotions. *Journal of Personality and Social Psychology*, *59*(5), 899–915. doi:10.1037/0022-3514.59.5.899 PMID:2348375

Sandıkcı, Ö., & Ekici, A. (2009). Politically motivated brand rejection. *Journal of Business Research*, *62*(2), 208–217. doi:10.1016/j.jbusres.2008.01.028

Scheier, M. F., & Carver, C. S. (1985). Optimism, coping, and health: Assessment and implications of generalized outcome expectancies. *Health Psychology*, *4*(3), 219–247. doi:10.1037/0278-6133.4.3.219 PMID:4029106

Schmitt, B. H. (1999). *Experiential Marketing: How to Get Customers to Sense, Feel, Think, Act, Relate to Your Company and Brands*. New York: The Free Press.

Sekaran, U. (1983). Methodological and theoretical issues and advancements in cross-cultural research. *Journal of International Business Studies*, *14*(2), 61–73. doi:10.1057/palgrave.jibs.8490519

Setmeyer, A. P. (2010). Consumerism, Catholicism, and Halls Theology of the Cross. *Dialog*, *49*(4), 306–314. doi:10.1111/j.1540-6385.2010.00557.x

Seyfang, G. (2004). Consuming values and contested cultures: A critical analysis of the UK strategy for sustainable consumption and production. *Review of Social Economy*, *62*(3), 323–338. doi:10.1080/0034676042000253936

Seyfang, G. (2006). Ecological citizenship and sustainable consumption: Examining local organic food networks. *Journal of Rural Studies*, *22*(4), 383–395. doi:10.1016/j.jrurstud.2006.01.003

Sharp, A., Høj, S., & Wheeler, M. (2010). Proscription and its impact on anti-consumption behaviour and attitudes: The case of plastic bags. *Journal of Consumer Behaviour*, *9*(6), 470–484. doi:10.1002/cb.335

Shaw, D., & Newholm, T. (2002). Voluntary simplicity and the ethics of consumption. *Psychology and Marketing*, *19*(2), 167–185. doi:10.1002/mar.10008

Sherry, J. F. Jr. (1989). Postmodern Alternatives: The Interpretive Turn in Consumer Research. In H. Kassarjian & T. Robertson (Eds.), *Handbook of Consumer Theory and Research*. Englewood Cliffs, N.J.: Prentice Hall.

Sheth, J. N., Sethia, N. K., & Srinivas, S. (2011). Mindful consumption: A customer-centric approach to sustainability. *Journal of the Academy of Marketing Science*, *39*(1), 21–39. doi:10.1007/s11747-010-0216-3

Shove, E. (2003a). *Comfort, Cleanliness & Convenience*. Oxford: Berg. Sidwell.

Shove, E. (2003b). Converging Conventions of Comfort, Cleanliness and Convenience. *Journal of Consumer Policy*, *26*(4), 395–418. Retrieved from http://www.lancs.ac.uk/sociology/research/publications/papers/shove-converging-conventions.pdf doi:10.1023/A:1026362829781

Sirgy, J. (1982). Self-Concept in Consumer Behavior: A Critical Review. *The Journal of Consumer Research*, *9*(3), 287–301. Retrieved from http://www.jstor.org/stable/2488624 doi:10.1086/208924

Sklair, L. (2010). Iconic Architecture and the Culture-ideology of Consumerism. *Theory, Culture & Society*, *27*(5), 135–159. doi:10.1177/0263276410374634

Snyder, C. R., Lassegard, M., & Ford, C. E. (1986). Distancing after group success and failure: Basking in reflected glory and cutting off reflected failure. *Journal of Personality and Social Psychology*, *51*(2), 382–388. doi:10.1037/0022-3514.51.2.382

Soper, K. (2008). Alternative hedonism, cultural theory and the role of aesthetic revisioning. *Cultural Studies*, *22*(5), 567–587. doi:10.1080/09502380802245829

Southerton, D., Chappells, H., & Van Vliet, B. (2004). *Sustainable Consumption*. Cheltenham: Edward Elgar.

Strongman, K. T. (1996). *The psychology of emotion: Theories of emotion in perspective* (4th ed.). New York, NY: John Wiley & Sons.

Sugden, J., & Tomlinson, A. (2000). Football, resentment and resistance in the break-up of the former Soviet Union. *Culture, Sport, Society*, *3*(2), 89–108. doi:10.1080/14610980008721872

Sussan, F., Hall, R., & Meamber, L. A. (2012). Introspecting the spiritual nature of a brand divorce. *Journal of Business Research*, *65*(4), 520–526. doi:10.1016/j.jbusres.2011.02.031

The Oxford English Dictionary. (1989). Oxford: Oxford University.

Theodorakis, N., Kaplanidou, K., & Karabaxoglou, J. (2015). Effect of Event Service Quality and Satisfaction on Happiness Among Runners of a Recurring Sport Event. *Leisure Sciences: An Interdisciplinary Journal*, *37*(1), 87–107. doi:10.1080/01490400.2014.938846

Thompson, C. J., & Coskuner-Balli, G. (2007). Enchanting ethical consumerism: The case of community supported agriculture. *Journal of Consumer Culture*, *7*(3), 275–303. doi:10.1177/1469540507081631

Thompson, J. (2005). The new visibility. *Theory, Culture & Society*, *22*(6), 31–51. doi:10.1177/0263276405059413

Tiwsakul, R. A., & Hackley, C. (2012). Postmodern paradoxes in Thai-Asian consumer identity. *Journal of Business Research*, *65*(4), 490–496. doi:10.1016/j.jbusres.2011.02.027

Tranfield, D., Denyer, D., & Smart, P. (2003). Towards a Methodology for Developing Evidence-Informed Management knowledge by means of Systematic Review. *British Journal of Management*, *14*(3), 207–222. Retrieved from http://www.cebma.org/wp-content/uploads/Tranfield-et-al-Towards-a-Methodology-for-Developing-Evidence-Informed-Management.pdf doi:10.1111/1467-8551.00375

Tuominen, P. (2007). Emerging metaphors in brand management: Towards a relational approach. *Journal of Communication Management*, *11*(2), 182–191. doi:10.1108/13632540710747398

Van Boven, L., & Gilovich, T. (2003). To Do or To Have: That is the Question. *Journal of Personality and Social Psychology*, *85*(December), 1193–1202. doi:10.1037/0022-3514.85.6.1193 PMID:14674824

Varman, R., & Belk, R. W. (2009). Nationalism and Ideology in an Anticonsumption Movement. *The Journal of Consumer Research*, *36*(4), 686–700. Retrieved from http://www.journals.uchicago.edu/doi/pdf/10.1086/600486 doi:10.1086/600486

Veblen, T. (1994). *The Theory of the Leisure Class*. New York: Dover.

Verme, P. (2009). Happiness, freedom and control. *Journal of Economic Behavior & Organization*, *71*(2), 146–161. doi:10.1016/j.jebo.2009.04.008

Walker, W. R., Skowronski, J. J., & Thomson, C. P. (1996). Life is pleasant – and memory helps to keep it that way! *Review of General Psychology*, *7*(2), 203–210. doi:10.1037/1089-2680.7.2.203

Wallendorf, M., & Arnould, E. J. (1988). My Favorite Things: A Cross-Cultural Inquiry into Object Attachment, Possessiveness, and Social Linkage. *The Journal of Consumer Research*, *14*(4), 531–547. doi:10.1086/209134

Wang, M., & Wong, M. C. (2014). Happiness and leisure across countries: Evidence from international survey data. *Journal of Happiness Studies*, *15*(1), 119–123. doi:10.1007/s10902-013-9417-z

Warde, A. (2005). Consumption and theories of practice. *Journal of Consumer Culture*, *5*(2), 131–153. doi:10.1177/1469540505053090

Waterman, A. S. (1993). Two conceptions of Happiness: Contrasts of personal expressiveness (Eudaimonia) and Hedonic Enjoyment. *Journal of Personality and Social Psychology*, *64*(4), 678–691. doi:10.1037/0022-3514.64.4.678

Watson, D., & Clark, L. A. (1984). Negative affectivity: The disposition to experience unpleasant emotional states. *Psychological Bulletin*, *67*(3), 465–490. doi:10.1037/0033-2909.96.3.465 PMID:6393179

Watson, D., Clark, L. A., & Tellegen, A. (1988). Development and validation of brief measures of positive and negative affect: The PANAS scales. *Journal of Personality and Social Psychology*, *47*(6), 1063–1070. doi:10.1037/0022-3514.54.6.1063 PMID:3397865

Wheeler, K. (2012). Change today, choose fairtrade. *Cultural Studies*, *26*(4), 492–515. doi:10.1080/09502386.2011.622780

White, A., & Schmidt, K. (2005). Systematic literature reviews. *Complementary Therapies in Medicine*, *13*(1), 54–60. doi:10.1016/j.ctim.2004.12.003 PMID:15907679

Wiedmann, K.-P., Hennigs, N., Pankalla, L., Kassubek, M., & Seegebarth, B. (2011). Adoption barriers and resistance to sustainable solutions in the automotive sector. *Journal of Business Research*, *64*(11), 1201–1206. doi:10.1016/j.jbusres.2011.06.023

Youngberg, Q. (2009). Mommys American Dream in Edward Albees The American Dream. *The Explicator*, *67*(2), 108–110. doi:10.3200/EXPL.67.2.108-110

Zavestoski, S. (2002). Guest Editorial: Anticonsumption Attitudes. *Psychology and Marketing*, *19*(2), 121–126. doi:10.1002/mar.10005

ADDITIONAL READING

Dolich, I. J. (1969). Congruence relationships between self images and product brands. *JMR, Journal of Marketing Research*, *6*(1), 80–84. doi:10.2307/3150001

Foucault, M. (1988). *The Care of the Self: The History of Sexuality* (Vol. 3). New York: Vintage.

Foucault, M. (1990). *The Use of Pleasure: The History of Sexuality* (Vol. 2). (R. Hurley, Trans.). New York: Vintage.

Fournier, S. (1998). Consumer Resistance: Societal Motivations, Consumer Manifestations, and Implications in the Marketing Domain. *Advances in Consumer Research. Association for Consumer Research (U. S.), 25*, 88–90. Retrieved from http://www.acrwebsite.org/search/view-conference-proceedings.aspx?Id=8130

Horowitz, D. L. (1985). *Ethnic Groups in Conflict*. Berkeley, CA: University of California Press.

Jenkins, R. (2004). *Social identity* (2nd ed.). London: Routledge. doi:10.4324/9780203463352

Levett, R., Christie, I., Jacobs, M., & Therivel, R. (2003). *A better choice of choice: Quality of life, consumption and economic growth* (Vol. 58). London: Fabian Society.

Levy, S. (1959). Symbols for Sale. *Harvard Business Review, 37*, 117–124. Retrieved from http://www.uibk.ac.at/smt/marketing/brandresearchlab2/files/symbolsforsale_levy.pdf

Ogilvie, D. M. (1987). The undesired self: A neglected variable in personality research. *Journal of Personality and Social Psychology, 52*(2), 379–385. doi:10.1037/0022-3514.52.2.379

KEY TERMS AND DEFINITIONS

Anti-Consumption: A resistance to, distaste of, or even resentment or rejection of consumption more generally (Zavestoski, 2002, p. 121).

Consumerism: A set of beliefs and values, integral but not exclusive to the system of capitalist globalization, intended to make people believe that human worth is best ensured and happiness is best achieved in terms of our consumption and possessions (Sklair, 2010, p. 135).

Consumption Communities: Consumption in online environments (social networking sites, websites, blogs and other online sites become the new marketplace), green and ethical consumption.

Consumption Society: Individualism and materialism have led individuals to purchase goods regardless of their usefulness; high degree of dependence on consumables (McCracken, 1990).

Consumption: Use of goods and services in which the object or activity becomes simultaneously a practice in the world and a form in which we construct our understandings of ourselves in the world (Miller, 1995, p. 30).

Happiness: The pursuit of pleasure (hedonism) and meaning in one's life (Eudaimonism).

Literature Review: Retrieve, appraise and summarise all the available evidence on a specific thematic (designed to reduce the effect of the reviewers' own bias; the appropriate resources should be in place before undertaking a review; identify relevant work; extract relevant data on outcomes and quality; summarise the evidence; and, interpret the evidence).

Subjective Well-Being: Three factor contributes to the concept- satisfaction with life, positive and negative affect.

Chapter 13
The Effect of the Marketing Strategy in Performance of the Pharmaceutical Sector

Irene Samanta
Piraeus University of Applied Sciences, Greece

ABSTRACT

The aim of this research is to examine the impact of Marketing Strategy possesses in pharmaceutical sector in Greece and define the competitive and organizational benefits accumulate from the procedure. A quantitative survey was conducted with a sample of pharmaceutical firms. The method used is Factor analysis and a Multivariable Regression Model in order to forecast the total performance of the organization. The importance of the Marketing Strategy in the current economic conditions provides a practical indication of marketing decision making and if managed carefully and closely monitored it can offer a number of direct competitive benefits to the industries.

INTRODUCTION

Over the recent decades, the dominant change in the world economy is the globalization of markets (Yip, 1992, Barlett and Ghoshal, 2000). The birth and adolescence of the global economy is the result of many other changes that the world has experienced during the last years. Advances in telecommunications (including the Internet revolution), advances in transport and production process advances have led the world toward a single converging commonality. Theodore Levitt (1983) recognizes the impact of the technological changes in the new reality of global economy. The enterprises in all over the world have modified their processes in order to thoroughly exploit the technological advances both in communication and information technology. During the last decade, spectacular changes have been notified in the international economic scene and multinational companies have been turned to a key player. Another sector where the enterprises have been focused in a world level are the commercial and financing transactions, which has led to an intensive growth of the world trade that has already exceeded the growth of world production. Even though the risk is too high day by day more and more companies are globalising since it has become a necessity in order for them to survive and grow. In their effort, they are supposed to face many obstacles and undertake enterprising risks. As a result of what so called global economy,

DOI: 10.4018/978-1-5225-2139-6.ch013

global mergers and acquisitions and furthermore investment activity and global merchandise exports are increasing rapidly.

The shift towards a more integrated and interdependent world economy has led to intensive competition (Kotler, 2000). Firms are challenging in the arena of the competitive battle that takes place in the international markets that once were thought to be safe. The need for enterprises to find tools that help them enhance their competitiveness towards other enterprises is urgent. In order for the companies to overcome the difficulties that may arise in the global scene and moreover to sustain their competitive position, firms should take into consideration a line of parameters such as: the nature of the product, strategic objectives of the enterprise (both in the short and long run), the external environment, the internal processes within the company, the strength of the competitors etc. The increased rivalry as well as the severe competitive pressure could be overcome with the appropriate Marketing Plan. Samanta &Kyriazopoulos (2014) states that the greater the implementation of marketing concepts and Planning, the greater the probability of long term profits and market dominance. At any rate, the Marketing Strategy has to be adopted as a Business Philosophy in order to help the company maintain and improve its position in a constantly turbulent, hostile and competitive environment. All the modern enterprises should recognize the importance of Marketing Strategy as a tool and stop facing it as being peripheral to the managerial function (Simkin, 2000).

The present research aims to identify the level of importance of the marketing strategy for the growth and survival of the Greek pharmaceutical industry. Furthermore, it will seek the terms that the pharmaceutical sector use for their Marketing Strategy in orders to enhance their competitiveness and their organizational benefits.

The aim in order to examine the case of Greek pharmaceutical sector was whether the Greek enterprises have recognized the necessity that marketing competency plays a significant role greater economy. Moreover, the contribution of the pharmaceutical sector in the development, employment and social coherence inside the European Union and Greece is substantial.

LITERATURE REVIEW

The Importance and Benefits of Marketing Strategy

In turbulent and sometimes hostile market conditions, businesses must respond to environmental changes and adjust their orientation to the new circumstances. Considering this, Paswan et al. (2011) underlined the importance of Marketing Plan. Nowadays businesses fail to succeed because of lack of marketing practice, including Strategy and implementation. It has underlined the importance of understanding the marketplace as a means to enable the industry to deal with the environmental changes and moreover and meet the customer's needs. Kotler (1998) underlines the problems that firms face with marketing and sales because their business-marketing concept is absent or pure. Considering this, the need to understand the effects of good Marketing Strategy on the Greek pharmaceutical companies is urgency.

Gray (1999) underlined the importance of differentiating the managerial techniques as not all of them are appropriate to all types of businesses. After the completion of this research, its findings will be of use to pharmaceuticals in the Greek market. Challenges multiply as companies are globalizing and their planning procedures are becoming the core of the strategic management process. Effective Marketing Strategy can therefore enable the company to become more reactive and flexible to the marketplace and this is what distinguishes the winners from the losers in the global economy scene (Yousefi et al, 2016). For the majority of the companies, development carries with it rigorous pressure for formalizing the Planning procedure. Startup companies need to conceptualise the market dynamics and its business opportunities; understand the differences between customer and product orientation; recognize the different needs and wants of customers; define their target group, conceptualize the importance of practicing a Marketing Plan. The tastes and needs of consumers change and they need to find a competitive advantage in order to survive to the changing reality

Marketing Strategy is a methodical procedure which involves measuring marketing opportunities and resources, determining marketing objectives and putting in action its execution and control. The rationale for planning has been underlined and emphasizes the necessity for a procedure that is thorough, carefully designed and strictly controlled (Rod et al., 2007; McDonald, 1992; Piercy, 2002; Piercy & Morgan, 1994).

Brassington and Pettitt (2000) argues Marketing Strategy may act as a catalyst between the market's needs and changes and resources and capabilities of the enterprise. An effective and efficient marketing Strategy should reflect the objectives and the main missions of the company. Possible wrong marketing directions and priorities of the company may have serious consequences regarding the position of the company in the marketplace. The most common threat is a serious loss in the market share of the company. Corporate planning after a detailed scanning on the external and internal business environment could integrate the various objectives among different Strategic Business Units of the company and help the company to gain a more competitive position in the market.

Marketers have to manage the complexity of the commercial environment in order to decide on critical issues such as: market positioning, product development, promotional activities, distribution channels, target markets, development strategies etc. According to McDonald (1992) better communication and cooperation between the various departments of the organization can be achieved.

The majority of the Marketing Plans are annual though their type varies on the type of the business. The Strategy can be brand based, regionally (division) based, business unit based or it can cover the entire organization. The review of the Marketing Strategy depends on the decision of the administration, it could be re-examined twice a year, when the circumstances require it, mid-way its duration or at the period it was meant to cover. Some of the companies faithfully apply the Marketing Strategy, other use it as an aid for the comprehension of the market dynamics without necessarily fully applying its content while others apply it partly or not at all, they just prepare it in order to satisfy the requirements of Administration.

The Marketing Strategy procedure encapsulates the fundamental elements of a marketing management: marketing analysis, strategic philosophy and determination of marketing mix plans intended to execute the recommended marketing strategy (Kotler, 1998). Marketing Strategy is a methodical procedure which involves measuring marketing opportunities and resources, determining marketing objectives and putting in action its execution and control (Pearson and Proctor, 1994). The rationale for planning has been underlined and emphasizes the necessity for a procedure that is thorough, carefully designed and strictly controlled (Chikweche,2013; McDonald, 1992; Goncharuk and Getman, 2014).

The output of Marketing Strategy and the mediator procedure contain major communication and relationship benefits states McDonald (1989). Therefore, as long as personnel are essentially involved and there is loyalty from administration the output of the Marketing Strategy can be an asset for the company.

According to Jobber (2001) is a beneficial process for the organization since it provides a crucial aim for decisions and activities and provides a practical indication of marketing decision making. Furthermore, it encourages people to set new objectives and motivates them to achieve more goals and raise their standards that otherwise would have lower standards. The Marketing Strategy process encourages the procedure of finding a competitive advantage via the scanning of the marketing mix of the company. In reference to McDonald (1992), the organizational adaptation to the business environment is encouraged through the Marketing Strategy procedure.

Moreover he states that since adaptive capability is linked to better performance the acceptance of the inevitability of changes is very important. Brassington et al. (2000) states that several benefits could be gained from a complete Marketing plan mainly attributed with the development, the control and the coordination of the marketing activity. In terms of the development helps to the better allocation of resources, recognizes available options and offers solutions in order to handle the continuously changing environment. An efficient Marketing Strategy raises fundamental issues regarding the resource allocation (issues concerning the build, hold, harvest and divest tactics). It supports the monitoring of changes by encouraging managers to review regularly the impact of changes in the business environment. Moreover, it helps to analyze the environment and identify the main strengths and weaknesses.

In terms of the co-ordination it makes clear of the objectives and makes specific what is expected. Inherent in this process is the reduction of internal rivalry and manages to integrate different areas. In addition, an important task is that it communicates the various goals and plans to the staff. Inherent to the process are as well improved internal communication and co-operation, advanced understanding of corporate priorities, enhanced confidence and motivation via the preparation and sequenced actions that have to be followed, along with the superior level of related marketing intelligence which helps decision making and progress of marketing strategies Kotler et al., (1998).

Finally, in terms of the control offered via Marketing Strategy it allows remedial evaluations to be taken soon, it can provides the management with warnings in case that something is not going the right way and in deed it can ensure that the targets are going to be achieved. According to Yip (1989) planning if managed carefully and closely monitored can offer a number of direct competitive benefits such as: enhanced market share performance, better communication among executives, and effectiveness in product development, improved product quality and declining manufacturing costs. Both competitive and organizational benefits should be viewed holistically. Moreover, Marketing Strategy can improve managers' comprehension of marketing and markets, offering them the capability to formulate strategic and tactical assessments (Leeflang and de Mortanges, 1996; Simkin, 1996, 2000).

Trends and Issues Affecting the Pharmaceutical Sector

Pharmaceutical markets differ in several critical issues from consumer markets. To illustrate the above we should refer that the patient that use the medicinal product in most of the cases is neither the buyer nor the decision maker. Moreover, in the pharmaceutical market issues such as regulatory, ethics and liability considerations are of major importance than in the case of super markets for example. In addition, price sensitivity and brand loyalty are not so important in the pharmaceutical market than in any other market taking into consideration that the product is a totally inelastic one. Many customers continue to purchase brands of medicines that they have been given in their childhood just because they trust the trademark. In many cases it is very difficult to persuade customers to switch to something different once they trust one brand and they believe that it works for them. As a result, companies are trying to maximize their brand loyalty by expanding brands into new areas. The consumer is the decision maker in the consumer market but in the pharmaceutical market this is not always true. It is the medicinal practitioners who have a unique and often multiple roles in the purchasing procedure of medicinal products even though the patient is the ultimate user. Medical practitioners are usually the decision makers who take the buying decision for their patients, or they might play the role of opinion leader, influencer or gatekeeper Karakaya and Yannopoulos (2010).

In the pharmaceutical market the degree of government regulation is advanced than in a common consumer market. Considerations regarding liability are also higher in the pharmaceutical market than in a consumer market. Ethical issues arise in the case of pharmaceutical market more regularly than in a consumer market. Regarding the R&D, in the case of pharmaceutical market without no doubt it is more complex and more costly than in a consumer market. Finally, in the pharmaceutical market the price sensitivity is lower than in a consumer market (Rod et al., 2007). The pharmaceutical market many issues arise that are of vital significance for the sector such as:

1. R&D necessity which leads to investments often exceeding the 20% of the total annual revenues of the company.
2. The responsive subject of patient rights.
3. More severe regulations compared to other markets.
4. Ethical issues (e.g. animal welfare and ecological protection), liability matters, and brand loyalty).
5. Price sensitivity topics.

The market of medicines can be influenced by many factors. Some of the factors are population trends, lifestyle, life expectancy, drug misuse, and employment trends and National Health System (NHS), which plays a very important role because it reimburses a major part of prescriptions and can also influence the OTC sales.

Lifestyle affects the market of the pharmaceutical products. Nowadays people seek a healthier way of life. This could lead to a fall in the demand of medicines. But the healthier people they become their expectations rise and this results again in more demand for medicines. Population trends have an important effect on most of the commercial markets, and indeed the pharmaceutical markets. Changes in population can affect the pharmaceutical market. The older people are more likely to need medicines than the younger ones.

Regarding the consumption and the expenditure on medicines in the countries of OECD (http://stats.oecd.org/pharmaceutical market), an augmentative tendency is observed during the last 20 years, with our country to constitute the exception. The total expense for medicines between the countries of OECD oscillates from 0, 7% to 2, 2% GNP with the mean in 1,2%. As part of the total expenditure on health the pharmaceutical expense represents an average of 15,4%. The share that corresponds in the GNP has been increased almost 50% from 1970, which means that in real terms the increase of the pharmaceutical expenditure each year was 1,5% more than the GNP.

However, since the early 1990s, the research-based pharmaceutical industry in Europe has been losing competitiveness with respect to the US. Data for 2002 and 2003 confirm the vulnerability of Europe's research-based pharmaceutical industry. Benchmarking and performance indicators show that the US has continued to increase its relative position as a focus of innovation. In 1990 the European market was the world's largest market with a 37. 8% share (against 31.1% for the North American market); in 2004, North America accounted for 49.2% of the world pharmaceutical market, against 27.8% for the European market. Apart from improving public health and driving medical progress the E The pharmaceutical industry is one of Europe's best performing high-technology sectors. It performs well on most standard measures, such as production, value added, high skill employment, R&D and trade surplus. Rapid as well, are the developments that are taking place in the international market of the pharmaceutical industry, taking into account the forecasted rise of market, the high technology of health, the publicity, the electronic trade, but also the economies of scale that are promoted after the big fusions that were observed in the world pharmaceutical market during the last decade. The pharmaceutical industry in Europe represents one of the most efficient and productive sectors of high technology. The European pharmaceutical sector has increased its production (almost over triple in 2003 comparing to 1990) while the commercial balance is positive.

The Greek Pharmaceutical Market

The pharmaceutical enterprise operates in the Greek market in three different ways, either as affiliated companies of multinational enterprises, or as Greek enterprises that collaborate in various ways with foreign pharmaceutical industries and finally as Greek enterprises that work independent and circulate generic medicines, in other words medicines whose patent has expired.

The increased consumption and expenditure on medicines are influenced by the following defining factors: The demographic structure of population of a country and mainly the ageing of population, the degree of cover of population and social teams from the pharmaceutical care, the increase of GNP, the available income and standard of living in general. In addition, some other very important factors that influence the pharmaceutical expenditure as well are: the appearance of new illnesses, the prices, the development of Medical science, the growth of new treatments and the high technology of health.

According to the Family Budget Survey which was conducted in 2014 the average monthly household expenditure regarding health and medication expenditure in Greece was 6.8% of the total household purchases. In more details, of this amount 24% was spent on physicians' services, 15% on pharmaceuticals, 32% on dentists' services, and 12% on expenditure for hospitalization.

Both vertical increase of parallel exports and increase in the consumption of medicinal products in Greece have resulted in a prominent increase over the last 6 years. There has been a 57% increase in total sales of medicinal products in DDDs per 1,000 inhabitants per day ranged from 704 in 1999 to 1,105 in 2004 (the most recent year of available data). The increase of the sales in value between 1999 and 2004 has reached a percentage of 115% in value and 36% in quantity.

Finally, the study realizes that in Greece correspond 1.143 residents per drugstore, the bigger proportion in the EU However, the proportion of pharmacist per drugstore is to contrary to other countries that are bigger. Also, Greek drugstores have the smaller medium surface in the EU, 47 tm. Regarding the quantity, the sales of medicinal products imported in 2004 reached 165 million units, a quantity analogous to 38% of the total sales volume. The quantities imported in 2003 and in 2004 varied by 12%. In 2004, the sales volume of the medicinal products manufactured in Greece were 223 million units (i.e. 51% of the total sales volume). The other 11% refers to medicinal products packaged in Greece (45 million units).

RESEARCH METHODOLOGY AND DATA ANALYSIS

For the present survey the Simple Random Sampling method was used and the sample size was fixed to 60 companies. For them 42 responded to the questionnaire (response rate 70%). For selecting the data personal interviews collection method was used. The questionnaire designed for the needs of this survey included 17 multiple choice and Likert scale questions. Each item is on a five-scale measure indicates: 1= (Strongly disagree) to 5= (Strongly agree). The questionnaire separated in four parts:

The first part includes questions about the company's profile:

- The size of the company,
- Company's performance,
- Responder's profile.

The second part includes questions about the company's strategy and business plan. These questions indicate:

- Company's Business Plan,
- Company's Strategic management.

The third part includes questions about the Marketing Plan. These questions indicate:

- The existence of Marketing Strategy within the company,
- The contains of Marketing Plan,
- The implementation of Marketing Strategy within the company,
- The control (review) of the Marketing Plan.

The last part includes questions about business environment. These questions indicate the changes that have taken place in the business environment and the reaction of the company towards them. The present research is conducted from May 2014 to September 2014.

A sample coming from 42 pharmaceutical companies was used. As far as the property status of the companies is concerned, the greater part of the sample is Purely Foreigner (26 cases) followed by the Purely Greek (15 cases) and only one case was Foreigner at majority. diversity The number of employees present a diversity (17%: less than 50 persons, 55%: 51 to 300 employees and 28%: more than 301 persons).

More than 50% of the Greek companies of the sample operate for more than 25 years and the respective mean value is about 23 years. For the Foreigner companies of the sample the corresponding numbers are 18 years and 16, 4 years, respectively.

More than 85% of the companies have a turnover of more than 15 million euros while in particular the 95% confidence interval of turn over for the Greek companies is between 32-64 million euros and the same confidence interval for the Foreigner companies is between 21-41 million euros.

An amount of 83% of the sample of the pharmaceutical companies that operate in Greece engage more than 51 employees, in which more than 50% have managed to remain at the sector for more than 25 years and almost 85% of the sample of companies have a turnover of 15 million euros.

For the purpose of the study we split the companies in two subgroups according to the turnover they had ("Large Companies": turnover more than 15.000.000 euros and number of employees more than 100, "Small Companies": turnover less than 15.000.000 euros and/or number of employees less than 100).

Asking the companies about the development of a Marketing Strategy and the main characteristics of this the 93% of the respondents answered that their company prepares a Marketing Plan. This result present that the Marketing Strategy has become a useful tool to their organizations. The duration of the Marketing Strategy for the 70% of the companies is less than three years, which is in accordance with the international practice. The average duration of the Marketing Strategy is 3,2 years, ranging from 3,3 years for the large companies to 2,8 years for the smaller ones, though this difference was not found to be statistically significant (t test, p value >0.05).

It should be mentioned that the largest proportion of the companies that evaluate their performance as successful, seem to prepare a Marketing Strategy with a duration of more than 3 years, though the results of the research do not verify a statistically significant connection (chi square test of independence, p- value >0.05).

The pharmaceutical sector, which is characterized by strong competition and high entrance barriers, the comparative advantage of the companies is derived not only from the monitoring and reaction to actions of rivalry but also from the level of customer satisfaction. The companies in order to achieve their strategic goals, they have developed specific internal procedures, measuring the level of customers' satisfaction, the development of after sales service and monitoring competitors' weaknesses and actions. Taking into account the size of the companies it has been observed a difference on the way that the large companies pay attention to the actions of their competitors from the smaller ones. The large companies addressed on various customer segments, serving their needs and requirements creating strategies with main purpose their satisfaction (Mann – Whitney, p-value= 0.017). The smaller businesses mainly due to cost restrictions compete to the main competitors cannot support equivalent marketing strategies.

Examining the reaction of the companies to the changes of the business environment there was not found any statistically significant differences (Kruskal Wallis and Mann - Whitney non parametric tests). Long term business plan reflects the mission and the vision of the company, something that should always be taken into account in the Planning process (more than 90% accept that point of view). Companies that take into account long term business plan while designing the Marketing Strategy appear to have positive performance regarding their profits and their sales growth compared to their competitors.

The budget set for the Marketing Strategy should be precise and flexible at the same time. Flexible enough to cope with changing circumstances but precise as well to justify the resources requested. The mainstream of the respondents (more than 80%, equally in large and small companies) support their Marketing Strategy is affected by the budget that has been set for the Marketing Plan. Companies that take under consideration the strict guidelines set concerning the Marketing Budget seem to have as well positive results in the performance of the company regarding the sales and the profits.

Examining the external strategic issues that may arise is another issue that should be done in a systematic base since the conditions in the external environment may change and therefore have an impact on the implementation of the Marketing Plan. The 70% of the respondents share the above opinion. A differentiation appears between large and small companies of the sector, indicating those large companies pay more attention to the external strategic issues than the smaller ones.

Again, companies that take examine the external strategic issues while designing their Marketing Strategy appear to have positive results in their performance in the field of sales and profits, though this factor cannot be determinant on its own. Marketing Strategy is a continuous, dynamic process and not a static one. Therefore, companies should adjust their strategies to the new environmental conditions and this should be reflected to the Marketing Strategy of the company. More than the half sample agrees with the above statement.

Companies that take under consideration this factor tend to have positive results in their sales and growth performance, though this factor doesn't seem to be statistically significant.

The performance of the company is closely linked to the level of customer satisfaction that the company offers, though it is mostly utilized by the customer oriented companies. Tracking and measuring customer satisfaction is of vital importance due to the existing intensive competition. Businesses that do take into account the customer satisfaction when designing their Marketing Strategy appear to have positive results (nearly 30%) mainly attributed to their profits and their sales but again in this occasion this aspect on its own cannot be determinant (statistically significant) for the performance of the company.

Furthermore, companies should focus on the Internal Company procedures since they reflect the dynamics of the company and the way operates. Therefore, Planning should comply with the existing internal company procedures, so as not to be a vague. Another imperative factor for the success of a Marketing Strategy is the control and the evaluation of the performance trends in order to ensure that the Marketing Strategy is well applied and that the outcomes will be the expected ones. However, a great percentage of the responding companies consider neither the existing internal procedures of the company nor the regular control of performance appears as of major importance for the design of the Marketing Plan. Nevertheless, the companies that do take into account the internal procedures while they design their Marketing Strategy appear to have a statistical significant benefit regarding the growth in the market share (but not in the growth of profit) and the 40% of the companies which pay attention to the monitoring of the performance trends, look to have better profit and market share performance.

The existence of reports that compare the results of each activity of the Marketing to the aforementioned objectives and resources is an imperative in order the Marketing Strategy to be efficient and effective. This is unfortunately followed only by the competitor oriented companies, while the customer oriented companies hardly take it into account when designing their Marketing Plan. To continue with the implementation of the Marketing Plan, a great extent of implementation to the companies (62% for the large companies and 57% for the small companies). The level of implementation and the performance of the Marketing Strategy is rather significant (especially among the large companies of the sector).

In a regular base the Marketing Strategy is redesigned twice a year for the 50% of the responders. It should be mentioned that the companies that re-examine their Marketing Strategy seem to have more successful implementation. Therefore, it can be concluded that the companies with organizational infrastructure, in most cases they manage to make better use of their marketing strategy.

CONCLUSION

According to the results of the research, regarding the existence of the Marketing Strategy the majority of the firms design and implement a Marketing Plan. Moreover, it is considered as a useful tool among the companies as the largest proportion of them companies prepares a more than 3 years Marketing Strategy. Customer satisfaction and actions of the rivalry are considered as main factors to the design of the Marketing Plan. The importance of the aforementioned factors is reflected in the internal procedures of the company. Regarding the environmental analysis the majority of the firms recognize several factors that result in various changes both in the internal and external business environment. For example, many barriers appear in the entrance and exit of competitors from the market, along with changes in sales and marketing strategies.

Moreover, it is underlined that during the preparation of the Marketing Strategy various issues are taken into consideration such as the existence of long term design within the Marketing Plan. The strict guidelines set regarding the Marketing Budget, the examination of various strategic issues, the Marketing Strategy as a continuous process, customer satisfaction as a priority, the effect of the existing internal company procedures in the design of the Marketing Plan, the performance trends of the Marketing activities along with the reports examining this performance. All the above factors are very important for the success of the company and bearing them in mind while designing and applying a Marketing Strategy seems to lead to better performance regarding the market share, the sales and growth. The result is that organizational benefits can be realized from the completion of the contents of the Marketing Plan. Regarding the revision and the implementation of the Marketing Strategy we concluded that the Marketing Strategy is not just a typical tool but it's been applied to a great extent.

The relation between the level of implementation and the performance of the Marketing Strategy is rather significant especially among the large companies of the sector. Moreover, it should be mentioned that the companies that re-examine their Marketing Strategy seem to have a greater level of implimentation. Therefore, the companies with organizational infrastructure and a philosophy to use tools such as Marketing Strategy in most of the cases they manage to make better use of it. The analysis underlined the importance of the Marketing Strategy and its ability to improve managers' comprehension of marketing and markets, offering them the capability to formulate strategic and tactical assessments. Planning if managed carefully and closely monitored can offer a number of direct competitive benefits. Moreover Marketing Strategy is a beneficial process for the organization since it provides a crucial aim for decisions and activities and provides a practical indication of marketing decision making. Via Marketing Strategy a deeper understanding of the marketing concept, philosophy and the basic ethos of marketing management can be achieved.

REFERENCES

Anatoliy, G. G., & Getman, M. (2014). *Benchmarking to improve a strategy and marketing in pharmaceuticals.* Benchmarking. *International Journal (Toronto, Ont.), 21*(3).

Barlett, C. A., & Ghoshal, S. (1995). *Transnational Management* (2nd ed.). Boston: Irwin.

Brassington, F., & Pettitt, S. (2000). *Principles of Marketing.* Prentice Hall.

Gray, H. P. (1999). *Global Economic Involvement.* Copenhagen: Copenhagen Business School Press. Hood, N.

Hellenic Republic Hellenic Statistical Authority. (2014). *Household Budget Survey.* Retrieved from http://www.statistics.gr/documents/20181/985039/Results+of+the+Household+Budget+Survey+(HBS)/338cb80b-6b5f-4d67-83d5-1f8fa77abf12?version=1.0

Jobber, D. (2001). Principles and practice of marketing (4th ed.). McGraw Hill.

Kotler, P., Armstrong, G., Saunders, J., & Wong, V. (1998). *Principles of Marketing.* Hemel Hempstead: Prentice-Hall.

Leeflang, P. S. H., & de Mortanges, C. P. (1996). An empirical investigation of Marketing Plan. *Journal of Euromarketing, 6*(1), 77–101. doi:10.1300/J037v06n01_06

Leidecker, J. K., & Bruno, A. V. (1984). Identifying and using critical success factors. *Long Range Planning, 17*(1), 23–31. doi:10.1016/0024-6301(84)90163-8

Levitt, T. (1975). Marketing Myopia: Retrospective Commentary. *Harvard Business Review.*

Levitt, T. (1983). The Globalization of markets. *Harvard Business Review*.

McDonald, M. (1992). Strategic Marketing Plan: A state-of-the-art review. *Marketing Intelligence & Planning*, *10*(4), 4–22. doi:10.1108/02634509210016632

McDonald, M. (1992). Ten barriers to Marketing Plan. *Journal of Business and Industrial Marketing*, *7*, 1, 5–18.

McDonald, M. (1992a). Strategic Marketing Plan: A state-of-the-art review. *Marketing Intelligence & Planning*, *10*(4), 4–22. doi:10.1108/02634509210016632

Michel, R., Nicholas, A. J., & Janet, C. (2007). Pharmaceutical marketing return-on-investment: A European perspective. *International Journal of Pharmaceutical and Healthcare Marketing, 1*(2).

Nazila, Y., Gholamhossein, M., Hamid, R.R., & Hossein, T. (2016). Pharmaceutical innovation and market share: Evidence from a generic market. *International Journal of Pharmaceutical and Healthcare Marketing, 10*(4).

O.E.C.D. (2015). *Pharmaceutical market.* Retrieved from http://stats.oecd.org

Paswan, A. K., Charles, B., & Francisco, G. (2011). Relationalism in marketing channels and marketing strategy. *European Journal of Marketing*, *45*(3), 311–333. doi:10.1108/03090561111107212

Pearson, G., & Proctor, T. (1994). The modern framework for Marketing Plan. *Marketing Intelligence & Planning*, *12*(4), 22–26. doi:10.1108/02634509410060712

Piercy, N., & Morgan, N. (1994). The Marketing Strategy process: Behavioural problems compared to analytical techniques in explaining Marketing Strategy credibility. *Journal of Business Research*, *29*(3), 167–178. doi:10.1016/0148-2963(94)90001-9

Piercy, N., & Morgan, N. (1994). The Marketing plan process: Behavioural problems compared with analytical techniques in explaining Marketing Strategy credibility. *Journal of Business Research*, *29*(3), 167–178. doi:10.1016/0148-2963(94)90001-9

Samanta, I., & Kyriazopoulos, P. (2014). *Applied Marketing*. Syghroni Ekdotiki Publications.

Simkin, L. (1996). The benefits of controlling implementation in Marketing Plan. *Journal of Marketing Management*, *12*, 375–390. doi:10.1080/0267257X.1996.9964423

Simkin, L. (2000). Delivering effective Marketing Plan. *Journal of Targeting, Measurement and Analysis for Marketing*, *8*(3), 1–16.

Chikweche Tendai, (2013). Benchmarking to improve a strategy and marketing in pharmaceuticals. *Marketing Intelligence & Planning*, *31*(7).

Yip, G. S. (1989). Global strategy. in a world of nations? *Sloan Management Review*, *31*, 29–41.

KEY TERMS AND DEFINITIONS

Competitive Environment: It refers to the number and types of companies against which a given business competes in its industry.

Marketing Plan: The process of analyzing one or more potentially interesting marketplaces in order to determine how a business can optimally compete in them, and process typically results in a marketing strategy that can be used to enhance sales for the business producing it.

Marketing Strategy: An organization's strategy that combines all of its marketing goals into one comprehensive plan and should be drawn from market research and focus on the right product mix in order to achieve the maximum profit potential and sustain the business.

Organizational Adaptation: The organization which is able to keep up with the rapid changes in its environment.

Strategic Implementation: The activity performed according to a plan in order to achieve an overall goal.

Chapter 14
The Aural Nature of Atmosphere in a Retail Setting

Sanda Renko
University of Zagreb, Croatia

Tomislav Gregur
University of Zagreb, Croatia

ABSTRACT

The potential influence of music in eliciting organic reactions has been appreciated since ancient times. Knowing that consumers typically receive exposure to many hours of music each day, scientists and marketers have recognized its potential in consumer behaviour and decision making. Literature suggests that customers like hearing music when they shop, and feel that the retailer providing music cares about them. Retailers have to work diligently to keep their stores favourable in the mind of consumers. Both practitioners and researchers supported the argument that music is a beneficial element in the use of atmospherics in business. Based on the empirical research this chapter provides an insight into the role of music as an important element in retail store atmosphere. The chapter explains the complex character of music, its classifications and key variables, and interaction with other atmospheric cues. The chapter concludes that music has a significant influence on consumer behavior, and that retailers must ensure that they are playing music that their target markets like in their stores.

INTRODUCTION

Along with the rapid development of new store formats, there has been growing recognition that product, services and salesmen are not enough to increase sales, extend consumer's time spent in the store, etc. Literature suggests (De Farias, 2010; Solomon, 2008) that until the 80's, buyers were thought to be exclusively rational beings, whose purchasing choices were made after logical processing of the available information into a stream that came from the detection of a problem to their satisfaction with the purchase. Consumers respond to more than just the core product or service being offered when making purchase decisions (Billings, 1990, p. 1) and the decision to enter a particular store, how much time to spend inside, and to buy or not to buy is heavily influenced by the shopping environment and its effect on customers' emotions (Bohl, 2012, p. 1). Many studies (e.g. Donovan and Rositer, 1982; Foxall, 1997;

DOI: 10.4018/978-1-5225-2139-6.ch014

Levy and Weitz, 2012) have found that the store environment significantly influences consumer's in-store behaviour in ways they might not be aware. A store's environment is comprised of a vast array of separate elements (such as colour, music, lighting, scent, etc.) which are highly interrelated and work together synergistically to affect consumers (Olahut et al., 2012, p. 319). Kotler (1973-74) was the first who encompassed all these elements under the term atmospherics, describing the conscious designing of space in store environments to produce certain effects in buyers. It is a multi-dimensional concept comprising the store's physical characteristics, such as architecture, layout, signs and displays, colours, lighting, temperature, sounds and smells (Levy and Weitz, 2012).

Among the wide array of atmospheric elements, music is one of the very first that attracted researchers' interest and has been shown to impact consumer behaviour (Michon and Chebat, 2004; Milliman, 1986). Burghelea et al. (2015) point out that their preliminary search on Business Source Complete for peer-reviewed journal articles, containing the word "music" resulted in a list of 1,516 titles. It has been identified as one of the most readily manipulated, influential and one of the most frequently used atmospheric factors to enhance the delivery of services to customers (Herrington and Capella, 1996; Yalch and Spangenberg, 1990). Support for the attractiveness of music as an atmospheric variable is evident in its potential to be more easily controlled by marketers than others (Broekemier et al., 2008, p. 60; Kellaris and Kent, 1992, p. 365). It is relatively inexpensive to provide, is easily changed, and is thought to have predictable appeals to individuals based on their ages and lifestyles (Yalch and Spangenberg, 1993, p. 632). Cheng and Hsieh (2011) narrate that music is an invisible language that stimulates emotions and internal feelings and, therefore, buyer shopping behaviour can be influenced by background music. The exposure to the right type of music can evoke a mood that can enhance purchase probability in consumers (Sullivan and Adcock, 2002, p. 156).

The main objective of this chapter is to explain the importance and buying influence of music in a retail setting. Namely, although customers are not paying attention to the background music, their actions can be subtly influenced by it (Peterson, 2016, p. 1). Following this introduction, the chapter begins with the theoretical background and the explanation of the complex character of music. A vast body of literature structured in a way that the historical development of using music to evoke customers' reactions, music classifications and key variables, and interaction with other atmospheric cues was given. For the purpose of getting a better insight into the role of music as an important element of retail store atmosphere, it has been explored in the selected retail context of the Republic of Croatia in a study on a sample of customers buying in supermarkets in the capital city. Croatia is a Southeast European country with modern retailing forms (supermarkets, hypermarkets and discounters) which accounted for 72 percent of grocery sales in 2014 (Gfk, 2015). The top 10 retailers hold almost 80 percent of the Croatian market, similar to situations in the markets of other developed Central and East European countries. The chapter concludes with a summary of the major findings of the study, where managerial implications are also discussed.

THEORETICAL BACKGROUND

Music is a complex, multidimensional stimulus with the potential to influence individual affect, cognition, and behaviour (Bruner, 1990). It is commonly defined (Zeesham and Hatem Obaid, 2015) as the art of organized sound, the purpose of which is to elicit an aesthetic response in listeners (Apel, 1973). In this section, the historical development of the interest for music as one of the key atmospheric variables is given. Moreover, music construct, properties and main genres with their variables are explained. In such a way, a comprehensive framework necessary for understanding the concept of store music is provided.

Historical Notions

Although it is generally accepted that music has received considerable scientific attention since Kotler's introduction of the term of atmospherics (1973-74), for centuries music has been known to have a powerful effect on human responses (Sweeney and Wyber, 2002), from the social science context, to marketing and retailing. Kellaris and Rice (1993) explain that the scientific investigation of music began in the second half of the 19th century in Germany in works of psychologists Fetchner (1876), Helmholtz (1862) and Stumpf (1883), while during the first half of the 20th century American psychologists (e.g. Gundlach, 1935; Hevner, 1935, etc.) intensified their interest in music. Lindberg (2009) notes that the use of music started as early as 1934, with the creation of Muzak one of the more well-known services that produced music playlists for stores nationwide.

It is traditionally believed that popular music research began with Adorno (1941) and in the 1970's continued its entry into the domain of marketing and consumer behaviour with the work of Smith and Curnow (1966) who examined the effect of music volume on the amount of time spent in stores. However, the experimental researches of Millman (1982; 1986) have notably turned the attention of consumer researchers to musical influences in marketing and retail contexts. According to Bruner (1990) more studies involving music and various aspects of marketing were needed since music has long been considered to be an efficient and effective means for triggering moods and communicating nonverbally.

Consumers' responses to advertising and to retail environments are influenced by music. There are a significant number of works on the relationships between music and advertising (Allan, 2014; Chou and Lien, 2010; Dunbar, 1990; Kellaris and Cox, 1989; Macklin, 1988; North et al., 2004; Stout and Leckenby, 1988; etc.). On the other hand, Sweeney and Wyber (2002) consider that studies focusing on the effects of music in the marketing domain have commonly been limited to either the effect of music on internal consumer evaluation or the effect of music on behavioral outcomes. Bruner (1990) also categorized studies on music on non-behavioural outcomes of music in the marketing context (e.g. Bitner, 1992; Kellaris and Rice, 1993; Kellaris and Kent, 1994; Oakes, 2000; Turley and Milliman, 2000; Wallace, 1994) and studies examining behavioural issues (e.g. Areni, 2003; Babin and Darden, 1996; Chebat et al., 2001; Day et al., 2009; Garlin and Owen, 2006; Lam, 2001; North et al., 1997; Oakes and North, 2008).

However, many attempts at explaining the effects of music are based on environmental psychology theory (Herrington and Capella, 1996, p. 27). Vida (2008), Herrington and Capella (1996) considered the parsimonious model of Mehrabian and Russell (1974) relevant in explaining individuals' reactions to environmental cues, e.g. music. Sweeney and Wyber (2002) extended the Mehrabian-Russell model including both emotional states and cognitive processing as mediators of the music-intended behaviour relationship. Gardner (1985) developed a conceptual model of mood states and consumer behaviour, and suggested that pleasant and happy music should lead to positive moods, which in turn should generate positive evaluations and behaviours. Bitner (1992) proposed the "Servicescapes" model which explored music as one of the elements in a service environment that has an effect on the cognitive, emotional, and physiological responses of both consumers and employees. In his "Musicscape" model Oakes (2000) extended Bitner's model by focusing in detail on the influence of a musical variable solely on customer response and behaviour within the service environment.

Key Dimensions

The definition of music is subtle and not well established since it has varied throughout history, in different regions and within society (Cervellin and Lippi, 2011, p. 371). Kellaris and Rice (1993) point out that music cannot be treated as a unidimensional stimulus because it could lead to inconsistent and conflicting findings. Music can be characterized in many ways, such as by type, tempo, and presence or absence of vocals (Yalch and Spanenberg, 1990, p. 57). Gjerdingen and Perrott (2008) are not talking about types, rather about genres of music which could be explained as an expressive style of music. In their music genre identification Gall (2004), Gjerdingen and Perrott (2008), and Kamien (2015) chose the following main genres of music:

1. **Jazz:** Born from a mix of European and African music traditions at the beginning of the 20th century among African American communities in southern areas of the United States. African undertones are evident in the mixture of blue notes, polyrhythms, improvisation, syncopation, and the swing note.
2. **Rock:** Began as a melting of the rhythm and blues and country western genres of the 1940s-50s. It was first called rock & roll, later shortened to rock. The backbeat is one of the essential elements of rock and roll music. Common features are vocals, hard driving beats and featured electric guitars.
3. **Rap:** Developed among young urban blacks as a part of hip-hop culture. It is generally not sung. The words are spoken with a backdrop of music borrowed from soul, funk and rock pieces. Musicians remix sounds, and rhythms with their own innovations and synthesized musical elements.
4. **Techno:** Has roots in the electronic house music made in Detroit in the mid-'80s. It is strictly electronic music, designed for a small, specific audience.
5. **Classical:** Has roots in the chant melodies of Medieval religious rites. Its contemporary incarnation encompasses everything from opera and the symphony orchestra. It is generally understood to be music rooted in Western European traditions performed by trained musicians in formal settings like concert halls, opera houses, and churches. Its key emphasis is the faithful interpretation of composers' written scores.
6. **Folk:** Each country has its own folk music. For the purpose of this research, and further methodology, Croatian music has been considered. There are different types of such a music: from a-cappella 'klapa'singing, vocal bands to light-entertainment music.
7. **Turbofolk:** Emerged in 1990s Serbia, often criticized because of its banality, its consumerism or its sexualized aesthetic quick enrichment, conspicuous consumption, masculinity realized through violence, and femininity realized through sexual availability (Baker, 2007).
8. **Popular:** Refers to the ever-changing music of all genres, favored by the public. Although not specifically applied until the middle of the 20th century, it can be traced by a few decades before that.

Shopper behavior tends to differ according to the type of music played (Herrington and Capella, 1996, p. 27). Music can influence both conscious and unconscious customer action (Oakes, 2003). There are interesting studies about the influence of genre on consumer behavior, such as Farnsworth's (1969) which suggests that those who love jazz have a taste of low order, while a higher order of taste is possessed by those who prefer clasical music. Moreover, a still higher status has been reached by those who are more attracted to the works of Beethoven and Bach than to those of Mendelssohn. Areni and Kim (1993), North and Hargreaves (1998), North et al. (2005), and Yalch and Spangenberg (1990) hypothesized about the influence of classical music on consumer behavior and did not find significant influence of classical music on consumption behavior or the time spent in the store, but that classical music led customers to purchase more expensive products. Accordingly, Yalch and Spangenberg (1990) point out that any retailer wishing to convey a high prestige, high price image should consider classical background music. Soothing, peaceful classical music, with the constant tempo was found to create positive moods and pleasurable atmosphere (Baker et al., 1992; Milliman, 1986). Moreover, classical background music usually communicates a sophisticated, upper class atmosphere (Areni and Kim, 1993).

Besides classical music, research (Andersson et al., 2012) has been done related to pop-music conditions, showing that consumers spent a significantly longer time in the store and spent significantly more on purchases during the pop-music condition compared to the no-music condition.

One of the most frequently used music classifications is (Yalch and Spangenberg, 1990, p. 57):

- **Foreground Music:** Which includes original artists and lyrics, and commands more attention from customers while they shop;
- **Background Music:** Which uses studio musicians playing instrumental, and tends to be more restricted in its range of tempos, frequencies, and volume.

It is the background music that was proven (Areni and Kim, 1993; Bruner, 1990; Garlin and Owen, 2006; Herrington and Capella, 1996; Oakes, 2000; Pham, 2014; Vida et al., 2007) to produce stronger effects on customers' perceptions and preferences. Linsen (1975) states that shoppers like hearing music when they shop, feel that they spend less time standing in the checking queue, and feel that stores providing background music care more about their customers.

Jain and Bagdare (2011) point out that the musical construct refers to musical variables which emit audio signals and interact with auditory receptors to create specific response (p.291), and they could be divided into two categories (Herrington and Capella, 1994):

1. **Structural Categories:** A structural category refers to the structural characteristics of music (Jain and Bagdare, 2011, p. 291) describing the objective and observable qualities of music composition. Bruner (1990) classified structural properties into three factors:

    a. Time,
    b. Pitch,
    c. Texture.

The time dimension includes (Jain and Bagdare, 2011, p. 291; Knoferle et al., 2012, p. 326) variables such as tempo (the speed or rate of the rhythm), rhythm (the pattern of accents given to beats or notes), and phrasing (the length of time a note sounds); while the pitch dimension consists of melody (the succession of notes occurring over time throughout a song), mode (the series of notes, arranged in a scale of ascending pitch), and harmony (the subjective reaction or pleasure). The third factor, texture, relates to timbre (the distinctiveness in tone), instrumentation (the weaving together of unique sonic properties of multiple instruments), and volume (loudness). Kellaris and Kent (1991) consider tempo and mode particularly important determinants of listeners' responses to music with regard to consumer behaviour, while Oakes's Musicscape (2000) highlights tempo, harmony, volume, and genre as musical variables that have the main and interactive effect on consumer behaviour.

Musical tempo, as the speed or rate at which a musical passage progresses (Oakes, 2000, p. 541), is measured in beats per minute. It is strongly correlated with arousal, when fast (slow) music has been shown to raise (lower) listeners' self-reported arousal levels (Husain et al., 2002). Oakes (2003) confirmed the relationship between the tempo of music and the time perception, because time spans filled with slower music are perceived to be shorter than those filled with faster music. Millman's (1982, 1986) studies reported increased purchase levels when slow tempo music was played compared to fast tempo music. Herrington and Capella (1996, p. 27) discovered that slower tempos and lower volumes tend to make retail patrons shop at a more leisurely pace and in certain instances spend more money than faster tempos and higher volumes. Literature (Webster and Weir, 2005) suggests that mode has also been shown to induce mood in listeners, but Knoferle et al. (2012) point out that although some evidence for an effect of mode exists, still there is a gap in theory and praxis to suggest specific effects of musical mode on consumer behavior. On the other hand, volume is the musical variable which is easiest to modify (Oakes, 2000, p. 543) because as with musical tempo, comparative, quantifiable measurement is possible. Studies concluded that the higher the volume of the music, the shorter the period of shopping (Smith and Curnow, 1966) and the longer the perception of waiting time duration (Baker et al., 2003; Baker and Cameron, 1996). Oakes (2000, p. 542) points out the problem of quantifying harmony and concludes that only the study of Kellaris and Kent (1992) acknowledged the possible interactive effects of other musical variables by choosing to alter the harmony of the same composition using digital technology, while holding other variables constant. Dragicevic and Rakidzija (2012, p. 668) concluded that combining melody, harmony and rhythm for the listener can act in many ways: by changing the mood, provoking a sense of balance, happiness, pleasure, or restlessness, anxiety and sadness It is difficult to determine exactly which musical structure causes a certain mood.

2. Affective Categories

The affective category relates to qualitative variables that are primarily described on the basis of a listeners' affective evaluation (Jain and Bagdare, 2011) such as liking, familiarity, and type (feeling and style).

While examining the relationship of liked music with the music emotion dimensions, the shopping experience, and return patronage intentions in retail and service settings, Vaccaro et al. (2011) and Broekemier et al. (2008) found that liked music was significantly related to prior shopping experiences and return patronage intentions. The findings of Sweeney and Wyber (2002) indicate that liked music has a major effect on consumers' evaluations (pleasure, arousal, etc.), while familiarity cannot explain these outcomes. Broekemier et al. (2008) investigated the effects of happy/sad or liked/disliked music on shopping intentions. Their findings indicated that when subjects are exposed to music perceived as happy music, purchase intentions were increasing.

Cameron et al. (2003) and Yalch and Spangenberg (2000) investigated whether customers' shopping times vary by degree of music likeability and familiarity. Contrary to expectations, they agree that the subjective shortening of time appears to be greater with the liked and familiar music due to increased arousal. Kellaris and Mantel (1994) suggest that disliked music produce shorter time duration estimates compared to liked music, and that managers can use this knowledge to manipulate consumer perceptions of time. Bailey and Areni (2006) discussed that perceived shopping time duration was shorter with familiar music.

Some researchers examined the influence of musical preferences on customers' patronage and evaluation of the service environment, such as restaurants, etc. For example, Caldwell and Hibbert (2002) found significant relationships between liked music in restaurants and intentions to return to the restaurant, while North and Hargreaves (1996) suggest the same outcomes in a student cafeteria.

Interactive/Holistic Character

The store environment is never neutral as it is a bundle of cues, messages and suggestions which communicate to shoppers (Markin et al., 1976, p. 43). Baker et al. (1992; 1994; 2002), Eroglu et al., (2005), Mower et al. (2012), and Teller and Dennis (2012) realized that it is important for the atmospheric elements to work together (Levy and Weitz, 2012, p. 490) in order to have a positive impact on buying behaviour and customer satisfaction. Literature review suggests that music and its interaction with other atmospheric elements can lead to more positive evaluation of the store environment (Baker et al., 1992; Eroglu et al., 2005; Mattila and Wirtz, 2001; Teller and Dennis, 2012).

Baker et al. (1992) examined the effects of ambience cues (lighting and music), and social cues (number/friendliness of employees) on customers' pleasure, arousal, and willingness to buy. In their later work, Baker et al. (2002) focused on the interaction between store design, employees and music on the retail store perception. Teller and Dennis (2012) showed that the interaction between music and aroma affected the pleasure and time spent in a store. Eroglu et al. (2005) investigated the effects of retail density and music tempo, and their impact on shopper responses and found that shopper hedonic and utilitarian evaluations of the shopping experience are highest under conditions of slow music/high density and fast music/low density. Matila and Wirtz (2001) examined the interactive effects of music and scents in a retail setting and concluded that when ambient scent and music were congruent in terms of their arousing qualities, consumers perceived the environment positively, with higher levels of approach and impulsive buying behaviour and satisfaction.

Yoo et al. (1998) examined how music, among various characteristics of retail environments influence consumers' emotional responses in the shopping environment, and how these emotions, in turn, influence consumers' store attitudes. Morrison's (2002) findings indicated that programmed music can play a role in a store stay and a personalised music strategy can support a retail brand making a connection with specific target markets.

METHODOLOGY

For the purpose of this chapter, a research study examining the influence of music on customers' intentions to purchase in a field setting was conducted. In concurrence with the recommendation by Donovan and Rossiter (1982) and Vaccaro et al. (2011) consumers were interviewed in the actual retail setting. The study was conducted in a retail supermarket chain in the city of Zagreb because it is the capital city with the most developed retail structure and concentration level.

Sampling Procedure

The data was collected using the store-intercept method as shoppers entered selected supermarkets in the city of Zagreb (supermarkets were selected as those retail types were chosen by 37% of the Croatian population respectively (Gfk, 2015)). The data collection period took place in August 2015 between the hours of 10 a.m. and 15.30 p.m., Monday through Friday.

The surveyed sample included 160 shoppers, but 10 of them declared that they had not paid attention to music in the store (due to time-consuming purchasing), the completed data was obtained from 150 shoppers. They represented the study sample with the largest percent of respondents (34%) were 46-60 years old and (22.7%) 26-35 years old. Other demographic characteristics indicate that the sample consists of 54.7 percent of females, and with 62.7 percent of at least high school education level.

Anonymity and confidentiality of responses in the introduction of the questionnaire were stressed.

Research Instruments' Design

The research instrument was based on a review of the pertinent literature on the use of music in retail and service environments. However, as our intention was to focus on those who had paid attention to the music while shopping, the research instrument began with the "introductory" question: "Did you pay attention to the music while shopping?" For those whose answer was negative, a question about the possible reason was given.

The rest of the questionnaire consisted of three parts. Part I included questions related to the respondents' perceptions about the music dimensions. Following Areni and Kim (1993) and Dragicevic and Rakidzija (2012), respondents could choose among various music genres: from classical to popular music. Musical preferences or "liking" the music was measured similar to Caldwell and Hibbert (2002) and Vaccaro et al. (2011) by asking respondents in a questionnaire to indicate their agreement with the statement "I like the music that was playing" on a 5-point rating scale (1 = strongly disagree; 5 = strongly agree). Besides music likeability, music dimensions, such as loudness and tempo were evaluated on a 5-point scale (1 = too slow; 5 = too fast) (Dube and Morin, 2001) and (1 = too silent; 5 = too loud) (Kellaris and Rice, 1993), respectively.

Part II related to the effects of music on respondents behavior in the store environment. The direct effect of music on retail repeat patronage was measured on a 5-point rating scale similar to Calldwell and Hibbert (2002), and Grewal et al. (2003). Two additional questions related to the effect of music on emotional states and store evaluation were adopted from Dube and Morin (2001) and Sweeney and Wyber (2002). In those questions respondents were asked to express the effect of music on their emotional state on a two-item, 3–point rating scale (e.g. unpleasant to pleasant; unsatisfied to satisfied), and to assess the effect of music on store evaluation on a 5-point scale (1 = not at all; 5 = very much).

Respondents' perception about music effects on purchasing intentions and the time spent in the store environment was operationalized by simply asking them to indicate their positive, neutral or negative opinion as suggested by Broekemier et al. (2008). For example, if music stimulates purchasing intentions, then respondents reported positive comments, and vice versa, if music discourages purchasing, then negative comments were given. Special attention in our research was devoted to the time spent in the store as it is strongly believed that a simple correlation between the time spent shopping and the amount purchased exists (Yalch and Spangenberg, 2000).

In order to investigate whether the music matches customers' demographic profile, and whether there is an interaction between music and demographic characteristics, Part III of the questionnaire focused on common characteristics of the sample such as gender, age, education, and employment status. The collected data was analysed using SPSS. Except from descriptive statistics calculations, the significance of the findings was explored using the Pearson correlation coefficient and chi-square tests, depending on the various types of combination of variables that occurred.

RESULTS AND DISCUSSION

In accordance with the research instrument, the analyses, as well as the results, first refer to the respondents' perceptions about music dimensions, then to the effects of music on the respondents' behavior. What follows is a short discussion of investigated themes and some interpretations.

Perceptions About Music Dimensions

Similar to Dragicevic and Rakidzija (2012), the largest percentage of respondents (48 percent) prefer folk music (Table 1). Such results were expected knowing the cultural characteristics of the investigated market and the fact that this "folk" genre includes a wide range of different types of music: from a-cappella 'klapa' singing, vocal bands to light-entertainment music. The explanation could also lie in the respondents' profile as the largest percentage of the sample (34 percent) were 46-60 years old customers.

Similar to Yalch and Spangenberg (1990) a statistically significant relationship was found between music genres and respondents' ages ($\chi 2 = 55{,}968$, df = 20, p = 0,000). The chi-square test suggests that among respondents who prefer folk music, the largest percentage of them (43.1 percent) are 46-60 years old. Our study showed that the range of ages did not only determine how shoppers responded to the store music. The chi-square test also shows significant relationships between the genres and employment status ($\chi 2 = 27{,}840$, df = 15, p = 0,023), and the largest percentage of respondents who prefer folk music are employed (62.5 percent). There are some interesting findings about music genres and respondents' profiles. Rock is popular for young employed respondents, classical music for older employed, turbofolk for students and young unemployed (16-25 years old), popular for employed 26-35 year olds, and jazz is preferred by young retired people.

Table 1. Preferred musical genres

Genre	Percentage
Rock	23.3
Classical	9.3
Folk	48.0
Turbofolk	1.3
Popular	16.0
Jazz	2.0
Total	100.0

However, contrary to Williams and Keen (2009) and Dragicevic and Rakidzija (2012) our research did not show gender differences in music preferences. Namely, there is not a statistically significant difference in the response to music between female and male shoppers.

Concerning other music dimensions, more than half of the sample (55.3 percent) liked the music in the supermarket, but there was also a high percentage of respondents (38.7 percent) who were not sure whether they liked the store music or not. However, no support was found for a statistically significant relationship between the respondents' liking music and the physical characteristics of the music, music complexity, and listener demographics as suggested by Herrington and Capella (1994). Thus, we can only report interesting findings that the largest percentage of respondents was neutral in responses to the music tempo and volume registered in the store. 76 percent of respondents did not consider the background music loud or silent, while 81.3 percent of the respondents did not think that the background music tempo was low or fast. Those findings can be explained alternatively in terms of environmental psychology (Donovan and Rossiter, 1982) and Musicscape theory (Oakes, 2000). Namely, in contrast to many previous studies (Milliman, 1982; Chebat et al., 2001; Dube and Morin, 2001; Roballey et al., 1985, etc.), slow tempo music has little arousing power and fails to stimulate cognitive processes (Michon and Chebat, 2004). The explanation should be also supported by the following:

1. The respondents are familiar with the specific store;
2. The research was conducted on the sample of respondents who usually shop in supermarkets;
3. The "grocery sector" (supermarkets, discount outlets, and so on) could be expected to provide mainly utilitarian value, prioritizing functional cues and managing aesthetic-ambience cues" (Massara, 2003, p. 52).

There is an important finding in the interaction between the liking of music and emotional states when the largest percentage of respondents (74.7 percent) expressed their pleasure and satisfaction with the background music in the retail setting. The chi-square test shows significant relationships between the liking of the music played in the store and the respondents' emotional state ($\chi 2 = 99{,}111$, df = 8, p = 0,000).

Effects of Music on Consumers' Behavior

Past research has indicated that musical preferences (e.g. liking) may explain the effects of music on consumers, more so than musical characteristics themselves (Sweeney and Wyber, 2002). In line with Areni and Kim (1993), Broekemier et al. (2008), Morrin et al. (2007), North and Hargreaves 1998, 2000), Yalch and Spangenberg (1990, 2000), etc. liking the music clearly affects consumer behaviour. Table 2 shows that there is a statistically significant relationship between liking music and store patronage, time spent in the store, purchasing intentions, and store evaluation. Based on the values set by Dancey and Reidy (2002, p. 166), in identifying the strength of those relationships only moderate to weak positive associations (Table 2) were found (with the correlation significant at the 0.01 level).

Although past research (Herrington and Capella, 1994; Hui et al., 1997) suggest that the preferential dimension of music, i.e. the degree to which the shopper likes/dislikes music has a positive impact on the amount of time spent in a store, the largest percentage of respondents in our study (72.3 percent) do not agree with the statement that liking music affects the tendency to spend more time in the store. In

Table 2. The strongest correlation coefficients for the effect of musical characteristics on consumers' behaviour

Item		Pearson Correlation Coefficient
Liking music	Retail repeat patronage	0,421**
	Time spent in the store	0,304**
	Purchasing intentions	0,329**
	Store evaluation	0,403**
Music volume	Store evaluation	-0,247**
Emotional states caused by music played	Retail repeat patronage	0,449**
	Time spent in the store	0,308**
	Purchasing intentions	0,377**
	Store evaluation	0,340**
Store attractiveness caused by music played	Retail repeat patronage	0,492**
	Time spent in the store	0,338**
	Purchasing intentions	0,337**

** Correlation is significant at the 0.01 level (2-tailed).

contrast, similar to Areni and Kim (1993) liked music does not influence the time spent in the store at all. Accordingly, we have the situation that a statistically significant relationship between liking store music and time spent in shopping was found but that the largest percentage of respondents think that liked music does not affect longer time spent shopping.

In addition, Broekemier et al. (2008) and Mattila and Wirtz (2001) have found that playing liked music produced the largest direct effect on customers' likelihood of shopping in the store, while our study confirmed a statistically significant relationship between liking music and shopping intentions with the largest percentage of respondents (35.4 percent) not agreeing that liking music has induced them to make more purchasing in the store. Our results support Vaccaro et al. (2011) findings about the effect of liked music on respondents' return patronage intentions. Namely a statistically significant relationship between liked music and a repeated visit to the store was found, and the largest percentage of respondents (36 percent) confirmed that music would influence their return patronage intentions.

Similar to Herrington and Capella (1996), no support for the effects of tempo and volume on shopping time, and intentions to return to the store was found. Neither the influence of gender on responses to music's loudness suggested in earlier studies (Kellaris and Rice, 1993; Smith and Curnow, 1966) was found. Instead, a statistically significant relationship between music volume and the evaluation of the store was found. There is a weak negative association between the customers' opinion of the store caused by the music played and the music volume because in loud music settings, respondents do not enjoy the store.

Our research confirmed the findings of Chebat et al. (2001), Dube and Morin (2001), and Kulkarni Vijay (2012) who demonstrated that music has an effect on the customer attitude towards the store. In line with Jain and Bagdare (2011), the intensity of pleasure induced by music exerts influence on store evaluation ($\chi2$ = 113,028, df = 16, p = 0,000). Additionally, there is a moderate positive association between the store attractiveness induced by music and revisit the store, time spent in the store, and purchasing intentions. Due to the pleasant experience created by music customers will recommend the store to others (Kulkarni Vijay, 2012) and tend to visit the store again.

Consistent with Bruner (1990) who considers music as a powerful emotional stimuli, this study reveals statistically significant relationships between customer's emotional states caused by music played and store patronage, time spent in the store, purchasing intentions, and store evaluation. However, as Table 2 shows, only moderate to weak positive associations (Table 2) were found (with the correlation significant at the 0.01 level).

LIMITATIONS AND FUTURE RESEARCH DIRECTION

Similar to any research, this study provides some useful findings but it has some limitations which have to be taken into account through future research. First, this study used actual consumers in actual marketplaces as subjects, with the purpose of studying the influence and stimulation that music has on consumers. The fact is that the research was conducted in a real retail setting but the music characteristics, such as tempo and loudness were held relatively constant. In such a way we face with the common practice in marketing studies that music is tested as a unidimensional stimulus (Kellaris and Rice, 1993), but it leads to conflicting findings. The previously mentioned statement is consistent with Broekemier et al. (2008) who point out that "with tempo held relatively constant, some of the emotional impact of music may have been lost" (p. 64). We did not use digital music technology to isolate the manipulation of tempo while maintaining the other musical variables as constants, as suggested by Oakes (2000). Thus, systemically varying the music played in retail settings similar to the procedure used by Yalch and Spangenberg (1990) is suggested.

Moreover, similar to many past studies (Pham, 2014), we did not consider the data on the individual characteristics of consumers. Further research should investigate consumers' personal music preferences to see if a similarity between them and music played in a store influence consumers' behaviour. The next limitation of this study is related to the setting, because the research was conducted only in one retail setting, a supermarket, and the music effects in other retail settings could be different. We also agree with Knoferle et al. (2012) that different levels of mode and music vary across specific departments and/or products categories. In order to improve the findings of the research, an experiment (which could take place in a lab or in a "simulated store") could be included. In such experiments respondents could be exposed to different levels of environmental cues and music dimensions (Sweeney and Wyber, 2002) in order to analyse their impact on consumers and their decision to shop in particular stores. Gilboa and Rafaeli (2003) point out that laboratory methods are preferred to enable control over multiple intervening variables such as noise, odour, interactions with employees or other consumers, etc.

Like Herrington and Capella (1996), the next limitation refers to the time period for data collection because data was collected only between the hours of 10 a.m. and 15.30 p.m., Monday through Friday when only certain groups of shoppers are shopping in the supermarket. Jain and Bagdare (2011) note that different groups of customers visit stores at different times of the day. Future research may include consumers who are working until 16 p.m. and who prefer to do late shopping and on Saturday/Sunday in order to find out the opinions of different demographic segments (North and Hargreaves, 1996).

Additionally, the examination of the interaction of music with other atmospheric cues is missing. The literature (Jain and Bagdare, 2011; Mower et al., 2012; Teller and Dennis, 2012) confirmed holistic character of music and realized that it is important for music to work together with other atmospheric elements (Levy and Weitz, 2012) in order to have a positive impact on buying behaviour and customer satisfaction. Therefore, we propose to further investigate the role of past and present experiences that customers had with the store, because it could affect their perception of the in-store environmental cues and their approach behaviour.

CONCLUSION

In making their purchase decisions, consumers respond to more than simply the tangible product or service being offered (Kotler, 1973-1974, p. 48) and store environmental factors can influence their subjective feelings experienced in the store and influence the shopping intention, consumption amount, perceived quality, satisfaction and shopping value (Babin and Attaway, 2000). On the other side, retailers need a framework which provides them with insights on how to improve customers' perceptions of the store in order to increase store loyalty; to improve customer's attitudes about the store in order to increase store visits, etc. Retailers have a certain amount of control over factors that influence customers' patronage decisions (Grewal et al., 2003, p. 264).

This chapter is focused on music as a powerful stimulus in shaping the retail experience (Jain and Bagdare, 2011). The potential influence of music in eliciting organic reactions has been appreciated (Cervellin and Lippi, 2011) since ancient cultures. Recognizing the potential for music to influence consumer behaviour, which in turn impacts their decision making, marketers invest substantial resources in an effort to effectively incorporate music into the design of the retail environment (Morrison and Beverland, 2003).) Stores use music as a marketing tool to influence the unconscious behaviours of shoppers, such as affecting their perceptions of how long they were shopping and encouraging them to linger in a store longer or to change their pace (Graves, 2010, p. 54). The study provides an exploratory examination of the impact of music on customers' behaviour in a retail setting, and in line with past research drew the general conclusion that music can be a critical component of store atmosphere and play a role in the purchase decision making process (Areni and Kim, 1993; Donavan and Rossiter, 1982; Smith and Curnow, 1966). However, some findings are contradictory to past studies.

A literature review suggests that music can positively affect store evaluation. It was observed that with liked music, perceptions about the store are positive. Statistically significant relationships between liking music and shopping intentions and repeated visits to the store were found. However, despite many past studies our research did not show gender differences in music preferences. Moreover, no support in our study for the effects of tempo and volume on shopping time, and intentions to return to the store were found. Although conducted on the small research sample, this study gave some theoretical and practical contributions. Theoretically, it suggests that music causes different behaviour among Southeastern European consumers comparing to consumers on some more developed markets. Contribution for the praxis lie in implications for retailers on investigated market who should not only rely on music rather in the interaction with other atmospheric cues.

Conclusively, despite widespread beliefs that music enhances a retail environment resulting in increased store traffic, greater customer satisfaction, and higher sales, there is a lack of direct evidence supporting these beliefs (Yalch and Spangenberg, 1990).

In line with the recommendations of Yalch and Spangenberg (1990, p. 61) and Herrington and Capella (1996), store music could be adapted according to the time of day, day of the week, and/or by departments. Store managers could think to offer a variety of different music genres, different music tempo and volume at different times for different departments, depending on the merchandise and the profile of each department's target customers. The setting is an important consideration when deciding on the type of music to play (Wood and Allen, 2012). For example, a supermarket seafood department might play a-cappella 'klapa'singing because this slow/soft music genre is the most appropriate for such merchandise and the target segment.

A personalised music strategy can support a retail brand and make a powerful connection with specific target markets by incorporating customer demographics (such as age, gender mix and income levels) and psychographics (such as preferences, lifestyles, personalty and attitudes)(Morrison, 2002). By understanding the demographics and psychographics of its target market, retailers can create an audio environment where their customers feel comfortable, relaxed and happy to spend time and money. The literature (Burghelea et al., 2015, p. 378) suggests that there is a relationship between music and memories evoked by the music which can be correlated with other atmospheric variables (smell, light or colour) and then all together can influence the shopping experience. Managers can use this knowledge to manipulate consumers' perception of time in the store (Burghelea et al., 2015), especially to make perceived waiting time seem shorter for consumers waiting in line, resulting in a reduction of the dissatisfaction level (p. 382). It is less expensive to pipe appropriate music into a store to entertain and distract than it is to hire more service people (Grewal et al., 2003).

REFERENCES

Adorno, T. W. (1941). On Popular Music. *Studies in Philosophy and Social Sciences*, *9*, 17–48.

Allan, D. (2014). Turn it up: That's my song in that ad. *International Journal of Music Business Research*, *3*(1), 26–51.

Andersson, P. K., Kristensson, P., Wastlund, E., & Gustafsson, A. (2012). Let the music play or not: The influence of background music on consumer behavior. *Journal of Retailing and Consumer Services*, *19*(6), 553–560. doi:10.1016/j.jretconser.2012.06.010

Apel, W. (1973). *Harvard dictionary of music*. Cambridge, MA: Belknap Press.

Areni, C. S. (2003). Exploring managers implicit theories of atmospheric music: Comparing academic analysis to industry insight. *Journal of Services Marketing*, *17*(2), 161–184. doi:10.1108/08876040310467925

Areni, C. S., & Kim, D. (1993). The Influence of Background Music on Shopping Behavior: Classical Versus Top-Forty Music in a Wine Store. *Advances in Consumer Research. Association for Consumer Research (U. S.)*, *20*, 336–340.

Babin, B.J., & Attaway, J.S. (2000). Atmospheric affect as a tool for creating value and gaining share of customer. *Journal of Business Research*, *49*(2), 91-99.

Babin, B. J., & Darden, W. R. (1996). Good and bad shopping vibes: Spending and patronage satisfaction. *Journal of Business Research*, *35*(3), 201–206. doi:10.1016/0148-2963(95)00125-5

Bailey, N., & Areni, C. S. (2006). When a few minutes sound like a lifetime: Does atmospheric music expand or contract perceived time? *Journal of Retailing*, *82*(3), 189–202. doi:10.1016/j.jretai.2006.05.003

Baker, C. (2007). *The concept of turbofolk in Croatia: inclusion/exclusion in the construction of national musical identity*. Nation in formation: inclusion and exclusion in Central and Eastern Europe, UCL School of Slavonic and East European Studies, London. Retrieved from http://eprints.soton.ac.uk/66293/1/Baker_-_turbofolk_2007.pdf

Baker, J., & Cameron, M. (1996). The effects of the service environment on affect and consumer perception of waiting time: An integrative review and research propositions. *Journal of the Academy of Marketing Science*, *24*(4), 338–349. doi:10.1177/0092070396244005

Baker, J., Grewal, D., Levy, M., & Voss, G. (2003). Wait Expectations, Store Atmosphere and Store Patronage Intentions. *Journal of Retailing*, *79*(4), 259–268. doi:10.1016/j.jretai.2003.09.006

Baker, J., Grewal, D., & Parasuraman, A. (1994). The Influence of Store Environment on Quality Inferences and Store Image. *Journal of the Academy of Marketing Science*, *22*(4), 328–339. doi:10.1177/0092070394224002

Baker, J., Levy, M., & Grewal, D. (1992). An Experimental Approach to Making Retail Store Environmental Decisions. *Journal of Retailing*, *68*(4), 445–460.

Baker, J., Parasuraman, A., Grewal, D., & Voss, G. B. (2002). The Influence of Multiple Store Environment Cues on Perceived Merchandise Value and Patronage Intentions. *Journal of Marketing*, *66*(April), 120–141. doi:10.1509/jmkg.66.2.120.18470

Billings, W. L. (1990), Effects of Store Atmosphere on Shopping Behaviour. *Honors Projects*. Retrieved from http://digitalcommons.iwu.edu/busadmin_honproj/16

Bitner, M. J. (1992). Servicescapes: The impact of physical surroundings on customers and employees. *Journal of Marketing*, *56*(2), 57–71. doi:10.2307/1252042

Bohl, P. (2012), The effects of store atmosphere on shopping behaviour': A literature review, *Corvinus Marketing Tanulmányok*, Retrieved from http://unipub.lib.uni-corvinus.hu/669/1/CMT_2012-1.pdf

Broekemier, G., Marquardt, R., & Gentry, J. W. (2008). An exploration of happy/sad and liked/disliked music effects on shopping intentions in a womens clothing store service setting. *Journal of Services Marketing*, *22*(1), 59–67. doi:10.1108/08876040810851969

Bruner, G. C. (1990). Music, mood, and marketing. *Journal of Marketing*, *54*(4), 94–104. doi:10.2307/1251762

Burghelea, M. R., Plaias, I., & El-Murad, J. (2015), The Effects of Music as an Atmospheric Variable on Consumer Behaviour in the Context of Retailing and Service Environments. *International Conference on Marketing and Business Development Journal*, 1(1), 377-392.

Caldwell, C., & Hibbert, S. A. (2002). The influence of music tempo and musical preference on restaurant patrons behavior. *Psychology and Marketing*, *19*(11), 895–917. doi:10.1002/mar.10043

Cameron, M. A., Baker, J., Peterson, M., & Braunsberger, K. (2003). The effect of music, wait-length evaluation, and mood on a low-cost wait experience. *Journal of Business Research*, *56*(6), 421–430. doi:10.1016/S0148-2963(01)00244-2

Cervellin, G., & Lippi, G. (2011). From music-beat to heart-beat: A journey in the complex interactions between music, brain and heart. *European Journal of Internal Medicine*, *22*(4), 371–374. doi:10.1016/j.ejim.2011.02.019 PMID:21767754

Chebat, J.-C., Gelinas Chebat, C., & Vaillant, D. (2001). Environmental background music and in-store selling. *Journal of Business Research*, *54*(2), 115–123. doi:10.1016/S0148-2963(99)00089-2

Chen, H.-S., & Hsieh, T. (2011). The effect of atmosphere on customer perceptions and customer behaviour responses in chain store supermarkets. *African Journal of Business Management*, *5*(24), 10054–10066. doi:10.5897/AJBM10.608

Chou, H. Y., & Lien, N. H. (2010). Advertising effects of songs nostalgia and lyrics relevance. *Asia Pacific Journal of Marketing and Logistics*, *22*(3), 314–329. doi:10.1108/13555851011062278

Dancey, C. P., & Reidy, J. (2002), Statistics Without Maths for Psychology (2 ed.). Dorchester: Pearson Education Ltd.

Day, R.-F., Lin, C.-H., Huang, W.-H., & Chuang, S.-H. (2009). Effects of music tempo and task difficulty on multi-attribute decision-making: An eye-tracking approach. *Computers in Human Behavior*, *25*(1), 130–143. doi:10.1016/j.chb.2008.08.001

De Farias, S. A. (2010, May 23-25), Store Atmospherics and Experiential Marketing: a conceptual framework and research propositions for an extraordinary customer experience. Proceedings of the IV Encontro de Marketing da ANPAD, Florianopolis/SC. Retrieved from http://www.anpad.org.br/diversos/trabalhos/EMA/ema_2010/2010_EMA27.pdf

Donovan, R. J., & Rossiter, J. R. (1982). Store Atmosphere: An Environmental Psychology Approach. *Journal of Retailing*, *58*(Spring), 34–57.

Dragicevic, M., & Rakidzija, I. (2012). The music as an element of physical evidence in service organizations. *Procedia Economics and Finance*, *3*, 666–671. doi:10.1016/S2212-5671(12)00212-2

Dube, L., & Morin, S. (2001). Background music pleasure and store evaluation: Intensity effects and psychological mechanisms. *Journal of Business Research*, *54*(2), 107–113. doi:10.1016/S0148-2963(99)00092-2

Dunbar, D. S. (1990). Music and Advertising. *International Journal of Advertising*, *9*, 197–203.

Eroglu, S. A., Machleit, K. A., & Chebat, J. C. (2005). The Interaction of Retail Density and Music Tempo: Effects on Shopper Responses. *Psychology and Marketing*, *22*(7), 577–589. doi:10.1002/mar.20074

Farnsworth, P. R. (1969). *The Social Psychology of Music*. Iowa City, Iowa: The University of Iowa Press.

Fetchner, G. T. (1876). *Vorschule der Asthetik*. Leipzig: Breithopf & Hartal.

Foxall, G. R. (1997). The Emotional Texture of Consumer Environments: A Systematic Approach to Atmospherics. *Journal of Economic Psychology*, *18*(4), 505–523. doi:10.1016/S0167-4870(97)00021-4

Gall, Z. (2004). *Glazbeni leksikon, Marjan Tisak, d.o.o.* Split: Hrvatska.

Gardner, M. P. (1985). Mood States and Consumer Behavior: A Critical Review. *The Journal of Consumer Research*, *12*(3), 281–300. doi:10.1086/208516

Garlin, F. V., & Owen, K. (2006). Setting the tone with the tune: "A meta-analytic review of the effect of background music in retail settings. *Journal of Business Research*, *59*(6), 755–764. doi:10.1016/j.jbusres.2006.01.013

GfK. (2015). SHOPPING MONITOR Croatia. Retrieved from http://progressive.com.hr/demo/2095-gfk-shoppingmonitor-hipermarketi-najpopularniji-oblik-trgovine-.html

Gilboa, S., & Rafaeli, A. (2003). Store Environment, Emotions and Approach Behavior: Applying Environmental Aesthetics to Retailing. *International Review of Retail, Distribution and Consumer research*, 13(2), 195-211. Retrieved from http://iew3.technion.ac.il/Home/Users/anatr/COMPLE-FINAL-20-11-02.pdf

Gjerdingen, R. O., & Perrott, D. (2008). Scanning the Dial: The Rapid Recognition of Music Genres. *Journal of New Music Research*, *37*(2), 93–100. doi:10.1080/09298210802479268

Graves, P. (2010). *Consumerology: The Market Research Myth, the Truth About Consumers, and the Psychology of Shopping*. Boston: Nicholas Brealey Publishing.

Grewal, D., Baker, J., Levy, M., & Voss, G. B. (2003). The effects of wait expectations and store atmosphere evaluations on patronage intentions in service-intensive retail stores. *Journal of Retailing*, *79*(4), 259–268. doi:10.1016/j.jretai.2003.09.006

Gundlach, R. C. (1935). Factors determining characterization of musical phrases. *The American Journal of Psychology*, *47*(4), 624–643. doi:10.2307/1416007

Helmholtz, H. (1862). Die Lehre von den Tonempfindunen. Verlag: Friedrich Vieweg & Sohn, Braunschweig.

Herrington, J. D., & Capella, L. M. (1994). Practical applications of music in service settings. *Journal of Services Marketing*, *8*(3), 50–65. doi:10.1108/08876049410065615

Herrington, J. D., & Capella, L. M. (1996). Effects of music in service environments: A field study. *Journal of Services Marketing*, *10*(2), 26–41. doi:10.1108/08876049610114249

Hevner, K. (1935). Expression in music: A discussion of experimental studies and theories. *Psychological Review*, *42*(2), 186–204. doi:10.1037/h0054832

Hui, M. K., Dube, L., & Chebat, J.-C. (1997). The impact of music on consumers reactions to waiting for services. *Journal of Retailing*, *73*(1), 87–104. doi:10.1016/S0022-4359(97)90016-6

Husain, G., Thompson, W. F., & Schellenberg, E. G. (2002). Effects of Musical Tempo and Mode on Arousal, Mood, and Spatial Abilities. *Music Perception*, *20*(2), 151–171. doi:10.1525/mp.2002.20.2.151

Jain, R., & Bagdare, S. (2011). Music and consumption experience: A review. *International Journal of Retail & Distribution Management*, *39*(4), 289–302. doi:10.1108/09590551111117554

Kamien, R. (2015). Music: An Appreciation (11 ed.). New York: McGraw-Hill Education.

Kellaris, J. J., & Cox, A. D. (1989). The Effects of Background Music in Advertising: A Reassessment. *The Journal of Consumer Research*, *16*(1), 113–118. doi:10.1086/209199

Kellaris, J. J., & Kent, R. J. (1991). Exploring tempo and modality effects, on consumer responses to music. *Advances in Consumer Research. Association for Consumer Research (U. S.)*, *18*, 243–248.

Kellaris, J. J., & Kent, R. J. (1992). The influence of music on consumers temporal perceptions: Does time fly when youre having fun. *Journal of Consumer Psychology*, *1*(4), 365–376. doi:10.1016/S1057-7408(08)80060-5

Kellaris, J. J., & Kent, R. J. (1994). An Exploratory Investigation of Responses Elicited by Music Varying in Tempo, Tonality, and Texture. *Journal of Consumer Psychology*, *2*(4), 381–401. doi:10.1016/S1057-7408(08)80068-X

Kellaris, J. J., & Mantel, S. P. (1994). The influence of mood and gender on consumer's time perceptions. *Advances in Consumer Research. Association for Consumer Research (U. S.)*, *21*, 514–518.

Kellaris, J. J., & Rice, R. C. (1993). The Influence of Tempo, Loudness, and Gender of Listener on Responses to Music. *Psychology and Marketing*, *10*(1), 15–29. doi:10.1002/mar.4220100103

Knoferle, K., Spangenberg, E., Herrmann, A., & Landwehr, J. (2012). It is all in the mix: The interactive effect of music tempo and mode on in-store sales. *Marketing Letters*, *23*(1), 325–337. doi:10.1007/s11002-011-9156-z

Kotler, P. (1973-1974). Atmospherics as a Marketing Tool. *Journal of Retailing*, *49*(4), 48–64.

Kulkarni, V.R. (2012). A study of impact of music on consumer buying behavior in retail. *International Journal of Management*, *3*(3), 152–159.

Lam, S.Y. (2001). The effects of store environment on shopping behavior: A critical review. *Advances in Consumer Research. Association for Consumer Research (U. S.)*, *28*, 190–197.

Levy, M., & Weitz, B. A. (2012). *Retailing Management* (8th ed.). Irwin, NY: McGraw-Hill.

Lindberg, P.J. (2009). Bad music in public spaces. *Travel+Leisure*. Retrieved from http://www.travelandleisure.com/articles/bad-music-in-public-spaces

Linsen, M.A. (1975). Like our music today Ms. shopper? Progressive Grocer, October, 156.

Macklin, M. C. (1988). The relationship between Music in Advertising and Children' Responses: An Experimental Investigation. In S. Hecker & D.W. Stewart (Eds.), Nonverbal Communication in Advertising (pp. 225-243). Lexington, MA: Lexington Books.

Markin, R. J., Lillis, C. M., & Narayana, C. L. (1976). Social-psychological significance of store space. *Journal of Retailing*, *52*(1), 43–54.

Massara, F. (2003). Store atmosphere: Still a fledgling art. *ECR Journal*, *3*(2), 47–52.

Mattila, A. S., & Wirtz, J. (2001). Congruency of scent and music as a driver of in-store evaluations and behaviour. *Journal of Retailing*, *77*(2), 273–289. doi:10.1016/S0022-4359(01)00042-2

Mehrabian, A., & Russel, J. A. (1974). *An approach to environmental psychology*. Cambridge, MA: MIT Press.

Michon, R., & Chebat, J. C. (2004). The Interaction Effect of Background Music and Ambient Scent on the Perception of Service Quality. *Paper presented at the 8th International Research Seminar in Service Management*, LA Londe-Les-Maures, Retrieved from http://www.ryerson.ca/~rmichon/Publications/Odour%20Music%20Service%20Quality.pdf

Milliman, R. (1982). Using background music to affect the behavior of supermarket shoppers. *Journal of Marketing*, *46*(3), 86–91. doi:10.2307/1251706

Milliman, R. (1986). The influence of background music on the behaviour of restaurant patrons. *The Journal of Consumer Research*, *13*(2), 286–289. doi:10.1086/209068

Morrison, M. (2002). The power of Music and its Influence on International Retail Brands and Shopper Behaviour: a Multi case Study Approach. *Paper presented at the Australia and New Zealand Marketing Academy Conference*, Auckland. Retrieved from http://www.evolvedsound.com.au/The_Power_of_Music_in_Retail.pdf

Morrison, M., & Beverland, M. (2003). In search of the right in-store music. *Business Horizons*, *46*(6), 77–82. doi:10.1016/S0007-6813(03)00092-2

Mower, J. F., Kim, M., & And Childs, M. L. (2012). Exterior atmospherics and consumer behaviour: Influence of landscaping and window display. *Journal of Fashion Marketing and Management*, *16*(4), 442–453. doi:10.1108/13612021211265836

North, A. C., & Hargreaves, D. J. (1996). The Effect of Music on Responses to a Dining Area. *Journal of Environmental Psychology*, *16*(1), 55–64. doi:10.1006/jevp.1996.0005

North, A. C., & Hargreaves, D. J. (1998). The effect of music on atmosphere and purchase intentions in cafeteria. *Journal of Applied Social Psychology*, *28*(24), 2254–2273. doi:10.1111/j.1559-1816.1998.tb01370.x

North, A. C., Hargreaves, D. J., & McKendrick, J. (1997). In-store music affects product choice. *Nature*, *390*(6656), 6656. doi:10.1038/36484

North, A. C., Mackenzie, L. C., Law, R. M., & Hargreaves, D. J. (2004). The Effects of Musical and Voice „Fit" on Responses to Advertisements. *Journal of Applied Social Psychology*, *34*(8), 1675–1708. doi:10.1111/j.1559-1816.2004.tb02793.x

North, A. C., Shilcock, A., & Hargreaves, D. J. (2005). The effect of musical style on restaurant customers spending. *Environment and Behavior*, *35*(5), 712–718. doi:10.1177/0013916503254749

Oakes, S. (2000). The Influence of the musicscape within service environment. *Journal of Services Marketing*, *14*(7), 539–556. doi:10.1108/08876040010352673

Oakes, S. (2003). Musical tempo and waiting perceptions. *Psychology and Marketing*, *20*(8), 685–705. doi:10.1002/mar.10092

Oakes, S., & North, A. C. (2008). Reviewing congruity effects in the service environment musicscape. *International Journal of Service Industry Management*, *19*(1), 63–82. doi:10.1108/09564230810855716

Olahut, M. R., El-Murad, J., & Plaias, I. (2012). Store atmosphere: conceptual issues and its impact on shopping behaviour, international conference. In Marketing – from information to decision (5th ed., pp. 317-343).

Peterson, G. (2016), The Impact Of Background Music On Spending Habits, Howl & Echoes. Retrieved from http://howlandechoes.com/

Pham, M. (2014), The Effects of Background Music on Consumer Behavior, University of California, Santa Barbara, Retrieved from http://www.writing.ucsb.edu/sites/secure.lsit.ucsb.edu.writ.d7/files/sitefiles/publications/2014%20Pham.pdf

Roballey, T. C., McGreevy, C., Rongo, R. R., Schwantes, M. L., Steger, P. J., Wininger, M. A., & Gardner, E. B. (1985). The effect of music on eating behaviour. *Bulletin of the Psychonomic Society*, *23*(3), 221–222. doi:10.3758/BF03329832

Smith, P. C., & Curnow, R. (1966). Arousal hypothesis and the effects of music on purchasing behavior. *The Journal of Applied Psychology*, *50*(3), 255–256. doi:10.1037/h0023326 PMID:5936035

Solomon, M.R. (2008), Consumer Behavior: buying, having and being (8th ed.). New York: Prentice Hall.

Stout, P., & Leckenby, J. D. (1988). Let the music play: Music as a nonverbal element in TV commercials. In S. Hecker, & D.W. Stewart (Eds.), Nonverbal Communication in Advertising (pp. 207-233). Lexington, MA, USA: Lexington Books.

Stumpf, C. (1883). *Grundzuge der Physiologischen Psychologie*. Leipzig: Engelmann.

Sullivan, M., & Adcock, D. (2002). *Retail marketing*. Hampshire, UK: Cengage Learning EMEA.

Sweeney, J. C., & Wyber, F. (2002). The role of cognitions and emotions in the music-approach-avoidance behaviour relationship. *Journal of Services Marketing*, *16*(1), 57–69. doi:10.1108/08876040210419415

Teller, C., & Dennis, C. (2012). The Effect of Ambient Scent on Consumers Perception, Emotions and Behaviour – a Critical Review. *Journal of Marketing Management*, *28*(1/2), 14–36. doi:10.1080/0267257X.2011.560719

Turley, L. W., & Milliman, R. E. (2000). Atmospheric effects on shopping behaviour: A review of the experimental evidence. *Journal of Business Research*, *49*, 193–211. doi:10.1016/S0148-2963(99)00010-7

Vaccaro, V. L., Yucetepe, V., Ahlawat, S., & Lee, M.-S. (2011). The Relationship of Liked Music with Music Emotion Dimensions, Shopping Experience, and Return Patronage Intentions in Retail and Service Settings. *Journal of Academy of Business and Economics*, *11*(4), 94–106.

Vida, I. (2008). The Impact of Atmospherics on Consumer Behaviour: The Case of the Music Fit in Retail Stores. *Economics and Business Review for Central and South-Eastern Europe*, *10*(1), 21–35.

Vida, I., Obadia, C., & Kunz, M. (2007). The Effects of Background Music on Consumer Responses in a High-end Supermarket. *International Review of Retail, Distribution and Consumer Research*, *17*(5), 469–482. doi:10.1080/09593960701631532

Wallace, W. T. (1994). Memory for Music: Effects of melody on recall of text. *Journal of Experimental Psychology*, *20*(6), 1471–1485.

Webster, G. D., & Weir, C. G. (2005). Emotional responses to music: Interactive effects of mode, texture, and tempo. *Motivation and Emotion*, *29*(1), 19–39. doi:10.1007/s11031-005-4414-0

Williams, K., & Keen, D. (2009). 2008 Survey of Public Participation in the Arts. In *National Endowment for the Arts, Personal Preferences & Leisure Activities – Musical Preferences* (Ch. 6, pp. 57-61). Retrieved from https://www.arts.gov/sites/default/files/2008-SPPA.pdf

Wood, W. W., & Allen, R. (2012). *The rock 'n' roll classroom: using music to manage mood, energy, and learning*. Thousand Oaks, CA: Corwin Press.

Yalch, R., & Spangenberg, E. (1990). Effects of Store Music on Shopping Behaviour. *Journal of Services Marketing*, *4*, 31–39.

Yalch, R., & Spangenberg, E. (1993). Using Store Music for Retail Zoning: A Field Experiment. *Advances in Consumer Research. Association for Consumer Research (U. S.)*, *20*, 632–636.

Yalch, R., & Spangenberg, E. (2000). The Effects of Music in a Retail Setting on Real and Perceived Shopping Times. *Journal of Business Research*, *49*(2), 139–147. doi:10.1016/S0148-2963(99)00003-X

Yoo, C., Park, J., & MacInnis, D. J. (1998). Effects of Store Characteristics and In-Store Emotional Experiences on Store Attitude. *Journal of Business Research*, *42*(3), 253–263. doi:10.1016/S0148-2963(97)00122-7

Zeeshan, M., & Hatem Obaid, M. (2015). Impact of Music on Consumer Behaviour: A Perspective on Retail Atmospheric. *Asian Journal of Business and Management Sciences*, *3*(2), 56–63.

ADDITIONAL READING

Backstrom, K., & Johansson, U. (2006). Creating and consuming experiences in retail store environments: Comparing retailer and consumer perspectives. *Journal of Retailing and Consumer Services*, *13*(6), 417–430. doi:10.1016/j.jretconser.2006.02.005

Berry, L. L., Carbone, L. P., & Haeckel, S. H. (2002) Managing the total customer experience, *Sloan Management Review*, Spring.

Bost, E. (1987). *Ladenatmosphare und Konsumentenverhalten (Retail atmospherics and consumer behaviour)*. Heidelberg: Physica-Verlag. doi:10.1007/978-3-642-51471-5

Chebat, J.-C., & Dube, L. (2000). Evolution and challenges facing retail atmospherics: The apprentice sorcerer is dying. *Journal of Business Research*, *49*(2), 89–90. doi:10.1016/S0148-2963(99)00012-0

d Astous, A. (2000). Irritating aspects of the shopping environment. *Journal of Business Research*, *49*(2), 149–156. doi:10.1016/S0148-2963(99)00002-8

Lewis, M., & Haviland, J. M. (1993). *Handbook of emotions*. New York: McGraw Hill.

Walsh, W. B., Craik, K. H., & Price, R. H. (2000). *Person-Environment Psychology: New Directions and Perspectives*. Mahwah, New Jersey: Lawrence Erlbaum Associates.

Wilson, M. (2005). Atmosphere key to well-being. *Chain Store Age*, *81*(10), 94.

KEY TERMS AND DEFINITIONS

Atmospherics: The conscious designing of space to create certain effects in buyers; the effort to design buying environments to produce specific emotional effects in the buyer that enhance his purchase probability.

Atmospheric Cues: Key dimensions (variables or elements) of an atmosphere such as colour, scent, layout, music, lighting, etc.

Mood: Emotional response produced by external stimulation, which in turn induces psychological change and response.

Music: The art of organized sound, the purpose of which is to elicit an aesthetic response in listeners.

Musical Construct: Musical variables which emit audio signals and interact with auditory receptors to create specific response.

Store Atmosphere: The design of in-store environment by stimulation of the five senses; the store's physical characteristics that project an image to customers.

Chapter 15
Enhancing Retailer–Consumers Relationship through Everyday Sustainability: McDonald's in Italy

Elena Candelo
University of Turin, Italy

Cecilia Casalegno
University of Turin, Italy

Chiara Civera
University of Turin, Italy

ABSTRACT

The chapter aims at investigating the effects that the Communication of Corporate Social Responsibility and Sustainability exerts on consumers' perception considering the fast food industry in Italy. the McDonald's case study has been developed through managerial interviews and formal documents analysis in order to report on its strategies for CSR activities implementation and their communication in Italy. Moreover, through surveys conducted in Italy, the case study has been tested on a particular group of young consumers - Generation Z - less influenced by the past McDonald's activity in order to demonstrate how communications of sustainability are better believed and perceived, when a brand has a long tradition of misperceptions.

INTRODUCTION

In the current market scenario, and mostly under the uncertain economical conditions driving customers towards their purchases, affirming that the more a business is conducted according to certain commonly recognized set of "good" rules and behaviours the more customers will be attracted to it, it is a sort of understatement.

DOI: 10.4018/978-1-5225-2139-6.ch015

This is directly linked to what the business and academic communities define as Corporate Social Responsibility, or, Corporate Sustainability and Responsibility (Visser, 2013), taking as granted that every company that wants to succeed among its customers and, in general, be better perceived by its stakeholders, does have to base its whole business on sustainable practices, regarding the social, the environmental and the economical spheres at the same time.

Consumers are greatly influenced by marketing communications that go beyond the points of sale, meaning that sustainable and responsible business models can sell more than any other marketing message, simply because they are in line with implicit practices and expectations of behaviours (De Pelsmacker *et al.*, 2005).

What said above is more valid when applied to certain business sectors, characterized by a lowered loyalty, increasing in criticisms and misperceptions by customers and stakeholders as well as doubts over the veracity of companies' spread communication messages based on responsible and sustainable practices. Some of these sectors (such as the grocery and the banking) have previously been investigated by the authors (Candelo et al., 2015; 2016) as far as those issues are concerned.

At this stage, the food industry is taken into consideration and, in particular, the retailing fast food industry, characterized by the so called "industry effect" that brings with it misperceptions and misjudgements among stakeholders that create difficulties in establishing, modifying and maintaining players' corporate image and so retain and attract new customers. The case of McDonalds' in Italy is investigated because of the intrinsic problems that the multinational has experienced over time connected to its rationalized and standardized production and sourcing methods, the quality of ingredients and overexploitation of lands and the evident drop in sales as consequence (Crawford et al., 2015). Moreover, the expansion in Italy since 1985 has been accompanied by several everyday challenges linked to the fact that Italy is widely acknowledged for the high quality of its food and the processing and sourcing of raw materials. As a result, McDonald's strategy has started to be shaped and communicated based on a new set of rules.

Understanding what these rules are, how they are communicated and how they, in fact, drive customers' perceptions in a challenging food market such Italy is the aim of the present chapter.

Many are the examples of virtuous fast food companies in different geographical markets (such as Chipotle or Panera Bread Company) that have strongly and proactively shifted their core business based on sustainability in an integrated approach (Freeman ct al., 2010) that overcomes the traditional attitude of giving back to the society only once profit is reached and sees Corporate Social Responsibility or Sustainability implementation as a mere response to the mounting pressures of stakeholders (Torres et al., 2012; De Pedro and Gilabert, 2012; Vallaster et al., 2012; Kuepfer and Papula, 2010; Neal and Cochran, 2008; Freeman et al., 2002; 2004; Macleod, 2001; Mohr et al., 2001).

The present chapter considers that even when CSR and Sustainability are implemented and communicated as responses to customers' or stakeholders' criticisms over a certain business, they can change perception and create higher customers' loyalty under certain conditions for the industry at issue, that are, for instance: the presence of a long-term view, the coherence between promises and performances of CSR and, the focus on a communication over products rather than ideas.

After analysing McDonald's case study in regards to its CSR and sustainability communication efforts into the Italian market, the authors have focused the study on a particular category of consumers in order to test theories and investigate their perception towards McDonald's communication strategies in Italy. Generation Z (people born after 1995 according to Montana and Petit, 2008) has been considered, as it represents the next generation of possible consumers and, at the same time, the future challenge for fast food companies. As it will be reported in the present chapter, this generation seems to be very keen to gather constant information over companies conduct and behaviour, especially about goods and services having a deep impact on human health and planet safety.

In order to achieve its purpose, the chapter is articulated into six sections: the literature review aims at providing an overview of the literature over Corporate Social Responsibility (CSR) and Sustainability, remarking common characteristics no matter the terminology used, the Communication of CSR and insights about the main characteristics of Generation Z, which is the one under investigation. The literature gap reports on the contribution that the research seeks to achieve in the academic debate. The methodology section describes the mixed adopted methodological approaches: McDonald's case study development and surveys on Generation Z to test their perception over CSR communication in the fast food industry. Result discussion is divided into two parts: the first reports the McDonald's case study elaborated by the authors in order to point out its CSR communications in Italy and its repositioning towards sustainability; the second one provides the results from the survey on Generation Z in Italy. The section on Managerial implications and conclusions reports the main findings and their usefulness from a management point of view. Ultimately, Limitations of the study and further researches are to point out the next steps of the investigation.

LITERATURE REVIEW

CSR and Its Communication

In the perspective of the present chapter, the authors refer to Corporate Social Responsibility and Sustainability as a set of non-business and business oriented actions that move forward the traditional mentality of managers who have always considered a trade-off between profitability and responsibility (Waddock and Smith, 2000) to combine together social, environmental, ethical and economical concerns.

Since the early 90's Corporate Social Responsibility (CSR) has strengthened its managerial implications (Carrol, 2008) and its relevance for companies' actions, to include the typical concepts and concerns of sustainability, ethics and environment into the business operations and communication, as concrete practices to implement, develop and spread inside and outside the business organization (Vallaster, Lindgreen, and Maon, 2012; Macleod, 2001; Mohr, Webb, and Harris, 2001; Kuepfer and Papula, 2010; Freeman and Phillips, 2002; Freeman, Wicks and Bidhan, 2004).

Nowadays CSR is largely being strengthened to include a concrete set of tools and planned activities addressed to solve social and environmental issues with positive repercussions on the reference community and ultimately on the existent and potential consumers.

Many authors have given their contribution to enrich CSR meanings according to its evolution in practice.

Corporate Social Responsibility, in its contemporary definition, is vast, complex and involves issues of different kind (Vallaster et al., 2012). Also, the business terminology utilized to indicate the responsibility of the business (no matter the size) has experienced variations. Under the umbrella of Corporate Social Responsibility, Corporate Responsibility, Company Stakeholder Responsibility (Freeman et al., 2006), Integrated Corporate Social Responsibility (Freeman et al., 2010) or Corporate Sustainability and Responsibility (Visser, 2013), it is possible to identify similar activities and practices of sustainability and responsible attitude that companies (depending on their size) carry out and implement with different impacts and implications for their stakeholders in general and consumers, in particular.

Nowadays, it is possible to state that CSR including sustainability implies a repositioning of the business, the creation of new products and services, which are sustainable, ethical and responsible in their value chain, processes, components, materials and, objectives and strives for long-term social, environmental and economic sustainability at the same time (Crane et al., 2013; Visser, 2012; Freeman et al., 2010; Pauli, 2010).

It is, in other words, a new way of positioning and re-positioning businesses and relations with community (Macleod, 2001; Mohr et al., 2001; Kuepfer and Papula, 2010; Freeman et al., 2002; 2004) and meet stakeholders and consumers' evolving expectations (De Pelsmacker et al., 2005; Lopez-De-Pedro and Gilabert, 2012; Waddock and Bodwell, 2007; Neal and Cochran, 2008; Kotler and Lee, 2005; Freeman et al., 2010; Freeman et al., 2002, 2004; Torres et al., 2012) that vary depending on the referred business sector.

The positive repercussions of implementing such strategy of integrated CSR can be seen at different levels: improved working environment affecting employees' productivity, reduced costs connected to waste management processes and lower carbon emissions and energy saving for instance, reduced social and environmental costs, access to new markets and consumers' niches through the development of innovative sustainable and ethical products and services, improved relationships with stakeholder in general, increased loyalty, trust and positive brand perception from consumers, enhanced corporate reputation (Brammer and Millington, 2005; Dawkins and Lewis, 2003; Werther and Chandler, 2005; Haanes et al., 2011; Hur, Kim, and Woo, 2014; Candelo et al., 2015).

Therefore, CSR has turned to a strategy with the aim of modifying and innovating business models according to a sustainable behaviour, for which it has become more and more of a requirement to measure qualitative and quantitative results and performances (Harrison and Freeman, 1999) and therefore, communicate them.

The communication of CSR might raise issues of different kind.

Along with the growth of inclusion and development of CSR strategies and practices within corporates' business, clearly companies have realized the strategic impact that those practices might exert on branding and marketing communication and, obviously, on their consumers. Literature and global researches show that customers' experiences define brand reputation (Uwins, 2014) and, customers' attitudes and purchase intentions are influenced by CSR initiatives – if consumers are aware of them (Pomering and Dolnicar, 2009).

As primary goal of any business, consumers influence and, are affected by, companies' values, beliefs, behaviours and their communication ultimately. Many factors (such as globalization, fast development of information and communication technologies, economic and financial crisis) have contributed, on one hand, to increase consumers' awareness and expectations towards products and services they buy and, on the other hand, have pushed companies to re-think about their offer, their social and environmental impacts and to build a new system of values which responds to the reference community and the society at large (Candelo *et al.*, 2014).

To this regard, CSR communication can positively impact on customers' preferences and perceptions that will ultimately produce better evaluation of the company (Sen and Bhattacharya, 2001; Pomering and Dolnicar, 2009); restoring of loyalty (Matute-Vallejo et al., 2011); creation of positive associations to corporates' brands which ultimately will strengthen corporate's reputation and its competitiveness on the market (Wheeler, 2009; Werther and Chandler, 2005; Hur et al., 2014; Candelo et al., 2014).

However, companies need to be very careful when linking their marketing communication to CSR, as consumers have dramatically lowered their trust towards the veracity of such messages and this is more true when consumers can actually "taste" if what stated reflects the reality, like in the food market, for instance.

In this scenario, consumers increase their confidence through CSR contents that are truly addressed to show results and performances of responsible actions and coherence with the business model; otherwise they seem to associate the communication just to a practice of self-celebration, raising cynics and doubts about the veracity of a certain activity of CSR.

CSR communication needs to be set transparently and show alignment between promises of CSR and achieved performances (de Ven, 2008; Hur et al., 2014).

Any message that does not meet this requirement is most likely to turn perceptions and brand associations in a negative way (Nascuddin and Bustami, 2007) with sever repercussions on customers' trust and confidence and the effectiveness of CSR is therefore uncertain as well (Pomering and Dolnicar, 2009).

The lack of communication barriers and the need of more transparency take to a global confidence crisis and intrinsic doubts about the conduct of fast food multinational companies. People are worried about their wealth and ask for more information to players, together with traceable raw materials and sustainable processes (Dabija and Postelnicu, 2025). In this scenario McDonald's has a hard job to do: the challenge is to turn, into reliable and effective communication, those messages that appear to be "too good to be true", by basing them not on promises but on facts. This strategy can lead to a better stakeholder engagement and customer experience and it is focused on avoiding further doubts about veracity of the various communications.

Accordingly, CSR communication – no matter if it is addressed to marketing purposes, PR, institutional or corporate, financial and organizational – needs to be transparent, homogeneous, coherent, and integrated in the way of reporting on ethics, sustainability, responsibility and environment. It establishes a multi-stakeholder and circular dialogue and, in case of retailers such McDonald's, it creates a connection at the point of sale (in this case restaurant) where consumers can experience what communicated and verify the alignment between their expectations and the company's actions (Siano et al., 2015). In this sense, CSR communication is focused on informing rather than persuading, that is why the communication of performances and concrete results and achievements is preferred to the merely statements of values and promises (de Ven, 2008; Hur et al., 2014) and, at the same time, product communication is most likely to be truly understood and verified by consumers.

According to the Consumer Trend for 2016 reported by Trendwatching (2), nowadays consumers want to experience and have a tangible proof of all the values and promises expressed by companies and strive for a more sustainable and ethical consumerism. In line with a tendency already reported by the Consumer Trend Report in 2013, products are asked to give back a specific set of expected sustainable and responsible values and go even further by showing alignment between promises of values and actual performances in products and services. In every industry, and especially in the food one, are required to be transparent to their audience, to become "naked" in communicating concrete and tangible benefits that go beyond the merely purpose a product is supposed to serve. "Brands' wishes will be consumers' command" (Consumer Trend Report, 2013) (3) and, in this sense, consumers can concretely drive a responsible and sustainable vision of new companies and well-established to shift to new business models and coherent ways of communicating.

Generation Z

Despite the aim and the characteristics of a certain kind of communication, it is important to analyse the target audience. In particular, differences among generations exist and shape their members' reactions to the same message. According to the literature, many definitions of generations exist. A first considers that people belonging to the same generation have lived deep economic and social changes in the environment they have experienced (Mannheim, 1952). A second one starts from the point that people living at the same time in the same environment share a system of patterns of perception, thought and action that are stably acquired and generated by objective conditions, but which tend to persist even after the change of these conditions (Bourdieu, 1990). According to what said above, despite the term generation traditionally wants to define an age difference about 25 year, it is not true in the modern society. In fact in the western societies, generations seem to have shortened the period of their succession and the final output is that the habitus of a generation changes every in less than two decades. Despite the definitions of generation coming from the Second World War are a lot, the authors consider the ones written by Kotler and Armstrong (2012), considering that the economical and societal development has begun in USA before that in UE. Baby booms were born between 1946 and 1964, the Generation X is composed by people born between 1965- 1976, while Generation Y is the sum of people born between 1977 and 1994 (also called Millenials or Echo Boomers). These two Generations differ each other form the fact that Gen Y is the first truly digital and networking Generation and it represents challenges for marketers since this is a fragmented generation in many thrives with distinctive life styles, dress codes, and associated music (Kotler and Armstrong, 2012). Despite the differences between the two generations, it is necessary to underline that they have something in common: they still believe that firms can be ethic and responsible and they give their confidence in organizations that tell them about their CSR results, because their idealism (Kotler *et al.*, 2009; Montana and Petit, 2008). Instead, literature (Harvey et al., 2014) and managerial studies concerning the Generation Z (coming after the Y one), according to our knowledge, don't consider enough attitudes and behaviours this Gen Z has towards organizations in general, even if this generation appears peculiar as it shows greater interest to the topics of sustainability and responsibility, to the concept of interaction and transparency as key elements of communication more than other previous generations. This is a Generation who, in most cases, is the offspring of Generation X, people are born after 1996 and who are also known as a Generation self-examining. Since Z people are more involved in environmental problems, when compared to the other generations, it is to underline that they are sceptic towards business organizations and they are more prone to quit their job if it doesn't respect sustainability standards they have in their mind (Korean Times, November 13, 2007). According to Monatana and Petit (2008), Gen Y is against a rigid working schedule, but appreciates a more flexible job, moreover it is very knee when it finds a working place in which ideas are respected and the personal initiative is spurred. In our opinion, this characteristics of Gen Y have an impact on Gen Z, which, in addiction, have developed an intrinsic curiosity towards the environment as the whole. The difference from Gen Y is that Z people want to be frequently evaluated in order to improve their skills, capabilities and knowledge. The major consequence of this habitus is the constant desire of receiving information also over corporations they get in touch with and their product.

The investigation over Generation Z is particularly interesting, considering that fat food players, like McDonalds', have made, in the latest years, first attempts of transformation both regarding products and communication. From the side of product, there is a stretching of the portfolio in terms of sustainability, whilst from the side of the communication, the effort is about to strengthen the relationships between the firm and its consumers. Moreover, Generation Z has been the youngest bunch of people having assisted to the strategic challenge in fast food markets. Since, for this reason, Z people has been less exposed to the original McDonalds' strategy, it represents the ideal panel to test the possible perception differences concerning the characterization of the player' s brand in terms of image, products and distribution formula.

LITERATURE GAP

Despite the academic literature and empirical researches on the use and the communication of Corporate Social Responsibility and Sustainability as strategies to turn consumers' perception positively and improve the corporate image are vast, little has been written on how to set up a communication for CSR when both the business sector and the company's image is critical and has been subjected to misperceptions and negative opinions about certain intrinsic characteristics of its business models for decades and since its foundation, throughout several geographical markets.

Moreover, the study seeks to fill a research gap as far as the investigation of a generation of consumers is concerned. Few are the current academic and managerial studies considering Generation Z and its perception over the CSR communication of multinational players in the food industry. Filling this gap means providing first results on how the CSR communication should be framed when related to traditional fast food retailers to better impact on young consumers and, potentially, show that a change of mind-set and perception is possible but only under certain conditions.

Accordingly, the purpose of the chapter is to respond to the following research questions:

Q1: How can a re-known brand among global fast food companies set up its CSR communication strategy more effectively in order to improve and solidify consumers' perception?
Q2: How the CSR communication affects Generation Z consumers?

In order to give answers to the research questions, as already said below, the authors have chosen to consider the global fast food chain McDonald's. It represents an interesting case of investigation for exploring and explaining the efforts in communication and the strategies undertaken in order to increase the customer experience and the engagement of stakeholders. Caused by the many intrinsic negative aspects connected to the American giant's core business. Critiques have been developed around the implemented processes damaging lands and territories, the use of substances potentially compromising the quality of both resources and products, until the employment policies (Candelo et al., 2016). It is to underline that this critiques are not just the output of buzzes, but they come from reference communities, researchers, academics, journalists, writers, internal and external clients, associations and environmental groups (Etzioni, 1986; Hawken, 2002; Blythe, 2005; Botteril and Kline, 2007). In particular, the case analysis wants to focus the attention on efforts spent by the re-known player in terms of sustainability and its responsibility towards the different communities involved in its business.

METHODOLOGY

The present research represents a step forward and it is part of a broaden research over the retail and fast food industry (Candelo et al., 2016). The chapter has adopted a mixed methodological approach:

the case study elaboration and the empirical stakeholder survey. The case study elaboration has been based on qualitative research of objective information over McDonald's and its integrated CSR communication strategies adopted in Italy only. The case study has considered both actions (such as products communication, point of sales communication and participation to events) and published documents and records from websites related to the company, company's institutional web site, press release, annual reports (Sustainability Reports, Social Reports, Code of Ethics). All the information has been collected through a period of 1 year starting from April 2015. The case study has been boosted by interviews to McDonald's Italian Top Management, who have provided a company's perspective and strategic insights over the developed communications and contributed to test the adopted methodology and the managerial implications.

From the side of the empirical survey, the authors have investigated from young stakeholders' perspective, the impact and effectiveness of different kinds of communications over sustainable products and processes, by testing groups over McDonald' CSR strategies (and communication) and the same strategies adopted by a factitious case.

Participants to survey have been asked to give their opinion around McDonald's case study and a factitious similar business case set up ad-hoc by the authors. Concerning the factitious case, the authors have utilized the role playing method in marketing research (Surprenant, and Churchill, 1984; Moncrief, 1991). The business case, named Etiristo & Co., has been built after having conducted researches over fast food best practices (Tencati and Zsolnai, 2012; Kojola, 2013; Shokri et al., 2014; Gerhardt et al., 2014) and new concepts restaurants trends.

Etiristo & Co. functions as opposite control case against McDonald's. Its business model is, accordingly, designed with intrinsic sustainable and responsible practices in the sourcing of materials, production, distribution and the approach to the target market. Etiristo & Co. is a local business reality, with no international investments and a brand positioning between a fast food and a traditional restaurant. On the other hand McDonald's, the principal considered case of fast food chain in our chapter, maintains its international positioning together with its "glocal" approach (Candelo et al., 2016).

The market research on people belonging to Gen Z has been conducted during the Autumn 2015 and first year university students composed the sample. This has been composed by a total of 546 Italian people (48% male, 52% female), consumers and non-consumers, aged from 18 to 19. The surveys on the sample have been structured online (Google Drive) and they were delivered through web platforms. They were presented to students in the classrooms and, at the same time, the two cases (McDondal's and Etiristo) were explained. In order to facilitate the moderation of results, half a sample was asked to fill the survey about McDonalds' - to monitor and measure their reactions to its CSR communication - and the other half the one concerning Etiristo & Co.

Two scenarios have been presented and explained to every group, which consisted in two different communication efforts in two different years: 2009 and 2015. The premise has been that it was necessary for all the participants to be aware of both the case histories.

The two scenarios are explained below:

1. **First Scenario:** The 2009. McDonald's communication efforts are ad-dressed to report on their ingredients controlled sourcing (Italian meet, for instance) and the introduction of fresh products in the menus. Moreover, in this year strategic future goals in terms of sustainability (both regarding the environment and the society) are more frequent. In a small town near Turin (Piedmont, Italy) a newly concept of fast food restaurant opens its doors to families: Etiristo & Co. From the

name to the business model, the restaurant is centred on sustainability, ethics and responsibility, with classical formula of hamburger and chips tailored also on vegans, vegetarians and celiac. The restaurant core business is based on controlled km 0 ingredients and a short supply chain, with physical evidence strictly linked to the territory tradition. Both products (meat, chips, vegetables and fruits) and processes are certified by National and International Standard to guarantee their sustainability.

2. **Second Scenario:** The 2015. This is the year old the Universal Exposition (Expo 2015, Milano) and McDonald's is one of the Official Sponsors of this event with a pavilion to promote its history and the evolution of McDonald's Italia. McDonald's has strengthened its efforts in order to meet emerged society trends concerning a healthier lifestyle. The green "new" layout is a visual output of this product and communication strategy. On the other hand, the fast food Etiristo & Co. continues its strategy by developing new products according to its business model and the ultimate concerns towards the sustainability. Its target market is still the Piedmont one, but Etiristo & Co. communicates its intention to open new restaurant in Italy and is evaluating a greenfield investment abroad, by maintaining the same business model.

Per each scenario people were interviewed towards their perception as a re-action to the two restaurants different communications. To do that, every group had to rank its level of confidence about the restaurant it had been assigned to. For the purpose, the authors have adopted a Likert scale going from 0 (being zero the lowest level of confidence) to 5 (being five the maximum level of confidence). In order to choose CSR communication KPIs to test, the literature review over the topic of CSR communication has been considered. Accordingly, elements resulting from the review of the literature have met other elements coming from the study of the case. The output has been a total of three different kinds of communications that the authors have tested. They are: product communication, sustainable communication and brand perception after having known sustainable results.

Moreover, every group has been interviewed on the colours of the McDonald's brand, per each scenario, in order to test the degree of perception towards the evolution of McDonald's brand communication strategy.

Eventually, every survey has been composed including a question concerning the total perception of the fast food player to which it refers.

RESULTS DISCUSSION

A Sustainable Repositioning: McDonald's in Italy

Over time, McDonald's has imposed its brand as one of the main symbols of globalization and characterized its production on rationalization of resources in order to achieve a cost-effective offer to meet mass target's demand for cheap food. Such strategy, which has been implemented since the very foundation of the multinational American company, brought with it several issues and divergent opinions from the community and general stakeholders about the influence and the negative impact over the cultural, societal and environmental spheres in each of the Countries the business has been developing.

As a matter of facts, the huge impact of McDonald's business model even on the life-style of its consumers has been one of the main reasons for the brand to be most likely attacked and criticized by the academic community by opinion leaders, environmental groups, consumers and non-consumers. The multinational's way of conducting its business has been seen and directly linked to typical characterizations of the fast capitalism growth, which has certainly worked in past and helped McDonald's reach a global success, while it is, lately, the object of many arguments and concerns about whether growing at any cost – especially in a sector like the food one – can be ineffective for the society, the land, the animals, the environment, and even for consumers' health.

Criticisms to McDonald's business model have dramatically spread their echo due to a global presence never really experienced before within the food retailers industry.

The core business of McDonald's sees its roots in the vision of Ray Kroc's, who was a Multimixer former sales representative for Richard and Maurice McDonald's restaurants chain and, who, fascinated by the business model based on self-service and drive-in, opened the first McDonald's restaurant in Des Plaines, Illinois on the 15th of April 1955. Based on low-cost hamburgers, he believed that such model of consumption would have become the future trend in the food retailing industry.

Since its foundation, McDonald's formula based its success on entry-level products chain selling affordable and convenient fast food, suitable and appealing for the mass market and their need of cheaper prices, quick meal and simple ingredients.

The American giant has created a 360° new experience inside the restaurant, which became soon a popular destination among families and also an innovative ready-to-go fast food place with the McDrive locations, where consumers can pass by, order and be delivered their food straight from the cars. These points of difference in the offer led to a quick growth in profits and market penetration.

The formal birth McDonald's Corporation - and its "Golden Arches" brand – happened in 1960, immediately as a company ready to take up the challenge of multinational presence. Not by chance, McDonald's has always been considered the very symbol of the American dream by exporting low-cost fast food for a growing target market with similar expectations, starting from meeting a demand of fast and cheap food by American baby boomers and working-women during the '60s (Mourdoukoutas, 2013).

Following a quick expansion all over the world in traditional and emerging markets facilitated by markets opening, integration, and globalization process happening in the '70s along with a mass marketing approach and communication and creating products that are still nowadays included in its the core offer and menu (such as the Big Mac since 1967), the American brand enters the Italian boundaries in 1985, approaching a more difficult and challenging market as far as food culture, quality and excellence are concerned.

The values pursued by Kroc 's idea of business model are based, since the creation of McDonald 's Corporation on pillars that nowadays the company uses as levers to strengthen its Social Responsibility Strategy: from a speech by Kroc 's "... If you love this business ... show it ... work at it ... show it with your employees and in your community..." The communication of a business taking care of the community its employees and its consumers has represented, on one hand, an element for a winning communication strategy, on the other hand, has made McDonald's more exposed to criticisms of various nature, coming from different stakeholders groups.

Combined to the stated attention to the community, there is the other side of the coin. What Ritzer in 2004 defines as McDonaldization refers to the set of managerial key principles leading to the Group's success on global markets, which are mainly based on rationalization and standardization and perceived as threats to the community wellbeing. First of all, the choice of materials and ingredients that are cost-efficient, necessary to offer low-priced hamburgers; secondly, strict controls on the production process and processes standardization in terms of workflow and main core products.

Not surprisingly, with a fast and impacting growth, the success has exposed McDonald's to criticisms impacting negatively on stakeholders' perception and, over time, deteriorating the market shares.

As already mentioned, due to intrinsic characteristics of the products, the service concept and the production processes, following the rules of resource rationalization and globalization, McDonald's business model and communication campaigns have been subjected, over the years, to strong criticisms coming from various sources: reference communities, researchers, academics, journalists, writers, external and internal customers, associations and environmental groups (Etzioni, 1986; Hawken, 2002; Blythe, 2005; Botteril e Kline, 2007). It is possible to affirm that the competitive advantages on which McDonald's business model and communications have been built on have represented, at the same time, limitations, which became more and more evident over the years. That is because of increasing awareness among the audience and public opinion about environmental and nutritional issues as well as sustainability and social responsibility matters, along with a cultural evolution and affirmation of new reference values especially in relation to the food sector (Candelo et al., 2016).

Standardization and globalization have been put under question and highly criticized that they started representing threats for the American multinational and, paradoxically, transforming its strengths into internal weaknesses. To report some of the most common criticisms: crops and livestock farming standardization have been accused to bring with it the destruction of biodiversity; the promotion and sale of food with an high fat content and sugar that is directed to a young target audience have been criticized to exert devastating nutritional effects (Hawken, 2002). Moreover, the competitive advantage in terms of efficiency is related to the highly criticized monoculture systems, intensive live storms, which cause deforestation and the increment in the use of antibiotics and artificial growth hormones for feeding chickens and cows (Botteril e Kline, 2007).

At the same time, the rationalization of labour force, which, on one hand, has meant substituting human resources in restaurants with technological resources and, on the other hand, has implied the increasing hiring of young people and immigrants with lower salaries, has represented one of the main issues of concerns for the public opinion associated with social problems. Accordingly, on the 24th of August 1986 Amita Etzioni (Professor at George Washington University) in her article "The Fast-Food Factory: McJobs are Bad for Kids", published on the Washington Post, coins the term "McJob", which will become part of the common language in the same year. The author defined the "McJob" as a routine job, supervised and controlled by managers who do not favour self-supervision and do not represent examples to emulate and therefore a job that does not succeed as educational opportunity. The term becomes part of the Oxford Dictionary in the same year (1986) as a synonym of "A low paid job with few prospects" (oxforddictionaries.com) (Candelo et al., 2016)

In response to the already mentioned drop in sales and profit since 1998 (Botteril and Kline, 2007), communication strategies at a global level have seen a shift – like a sort of response – to include sustainability, ethics and environment as main contents and matters of concerns. Moreover, this appears to represent an alignment to the main global competitors' actions and communications. In America, for instance, McDonald's reputation has been put under risk also by the intense growth of players like Chipotle Mexican Grill (the Mexican chain that has won McDonald's sales over) (Wood, 2014; Wong, 2014), Five Guys and Panera Bread, that are innovating their business models including organic, bio, fresh, healthy and sustainable choices of products in their offer and extensively communicating about this (Candelo et al., 2016).

It is clear that McDonald's did not respond as quick as some of its competitors in the implementation of CSR activities and sustainable practices and neither in their communication, mostly because of the size of its business, which made the reaction slower and the change in perception probably even more.

The effort put by McDonald's in implementing sustainable and responsible practices related to its food production, its delivery and the whole supply chain started to be formally communicated in the early 2002, precisely in 2002, the American Giant publishes the first Social Responsibility Report, with the aim of underlying increasing attention towards the environment, ethics and food quality and healthier solutions for its consumers.

In the Report the Group highlights three strategies which they declare to base their business on from that moment onwards: the attention to human resources in terms of salaries and contracts, the focus on consumers in order to guarantee excellence in ingredients and operations, and the growth in profits in regards to the Company and all the partners throughout the supply chain (intermediaries and suppliers). The communication strategy is articulated around 4 macro areas in which McDonald's states to be creating value with honesty, integrity and ethical standards: the Community, the Environment, People (internal human resources and staff), and the Market (intended as suppliers and consumers). Despite the Social Responsibility Report has contributed to formalize the communication of new values driving the business, audience's perception over the veracity of such information still was not aligned with McDonald's intentions. Some criticisms form the academic community, for instance, are built around the fact that the Report would represent just an attempt of communication in order to merely respond to reputation crises, without representing a concrete shift of actions, goals and strategies (Hawken, 2002) (Candelo et al., 2016).

In some years later when McDonald's concretely tackles the challenge of a strategic repositioning, modifying marketing and communication levers in crucial markets, where reputation crises have strongly shaped specific needs and expectations around the American multinational's business. Accordingly, embracing a more sustainable route and giving attention to food quality and taste represent the main goals of such strategy, with a strong reshaping of communication.

Since 2007, the Group has announced, in the press and on its website, the concrete initiative to foresee the recycling of used oils for cooking and frying, which would be used for the production of biofuel, part of which is intended for transportation of materials and drinks from the distribution centres to the McDonald's restaurants.

Such sustainable strategy takes shape on the fact that once the multinational achieved a strong capillarity they started thinking about adapting more to the reference territory, by innovating their business model and tailoring offers and communications in order to meet consumers' habits and expectations all over the world.

The repositioning strategy has started from France in 2008, involving firstly the Mediterranean countries, including Italy, where the need of restoring a more valuable reputation and responding to on-going needs for quality and sustainability have been felt necessary to maintain the growth for the upcoming 10 years. The rebranding, shifting the typical red colour to the green is a strong sign of communication, on the press, the websites and on the point of sale.

As reported by the Chief Executive Officer at McDonald's Italy, the repositioning strategy has been set up around more than 10 strategic levers, by re-thinking products, ingredients, service, processes, consumption models, supply chain, workplace, restaurants layout, brand, websites, relations with the local communities. In all these areas, both marketing and integrated communication (institutional or corporate, PR, financial and organizational) have played a key role to gradually and positively modify and affect stakeholders' perception.

Clearly, the implementation of such actions needs time and lots of efforts, especially when it comes to a giant and well-established company like McDonald's.

That is why it is worthy and interesting to point out how this process of repositioning has been integrated with the existent strategies and which communications have been put a stronger accent in order to change stakeholders' perception and in which period of time the expected results can be achieved.

The focus of the chapter is put on the Italian market as it is considered very challenging in regards to the new McDonald's strategy and constitutes an example of food culture that has imposed considerable modifications in the multinational's approach to consumers, who are confirming specific and healthy food choices (such as vegetarian, vegan and, bio), and want to see reflection of this in a coherent and transparent communication activity.

The repositioning strategy in Italy has been developed gradually by implementing and communicating one topic at a time in order not to create confusion in stakeholders' minds and it is expected to take more than 10 years to orientate their perception towards McDonald's as a good food fast destination. In particular, the strategy has been articulated in seven areas, considered key for the Italian audience.

1. **Placement/Layout:** Restaurants were originally born in American style, serving cheap and standardized food. The aim of the strategy is to turn them into contemporary, modern, more spacious food destinations, characterized by better aesthetics and new characterizations of food, which is now thought to bring people together, enjoying a longer staying for pleasure and leisure.
2. **Integration with the Urban Context:** This concept refers to Corporate Social Responsibility in the sense that restaurants are being renovated to match with their reference environment with less impacting material, with a challenging goal of reusing the oil for transportations and rely on solar panel energy in most of the Italian restaurants. Moreover, plants and flowers are being introduced outdoors within wood decorations. Layout is set up more with restaurant logic than a distributor one, like it was in the past. This change is considered a consistent upgrade addressed to concretely influence perception towards sustainability and community engagement, as it is based on experience.
3. **Products and Ingredients:** The aim of McDonald's is not to modify their core products, instead to extend the line in order to match with specific tastes and local needs. The increase in the use of chicken as well as local and bio ingredients, the reduction in the use of antibiotics, respond to a greater demand from Italian consumers, who would rather sacrifice higher price to being delivered local products.
4. **Re-Shoring:** Localization is achieved by re-shoring the main sources for production. In particular, the cows are grown in Italy (75% from Amadori, for instance), milk its derivatives come from Brescia and, parmesan is the real Italian "Parmigiano Reggiano".
5. **Re-Branding:** The original red colour as background of the "Golden Arches" of McDonald's logo has been substituted by the green colour with the aim of communicating a change of attitude towards more sustainable practices.
6. **New Consumption Model:** the "Cafeteria service" has been introduced in Italy to test its potentials and nowadays McDonald's owns 280 Italian style cafeterias between Italy and abroad placed inside the existent restaurants. The implementation and strong communication about "breakfast at McDonald's" aimed at attracting new consumers and make the current offer more appealing by taking advantage of the exclusive quality coffee McDonald's is serving. The combination of newly introduced products (such as the coffee) with core ones creates a "halo effect" increasing the perception of the existent.

7. **Inclusion of CSR Contents in Communication:** Communication strategy has been developed around pillars reflecting sustainability and responsibility. First of all, familiar products are implemented and communicated in order to fight junk food perception, especially among younger generations. Secondly, misperceptions related to the "Mcjob" issues are dealt with by communicating a growing attention towards job market and young people employment. The multinational places itself as entry level job place for students and communication is set up around their commitment to the company. The activation of the McItaly Job Tour (through which McDonald's recruits people in public squares) represents one of the strongest and most concrete communication tools to activate a positive word of mouth and fight the prejudgements of working at McDonald's. Such campaign has taken advantage of the crisis period and high unemployment rate in Italy to communicate that the Company was creating more than 1000 job positions per year and that they were one of the biggest employers in Italy. Investments in such communications have been positively reflected also in an increased commitment from people already working at McDonald's. Thirdly and eventually, the focus on young generations well-being has driven the Company to communicate over nutritional values and lower the percentage of fat and sugar in their products, with a strong commitment to include in the Happy Meal menus juices, milk and water as core products by 2020, (4).

Results from The Survey on Generation Z in Italy

A total of 435 people filled the online survey and, precisely, the 45% of the respondents answered to the McDonald's survey, whilst the 55% to the Etiristo & Co. one. The differences concerning the rate of the answers were not remarkable. Per each scenario the authors have asked the groups to rate their perception towards the two restaurant chains. As the Table 1 shows, the 51% of the analysed sample does not usually consume fast food at all. On the other side, the 35% of the sample asserts to be a strong McDonald's consumer. This shows that the brand McDonald's has a large awareness, because the brand was strongly recognized by every interviewed person.

People in every group were tested about the colours of the brand McDonald's and, as shown below (Table 2), few of them have realized that the restaurant layout, together with the background of the brand design, have changed turning from red to green. The interesting result is that people didn't recognize the green background even after the Expo period, in which the logo exposition was huge and frequent.

Concerning the comparison between McDonald's and the factitious case (Etiristo & Co.), it is interesting to underline that the two cases have different business models, histories and brand heritage. First of all, this is a global multinational company with a high brand awareness, very known by young people (Generation Z as well) not just as a restaurant, but also as an entertainment and a meeting place. This is the reason why the consumption experience mean is very high; in 2009 the mean is 4 out of 5 and this is due to the fact that teenagers usually perceive McDonald's as place though which they can meet friends without any food concerns. When people grow, their concerns about food and environmental problems grow as well as stated by Montana and Petit (2008) and this is the reason why their consumption experience decreases to 3.6 in 2015.

From the side of Etiristo & Co., the consumption experience lightly decreases to 3.3 from the beginning of its business (2009) to the 2015, due to the territorial expansion, which could bring to a target dilution and modify the brand identity by adding the international meaning. This could cause the partial lost of sustainable basis of the original business model and this could confuse the target.

On the other hand, what is communicated and how has an impact on the brand perception and this is proved by the results gathered towards the product communication and the sustainable one. McDonald's results show that the increasing of product perception is incremental among the considered years, passing from 1.4 in 2009 to 1.8 in 2015, whilst it is lightly incremental the perception of the business sustainability after the communication of the future activities: promises are not sufficient for the audience, at least they are not enough to effectively increase the sustainability perception by the audience. McDonald's passes from a mean of 2.4 to a result of 2.7 in 2015. Accordingly, the brand perception after being aware of sustainable results reports a major augment from a mean of 2.4 to a mean of 2.9 in 2015. This result shows that tangible results can shape the perception better that promises can do: even in this case the way is long for a multinational company which for years has been carrying on its shoulders the weight of being the industry leader and a symbol of the American business culture. This last result is reinforced by the one concerning Etiristo: in this case the restaurant maintains its promises by showing results during time and it takes to a light increase of brand perception up to 3.8.

Table 1. Consumer/non-consumers at the time of the research

	Fast Food	McDonald's
Consumers	51%	36%
Non-consumers	49%	64%

Source: authors' personal processing.

Table 2. McDonald's brand colours perception during the years

Brand Colours	Answers 2009	Answers 2015
Red and gold	92.5%	58.5%
Green and gold	7.5%	41.5%
Blue and gold	-	-

Source: authors' personal processing.

Table 3. Z generation McDonald's perception at the time of the research

McDonald's Perception in 2015	%
American multinational company, symbol of consumerism	47.4
Multinational company worrying about sustainability	17.5
Meeting place to have fun	13.4
Not real behavioural change from the past	21.6

Source: authors' personal processing.

Table 4. Z Generation Etiristo & Co. perception at the time of the research

Etiristo & Co. Perception in 2015	%
Sustainable local restaurant	25.7
Restaurant worrying to improve the community	28.6
Meeting place to have fun	5.7
Keeps its promises	7.1
Just the usual fast food	32.9

Source: authors' personal processing.

Table 5. Young stakeholder perception evolution

	2009		2015	
	Mc	Eti	Mc	Eti
Product communication	1.4	3.3	1.8	4.5
Sustainable communication	2.4	4.1	2.7	4
Brand perception after having known sustainable results	2.4	3.5	2.9	3.8
Consumption experience	4.2	3.5	3.6	3.3

Source: authors' personal processing.

CONCLUSION

The analysis of the consider sample, together with its attitudes towards fast food players, confirms what literature states: youngest people are skeptical about multinational organizations behaviours and, above all, their CSR communication. At the same time, their brand perception can be improved with the communication about real results in terms of sustainability. Nevertheless, the CSR results and product communication is not positively related with the consumption experience. In fact, considering the McDonald's case, it seems that the answers are influenced by the global image of the player as a symbol of American capitalism (47.4% of the tested sample). The analysis of McDonald's communication strategies, together with the results of the investigation on Generation Z, led the authors to suggest some considerations in order to give an answer to the two research questions. This can represent a sum of tips, which can be generally adapted to large multinational companies in the form of restaurant chains targeting Z Generations above all. Two premises are required: first of all, clearly, for these companies, is hard to maintain the same level of product and service quality in the long while and in every country, they are and eventually to drive differently. Secondly, results from communication activity are under a longer gestation process.

Since the first research question (RQ1) of the present chapter is about how to implement the CSR communication strategy to do so that it can have a positive impact on the brand perception, the case study shows that: the stronger the brand awareness and exposition is, the longer is the strategic repositioning; the transformation of soft skills - such as sustainability and responsibility - into core activities, both concrete and communicated, requires a long period to positively turn the brand perception; it is fundamental to choose one topic of communication at a time, in order not to create confusion in stakeholders' mind, even when the target is willing to embrace multiple inputs.

On the other side, the research done in order to give answers to the second question (RQ2) led the authors to consider that differently form the past, standardization has shifted to new meanings concerning sustainable communication and strategies are required to be shaped according to the cultural environment they refer to. Not all the Countries are in the same stage of understanding and applying CSR and sustainability practices. In particular, Generation Z in Italy appears to be highly committed to CSR and sustainability as drivers in the food industry, especially in a future perspective. Moreover, being CSR and Communication integrated strategically, communication strategy needs to be oriented to report on results and performances rather that promises and values. Generation Z is, in fact, more receptive to achievements that are evident in the point of sale and proved by the media. Eventually, Generation Z is better influenced by coherence and sustainability in communication. The factious case study suggests that changes in a business model, which is sustainable itself and bases its communication on that, requires more prudency. The increase in number of restaurants (for instance related to internationalization strategy) could bring with it issues of different kind. First, attracting a different target with difficulties connected to the coexistence of heterogeneous groups experiencing the same consumption model and could also impact on misperception of a homogeneous communication strategies oriented to sustainability.

Both the case studies and the surveys over young stakeholder brand perception confirm that, in order to see concrete benefits from a repositioning strategy of such giant player, communication efforts have to be implemented for a long period of time. However, considering that Generation Z, being born after 1996, does not have a well-established positioning of McDonald's in their minds, given their very young age, it might take less time to create new perceptions. According to the results of the surveys, on one hand, Generation Z is more receptive to changes in communication, on the other hand, it appears to be more judgemental regarding CSR strategies stated by multinational companies.

Limitations of the Study and Further Research

The study is focused on the CSR communication strategies and consumers' perceptions over those in a limited geographical area: Italy. Moreover, McDonald's case study has been tested through surveys on the sample of Generation Z consumers by comparing it to a factitious case study. The elaboration of a factitious case study that the authors have based on sustainability at the core of the business might, therefore, have influenced the sample of tested consumers to turn their perception more positively towards the factitious brand.

To this regard, the authors plan two extensions of the research. The first will be to include wider geographical areas in the testing of Generation Z perception towards CSR communication of fast food players in order to point out both McDonald's differentiated CSR communication strategies and variations in perceptions based on different cultural and market conditions. The second evolution of the study will be to compare McDonald's CSR communication strategies to competitors, which have implemented a sustainability-oriented business and base their selling proposal and their success on it.

REFERENCES

Barriaux, M. (2007, July 5). McDonald's goes green–but not all customers are lovin' it. *The Guardian.*

Blythe, J. (2005). *Essentials of marketing*. Pearson Education.

Botterill, J., & Kline, S. (2007). From McLibel to McLettuce: Childhood, spin and re-branding. *Society and Business Review*, *2*(1), 74–97. doi:10.1108/17465680710725281

Bourdieu, P. (1990). *The Logic of Practice*. Cambridge: Polity Press.

Brammer, S., & Millington, A. I. (2005). Corporate Reputation and philanthropy: An empirical analysis. *Journal of Business Ethics*, *61*(1), 29–44. doi:10.1007/s10551-005-7443-4

Candelo, E., Casalegno, C., & Civera, C. (2014). Meanings and implications of corporate social responsibility and branding in grocer retailers: A comparative study over Italy and the UK. In Handbook of Research on Retailer-Consumer Relationship Development (p. 351).

Candelo, E., Casalegno, C., & Civera, C. (2015). Towards Corporate Shared Value in Retail Sector: A Comparative Study over Grocery and Banking Between Italy and the UK. *The International Journal of Economic Behavior-IJEB*, *5*(1), 105–120.

Candelo, E., Civera, C., & Casalegno, C. (2016). Communication for preventing reputational risk. McDonald's strategy and its impact on the Italian market. In *V. Cantino, P. Devincentiis & D. Racca (2016). Risk Management: Perspectives and Open Issues* (pp. 461–476). McGraw-Hill.

Carrol, A. B. (2008). A History of Corporate Social Responsibility, Concepts and Practices. In A. Crane, D. Matten, A. McWilliams, J. Moon, & D. S. Siegel (Eds.), *The Oxford Handbook of Corporate Social Responsibility*. OUP Oxford.

Crane, A., Matten, D., & Spence, L. J. (2013). Corporate Social Responsibility: in a global context. In A. Crane, D. Matten, & L. J. Spence (Eds.), *Corporate social responsibility: readings and cases in a global context*. Abingdon: Routledge.

Crawford, A. (2015). McDonald's: A Case Study in Glocalization. *Journal of Global Business Issues, 9*(1), 11.

Dabija, D. C., & Postelnicu, C. (2015). McDonald's-between Internationalization and Regionalization of Restaurant's Value. *Review of Management & Economic Engineering, 14*(1).

Dawkins, J., & Lewis, S. (2003). CSR in stakeholder expectations: And their implication for company strategy. *Journal of Business Ethics, 44*(2), 185–193. doi:10.1023/A:1023399732720

De Pelsmaker, P., Janssen, W., & Mielants, C. (2005). Consumer values and fair-trade beliefs, attitudes and buying behaviour. *International Review on Public and Non Profit Marketing*, *2*(2), 50–69.

De Ven, B. (2008). An Ethical Framework for the Marketing of Corporate Social Responsibility. *Journal of Business Ethics, 82*(2), 339–352. doi:10.1007/s10551-008-9890-1

Duncan, T. (2001). *IMC: Using Advertising & Promotion to Build Brands*. Boston: McGrawHill.

Duncan, T., & Mulhern, F. (2004). A White Paper on the Status, Scope and Future of IMC. New York: McGraw-Hill

Etzioni, A. (1986, August 24). The Fast-Food Factories: McJobs are Bad for Kids. *The Washington Post.*

Freeman, R. E., & Phillips, R. A. (2002). Stakeholder theory: A libertarian defence. *Business Ethics Quarterly, 12*(3), 333. doi:10.2307/3858020

Freeman, R. E., & Velamuri, S. R. (2006). A new approach to CSR: Company stakeholder responsibility. In Corporate social responsibility (pp. 9-23). UK: Palgrave Macmillan.

Freeman, R. E., Wicks, A., Harrison, J., Parmar, B., & de Colle, S. (2010). *Stakeholder Theory: The State of The Art*. Cambridge University Press. doi:10.1017/CBO9780511815768

Freeman, R. E., Wicks, A. C., & Parmar, B. (2004, May-June). Stakeholder Theory and The Corporate Objective Revisited. *Organization Science, 15*(3), 364–369. doi:10.1287/orsc.1040.0066

Gasca P. (2014, July 29). McDonald's Rebranding Strategy: Why the World's Biggest Restaurant Thinks It's Time to Tweak Its Recipe. *Inc.com.*

Gerhardt, S., Hazen, S., & Lewis, S. (2014). Small Business Marketing Strategy Based on McDonald's. *ASBBS Proceedings, 21*(1), 271.

Haanaes, K., Balagopal, B., Arthur, D., Kong, M. T., Velken, I., Kruschwitz, N., & Hopkins, M. S. (2011). First Look: The Second Annual Sustainability & Innovation Survey. *Sloan Management Review*, *52*(2).

Harrison, J. S., & Freeman, R. E. (1999). Stakeholders, Social Responsibility, and Performance: Empirical Evidence and Theoretical Perspectives. *Academy of Management Journal*, *42*(5), 479–485. doi:10.2307/256971

Harvey, J. K., & Nancy, L. G. (2014). Work values and beliefs of Generation X and Generation Y. *Journal of Youth Studies*, *17*(1), 92–112. doi:10.1080/13676261.2013.815701

Hawken, P. (2002). McDonald's and Corporate Social Responsibility, Press Release from Food First. *Institute for Food and Development Policy.*

Hur, W. M., Kim, H., & Woo, J. (2014). How CSR Leads to Corporate Brand Equity: Mediating Mechanisms of Corporate Brand Credibility and Reputation. *Journal of Business Ethics*, *125*(1), 75–86. doi:10.1007/s10551-013-1910-0

Jackson, K. T. (2004). *Building reputational capital: Strategies for integrity and fair play that improve the bottom line*. Oxford University Press.

Kliatchko, J. (2008). Revisiting the IMC construct: A revised definition and four pillars. *International Journal of Advertising*, *27*(1), 133–160.

Kojola, E. (2013). Serving Food Justice: A Union Campaign for Fresh Food, Health, and Sustainability. *Journal of Workplace Rights*, *17*(2), 175–191. doi:10.2190/WR.17.2.d

Kotler, P., & Armstrong, G. (2012). *Principles of marketing*. Prentice Hall Inc.

Kotler, P., Armstrong, G., Saunders, J., & Wong, V. (2009). *Principles of Marketing*. Prentice Hall.

Kotler, P., & Lee, N. (2005). *Corporate Social Responsibility. Doing the Most Good for Your Company and Your Cause*. Hoboken: Wiley.

Kuepfer, J., & Papula, J. (2010). Corporate social responsibility – the dilemmas behind the popular concept and how to best address them. *International Journal of Sustainable Society*, *2*(3), 291. doi:10.1504/IJSSOC.2010.034765

Lopez-De-Pedro, J. M., & Rimbau Gilabert, E. (2012). Stakeholder Approach: What Effects Should We Take into Account in Contemporary Societies. *Journal of Business Ethics*, *107*(2), 147–158. doi:10.1007/s10551-011-1029-0

Macleod, S. (2001). Why worry about CSR? *Strategic Communication Management*, *5*(5), 8–9.

Mannheim, K. (1952). On the Problem of Generations. In P. Kecskemeti (Ed.), Essays on the Sociology of Knowledge (pp. 276-322). London: Routledge.

Matute-Vallejo, J., Bravo, R. & Pina, J.M. (2011). The influence of Corporate Social Responsibility and Price Fairness on Customer Behaviour: Evidence from the Financial Sector. In *Corporate Social Responsibility and Environmental Management, 18*. doi:10.1002/csr.247

Mohr, B. A., Webb, D. J., & Harris, K. E. (2001). Do consumers expect companies to be socially responsible? The impact of corporate social responsibility on buying behavior. *The Journal of Consumer Affairs*, *35*(1), 45–72. doi:10.1111/j.1745-6606.2001.tb00102.x

Moncrief, W. C. (1991). The use of sales management role playing exercises. *Marketing Education Review*, *1*(3), 46–55. doi:10.1080/10528008.1991.11488319

Montana, P. J., & Petit, F. (2008). Motivating Generation X and Y on the job and preparing Z. *Global Journal of Business Research*, *2*(2), 139–148.

Mourdoukoutas P. (2013, November 23). McDonald's: three strategies to reignite sales growth. *Forbes.*

Nascuddin, E., & Bustami, R. (2007). The Yin and Yang of CSR Ethical Branding. *Asian Academy of Management Journal*, *12*(2), 83–100.

Neal, R., & Cochran, L. P. (2008). Corporate Social Responsibility, Corporate Governance, and Financial Performance: Lesson from Finance. *Business Horizons*, *51*(6), 535–540. doi:10.1016/j.bushor.2008.07.002

Pauli, G. (2010). *The blue economy: 10 years, 100 innovations, 100 million jobs*. Paradigm Publications.

Pomering, A., & Dolnicar, S. (2009). Assessing the Prerequisite of Successful CSR Implementation: Are Consumers Aware of CSR Initiatives? *Journal of Business Ethics*, *85*(2), 285–301. doi:10.1007/s10551-008-9729-9

Ritzer, G. (2004). *The McDonaldization of Society* (Rev. New Century ed.). *Thousand Oaks*, CA, USA: *Pine Forge Press..*

Roberts, P. W., & Dowling, G. R. (2002). Corporate Reputation and Sustained Superior Financial Performance. *Strategic Management Journal*, *23*(12), 1077–1093. doi:10.1002/smj.274

Sen, S., & Bhattacharya, C. B. (2001). Does doing good always lead to doing better? Consumer reactions to corporate social responsibility. *JMR, Journal of Marketing Research*, *38*(2), 225–243. doi:10.1509/jmkr.38.2.225.18838

Shokri, A., Oglethorpe, D., & Nabhani, F. (2014). Evaluating sustainability in the UK fast food supply chain. *Journal of Manufacturing Technology Management*, *25*(8), 1224–1245. doi:10.1108/JMTM-04-2013-0031

Siano, A., Vollero, A., & Siglioccolo, M. (2015). *Corporate Communication Management. Accrescere la reputazione per attrarre risorse*. Torino: Giappichelli.

Surprenant, C., & Churchill, G. A. Jr. (1984). Can Role Playing be Substituted for Actual Consumption? *Advances in Consumer Research. Association for Consumer Research (U. S.)*, *11*(1), 122–126.

Tencati, A., & Zsolnai, L. (2012). Collaborative Enterprise and Sustainability: The Case of Slow Food. *Journal of Business Ethics*, *110*(3), 345–355. doi:10.1007/s10551-011-1178-1

Torres, A., Bijmolt, T. H. A., Tribó, J. A., & Verhoef, P. (2012, March). Generating global brand equity through corporate social responsibility to key stakeholders. *International Journal of Research in Marketing*, *29*(1), 13–24. doi:10.1016/j.ijresmar.2011.10.002

Uwins, S. (2014). *Creating Loyal Brands. A guide to earning loyalty in a connected world*. Publish Green.

Vallaster, C., Lindgreen, A., & Maon, F. (2012). Strategically Leveraging Corporate Social Responsibility: A Corporate Brand Perspective. *California Management Review*, *54*(3), 34–60. doi:10.1525/cmr.2012.54.3.34

Visser, W. (2012). The Future of CSR: Towards Transformative CSR, or CSR 2.0.

Visser, W. (2013). *CSR 2.0: Transforming corporate sustainability and responsibility*. Springer.

Waddock, S., & Bodwell, C. (2007). What is Responsibility Management? And why bother? In Total Responsibility Management: The Manual (pp. 9–25). doi:10.9774/GLEAF.978-1-907643-01-9_2

Waddock, S., & Smith, N. (2000). Corporate Responsibility Audits: Doing Well by Doing Good. *MIT Sloan Management Review, 42*(2).

Webley, S. (2003). Risk, Reputation and Trust. *Journal of Communication Management*, *8*(1), 9–12. doi:10.1108/13632540410807501

Werther, W. B. Jr, & Chandler, B. (2005). Strategic Corporate Social Responsibility as Global Brand Insurance. *Business Horizons*, *48*(4), 317–324. doi:10.1016/j.bushor.2004.11.009

Wheeler, A. (2009). *Designing Brand Identity: An Essential Guide for the Whole Branding Team*. New York: Wiley.

Wong, V. (2014, July 23). McDonald's gives itself a year and half to get into chipotl Fighting shape. *Bloomberg.com.*

Wood, S.P. (2014, July 24). McDonald's has 18 months to rebrand… or else. *Adweek.com.*

ADDITIONAL READING

Christodoulides, G., Jevons, C., & Blackshaw, P. (2011). The voice of the consumer speaks forcefully in brand identity. *Journal of Advertising Research*, 51(1 50th Anniversary Suppl.), 101-111.

Eberele, D., Berens, G., & Li, T. (2013). The impact of interactive corporate social responsibility communication on corporate reputation. *Journal of Business Ethics*, *118*(4), 731–746. doi:10.1007/s10551-013-1957-y

Frostenson, M., Helin, S., & Sandstrom, J. (2011). Organizing Corporate Responsibility Communication Through Filtration: A Study of Web Communication Patterns in Swedish Retail. *Journal of Business Ethics*, *100*(1), 31–43. doi:10.1007/s10551-011-0771-7

Love, J. F. (1986). *Mcdonald's Behind the Arches*. New York, NY: Bantam Books.

MacPherson Lane, M. (2010, March 18). *McDonald's Logo to Go "Green" in Europe*, Huffingtonpost.com, 18th of March 2010

Porter, E. M., & Kramer, R. M. (2002). The Competitive Advantage of Corporate Philanthropy. *Harvard Business Review*, *80*(12), 57–68. PMID:12510538

Porter, M., & Kramer, M. (2011). Creating Shared Value. How to reinvent capitalism and unleash a wave of innovation and growth. *Harvard Business Review*, *89*(1/2), 62–77.

Small, L. (2011). Corporate Responsibility, Marketing and Economic Development in Emerging Markets. Retrieved from www.accountability.org/about-us/news/accountability-1/accountability.html

Smith, N. C. (2003). Corporate social responsibility: Not whether, but how. *Center for Marketing Working Paper*.

Takano, K. (2013). McDonalds Japan: A case study of effective public relations. *Public Relations Review*, *39*(1), 60–62. doi:10.1016/j.pubrev.2012.09.007

Winfrey G. (2009, November 23). McDonald's Making New Sign to Tell You How Eco-Friendly It Is. *Businessinsider.com*.

KEY TERMS AND DEFINITIONS

Branding: The strategy used to create a unique name and image for a product in consumers' mind.

Generation Z: Group of people born after 1995. It comes after Baby boomers (born between 1946 and 1964), Generation X (people born between 1965- 1976), and Generation Y, also called Millennials (people born between 1977 and 1994).

Integrated Corporate Social Responsibility: Part of core management concepts and processes; it represents an integration of economic with social, ethical and environmental decision-making criteria for corporate strategy.

Sustainability: The combination of environmental, societal and ethical concerns in processes, goods/ products and services development.

ENDNOTES

1. The Authors own full responsibility of the contents of the paper. Anyway paragraphs named, 'Introduction', 'CSR and its communication' and 'A sustainable repositioning: McDonald's case study' have been attributed to Dr. Civera; while paragraphs named 'Generation Z', 'Literature gap' and 'Methodology' must be attributed to Professor Elena Candelo'. Eventually, 'Results from the survey', 'Managerial implication and conclusion' and 'Further implications' are attributed to Dr. Cecilia Casalegno.
2. For the report see http://trendwatching.com/trends/5-trends-for-2016/
3. For the full report see trendwatching.com/consumer/report/2013
4. The results from the interview to the Chief Executive Officer at McDonald's Italy appeared in a previous publications from the authors titled: Candelo, E., Civera C., & Casalegno C. (2016). Communication for preventing reputational risk. McDonald's strategy and its impact on the Italian market. In V. Cantino, P. Devincentiis & D. Racca (Eds.), *Risk Management: Perspectives and Open Issues* (pp. 461-476). McGraw-Hill.

Chapter 16
Conquering the Digital Customer:
How Zara Is Confronting the Digital Innovation Revolution

Eric Viardot
EADA Business School, Spain

Petra A. Nylund
University of Vic, Spain

ABSTRACT

This case study illustrates the effectiveness of pursuing a customer centric marketing approach in order to achieve long term strategic success and global market leadership in the fashion industry. The case study provides the most significant elements of Zara's history. Then it describes the competitive environment. Next it reveals how Zara has set up a unique, lean, and agile supply chain strategy in order to deliver new products on a very frequent basis and faster than any of its competitors, as fashion customers expect constant changes. Then the case study details the customer centric marketing strategy, with the use of customers as the source of the inspiration for fashion design, the central role of the stores to build a very high level of trust with its customers, which is used by Zara to make a distinctive brand strategy. Finally, the case study discusses the new challenges of Zara to adapt its customer centric marketing strategy to the digital market.

INTRODUCTION

On March 9, 2016, Pablo Isla, chairman and CEO of Inditex, looked up at his CFO Ignacio Fernández, after finishing the webcast conference call of the company results for the fiscal year 2015, which had ended on January 31st. The revenues were €20.900 million, up by 15% compared to the previous year, as expected by the analysts. Net margin at 13.8% was beating that of archrival H&M which had fallen to 11.6%. This was just the confirmation that Inditex, with its flagship brand, was now the unconditional worldwide leader in the apparel industry.

DOI: 10.4018/978-1-5225-2139-6.ch016

Zara, the oldest brand – or concept as described by Inditex – was the most important for the group. With 2002 stores in 88 countries, Zara represented 65% of the revenues and 67% of the margin.

BACKGROUND

The amazing success of Zara -and Inditex- is closely linked with his founder, Amancio Ortega Gaona. He began his career in 1963 as a clothing manufacturer. The business grows steadily over the decade until Ortega owns several factories, which distribute their merchandise to other European countries.

In 1975, Amancio Ortega opened the first Zara store on a street in downtown La Coruña, Spain in 1975. The expansion strategy which made a small Spanish clothing firm into the undisputed worldwide leader in apparel can be described in three phases: First came the national development in Spain, then the international expansion in Europe and in the US and Latin America (1988-2003), and finally the global surge in Asia and the rest of the world.

As illustrated in Figure 1 the rise of Zara and Inditex has been extraordinary. From 1991 to 2015, the compound average growth rate was about 18.5%, from €257 million to €20.900 million meaning that Zara has managed to double its size almost every four years! This commercial success reflects the importance of growth in the Zara culture. The founder Ortega likes to repeat that "a company that does not grow will die." Ortega stepped down as CEO in 2011 leaving the place to Pablo Isla, but he is still very involved in the strategic decision making of the company and owns nearly 60 percent of Inditex shares.

Figure 1. Inditex sales and net profit from 1975 to 2015 (million EUR)
Source: Inditex annual reports and documents complied by authors.

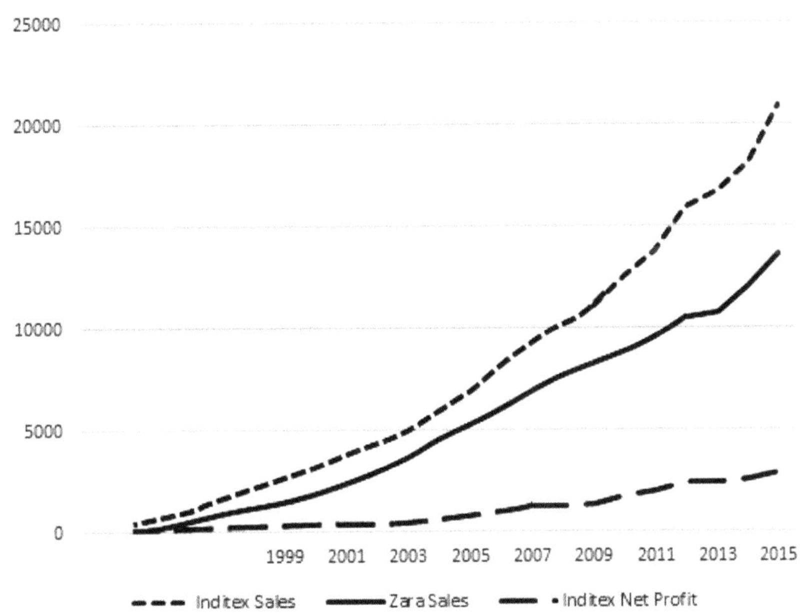

THE INDUSTRY AND THE COMPETITION

In the apparel industry, Zara's main global competitors are H&M and Gap. In addition, new competitors born online are emerging using the Internet as their only or primary sales channel such as Zalando and Asos. Figure 2 shows the sales of each competitor compared to the sales of Inditex. Whereas H&M and Gap have taken a drop in sales during 2015, Inditex has experienced continued growth. Zalando and Asos are still far from the sales of the incumbents, but are growing at a steady pace.

Hennes & Mauritz AB, also known as H&M, is an apparel and accessory store founded in 1947 in Sweden known for offering the latest fashion trends. H&M is the world's second biggest-selling clothing retailer and has proven to be a very aggressive competitor for Zara. H&M specializes in taking advantage of the season's latest looks inspired by design houses around the world and providing women, men, and children contemporary clothing styles at low prices. Targeting the 18 to 34-year-old market, the company manufactures affordable, stylish clothing. H&M operates more than 4,000 stores in 62 countries, with online presence in 32 of these markets. The H&M brand has a strong recognition worldwide. The H&M group also includes brands COS, Monki, Weekday, Cheap Monday and & Other Stories, as well as H&M Home. Stefan Persson, chairman of H&M and son of the founder Erling Persson, is the largest shareholder with a 28 percent holding

Gap built its iconic casual brand on basics for men, women, and children first by providing jeans, khakis, and T-shirts which had become the standard fashion in the U.S. in the 1990's. The founding Fisher family now owns 45 percent of the company. The group expanded with the urban chic chain Banana Republic and chic at a discount Old Navy. The diversification was initially successful but entered into trouble in the mid 2000's as the brands went too deep in their concept and frustrated the clients who switched to fresher competitors. Gap experienced a decrease in revenues and market share as well as financial losses. though it has some hit products like the Perfect Black Trousers in 2010 or the special collections in collaboration with Stella McCartney. In an attempt to compete with online fashion retailers, Gap acquired online fitness apparel brand Athleta in 2008, and the multi-brand platform Intermix in 2013. In 2016, Gap operates about 3,700 stores in 52 markets. Intermix ships to 213 countries and

Figure 2. Sales of Inditex, H&M, Gap, Zalando, and Asos from 2011 to 2015 (million (EUR)
Source: Factiva, complied by authors.

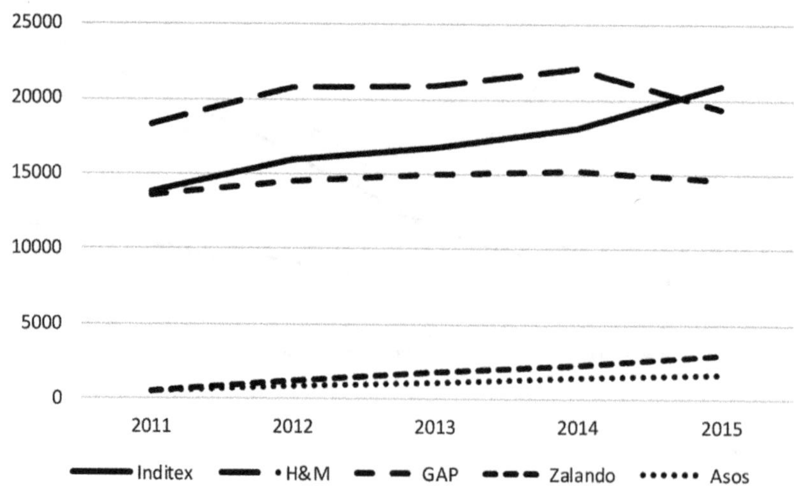

the other Gap brands to 93 countries. However, Gap does not operate separate online stores for different countries similar to its competitors.

Zalando was born online in 2008, then as a shoe store run from Germany. Today, Swedish investment company Kinnevik is the largest shareholder with a 32 percent ownership. With a business model inspired by US online retailer Zappo, it currently serves customers in 15 European countries. With a logistics systems centered on three German hubs and a recent Italian facility, and in partnership with DHL, the chain offers free delivery within two days and free returns within 100 days. The company manages outsources design and manufacturing from a buying office in Paris. It operates two outlet stores located in Berlin and Frankfurt.

Asos is another online-only competitor which was founded in the London in 2000. It has online stores in the UK, France, Germany, Italy, Spain, Australia, US, Russia and China, and ships to a total of 240 countries. With outsourced manufacturing of its own brand, Asos also sells 850 other brands. The Danish retailer Bestseller is currently the largest owner of Asos with 27 percent of shares.

The apparel industry is far from being only global and it is still very fragmented geographically. Thus, Zara is also facing many local champions such as American Apparel (US), Kookai (France), Next (UK), C&A (Germany-Belgium), Uniqlo (Japan), or Lojas Renner (Brazil).

ZARA'S BUSINESS MODEL: BUILT TO BE FAST

Fashion customers expect constant changes so new products have to be available on a frequent basis (Bruce and Daly, 2006). Thus, fashion companies are using time as a factor of competitive differentiation. And on that matter, one of the characteristics of Zara is its ability to be the fastest among its competitors. The typical retailer used to need an average of six months to design a new collection and then another three months to manufacture it. But the average time for a Zara concept to go from idea to appearance in store is 2 to 3 weeks. In 2008, when considering the time from creation to delivery, Zara was 12 times faster than Gap and five times faster than H&M (the second best in class in the apparel industry). Furthermore, Zara is not only faster but also "fresher", as it is also able to offer ten times more unique products, as the collection are changing every three weeks.

Such amazing results are made possible by the unique approach of the supply chain. Zara is able to be so alert because it is vertically integrated and it has a deep symbiosis with its-mostly locals-suppliers; it is also making a very effective use of the technology for just-in-time manufacturing, and finely it has set up a world class logistics to swiftly deliver its products to the stores. While H&M has 900 suppliers and no factories, nearly 60% of Zara's merchandise is produced in-house in 23 highly automated factories which are located in Galicia, a remote location in North West Spain with no special tradition in clothing.

Zara attempts to keep its offering simple, with usually just three sizes and three colors. The raw material is bought in large volume to save cost. The cloths are cut by computer-guided cutting tools which follow the patterns made from selected designs. About half of the clothes are made undyed so the firm can respond quickly if there are some fashion shifts at mid-season. The dyes come from Zara's own subsidiary and the dying is performed by robots. Inventory optimization models help the firm determine how many of which items in which sizes should be delivered to stores during twice-a-week shipments, ensuring stores are stocked with just what they need.

Then the prepared fabric pieces are sent for the sewing of the garments to local subcontractors located close to the main central facility of Zara in La Coruña. They have worked with Inditex so long they are not even written contracts. They receive a flat fee per type of garment, and they operate on short lead times and a fast turnaround so that Zara has a better control on transportation delays, quality management, and costs than if it was sourcing overseas. Pablo Isla, the CEO, says "Proximity sourcing is extremely relevant to us, to be able to react during the season and to maintain flexibility."

Zara relies also on third parties in low-cost manufacturing locations, mostly in Turkey and Asia, for its "staple" collection items with minimal fashion content, such as t-shirts, jeans, lingerie, and woolens. They usually have a longer shelf life than the fashion driven garments and this outsourcing policy is made in order to save costs. Those items represent 40% of the total volume but only 15% of the total value of Zara products.

Zara manufactures only 15 to 20 percent of production before the season begins. 50 percent is made at the start of the season and the remainder is manufactured in season. In comparison, most of the other apparel companies are committing 80% to 90% of their production in advance of the season.

Furthermore, Zara has managed to change the timing of the collection. Luis Lara, a former commercial Director at Zara, says, "the season used to start in September, but we moved it to August, and then to July so we could get more information from the customers about their desires and incorporate them earlier in our production planning."

All the items are then sent to one of the nine distribution centers located in Spain with a total of more than 1,000,000 square meters. The biggest one is in La Coruña and sizes 500,000 square meters, about the size of 65 soccer fields. The facilities move about 2.5 million items a day, with no item staying in-house for more than 72 hours. Using renewable energy systems, the logistics centers are heavily automated with ceiling-mounted racks and customized sorting machines. All garments are ironed in advance, packed on hangers, attached with security and price tags, and finally sorted out to be prepared for shipping.

All the shops that can be reached overnight all over Europe (about 75 per cent of deliveries) are served by the firm's trucking fleet powered by biodiesel. Farther destinations (about 25 per cent) are supplied by chartered cargo flights from Air France-KLM Cargo and Emirates Air. Flights are coordinated so that after the outbound shipment of Inditex products, the return legs are loaded with raw materials and half-finished clothes items from locations outside of Spain. "This system enables a product to get from the distribution centers to the European stores in an average of 24 hours, 48 hours in America and Asia" (AR 2010). Shipments tend to have almost zero flaws, with 98.9 per cent accuracy and under 0.5 per cent shrinkage.

Thus, Zara's supply chain can be described as "leagile" (Bruce et al., 2004) as it combines the lean and agile supply chain management to respond to changing markets (Abernathy, 2000). With such a configuration, the use of information technology is essential to share data for fast and accurate data in order to improve the visibility of the requirements. On that matter, Zara relies on its own information technology (IT) system, which is completely proprietary and far from the standards of the IT market. In fact, Zara's IT infrastructure is relatively simple but completely in line with the needs of the company. This means that for the same level of performance – or even better – its IT expenditure is less than one fourth the fashion industry average (Sull & Turconi, 2008).

FASHION FOR CUSTOMERS

It is often said that Zara is about Fast Fashion, but actually Zara is about Customer Centric Fashion. Zara is fast because fashion shoppers like to change and Amancio Ortega was the first to create a company which listens to its customers and does not try to impose a model created by some "iconic" or "creative" designers. Zara´s total orientation to the customer is the origin of its fabulous development.

Amancio Ortega says: "the customer must continue to be our main centre of attention, both in the creation of our fashion collections and in the design of our shops, of our logistical system and of any other activity." The strategic supremacy of customers in the Zara business model is engrained in the mission and vision of the company: "Zara is in tune with its customers, who help it give shape to the ideas, trends and tastes developing in the world. This is the secret to its success among a wide range of people, cultures and generations, who, despite their differences, all share a special fondness for fashion."

The typical Zara customer as identified by the company is a person who is up to date with the latest developments in the fashion industry and wants fashionable, trendy, and unique outfits at affordable prices. There is no geographic, demographic, or economical element in this understanding of the customer. Years ago, the typical Zara customer would have been described as the "chica" Zara, the typical Spanish woman between 25 to 40 years old. Yet, today the Zara shopper can be a man, a woman, a teenager, or even a child, located in every place of the world where fashion is important, typically large cities where people do have a reasonable purchasing power and an appetence for style and mode.

One key consequence of the customer centricity of the Zara business model is that Ortega has turned the basic rules of fashion upside down. Since the time of "haute couture" in France and then Italy, the business has been dominated by powerful – and often- talented designers who were "deciding" what would be the fashion of the year. Top designers of today such as Tom Ford, John Galliano, Stella McCartney, or Ralph Lauren are influencing the trends in fashion. They work also for retailers which are using their design to manufacture massively the same model, outsourcing the materials and the manufacturing, before piling the clothes in thousands of distribution outlets while spending millions of euros or dollars to advertise their product and influence the consumers and drive it to the shop.

Zara sells accessible, wearable, and instant fashion that the customers have either seen the look on the catwalk and can't afford it, or they want new fashion at a mid-range price. Zara was described once by a Goldman analyst as "Armani at moderate prices". Zara's garments look like high fashion, but are significantly less expensive. The quality of the product is good and if Zara's offering is sometimes referred to as clothing to be worn six to ten times; it is due to the ever changing tastes of Zara customers not because of the poor quality of the items.

Using its customers as a source of ideas and inspiration, Zara is skilled at picking up the latest trends in fashion. Its team of almost 300 young and unknown designers creates designs based on the latest styles from the catwalk and other fashion hotspots, which are effortlessly adjustable to the mass market.

For instance, stories abound about the fact that some years ago after Madonna's first concert date in Spain during a recent tour, her outfit was copied by Zara designers. By the time she performed her last concert in Spain, some members of the audience were wearing the same outfit (Kumar & Linguri, 2006). In 2003, when the Crown Prince of Spain announced his engagement to Letizia Ortiz, she wore a white trouser-suit for the occasion. In just three weeks, the same white trouser-suit was available in all European Zara shops where it was snatched up by hundreds of European women.

On an average, Zara generates an amazing 40,000 items a year versus 2,000 to 4,000 items presented at other large chains like H&M and Gap. And those products fit extremely well with the fashion-conscious customers of Zara. Take a recent testimonial about Zara from Liz Jones (2012), one of the leading fashion trend setters in the UK press: "The brand has executed all the key trends extremely well. The bags are brilliant as are the shoes. When once there were rows and rows of black courts, there are myriad funky flats on offer and peep-toe platforms in hot pink and orange. The accessories beat Marks & Spencer hands down. Yes, Gap does swimwear better, M&S does better undies, Banana Republic does better workwear, and Cos does simple sporty separates extremely well, but if you are looking for a few pieces to take on holiday, there are colorful kaftan shirts, drawstring silk or linen trousers, and wacky T-shirts…" Those are the typical comments of Zara's clients.

With its global expansion, Zara pays close attention to catering to the various climates and weather-based trends of each geography. Some apparel retailers recycle their European or North American seasonal collection six months later in Australia, South Africa, or South America. But Zara produces separate collections targeted specifically for its northern and southern hemisphere stores.

Once the garments are made, Zara sends them out quickly to all its stores in the world. As the CEO, Pablo Isla comments: "The vertical integration of our production system allows us to place a garment in any store around the world in a period between two to three weeks." Actually, if an item is demanded by enough customers, it can be in their Zara stores to accommodate that request within 10 days.

This unique combination of a large number of customer driven references and the ability to manufacture and delivered them quickly provides another unique and valuable competitive advantage to Zara: its ability to have a new collection every three weeks in the store. This is extremely appealing to "fashionistas". Actually, Zara has a global average of 17 visits per customer per year, much higher than the average five to six annual visits to its competitors.

With this fast fashion model Zara manages to create a climate of exclusivity, opportunity, and scarcity, which is exactly what fashion shoppers are looking for. It brings customers into stores to see what is new, what they must not miss, and what they must own before it's gone forever. What is truly extraordinary is that Zara was the first fashion apparel to come with this new disruptive approach.

For instance, when Zara opened its first store in the United Kingdom, on London's trendy Regent Street, shoppers went browsing without shopping, thinking they would come back later to buy during a discount sale. Then the store assistants explained that the collections were changed every two weeks, and the style liked by the customer would very likely not be available later or even ever. Thus, if they wanted something, they had to buy it now. Customers got the message and Regent Street became one of Zara's most profitable stores while more stores opened in the UK.

Some customers are getting so hooked to the Zara style that they get up early at the date when the next collection is delivered by the "Zara truck" in order to be the first to enjoy the wider choice of new offers that may not last long. And when they enter the store they know the newest items arrive on black plastic hangers before store staff transfer items to wooden hangers afterward. In some cases, there are stores which are running out of stock. However, Zara does not view this as a negative since it reinforces the shoppers' perception of the uniqueness of their purchase.

Zara's objective is not that consumers purchase a lot, but that they purchase often. To do so they have to find something fresh every time they enter the store. Hence Zara changes its designs very quickly and offers only limited quantity during a restricted amount of time. An additional benefit of producing in small quantities is that Zara saves on cost, should a design not be very well-received.

Zara customer centric model is to be responsive to fashion items that are selling well during the season, and to discontinue those that are not. Says Jesus Echevarria, Director of Communication: "There is no point in sticking to one set of designs if customer feedback is that certain pieces are not popular. We only want to put pieces in-store that customers are happy with, and that suit their current and changing styles and taste."

With such a policy of scarcity and just-in-time, Zara does not have to rely heavily on discount prices like its competitors: Zara's unsold items account for only 10% of the total stock while the average for the industry is between 17 to 20%.

THE IMPORTANCE OF THE STORE AS THE POINT OF CONTACT WITH THE CUSTOMER

The store is the cornerstone of the Zara customer centric approach. The store is where the company´s business model starts and ends, with the customer as its main asset. In January 2016, Zara reported 2,002 stores in 88 countries, with a net addition of 79 new stores in 2015, compared to 96 stores opened in 2014, 76 in 2013, and 120 in 212. The Inditex group then had over 7,000 stores worldwide.

Everything is made at the store to welcome the fashion customers. This includes a privileged location in main cities, meticulously planned show windows and a uniquely conceived architecture inside and out, a precise product coordination, and an excellent customer service.

Privileged Locations

Like for any retail business, location is a key success factor in order to get the maximum traffic of prospects and customers. In the case of Zara, this is even more critical as the store is the only way where Zara is connecting with its customers. This is due to the fact that since its creation and contrary to the rest of its competitors, Zara has never invested in advertising especially at the level of brand building. Its brand strategy is based only on word-of-mouth which reinforces the sense of exclusivity and scarcity. Zara products are never advertised: the customer has to enter the store to see them. If they like the collection, they will tell their friends and social relations to hurry before it goes out of stock!

Zara spends just 0.5 percent on advertising while other clothing retailers spend 4-5 percent of sales. Thc little it does spend goes to reinforcing its identity as a clothing retailer whose goal is to 'democratize fashion'. While competitors will use high-profile celebrities to endorse their product and generate sales, Zara relies only on its stores to communicate its brand image. Consequently, Zara locates its stores in busy, prestigious, and city center shopping streets.

More specifically, the first store in a new country acts as a flagship for the future stores to be opened. So Zara looks for upscale locations in the world's largest cities such as the Champs Elysée, in Paris, France, the most expensive commercial location in Europe which sees 500,000 people per day during the week and up to 750,000 on the week-end.

The inauguration of a new Zara store is always a wonderful event for public relations as huge crowds of aspirant shoppers are waiting for the opening of the new shop and then grabbing what they can get before it is sold out. Recent inaugurations in London's Oxford Street, Brisbane's Queen Street Mall, and a 4,400 square meter flagship store in New York's SoHo, have been incredibly popular and have generated –for free- a high exposure of the Zara brand name in all the media, the traditional ones as well as the digital ones.

Zara has a special organization in charge of scouting for prime real estate along established shopping corridors. Zara plans its arrival in various countries over a long period of time, and is patient in waiting for the right opportunities. Says Echevarria: "Wherever we plan to open a new Zara store, we will do research into the areas we feel are suitable for our brand, and choose locations that are prominent in each city. We are patient in this process and, if nothing comes up, we will not compromise, but, instead, wait until a good opportunity arises".

Meticulously Planned Shop Windows and Interior Architecture

Beside locations, shop windows – shop fronts in Zara terminology – are the second element that Zara uses to communicate its brand image. Zara communication strategy is based on the belief that an iconic physical store well located and a well-designed window front are very effective at attracting shoppers. Store windows are critical for Zara to remain visible and entice customers to visit, enter, and buy.

The displays are changed regularly, in synchronization with the arrival of the new collection. The goal is that all people walking past a Zara store should be greeted by a beautiful window display where the latest designs are exposed so that they would instinctively want to enter the store, browse through the collections, and try on a few outfits.

All the store windows are designed centrally in La Coruña. Zara has a full team of window front designers who constantly travel around to its international locations to understand the culture and customers of each store. They then come back and create the window design that is unique to the store in an artistic and attention grabbing way. Next, all the props and details are then shipped to each store manager and are put up under strict guidelines.

Though the shop front is centrally designed and managed, the store manager is allowed to change the displays on the shop mannequins which are at the entrance and within the store. On average, those mannequins are changed every two to three days; it gives the impression to the customers that something has changed within the Zara store and may lure them to enter.

The same kind organization is used for the design of the lay-out of each store. A centralized dedicated team mixing designers and merchandisers aggregate all the information from the inside and the outside in order to create the most truly attractive arrangement for the Zara customers so that they get a unique and rewarding experience.

This centralized organization is made to save time to the store manager and employees which do not have to think about the lay out and the equipment of the store windows and can focus on more productive activity. This makes even more sense when one considers that a typical Zara shop will change its shop windows and the store lay-out between 18 to 26 times in a year, in line with the arrival of new collections. Furthermore, the centralization is a good way to ensure the same level of quality in all the shops all over the world. It also reduces costs in sourcing and production of all the accessories as the centralization allows economies of scale. The central designers' team can also build knowledge as it consolidates all the feedback coming from the stores about the commercial impact of a new concept of window. The errors are quickly acknowledged and not repeated while the successful concepts are extended to other shops in other markets.

Precise Product Coordination and Customer Feedback

Being customer centric, Zara has managed to become an expert in figuring out the kind of products that fashion-enthusiast customers are looking for. And it all starts at the store with the collection of information through a mix of quantitative and qualitative methods.

Zara has equipped all the store managers with handheld Personal Digital Assistant (PDA) devices that are linked to the store's Point-Of-Sale (POS) system and show how garments rank by sales. The PDAs are also used to gather clients input as staff regularly chats with customers to gain feedback on what they'd like to see more, asking about the preferred length of a shirt or the desired color for a trouser, or the most desired neck for a kind of shirt. They also casually check which outfit on the catwalk do they like, or which celebrity's get-up are they coveting.

At the end of the day, when doors are closed, the staff finds other customer information in analyzing the piles of unsold items that customers tried on but didn't buy. They often reveal if there are any preferences or disappointment in cloth, color, or styles offered.

Then, in less than an hour, managers can send updates that combine the hard data captured at the cash register combined with insights on what customers would like to see. The data is compiled at a central analytics facility using a sophisticated but robust proprietary software program, designed especially by and for the company. Analysts look for patterns in customers' shopping trends and use their findings to advise store managers on how to adjust merchandise layouts to maximize sales and product turnaround.

The PDAs are also used for the ordering by each store, both for replenishment items as well as new products. This is critical for the company as the goal is to deliver just what the customers want and to have the lowest stock possible. It is also important for the store managers, as a part of their remuneration depends on the accuracy of their sales forecasts and sales growth.

Each evening the newest designs which are available for order are sent digitally by headquarters. Order deadlines are twice weekly, and are issued via the PDAs. Store managers who fail to order by the deadline receive replenishment items only. Deliveries arrive at stores twice per week from Zara headquarters a few days after the order is made.

Zara store operations are designed so that the store staff is completely dedicated to sell and help customers find what they want. All store logistical operations are centralized to save time. Similarly, all garments are ironed in advanced, packed on hangers, with security attached directly at the central logistical centers in Spain. Thus employees in Zara stores have only to move items from shipping box to store racks and spend the rest of the time catering the customers. Efforts like this help store staff regain as much as three hours in prime selling time.

Zara knows that retailers are only as successful as their sales staff and is not thrifty in terms of resources. In 2015, 15,800 new jobs were created by Inditex. Out of the 152,854 employees, 78,000 where already included in a profit-sharing scheme. The company invests also significantly in training as more than 80% of the Group's training investment targets store staff which represent 87% of the total employees.

Store training plans have an extremely practical focus on subjects such as customer service, product, and recent fashion trends. The training concentrates also on the capacity to capture and formalize the information received from clients each day. In order to have standard quality training of store personnel, Zara has specific instruction materials with guidelines, advice, and periodic evaluations in addition to other content that helps both trainers and apprentices. Among these materials, the Zara store organization manuals are particularly important and are constantly updated. They include detailed information on all aspects of the in-store work and detailed information on Zara and Inditex.

Zara employees are also self-motivated with a strong commercial culture which was set up by the founder. Luis Lara says, "Zara has a very powerful customer oriented culture: everything is made for the customer. The stores are there to welcome the customers and the central operations are there to support the store. I have never seen at Zara the kind of conflict which is so typical in retail, between the shops and the central, them vs. us. The commercial corporate culture is very strong and those who cannot fit in do not stay very long". Another important element of the Zara culture is autonomy and common sense. Zara employees like to try things, they're not afraid to make a mistake, and they react fast in order to try to improve.

Excellent Customer Service

Attention to the customer is another area to which Zara pays most attention, mainly as the content of periodical training for the teams in the stores. Zara sees customer service as the key enabling chain to attend to customer desires as swiftly as possible.

In addition, customers have other communication channels with Zara for resolving any questions regarding products or the organization that could not be dealt with in the store. A specialized professional team offers personalized service to all customers who require it, by phone, e-mail, or post and in several languages, so as to make the query easier.

Furthermore, all the Zara store teams and the regional management teams of stores or offices in the countries in which the online store is operative have received specific training in online customer services, as the customer who shops at Zara.com can pick up his or her order at any store in the chain in these countries.

The unique approach of "fashion for customers" combined with the pivotal role of the store allows Zara to build a very high level of trust with its customers which then generates customer loyalty (Lombart and Louis, 2016).

A DISTINCTIVE BRANDING STRATEGY

In another striking difference with the rest of the fashion industry, Zara spends very little money on advertising. Its budget is about 0,5% of annual sales while the average advertising budget for its competitors is between 4 to 5%. "Advertising is about building up expectations, and telling customers what they can expect and what we can deliver. At Zara, we want expectations to come from the in-store experience and to come from the customer's personal journey and satisfaction from shopping at Zara" says Echevarria.

With such a customer centric branding strategy, there is no opportunity for disappointment and there is no way for Zara to give false promises. The brand name is built essentially with the word of mouth of satisfied customers telling, and showing, their family, friends and social relation how pleased they are to shop at Zara. And it works! Indeed, in the 2016 BrandZ™ Top 100 Global Brands by Millward Brown and WPP, Zara is ranked 35 and it stands out as the second most valuable brand in the apparel category, behind Nike ranked 24, and ahead of H&M ranked 79. Even more interestingly, the brand value of Zara is evaluated at $M 25,221, nearly twice that of H&M, as shown in Table 1.

Thus, Zara has managed to enlarge the trust related to individual shop or employees to the trust towards the entire company through positive word of mouth and smart public relation communication. This trust in the entire company is particularly relevant in service chains where the service is performed by changing personnel (Kandampully, 2002). Then consumer trust can be converted into value and loyalty in relational exchanges (Sirdeshmukh et al., 2002; Grayson et al., 2006; Brodie et al., 2009).

The powerful brand image of Zara is an important asset as the trust generated between a customer and a brand is central to a mutually beneficial relationship (Lymperopoulos et al., 2010) that leads to customer satisfaction and loyalty (Ball et al., 2004; Kenning, 2008). For instance, the Reputation Insti-

Table 1. Value of the leading worldwide apparel brands

#	Brand Name	Brand Value $M	#	Brand Name	Brand Value $M
1	Nike	37,472	6	Victoria's Secret	6,245
2	Zara	25,221	7	Adidas	5,257
3	H&M	12,665	8	Next	5206
4	Uniqlo	8,625	9	Ralph Lauren	3,497
5	Under Armour	6,698	10	Lulemon	3,047

Source: 2016 BrandZ™ Top 100 Global Brands.

tute estimates that if a company improves its reputation by five points, the number of people who would definitely recommend the company goes up by 7,1%. The brand also contributes to a steady price policy as in times of pressure to discount, Zara –and H&M- were the two companies which managed to get most of the full mark up for their products because consumers, perceiving value, switched to these brands.

A CUSTOMER CENTRIC PRICING STRATEGY

In order to reinforce its image of leader in the democratization of fashion, Zara offers affordable prices in order to encourage purchases. But its pricing policy differs by country markets. For instance, Zara products are low-priced in Spain, while in China, Australia, and Japan, they are priced as a luxury fashion items, as illustrated in Table 2 which indicates the price of a Zara Summer dress in various locations. Figure 3 provides another price comparison of 12 different items in 7 countries.

Similarly, the price will vary from one location to another. Fashionista.com, a famous fashion news site, reports that the average spending at Zara is $92.03 in New York and $68.05 in Miami on the basis of data collected from customer credit card transactions.

Being a customer centric company with an intimate knowledge of the client reaction, Zara sets prices according to individual market conditions, rather than using the "cost plus margin" like most of its competitors. When it comes to competition, Zara generally prices its products somewhat higher than C&A and H&M, but below Gap and Next.

Prices are managed centrally: they are marked in the stores with a device that reads the bar code, gets the correct local price from the headquarter information system, and prints the label before it is put on the item.

THE ROUTES TO EXPANSION

Table 3 clearly shows the avenues for Zara's future expansion. While the relative importance of Zara's home market is declining, the rest of Europe and America stays unchanged and Asia continues to grow. Consequently, Zara has recently increased its focus on two markets: China and online sales. China is identified as one of the key market for the future and as the leading territory for Zara expansion in Asia. On the other hand, Zara sees the development of the digital market as a way to revitalize the mature European market and a solution to accelerate its penetration of the US market Its online offer is also

Table 2. Price of one summer dress in a Zara chain store

Barcelona	26	Euro
Madrid	29	Euro
Paris	35	Euro
London	43	Euro
Los Angeles	37	$
Seoul	40	$
New York City	43	$
Milan	45	$
Shanghai	51	$
Mexico City	51	$
Beijing	58	$
Sydney	72	$
Tokyo	74	$

Source: www.numbeo.com.

Figure 3. Price differences of 12 Zara products in different countries
Source: Gothenburg University Publications Electronic Archive, n.d.

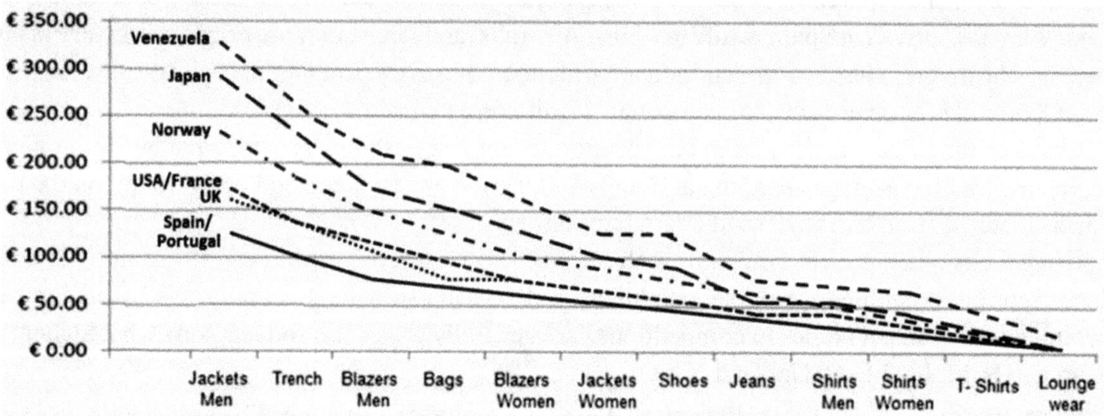

a diversification in order to reach digital fashionistas who are living outside of the affluent cities that Zara is targeting. Thus Zara launched its Zara online in China in September 2012, ahead of other Asian countries.

Zara in China

Zara was the first brand with which Inditex entered the Chinese market in 2006. Since that date, it has been increasing its number of stores at a steady pace and ten years later it had 566 stores in China, of which 179 were Zara stores. Table 4 shows the evolution of the Zara stores opening in China.

Zara was one of the first apparel makers to go to China, following Uniqlo which first came to the Chinese market in 2002; H&M followed in 2007 and Gap in 2010. All of them have just begun to tap the market and have still room for growth. As indicated in Table 5, Zara has 179 stores in China, while Uniqlo has 449, H&M has 353, and Gap has five. By contrast, Nike and Adidas, which entered in the early 1980s for the former and in the early 1990s for the later have about 6,000 stores each in the country, many of them franchises.

When Zara came into China, it had to adapt to the specificities of this appealing but sometimes difficult market for western companies. There was a strong potential as the growth of the Chinese economy had been fueled by a burgeoning demography combined with the political stability of its one-party system and the deregulation of most sectors including a new textile policy. The country is gigantic, with a clear difference between rural and urban culture. There are also differences at the urban level between people living in the six large megacities of more than 10 million people (Beijing, Shanghai, Chongqing, Guangzhou, Shenzhen and Tianjin), those living in the 120 cities that have more than 1 million people, and the 440 other cities. The cultural Confucian conflict between status projection and self- protection, between upward mobility and fear-based conformism is also typical of the Chinese society, especially since the late nineties where increasing wealth and the opening society has allowed the Chinese to express their individuality through fashion.

Table 3. Relative evolution of Inditex revenues 2010-2015 by geographical area and perspectives

Area	2010	2015	Trend
Spain	28%	18%	↘
Rest of Europe	45%	44%	→
Americas	12%	15%	↗
Asia and Rest of the World	15%	23%	↗
Total	100%	100%	

Source: Inditex Annual report, compiled by the authors.

Table 4. Evolution of Zara stores opening in China

Year	Number of Openings	Total Stores
2006	1	1
2007	12	13
2008	10	23
2009	21	44
2010	21	65
2011	55	120
2012	18	138
2013	14	152
2014	13	165
2015	14	179

Source: Inditex Annual Reports compiled by the authors.

Table 5. Relative stores presence of foreign apparel retailers in China in 2016

	GAP	H&M	Zara	Uniqlo
China	5	353	179	449
Total	3700	4000	2002	1360
%	0.01%	8.83%	8.94%	33.01%

Source: Annual Reports, compiled by the authors.

But Zara is doing well in China. It has found that urban Chinese fashionistas are not that different from the European Zara girl. Chinese office ladies prefer Zara's slim fits more and Chinese women choose pastels to flatter their pale skin rather than the stronger colors Europeans prefer; but otherwise they have surprisingly similar tastes, says Zara designer Iria Campos. The Zara brand appears also to be one of those brands which helps customers resolve their Confucian inner conflict by allowing them to simultaneously stand out and fit in.

The apparel market perspective in China looks very promising as Chinese consumers are expected to continue to grow in strength and sophistication according to a recent report from the Boston Consulting Group. Fashion shoppers in their 20s and 30s, who were born after the Cultural Revolution, already outspend the urban average by 18 percent. They are ignorant of the rough conditions that their parents had lived when they were their age and many of them have a good job at a foreign or local company; accordingly, they are much more optimistic and prone to spend for themselves. In addition, women living inland or in "low-tier" cities are also expected to spend more on fashion over the coming decade. Consequently, annual fashion expenditures should triple from $67 billion in 2011 to 200.7 billion in 2020.

Zara is ready to grab a good piece of this market with its customer centric approach. It will keep up by opening new stores but it will also adapt its offer. Says Echevarria: "Zara is a constantly evolving brand and with our designers travelling to Asia and learning the trends and fashion preferences of our new consumers, this will definitely influence our future collections".

Digital Expansion

As Internet is becoming an integrated part of everyday life, an increasing number of purchases are made on the go. According to Criteo, over 40 percent of digital retail purchases are made from smartphones in Asian markets such as South Korea and Japan, whereas smartphone purchases account for 8-18 percent in e.g. the UK, the U.S., Turkey, Germany, Italy, Brazil, France, and Russia. New shopping apps with improved functionality compared to today's online stores are cropping up and forces Zara to constantly develop shopping options and to explore new opportunities for integrating the online and offline experience.

Online shopping has also brought an increased focus on specific shopping days. Following the success of Black Friday as a day for physical discount shopping, Cyber Monday had been launched by online retailers in the U.S. and is now bigger than Black Friday with an estimated 9.3 bn USD. In China, Singles Day on November 11, 2015, was the biggest shopping day of the year with online retailer Alibaba reaching 14.3 bn USD sales in just one day, thereby increasing sales with 60 percent compared to the same day the previous year, according to Criteo. As customers can shop from wherever they happen to be, they have become more prone to adopt discount days. There's no longer a need to rearrange one's agenda or feel uncomfortable in crowded stores. Still, discount days entice customers to anticipate buying decisions and to increase total spending.

Using the store as its primary point of interface with the customer, Zara has been deliberately slow in embracing the Internet. Its first online experience came with after-sales services. It proved to be extremely successful: in 2009 more than 85% of the total customer queries were made on-line.

Zara online was officially launched in September 2010 and was made available in eleven countries and 14 languages. In 2016, Zara online was available in 29 markets. Zara online has been designed as a support to the physical store, and not as a replacement. It has been conceived as a showcase for Zara to demonstrate its fashion options and maintain a close and direct relationship with its customers. The main reason is that the absence of physical contact with the merchandise tend to make more traditional fashionistas uncomfortable. Conversely, teens and young women do not have those inhibitions: they go shopping online or offline at their whim.

Pablo Isla explained: "Our online business would not be what it is without the stores. We also see that online is contributing also to the store sales because we have more than 6 million people seeing our products every day on our web pages and online pages".

The goal is to provide a new service to Zara customers and with a purchasing experience that is as close as possible to the physical store. In fact, a third of the online customers choose to receive their delivery in a Zara store, and two thirds of those customers who return purchases do that in physical stores, often while buying the same item in a different size. Thus, Zara focuses on an integrated business model where online and offline sales complement each other in creating a close and continuous bond with the customer. Instead of losing customer contact as customers go online, Zara is thickening customer contact through multiple channels.

With its combined online strategy, covering different media and devices, Zara wanted first to rejuvenate its customer base in its European mature markets. In the U.S., Zara online should allow the company to expand faster in order to reach its target market of fashion conscious young women aged 18 to 25 who have the Zara brand in high regard, are digitally agile and do not have any kind of reluctance to shop over the net. As Zara is nationally recognized, it is much cheaper to launch a web store than to invest in real estate in 50 more malls in the U.S.

In 2015, despite the slowdown of the Chinese economy, China became the largest e-commerce market in the world, surpassing the US. The Chinese online marketplace is dominated by Alibaba with USD 3.7 bn in revenues in 2016. Alibaba's main vehicle is the primarily c2c-oriented marketplace Taobao, but Alibaba has also launched the b2c-platform Tmall for companies to approach customers under their own brand. In late 2014 Zara opened a store in Tmall, in addition to the zara.cn site launched in 2012. "It is like opening a store in a shopping mall", said Pablo Isla. "In terms of how it works it is no different from our online sales through our own web site." Some of Zara's competitors were already present at Tmall, such as Gap, Uniqlo, and Forever 21, whereas H&M was pursuing a solo strategy.

As evidenced in Figure 4, Inditex and Zara maintain a high number of physical stores while simultaneously creating an important online presence. Inditex however decreased the growth target for physical stores from a previous 8-10 percent to 6-8 percent in 2016. H&M maintains an aggressive physical store expansion targeting 10-15 percent store growth. It has also launched slightly more online stores and it is steering clear of third-party sites such as Tmall. GAP on the other hand is following a U.S.-centric online strategy with little adaptation of online stores to markets in other countries. Zalando and Asos are still smaller than Zara and Inditex both online and offline, but exhibit considerable growth as seen in Figure 2.

Figure 4. Bricks vs. clicks: physical versus online stores of Inditex, H&M, Gap, Zalando, and Asos, size of circles represents 2015 sales
Source: Annual Reports, complied by the authors.

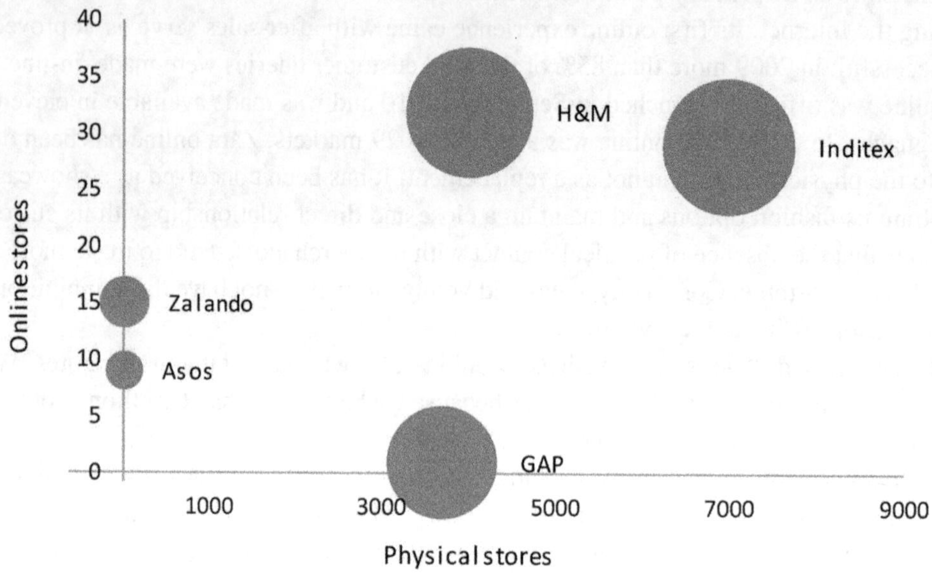

An examination of the retail website demonstrated that as much as 96 percent of customer visits do not result in a purchase, with customers leaving the online store empty handed. Consequently, retailers must create flow, a state of full immersion in the shopping experience to increase conversion of visitors to paying customers, (McDowell, Wilson, & Kile, 2016). The web design is therefore an essential driver of online revenue and Zara has understood it very clearly.

The Zara online stores have been designed to make online shopping as consumer friendly as possible. Zara's garment search function has been enhanced by a number of filter options (by garment characteristics, colors, sizes, prices, etc.). Shoppers can also find specific items by reference number, garment description, category, and so forth. The company operates separate pages for mobile devices and also has a shopping app available on App Store and Google Play. Garment prices are identical online and in stores. Customers can view their shopping baskets at any time while browsing, editing their product selections right away. Clients can either have the products delivered at home or pick up their orders at a conveniently located store choice within a period of three to five days. In the latter case, the website provides a store search and mapping tool in order to help them to automatically locate the nearest Zara store. For home delivery, clients can choose between three options: Standard, Express, and Defined Date Delivery. Shoppers opting for standard delivery receive their orders at home within two to four days. With the express delivery, the orders are delivered within 24-48 hours, except specific areas. The Defined Date Delivery is a special option in which shoppers can choose the date and time of delivery at no extra charge. All product orders are wrapped in purpose-designed eco-friendly packaging which keeps purchased garments in an optimal state until delivery. Payments can be made using major credit cards.

The exchange and return policy is identical to that offered in-store: during a 30-day period any unwanted items can be picked up at home or returned to Zara stores. In each country where the online store is available, Zara has hired a logistics operator with a proven track record in the field to handle nationwide distribution. Site users can also call toll-free customer service or write to a dedicated e-mail address for help with order-related queries or problems.

Additionally, Zara's online website displays visual content of the collections with photos, lookbooks, videos, and a fashion collaboration section called "People!" so that shoppers can get an overall impression of the current range. Moreover, this content can be shared on the various social networks. Users can also sign up for a newsletter to stay abreast of the latest fashion trends.

Zara online had more than three hundred people (graphic designers, retouchers, sales people, models, stylists, IT people, customer service, and logistics people, among others). It also has the unconditional and permanent support of all Zara teams, especially the stores team, which have had specific training regarding the new channel in order to give better customer service at the point of sale.

The online store team work closely with the Zara design and sales teams, as well as with the chain coordination and show window teams. This is essential given that it has become one of the prime fashion show windows.

Regarding delivery time to digital customers, the Zara logistic model is better tuned to its digital strategy than its competitors and is likely to be more profitable than rival H&M´s. Zara can deliver products from its distribution centers in Spain to the U.S. within 48 hours while H&M has to invest in distribution in the U.S., since it doesn't make its own clothing and relies exclusively on suppliers. However, all over the world, online retailers are pushing down delivery times. Amazon is currently offering free two-hour delivery on some items with their Prime Now service. The initiative has received much attention and has gained Amazon additional market share in digital retail. According to the Deloitte 2015 Holiday Survey, 92 percent of consumers now consider two-day delivery fast, whereas 3 to 4-day delivery is seen as fast shipping by only 63 percent.

Zara is also increasing visibility towards customers through building popularity in social networks. For instance, in June 2016, Zara had 11 million followers on Instagram, compared to H&M's 15 million, Gap's 1 million, Zalando's 300.000, and Asos' 4.5 million. On Facebook, Zara had 24 million likes, compared to over 27 million for H&M, 8 million for Gap, and 4 million each for Zalando and Asos. Although Zara was doing very well on social networks, H&M had a leading edge which required further improvement of Zara's social media strategy.

CONCLUSION

Looking forward, Zara has some clear challenges to meet in order to keep its number one position in the apparel industry and continue to grow. First, the Zara formula has not worked everywhere, like in America, for instance, where Zara has struggled. The company has reacted with the launching of its online store and the inauguration on New York City's Fifth Avenue of the New Zara Global Concept Store which is going to become the global standard for all the Zara stores in the world.

Zara is also susceptible to conditions to the Spanish market which is still making 18 percent of corporate revenues. The continued strained situation of the Spanish economy is expected to have an impact on Zara sales for the next coming years.

In addition, being a worldwide leader generates also political issues. In 2011, China's consumer watchdog attacked Zara for poor quality. The firm denies that it was singled out for political reasons but the Chinese government routinely targets large foreign firms for minor lapses, as in other cases such as Google, McDonald's, Danone, or Carrefour. Also in 2011, Zara was accused in Brazil of using suppliers who were running sweatshops with Bolivian workers brought illegally to Brazil for their outsourced production. Since that date, Inditex has strengthened the supervision of all its outsourced production operations and had produced a code of ethics with strict conditions mandatory for all its suppliers. Still, a report released by the India Committee of the Netherlands in 2016 pointed to poor living conditions and restricted freedom of movement among workers in Bangalore.

Moreover, competitors do not stay idle and are catching up. Though they cannot break their company and rebuild it from scratch in order to duplicate Zara, they have reduced the gulf between them and Zara. Gap has moved production away from Asia and closer to home. Adopting Zara's commercial approach, H&M has increased the frequency of new items in stores. Other fast fashion rivals like Renner rolls out mini-collections every two months while Forever 21 and Uniqlo stores get new looks within 6 weeks.

Finally, competition is increasing from new born-online business models such as those of Zalando and Asos that take advantage of network effects in the widely distributed customer base (Nair, Wierman, and Zwart, 2015). The scale of customers that can be reached by an online business model allows for a much more varied offering in order to take full advantage of the resources dedicated to create an efficient distribution model. The born-onlines have tended to begin by launching their own brand to build recognition, and are now at a point where they can begin to cash in on the demand-side effects of scale through offering multiple brands as a complement to their own brand. Zalando has launched an online platform to sell not only their own apparel but a wide range of brands. They are working with in-store delivery with several brands, and have invited Zara to join the platform. The platform does not accommodate separate brand stores, but offers brand-specific garment searches. Still, the visual brand image is not prominent in searches, and the image of the participating brand is subordinate to that of the Zalando platform. Joining Zalando and other multi-brand platforms would increase the visibility of Zara to the digital customer, but would offer little control over the brand image and the customer relationship that is so important to the company. In addition, feedback about customer behavior was not as readily available as for Zara's own stores.

Nevertheless, Zara is confident in that its customer centric model is the best way for continuing growth and profitability in both real and virtual markets. Concludes Echevarria: "In the last 40-over years, Zara and Inditex have risen to where we are based on flexibility and understanding our consumers. This will continue to be our principle and, if changes are necessary, we will respond with what is best for the company and for our customers".

REFERENCES

Abernathy, F. H., Dunlop, J. T., Hammond, J. H., & Weil, D. (2000). Retailing and supply chains in the information age. *Technology in Society*, *22*(1), 5–31. doi:10.1016/S0160-791X(99)00039-1

Ball, D., Coelho, P. S., & Machas, A. (2004). The role of communication and trust in explaining customer loyalty. *European Journal of Marketing*, *38*(9/10), 1272–1293. doi:10.1108/03090560410548979

Brodie, R. J., Whittome, J. R. M., & Brush, G. J. (2009). Investigating the service brand: A customer value perspective. *Journal of Business Research*, *62*(3), 345–355. doi:10.1016/j.jbusres.2008.06.008

Bruce, M., & Daly, L. (2006). Buyer behaviour for fast fashion. *Journal of Fashion Marketing and Management*, *10*(3), 329–344. doi:10.1108/13612020610679303

Bruce, M., Moore, C., & Birtwistle, G. (Eds.). (2004). *International retail marketing: A case study approach*. Oxford, UK: Butterworth-Heinemann.

Grayson, K., Johnson, D., & Chen, D.-F. R. (2008). Is firm trust essential in a trusted environment? How trust in the business context influences customers. *JMR, Journal of Marketing Research, 45*(2), 241–256. doi:10.1509/jmkr.45.2.241

Jones, L. (2012). *Fashion therapy, Daily mail.* Retrieved from http://www.dailymail.co.uk/femail/article-2160686/LIZ-JONES-FASHION-THERAPY--Why-Zaras-stepahead.html#ixzz1z5C003rV

Kandampully, J. (2002), Services management: The new paradigm in hospitality. Melbourne, Australia: Pearson Education.

Kenning, P. (2008). The influence of general trust and specific trust on buying behavior. *International Journal of Retail & Distribution Management, 36*(6), 461–476. doi:10.1108/09590550810873938

Kumar, N., & Linguri, S. (2006). Zara fashion sense. *Business Strategy Review, 17*(2), 81–84. doi:10.1111/j.0955-6419.2006.00409.x

Lombart, C., & Louis, D. (2016). Sources of retailer personality: Private brand perceptions. *Journal of Retailing and Consumer Services, 28*, 117–125. doi:10.1016/j.jretconser.2015.09.002

Lymperopoulos, C., Chaniotakis, I. E., & Rigopoulou, I. D. (2010). Acceptance of detergent-retail brands: The role of consumer confidence and trust. *International Journal of Retail & Distribution Management, 38*(9), 719–736. doi:10.1108/09590551011062457

McDowell, W. C., Wilson, R. C., & Kile, C. O. (2016). An examination of retail website design and conversion rate. *Journal of Business Research*. doi:10.1016/j.jbusres.2016.04.040

Nair, J., Wierman, A., & Zwart, B. (2015). Provisioning of large-scale systems: The interplay between network effects and strategic behavior in the user base. *Management Science, 62*(6), 1830–1841. doi:10.1287/mnsc.2015.2210

Naylor, J. B., Naim, M. M., & Berry, D. (1999). Leagility: Integrating the lean and agile manufacturing paradigms in the total supply chain. *International Journal of Production Economics, 62*(1-2), 107–118. doi:10.1016/S0925-5273(98)00223-0

Sirdeshmukh, D., Singh, J., & Sabol, B. (2002). Consumer trust, value, and loyalty in relational exchanges. *Journal of Marketing, 66*(1), 15–37. doi:10.1509/jmkg.66.1.15.18449

Sull, D., & Turconi, S. (2008). Fast Fashion Lessons. *Business Strategy Review, 19*(2), 4–11. doi:10.1111/j.1467-8616.2008.00527.x

ADDITIONAL READING

Agarwal, R., Selen, W., Roos, G., & Green, R. (2015). *The Handbook of Service Innovation*. Springer. doi:10.1007/978-1-4471-6590-3

Bendoni, W. (2017). *Social Media for Fashion Marketing: Storytelling in a Digital World.* Bloomsbury Visual Art.

Brem, A., & Viardot, E. (2015). *Adoption of Innovation: Balancing Internal and External Stakeholders in the Marketing of Innovation.* Springer International Publishing. doi:10.1007/978-3-319-14523-5

Clodfelte, R. (2014). *Retail Buying: From Basics to Fashion.* Fairchild Books.

Cuthbertson, R., Furseth, P. I., & Ezell, S. J. (2015). *Innovating in a Service-Driven Economy: Insights, Application, and Practice.* Springer. doi:10.1057/9781137409034

Easey, M. (2008). *Fashion Marketing.* Wiley.

Greenstein, S., Goldfarb, A., & Tucker, C. (2013). *The Economics of Digitization.* Edward Elgar Publishing. doi:10.4337/9781784710408

Lea-Greenwood, G. (2013). *Fashion Marketing Communications.* Wiley.

Mink Rath, P., Bay, S., Gill, P., & Petrizzi, R. (2014). *The Why of the Buy: Consumer Behavior and Fashion Marketing.* Fairchild Books.

Sherman, G. J., & Perlman, S. (2014). *The Real World Guide to Fashion Selling and Management.* Fairchild Books.

KEY TERMS AND DEFINITIONS

Apparel Industry: The sum of companies producing and distributing clothing, accessories and footwear.

Customer Centric: Focused on the needs of the customer.

Digital Customer: Customer who makes purchases online.

Digital Innovation Revolution: The radical increase in innovation driven by the emergence of the Internet and of the digitization of information.

Digital Market: The sum of digital customers.

Fast Fashion: Apparel that follows swiftly changing trends.

Online Store: Sales channel that operates on the Internet.

PDA (Personal Digital Assistant): Handheld mobile digital device connected to the Internet.

Compilation of References

(1994). OECD Tourism Policy and International Tourism. InOECD (Ed.), *Countries: 1991–1992*. Organization for Economic Co-Operation and Development.

Aaker, D. A. (1996). *Building Strong Brands*. N.Y.: Free Press.

Abela, A. (2006). Marketing and consumerism: a response to O'Shaughnessy and O'Shaughnessy. *European Journal of Marketing*, *40*(1 & 2), 5-16.

Abernathy, F. H., Dunlop, J. T., Hammond, J. H., & Weil, D. (2000). Retailing and supply chains in the information age. *Technology in Society*, *22*(1), 5–31. doi:10.1016/S0160-791X(99)00039-1

Adorno, T. W. (1941). On Popular Music. *Studies in Philosophy and Social Sciences*, *9*, 17–48.

Agarwal, R., & Karahanna, E. (2000). Time flies when youre having fun: Cognitive absorption and beliefs about information technology usage. *Management Information Systems Quarterly*, *24*(4), 665–694. doi:10.2307/3250951

Age, A. (1991). Spurts and Starts: Corporate Role in '90s Environmentalism Hardly Consistent. *Advertising Age*, *62*(46), GR14–GR16.

Agyeman, C. M. (2014). Consumers' buying behavior towards green products: An exploratory study. *International Journal of Management Research and Business Strategy*, *3*(1), 189.

Ahmad, A. & Thyagaraj, K. S. (2015). Consumer's Intention to Purchase Green Brands: The Roles of Environmental Concern, Environmental Knowledge and Self Expressive Benefits. *Current World Environment*, 10(3), 879-889.

Ahmadi, L., Croiset, E., Elkamel, A., Douglas, P. L., Entchev, E., Abdul-Wahab, S. A., & Yazdanpanah, P. (2015). Effect of socio-economic factors on EV/HEV/PHEV adoption rate in Ontario. *Technological Forecasting and Social Change*, *98*, 93–104. doi:10.1016/j.techfore.2015.06.012

Ahuvia, A. (2008). If money doesnt make us happy, why do we act as if it does? *Journal of Economic Psychology*, *29*(4), 491–507. doi:10.1016/j.joep.2007.11.005

Ajanovic, A. (2014). Promoting environmentally benign electric vehicles. *Energy Procedia*, *57*, 807–816. doi:10.1016/j.egypro.2014.10.289

Ajzen, I. (1991). The theory of planned behavior. *Organizational Behavior and Human Decision Processes*, *50*(2), 179–211. doi:10.1016/0749-5978(91)90020-T

Ajzen, I. (2002). Residual effects of past on later behavior: Habituation and reasoned action perspectives. *Personality and Social Psychology Review*, *6*(2), 107–122. doi:10.1207/S15327957PSPR0602_02

Aktan, B., Mandacı, P. E., Kopurlu, B. S., & Ersener, B. (2009). Behaviour of emerging stock markets in the global financial meltdown: Evidence from bric-a. *African Journal of Business Management*, *3*, 396–404.

Al-Alawi, B. M., & Bradley, T. H. (2013a). Review of hybrid, plug-in hybrid, and electric vehicle market modeling studies. *Renewable & Sustainable Energy Reviews*, *21*, 190–203. doi:10.1016/j.rser.2012.12.048

Al-Alawi, B. M., & Bradley, T. H. (2013b). Total cost of ownership, payback, and consumer preference modeling of plug-in hybrid electric vehicles. *Applied Energy*, *103*, 488–506. doi:10.1016/j.apenergy.2012.10.009

Albinsson, P. A., & Yasanthi Perera, B. (2012). Alternative marketplaces in the 21st century: Building community through sharing events. *Journal of Consumer Behaviour*, *11*(4), 303–315. doi:10.1002/cb.1389

AlGhamdi, R., Nguyen, J., Nguyen, A., & Drew, S. (2012). Factors Influencing e-commerce Adoption by Retailers in Saudi Arabia: A quantitative analysis. *International Journal of Electronic Commerce Studies*, *3*(1), 83–100.

Ali, S., Butt, B. Z., & Rehman, K. (2011). Comovement between emerging and developed stock markets: An investigation through cointegration analysis. *World Applied Sciences Journal*, *12*, 395–403.

Allan, D. (2014). Turn it up: That's my song in that ad. *International Journal of Music Business Research*, *3*(1), 26–51.

Allen, M. (2012). What was Web 2.0? Versions as the dominant mode of internet history. *New Media & Society*, *15*(2), 260–275. doi:10.1177/1461444812451567

Al-Shebil, S., Rasheed, A., & Al-Shammari, H. (2011). Coping with boycotts: An analysis and framework. *Journal of Management & Organization*, *17*(03), 383–397. doi:10.1017/S183336720000153X

Alvarez-Lois, P. (2000). Capacity utilization and monetary policy (Working Paper). Banco de Espana Documento de Trabajo No: 0306.

Anatoliy, G. G., & Getman, M. (2014). *Benchmarking to improve a strategy and marketing in pharmaceuticals.* Benchmarking. *International Journal (Toronto, Ont.)*, *21*(3).

Anderson, E.W., Fornell, C., & Lehmann, D.R. (1994). Customer satisfaction, market share and profitability: Findings from Sweden. *Journal of Marketing*, *58*, 53-66.

Anderson, C. (2006). *The Long Tail: Why the Future of Business Is Selling Less of More*. Hyperion.

Anderson, W. T., & Cunningham, W. H. (1972). The social conscious consumer. *Journal of Marketing*, *36*(3), 23. doi:10.2307/1251036

Andersson, P. K., Kristensson, P., Wastlund, E., & Gustafsson, A. (2012). Let the music play or not: The influence of background music on consumer behavior. *Journal of Retailing and Consumer Services*, *19*(6), 553–560. doi:10.1016/j.jretconser.2012.06.010

Andidas.com (2003). *Toyota Prius: Marketing Communications Plan.*

Andreasen, A. R. (1995). *Marketing social change*. San Francisco: Jossey Bass.

Andreasen, A. R. (2002). Commercial marketing and social change. *Social Marketing Quarterly*, *8*(2), 41–45. doi:10.1080/15245000212552

Andrews, F. M., & Withey, S. B. (1976). *Social indicators of well-being: America 's perception of life quality*. New York: Plenum Press. doi:10.1007/978-1-4684-2253-5

Anon. (2003). Adulteration of edible oils. Food safety and Security, May, 14.

Antil, J. H. (1984). Socially Responsible Consumers: Profile and Implications for Public Policy. *Journal of Macromarketing,* 4(2), 18-39.

Antioco, M., Moenaert, R. K., Feinberg, R. A., & Wetzels, M. G. M. (2008). Integrating service and design: The influences of organizational and communication factors on relative product and service characteristics. *Journal of the Academy of Marketing Science, 36*(4), 501–521. doi:10.1007/s11747-008-0097-x

Antonies, G., & Raaij, V. W. (1998). *Consumer Behavior: A European Perspective.* West Sussex, England: John Wiley & Sons Ltd.

Apel, W. (1973). *Harvard dictionary of music.* Cambridge, MA: Belknap Press.

Arabacı, Ö., & Arabacı, R. Y. (2008). Kapasite kullanım oranları ve enflasyon ilişkisi: Türkiye örneği. *Uludağ Üniversitesi İktisadi ve İdari Bilimler Fakülte Dergisi, 27*(2), 93–109.

Arabacı, Ö., & Eryiğit, K. Y. (2012). A threshold regression estimation of philips curve: Turkey Case. *Eskişehir Osmangazi Üniversitesi İİBF Dergisi, 7,* 29–47.

Aranyossy, M. (2011). Resource-based Analysis of E-commerce Business Value (Working paper).

Areni, C. S. (2003). Exploring managers implicit theories of atmospheric music: Comparing academic analysis to industry insight. *Journal of Services Marketing, 17*(2), 161–184. doi:10.1108/08876040310467925

Areni, C. S., & Kim, D. (1993). The Influence of Background Music on Shopping Behavior: Classical Versus Top-Forty Music in a Wine Store. *Advances in Consumer Research. Association for Consumer Research (U. S.), 20,* 336–340.

Argo, J. J., Dahl, D. W., & Machanda, R. V. (2005). The influence of a mere social presence in a retail context. *The Journal of Consumer Research, 32*(2), 207–212. doi:10.1086/432230

Argyle, M. (1987). *The Philosophy of Happiness.* New York: Methuen.

Arndt, J., Barksdale, H., & Perreault, W. (1980). Comparative study of attitudes toward marketing, consumerism and Government regulation: The United States versus Norway and Venezuela. In R. Day & H. K. Hunt (Eds.), *New Findings in Consumer Satisfaction and Campaigning* (pp. 66–72). Bloomington, IN: Indiana University.

Arnould, E. J., & Thompson, C. J. (2005). Consumer Culture Theory (CCT): Twenty Years of Research. *The Journal of Consumer Research, 31*(4), 868–882. doi:10.1086/426626

Ashenfelter, O., Ciccarella, S., & Shatz, H. J. (2007). French wine and the U.S. boycott of 2003: Does politics really affect commerce? *Journal of Wine Economics, 2*(1), 55–74. doi:10.1017/S1931436100000298

Assad, S.W. (2007). The rise of consumerism in Saudi Arabian society. *International Journal of Commerce & Management,* 17(1/2), 73-104.

Atiq, A., Srinivasan, A., & Gardner, L. (2013). Service System Design (SSD) Innovation through Consumer Participation.

Axsen, J., Bailey, J., & Castro, M. A. (2015). Preference and lifestyle heterogeneity among potential plug-in electric vehicle buyers. *Energy Economics, 50,* 190–201. doi:10.1016/j.eneco.2015.05.003

Baba, S., & Fedorikhin, A. (1999). Heart and Mind in Conflict: The Interplay of Affect and Cognition in Consumer Decision Making. *The Journal of Consumer Research, 26*(3), 278–292. doi:10.1086/209563

Babin, B.J., & Attaway, J.S. (2000). Atmospheric affect as a tool for creating value and gaining share of customer. *Journal of Business Research, 49*(2), 91-99.

Babin, B. J., & Darden, W. R. (1996). Good and bad shopping vibes: Spending and patronage satisfaction. *Journal of Business Research*, *35*(3), 201–206. doi:10.1016/0148-2963(95)00125-5

Baccarani, C., & Brunetti, F. (2011). The Need for Customer Education in High People-Density Services: A New Role for Service Providers? *Proceedings of the14th Toulon-Verona Conference* (pp. 115-131). Alicante, Spain: University of Alicante.

Baccarani, C., Ugolini, M., & Bonfanti, A. (2010). A Conceptual Service Quality Map: The Value of a Wide Opened Perspective. *Proceedings of the13th Toulon-Verona Conference* (pp. 873-892). Coimbra, Portugal: University of Coimbra.

Baccarani, C., & Golinelli, G. M. (2009). *Leadership for Excellence in Services. Sinergie, 78(Gennaio-Maggio).* VII-XVI.

Bailey, J., Miele, A., & Axsen, J. (2015). Is awareness of public charging associated with consumer interest in plug-in electric vehicles? *Transportation Research Part D, Transport and Environment*, *36*, 1–9. doi:10.1016/j.trd.2015.02.001

Bailey, N., & Areni, C. S. (2006). When a few minutes sound like a lifetime: Does atmospheric music expand or contract perceived time? *Journal of Retailing*, *82*(3), 189–202. doi:10.1016/j.jretai.2006.05.003

Baines, T. S., Lightfoot, H. W., Benedettini, O., & Kay, J. M. (2009). The Servitization of Manufacturing A Review of Literature and Reflection on Future Challenges. *Journal of Manufacturing Technology Management*, *20*(5), 547–567. doi:10.1108/17410380910960984

Baker, C. (2007). *The concept of turbofolk in Croatia: inclusion/exclusion in the construction of national musical identity*. Nation in formation: inclusion and exclusion in Central and Eastern Europe, UCL School of Slavonic and East European Studies, London. Retrieved from http://eprints.soton.ac.uk/66293/1/Baker_-_turbofolk_2007.pdf

Baker, E., Al-Gahtani, S., & Hubona, G. (2007). The effects of gender and age on new technology implementation in a developing country: Testing the theory of planned behavior (TPB). *Information Technology & People*, *20*(4), 352–375. doi:10.1108/09593840710839798

Baker, J. A., Parasuraman, A., Grewal, D., & Voss, G. B. (2002). The Influence of Multiple Store Environment Cues on Perceived Merchandise Value and Patronage Intentions. *Journal of Marketing*, *66*(2), 120–141. doi:10.1509/jmkg.66.2.120.18470

Baker, J., & Cameron, M. (1996). The effects of the service environment on affect and consumer perception of waiting time: An integrative review and research propositions. *Journal of the Academy of Marketing Science*, *24*(4), 338–349. doi:10.1177/0092070396244005

Baker, J., Grewal, D., Levy, M., & Voss, G. (2003). Wait Expectations, Store Atmosphere and Store Patronage Intentions. *Journal of Retailing*, *79*(4), 259–268. doi:10.1016/j.jretai.2003.09.006

Baker, J., Grewal, D., & Parasuraman, A. (1994). The Influence of Store Environment on Quality Inferences and Store Image. *Journal of the Academy of Marketing Science*, *22*(4), 328–339. doi:10.1177/0092070394224002

Baker, J., Levy, M., & Grewal, D. (1992). An Experimental Approach to Making Retail Store Environmental Decisions. *Journal of Retailing*, *68*(4), 445–460.

Bakos, Y. (2001). The emerging landscape for retail e-commerce. *The Journal of Economic Perspectives*, *15*(1), 69–80. doi:10.1257/jep.15.1.69

Baldwin, C. Y., & Clark, K. B. (2000). *Design Rules: The Power of Modularity*. MIT Press.

Ball, D., Coelho, P. S., & Machas, A. (2004). The role of communication and trust in explaining customer loyalty. *European Journal of Marketing*, *38*(9/10), 1272–1293. doi:10.1108/03090560410548979

Bamberg, S. (2003). How does environmental concern influence specific environmentally related behaviors? A new answer to an old question. *Journal of Environmental Psychology*, *23*(1), 21–32. doi:10.1016/S0272-4944(02)00078-6

Bamfield, J.A.N. (2012). *Shopping and Crime*. New York: Palgrave Macmillan. doi:10.1057/9780230393554

Banbury, C., Stinerock, R., & Subrahmanyan, S. (2012). Sustainable consumption: Introspecting across multiple lived cultures. *Journal of Business Research*, *65*(4), 497–503. doi:10.1016/j.jbusres.2011.02.028

Bandura, A. (1986). *Social foundations of thought and actions: a social cognitive theory*. Englewood Cliffs, NJ: Prentice–Hall.

Banerjee, B., & McKeague, K. (1994). How green is my value: Exploring the relationship between environmentalism and materialism. In C. T. Allen & D. R. John (Eds.), *Advances in Consumer Research* (Vol. 21, pp. 147–152). Provo, Utah: Association for Consumer Research.

Banerjee, S. B. (2002). Corporate environmentalism: The construct and its measurement. *Journal of Business Research*, *55*(1), 177–191. doi:10.1016/S0148-2963(00)00135-1

Banister, E. N., & Hogg, M. K. (2004). Negative symbolic consumption and consumers drive for self-esteem: The case of the fashion industry. *European Journal of Marketing*, *38*(7), 850–868. doi:10.1108/03090560410539285

Barke, R. L., Clouse, R., Stout, T. G., & Stout, G. R. (2009). The Economics of Buying a More Fuel-Efficient Automobile: An Interactive Analysis. *Journal of Financial Planning*, *22*(6), 62–71.

Barksdale, H. C., & Darden, W. R. (1972). Consumer attitudes toward marketing and consumerism. *Journal of Marketing*, *36*(4), 28–35. doi:10.2307/1250423

Barksdale, H. C., Perreault, W. D., Arndt, J., Barnhill, J., French, W., Halliday, M., & Zif, J. (1982). A cross national survey of consumer attitudes towards marketing practices, consumerism and Government regulations. *The Columbia Journal of World Business*, *17*, 71–86.

Barlett, C. A., & Ghoshal, S. (1995). *Transnational Management* (2nd ed.). Boston: Irwin.

Barnett, C., Cloke, P., Clarke, N., & Malpass, A. (2005). Consuming Ethics: Articulating the Subjects and Spaces of Ethical Consumption. *Antipode*, *37*(1), 23–45. doi:10.1111/j.0066-4812.2005.00472.x

Barriaux, M. (2007, July 5). McDonald's goes green–but not all customers are lovin' it. *The Guardian*.

Barry, D., Helstrom, B., and Potter, J. (2016). and Related Technology. *Asset Management Excellence: Optimizing Equipment Life-Cycle Decisions*, 89.

Barth, M., Jugert, P., & Fritsche, I. (2016). Still underdetected–Social norms and collective efficacy predict the acceptance of electric vehicles in Germany. *Transportation Research Part F: Traffic Psychology and Behaviour*, *37*, 64–77. doi:10.1016/j.trf.2015.11.011

Barunik, J., Vacha, L., & Kristoufek, L. (2011). Comovement of Central European stock markets using wavelet coherence: evidence from high-frequency data (Working paper). Charles University Prague, Faculty of Social Sciences.

Bask, A., Lipponen, M., Rajahonka, M., & Tinnilä, M. (2010). The Concept of Modularity: Diffusion from Manufacturing to Service Production. *Journal of Manufacturing Technology Management*, *21*(3), 355–375. doi:10.1108/17410381011024331

Basset, R. L., & Latane, B. (1976). Social Influences and News Stories. Paper presented at American Psychological Association, Washington DC.

Bastek, M., Tuunanen, T., & Gardner, L. (2008). *Consumer Information Systems Service Families*. The University of Auckland Business School.

Batra, R., Ahuvia, A., & Bagozzi, R. P. (2012). Brand love. *Journal of Marketing*, *76*(2), 1–16. doi:10.1509/jm.09.0339

Bauer, H.H., Albrect C.M, Bryant M.D., & Haber T.E. (2008). The consumer strikes back: Assessing antecedents to boycott participation. *American Marketing Association,* Winter, 350-351.

Baxter, S. (2007). Is it worth the cost? Marketing to negatively perceived consumer groups. *Global Journal of Business Research*, *1*(1), 87–96.

BBMG. (n. d.). The 2009 BBMG Conscious Consumer Report: Redefining Value in a New Economy. Retrieved from http://bbmg.com/

BCG.com. (2008). Creating People Advantage Summary. Retrieved from http://www.bcg.com/impact_expertise/publications/files/Creating_People_Advantage_Summary_May_2008.pdf

Beach-Larsen, T. (1996). Danish consumers attitudes to the functional and environmental characteristics of food packaging. *Journal of Consumer Policy*, *19*(3), 339–363. doi:10.1007/BF00411413

Beastfeeding.com. (2011). The Nestlé Boycott. Retrieved from http://www.breastfeeding.com/advocacy/advocacy_boycott.html

Beatley, T. (2000). *Green Urbanism: Learning from European Cities* (p. 17). Washington: Island Press.

Beck, M. J., Rose, J. M., & Hensher, D. A. (2013). Environmental attitudes and emissions charging: An example of policy implications for vehicle choice. *Transportation Research Part A, Policy and Practice*, *50*, 171–182. doi:10.1016/j.tra.2013.01.015

Beck, U. (2015). *What is globalization?* John Wiley & Sons.

Belk, R. W. (1988). Possessions and the Extended Self. *The Journal of Consumer Research*, *15*(2), 139–168. Retrieved from http://www.jstor.org/stable/2489522 doi:10.1086/209154

Belk, R. W., & Pollay, R. W. (1985). Images of Ourselves: The Good Life in Twentieth Century Advertising. *The Journal of Consumer Research*, *11*(4), 887–897. doi:10.1086/209024

Belton, W. J. Jr, & Cebula, R. J. (2000). Capacity utilization rates and unemployment rates: Are they complements or substitutes in warning about future inflation? *Applied Economics*, *32*(14), 1853–1864. doi:10.1080/000368400425071

Bemporad, R. & Baranowski, M. (2010). *Marketing to Conscious Consumers: Identify, Engage and Leverage Your Most Passionate Customers*. John Wiley & Sons.

Benbasat, I., Goldstein, D. K., & Mead, M. (1987). The Case Research Strategy in Studies of Information Systems. *Management Information Systems Quarterly*, *11*(3), 369–386. doi:10.2307/248684

Bendapudi, N., & Leone, R. P. (2003). Psychological Implications of Customer Participation in Coproduction. *Journal of Marketing*, *67*(1), 14–28. doi:10.1509/jmkg.67.1.14.18592

Bennett, K., Layzell, P., Budgen, D., Brereton, P., Macaulay, L., & Munro, M. (2000, 5-8 December). Service-based software: the future for flexible software. *Paper presented at the7th Asia-Pacific Software Engineering Conference*. doi:10.1109/APSEC.2000.896702

Beresteanu, A., & Li, S. (2011). Gasoline prices, government support, and the demand for hybrid vehicles in the United States. *International Economic Review*, *52*(1), 161–182. doi:10.1111/j.1468-2354.2010.00623.x

Bergman, M., King, J. L., & Lyytinen, K. (2002). Large scale requirements analysis revisited: The need for understanding the political ecology of requirements engineering. *Requirements Engineering*, *7*(3), 152–171. doi:10.1007/s007660200011

Berkowitz, L., & Lutterman, K. G. (1968). The traditional socially responsible personality. *Public Opinion Quarterly*, *32*(2), 169. doi:10.1086/267597

Berry, L. L., Parasuraman, A., & Zeithaml, V. A. (1988). The Service Quality-Puzzle. *Business Horizons*, *31*(5), 35–43. doi:10.1016/0007-6813(88)90053-5

Berry, L. L., & Seiders, K. (2008). Serving Unfair Customers. *Business Horizons*, *51*(1), 29–37. doi:10.1016/j.bushor.2007.09.002

Berry, L., Carbone, L., & Haeckel, S. (2002). Managing the Total Customer Experience. *MIT Sloan Management Review*, *43*(3), 85–89.

Bettencourt, L., Ostrom, A. L., Brown, S. W., & Roundtree, R. I. (2002). Client Co-Production in Knowledge-Intensive Business Services. *California Management Review*, *44*(4), 100–128. doi:10.2307/41166145

Beynon-Davies, P. (2002). *Information systems - an introduction to informatics in organizations*. Houndmills: Palgrave.

Bhatia, M, and Jain, A. (2013). Green Marketing: A Study of Consumer Perception and Preference in India. *Electronic Green Journal*, 1(36).

Bhide, M., Deolasee, P., Katkar, A., Panchbudhe, A., Ramamritham, K., & Shenoy, P. (2002). Adaptive Push-Pull: Disseminating dynamic web data. *IEEE Transactions on* Computers, *51*(6), 652–668.

Bhuian, S. N., Abdul-Muhmin, A. G., & Kim, D. (2001). Business education and its influence on attitudes to business, consumerism, and Government in Saudi Arabia. *Journal of Education for Business*, *76*(4), 226–230. doi:10.1080/08832320109601315

Bhushan, R. (2003, October 2). A Question of Quality. *The Hindu.*

Billings, W. L. (1990), Effects of Store Atmosphere on Shopping Behaviour. *Honors Projects.* Retrieved from http://digitalcommons.iwu.edu/busadmin_honproj/16

Bilotkach, V., & Mills, M. (2012). Simple Economics of Electric Vehicle Adoption. *Procedia: Social and Behavioral Sciences*, *54*, 979–988. doi:10.1016/j.sbspro.2012.09.813

Bimonte, S., & Faralla, V. (2012). Tourist Types and Happiness a Comparative Study in Maremma, Italy. *Annals of Tourism Research*, *39*(4), 1929–1950. doi:10.1016/j.annals.2012.05.026

Bimonte, S., & Faralla, V. (2014). Happiness and nature-based vacations. *Annals of Tourism Research*, *46*, 163–184. doi:10.1016/j.annals.2014.02.002

Biswas, A., Licata, J.W., McKee, D., Pullig, C., and Daughtridge, C. (2000). The recycling cycle: An empirical examination of consumer waste recycling and recycling shopping behaviors. *Advertising and Environmental issues, 19*(1), 93-115.

Biswas, A., & Roy, M. (2015). Green products: An exploratory study on the consumer behaviour in emerging economies of the East. *Journal of Cleaner Production*, *87*, 463–468. doi:10.1016/j.jclepro.2014.09.075

Bitner, M. J. (1992). Servicescapes: The Impact of Physical Surroundings on Customers and Employees. *Journal of Marketing*, *56*(2), 57–71. doi:10.2307/1252042

Bitner, M. J., Booms, B. H., & Mohr, L. A. (1994). Critical Service Encounters: The Employees Viewpoint. *Journal of Marketing*, *58*(4), 95–106. doi:10.2307/1251919

Bitner, M. J., Brown, S., & Meuter, M. L. (2000). Technology Infusion in Service Encounters. *Journal of the Academy of Marketing Science*, *28*(1), 138–149. doi:10.1177/0092070300281013

Bjerkan, K. Y., Nørbech, T. E., & Nordtømme, M. E. (2016). Incentives for promoting Battery Electric Vehicle (BEV) adoption in Norway. *Transportation Research Part D, Transport and Environment*, *43*, 169–180. doi:10.1016/j.trd.2015.12.002

Blackburn, W. D., & Chidambaran, N. K. (2013). Is the world stock market comovement changing? (Working paper). University of Massachusetts.

Black, I. R., & Cherrier, H. (2010). Anti-consumption as part of living a sustainable lifestyle: Daily practices, contextual motivations and subjective values. *Journal of Consumer Behaviour*, *9*(6), 437–453. doi:10.1002/cb.337

Bleuel, W. H., & Patton, J. D. Jr. (1994). *Service Management: Principles and Practices*. North Carolina: ISA Press.

Bloom, P. N., & Greyser, S. A. (1981). The Maturing of Consumerism. *Harvard Business Review*, *59*(November-December), 130–139. PMID:10252236

Bloom, P. N., & Smith, R. B. (1986). *The Future of Consumerism*. Lexington, Mass: Lexington Books.

Blythe, J. (2005). *Essentials of marketing*. Pearson Education.

Böckle, G., Munoz, J.B., Knauber, P., Krueger, C.W., do Prado Leite, J.C.S., van der Linden, F., … Weiss, D. (2002, August 19-22). Adopting and Institutionalizing a Product Line Culture. *Proceedings of the Second International Conference on Software Product Lines SPLC 2*, San Diego, CA, USA (pp. 49-59).

Boehm, B. (1988). A Spiral model of software development and enhancement. *IEEE Computer*, *21*(5), 61–72. doi:10.1109/2.59

Bohl, P. (2012), The effects of store atmosphere on shopping behaviour': A literature review, *Corvinus Marketing Tanulmányok*, Retrieved from http://unipub.lib.uni-corvinus.hu/669/1/CMT_2012-1.pdf

Bohnsack, R., Kolk, A., & Pinkse, J. (2015). Catching recurring waves: Low-emission vehicles, international policy developments and firm innovation strategies. *Technological Forecasting and Social Change*, *98*, 71–87. doi:10.1016/j.techfore.2015.06.020

Boileau and Normandin. (1999). Capacity utilization and the dynamics of business cycle fluctuations (working paper). University of Colorado at Boulder.

Bolton, R. N., & Saxena-Iyer, S. (2009). Interactive Services: A Framework, Synthesis and Research Directions. *Journal of Interactive Marketing*, *23*(1), 91–104. doi:10.1016/j.intmar.2008.11.002

Bonfanti, A. (2014). A Dilemma for Retailers: How to Make Store Surveillance Secure and Appealing to Shoppers? In F. Musso & E. Druica (Eds.), *Handbook of Research on Retailer-Consumer Relationship Development* (pp. 297–317). Hershey, PA, USA: IGI Global. doi:10.4018/978-1-4666-6074-8.ch016

Bonfanti, A. (2016). Customers Needs and Expectations on Servicescape Surveillance Management. *The TQM Journal*, *28*(6), 887–906. doi:10.1108/TQM-05-2015-0067

Bonges, H. A. III, & Lusk, A. C. (2016). Addressing electric vehicle (EV) sales and range anxiety through parking layout, policy and regulation. *Transportation Research Part A, Policy and Practice*, *83*, 63–73. doi:10.1016/j.tra.2015.09.011

Boonman, M., Huisman, W., Sarrucco-Fedorovtsjv, E., & Sarrucco, T. (2010). A success story for Producers and Consumers. *Dutch Association of Workshops*.

Borgmann, A. (2000). Reflections and Reviews: The moral complexion of consumption. *The Journal of Consumer Research*, *26*(4), 418–422. doi:10.1086/209572

Bosnjak, M., Brown, C. A., Lee, D. J., Yu, G. B., & Sirgy, M. J. (2014). Self-Expressiveness in Sport Tourism: Determinants and Consequences. *Journal of Travel Research*, *19*, 1–10. doi:10.1177/0047287514535845

Bostan, I., Burciu, A., & Grosu, V. (2010). The consumerism and consumer protection policies in the European Community. *Theoretical and Applied Economics*, *17*(4), 19–34.

Botsman, R., & Rogers, R. (2010). *What's mine is yours: How collaborative consumption is changing the way we live*. N.Y.: Harper Collins Publisher.

Botsman, R., & Rogers, R. (2010). *What's Mine Is Yours: The Rise of Collaborative Consumption*. New York: HarperCollins.

Botterill, J., & Kline, S. (2007). From McLibel to McLettuce: Childhood, spin and re-branding. *Society and Business Review*, *2*(1), 74–97. doi:10.1108/17465680710725281

Bourdieu, P. (1990). *The Logic of Practice*. Cambridge: Polity Press.

Bourgeois, J. C., & Barnes, J. G. (1979). Viability and profile of the consumerist segment. *The Journal of Consumer Research*, *5*(March), 217–227. doi:10.1086/208734

Bowen, D. E., Siehl, C., & Schneider, B. (1989). A Framework for Analyzing Customer Service Orientations in Manufacturing. *Academy of Management Review*, *14*(1), 75–95.

Boyatzis, R. E. (1998). *Transforming Qualitative Information - Thematic Analysis and Code Development*. Thousand Oaks, CA: Sage.

Boztepe, A. (2016). Green marketing and its impact on consumer buying behavior. *European Journal of Economic and Political Studies*, *5*(1), 5–21.

Brammer, S., & Millington, A. I. (2005). Corporate Reputation and philanthropy: An empirical analysis. *Journal of Business Ethics*, *61*(1), 29–44. doi:10.1007/s10551-005-7443-4

Brassington, F., & Pettitt, S. (2000). *Principles of Marketing*. Prentice Hall.

Braunsberger, K., & Buckler, B. (2011). What motivates consumers to participate in boycotts: Lessons from the ongoing Canadian seafood boycott. *Journal of Business Research*, *64*(1), 96–102. doi:10.1016/j.jbusres.2009.12.008

Breitung, J., & Candelon, B. (2006). Testing for short and long-run causality: A frequency domain approach. *Journal of Econometrics*, *132*(2), 363–378. doi:10.1016/j.jeconom.2005.02.004

Brickman, P., & Campbell, D. T. (1971). Hedonic relativism and planning the good society. In M.H. Appley (Ed.), *Adaptation Level Theory: A Symposium* (pp. 287-304). New York: Academic Press.

Brodie, R. J., Whittome, J. R. M., & Brush, G. J. (2009). Investigating the service brand: A customer value perspective. *Journal of Business Research*, *62*(3), 345–355. doi:10.1016/j.jbusres.2008.06.008

Broekemier, G., Marquardt, R., & Gentry, J. W. (2008). An exploration of happy/sad and liked/disliked music effects on shopping intentions in a womens clothing store service setting. *Journal of Services Marketing*, *22*(1), 59–67. doi:10.1108/08876040810851969

Brooks, F. (1975). *The Mythical Man Month: Essays on Software Engineering*. Reading, Mass, USA: Addison-Wesley. doi:10.1145/800027.808439

Brown, C., & Vessey, I. (2003). Managing the next wave of enterprise systems: Leveraging lessons from ERP. *MIS Quarterly Executive*, *2*(1), 45–57.

Brown, L. R. (2001). *Eco-Economy* (1st ed.). W. W. Norton & Company.

Brownsword, L., & Clements, P. (1996). A Case Study in Successful Product Line Development.

Bruce, M., & Daly, L. (2006). Buyer behaviour for fast fashion. *Journal of Fashion Marketing and Management*, *10*(3), 329–344. doi:10.1108/13612020610679303

Bruce, M., Moore, C., & Birtwistle, G. (Eds.). (2004). *International retail marketing: A case study approach*. Oxford, UK: Butterworth-Heinemann.

Bruner, G. C. (1990). Music, mood, and marketing. *Journal of Marketing*, *54*(4), 94–104. doi:10.2307/1251762

Brunk, M. E. (1973). The anatomy of consumerism. *Journal of Advertising*, *2*(1), 9–12. doi:10.1080/00913367.1973.10672477

Brunner, F. M. (1996). *A Psychological rendering of consumerism* [Unpublished Doctorate Thesis]. Pacifica Graduate Institute.

Buhalis, D., & Main, H. (1998). Information technology in peripheral small and medium hospitality enterprises: Strategic analysis and critical factors. *International Journal of Contemporary Hospitality Management*, *10*(5), 198–202. doi:10.1108/09596119810227811

Burghelea, M. R., Plaias, I., & El-Murad, J. (2015), The Effects of Music as an Atmospheric Variable on Consumer Behaviour in the Context of Retailing and Service Environments. *International Conference on Marketing and Business Development Journal*, 1(1), 377-392.

Burns, D. J., Manolis, C., & Keep, W. W. (2010). Fear of Crime on Shopping Intentions: An Examination. *International Journal of Retail & Distribution Management*, *38*(1), 45–56. doi:10.1108/09590551011016322

Burroughs, J. E., & Rindfleisch, A. (2002). Materialism and well-being: A conflicting values perspective. *The Journal of Consumer Research*, *29*(3), 348–370. doi:10.1086/344429

Byrd, T. A., Cossick, K. L., & Zmud, R. W. (1992). A synthesis of research on requirements analysis and knowledge acquisition techniques. *Management Information Systems Quarterly*, *16*(1), 117–138. doi:10.2307/249704

Caldwell, C., & Hibbert, S. A. (2002). The influence of music tempo and musical preference on restaurant patrons behavior. *Psychology and Marketing*, *19*(11), 895–917. doi:10.1002/mar.10043

Caldwell, K., Henshaw, L., & Taylor, G. (2011). Developing a framework for critiquing health research: An early evaluation. *Nurse Education Today*, *31*(8), e1–e7. doi:10.1016/j.nedt.2010.11.025 PMID:21185111

Cameron, M. A., Baker, J., Peterson, M., & Braunsberger, K. (2003). The effect of music, wait-length evaluation, and mood on a low-cost wait experience. *Journal of Business Research*, *56*(6), 421–430. doi:10.1016/S0148-2963(01)00244-2

Campbell, C. (2005b). *The romantic ethic and the spirit of modern consumerism*. UK: WritersPrintShop.

Campbell, C. (1995). The sociology of consumption. In D. Miller (Ed.), *Acknowledging Consumption* (pp. 96–126). London: Routledge.

Campbell, C. (2004). I shop therefore I know that I am: the metaphysical basis of modern consumerism. In K. M. Ekstrom & H. Brembeck (Eds.), *Elusive Consumption* (pp. 27–43). Oxford: Berg.

Campbell, C. (2005a). The Craft Consumer: Culture, craft and consumption in a postmodern society. *Journal of Consumer Culture*, *5*(1), 23–42. doi:10.1177/1469540505049843

Candelo, E., Casalegno, C., & Civera, C. (2014). Meanings and implications of corporate social responsibility and branding in grocer retailers: A comparative study over Italy and the UK. In Handbook of Research on Retailer-Consumer Relationship Development (p. 351).

Candelo, E., Casalegno, C., & Civera, C. (2015). Towards Corporate Shared Value in Retail Sector: A Comparative Study over Grocery and Banking Between Italy and the UK. *The International Journal of Economic Behavior-IJEB*, *5*(1), 105–120.

Candelo, E., Civera, C., & Casalegno, C. (2016). Communication for preventing reputational risk. McDonald's strategy and its impact on the Italian market. In *V. Cantino, P. Devincentiis & D. Racca (2016). Risk Management: Perspectives and Open Issues* (pp. 461–476). McGraw-Hill.

Caporale, M. G., & Spagnolo, N. (2010). Stock market integration between three CEECs, Russia and the UK (working paper). CESIFO.

Carley, S., Krause, R. M., Lane, B. W., & Graham, J. D. (2013). Intent to purchase a plug-in electric vehicle: A survey of early impressions in large US cites. *Transportation Research Part D, Transport and Environment*, *18*, 39–45. doi:10.1016/j.trd.2012.09.007

Carrol, A. B. (2008). A History of Corporate Social Responsibility, Concepts and Practices. In A. Crane, D. Matten, A. McWilliams, J. Moon, & D. S. Siegel (Eds.), *The Oxford Handbook of Corporate Social Responsibility*. OUP Oxford.

Caulfield, B., Farrell, S., & McMahon, B. (2010). Examining individuals preferences for hybrid electric and alternatively fuelled vehicles. *Transport Policy*, *17*(6), 381–387. doi:10.1016/j.tranpol.2010.04.005

Cecchetti, S.G. (1995). Inflation indicators and inflation policy. In *NBER Macroeconomics Annual* (pp. 189–219).

Çelik, S., & Haug, K. (2012, September). Revisiting the link between consumers sentiment and economic activity. *Paper presented at the 31st CIRET Conference*, Vienna.

Cervellin, G., & Lippi, G. (2011). From music-beat to heart-beat: A journey in the complex interactions between music, brain and heart. *European Journal of Internal Medicine*, *22*(4), 371–374. doi:10.1016/j.ejim.2011.02.019 PMID:21767754

Chakrabarti, R., & Berthon, P. (2012). Gift giving and social emotions: Experience as content. *Journal of Public Affairs*, *12*(2), 154–161. doi:10.1002/pa.1417

Champniss, G., Wilson, H. N., & Macdonald, E. K. (2015). Why your customers' social identities matter. *Harvard Business Review*, *93*(1/2), 88–96.

Chandra, A., Gulati, S., & Kandlikar, M. (2010). Green drivers or free riders? An analysis of tax rebates for hybrid vehicles. *Journal of Environmental Economics and Management*, *60*(2), 78–93. doi:10.1016/j.jeem.2010.04.003

Charles, H., & Schwepker, C. H. Jr. (2003). Customer-Orientated Selling: A Review, Extension, and Directions for Future Research. *Journal of Personal Selling & Sales Management*, *23*(2), 151–171.

Chase, D., & Smith, T. K. (1992). Consumers keen on green but marketers don't deliver. *Advertising Age*, *63*(29), 2–4.

Chebat, J.-C., Gelinas Chebat, C., & Vaillant, D. (2001). Environmental background music and in-store selling. *Journal of Business Research*, *54*(2), 115–123. doi:10.1016/S0148-2963(99)00089-2

Chen, G., Firth, M., & Rui, O. M. (2002). Stock market linkages: Evidence from Latin America. *Journal of Banking & Finance*, *26*(6), 113–1141. doi:10.1016/S0378-4266(01)00160-1

Cheng, S., Lam, T., & Hsu, C. H. C. (2006). Negative Word-of-Mouth Communication Intention: An Application of the Theory of Planned Behavior. *Journal of Hospitality & Tourism Research (Washington, D.C.)*, *30*(1), 95–116. doi:10.1177/1096348005284269

Chen, H.-S., & Hsieh, T. (2011). The effect of atmosphere on customer perceptions and customer behaviour responses in chain store supermarkets. *African Journal of Business Management*, *5*(24), 10054–10066. doi:10.5897/AJBM10.608

Cherrier, H. (2009). Anti-Consumption Discourses and Consumer Resistant-Identities. *Journal of Business Research*, *62*(2), 181–190. doi:10.1016/j.jbusres.2008.01.025

Cherrier, H., Russell, S. V., & Fielding, K. (2012). Corporate environmentalism and top management identity negotiation. *Journal of Organizational Change Management*, *25*(4), 518–534. doi:10.1108/09534811211239209

Chikweche Tendai, (2013). Benchmarking to improve a strategy and marketing in pharmaceuticals. *Marketing Intelligence & Planning*, *31*(7).

Cho, J. O., & Cooley, T. F. (1992). *The business cycle with nominal contracts. Manuscript*. University of Rochester.

Chong, F., & Carraro, G. (2006). Architecture Strategies for Catching the Long Tail.

Choo, S., & Mokhtarian, P. L. (2002). The relationship of vehicle type choice to personality, lifestyle, attitudinal, and demographic variables (Research Report UCD-ITS-RR-02-060. Institute of Transportation Studies, University of California. Retrieved from its.ucdavis.edu/publications/2002/RR-02-06.pdf

Choo, C. W., Detlor, B., & Turnbull, D. (2013). *Web work: Information seeking and knowledge work on the World Wide Web* (Vol. 1). Springer Science & Business Media.

Choo, S., & Mokhtarian, P. L. (2004). What type of vehicle do people drive? The role of attitude and lifestyle in influencing vehicle type choice. *Transportation Research*, *38*(3), 201–222.

Chou, H. Y., & Lien, N. H. (2010). Advertising effects of songs nostalgia and lyrics relevance. *Asia Pacific Journal of Marketing and Logistics*, *22*(3), 314–329. doi:10.1108/13555851011062278

Choy, D., & Prizzia, R. (2010). Environmental Consumerism and the Role of the Hybrid Auto in Hawaii. *International Management Review*, *6*(1), 58.

Christodoulides, G. (2009). Branding in the post-internet era, *Marketing Theory*, 9(1). Retrieved from http://mtq.sagepub.com/content/9/1/141

Chui, K. C. (1992). *An introduction to wavelets: Wavelet analysis and its applications*. San Diego: Academic Press.

Cissé-Depardon, K., & NGoala, G. (2009). The effects of satisfaction, trust and brand commitment on consumers decision to boycott[English Edition]. *Recherche et Applications en Marketing*, *24*, 43–66. doi:10.1177/076737010902400103

Citrin, A. V., Stern, D. E., Spangenberg, E. R., & Clark, M. J. (2003). Consumer Need for Tactile Input: An Internet Retailing Challenge. *Journal of Business Research*, *56*(11), 915–922. doi:10.1016/S0148-2963(01)00278-8

Clark, D. (2006). *The Rough Guide to Ethical Living*. London: Rough Guides.

Clarke, N., Barnett, C., Cloke, P., & Malpass, A. (2007). Globalising the consumer: Doing politics in an ethical register. *Political Geography*, *26*(3), 231–249. doi:10.1016/j.polgeo.2006.10.009

Clarke, N., Cloke, P., Barnett, C., & Malpass, A. (2008). The spaces and ethics of organic food. *Journal of Rural Studies*, *24*(3), 219–230. doi:10.1016/j.jrurstud.2007.12.008

Claudy, M. (2011). *An empirical investigation of consumer resistance to green product innovation* [Unpublished Doctoral Thesis]. Dublin Institute of Technology.

Claussen, D. (2006). On foolishness in football. *Análise Social*, *179*(41), 583–592. Retrieved from http://analisesocial.ics.ul.pt/?page_id=16

Clements, P., & Northrop, L. (2002). *Software Product Lines - Practices and Patterns*. Boston: Addison-Wesley.

Clemont, A., & Besselaar, O. (1993). A retrospective look at PD projects. *Communications of the ACM*, *36*(4), 29–39. doi:10.1145/153571.163264

Coddington, W. (1990). It's no fad: Environmentalism is now a fact in corporate life. *Marketing News*, *15*(Oct), 7.

Coe, N.M. and Wrigley, N. (2009). The Globalization of Retailing (Vol. I and II). Cheltenham, MA: Edward Elgar Publishing Ltd.

Coleman, P. (2006). *Shopping Environments: Evolution, Planning and Design*. Oxford: *Elsevier*.

Colon, R. M. (1997). *Causal Relationships of Familial Influence and Adolescents' Attitude toward Substance Use in the Theory of Planned Behavior: A Social Impact Model* [Unpublished PhD Thesis]. University of Houston.

Coninx, P. (2004). Hybrid vehicles - Targeting Incentives for the Next Step Forward. Report by Automobile Consumer Coalition.

Conner, M., & Norman, P. (Eds.), (2005). *Predicting Health Behaviour: Research and Practice with Social Cognition Models* (2nd ed., pp. 170–222). Maidenhead: Open University Press.

Consulting, D. (2008). Green Thinking, prepared for Green Report. Retrieved from http://www.green-report.ro/dynamic/studii/sondaje/daedalus-consulting-green-thinking-sondaj-pe-teme-de-mediu-printre-romani---9288.htm

Consumer, E. (n. d.). Product Guides. Retrieved from http://www.ethicalconsumer.org/ethicalreports/internetreport/activism.aspx

Copeland, M.V & Malik, O. (2005). How to Ride the Fifth Wave. *Business 2.0*, July.

Cornish, D., & Clarke, R. (1986). *The Reasoning Criminal: Rational Choice Perspectives on Offending*. New York: Springer-Verlag. doi:10.1007/978-1-4613-8625-4

Corrado, C., & Mattey, J. (1997). Capacity utilization. *The Journal of Economic Perspectives*, *11*(1), 151–167. doi:10.1257/jep.11.1.151

Corstjens, M. and Lal, R. (2012). Retail Doesn't Cross Borders: Here's Why and What to Do About It. *Harvard Business Review*, *90*(4), 104-111.

Cowe, R. (1993). Companies find ethics makes commercial sense. *The Guardian*, 27 April.

Cowper, R. J. (1992). Shopping Centre Management for the Nineties. *Property Management*, *10*(4), 329–337. doi:10.1108/02637479210030466

Cozens, P., Saville, G., & Hillier, D. (2005). Crime Prevention through Environmental Design (CPTED): Are View and Modern Bibliography. *Journal of Property Management*, *23*(5), 328–356. doi:10.1108/02637470510631483

Craig-Lees, M., & Hill, C. (2006, June 20-21). Anti-consumption: concept clarification and changing consumption behaviour. *Proceedings of the International Centre for Anti-Consumption Research (ICAR) Symposium*, Auckland, New Zealand.

Cran, D. J. (1994). Towards Validation of the Service Orientation Construct. *Service Industries Journal, 14*(1), 34–44. doi:10.1080/02642069400000003

Crane, A., Matten, D., & Spence, L. J. (2013). Corporate Social Responsibility: in a global context. In A. Crane, D. Matten, & L. J. Spence (Eds.), *Corporate social responsibility: readings and cases in a global context*. Abingdon: Routledge.

Crawford, A. (2015). McDonald's: A Case Study in Glocalization. *Journal of Global Business Issues, 9*(1), 11.

Crocker, D. A., & Linden, T. (Eds.). (1998). *Ethics of consumption: The good life, justice and global stewardship*. Lanham, MD: Rowman and Littlefield.

Cromie, J. G., & Ewing, M. T. (2009). The rejection of brand hegemony. *Journal of Business Research, 62*(2), 218–230. doi:10.1016/j.jbusres.2008.01.029

Cronan, T. P., & Al-Rafee, S. (2008). *Factors that influence the intention to pirate software and media*. *Journal of Business Ethics, 78*(4), 527–545. doi:10.1007/s10551-007-9366-8

Csikszentmihalyi, M. (1990). *Flow: The psychology of optimal experience*. New York: Harper and Row.

Csikszentmihaly, M. (1991). *Flow: the psychology of optimal experience*. New York, USA: Harper Collins.

Dabija, D. C., & Postelnicu, C. (2015). McDonald's-between Internationalization and Regionalization of Restaurant's Value. *Review of Management & Economic Engineering, 14*(1).

Dancey, C. P., & Reidy, J. (2002), Statistics Without Maths for Psychology (2 ed.). Dorchester: Pearson Education Ltd.

Darley, W. K., & Johnson, D. M. (1993). Cross-national comparison of consumer attitudes toward consumerism in four developing countries. *The Journal of Consumer Affairs, 27*(1), 37–54. doi:10.1111/j.1745-6606.1993.tb00736.x

Darling, R. J., Heller, V. L., & Tablada, D. M. (2009). Positioning a firms initial market offering: A strategic application of a consumer-oriented model. *European Business Review, 21*(6), 516–530. doi:10.1108/09555340910998814

Daubechies, I. (1992). *Ten lectures on wavelet. CBMS-NSF Regional Conference Series in Applied Mathematics* (Vol. 61). Philadelphia: Society for Industrial and Applied Mathematics.

Daunt, K. L., & Harris, L. C. (2012b). Exploring the Forms of Dysfunctional Customer Behaviour: A Study of Differences in Servicescape and Customer Disaffection with Service. *Journal of Marketing Management, 28*(1/2), 129–153. doi:10.1080/0267257X.2011.619149

Daunt, K., & Harris, L. C. (2012a). Motives of Dysfunctional Customer Behavior: An Empirical Study. *Journal of Services Marketing, 26*(4), 293–308. doi:10.1108/08876041211237587

Dauvergne, P. (2008). *The Shadows of Consumption: Consequences for the Global Environment*. Cambridge, MA: The MIT Press.

Dave, C. (2006). Why is high capacity utilization no longer inflationary in Canada? (Working Paper). Department of Finance, Canada.

Davies, H. (2011). Why I like my pleasures one at a time. *New Statesman*. Retrieved from http://www.newstatesman.com/sport/2011/03/cup-final-football-madrid

Davis, G. (1982). Strategies for information requirements determination. *IBM Systems Journal, 21*(1), 4–31. doi:10.1147/sj.211.0004

Davis, S. C., Diegel, S. W., & Boundy, R. G. (2015). *Transportation Energy Data Book* (34th ed.). Vehicle Technologies Office, Office of Energy Efficiency and Renewable Energy, U.S. Department of Energy.

Dawkins, J., & Lewis, S. (2003). CSR in stakeholder expectations: And their implication for company strategy. *Journal of Business Ethics*, *44*(2), 185–193. doi:10.1023/A:1023399732720

Day, R.-F., Lin, C.-H., Huang, W.-H., & Chuang, S.-H. (2009). Effects of music tempo and task difficulty on multi-attribute decision-making: An eye-tracking approach. *Computers in Human Behavior*, *25*(1), 130–143. doi:10.1016/j.chb.2008.08.001

Daziano, R. A. (2013). Conditional-logit Bayes estimators for consumer valuation of electric vehicle driving range. *Resource and Energy Economics*, *35*(3), 429–450. doi:10.1016/j.reseneeco.2013.05.001

De Farias, S. A. (2010, May 23-25), Store Atmospherics and Experiential Marketing: a conceptual framework and research propositions for an extraordinary customer experience. Proceedings of the IV Encontro de Marketing da AN-PAD, Florianopolis/SC. Retrieved from http://www.anpad.org.br/diversos/trabalhos/EMA/ema_2010/2010_EMA27.pdf

de Haan, P., Duthaler, C., Peters, A., & Smieszek, T. (2006). Characteristics of buyers of hybrid Honda Civic IMA: Preferences, decision process, vehicle ownership, and willingness-to-pay [Bericht zum Schweizer Autokaufverhalten]. ETH Zurich.

De Pelsmaker, P., Janssen, W., & Mielants, C. (2005). Consumer values and fair-trade beliefs, attitudes and buying behaviour. *International Review on Public and Non Profit Marketing*, *2*(2), 50–69.

De Ven, B. (2008). An Ethical Framework for the Marketing of Corporate Social Responsibility. *Journal of Business Ethics*, *82*(2), 339–352. doi:10.1007/s10551-008-9890-1

Decima Research Inc. (2004). Automotive Purchase Considerations in Canada (Report 23496-052112/001/CY).

DEFRA. (2008, January). A Framework for Pro-Environmental Behaviors Report by Department for Environment, Food and Rural Affairs.

Delacote, P. (2009). On the sources of consumer boycotts ineffectiveness. *Journal of Environment & Development*, *18*(3), 306–322. doi:10.1177/1070496509338849

Delgado, M. S., Harriger, J. L., & Khanna, N. (2015). The value of environmental status signaling. *Ecological Economics*, *111*, 1–11. doi:10.1016/j.ecolecon.2014.12.021

Dell. (n. d.). DFS home page. Retrieved from http://www.dell.com/learn/us

Demiroglu, U., & Sarıkaya, C. (2013). *The capacity buildup over the past decade and the capacity utilization rate in Turkey. CBT Research Notes in Economics 1312*. Research and Monetary Policy Department, Central Bank of the Republic of Turkey.

Devinney, T. (2006). The other CSR, FLO. Retrieved from http://www.fairtrade.net

Diamond, D. (2009). The impact of government incentives for hybrid-electric vehicles: Evidence from US states. *Energy Policy*, *37*(3), 972–983. doi:10.1016/j.enpol.2008.09.094

Diener, E., Emmons, R. A., Larson, R. J., & Griffin, S. (1985). The satisfaction with life scale. *Journal of Personality Assessment*, *49*(1), 71–75. doi:10.1207/s15327752jpa4901_13 PMID:16367493

Diener, E., & Lucas, R. (1999). Personality and Subjective Well-being. In D. Kahneman, E. Diener, & N. Schwarz (Eds.), *Well-being: The Foundations of Hedonic Psychology*. New York: Russell Sage Foundation.

Diener, E., Oishi, S., & Lucas, R. E. (2002). Subjective well-being: The science of happiness and life satisfaction. In C. R. Snyder & S. J. Lopez (Eds.), *Handbook of Positive Psychology*. Oxford, New York: Oxford University Press.

Djurdjevic, E. (2013). *The Effects of Social Contextual Factors on Rater Motivation and Performance Ratings* [Unpublished PhD Thesis]. University of Arkansas.

Dolan, C. S. (2008). Arbitrating risk through moral values: The case of Kenyan Fairtrade. *Research in Economic Anthropology, 28*, 271–296. doi:10.1016/S0190-1281(08)28012-1

Dombos, T. (2008). Longing for the West: The geo-symbolics of the ethical consumption discourse in Hungary. *Research in Economic Anthropology, 28*, 123–141. doi:10.1016/S0190-1281(08)28006-6

Dong, B., Evans, K. R., & Zou, S. (2008). The effects of customer participation in co-created service recovery. *Journal of the Academy of Marketing Science, 36*(1), 123–137. doi:10.1007/s11747-007-0059-8

Donnelly, C., Simmons, G., Armstrong, G., & Fearne, A. (2015). Digital loyalty card 'big data and small business marketing: Formal versus informal or complementary? *International Small Business Journal, 33*(4), 422–442. doi:10.1177/0266242613502691

Donovan, R. J., & Rossiter, J. R. (1982). Store Atmosphere: An Environmental Psychology Approach. *Journal of Retailing, 58*(Spring), 34–57.

Dörbecker, R., & Böhmann, T. (2013). The Concept and Effects of Service Modularity--A Literature Review. *Paper presented at the 2013 46th Hawaii International Conference on System Sciences (HICSS).*

Dragicevic, M., & Rakidzija, I. (2012). The music as an element of physical evidence in service organizations. *Procedia Economics and Finance, 3*, 666–671. doi:10.1016/S2212-5671(12)00212-2

Drew, S. (2003). Strategic uses of e-commerce by SMEs in the east of England. *European Management Journal, 21*(1), 79–88. doi:10.1016/S0263-2373(02)00148-2

DSouza, C., Taghian, M., & Khosla, R. (2007). Examination of Environmental Beliefs an its Impact on the Influence of Price, Quality and Demographic Characteristics with respect to Green Purchase Intention. *Journal of Targeting. Measurement and Analysis for Marketing, 15*(2), 69–78. doi:10.1057/palgrave.jt.5750039

Dube, L., & Morin, S. (2001). Background music pleasure and store evaluation: Intensity effects and psychological mechanisms. *Journal of Business Research, 54*(2), 107–113. doi:10.1016/S0148-2963(99)00092-2

Dubinsky, A. J., & Hensel, P. J. (1984). Marketing student attitudes toward advertising: Implications for marketing education. *Journal of Marketing Education, 6*(Summer), 22–26. doi:10.1177/027347538400600206

Dubois, E., & Pohl, K. (2003). RE 02: A major step toward a mature requirements engineering community. *IEEE Software, 20*(1), 14–15. doi:10.1109/MS.2003.1159024

Duclos, L. K., Siha, S. M., & Lummus, R. R. (1995). JIT in Services: A Review of Current Practices and Future Directions for Research. *International Journal of Service Industry Management, 6*(5), 36–52. doi:10.1108/09564239510101518

Dumortier, J., Siddiki, S., Carley, S., Cisney, J., Krause, R. M., Lane, B. W., & Graham, J. D. et al. (2015). Effects of providing total cost of ownership information on consumers intent to purchase a hybrid or plug-in electric vehicle. *Transportation Research Part A, Policy and Practice, 72*, 71–86. doi:10.1016/j.tra.2014.12.005

Dunbar, D. S. (1990). Music and Advertising. *International Journal of Advertising, 9*, 197–203.

Duncan, T., & Mulhern, F. (2004). A White Paper on the Status, Scope and Future of IMC. New York: McGraw-Hill

Duncan, T. (2001). *IMC: Using Advertising & Promotion to Build Brands*. Boston: McGrawHill.

Dunn, K. (2015). Globalization and consumer: What marketer needs to know. *The Neumann Business Review*, 2015, 16-30.

Du, X., Jiao, J., & Tseng, M. M. (2001). Architecture of Product Family: Fundamentals and Methodology. *Concurrent Engineering*, *9*(4), 309–325. doi:10.1177/1063293X0100900407

Dwyer, W. O., Leeming, F. C., Cobern, M. K., Porter, B. E., & Jackson, J. M. (1993). Critical review of behavioral interventions to preserve the environment: Research since 1980. *Environment and Behavior*, *25*(5), 275–321. doi:10.1177/0013916593255001

Eagly, A. H., & Kulesa, P. (1997). Attitudes, attitude structure, the resistance to change. In M.H. Bazermann, D.M. Messick, A.E. Tenbrunsel et al. (Eds.), Environment, Ethics, and Behavior (pp. 122-153). San Francisco, CA: The New Lexington Press.

Echeverri, P., Salomonson, N., & Åberg, A. (2012). Dealing with Customer Misbehaviour: Employees Tactics, Practical Judgement and Implicit Knowledge. *Marketing Theory*, *12*(4), 427–449. doi:10.1177/1470593112457741

Edgar, B., Doherty, J., & Meert, H. (2004). *Immigration and homelessness in Europe*. Policy Pr.

Edvardsson, B. (2005). Service Quality: Beyond Cognitive Assessment. *Managing Service Quality*, *15*(2), 127–131. doi:10.1108/09604520510585316

Edwards, S. M. (2011). A social media mindset. *Journal of Interactive Advertising*, *12*(1), 1–3. doi:10.1080/15252019.2011.10722186

Eisenhardt, K. M. (1989). Building Theories from Case Study Research. *Academy of Management Review*, *14*(4), 532–550.

El Dief, M., & Font, X. (2010). The determinants of hotels marketing managers green marketing behaviour. *Journal of Sustainable Tourism*, *18*(2), 157–174. doi:10.1080/09669580903464232

Elliott, R. (1997). Existential consumption and irrational desire. *European Journal of Marketing*, *31*(3/4), 285–296. doi:10.1108/03090569710162371

Elyasiani, E., Priyal, P., & Puri, T. N. (1998). Interdependence and dynamic linkages between stock markets of Sri Lanka and its trading partners. *Journal of Multinational Finance Management*, *8*(1), 89–101. doi:10.1016/S1042-444X(98)00020-6

Emery, K. M., & Chang, C. P. (1997). *Is there a stable relationship between capacity utilization and inflation?* Federal Reserve Bank of Dallas Economic Review First Quarter.

Environics Research Group. (2005). *Development of a New Vehicle Rating System: Psychographic Segmentation and Consumer Consultations*. Report prepared for Natural Resources Canada.

Eres, B. (2011). Alternative measures of rate of capacity utilization for the Turkish economy: A Comparative Analysis in Means of Adequacy for Empirical Investigation and Growth Models. *Sosyoekonomi*, *2011-12*, 110211.

Eriksson, P., & Kovalainen, A. (2008). Qualitative methods in business research. *Sage*.

Ernst, H., Hoyer, W. D., Krafft, M., & Soll, J.-H. (2010). Consumer Idea Generation (working paper). WHU, Vallendar.

Eroglu, S. A., Machleit, K. A., & Chebat, J. C. (2005). The Interaction of Retail Density and Music Tempo: Effects on Shopper Responses. *Psychology and Marketing*, *22*(7), 577–589. doi:10.1002/mar.20074

Estes, R. M. (1971). Consumerism & Business. *California Management Review*, *14*(2), 5–11. doi:10.2307/41164327

Etgar, M. (2008). A Descriptive Model of the Consumer Co-Production Process. *Journal of the Academy of Marketing Science*, *36*(Spring), 97–108. doi:10.1007/s11747-007-0061-1

EthicalConsumer. (n. d.). Successful Consumer Boycotts: Ethical Consumer. Retrieved from http://www.ethicalconsumer.org/boycotts/successfulboycotts.aspx

Ettenson, R., & Klein, J. G. (2005). The fallout from French nuclear testing in the South Pacific: A longitudinal study of consumer boycotts. *International Marketing Review*, *22*(2), 199–224. doi:10.1108/02651330510593278

Etzioni, A. (1986, August 24). The Fast-Food Factories: McJobs are Bad for Kids. *The Washington Post.*

Etzioni, A. (1998). Voluntary simplicity characterization, select psychological implications, and social consequences. *Journal of Economic Psychology*, *19*(5), 619–643.

European Commission. (2012a). Retail Forum. Retrieved from http://ec.europa.eu/environment/industry/retail/indexen.html

European Fair Trade Association. (n. d.). Retrieved from http://www.european-fair-trade-association.org/efta/index.php

Fairtrade Labelling Organizations International. (n. d.). What is FairTrade? Retrieved from http://www.fairtrade.net/about-fairtrade/what-is-fairtrade.html

Farah, M. F., & Newman, A. J. (2009). Exploring consumer boycott intelligence using a socio -cognitive approach. *Journal of Business Research.*

Farnsworth, P. R. (1969). *The Social Psychology of Music*. Iowa City, Iowa: The University of Iowa Press.

Feick, L., & Price, L. (1987). The Market Maven: A Dif-fuser of Marketplace Information. *Journal of Marketing*, *51*(1), 83–97. doi:10.2307/1251146

Fershtman, C., & Gandal, N. (1998). The effect of the Arab boycott on Israel: The automobile market. *The Rand Journal of Economics*, *29*(1), 193–214. doi:10.2307/2555822

Fetchner, G. T. (1876). *Vorschule der Asthetik*. Leipzig: Breithopf & Hartal.

Fichtenbaum, R. (2003). Is there a natural level of capacity utilization? *Forum for Social Economics*, *33*(1), 45–62. doi:10.1007/BF02778965

Finn, M. G. (1995). Is 'high' capacity utilization inflationary? *Economic Quarterly, Federal Reserve Bank of Richmond.*

Firat, A. F., & Dholakia, N. (1982). Consumption Choices at the Macro Level. *Journal of Macromarketing*, *2*(2), 6–15. doi:10.1177/027614678200200202

Fisk, R., Grove, S., Harris, L. C., Keeffe, D., Daunt, K. L., Russell-Bennett, R., & Wirtz, J. (2010). Customers Behaving Badly: A State of the Art Review, Research Agenda and Implications for Practitioners. *Journal of Services Marketing*, *24*(6), 417–429. doi:10.1108/08876041011072537

Forbes, (2011). 3 Steps to More Honest Business. Retrieved from http://www.forbes.com/sites/thebigenoughcompany/2011/09/21/3-steps-to-a-more-honest-business/

Fornell, C. (1992, January). A national customer satisfaction barometer: The Swedish experience. *Journal of Marketing*, *56*(1), 6–21. doi:10.2307/1252129

Fotis, J. N. (2015). *The Use of social media and its impacts on consumer behaviour: the context of holiday travel* [Doctoral dissertation]. Bournemouth University.

Foxall, G. R. (1997). The Emotional Texture of Consumer Environments: A Systematic Approach to Atmospherics. *Journal of Economic Psychology*, *18*(4), 505–523. doi:10.1016/S0167-4870(97)00021-4

Foxall, G. R., & Greenley, G. E. (1999). Consumers Emotional Responses to Service Environments. *Journal of Business Research*, *46*(2), 149–158. doi:10.1016/S0148-2963(98)00018-6

Foxall, G. R., & Greenley, G. E. (2000). Predicting and Explaining Responses to Consumer Environments: An Empirical Test and Theoretical Extension of the Behavioural Perspective Model. *Service Industries Journal*, *20*(2), 39–63. doi:10.1080/02642060000000019

Frank, B. (2012). How can customer-based brand equity be increased through sports sponsorship? Master of International Business in Strategic Marketing. Netherlands: Maastricht University. Retrieved from http://pt.scribd.com/doc/86734653/How-Can-Customer-Based-Brand-Equity-Be-Increased-Throug-Sports-Sponsorship

Freeman, R. E., & Velamuri, S. R. (2006). A new approach to CSR: Company stakeholder responsibility. In Corporate social responsibility (pp. 9-23). UK: Palgrave Macmillan.

Freeman, R. E., & Phillips, R. A. (2002). Stakeholder theory: A libertarian defence. *Business Ethics Quarterly*, *12*(3), 333. doi:10.2307/3858020

Freeman, R. E., Wicks, A. C., & Parmar, B. (2004, May-June). Stakeholder Theory and The Corporate Objective Revisited. *Organization Science*, *15*(3), 364–369. doi:10.1287/orsc.1040.0066

Freeman, R. E., Wicks, A., Harrison, J., Parmar, B., & de Colle, S. (2010). *Stakeholder Theory: The State of The Art*. Cambridge University Press. doi:10.1017/CBO9780511815768

French, W. A., Barksdale, H. C., & Perreault, W. D. (1982). Consumer attitudes towards marketing in England and the United States. *European Journal of Marketing*, *16*(6), 20–30. doi:10.1108/EUM0000000004853

Frey, B. S., & Stutzer, A. (2002). *Happiness and Economics: How the Economy and Institutions Effect Human Well Being*. Princeton, NJ: Princeton University Press.

Friedman, M. (1985). Consumer boycotts in the United States, 1970-1980: Contemporary events in historical perspective. *The Journal of Consumer Affairs*, 19(1), 96-117.

Friedman, M. (1996). A positive approach to organized consumer action: The buycott as an alternative to the boycott. *Journal of Consumer Policy*, *19*(4), 439–451. doi:10.1007/BF00411502

Friend, L. A., Costley, C. L., & Brown, C. (2010). Spirals of Distrust vs Spirals of Trust in Retail Customer Service: Consumers as Victims or Allies. *Journal of Services Marketing*, *24*(6), 458–467. doi:10.1108/08876041011072573

Ftiti, Z., Tiwari, A., Belanes, A., & Guesmi, K. (2015). Tests of financial market contagion: Evolutionary cospectral analysis vs. wavelet analysis. *Computational Economics*, *46*(4), 575–611. doi:10.1007/s10614-014-9461-8

Fullerton, R. A., & Punj, G. (1993). Choosing to Misbehave: A Structural Model of Aberrant Consumer Behavior. *Advances in Consumer Research. Association for Consumer Research (U. S.)*, *20*, 570–574.

Fullerton, R. A., & Punj, G. (1997). What is Consumer Misbehavior? *Advances in Consumer Research. Association for Consumer Research (U. S.)*, *24*, 336–339.

Fullerton, R. A., & Punj, G. (2004). Repercussions of Promoting an Ideology of Consumption: Consumer Misbehavior. *Journal of Business Research*, *57*(11), 1239–1249. doi:10.1016/S0148-2963(02)00455-1

Funk, D. C., & James, J. D. (2004). The Fan Attitude Network (FAN) Model: Exploring attitude formation and change among sport consumers. *Sport Management Review*, *7*(1), 1–26. doi:10.1016/S1441-3523(04)70043-1

Gallagher, K. S., & Muehlegger, E. (2011). Giving green to get green? Incentives and consumer adoption of hybrid vehicle technology. *Journal of Environmental Economics and Management*, *61*(1), 1–15. doi:10.1016/j.jeem.2010.05.004

Gallaugher, J. M. (2002). E-commerce and the undulating distribution channel. *Communications of the ACM*, *45*(7), 89–95. doi:10.1145/514236.514240

Gallegati, M. (2005). A wavelet analysis of MENA stock markets.

Gallegati, M. (2012). A wavelet-based approach to test for financial market contagion. *Computational Statistics & Data Analysis*, *56*(11), 3491–3497. doi:10.1016/j.csda.2010.11.003

Gall, Z. (2004). *Glazbeni leksikon, Marjan Tisak, d.o.o.* Split: Hrvatska.

Garcia, R., & Balbaky, S. (2006). Vehicle choice decision-making: What are the factors with which consumers choose their automobile purchases? (working paper). Northeastern University.

Gardner, M. P. (1985). Mood States and Consumer Behavior: A Critical Review. *The Journal of Consumer Research*, *12*(3), 281–300. doi:10.1086/208516

Garlin, F. V., & Owen, K. (2006). Setting the tone with the tune: "A meta-analytic review of the effect of background music in retail settings. *Journal of Business Research*, *59*(6), 755–764. doi:10.1016/j.jbusres.2006.01.013

Garner, A.C. (1994). Capacity utilization and U.S. inflation. *Federal Reserve Bank of Kansas City Economic Review*, Fourth Quarter, 1–21.

Garrett, D. (1987). The effectiveness of marketing policy boycotts: Environmental opposition to marketing. *Journal of Marketing*, *51*(April), 46–57. doi:10.2307/1251128

Gasca P. (2014, July 29). McDonald's Rebranding Strategy: Why the World's Biggest Restaurant Thinks It's Time to Tweak Its Recipe. *Inc.com.*

Gaski, J. F., & Etzel, M. J. (1986, July). The Index of Consumer Sentiment toward Marketing. *Journal of Marketing*, *50*(3), 71–81. doi:10.2307/1251586

Gawlinski, M. (2003). *Interactive television production.* Oxford: Focal Press.

Gefen, D., & Straub, D. W. (2004). Consumer trust in B2C e-Commerce and the importance of social presence: Experiments in e-Products and e-Services. *Omega*, *32*(6), 407–424. doi:10.1016/j.omega.2004.01.006

Gelb, B. D. (1995). More boycotts ahead? Some implications. *Business Horizons*, *38*(2), 70–77. doi:10.1016/0007-6813(95)90058-6

Gelos, G., & Sahay, R. (2000). Financial market spillovers in transition economies. *IMF Working Paper*, *2000*(71).

Gençay, R., Selçuk, F., & Witcher, B. (2001). Differentiating intraday seasonalities through wavelet multi-scaling. *Physica A*, *289*(3-4), 543–556. doi:10.1016/S0378-4371(00)00463-5

Gerhardt, S., Hazen, S., & Lewis, S. (2014). Small Business Marketing Strategy Based on McDonald's. *ASBBS Proceedings, 21*(1), 271.

GfK. (2015). SHOPPING MONITOR Croatia. Retrieved from http://progressive.com.hr/demo/2095-gfk-shoppingmonitor-hipermarketi-najpopularniji-oblik-trgovine-.html

Ghemawat, P. (2007). Managing Differences: The Central Challenge of Global Strategy. *Harvard Business Review*, 85(3), 58-68.

Giddens, A. (1991). *Modernity and Self-identity.* Stanford, CA: Stanford University Press.

Giese, J. L., & Cote, J. A. (2000). *Defining customer satisfaction.* Academy of Marketing Science Review. Retrieved from www.amsreview.org/articles/giese01-2000.pdf

Gifford B. (1991, August 19). The Greening of the Golden Arches-McDonald's Teams With Environmental Group to Cut Waste. *The San Diego Union*, C1 & C4.

Gilboa, S., & Rafaeli, A. (2003). Store Environment, Emotions and Approach Behavior: Applying Environmental Aesthetics to Retailing. *International Review of Retail, Distribution and Consumer research*, 13(2), 195-211. Retrieved from http://iew3.technion.ac.il/Home/Users/anatr/COMPLE-FINAL-20-11-02.pdf

Gilmore, E. A., & Lave, L. B. (2013). Comparing resale prices and total cost of ownership for gasoline, hybrid and diesel passenger cars and trucks. *Transport Policy*, *27*, 200–208. doi:10.1016/j.tranpol.2012.12.007

Ginsberg, J. M., & Bloom, P. N. (2004). Choosing the right green marketing strategy. *MIT Sloan Management Review*, *46*(1), 79–84.

Gjerdingen, R. O., & Perrott, D. (2008). Scanning the Dial: The Rapid Recognition of Music Genres. *Journal of New Music Research*, *37*(2), 93–100. doi:10.1080/09298210802479268

Godazgar, H. (2007). Islam versus consumerism and postmodernism in the context of Iran. *Social Compass*, *54*(3), 389–418. doi:10.1177/0037768607080835

Gordon, J. (2013). Big Data, Analytics and The Future Of Marketing And Sales. *Forbes*. Retrieved from http://www.forbes.com/sites/mckinsey/2013/07/22/big-data-analytics-and-the-future-of-marketing-sales/#1a9591ae344d

Graham-Rowe, E., Gardner, B., Abraham, C., Skippon, S., Dittmar, H., Hutchins, R., & Stannard, J. (2012). Mainstream consumers driving plug-in battery-electric and plug-in hybrid electric cars: A qualitative analysis of responses and evaluations. *Transportation Research Part A, Policy and Practice*, *46*(1), 140–153. doi:10.1016/j.tra.2011.09.008

Grandey, A. A., Dickter, D. N., & Sin, H. (2004). The Customer is not Always Right: Customer Aggression and Emotion Regulation of Service Employees. *Journal of Organizational Behavior*, *25*(3), 397–418. doi:10.1002/job.252

Grandon, E. E., & Pearson, J. M. (2004). Electronic commerce adoption: An empirical study of small and medium US businesses. *Information & Management*, *42*(1), 197–216. doi:10.1016/j.im.2003.12.010

Graves, P. (2010). *Consumerology: The Market Research Myth, the Truth About Consumers, and the Psychology of Shopping*. Boston: Nicholas Brealey Publishing.

Gray, H. P. (1999). *Global Economic Involvement*. Copenhagen: Copenhagen Business School Press. Hood, N.

Gray, J. (1985). *Ecological Beliefs and Behaviour*. London: Greenwood Press.

Grayson, K., Johnson, D., & Chen, D.-F. R. (2008). Is firm trust essential in a trusted environment? How trust in the business context influences customers. *JMR, Journal of Marketing Research*, *45*(2), 241–256. doi:10.1509/jmkr.45.2.241

Greenwood, J., Hercowitz, Z., & Huffman, W. (1988). Investment, capacity utilization and the real business cycle. *American Economic Association*, *78*(3), 402–417.

Greyser, S. A. (1977). Public Attitudes and Consumerism. In Cady, J.F. (Ed.), *Marketing and Public Interest:Proceedings of Symposium*, Cambridge, Mass. (pp. 299-309).

Greyser, S. A., & Diamond, S. L. (1974). Business in Adapting to Consumerism. *Harvard Business Review*, *52*(September-October), 38–58.

Grönroos, C. (2000). *Service Management and Marketing. A Consumer Relationship Management Approach*. Chichester: John Wiley & Sons.

Grönroos, C. (2007). *Service management and marketing - customer management in service competition*. Chichester: Wiley.

Grönroos, C. (2007a). *Service Management and Marketing - Customer Management in Service Competition*. Chichester: Wiley.

Grönroos, C., Heinonen, F., Isoniemi, K., & Lindholm, M. (2000). The NetOffer Model: A Case Example from the Virtual Marketspace. *Management Decision*, *38*(4), 243–252. doi:10.1108/00251740010326252

Gummesson, E. (1994). *Relationship Marketing: From 4Ps to 30Rs*. Stockholm, Sweden: Stockholm University.

Gummesson, E. (2002). *Total Relationship Marketing*. Oxford: Butterworth-Heinemann.

Gundlach, R. C. (1935). Factors determining characterization of musical phrases. *The American Journal of Psychology*, *47*(4), 624–643. doi:10.2307/1416007

Gupta, S., & Ogden, D. T. (2009). To buy or not to buy? A social dilemma perspective on green buying. *Journal of Consumer Marketing*, *26*(6), 376–391. doi:10.1108/07363760910988201

Haanaes, K., Balagopal, B., Arthur, D., Kong, M. T., Velken, I., Kruschwitz, N., & Hopkins, M. S. (2011). First Look: The Second Annual Sustainability & Innovation Survey. *Sloan Management Review*, *52*(2).

Hackbarth, A., & Madlener, R. (2013). Consumer preferences for alternative fuel vehicles: A discrete choice analysis. *Transportation Research Part D, Transport and Environment*, *25*, 5–17. doi:10.1016/j.trd.2013.07.002

Haddadian, G., Khodayar, M., & Shahidehpour, M. (2015). Accelerating the Global Adoption of Electric Vehicles: Barriers and Drivers. *The Electricity Journal*, *28*(10), 53–68. doi:10.1016/j.tej.2015.11.011

Hagman, J., Ritzén, S., Stier, J. J., & Susilo, Y. (2016). Total cost of ownership and its potential implications for battery electric vehicle diffusion. *Research in Transportation Business & Management*.

Hakanen, T., & Jaakkola, E. (2012). Co-creating customer-focused solutions within business networks: A service perspective. *Journal of Service Management*, *23*(4), 593–611. doi:10.1108/09564231211260431

Halkier, B. (2010). *Consumption Challenged*. Surrey: Ashgate.

Hall, S. M. (2011). Exploring the ethical everyday: An ethnography of the ethics of family consumption. *Geoforum*, *42*(6), 627–637. doi:10.1016/j.geoforum.2011.06.009

Hamilton, C., & Mail, E. (2003). *Downshifting in Australia: A Sea-Change in the Pursuit of Happiness*. Australia Institute, Canberra.

Hänninen, J., Tuunanen, T., & Vartiainen, T. (2015). Value Co-Creation for Cyber-Physical Systems in Mining and Construction Industry.

Hänninen, J., Tuunanen, T., & Vartiainen, T. (2015, August 13-15). Value Co-Creation for Cyber-Physical Systems in Mining and Construction Industry. *Paper presented at theAmericas Conference on Information Systems (AMCIS)*, Puerto Rico.

Hansen, G. D., & Prescott, E. C. (2005). Capacity constraints, asymmetries, and the business cycle. *Review of Economic Dynamics*, *8*(4), 850–865. doi:10.1016/j.red.2005.08.001

Hansla, A., Gamble, A., Juliusson, A., & Gärling, T. (2007). The relationships between awareness of consequences, environmental concern, and value orientations. *Journal of Environmental Psychology*, *28*(10), 1–9.

Hargreeves, D. (1994). The cost of a fair deal. *Financial Times*, 17 March.

Harker, P. T. (1995). *Introduction* (pp. 1–10). The Service Productivity and Quality Challenge.

Harris, L. C., & Daunt, K. (2013). Managing Customer Misbehavior: Challenges and Strategies. *Journal of Services Marketing*, *27*(4), 281–293. doi:10.1108/08876041311330762

Harris, L. C., & Daunt, K. L. (2011). Deviant Customer Behaviour: A Study of Techniques of Neutralization. *Journal of Marketing Management*, *27*(7-8), 834–853. doi:10.1080/0267257X.2010.498149

Harris, L. C., & Reynolds, K. (2003). The Consequences of Dysfunctional Consumer Behavior. *Journal of Service Research*, *6*(2), 144–161. doi:10.1177/1094670503257044

Harris, L. C., & Reynolds, K. L. (2004). Jaycustomer Behavior: An Exploration into the Types and Motives in the Hospitality Industry. *Journal of Services Marketing*, *18*(5), 339–357. doi:10.1108/08876040410548276

Harrison, J. S., & Freeman, R. E. (1999). Stakeholders, Social Responsibility, and Performance: Empirical Evidence and Theoretical Perspectives. *Academy of Management Journal*, *42*(5), 479–485. doi:10.2307/256971

Harrison, R., Newholm, T., & Shaw, D. (2005). *The ethical consumer*. London: Sage.

Harton, H. C., Green, L. R., Jackson, C., & Latane, B. (1998). Demonstrating dynamic social impact: Consolidation, clustering, correlation and (sometimes) the correct answer. *Teaching of Psychology*, *25*(1), 31–35. doi:10.1207/s15328023top2501_9

Harvey, J. K., & Nancy, L. G. (2014). Work values and beliefs of Generation X and Generation Y. *Journal of Youth Studies*, *17*(1), 92–112. doi:10.1080/13676261.2013.815701

Ha, S., & Stoel, L. (2009). Consumer e-shopping acceptance: Antecedents in a technology acceptance model. *Journal of Business Research*, *62*(5), 565–571. doi:10.1016/j.jbusres.2008.06.016

Hauser, J., Tellis, G. J., & Griffin, A. (2006). Research on Innovation: A Review and Agenda for Marketing Science. *Marketing Science*, *25*(6), 686–717. doi:10.1287/mksc.1050.0144

Hausknecht, D. R. (1990). *Measurement scales in consumer satisfaction/dissatisfaction*. Journal of Consumer Satisfaction. *Dissatisfaction and Complaining Behavior*, *3*, 1–11.

Hawken, P. (2002). McDonald's and Corporate Social Responsibility, Press Release from Food First. *Institute for Food and Development Policy*.

Hayes, R., & Blackwood, R. (2006). Evaluating the Effects of EAS on Product Sales and Loss: Results of a Large-Scale Field Experiment. *Security Journal*, *19*(4), 262–276. doi:10.1057/palgrave.sj.8350025

Hayes, R., & Downs, D. M. (2011). Controlling Retail Theft with CCTV Domes, CCTV Public View Monitors, and Protective Containers: A Randomized Controlled Trial. *Security Journal*, *24*(3), 237–250. doi:10.1057/sj.2011.12

Hayes, R., Johns, T., Scicchitano, M., Downs, D., & Pietrawska, B. (2011). Evaluating the Effects of Protective Keeper Boxes on Hot Product Loss and Sales: A Randomized Controlled Trial. *Security Journal*, *24*(3), 357–369. doi:10.1057/sj.2011.2

Headey, B., & Wearing, A. (1992). *Understanding Happiness*. Melbourne, Australia: Longman Chesire.

Heaven, P. C. L., & Ciarrochi, J. (2012). When IQ is not everything: Intelligence, personality and academic performance at school. *Personality and Individual Differences*, *53*(4), 518–522. doi:10.1016/j.paid.2012.04.024

Heffner, R., Turrentine, T., & Kurani, K. (2006). *A Primer on Automobile Semiotics*. Institute of Transportation Studies. University of California.

He, L., Wang, M., Chen, W., & Conzelmann, G. (2014). Incorporating social impact on new product adoption in choice modeling: A case study in green vehicles. *Transportation Research Part D, Transport and Environment*, *32*, 421–434. doi:10.1016/j.trd.2014.08.007

Helkkula, A. (2011). Characterising the Concept of Service Experience. *Journal of Service Management*, *22*(3), 367–389. doi:10.1108/09564231111136872

Hellenic Republic Hellenic Statistical Authority. (2014). *Household Budget Survey.* Retrieved from http://www.statistics.gr/documents/20181/985039/Results+of+the+Household+Budget+Survey+(HBS)/338cb80b-6b5f-4d67-83d5-1f8fa77abf12?version=1.0

Helmholtz, H. (1862). Die Lehre von den Tonempfindunen. Verlag: Friedrich Vieweg & Sohn, Braunschweig.

Henion, K. E., & Kinnear, T. C. (1976). *Measuring the Effect of Ecological Information and Social Class on Selected Product Choice Criteria Importance Ratings, Ecological Marketing* (pp. 145–156). Chicago: American Marketing Association.

Hennig-Thurau, T., Gwinner, K. P., & Gremler, D. D. (2002). U*nderstanding relationship marketing outcomes: An integration of relational benefits and relationship quality. Journal of Service Research*, *4*(3), 230–247. doi:10.1177/1094670502004003006

Herrington, J. D., & Capella, L. M. (1994). Practical applications of music in service settings. *Journal of Services Marketing*, *8*(3), 50–65. doi:10.1108/08876049410065615

Herrington, J. D., & Capella, L. M. (1996). Effects of music in service environments: A field study. *Journal of Services Marketing*, *10*(2), 26–41. doi:10.1108/08876049610114249

Hertz, N. (2001). *The Silent Takeover. Global Capitalism and The Death of Democracy.* London: William Heinemann.

Hevner, A. R., March, S. T., & Park, J. (2004). Design Research in Information Systems Research. *Management Information Systems Quarterly*, *28*(1), 75–105.

Hevner, K. (1935). Expression in music: A discussion of experimental studies and theories. *Psychological Review*, *42*(2), 186–204. doi:10.1037/h0054832

Hill, A. V., Collier, D. A., Froehle, C. M., Goodale, J. C., Metters, R. D., & Verma, R. (2002). Research opportunities in service process design. *Journal of Operations Management*, *20*(2), 189–202. doi:10.1016/S0272-6963(01)00092-4

Hilton, M. (2003). *Consumerism in twentieth-century Britain: The search for a historical movement.* Cambridge: Cambridge University Press. doi:10.1017/CBO9780511610097

Hines, J. M., Hungerford, H. R., & Tomera, A. N. (1986). Analysis and synthesis of research on responsible pro-environmental behavior: A meta-analysis. *The Journal of Environmental Education*, *18*(2), 1–8. doi:10.1080/00958964.1987.9943482

Hirschheim, R., Heinzl, K. K., & Lyytinen, K. (1995). *Information Systems Development and Data Modelling.* Cambridge University Press. doi:10.1017/CBO9780511895425

Hirschheim, R., Klein, H. K., & Lyytinen, K. (2003). *Information Systems Development and Data Modeling: Conceptual and Philosophical Foundations.* Cambridge University Press.

Hobson, K. (2006). Environmental responsibility and the possibilities of pragmatist orientated research. *Social & Cultural Geography*, *7*(2), 283–298. doi:10.1080/14649360600600734

Hoffman, D. L., Kopalle, P. K., & Novak, T. P. (2010). The "Right" Consumers for Better Concepts: Identifying and Using Consumers High in Emergent Nature to Further Develop New Product Concepts. Journal of Marketing Research Insider. Retrieved from http://www.mediacom.com/media/2088012/mediacom%20the%20insider_the%20empowered%20 consumer_whitepaper.pdf

Hoffman, K. D., & Bateson, J. E. G. (1997). *Essentials of Services Marketing*. Fort Worth: Dryden Press.

Hoffman, S., & Müller, S. (2009). Consumer boycotts due to factory relocation. *Journal of Business Research, 62*(2), 239–247. doi:10.1016/j.jbusres.2008.01.031

Hogan, J., Hogan, R., & Busch, C. M. (1984). How to Measure Service Orientation. *The Journal of Applied Psychology, 69*(1), 167–173. doi:10.1037/0021-9010.69.1.167 PMID:6698916

Hogg, M. K., Banister, E. N., & Stephenson, C. A. (2009). Mapping symbolic (anti-) consumption. *Journal of Business Research, 62*(2), 148–159. doi:10.1016/j.jbusres.2008.01.022

Holbrook, M. B. (1987). O, Consumer, How You've Changed: Some Radical Reflections on the Roots of Consumption. In A. F. Firat, N. Dholakia, & R. P. Bagozzi (Eds.), *Philosophical and Radical Thought in Marketing* (pp. 156–177). Lexington, MA: Lexington Books.

Holbrook, M. B., & Hirschman, E. C. (1982). The Experiential Aspects of Consumption: Consumer Fantasies, Feelings and Fun. *The Journal of Consumer Research, 9*(2), 132–140. Retrieved from http://www.jstor.org/stable/2489122 doi:10.1086/208906

Hollenbeck, C. R., & Zinkhan, G. M. (2006). Consumer Activism on the Internet: The Role of Anti-brand Communities. *Advances in Consumer Research*, 33, 479-485. Retrieved from http://www.acrwebsite.org/volumes/v33/v33_10337.pdf

Holt, D. B. (2004). *How Brands Become Icons: The Principles of Cultural Branding*. Boston: Harvard Business School Press.

Homburg, C., Hoyer, W. D., & Fassnacht, M. (2002). Service Orientation of a Retailers Business Strategy: Dimensions, Antecedents, and Performance Outcomes. *Journal of Marketing, 66*(4), 86–101. doi:10.1509/jmkg.66.4.86.18511

Hopwood, M. (2007). It's football but not as you know it: Using public relations to promote the world game in Australia. *Humanities & Social Sciences Papers*. Retrieved from http://epublications.bond.edu.au/hss_pubs/164

Hosany, S. (2012). Appraisal Determinants of Tourist Emotional Responses. *Journal of Travel Research, 51*(3), 303–314. doi:10.1177/0047287511410320

Hoyer, W. D., Chandy, R., Dorotic, M., Kraff, M., & Singh, S. S. (2010). Consumer Cocreation in New Product Development. *Journal of Service Research, 13*(3), 283–296. doi:10.1177/1094670510375604

Hsu, C. I., Li, H. C., & Lu, S. M. (2013). A dynamic marketing model for hybrid electric vehicles: A case study of Taiwan. *Transportation Research Part D, Transport and Environment, 20*, 21–29. doi:10.1016/j.trd.2013.01.001

Huefner, J. C., & Hunt, H. K. (2000). Consumer Retaliation as a Response to Dissatisfaction. *Journal of Consumer Satisfaction. Dissatisfaction and Complaining Behavior, 13*, 61–82.

Hui, M. K., Dube, L., & Chebat, J.-C. (1997). The impact of music on consumers reactions to waiting for services. *Journal of Retailing, 73*(1), 87–104. doi:10.1016/S0022-4359(97)90016-6

Hultén, B. (2012). Sensory Cues and Shoppers Touching Behaviour: The Case of IKEA. *International Journal of Retail & Distribution Management, 40*(4), 273–289. doi:10.1108/09590551211211774

Hume, S. (1991). McDonald's: Case Study. *Advertising Age, 62*(5), 32.

Humphery, K. (1998). *Shelf Life: Supermarkets and the Changing Cultures of Consumption*. Melbourne: Cambridge University Press.

Hur, W. M., Kim, H., & Woo, J. (2014). How CSR Leads to Corporate Brand Equity: Mediating Mechanisms of Corporate Brand Credibility and Reputation. *Journal of Business Ethics*, *125*(1), 75–86. doi:10.1007/s10551-013-1910-0

Husain, F., & Saidi, R. (2000). The integration of the Pakistani equity market with internatioanl equity markets: An investigation. *Journal of International Development*, *12*(2), 207–218. doi:10.1002/(SICI)1099-1328(200003)12:2<207::AID-JID636>3.0.CO;2-Z

Husain, G., Thompson, W. F., & Schellenberg, E. G. (2002). Effects of Musical Tempo and Mode on Arousal, Mood, and Spatial Abilities. *Music Perception*, *20*(2), 151–171. doi:10.1525/mp.2002.20.2.151

Hustad, T. P., & Pessemier, E. A. (1973). Will the real consumer activist please stand up: An examination of consumers opinions about marketing practices? *JMR, Journal of Marketing Research*, *10*(Nov), 319–324. Retrieved from http://www.ethicalconsumer.org/boycotts/successfulboycotts.aspx doi:10.2307/3149703

Iivari, J. (1990a). Hierarchical Spiral Model for Information-System and Software- Development. 1. Theoretical Background. *Information and Software Technology*, *32*(6), 386–399. doi:10.1016/0950-5849(90)90125-B

Iivari, J. (1990b). Hierarchical Spiral Model for Information-System and Software- Development. 2. Design Process. *Information and Software Technology*, *32*(7), 450–458. doi:10.1016/0950-5849(90)90160-S

Iivari, J., & Lyytinen, K. (1999). Research on Information Systems Development in Scandinavia- Unity in Plurality. *Scandinavian Journal of Information Systems*, *10*(1-2), 135–185.

Ireland, P. N. (1994). *Monetary policy with nominal price rigidity. Manuscript*. Federal Reserve Bank of Richmond.

Ismail, H. B., & Panni, M. F. A. K. (2008). Consumer perceptions on the consumerism issues and its influence on their purchasing behavior: A view from Malaysian food industry. *Journal of Legal, Ethical and Regulatory Issues*, *11*(1), 43–64.

Ismail, H. B., & Panni, M. F. A. K. (2008). Consumer perceptions on the consumerism issues and its influence on their purchasing behaviour: A view from Malaysian food industry. *Journal of Legal. Ethical and Regulatory Issues*, *11*(1), 43–64.

Iyer, R., & Muncy, J. A. (2009). Purpose and object of anti-consumption. *Journal of Business Research*, *62*(2), 160–168. doi:10.1016/j.jbusres.2008.01.023

Jackson, T. (2006). Prosperity without growth? Sustainability Development Commission. Retrieved from http://www.sd-commission.org.uk/publications/downloads/prosperitywithoutgrowthreport.pdf

Jackson, J. M. (1986). In defense of social impact theory: Comment on Mullen. *Journal of Personality and Social Psychology*, *50*(3), 511–513. doi:10.1037/0022-3514.50.3.511

Jackson, J. M., & Latane, B. (1981). Strength and Number of Solicitors and the Urge Toward Alturism. *Personality and Social Psychology Bulletin*, *7*(3), 414–422. doi:10.1177/014616728173009

Jackson, K. T. (2004). *Building reputational capital: Strategies for integrity and fair play that improve the bottom line*. Oxford University Press.

Jacobsen, E., & Dulsrud, A. A. (2007). Will consumers save the world? The framing of political consumerism. Journal of Agricultural and Environmental Ethics, 20, 469–482.

Jain, R., & Bagdare, S. (2011). Music and consumption experience: A review. *International Journal of Retail & Distribution Management*, *39*(4), 289–302. doi:10.1108/09590551111117554

Jarke, M., & Pohl, K. (1994). Requirements Engineering in 2001 - (Virtually) Managing a Changing Reality. *Software Engineering Journal*, *9*(6), 257–266. doi:10.1049/sej.1994.0035

Järvinen, P. (2007). Action research is similar to design science. *Quality & Quantity*, *41*(1), 37–54. doi:10.1007/s11135-005-5427-1

Jenn, A., Azevedo, I. L., & Ferreira, P. (2013). The impact of federal incentives on the adoption of hybrid electric vehicles in the United States. *Energy Economics*, *40*, 936–942. doi:10.1016/j.eneco.2013.07.025

Jiao, J., Ma, Q., & Tseng, M. M. (2003). Towards High Value-Added Products and Services: Mass Customization and Beyond. *Technovation*, *23*(10), 809–821. doi:10.1016/S0166-4972(02)00023-8

Jirotka, M., & Goguen, J. (Eds.). (1994). *Requirements Engineering: Social and Technical Issues*. Academic Press.

Jobber, D. (2001). Principles and practice of marketing (4th ed.). McGraw Hill.

John, A., & Klein, J. (2003). The boycott puzzle: Consumer motivations for purchase sacrifice. *Management Science*, *49*(9), 1196–1209. doi:10.1287/mnsc.49.9.1196.16569

Johnson, M. D., & Ettlie, J. E. (2001). Technology, customization, and reliability. *Journal of Quality Management*, *6*(2), 193–210. doi:10.1016/S1084-8568(01)00037-2

Jones, L. (2012). *Fashion therapy, Daily mail.* Retrieved from http://www.dailymail.co.uk/femail/article-2160686/LIZ-JONES-FASHION-THERAPY--Why-Zaras-stepahead.html#ixzz1z5C003rV

Jones, M. A. (1999). Entertaining Shopping Experiences: An Exploratory Investigation. *Journal of Retailing and Consumer Services*, *6*(3), 129–139. doi:10.1016/S0969-6989(98)00028-9

Jones, P., Clarke-Hill, C., Shears, P., Comfort, D., & Hillier, D. (2004). Radio Frequency Identification in the UK: Opportunities and Challenges. *International Journal of Retail & Distribution Management*, *32*(3), 164–171. doi:10.1108/09590550410524957

Jones, P., Hillier, D., Comfort, D., & Eastwood, I. (2005). Sustainable retailing and consumerism. *Management Research News*, *28*(1), 34–44. doi:10.1108/01409170510784760

Jose, A., & Tollenaere, M. (2005). Modular and platform methods for product family design: Literature analysis. *Journal of Intelligent Manufacturing*, *16*(3), 371–390. doi:10.1007/s10845-005-7030-7

Jüttner, U., Schaffner, D., Windler, K., & Maklan, S. (2013). Customer Service Experiences. Developing and Applying a Sequential Incident Laddering Technique. *European Journal of Marketing*, *47*(5/6), 738–768. doi:10.1108/03090561311306769

Kacker, M. (1986). Coming to Terms with Global Retailing. *International Marketing Review*, *3*(1), 7.

Kajalo, S., & Lindblom, A. (2010a). The Perceived Effectiveness of Surveillance in Reducing Crime at Shopping Centers in Finland. *Property Management*, *28*(1), 47–59. doi:10.1108/02637471011017172

Kajalo, S., & Lindblom, A. (2010b). Surveillance Investments in Store Environment and Sense of Security. *Facilities*, *28*(9/10), 465–474. doi:10.1108/02632771011057198

Kajalo, S., & Lindblom, A. (2011). Effectiveness of Formal and Informal Surveillance in Reducing Crime at Grocery Stores. *Journal of Small Business and Enterprise Development*, *18*(1), 157–169. doi:10.1108/14626001111106488

Kajalo, S., & Lindblom, A. (2012). Evaluating the Effects of Formal and Informal Surveillance: A Retailer's View. *Proceedings of ASBBS Annual Conference* (Vol. 19, pp. 461-471). Las Vegas.

Kajalo, S., & Lindblom, A. (2015). Creating a Safe and Pleasant Shopping Environment: A Retailers View. *Property Management*, *33*(3), 275–286. doi:10.1108/PM-10-2014-0042

Kajalo, S., & Lindblom, A. (2016). The Role of Formal and Informal Surveillance in Creating a Safe and Entertaining Retail Environment. *Facilities*, *34*(3/4), 219–232. doi:10.1108/F-06-2014-0055

Kalafatis, S. P., Pollard, M., East, R., & Tsogas, M. H. (1999). Green marketing and Ajzens theory of planned behavior: A cross-market examination. *Journal of Consumer Marketing*, *16*(5), 441–460. doi:10.1108/07363769910289550

Kamien, R. (2015). Music: An Appreciation (11 ed.). New York: McGraw-Hill Education.

Kandampully, J. (2002), Services management: The new paradigm in hospitality. Melbourne, Australia: Pearson Education.

Kandil (1998). Supply-side asymmetry and the non-neutrality of demand fluctuations. *Journal of Macroeconomics*, *20*(4), 785-809.

Kano, N., Seraku, N., Takahashi, F., & Tsuji, S. (1984). Attractive Quality and Must-Be Quality. *Journal of Japanese Society for Quality Control*, *14*(2), 39–48.

Kaplan, A. M., & Haenlein, M. (2010). Users of the world, unite! The challenges and opportunities of Social Media. *Business Horizons*, *53*(1), 59–68. doi:10.1016/j.bushor.2009.09.003

Karim, A. B., Majid, M. S. A. & Karim, S. A. A. (2009). Financial integration between Indonesia and its major trading partners. MPRA.

Kautz, K. (2001). Trends in the research on software process improvement in Scandinavia. *Scandinavian Journal of Information Systems*, *13*, 3–6.

Kavalec, C. (1999). Vehicle choice in an aging population: Some insights from a stated preference survey from California. *The Energy Journal (Cambridge, Mass.)*, *20*(3), 123–138. doi:10.5547/ISSN0195-6574-EJ-Vol20-No3-5

Kaynak, E. (1985). Some thoughts on consumerism in developed and less developed countries. *International Marketing Review*, *2*(2), 15–31. doi:10.1108/eb008273

Kaynak, E., Kucukemiroglu, O., & Odabasi, Y. (1992). Consumer complaint handling in an advanced developing economy: An empirical investigation. *Journal of Business Ethics*, *11*(11), 813–829. doi:10.1007/BF00872359

Keil, M., & Carmel, E. (1995). Customer developer links in software-development. *Communications of the ACM*, *38*(5), 33–44. doi:10.1145/203356.203363

Kellaris, J. J., & Cox, A. D. (1989). The Effects of Background Music in Advertising: A Reassessment. *The Journal of Consumer Research*, *16*(1), 113–118. doi:10.1086/209199

Kellaris, J. J., & Kent, R. J. (1991). Exploring tempo and modality effects, on consumer responses to music. *Advances in Consumer Research. Association for Consumer Research (U. S.)*, *18*, 243–248.

Kellaris, J. J., & Kent, R. J. (1992). The influence of music on consumers temporal perceptions: Does time fly when youre having fun. *Journal of Consumer Psychology*, *1*(4), 365–376. doi:10.1016/S1057-7408(08)80060-5

Kellaris, J. J., & Kent, R. J. (1994). An Exploratory Investigation of Responses Elicited by Music Varying in Tempo, Tonality, and Texture. *Journal of Consumer Psychology*, *2*(4), 381–401. doi:10.1016/S1057-7408(08)80068-X

Kellaris, J. J., & Mantel, S. P. (1994). The influence of mood and gender on consumer's time perceptions. *Advances in Consumer Research. Association for Consumer Research (U. S.)*, *21*, 514–518.

Kellaris, J. J., & Rice, R. C. (1993). The Influence of Tempo, Loudness, and Gender of Listener on Responses to Music. *Psychology and Marketing*, *10*(1), 15–29. doi:10.1002/mar.4220100103

Keng, C.-J., Huang, T.-L., Zheng, L.-J., & Hsu, M. K. (2007). Modeling Service Encounters and Customer Experiential Value in Retailing. An Empirical Investigation of Shopping Mall Customers in Taiwan. *International Journal of Service Industry Management*, *18*(4), 349–367. doi:10.1108/09564230710778137

Kenning, P. (2008). The influence of general trust and specific trust on buying behavior. *International Journal of Retail & Distribution Management*, *36*(6), 461–476. doi:10.1108/09590550810873938

Keown, C. F. (1982). Attitudes of practitioners and students toward marketing. *Journal of Marketing Education*, *4*(Fall), 14–20. doi:10.1177/027347538200400203

Kesebir, B., & Diener, E. (2008). In Pursuit of Happiness Empirical Answers to Philosophical Questions. *Perspectives on Psychological Science*, *3*(2), 117–125. doi:10.1111/j.1745-6916.2008.00069.x PMID:26158878

Khan, M., & Kar, N. C. (2009). Hybrid electric vehicles for sustainable transportation: A Canadian perspective. *World Electric Vehicle Journal*, *3*, 1–12.

Khan, S. (2012). Enlightenment through play. *New Statesman (London, England)*, *141*(5087), 13–20.

Kilbourne, W. E. (1995). Green Advertising: Salvation or Oxymoron? *Journal of Advertising*, *24*(2), 7–19. doi:10.1080/00913367.1995.10673472

Kilbourne, W. E., Beckman, S. D., & Thelen, E. (2002). The role of the dominant social paradigm in environmental attitudes: A multinational examination. *Journal of Business Research*, *55*(3), 193–204. doi:10.1016/S0148-2963(00)00141-7

Kim (1999). Economic capacity utilization and its determinants: theory and evidence. *Review of Industrial Organization*, *15*, 321-229.

Kim, D. J., Ferrin, D. L., & Rao, H. R. (2008). A trust-based consumer decision-making model in electronic commerce: The role of trust, perceived risk, and their antecedents. *Decision Support Systems*, *44*(2), 544–564. doi:10.1016/j.dss.2007.07.001

Kinnear, T. C., Taylor, J. R., & Ahmed, S. A. (1974). Ecologically concerned consumers: Who are they? *Journal of Marketing*, *38*(April), 20–24. doi:10.2307/1250192

Klaus, P., & Maklan, S. (2012). EXQ: A Multiple-Scale for Assessing Service Experience. *Journal of Service Management*, *23*(1), 5–33. doi:10.1108/09564231211208952

Klaus, P., & Maklan, S. (2013). Towards a Better Measure of Customer Experience. *International Journal of Market Research*, *55*(2), 227–246. doi:10.2501/IJMR-2013-021

Klein, N. (2000). No Logo (pp. 3-26 and pp. 325-343). London. Flamingo

Klein, J. G., Smith, N. C., & John, A. (2004). Why we boycott: Consumer motivations for boycott participation. *Journal of Marketing*, *68*(3), 92–109. doi:10.1509/jmkg.68.3.92.34770

Kliatchko, J. (2008). Revisiting the IMC construct: A revised definition and four pillars. *International Journal of Advertising*, *27*(1), 133–160.

Klingebiel, R., & De Meyer, A. (2013). Becoming aware of the unknown: Decision making during the implementation of a strategic initiative. *Organization Science*, *24*(1), 133–153. doi:10.1287/orsc.1110.0726

Knauer, V. (1971, April 21). Special assistant for consumer affairs to the president of the United States, in an address to National Application and Radio- TV Dealers Association, Chicago.

Knoferle, K., Spangenberg, E., Herrmann, A., & Landwehr, J. (2012). It is all in the mix: The interactive effect of music tempo and mode on in-store sales. *Marketing Letters*, *23*(1), 325–337. doi:10.1007/s11002-011-9156-z

Koh, J., & Kim, Y. G. (2004). Knowledge sharing in virtual communities: An e-business perspective. *Expert Systems with Applications*, *26*(2), 155–166. doi:10.1016/S0957-4174(03)00116-7

Kojola, E. (2013). Serving Food Justice: A Union Campaign for Fresh Food, Health, and Sustainability. *Journal of Workplace Rights*, *17*(2), 175–191. doi:10.2190/WR.17.2.d

Kollmuss, A., & Agyeman, J. (2002). Mind the Gap: Why do people act environmentally and what are the barriers to pro-environmental behavior? *Environmental Education Research*, *8*(3), 239–260. doi:10.1080/13504620220145401

Korajczyk, A. R. (1996). A measure of stock market integration for developed and emerging markets. *The World Bank Economic Review*, *10*(2), 267–289. doi:10.1093/wber/10.2.267

Koslow, S. (2000). Can the truth hurt? How honest and persuasive advertising can unintentionally lead to increased consumer skepticism. *The Journal of Consumer Affairs*, *34*(2), 16–32. doi:10.1111/j.1745-6606.2000.tb00093.x

Kotler, P., & Keller, K. L. (2006). Marketing Management (12thed.). Upper Saddle River, NJ: Pearson Education.

Kotler, P. (1972). What consumerism means for marketers. *Harvard Business Review*, *3*, 48–57.

Kotler, P. (1973-1974). Atmospherics as a Marketing Tool. *Journal of Retailing*, *49*(4), 48–64.

Kotler, P. (2000). *Marketing Management*. New York, NY: Prentice Hall.

Kotler, P. (2011). Reinventing marketing to manage the environmental imperative. *Journal of Marketing*, *75*(4), 132–135. doi:10.1509/jmkg.75.4.132

Kotler, P., & Armstrong, G. (2012). *Principles of marketing*. Prentice Hall Inc.

Kotler, P., Armstrong, G., Harris, L., & Piercy, N. (2013). *Principles of Marketing*. Essex: Pearson Education.

Kotler, P., Kartajaya, H., & Setiawan, I. (2010). *Marketing 3.0: From Products To Customers To The Human Spirit*. New York: John Wiley & Sons Inc. doi:10.1002/9781118257883

Kotler, P., & Lee, N. (2005). *Corporate Social Responsibility. Doing the Most Good for Your Company and Your Cause*. Hoboken: Wiley.

Kotler, P., Roberto, N., & Lee, N. R. (2002). *Social marketing: Improving the quality of life*. London: Sage.

Kozinets, R. V., & Handelman, J. (1998). Ensouling consumption: A netnographic exploration of the meaning of boycotting behaviour. Advances in Consumer Research, 25, 475-480.

Kozinets, R. V. (2002). Can consumers escape the market? Emancipatory illuminations from burning man. *The Journal of Consumer Research*, *29*(1), 20–38. doi:10.1086/339919

Kozinets, R. V., & Handelman, J. M. (2004). Adversaries of consumption: Consumer movements, activism, and ideology. *The Journal of Consumer Research*, *31*(3), 691–704. doi:10.1086/425104

Kozlowski, A., Bardecki, M., & Searcy, C. (2012). Environmental Impacts in the Fashion Industry: A Life-cycle and Stakeholder Framework. *Journal of Corporate Citizenship*, *45*, 17–37. Retrieved from http://connection.ebscohost.com/c/articles/79191008/environmental-impacts-fashion-industry-life-cycle-stakeholder-framework

Kreidler, N. B., & Joseph, M. S. (2009). *How green should you go? Understanding the role of green atmospherics in service environment evaluations*. International Journal of Culture. *Tourism and Hospitality Research, 3*(3), 228–245.

Krishnamurth, S., & Kucuk, S. U. (2009). Anti-branding on the Internet, *Journal of Business Research,* 62, 1119-1126, Retrieved from http://www.ehl.lu.se/biblioteket

Krishnamurthy, S., & Kucuk, S. U. (2009). Anti-branding on the internet. *Journal of Business Research, 62*(11), 1119–1126. doi:10.1016/j.jbusres.2008.09.003

Krishnan, M. S. (2013). Green Consumerism. Retrieved from http://slideshare.net/subudhrakrishnan3/the-green-consumer

Kristensen, K., Martensen, A., & Grønholdt, L. (2000). Customer satisfaction measurement at post Denmark: Results of application of the European Customer Satisfaction Index methodology. *Total Quality Management, 11*(7), 1007–1015. doi:10.1080/09544120050135533

Krupa, J. S., Rizzo, D. M., Eppstein, M. J., Lanute, D. B., Gaalema, D. E., Lakkaraju, K., & Warrender, C. E. (2014). Analysis of a consumer survey on plug-in hybrid electric vehicles. *Transportation Research Part A, Policy and Practice, 64*, 14–31. doi:10.1016/j.tra.2014.02.019

Kucuk, S. U. (2008). Negative Double Jeopardy: The role if anti-brand sites on the internet, *Journal of Brand Management*, 15, 209–222. Retrieved from http://www.palgrave-journals.com/bm/journal/v15/n3/abs/2550100a.html

Kuepfer, J., & Papula, J. (2010). Corporate social responsibility – the dilemmas behind the popular concept and how to best address them. *International Journal of Sustainable Society*, 2(3), 291. doi:10.1504/IJSSOC.2010.034765

Kulas, J. T., Mcinnerney, J. E., Demuth, R. F., & Jadwinski, V. (2007). Employee Satisfaction and Theft: Testing Climate Perceptions as a Mediator. *The Journal of Psychology, 141*(4), 389–402. doi:10.3200/JRLP.141.4.389-402 PMID:17725072

Kulkarni, V.R. (2012). A study of impact of music on consumer buying behavior in retail. *International Journal of Management, 3*(3), 152–159.

Kumar, N., & Linguri, S. (2006). Zara fashion sense. *Business Strategy Review, 17*(2), 81–84. doi:10.1111/j.0955-6419.2006.00409.x

Kurkovsky, S., & Harihar, K. (2006). Using ubiquitous computing in interactive mobile marketing. *Personal and Ubiquitous Computing, 10*(4), 227–240. doi:10.1007/s00779-005-0044-5

Lamb, R., & Kling, R. (2003). Reconceptualizing users as social actors in information systems research. *Management Information Systems Quarterly, 27*(2), 197–235.

Lamb, R., & Kling, R. (2003). Reconceptualizing Users as Social Actors in Information Systems Research. *Management Information Systems Quarterly, 27*(2), 197–235.

Lampman, R. J. (1988). JFK's four consumer rights: a retrospective view. In E. S. Maynes (Ed.), *The Frontier of Research in the Consumer Interest* (pp. 19–33). Columbia, MO: American Council of Consumer Interests.

Lam, S.Y. (2001). The effects of store environment on shopping behavior: A critical review. *Advances in Consumer Research. Association for Consumer Research (U. S.), 28*, 190–197.

Lane, B. (2005). *Car Buyer Research Report: Consumer Attitudes to Low Carbon and Fuel-efficient Passenger Cars.* Report prepared for the Low Carbon Vehicle Partnership.

Langer, E. J. (2004). *Langer Mindfulness Scale User Guide and Technical Manual.* Worthington, OH: IDS Publishing Corporation.

Lang, T., & Yiannis, G. (2005). A brief history of consumer activism. In R. Harrison, T. Newholm, & D. Shaw (Eds.), *The ethical consumer* (pp. 39–53). London: Sage. doi:10.4135/9781446211991.n4

Laroche, M., Bergeron, J., & Barbaro-Forleo, G. (2001). Targeting consumers who are willing to pay more for environmentally friendly products. *Journal of Consumer Marketing*, *18*(6), 503–520. doi:10.1108/EUM0000000006155

Larson, P. D., Viáfara, J., Parsons, R. V., & Elias, A. (2014). Consumer attitudes about electric cars: Pricing analysis and policy implications. *Transportation Research Part A, Policy and Practice*, *69*, 299–314. doi:10.1016/j.tra.2014.09.002

Latane, B., & Nida, S. (1980). Social impact theory and group influence: A social engineering perspective. In P.B. Paulus (Ed.), Psychology of group influence (pp. 3-34).

Latane, B. (1981). The Psychology of Social Impact. *The American Psychologist*, *36*(4), 343–356. doi:10.1037/0003-066X.36.4.343

Layard, R. (2005). *Happiness: Lessons from a New Science*. London: Allen Lane.

Leeflang, P. S. H., & de Mortanges, C. P. (1996). An empirical investigation of Marketing Plan. *Journal of Euromarketing*, *6*(1), 77–101. doi:10.1300/J037v06n01_06

Lee, H. S., & Lee, H. J. (2014). Factors Influencing Online Trust. *Academy of Marketing Studies Journal*, *18*(1), 41–50.

Lee, M. S. W., Motion, J., & Conroy, D. (2009a). Anti-consumption and brand avoidance. *Journal of Business Research*, *62*(2), 169–180. doi:10.1016/j.jbusres.2008.01.024

Leidecker, J. K., & Bruno, A. V. (1984). Identifying and using critical success factors. *Long Range Planning*, *17*(1), 23–31. doi:10.1016/0024-6301(84)90163-8

Lemke, F., Clark, M., & Wilson, H. (2010). Customer Experience Quality: An Exploration in Business and Consumer Contexts Using Repertory Grid Technique. *Journal of the Academy of Marketing Science*, *39*(6), 846–869. doi:10.1007/s11747-010-0219-0

LEtang, J., & Hopwood, M. (2008). Sports public relations. *Public Relations Review*, *34*(2), 87–89. doi:10.1016/j.pubrev.2008.05.001

Levitt, T. (1983). The Globalization of markets. *Harvard Business Review*.

Levitt, T. (1975). Marketing Myopia: Retrospective Commentary. *Harvard Business Review*.

Levy, M., & Powell, P. (2003). Exploring SME internet adoption: Towards a contingent model. *Electronic Markets*, *13*(2), 173–181. doi:10.1080/1019678032000067163

Levy, M., & Weitz, B. A. (2012). *Retailing Management* (8th ed.). Irwin, NY: McGraw-Hill.

Liljander, V., & Strandvik, T. (1997). Emotions in Service Satisfaction. *International Journal of Service Industry Management*, *8*(2), 148–169. doi:10.1108/09564239710166272

Lim, W. C. (1994). Effects of Reuse on Quality, Productivity, and Economics. *Software*, *11*(5), 23–30. doi:10.1109/52.311048

Lindberg, P.J. (2009). Bad music in public spaces. *Travel+Leisure*. Retrieved from http://www.travelandleisure.com/articles/bad-music-in-public-spaces

Lindblom, A., & Kajalo, S. (2011). The Use and Effectiveness of Formal and Informal Surveillance in Reducing Shoplifting: A Survey in Sweden, Norway, and Finland. *International Review of Retail, Distribution and Consumer Research*, *21*(2), 111–128. doi:10.1080/09593969.2011.562677

Linsen, M.A. (1975). Like our music today Ms. shopper? Progressive Grocer, October, 156.

Lisa, A. (2004). Is it unfair pricing? *Tire Business*, *22*(14), 15.

Liu, T.-C., & Chen, C.-F. (2011). Please Smile, the CCTV Is Running! *Service Industries Journal*, *31*(7), 1075–1092. doi:10.1080/02642060903108342

Liu, Y. (2014). Household demand and willingness to pay for hybrid vehicles. *Energy Economics*, *44*, 191–197. doi:10.1016/j.eneco.2014.03.027

Li, X., Clark, C. D., Jensen, K. L., Yen, S. T., & English, B. C. (2013). Consumer purchase intentions for flexible-fuel and hybrid-electric vehicles. *Transportation Research Part D, Transport and Environment*, *18*, 9–15. doi:10.1016/j.trd.2012.08.001

Lohman, P. (2012). Consumer Activism: Reinforcing Moral Identity through fair trade coffee. Retrieved from http://www.e-ir.info/2012/05/24/consumer-activism-reinforcing-moral-identity-through-fair-trade-coffee/

Lombart, C., & Louis, D. (2016). Sources of retailer personality: Private brand perceptions. *Journal of Retailing and Consumer Services*, *28*, 117–125. doi:10.1016/j.jretconser.2015.09.002

Lopez-De-Pedro, J. M., & Rimbau Gilabert, E. (2012). Stakeholder Approach: What Effects Should We Take into Account in Contemporary Societies. *Journal of Business Ethics*, *107*(2), 147–158. doi:10.1007/s10551-011-1029-0

Loureiro, S. M. C. (2014). The role of the rural tourism experience economy in place attachment and behavioral intentions. *International Journal of Hospitality Management*, *40*, 1–9. doi:10.1016/j.ijhm.2014.02.010

Loureiro, S. M. C., & Kastenholz, E. (2011). Corporate reputation, satisfaction, delight, and loyalty towards rural lodging units. *International Journal of Hospitality Management*, *30*(3), 575–583. doi:10.1016/j.ijhm.2010.10.007

Lovelock, C. (1994). *Product Plus: How Product + Service = Competitive Advantage*. New York: McGraw-Hill.

Lovelock, C. (2001). *Services Marketing: People, Technology, Strategy* (4th ed.). Upper Saddle River, NJ: Prentice Hall.

Lovelock, C. H. (1983). Classifying Services to Gain Strategic Marketing Insights. *Journal of Marketing*, *47*(3), 9–20. doi:10.2307/1251193

Lucas, R. E., & Dyrenforth, P. S. (2006). Does the existence of social relationships matter for subjective well-being? In K. D. Vohs & E. J. Finkel (Eds.), *Self and Relationships: Connecting Intrapersonal and Interpersonal Processes* (pp. 254–273). New York: Guildford Press.

Lucas, R. E. Jr. (1975). An equilibrium model of the business cycle. *Journal of Political Economy*, *83*(6), 1113–1144. doi:10.1086/260386

Lunt, P. K., & Livingstone, S. M. (1992). *Mass Consumption and Personal Identity: Everyday economic experience*. Buckingham, U.K.: Open University Press.

Lusch, R. F., & Nambisan, S. (2015). Service innovation: a service-dominant logic perspective. *Management Information Systems Quarterly*, *39*(1), 155–175.

Lusch, R. F., & Nambisan, S. (2015). Service Innovation: A Service-Dominant Logic Perspective. *Management Information Systems Quarterly*, *39*(1), 155–175.

Lymperopoulos, C., Chaniotakis, I. E., & Rigopoulou, I. D. (2010). Acceptance of detergent-retail brands: The role of consumer confidence and trust. *International Journal of Retail & Distribution Management*, *38*(9), 719–736. doi:10.1108/09590551011062457

Lysonski, S., Durvasula, S. and Watson, J. (2003). Should marketing managers be concerned about attitudes towards marketing and consumerism in New Zealand? A longitudinal study. *European Journal of Marketing*, 37(3 & 4), 385-406.

Lytle, R. S., & Timmerman, J. E. (2006). Service Orientation and Performance: An Organizational Perspective. *Journal of Services Marketing, 20*(2), 136–147. doi:10.1108/08876040610657066

Lytle, R., Hom, P., & Mokwa, M. (1998). SERV OR: A Managerial Measure of Organizational Service Orientation. *Journal of Retailing, 74*(4), 455–475. doi:10.1016/S0022-4359(99)80104-3

MacCarthy, B. L., Brabazon, P. G., & Bramham, J. (2002). *Key Value Attributes in Mass Customization.* In *Moving into Mass Customization - Information Systems and Management Principles*(pp. 71–87).

Macklin, M. C. (1988). The relationship between Music in Advertising and Children' Responses: An Experimental Investigation. In S. Hecker & D.W. Stewart (Eds.), Nonverbal Communication in Advertising (pp. 225-243). Lexington, MA: Lexington Books.

Macleod, S. (2001). Why worry about CSR? *Strategic Communication Management, 5*(5), 8–9.

Madaleno, M., & Pinho, C. (2012). International stock market indices comovements: A new look. *International Journal of Finance & Economics, 17*(1), 89–102. doi:10.1002/ijfe.448

Madrigal, R. (1995). Cognitive and Affective Determinants of Fan Satisfaction with Sporting Event Attendance. *Journal of Leisure Research, 27*(3), 205–227. Retrieved from http://js.sagamorepub.com/jlr/article/view/857

Mady, T. T. (2011). Sentiment toward marketing: Should we care about consumer alienation and readiness to use technology? *Journal of Consumer Behaviour, 10*(4), 192–204. doi:10.1002/cb.329

Magarey, M. J. (2001). Elements of a systematic review. *The Journal for Nurse Practitioners, 7*(6), 376–382. doi:10.1046/j.1440-172X.2001.00295.x PMID:11785440

Magnusson, P. R., Matthing, J., & Kristensson, P. (2003). Managing user involvement in service innovation: Experiments with innovating end users. *Journal of Service Research, 6*(2), 111–124. doi:10.1177/1094670503257028

Mahony, D. F., Madrigal, R., & Howard, D. R. (2000). Using the Psychological Commitment to Team (PCT) Scale to Segment Sport Consumers Based on Loyalty. *Sport Marketing Quarterly, 9*(1), 15-25. Retrieved from http://epay.wvsto.com/WVU/WVFITSportBooks/Using-the-Psychological-Commitment-to-Team-PCT-Scale-to-Segment-Sport-Consumers-Based-on-Loyalty-P10550.aspx

Mainieri, T., Barnett, E. G., Unipan, J. B., & Oskamp, S. (1997). Green buying: The influence of environmental concern on consumer behavior. *The Journal of Social Psychology, 137*(2), 189–204. doi:10.1080/00224549709595430

Majfud, J. (2009). The pandemic of consumerism. *UN chronicle*. Retrieved from http://institucional.us.es/araucaria/otras_res/2009_11/resegna_1109_6.htm#_ftn1

Majid, K. A., & Russell, C. A. (2015). Giving green a second thought: Modeling the value retention of green products in the secondary market. *Journal of Business Research, 68*(5), 994–1002. doi:10.1016/j.jbusres.2014.10.001

Mannheim, K. (1952). On the Problem of Generations. In P. Kecskemeti (Ed.), Essays on the Sociology of Knowledge (pp. 276-322). London: Routledge.

Mann, T. (1992). Security Services Under Fire. *Management Services, 36*(1), 28–30.

March, S., & Smith, G. (1995). Design and natural science research on information technology. *Decision Support Systems, 15*(4), 251–266. doi:10.1016/0167-9236(94)00041-2

Markin, R. J., Lillis, C. M., & Narayana, C. L. (1976). Social-psychological significance of store space. *Journal of Retailing*, *52*(1), 43–54.

Markowitz, H. (1952). Portfolio selection. *The Journal of Finance*, *7*, 77–91.

Marques, C. P., & Almeida, D. (2013). A Path Model of Attitudinal Antecedents of Green Purchase Behaviour. *Economia e Sociologia (Evora, Portugal)*, *6*(2), 135–144.

Massara, F. (2003). Store atmosphere: Still a fledgling art. *ECR Journal*, *3*(2), 47–52.

Mathiassen, L., Saarinen, T., Tuunanen, T., & Rossi, M. (2007). A Contingency Model for Requirements Development. *Journal of the Association for Information Systems*, *8*(11), 569–597.

Matthews, V. (1994). Give farmers a coffee break. *Marketing Week*, *13*(May), 26.

Mattila, A. S., & Wirtz, J. (2001). Congruency of scent and music as a driver of in-store evaluations and behaviour. *Journal of Retailing*, *77*(2), 273–289. doi:10.1016/S0022-4359(01)00042-2

Matute-Vallejo, J., Bravo, R. & Pina, J.M. (2011). The influence of Corporate Social Responsibility and Price Fairness on Customer Behaviour: Evidence from the Financial Sector. In *Corporate Social Responsibility and Environmental Management, 18*. doi:10.1002/csr.247

Mavlanova, T., Benbunan-Fich, R., & Koufaris, M. (2012). Signaling theory and information asymmetry in online commerce. *Information & Management*, *49*(5), 240–247. doi:10.1016/j.im.2012.05.004

McAfee, A. (2009). Enterprise 2.0: New Collaborative Tools for Your Organization's Toughest Challenges. Boston (Massachussetts): Harvard Business Press.

McAfee, A. (2006). Enterprise 2.0: The Dawn of Emergence Collaboration. Reprint 47306. *MIT Sloan Management Review*, *47*(3), 21–28.

McAfee, A., Brynjolfsson, E., Davenport, T. H., Patil, D. J., & Barton, D. (2012). Big data. *The management revolution. Harvard Business Review*, *90*(10), 61–67. PMID:23074865

McCabe, S., & Johnson, S. (2013). The happiness factor in tourism: Subjective well-being and social tourism. *Annals of Tourism Research*, *41*, 42–65. doi:10.1016/j.annals.2012.12.001

McCarty, J. A., & Shrum, L. J. (1994). The recycling of solid wastes: Personal values, value orientations, and attitudes about recycling as antecedents of recycling behavior. *Journal of Business Research*, *30*(1), 53–62. doi:10.1016/0148-2963(94)90068-X

McCracken, G. (1988). *Culture and Consumption: New Approaches to the Symbolic Character of Consumer Goods and Advertising*. Bloomington, IN: Indiana University Press.

McCracken, G. (1989). Who is the Celebrity Endorser? Cultural Foundations of the Endorsement Process. *The Journal of Consumer Research*, *16*(3), 310–321. doi:10.1086/209217

McCracken, G. (1990). *Culture and Consumption: New Approaches to the Symbolic Character of Consumer Goods and Activities*. Bloomington: Indiana University Press.

McDaniel, S. W., & Rylander, D. H. (1993). Strategic Green Marketing. *Journal of Consumer Marketing*, *10*(3), 4–10. doi:10.1108/07363769310041929

McDonagh, P., Olariu, C., Hava, A., & Thorpe, C. (2013). Enabling IPTV service assurance using openflow. *Paper presented at the 2013 27th International Conference on Advanced Information Networking and Applications Workshops (WAINA)*. doi:10.1109/WAINA.2013.91

McDonald, S., & Oates, C.J. (2006). Sustainability: Consumer Perceptions and Marketing Strategies. Business Strategy and the Environment, 15, 157-170.

McDonald, M. (1992). Strategic Marketing Plan: A state-of-the-art review. *Marketing Intelligence & Planning*, *10*(4), 4–22. doi:10.1108/02634509210016632

McDonald, M. (1992). Ten barriers to Marketing Plan. *Journal of Business and Industrial Marketing*, *7*, 1, 5–18.

McDowell, W. C., Wilson, R. C., & Kile, C. O. (2016). An examination of retail website design and conversion rate. *Journal of Business Research*. doi:10.1016/j.jbusres.2016.04.040

McElhattan, R. (1985). Inflation, supply shocks and the stable inflation rate of capacity utilization, Economic Review. Federal Reserve Bank of San Francisco.

McGinnis, L. P., & Gentry, J. W. (2009). Underdog consumption: An exploration into meanings and motives. *Journal of Business Research*, *62*(2), 191–199. doi:10.1016/j.jbusres.2008.01.026

McGowan, P., Durkin, M. G., Allen, L., Dougan, C., & Nixon, S. (2001). Developing competencies in the entrepreneurial small firm for use of the internet in the management of customer relationships. *Journal of European Industrial Training*, 25(2/3/4), 126-136.

McIllhenny, J.H. (1990). The new consumerism: how will business respond. *At Home with Consumers*, 11(5), 9-10.

McKenna, B., Tuunanen, T., & Gardner, L. (2013). Consumers adoption of information services. *Information & Management*, *50*(5), 248–257. doi:10.1016/j.im.2013.04.004

Mehrabian, A., & Russel, J. A. (1974). *An approach to environmental psychology*. Cambridge, MA: MIT Press.

Mendleson, N. (1994). Environmental marketing business partnering at AFC developing strategic, Environmental Marketing: Critical Success Strategies for Reaching the Green Consumer. *Proceedings of The 1994 Conference* (pp. 87-103).

Mendo, F. A., & Fitzgerald, G. (2005). A multidimensional framework for SME e-business progression. *Journal of Enterprise Information Management*, *18*(6), 678–696. doi:10.1108/17410390510628382

Menor, L. J., Takikonda, M. V., & Sampson, S. E. (2002). New service development: Areas for exploitation and exploration. *Journal of Operations Management*, *20*(2), 135–157. doi:10.1016/S0272-6963(01)00091-2

Merisalo-Rantanen, H., Tuunanen, T., & Rossi, M. (2005). Is extreme programming just old wine in new bottles: A comparison of two cases. *Journal of Database Management*, *16*(4), 41–61. doi:10.4018/jdm.2005100103

Merriam-Webster Dictionary. (n. d.). Boycott. Retrieved from http://www.merriam-webster.com/dictionary/boycott

Meyer, C., & Schwager, A. (2007). Understanding Customer Experience. *Harvard Business Review*, *85*(2), 116–126. PMID:17345685

Meyer-Waarden, L. (2004, October 27-28). in Brătianu, C., Lixăndroiu D., Pop Nicolae Al. (Eds.), (2006). Business Excellence. *Proceedings of the International Conference on Business Excellence ICBE*, Braşov, România.

Miao, L. (2008). *Consumers' Emotional Responses to Service Encounters: The Influence of Other Consumers* [Unpublished PhD Thesis]. The Pennsylvania State University.

Michel, R., Nicholas, A. J., & Janet, C. (2007). Pharmaceutical marketing return-on-investment: A European perspective. *International Journal of Pharmaceutical and Healthcare Marketing, 1*(2).

Michon, R., & Chebat, J. C. (2004). The Interaction Effect of Background Music and Ambient Scent on the Perception of Service Quality. *Paper presented at the 8th International Research Seminar in Service Management*, LA Londe-Les-Maures, Retrieved from http://www.ryerson.ca/~rmichon/Publications/Odour%20Music%20Service%20Quality.pdf

Mick, D. G. (1988). Contributions to the Semiotics of Marketing and Consumer Behavior. In T. Sebeok & J. Umiker-Sebeok (Eds.), *The Semiotic Web: A Yearbook of Semiotics*. Berlin: Mouton de Gruyter.

Mick, D. G. (2006). Presidential Address: Meaning and Mattering Through Transformative Consumer Research. In C. Pechmann & L. Price (Eds.), *NA - Advances in Consumer Research* (Vol. 33, pp. 1–4). Duluth, MN: Association for Consumer Research.

Miles, M. B., & Huberman, A. M. (1994). *Qualitative Data Analysis: An Expanded Sourcebook*. Thousand Oaks, CA: Sage.

Miller, D. (1995). Consumption as the vanguard of history. In D. Miller (Ed.), *Acknowledging Consumption: A Review of New Studies* (pp. 1–57). London: Routledge.

Miller, D. (1998). *A Theory of Shopping. Cambridge*. Cambridge: Polity Press.

Milliman, R. (1982). Using background music to affect the behavior of supermarket shoppers. *Journal of Marketing, 46*(3), 86–91. doi:10.2307/1251706

Milliman, R. (1986). The influence of background music on the behaviour of restaurant patrons. *The Journal of Consumer Research, 13*(2), 286–289. doi:10.1086/209068

Mills, M. K., & Bonoma, T. V. (1979). Deviant Consumer Behavior: New Challenge for Marketing Research. *Proceedings of the Educators'Conference* (pp. 445-449). Chicago, IL: American Marketing Association.

Mills, M. K. (1981). Deviance and Dissatisfaction: An Exploration Study. *Advances in Consumer Research. Association for Consumer Research (U. S.), 8*, 682–686.

Mingers, J., & Harzing, W. A. (2007). Ranking Journals in Business and Management: A Statistical Analysis of the Harzing Data Set. *European Journal of Information Systems, 16*(4), 303–316. doi:10.1057/palgrave.ejis.3000696

Mintzberg, H., Ahlstrand, B. W., & Lampel, J. (1998). *Strategy Safari: the Complete Guide Trough the Wilds of Strategic Management*. London: Financial Times Prentice Hall.

Mirchevska, T. P., & Markova, S. (2011). Emergence of the social consumer – The impact of personalization, localization and social collaboration on consumerism. *Annals of the University of Petrosani Economics, 11*(3), 229–236.

Miremadi, M. (2012). How much will consumers pay to go green. Retrieved from http://www.mckinsey.com/insights/manufacturing/how_much_will_consumers_pay_to_go_green

Mitchell, V.-W., & Chan, J. K. L. (2002). Investigating UK Consumers Unethical Attitudes and Behaviours. *Journal of Marketing Management, 18*(1/2), 5–26. doi:10.1362/0267257022775873

Modi, A. G., Patel, B. K., & Patel, N. R. (2010). The study on co-movement of selected stock markets. *International Research Journal of Finance and Economics, 47*, 170–185.

Mohan, K., & Ramesh, B. (2003). Ontology-Based Support for Variability Management in Product and Service Families. *Proceedings of the 36th Annual Hawaii International Conference on System Sciences (HICSS'03)*.

Mohr, B. A., Webb, D. J., & Harris, K. E. (2001). Do consumers expect companies to be socially responsible? The impact of corporate social responsibility on buying behavior. *The Journal of Consumer Affairs*, *35*(1), 45–72. doi:10.1111/j.1745-6606.2001.tb00102.x

Moisander, J. (2007). Motivational complexity of green consumerism. *International Journal of Consumer Studies*, *31*(4), 404–409. doi:10.1111/j.1470-6431.2007.00586.x

Moncrief, W. C. (1991). The use of sales management role playing exercises. *Marketing Education Review*, *1*(3), 46–55. doi:10.1080/10528008.1991.11488319

Montana, P. J., & Petit, F. (2008). Motivating Generation X and Y on the job and preparing Z. *Global Journal of Business Research*, *2*(2), 139–148.

Moore, G. (1991). *Crossing the Chasm: Marketing and Selling High-Tech Products to Mainstream Customers*. New York, NY: Harper Business Essentials.

Moraes, C., Szmigin, I., & Carrigan, M. (2010). Living production-engaged alternatives: An examination of new consumption communities. *Consumption Markets & Culture*, *13*(3), 273–298. doi:10.1080/10253861003787015

Morana, C., & Beltratti, A. (2008). Comovements in international stock markets. *International Financial Markets. Institutions and Money*, *18*(1), 31–45. doi:10.1016/j.intfin.2006.05.001

Morck, R., Yeung, B., & Yu, W. (2000). The information content of stock markets: Why do emerging markets have synchronous stock price movements? *Journal of Financial Economics*, *58*(1-2), 215–238. doi:10.1016/S0304-405X(00)00071-4

Morrison, M. (2002). The power of Music and its Influence on International Retail Brands and Shopper Behaviour: a Multi case Study Approach. *Paper presented at the Australia and New Zealand Marketing Academy Conference*, Auckland. Retrieved from http://www.evolvedsound.com.au/The_Power_of_Music_in_Retail.pdf

Morrison, M., & Beverland, M. (2003). In search of the right in-store music. *Business Horizons*, *46*(6), 77–82. doi:10.1016/S0007-6813(03)00092-2

Morrison, S., & Crane, F. G. (2007). Building the service brand by creating and managing an emotional brand experience. *Journal of Brand Management*, *14*(5), 410–421. doi:10.1057/palgrave.bm.2550080

Moschis, G. P., & Cox, D. (1989). Deviant Consumer Behavior. *Advances in Consumer Research. Association for Consumer Research (U. S.)*, *16*(1), 732–737.

Mostafa, M. M. (2007). A hierarchical analysis of the green consciousness of the Egyptian consumer. *Psychology and Marketing*, *24*(5), 445–473. doi:10.1002/mar.20168

Mostafa, M. M. (2007). Antecedents of Egyptian Consumers Green Purchase Intentions. *Journal of International Consumer Marketing*, *19*(2), 97–126. doi:10.1300/J046v19n02_06

Mourali, M., & Yang, Z. (2013). The Dual Role Of Power In Resisting Social Influence. *The Journal of Consumer Research*, *40*(3), 539–554. doi:10.1086/671139

Mourdoukoutas P. (2013, November 23). McDonald's: three strategies to reignite sales growth. *Forbes.*

Mower, J. F., Kim, M., & And Childs, M. L. (2012). Exterior atmospherics and consumer behaviour: Influence of landscaping and window display. *Journal of Fashion Marketing and Management*, *16*(4), 442–453. doi:10.1108/13612021211265836

Muniz, A. M. Jr, & OGuinn, T. C. (2001). Brand Community. *The Journal of Consumer Research*, *27*(4), 412–433. doi:10.1086/319618

Murillo Viu, J., Romani Fernandez, J., & Surinach Caralt, J. (2008). The impact of heritage tourism on an urban economy: The case of Granada and the Alhambra. *Tourism Economics*, *14*(2), 361–376. doi:10.5367/000000008784460481

Murphy, P. (1985). *Tourism: A Community Approach*. New York: Methuen Inc.

Murphy, P. (2000). The commodified self in consumer culture: A cross-cultural perspective. *The Journal of Social Psychology*, *40*(October), 636–647. doi:10.1080/00224540009600504 PMID:11059210

Murtagh, C., & Lukehart, C. (1994). *Boycott organizer's guide*. Retrieved from http://www.greenamerica.org/PDF/GuideBoycottOrganizers.pdf

Myburgh-Louw, J., & O'Shaughnessy, N. J. (1994). Consumer perception of misleading and deceptive claims on the packaging of green fast moving consumer goods. In R. Achrol, & A. Mitchell, (Eds.) *American Marketing Association Summer Educators' Conference Proceedings*, Chicago, Ill., USA (Vol. 5, pp. 344-353).

Nair, J., Wierman, A., & Zwart, B. (2015). Provisioning of large-scale systems: The interplay between network effects and strategic behavior in the user base. *Management Science*, *62*(6), 1830–1841. doi:10.1287/mnsc.2015.2210

Nambisan, S., & Baron, R. A. (2009). Virtual Customer Environments: Testing a Model of Voluntary Participation in Value Co-creation Activities. *Journal of Product Innovation Management*, *26*(4), 388–406. doi:10.1111/j.1540-5885.2009.00667.x

Nascuddin, E., & Bustami, R. (2007). The Yin and Yang of CSR Ethical Branding. *Asian Academy of Management Journal*, *12*(2), 83–100.

Nawijn, J. (2011a). Determinants of daily happiness on vacation. *Journal of Travel Research*, *50*(5), 559–566. doi:10.1177/0047287510379164

Nawijn, J. (2011b). Happiness Through Vacationing: Just a Temporary Boost or Long-Term Benefits? *Journal of Happiness Studies*, *12*(4), 651–665. doi:10.1007/s10902-010-9221-y

Nawijn, J., & Peeters, P. M. (2010). Travelling green: Is tourists happiness at stake? *Current Issues in Tourism*, *13*(4), 381–392. doi:10.1080/13683500903215016

Naylor, J. B., Naim, M. M., & Berry, D. (1999). Leagility: Integrating the lean and agile manufacturing paradigms in the total supply chain. *International Journal of Production Economics*, *62*(1-2), 107–118. doi:10.1016/S0925-5273(98)00223-0

Nazila, Y., Gholamhossein, M., Hamid, R.R., & Hossein, T. (2016). Pharmaceutical innovation and market share: Evidence from a generic market. *International Journal of Pharmaceutical and Healthcare Marketing*, *10*(4).

Neal, R., & Cochran, L. P. (2008). Corporate Social Responsibility, Corporate Governance, and Financial Performance: Lesson from Finance. *Business Horizons*, *51*(6), 535–540. doi:10.1016/j.bushor.2008.07.002

Nenycz-Thiel, M., Beal, V., Ludwichowska, G., & Romaniuk, J. (2013). Investigating the accuracy of self-reports of brand usage behavior. *Journal of Business Research*, *66*(2), 224–232. doi:10.1016/j.jbusres.2012.07.016

Neslin, S. A., Grewal, D., Leghorn, R., Shankar, V., Teerling, M. L., Thomas, J. S., & Verhoef, P. C. (2006). Challenges and opportunities in multichannel customer management. *Journal of Service Research*, *9*(2), 95–112. doi:10.1177/1094670506293559

Nettle, D. (1999). Using Social Impact Theory to simulate language change. *Lingua*, *108*(2-3), 95–117. doi:10.1016/S0024-3841(98)00046-1

Ng, H. T. (2002). Stock market linkages in South-East Asia. *Asian Economic Journal*, *16*(4), 353–377. doi:10.1111/1467-8381.00157

Normann, R. (2000). *Service Management - Strategy and Leadership in Service Business.* Chichester: Wiley.

North, A. C., & Hargreaves, D. J. (1996). The Effect of Music on Responses to a Dining Area. *Journal of Environmental Psychology, 16*(1), 55–64. doi:10.1006/jevp.1996.0005

North, A. C., & Hargreaves, D. J. (1998). The effect of music on atmosphere and purchase intentions in cafeteria. *Journal of Applied Social Psychology, 28*(24), 2254–2273. doi:10.1111/j.1559-1816.1998.tb01370.x

North, A. C., Hargreaves, D. J., & McKendrick, J. (1997). In-store music affects product choice. *Nature, 390*(6656), 6656. doi:10.1038/36484

North, A. C., Mackenzie, L. C., Law, R. M., & Hargreaves, D. J. (2004). The Effects of Musical and Voice „Fit" on Responses to Advertisements. *Journal of Applied Social Psychology, 34*(8), 1675–1708. doi:10.1111/j.1559-1816.2004.tb02793.x

North, A. C., Shilcock, A., & Hargreaves, D. J. (2005). The effect of musical style on restaurant customers spending. *Environment and Behavior, 35*(5), 712–718. doi:10.1177/0013916503254749

O.E.C.D. (2015). *Pharmaceutical market.* Retrieved from http://stats.oecd.org

O'Hern. M.S., & Rindfleisch, A. (2009). Customer Co-Creation: A Typology and Research Agenda. Review of Marketing Research, 6, 84-106.

Oakes, S. (2000). The Influence of the musicscape within service environment. *Journal of Services Marketing, 14*(7), 539–556. doi:10.1108/08876040010352673

Oakes, S. (2003). Musical tempo and waiting perceptions. *Psychology and Marketing, 20*(8), 685–705. doi:10.1002/mar.10092

Oakes, S., & North, A. C. (2008). Reviewing congruity effects in the service environment musicscape. *International Journal of Service Industry Management, 19*(1), 63–82. doi:10.1108/09564230810855716

Obermiller, C., & Spangenberg, E. R. (1998). Development of a Scale to Measure Consumer Skepticism Toward Advertising. *Journal of Consumer Psychology, 7*(2), 159–186. doi:10.1207/s15327663jcp0702_03

OBrien, C. (2008). Sustainable Happiness: How Happiness Studies Can Contribute to a More Sustainable Future. *Canadian Psychology, 49*(4), 289–295. doi:10.1037/a0013235

Ogawa, S., & Piller, F. T. (2006). Reducing the Risks of New Product Development. *Sloan Management Review, 47*, 65–72.

Oh, H., Fiore, A. M., & Jeoung, M. (2007). Measuring experience economy concepts: Tourism applications. *Journal of Travel Research, 46*(2), 119–132. doi:10.1177/0047287507304039

Oishi, Sh., Graham, J., Kesebir, S., & Galinha, I. C. (2013). Concepts of Happiness Across Time and Cultures. *Personality and Social Psychology Bulletin, 39*(5), 559–577. doi:10.1177/0146167213480042 PMID:23599280

Olahut, M. R., El-Murad, J., & Plaias, I. (2012). Store atmosphere: conceptual issues and its impact on shopping behaviour, international conference. In Marketing – from information to decision (5th ed., pp. 317-343).

Olander, F., & Thøgersen, J. (1995). Understanding of consumer behavior as a prerequisite for environmental protection. *Journal of Consumer Policy, 18*, 345–385. doi:10.1007/BF01024160

Oliver, R. L. (1997). *Satisfaction: A behavioral perspective on the consumer.* New York: McGraw Hill.

Oliver, R. L. (2006). *Customer satisfaction research. The handbook of marketing research.* California: Sage.

Orel, F. D., & Zeren, D. (2009). Pazarlama ve tüketici yandaşlığı anlayışına yönelik tüketici tutumları: Boylamsal bir çalışma. *Finans Politik & Ekonomik Yorumlar*, *46*(536), 65–78.

Ostrom, A. L., Parasuraman, A., Bowen, D. E., Patricio, L., Voss, C. A., & Lemon, K. (2015). Service research priorities in a rapidly changing context. *Journal of Service Research*, *18*(2), 127–159. doi:10.1177/1094670515576315

Ottman, J. A. (1993). *Green Marketing: Challenges & Opportunities for the New Marketing Age*. Chicago: NTC Publishing Group.

Ottman, J. A. et al.. (2006). *Avoiding GreenMarketing Myopia. Issue of Environment*, *48*(5), 22–36.

Overstreet, J., & Clodfelter, R. (1995). Safety and Security Concerns of Shopping Center Consumers and the Effect of these Concerns on Shopping Behavior. *Journal of Shopping Center Research*, *2*(1), 91–109.

Ozaki, R., & Sevastyanova, K. (2011). Going hybrid: An analysis of consumer purchase motivations. *Energy Policy*, *39*(5), 2217–2227. doi:10.1016/j.enpol.2010.04.024

Ozanne, L. K., & Ballantine, P. W. (2010). Sharing as a form of anti-consumption? An examination of toy library users. *Journal of Consumer Behaviour*, *9*(6), 485–498. doi:10.1002/cb.334

Ozcaglar-Toulouse, N., Shiu, E., & Shaw, D. (2006). In search of fair trade: Ethical consumer decision making in France. *International Journal of Consumer Studies*, *30*(5), 502–514. doi:10.1111/j.1470-6431.2006.00532.x

Packard, V. (1957). *The Hidden Persuaders*. London: Longman.

Panni, M. F. A. K. (2006). *The Effect of Consumerism towards customer attitudinal behavior in food insustry in Malaysia* [Unpublished Master's Thesis]. Multimedia University, Melaka, Malaysia.

Panpura, D., Patel, B. K., & Patel, N. (2011). Study of comovement and interdependence of Indian stock market with selected foreign stock markets. *Asian Journal of Research in Banking and Finance*, *1*, 74–92.

Parasuraman, A., Zeithaml, V. A., & Berry, L. L. (1985). A Conceptual Model of Service Quality and Its Implications for Future Research. *Journal of Marketing*, *49*(4), 41–50. doi:10.2307/1251430

Paswan, A. K., Charles, B., & Francisco, G. (2011). Relationalism in marketing channels and marketing strategy. *European Journal of Marketing*, *45*(3), 311–333. doi:10.1108/03090561111107212

Pauli, G. (2010). *The blue economy: 10 years, 100 innovations, 100 million jobs*. Paradigm Publications.

Paulikaite, M. (2015). Anti-branding: a way to destroy brands? Case of Apple Inc. Oct. http://www.brandba.se/blog/2015 (accessed 17 April 2016).

Pavot, W., & Diener, E. (1993). Review of the Satisfaction with Life Scale. *Psychological Assessment*, *5*(2), 164–172. doi:10.1037/1040-3590.5.2.164

Pearson, G., & Proctor, T. (1994). The modern framework for Marketing Plan. *Marketing Intelligence & Planning*, *12*(4), 22–26. doi:10.1108/02634509410060712

Peattie, K. (1992). *Green Marketing*. Pitman.

Peattie, K. (2001). Golden Goose or Wild Goose? The Hunt for the Green Consumer. *Business Strategy and the Environment*, *10*(4), 187–199. doi:10.1002/bse.292

Peattie, K., & Crane, A. (2005). Green Marketing: Legend, myth, farce or prophesy. *Qualitative Market Research*, *8*(4), 357–370. doi:10.1108/13522750510619733

Peattie, K., & Peattie, S. (2009). Social marketing: A pathway to consumption reduction? *Journal of Business Research*, *62*(2), 260–268. doi:10.1016/j.jbusres.2008.01.033

Peck, J., & Childers, T. L. (2003). To Have and to Hold: The Influence of Haptic Information on Product Judgements. *Journal of Marketing*, *67*(April), 35–48. doi:10.1509/jmkg.67.2.35.18612

Peek-Asa, C., Casteel, C., Kraus, J. F., & Whitten, P. (2006). Employee and Customer Injury during Violent Crimes in Retail and Service Businesses. *American Journal of Public Health*, *96*(10), 1867–1872. doi:10.2105/AJPH.2005.071365 PMID:17008585

Peffers, K., Tuunanen, T., Rothenberger, M., & Chatterjee, S. (2008). A design science research methodology for information systems research. *Journal of Management Information Systems*, *24*(3), 45–78. doi:10.2753/MIS0742-1222240302

Penaloza, L., & Price, L. L. (1993). Consumer resistance: A conceptual overview. *Advances in Consumer Research. Association for Consumer Research (U. S.)*, *20*, 123–128.

Penny, L. (2012). Hate capitalism, love shopping. *New Statesman (London, England)*, *141*(5087), 13–13.

Penttinen, E. (2007). *Transition from products to services within the manufacturing business* [Unpublished Doctoral dissertation]. Helsinki School of Economics, Helsinki.

Percival, B. D., & Walden, A. T. (2000). *Wavelet methods for time series analysis*. Cambridge University Press. doi:10.1017/CBO9780511841040

Perks, H., Gruber, T., & Edvardsson, B. (2012). Co-creation in radical service innovation: A systematic analysis of microlevel processes. *Journal of Product Innovation Management*, *29*(6), 935–951. doi:10.1111/j.1540-5885.2012.00971.x

Perlman, Y., & Ozinci, Y. (2014). Reducing Shoplifting by Investment in Security. *The Journal of the Operational Research Society*, *65*(5), 685–693. doi:10.1057/jors.2013.37

Peters, C., Maglio, P., Badinelli, R., Harmon, R. R., Maull, R., Spohrer, J. C., & Demirkan, H. et al. (2016). Emerging Digital Frontiers for Service Innovation. *Communications of the Association for Information Systems*, *39*(1).

Peterson, G. (2016), The Impact Of Background Music On Spending Habits, Howl & Echoes. Retrieved from http://howlandechoes.com/

Peterson, R. A., & Wilson, W. R. (1992). Measuring customer satisfaction: Fact and artefact. *Journal of the Academy of Marketing Science*, *20*(1), 61–71. doi:10.1007/BF02723476

Petty, R. D. (2012). Using the law to protect the brand on social media sites: A three "M"s framework for marketing managers, *Management Research Review*, 35(9), 758 – 769. Retrieved from http://www.emeraldinsight.com/journals.htm?issn=20408269&volume=35&issue=9&articleid=17044169&show=html

Pham, M. (2014), The Effects of Background Music on Consumer Behavior, University of California, Santa Barbara, Retrieved from http://www.writing.ucsb.edu/sites/secure.lsit.ucsb.edu.writ.d7/files/sitefiles/publications/2014%20Pham.pdf

Phau, I., & Ong, D. (2007). An Investigation of the Effects of Environmental Claims in Promotional Messages for Clothing Brands. *Marketing Intelligence & Planning*, *25*(7), 772–788. doi:10.1108/02634500710834214

Phelps, E. S. (1967). Phillips curves, expectations of inflation and optimal unemployment over time. *Economica*, *34*(135), 254–281. doi:10.2307/2552025

Phipps, M., Ozanne, L. K., Luchs, M. G., Subrahmanyan, S., Kapitan, S., Catlin, J. R., & Weaver, T. et al. (2013). Understanding the inherent complexity of sustainable consumption: A social cognitive framework. *Journal of Business Research*, *66*(8), 1227–1234. doi:10.1016/j.jbusres.2012.08.016

Pickett, G. M., Grove, S. J., & Kangun, N. (1993). An analysis of the conserving consumer: A public policy perspective. In C.T. Allen, et al. (Eds.) *American Marketing Association Winter Educator's Conference Proceedings*, Chicago, IL, USA (Vol. 3, pp. 151-153). American Marketing Association.

Pickett, B. J. (2008). Pro-environmental products: Marketing influence on consumer purchase decision. *Journal of Consumer Marketing*, *25*(5), 281–293. doi:10.1108/07363760810890516

Piercy, N., & Morgan, N. (1994). The Marketing Strategy process: Behavioural problems compared to analytical techniques in explaining Marketing Strategy credibility. *Journal of Business Research*, *29*(3), 167–178. doi:10.1016/0148-2963(94)90001-9

Pihlström, M. (2007). Committed to content provider or mobile channel? determinants of continuous mobile multimedia service use. *Journal of Information Technology Theory and Application*, *9*(1), 1–23.

Piven, I., Davis, R., & Lim, M. (2012). Conceptualising the Brand Relationship in Social Media Consumption. *Paper presented at the ANZMAC '12*, Adelaide, Australia.

Planas, C., Roeger, W., & Rossi, A. (2013). The information content of capacity utilization for detrending total factor productivity. *Journal of Economic Dynamics & Control*, *37*(3), 577–590. doi:10.1016/j.jedc.2012.09.005

Pohl, K., Böckle, G., & van der Linden, F. (2005). *Software Product Line Engineering - Foundations, Principles, and Techniques*. Berlin: Springer. doi:10.1007/3-540-28901-1

Polonsky, M. J. (1994a). A Stakeholder Theory Approach to Designing Environmental Marketing Strategy (Unpublished Working Paper).

Polonsky, M. J. (1994b, November). An introduction to Green Marketing. *Electronic Green Journal*, *1*(2).

Polonsky, M. J., Vocino, A., Grimmer, M., & Miles, M. (2016). Past and Future Orientation, Environmental Attitudes and Green Consumer Behaviour. In Looking Forward, Looking Back: Drawing on the Past to Shape the Future of Marketing (pp. 654-654). Springer International Publishing.

Pomering, A., & Dolnicar, S. (2009). Assessing the Prerequisite of Successful CSR Implementation: Are Consumers Aware of CSR Initiatives? *Journal of Business Ethics*, *85*(2), 285–301. doi:10.1007/s10551-008-9729-9

Portwood-Stacer, L. (2012). Anti-consumption as tactical resistance: Anarchists, subculture, and activist strategy. *Journal of Consumer Culture*, *12*(1), 87–105. doi:10.1177/1469540512442029

Potoglou, D., & Kanaroglou, P. S. (2007). Household demand and willingness to pay for clean vehicles. *Transportation Research Part D, Transport and Environment*, *12*(4), 264–274. doi:10.1016/j.trd.2007.03.001

Prahalad, C. K., & Ramaswamy, V. (2004). *The Future of Competition: Co-creating Unique Value with Consumers*. Boston: Harvard Business School Press.

Pratt, J. (2008). Food values: The local and the authentic. In G. De Neve, L. Peter, J. Pratt, D. C. Wood (Eds.), Hidden Hands in the Market: Ethnographies of Fair Trade, Ethical Consumption, and Corporate Social Responsibility, Research in Economic Anthropology (Vol. 28, pp. 53-70). Emerald Group Publishing Limited. doi:10.1016/S0190-1281(08)28003-0

Pretious, M., Stewart, R., & Logan, D. (1995). Retail Security: A Survey of Methods and Management in Dundee. *International Journal of Retail & Distribution Management*, *23*(9), 28–35. doi:10.1108/09590559510098681

PSBresearch. (2009). Retrieved from http://www.psbresearch.com/green_2009.htm#top

PSBresearch. (n. d.). Retrieved from http://www.psbresearch.com/green_JWT.htm

Qian, H., Haynes, K. E., & Riggle, J. D. (2011). Incubation push or business pull? Investigating the geography of US business incubators. *Economic Development Quarterly*, *25*(1), 79–90. doi:10.1177/0891242410383275

Ramesh, B., Tiwana, A., & Mohan, K. (2002, October 3-5). Supporting Information Product and Service Families with Traceability. *Proceedings of the 4th International Workshop on Software Product-Family Engineering PFE '01*, Bilbao, Spain (pp. 353-363).

Ram, Y., Nawijn, J., & Peeters, P. (2013). Happiness and limits to sustainable tourism mobility: A new conceptual model. *Journal of Sustainable Tourism*, *21*(7), 1017–1035. doi:10.1080/09669582.2013.826233

Ranjan, K. R., & Read, S. (2016). Value co-creation: Concept and measurement. *Journal of the Academy of Marketing Science*, *44*(3), 290–315. doi:10.1007/s11747-014-0397-2

Rao, S. S., Metts, G., & Monge, C. A. M. (2003). Electronic commerce development in small and medium sized enterprises: A stage model and its implications. *Business Process Management Journal*, *9*(1), 11–32. doi:10.1108/14637150310461378

Rapoport, R. N. (1970). Three dilemmas of action research. *Human Relations*, *23*(6), 499–513. doi:10.1177/001872677002300601

Ravald, A., & Grönroos, C. (1996). The value concept and relationship marketing. *European Journal of Marketing*, *30*(2), 19–30. doi:10.1108/03090569610106626

Reddy, A. C., & Campell, D. P. (1994). *Marketing's role in Economic Development*. London: Quorum Books.

Redlynx. (2009). TV-centered Cross-Media Games and Entertainment. Retrieved from http://www.redlynx.com

Redmond, L. (2000*). Identifying and Analysing Travel-related Attitudinal, Personality and Lifestyle Clusters in the San Francisco Bay Area* [MSc Thesis]. University of California, Davis.

Reingold, R. N., & Lansing, P. (1994). An ethical analysis of Japans response to the Arab boycott of Israel. *Business Ethics Quarterly*, *4*(3), 335–353. doi:10.2307/3857451

Reynolds, K. L., & Harris, L. C. (2009). Dysfunctional Customer Behavior Severity: An Empirical Examination. *Journal of Retailing*, *85*(3), 321–355. doi:10.1016/j.jretai.2009.05.005

Rezvani, Z., Jansson, J., & Bodin, J. (2015). Advances in consumer electric vehicle adoption research: A review and research agenda. *Transportation Research Part D, Transport and Environment*, *34*, 122–136. doi:10.1016/j.trd.2014.10.010

Ritzer, G. (2004). *The McDonaldization of Society* (Rev. New Century ed.) . *Thousand Oaks*, CA, USA: *Pine Forge Press.* .

Roballey, T. C., McGreevy, C., Rongo, R. R., Schwantes, M. L., Steger, P. J., Wininger, M. A., & Gardner, E. B. (1985). The effect of music on eating behaviour. *Bulletin of the Psychonomic Society*, *23*(3), 221–222. doi:10.3758/BF03329832

Roberts, J. (1996). Green consumers in the1990s: Profile and implications for advertising. *Journal of Business Research*, *36*(3), 217–232. doi:10.1016/0148-2963(95)00150-6

Robertson, D., & Ulrich, K. (1998). Planning for Product Platforms. *MIT Sloan Management Review*, *39*(4), 19–31.

Roberts, P. W., & Dowling, G. R. (2002). Corporate Reputation and Sustained Superior Financial Performance. *Strategic Management Journal*, *23*(12), 1077–1093. doi:10.1002/smj.274

Rohm, A., & Swaminathan, V. (2004). A typology of online shoppers based on shopping motivations. *Journal of Business Research*, *57*(7), 748–757. doi:10.1016/S0148-2963(02)00351-X

Roseman, I. J., Spindel, M. S., & Jose, P. E. (1990). Appraisals of Emotion-Eliciting Events: Testing a Theory of Discrete Emotions. *Journal of Personality and Social Psychology*, *59*(5), 899–915. doi:10.1037/0022-3514.59.5.899 PMID:2348375

Rose, R. L., & Neidermeyer, M. (1999). From Rudeness to Roadrage: The Antecedents and Consequences of Consumer Aggression. *Advances in Consumer Research. Association for Consumer Research (U. S.), 26*, 12–17.

Rospigliosi, A., & Greener, S. (2015) (Ed.), Leading Issues in Social Media Research. Academic Publishing Ltd.

Rothschild, M. L. (1999). Carrots, sticks and promises: A conceptual framework for the management of public health and social issues behaviors. *Journal of Marketing, 63*(4), 24–37. doi:10.2307/1251972

Rothschild, M. L. (2002). Accommodating self-interest. *Social Marketing Quarterly, 8*(2), 32–35. doi:10.1080/15245000212559

Roux, D. (2007). Consumer resistance: Proposal for an integrative framework. *Recherche et Applications en Marketing, 22*(4), 59–79. doi:10.1177/076737010702200403

Rowlands, I. H., Parker, P., & Scott, D. (2002). Consumer perceptions of green power. *Journal of Consumer Marketing, 19*(2), 112–127. doi:10.1108/07363760210420540

Rowley, J. (2004). Online branding, *Online Information Review*, 28(2), 131–138. Retrieved from http://www.emeraldinsight.com/journals.htm?issn=1468-4527&volume=28&issue=2&articleid=862248&show=html&PHPSESSID=ufafb m4asi1f8kfsedv58qea12 13)

Rua, A. (2012). Wavelets in economics. *Banco De Portugal Economic Bulletin, Summer,* 71-79.

Rua, A. (2010). Measuring comovement in the time-frequency space. *Journal of Macroeconomics, 32*(2), 685–691. doi:10.1016/j.jmacro.2009.12.005

Rua, A., & Nunes, L. C. (2009). International comovement of stock market returns: A wavelet analysis. *Journal of Empirical Finance, 16*(4), 632–639. doi:10.1016/j.jempfin.2009.02.002

Ruiz, S., Arcas, N., & Cuestas, P. (2001). Consumer attitudes towards ecological agrarian fruits and vegetables in Spain. A Segmentation Approach. *Acta Horticulturae, 559*(559), 681–686. doi:10.17660/ActaHortic.2001.559.100

Rusko, R. (2011). Virtual Business Incubations: An Alternative Way to Develop and Service Peripheral Areas.[IJIDE]. *International Journal of Innovation in the Digital Economy, 2*(3), 48–64. doi:10.4018/jide.2011070104

Rusko, R. (2012). Strategic Processes and Turning Points in ICT Business: Case Nokia. *International Journal of Innovation in the Digital Economy, 3*(3), 25–34. doi:10.4018/jide.2012070103

Rust, R. T., & Oliver, R. L. (1994). Service quality: insights and managerial implications from the frontier. In R. T. Rust & R. L. Oliver (Eds.), *Service Quality: New Directions in Theory and Practice* (pp. 1–19). London: Sage. doi:10.4135/9781452229102.n1

Ryan, T. (2014). Green Intentions: An Exploratory Study on Advertising and the Environmental Movement. *Journal of Research for Consumers*, 26, 13.

Samanta, I., & Kyriazopoulos, P. (2014). *Applied Marketing*. Syghroni Ekdotiki Publications.

Sandberg, J., & Alvesson, M. (2011). Ways of Constructing Research Questions: Gap-Spotting or Problematization? *Organization, 18*(1), 23–44. doi:10.1177/1350508410372151

Sandıkcı, Ö., & Ekici, A. (2009). Politically motivated brand rejection. *Journal of Business Research, 62*(2), 208–217. doi:10.1016/j.jbusres.2008.01.028

Sashi, C. M. (2012). Customer engagement, buyer-seller relationships, and social media. *Management Decision, 50*(2), 253–272. doi:10.1108/00251741211203551

Scheier, M. F., & Carver, C. S. (1985). Optimism, coping, and health: Assessment and implications of generalized outcome expectancies. *Health Psychology*, *4*(3), 219–247. doi:10.1037/0278-6133.4.3.219 PMID:4029106

Schembri, S. (2006). Rationalizing Service Logic, or Understanding Services as Experience? *Marketing Theory*, *6*(3), 381–392. doi:10.1177/1470593106066798

Schendler, A. (2009). *Getting green done: Hard truths from the front lines of the sustainability revolution*. New York, NY: Public Affairs.

Schmitt, B. H. (1999). *Experiential Marketing: How to Get Customers to Sense, Feel, Think, Act, Relate to Your Company and Brands*. New York: The Free Press.

Schor, J. B., & Holt, D. B. (Eds.). (2000). *The Consumer Society Reader*. New Press.

Schultze, C. L. (1963). Uses of capacity measures for short-run economic analysis. *The American Economic Review*, *53*, 76–85.

Schwenk, C. R. (1984). Cognitive simplification processes in strategic decision-making. *Strategic Management Journal*, *5*(2), 111–128. doi:10.1002/smj.4250050203

Schwepker, C. H., & Cornwell, R. B. (1991). An examination of ecologically concerned consumers and their intention to purchase ecologically packaged products. *Journal of Public Policy & Marketing*, *10*(2), 77–101.

Schwepker-Jr, C. H., & Cornwell, T. B. (1991). An Examination of Ecologically Concerned Consumers and their Intention to Purchase Ecologically Packaged Products. *Journal of Public Policy & Marketing*, *10*(2), 77–101.

Scott, M. S. (2007). How to Measure Customer Satisfaction: Satisfaction Measurement and Theory. Retrieved from http://www.aboutsurveys.com/how-to-measure-customer-satisfaction-satisfaction-measurement-and-theory/

Sedikides, C., & Jackson, J. M. (1990). Social impact theory: A field test of source strength, source immediacy and number of targets. *Basic and Applied Social Psychology*, *11*(3), 273–281. doi:10.1207/s15324834basp1103_4

Sekaran, U. (1983). Methodological and theoretical issues and advancements in cross-cultural research. *Journal of International Business Studies*, *14*(2), 61–73. doi:10.1057/palgrave.jibs.8490519

Sen, S., & Bhattacharya, C. B. (2001). Does doing good always lead to doing better? Consumer reactions to corporate social responsibility. *JMR, Journal of Marketing Research*, *38*(2), 225–243. doi:10.1509/jmkr.38.2.225.18838

Sen, S., Gürhan-Canlı, Z., & Morwitz, V. (2001). Withholding consumption: A social dilemma perspective on consumer boycotts. *The Journal of Consumer Research*, *28*(3), 399–417. doi:10.1086/323729

Setmeyer, A. P. (2010). Consumerism, Catholicism, and Halls Theology of the Cross. *Dialog*, *49*(4), 306–314. doi:10.1111/j.1540-6385.2010.00557.x

Seyfang, G. (2004). Consuming values and contested cultures: A critical analysis of the UK strategy for sustainable consumption and production. *Review of Social Economy*, *62*(3), 323–338. doi:10.1080/0034676042000253936

Seyfang, G. (2006). Ecological citizenship and sustainable consumption: Examining local organic food networks. *Journal of Rural Studies*, *22*(4), 383–395. doi:10.1016/j.jrurstud.2006.01.003

Shapiro, M. D., Gordon, R. J., & Summers, L. H. (1989). Assessing the federal reserve measure of capacity and utilization. *Brookings Papers on Economic Activity*, *1*(1), 181–241. doi:10.2307/2534498

Sharp, A., Høj, S., & Wheeler, M. (2010). Proscription and its impact on anti-consumption behaviour and attitudes: The case of plastic bags. *Journal of Consumer Behaviour*, *9*(6), 470–484. doi:10.1002/cb.335

Shaw, D., & Newholm, T. (2002). Voluntary simplicity and the ethics of consumption. *Psychology and Marketing, 19*(2), 167–185. doi:10.1002/mar.10008

Sherry, J. F. Jr. (1989). Postmodern Alternatives: The Interpretive Turn in Consumer Research. In H. Kassarjian & T. Robertson (Eds.), *Handbook of Consumer Theory and Research*. Englewood Cliffs, N.J.: Prentice Hall.

Sheth, J. N., Sethia, N. K., & Srinivas, S. (2011). Mindful consumption: A customer-centric approach to sustainability. *Journal of the Academy of Marketing Science, 39*(1), 21–39. doi:10.1007/s11747-010-0216-3

Shewmake, S., & Jarvis, L. (2014). Hybrid cars and HOV lanes. *Transportation Research Part A, Policy and Practice, 67*, 304–319. doi:10.1016/j.tra.2014.07.004

Shokri, A., Oglethorpe, D., & Nabhani, F. (2014). Evaluating sustainability in the UK fast food supply chain. *Journal of Manufacturing Technology Management, 25*(8), 1224–1245. doi:10.1108/JMTM-04-2013-0031

Shove, E. (2003a). *Comfort, Cleanliness & Convenience*. Oxford: Berg. Sidwell.

Shove, E. (2003b). Converging Conventions of Comfort, Cleanliness and Convenience. *Journal of Consumer Policy, 26*(4), 395–418. Retrieved from http://www.lancs.ac.uk/sociology/research/publications/papers/shove-converging-conventions.pdf doi:10.1023/A:1026362829781

Shrivastava, P., & Grant, J. H. (1985). Empirically derived models of strategic decision-making processes. *Strategic Management Journal, 6*(2), 97–113. doi:10.1002/smj.4250060202

Siano, A., Vollero, A., & Siglioccolo, M. (2015). *Corporate Communication Management. Accrescere la reputazione per attrarre risorse*. Torino: Giappichelli.

Silveira, G. D., Borenstein, D., & Fogliatto, F. S. (2001). Mass Customization: Literature Review and Research Directions. *International Journal of Production Economics, 72*(1), 1–13. doi:10.1016/S0925-5273(00)00079-7

Sima, V., & Gheorghe, I. (2009). Eco-Efficiency – A Romanian Perspective. *Proceedings of the 11th IBIMA Conference, Creating Global Economies through Innovation and Knowledge Management* (pp. 1642-1650).

Sima, V., & Gheorghe, I. (2009). The Green Strategy Mix – A New Marketing Approach, *Proceedings of the 13th IBIMA Conference on Knowledge Management and Innovation in Advancing Economies, Analyses & Solutions* (pp. 1344-1347).

Sima, V., & Gheorghe, I. G. (2009). The 'Green Dimension' of Customer satisfaction. *Proceedings of the 11th IBIMA Conference, Creating Global Economies through Innovation and Knowledge Management* (pp. 1638-1641).

Sima, V. (2010). Motivations for a Systemic Approach of the Innovative Strategies for a "Green" Product. *Petroleum-Gas University of Ploieşti Bulletin, 12*(3), 104–111.

Sima, V., & Gheorghe, I. G. (2007). The Corporate Social Responsibility – a Modern Marketing Concept. *Annals Of The Oradea University, Fascicle of Management and Technological Engineering, 6*(14), 2592–2596.

Sima, V., & Gheorghe, I. G. (2009). The Opportunity for a Reconsideration of the Dimensions of the Assessment Model of the Customers Satisfaction. *Communications of the IBIMA, 9*, 64–68.

Simkin, L. (1996). The benefits of controlling implementation in Marketing Plan. *Journal of Marketing Management, 12*, 375–390. doi:10.1080/0267257X.1996.9964423

Simkin, L. (2000). Delivering effective Marketing Plan. *Journal of Targeting, Measurement and Analysis for Marketing, 8*(3), 1–16.

Singer, A., Hardwick, S. W., & Brettell, C. B. (2009). *Twenty-first century gateways: Immigrant incorporation in suburban America*. Brookings Institution Press.

Sirdeshmukh, D., Singh, J., & Sabol, B. (2002). Consumer trust, value, and loyalty in relational exchanges. *Journal of Marketing*, *66*(1), 15–37. doi:10.1509/jmkg.66.1.15.18449

Sirgy, J. (1982). Self-Concept in Consumer Behavior: A Critical Review. *The Journal of Consumer Research*, *9*(3), 287–301. Retrieved from http://www.jstor.org/stable/2488624 doi:10.1086/208924

Sklair, L. (2010). Iconic Architecture and the Culture-ideology of Consumerism. *Theory, Culture & Society*, *27*(5), 135–159. doi:10.1177/0263276410374634

Slater, D. (1997). *Consumer, Culture and Modernity*. Cambridge: Policy Press.

Smart, K. L., & Whiting, M. E. (2001). Designing Systems that support learning and use: A Customer-centered approach. *Information & Management*, *39*(3), 177–190. doi:10.1016/S0378-7206(01)00089-1

Smith, P. C., & Curnow, R. (1966). Arousal hypothesis and the effects of music on purchasing behavior. *The Journal of Applied Psychology*, *50*(3), 255–256. doi:10.1037/h0023326 PMID:5936035

Snyder, C. R., Lassegard, M., & Ford, C. E. (1986). Distancing after group success and failure: Basking in reflected glory and cutting off reflected failure. *Journal of Personality and Social Psychology*, *51*(2), 382–388. doi:10.1037/0022-3514.51.2.382

Soanes, C., & Stevenson, A. (Eds.). (2004). *Concise Oxford English Dictionary* (11th ed.). Oxford: Oxford University Press.

Soars, B. (2009). Driving Sales through Shoppers Sense of Sound, Sight, Smell and Touch. *International Journal of Retail & Distribution Management*, *37*(3), 286–298. doi:10.1108/09590550910941535

Solomon, M.R. (2008), Consumer Behavior: buying, having and being (8th ed.). New York: Prentice Hall.

Sommerville, I. (2001). *Software Engineering* (6th ed.). Addison-Wesley.

Soper, K. (2008). Alternative hedonism, cultural theory and the role of aesthetic revisioning. *Cultural Studies*, *22*(5), 567–587. doi:10.1080/09502380802245829

Southerton, D., Chappells, H., & Van Vliet, B. (2004). *Sustainable Consumption*. Cheltenham: Edward Elgar.

SpannerWorks. (2007). *What is social media*. Retrieved from www.spannerworks.com/ebooks

Stanciu, M. (2006). Metode de cercetare a modelelor de consum. Studii şi Cercetări Economice, 42.

Stern, P. C. (2000). Toward a coherent theory of environmentally significant behavior. *The Journal of Social Issues*, *56*(3), 407–424. doi:10.1111/0022-4537.00175

Stern, P. C., Dietz, T., Kalof, L., & Guagnano, G. A. (1995). Values, beliefs and pro environmental action: Attitude formation toward emergent attitude objects. *Journal of Applied Social Psychology*, *25*(18), 1611–1636. doi:10.1111/j.1559-1816.1995.tb02636.x

Stout, P., & Leckenby, J. D. (1988). Let the music play: Music as a nonverbal element in TV commercials. In S. Hecker, & D.W. Stewart (Eds.), Nonverbal Communication in Advertising (pp. 207-233). Lexington, MA, USA: Lexington Books.

Strandvik, T., Rindell, A., & Wilen, K. (2013). Ethical consumers brand avoidance. *Journal of Product and Brand Management*, *22*(7), 484–490. doi:10.1108/JPBM-09-2013-0392

Straughan, R. D., & Roberts, J. A. (1999). Environmental segmentation alternatives: A look at green consumer behavior in the new millennium. *Journal of Consumer Marketing*, *16*(6), 558–575. doi:10.1108/07363769910297506

Strongman, K. T. (1996). *The psychology of emotion: Theories of emotion in perspective* (4th ed.). New York, NY: John Wiley & Sons.

Stuart, F. I., & Tax, S. (2004). Toward an integrative approach to designing service experiences Lessons learned from theatre. *Journal of Operations Management*, *22*(6), 690–627.

Stumpf, C. (1883). *Grundzuge der Physiologischen Psychologie*. Leipzig: Engelmann.

Suchard, H. T., & Polonsky, M. J. (1991). A theory of environmental buyer behavior and its validity: The Environmental Action-Behavior Model. In M.C. Gilly et al. (Eds.), *American Marketing Association Summer Educator's Conference Proceedings*, Chicago, IL., USA (Vol. 2, pp. 187-201). American Marketing Association.

Sugden, J., & Tomlinson, A. (2000). Football, resentment and resistance in the break-up of the former Soviet Union. *Culture, Sport, Society*, *3*(2), 89–108. doi:10.1080/14610980008721872

Sull, D., & Turconi, S. (2008). Fast Fashion Lessons. *Business Strategy Review*, *19*(2), 4–11. doi:10.1111/j.1467-8616.2008.00527.x

Sullivan, M., & Adcock, D. (2002). *Retail marketing*. Hampshire, UK: Cengage Learning EMEA.

Surprenant, C., & Churchill, G. A. Jr. (1984). Can Role Playing be Substituted for Actual Consumption? *Advances in Consumer Research. Association for Consumer Research (U. S.)*, *11*(1), 122–126.

Sussan, F., Hall, R., & Meamber, L. A. (2012). Introspecting the spiritual nature of a brand divorce. *Journal of Business Research*, *65*(4), 520–526. doi:10.1016/j.jbusres.2011.02.031

Sweeney, J. C., & Wyber, F. (2002). The role of cognitions and emotions in the music-approach-avoidance behaviour relationship. *Journal of Services Marketing*, *16*(1), 57–69. doi:10.1108/08876040210419415

Swenson, M. R., & Wells, W. D. (1997). Useful correlates of per-environmental behavior, Goldberg. In M.E., Fishbein, M. Middlestadt, S.E. (Eds.), Social Marketing: Theoretical and Practical Perspectives (pp. 91-109). Mahwah, NJ: Lawrence Erlbaum.

Swimberghe, K., Flurry, L. A., & Parker, J. M. (2011). Consumer religiosity: Consequences for consumer activism in the United States. *Journal of Business Ethics*, *103*(3), 453–467. doi:10.1007/s10551-011-0873-2

Tapscott, D., Williams, A. D., and Herman, D. (2007). Government 2.0: Transforming government and governance for the twenty-first century. *New Paradigm*.

Taş, O., & Tokmakçıoğlu, K. (2010). Efficient market hypothesis and comovement among emerging markets. *Dogus University Journal*, *11*, 286–301.

Tata, R. J. (1977). Uruguay: Population geography of a troubled welfare state. *The Journal of Geography*, *76*(2), 46–51. doi:10.1080/00221347708980880

Tax, S. S., & Brown, S. W. (1998). Recovering and Learning from Service Failure. *Sloan Management Review*, (Fall): 75–88.

Teller, C., & Dennis, C. (2012). The Effect of Ambient Scent on Consumers Perception, Emotions and Behaviour – a Critical Review. *Journal of Marketing Management*, *28*(1/2), 14–36. doi:10.1080/0267257X.2011.560719

Tencati, A., & Zsolnai, L. (2012). Collaborative Enterprise and Sustainability: The Case of Slow Food. *Journal of Business Ethics*, *110*(3), 345–355. doi:10.1007/s10551-011-1178-1

Teng, C.-C., & Barrows, C. W. (2009). Service Orientation: Antecedents, Outcomes, and Implications for Hospitality Research and Practice. *Service Industries Journal*, *29*(10), 1413–1435. doi:10.1080/02642060903026247

TGI surveys. (n. d.). Retrieved from http://www.tgisurveys.com/knowledgehub/reports/KMR_TGI_Green_Values.pdf

The Economist. (2016, January 23). The oil conundrum.

The Guardian. (2010). Nestlé hit by Facebook "anti-social" media surge. Retrieved from http://www.guardian.co.uk/sustainable-business/nestle-facebook

The Guardian. (21014) Smart meters: everything you need to know. Retrieved from https://www.theguardian.com/british-gas-smart-meter-challenge/2014/aug/26/smart-meters-everything-you-need-to-know

The Oxford English Dictionary. (1989). Oxford: Oxford University.

The Roper Organization. (1971). *The cost of cleaner Air: How much do people want it?* (6th ed.). Ames, IA: Iowa State University Press.

Theodorakis, N., Kaplanidou, K., & Karabaxoglou, J. (2015). Effect of Event Service Quality and Satisfaction on Happiness Among Runners of a Recurring Sport Event. *Leisure Sciences: An Interdisciplinary Journal*, *37*(1), 87–107. doi:10.1080/01490400.2014.938846

Thøgersen, J. (2000). Psychological Determinants of Paying Attention to Ecolabels in Purchase Decisions: Model Development and Multinational Validation. *Journal of Consumer Policy*, *23*(3), 285–313. doi:10.1023/A:1007122319675

Thomke, S., & von Hippel, E. (2002). Customers as innovators - A new way to create value. *Harvard Business Review*, *80*(4), 74. PMID:12024760

Thompson, C. J., & Coskuner-Balli, G. (2007). Enchanting ethical consumerism: The case of community supported agriculture. *Journal of Consumer Culture*, *7*(3), 275–303. doi:10.1177/1469540507081631

Thompson, J. (2005). The new visibility. *Theory, Culture & Society*, *22*(6), 31–51. doi:10.1177/0263276405059413

Tiwsakul, R. A., & Hackley, C. (2012). Postmodern paradoxes in Thai-Asian consumer identity. *Journal of Business Research*, *65*(4), 490–496. doi:10.1016/j.jbusres.2011.02.027

Toffler, A. (1980). *The Third Wave*. New York: William Morrow and Co.

Tonglet, M. (2000). Consumer Misbehaviour: Consumers Perceptions of Shoplifting and Retail Security. *Security Journal*, *13*(4), 107–122. doi:10.1057/palgrave.sj.8340063

Tonglet, M. (2002). Consumer Misbehaviour: An Exploratory Study of Shoplifting. *Journal of Consumer Behaviour*, *1*(4), 336–354. doi:10.1002/cb.79

Torres, A., Bijmolt, T. H. A., Tribó, J. A., & Verhoef, P. (2012, March). Generating global brand equity through corporate social responsibility to key stakeholders. *International Journal of Research in Marketing*, *29*(1), 13–24. doi:10.1016/j.ijresmar.2011.10.002

Tranfield, D., Denyer, D., & Smart, P. (2003). Towards a Methodology for Developing Evidence-Informed Management knowledge by means of Systematic Review. *British Journal of Management*, *14*(3), 207–222. Retrieved from http://www.cebma.org/wp-content/uploads/Tranfield-et-al-Towards-a-Methodology-for-Developing-Evidence-Informed-Management.pdf doi:10.1111/1467-8551.00375

Tuna, Y., & Özkoçak, L. (2012). The First Step to Communication with Environmentally Responsible Consumer: Measuring Environmental Consciousness of Turkish Consumers. *Online Journal of Communication and Media Technologies*, *2*(3), 145.

Tuominen, P. (2007). Emerging metaphors in brand management: Towards a relational approach. *Journal of Communication Management*, *11*(2), 182–191. doi:10.1108/13632540710747398

Turban, E., King, D., Lee, J. K., Liang, T. P., & Turban, D. C. (2015). Overview of Electronic Commerce. In *Electronic Commerce* (pp. 3–49). Springer International Publishing. doi:10.1007/978-3-319-10091-3_1

Turley, L. W., & Milliman, R. E. (2000). Atmospheric effects on shopping behaviour: A review of the experimental evidence. *Journal of Business Research*, *49*, 193–211. doi:10.1016/S0148-2963(99)00010-7

Turrentine, T., Kurani, K., & Heffner, R. (2007). Fuel economy: What drives consumer choice? *Access*, *31*(Fall), 14–19.

Tuunainen, V. K., & Tuunanen, T. (2011). IISIn-A model for analyzing ICT Intensive Service Innovations in n-sided Markets. *Paper presented at the 2011 44th Hawaii International Conference on System Sciences (HICSS)*. doi:10.1109/HICSS.2011.234

Tuunainen, V. K., Tuunanen, T., & Bastek, M. (2009). A Model for ICT Intensive Service Innovations in two-sided markets–Case Study of IPTV in a National TV Broadcasting Company. *Paper presented at the International Conference on New Trends in Information and Service Science NISS'09*. doi:10.1109/NISS.2009.161

Tuunainen, V. K., Tuunanen, T., & Piispanen, J. (2011). Mobile service platforms: Comparing nokia ovi and apple app store with the iisin model. *Paper presented at the 2011 10th International Conference on Mobile Business*. doi:10.1109/ICMB.2011.42

Tuunanen, T. (2009). The Future of Services is Changing (Video). Retrieved from http://www.tuunanen.fi

Tuunanen, T., Peffers, K., & Gengler, C. (2004). Wide audience requirements engineering (WARE): a practical method and case study. Helsinki School of Economics.

Tuunanen, T. (2003). A New Perspective on Requirements Elicitation Methods. *Journal of Information Technology Theory and Application*, *5*(3), 45–62.

Tuunanen, T., Bask, A., & Merisalo-Rantanen, H. (2012). Typology for modular service design: Review of literature. *International Journal of Service Science, Management, Engineering, and Technology*, *3*(3), 99–112. doi:10.4018/jssmet.2012070107

Tuunanen, T., & Cassab, H. (2011). Service process modularization: Reuse versus variation in service extensions. *Journal of Service Research*, *14*(3), 340–354. doi:10.1177/1094670511413912

Tuunanen, T., & Govindji, H. (2016). Understanding flow experience from users requirements. *Behaviour & Information Technology*, *35*(2), 134–150. doi:10.1080/0144929X.2015.1015167

Tuunanen, T., & Kuo, I. T. (2015). The effect of culture on requirements: A value-based view of prioritization. *European Journal of Information Systems*, *24*(3), 295–313. doi:10.1057/ejis.2014.29

Tuunanen, T., Myers, M., & Cassab, H. (2010). A conceptual framework for consumer information systems development. *Pacific Asia Journal of the Association for Information Systems*, *2*(1), 5.

Tuunanen, T., Myers, M., & Cassab, H. (2010). A Conceptual Framework for Consumer Information Systems Development. *Pacific Asia Journal of the Association for Information Systems*, *2*(1), 5.

Ugolini, M. M., Rossato, C., & Baccarani, C. (2014). A Five-Senses Perspective to Quality in Hospitals. *The TQM Journal*, *26*(3), 284–299. doi:10.1108/TQM-01-2014-0010

Uhl, Ch. (2004). *Developing Ecological Consciousness: Path to a Sustainable World*. Rowman & Littlefield Publisher, Inc.

Ungar, S. (1994). Apples and oranges: Probing the attitude behavior relationship for the environment. *The Canadian Review of Sociology and Anthropology. La Revue Canadienne de Sociologie et dAnthropologie*, *31*(3), 288–304. doi:10.1111/j.1755-618X.1994.tb00950.x

United Nations. (n. d.). Transforming our world: the 2030 Agenda for Sustainable Development. Retrieved from https://sustainabledevelopment.un.org/post2015/transformingourworld

Unpublished doctoral dissertation or master's theses:

Uray, N., & Menguc, B. (1996). Testing the cross-cultural generalizability of the scale of consumer attitudes toward marketing and consumerism. *Journal of International Consumer Marketing*, *9*(2), 65–93. doi:10.1300/J046v09n02_04

Uwins, S. (2014). *Creating Loyal Brands. A guide to earning loyalty in a connected world*. Publish Green.

Vaccaro, V. L., Yucetepe, V., Ahlawat, S., & Lee, M.-S. (2011). The Relationship of Liked Music with Music Emotion Dimensions, Shopping Experience, and Return Patronage Intentions in Retail and Service Settings. *Journal of Academy of Business and Economics*, *11*(4), 94–106.

Valkonen, K., Lindström, N., Natunen, L., Isoviita, R., & Tuunanen, T. (2015, August). Balance of Hedonic and Utilitarian Values in Information Systems Use. *Proceedings of theScandinavian Conference on Information Systems* (pp. 165-176). Springer International Publishing. doi:10.1007/978-3-319-21783-3_12

Valkonen, K., Lindström, N., Natunen, L., Isoviita, R., & Tuunanen, T. (2015). *Balance of Hedonic and Utilitarian Values in Information Systems Use Nordic Contributions in IS Research* (pp. 165–176). Springer.

Vallaster, C., Lindgreen, A., & Maon, F. (2012). Strategically Leveraging Corporate Social Responsibility: A Corporate Brand Perspective. *California Management Review*, *54*(3), 34–60. doi:10.1525/cmr.2012.54.3.34

van Aken, J. E. (2004). Management research based on the paradigm of the design sciences: The quest for field-tested and grounded technological rules. *Journal of Management Studies*, *41*(2), 219–246. doi:10.1111/j.1467-6486.2004.00430.x

Van Boven, L., & Gilovich, T. (2003). To Do or To Have: That is the Question. *Journal of Personality and Social Psychology*, *85*(December), 1193–1202. doi:10.1037/0022-3514.85.6.1193 PMID:14674824

Van der Linden, F. (2002). Software product families in Europe: The Esaps & Cafe projects. *IEEE Software*, *19*(4), 41–49. doi:10.1109/MS.2002.1020286

van Liere, D. W., Hagdorn, L., Hoogeweegen, M. R., & Vervest, P. H. (2004). Embedded coordination in a business network. *Journal of Information Technology*, *19*(4), 261–269. doi:10.1057/palgrave.jit.2000026

van Ommering, R., & Bosch, J. (2002, August 19-22). Widening the Scope of Software Product Lines - From Variation to Composition. *Proceedings of the Second International Conference on Software Product Lines SPLC 2*, San Diego, CA, USA (pp. 328-3470.

Varadarajan, P., Rajan, P., & Thirunarayana, P. (1990). Consumers attitudes towards marketing practices, consumerism, and government relations: Cross-national perspective. *European Journal of Marketing*, *24*(6), 6–24. doi:10.1108/03090569010137934

Vargo, S. L., & Lusch, R. F. (2004). Evolving to a new dominant logic for marketing. *Journal of Marketing*, *68*(1), 1–17. doi:10.1509/jmkg.68.1.1.24036

Vargo, S. L., Maglio, P. P., & Akaka, M. A. (2008). On value and value co-creation: A service systems and service logic perspective. *European Management Journal*, *26*(3), 145–152. doi:10.1016/j.emj.2008.04.003

Varman, R., & Belk, R. W. (2009). Nationalism and Ideology in an Anticonsumption Movement. *The Journal of Consumer Research*, *36*(4), 686–700. Retrieved from http://www.journals.uchicago.edu/doi/pdf/10.1086/600486 doi:10.1086/600486

Vartiainen, T., & Tuunanen, T. (2016). Value Co-Creation and Co-Destruction in an IS Artifact: Contradictions of Geocaching. *Paper presented at theHawaii International Conference on System Sciences*, Hawaii. doi:10.1109/HICSS.2016.160

Vavra, T. G. (1997). *Improving Your Measurement of Customer Satisfaction: A Guide to Creating, Conducting, Analyzing, and Reporting Customer Satisfaction Measurement Programs*. ASQ Quality Press.

Veblen, T. (1899): The Theory of the Leisure Class: an economic study of institutions. Mineola, NY: Dover Publications.

Veblen, T. (1994). *The Theory of the Leisure Class*. New York: Dover.

Verhoef, P. C. (2001). *Analysing customer relationships: Linking relational constructs and marketing instruments to customer behavior* [Unpublished doctoral dissertation]. Erasmus University, Rotterdam.

Verme, P. (2009). Happiness, freedom and control. *Journal of Economic Behavior & Organization*, *71*(2), 146–161. doi:10.1016/j.jebo.2009.04.008

Vida, I. (2008). The Impact of Atmospherics on Consumer Behaviour: The Case of the Music Fit in Retail Stores. *Economics and Business Review for Central and South-Eastern Europe*, *10*(1), 21–35.

Vida, I., Obadia, C., & Kunz, M. (2007). The Effects of Background Music on Consumer Responses in a High-end Supermarket. *International Review of Retail, Distribution and Consumer Research*, *17*(5), 469–482. doi:10.1080/09593960701631532

Visser, W. (2012). The Future of CSR: Towards Transformative CSR, or CSR 2.0.

Visser, W. (2013). *CSR 2.0: Transforming corporate sustainability and responsibility*. Springer.

von Hippel, E. (1986). Lead Users: A Source of Novel Product Concepts. *Management Science*, *32*(July), 791–805. doi:10.1287/mnsc.32.7.791

Voss, C. A., & Hsuan, J. (2009). Service architecture and modularity. *Decision Sciences*, *40*(3), 541–569. doi:10.1111/j.1540-5915.2009.00241.x

Vredenburg, K., Mao, J., Smith, P. W., & Carey, T. (2002). A survey of user-centered design practise. *CHI Letters, 12*(2).

Waddock, S., & Bodwell, C. (2007). What is Responsibility Management? And why bother? In Total Responsibility Management: The Manual (pp. 9–25). doi:10.9774/GLEAF.978-1-907643-01-9_2

Waddock, S., & Smith, N. (2000). Corporate Responsibility Audits: Doing Well by Doing Good. *MIT Sloan Management Review, 42*(2).

Walker, W. R., Skowronski, J. J., & Thomson, C. P. (1996). Life is pleasant – and memory helps to keep it that way! *Review of General Psychology*, *7*(2), 203–210. doi:10.1037/1089-2680.7.2.203

Wallace, W. T. (1994). Memory for Music: Effects of melody on recall of text. *Journal of Experimental Psychology*, *20*(6), 1471–1485.

Wallendorf, M., & Arnould, E. J. (1988). My Favorite Things: A Cross-Cultural Inquiry into Object Attachment, Possessiveness, and Social Linkage. *The Journal of Consumer Research*, *14*(4), 531–547. doi:10.1086/209134

Walls, J., Widmeyer, G., & El Sawy, O. (1992). Building an Information System Design Theory for Vigilant EIS. *Information Systems Research*, *3*(1), 36–59. doi:10.1287/isre.3.1.36

Walsh, P. D. (1994). Training Security Personnel. *Journal of Property Management*, *59*(2), 60–62.

Wang, M., & Wong, M. C. (2014). Happiness and leisure across countries: Evidence from international survey data. *Journal of Happiness Studies*, *15*(1), 119–123. doi:10.1007/s10902-013-9417-z

Want, R., Schilit, B. N., & Jenson, S. (2015). Enabling the Internet of Things. *IEEE Computer*, *48*(1), 28–35. doi:10.1109/MC.2015.12

Warde, A. (2005). Consumption and theories of practice. *Journal of Consumer Culture*, *5*(2), 131–153. doi:10.1177/1469540505053090

Waterman, A. S. (1993). Two conceptions of Happiness: Contrasts of personal expressiveness (Eudaimonia) and Hedonic Enjoyment. *Journal of Personality and Social Psychology*, *64*(4), 678–691. doi:10.1037/0022-3514.64.4.678

Watson, D., & Clark, L. A. (1984). Negative affectivity: The disposition to experience unpleasant emotional states. *Psychological Bulletin*, *67*(3), 465–490. doi:10.1037/0033-2909.96.3.465 PMID:6393179

Watson, D., Clark, L. A., & Tellegen, A. (1988). Development and validation of brief measures of positive and negative affect: The PANAS scales. *Journal of Personality and Social Psychology*, *47*(6), 1063–1070. doi:10.1037/0022-3514.54.6.1063 PMID:3397865

Watson, R. T., Pitt, L. F., Berthon, P., & Zinkhan, G. M. (2002). U-commerce: Expanding the universe of marketing. *Journal of the Academy of Marketing Science*, *30*(4), 333–347. doi:10.1177/009207002236909

WBCSD. (1996). A Changing Future for Paper. Retrieved from http://pubs.iied.org/pdfs/X136IIED.pdf

WBCSD. (n. d.). Corporate social responsibility. Retrieved from http://www.wbcsd.org/work-program/business-role/previous-work/corporate-social-responsibility.aspx

Webley, S. (2003). Risk, Reputation and Trust. *Journal of Communication Management*, *8*(1), 9–12. doi:10.1108/13632540410807501

Webster, G. D., & Weir, C. G. (2005). Emotional responses to music: Interactive effects of mode, texture, and tempo. *Motivation and Emotion*, *29*(1), 19–39. doi:10.1007/s11031-005-4414-0

Wee, C. H., & Chan, M. (1989). Consumer sentiment towards marketing in Hong Kong. *Asia Pacific International Journal of Marketing*, *1*(1), 25–29.

Weiner, J. L., & Doescher, T. A. (1991). A Framework for Promoting Cooperation. *Journal of Marketing*, *55*(2), 38–47. doi:10.2307/1252236

Wellhoff, A., & Masson, J. E. (2005). *Le Merchandising: Bases, Techniques, Nouvelles Tendances*. Paris: Dunod.

Werther, W. B. Jr, & Chandler, B. (2005). Strategic Corporate Social Responsibility as Global Brand Insurance. *Business Horizons*, *48*(4), 317–324. doi:10.1016/j.bushor.2004.11.009

West, S. (2007). The effect of gasoline prices on the demand for sport utility vehicles. Working Paper prepared for the "Demand Estimation in Environmental Economics" session, 2007 Midwest Economics Association Meetings.

Westbrook, R. A., & Oliver, R. L. (1981). Developing better measures of consumer satisfaction: Some preliminary results. In K. B. Monroe (Ed.), *Advances in consumer research* (8th ed., pp. 94–99). MI: Association for Consumer Research.

Wheeler, A. (2009). *Designing Brand Identity: An Essential Guide for the Whole Branding Team*. New York: Wiley.

Wheeler, K. (2012). Change today, choose fairtrade. *Cultural Studies*, *26*(4), 492–515. doi:10.1080/09502386.2011.622780

White, S. (2011). Defining Green Marketing. Retrieved from http://dstevenwhite.com/2010/08/04/defining-green-marketing

White, A., & Schmidt, K. (2005). Systematic literature reviews. *Complementary Therapies in Medicine*, *13*(1), 54–60. doi:10.1016/j.ctim.2004.12.003 PMID:15907679

Wiedmann, K.-P., Hennigs, N., Pankalla, L., Kassubek, M., & Seegebarth, B. (2011). Adoption barriers and resistance to sustainable solutions in the automotive sector. *Journal of Business Research*, *64*(11), 1201–1206. doi:10.1016/j.jbusres.2011.06.023

Wikipedia. (2012). European Environment Agency. Retrieved from http://en.wikipedia.org/wiki/European_environmnet_agency

Wikipedia. (n. d.). Internet activism. Retrieved from https://en.wikipedia.org/wiki/Internet_activism

Williams, K., & Keen, D. (2009). 2008 Survey of Public Participation in the Arts. In *National Endowment for the Arts, Personal Preferences & Leisure Activities – Musical Preferences* (Ch. 6, pp. 57-61). Retrieved from https://www.arts.gov/sites/default/files/2008-SPPA.pdf

Wirtz, J., & Lee, M.C. (2003). An examination of the quality and context-specific applicability of commonly customer satisfaction measures. *Journal of Service Research*, *5*, 345–355. doi:10.1177/1094670503005004006

Wiser, R. H. (1998). Green power marketing: Increasing customer demand for renewable energy. *Utilities Policy*, *7*(2), 107–119. doi:10.1016/S0957-1787(98)00005-8

Wong, V. (2014, July 23). McDonald's gives itself a year and half to get into chipotl Fighting shape. *Bloomberg.com.*

Wong, W., Penm, J., Terrell, R. D., & Lim, K. Y. C. (2004). The relationship between stock markets of major developed countries and Asian emerging markets. *Journal of Applied Mathematics and Decision Sciences*, *8*(4), 201–218. doi:10.1155/S1173912604000136

Wood, S.P. (2014, July 24). McDonald's has 18 months to rebrand… or else. *Adweek.com.*

Wood, W. W., & Allen, R. (2012). *The rock 'n' roll classroom: using music to manage mood, energy, and learning.* Thousand Oaks, CA: Corwin Press.

Wood, W., & Neal, D. T. (2009). The habitual consumer. *Journal of Consumer Psychology*, *19*(4), 579–592. doi:10.1016/j.jcps.2009.08.003

Woo, K., & Fock, H. K. Y. (2004). Retaining and Divesting Customers: An Exploratory Study of Right Customers, At-Risk Right Customer, and Wrong Customers. *Journal of Services Marketing*, *18*(3), 187–197. doi:10.1108/08876040410536495

World Economic Forum. (2012). More with less: Scaling Sustainable Consumption and Resource Efficiency. Retrieved from http://www3.weforum.org/docs/IP/CO/WEFCoScalingSustainableConsumpionResourceEfficiencyReport2012.pdf

Worthington, C. A., Katsuura, M., & Higg, H. (2003). Price linkages in Asian equity markets: Evidence bordering the Asian economic, currency and financial crises. *Asia-Pacific Financial Markets*, *10*(1), 29–44. doi:10.1023/B:FEJM.0000039873.53973.3c

Wortmann, F., & Flüchter, K. (2015). Internet of things. *Business & Information Systems Engineering*, *57*(3), 221–224. doi:10.1007/s12599-015-0383-3

Wu, S.-I. & Chen, J.-Y. (2014). A Model of Green Consumption Behavior Constructed by the Theory of Planned Behavior. *International Journal of Marketing Studies*, *6*(5), 128.

Wu, C. H.-J., Liang, R.-D., Tung, W., & Chang, C.-S. (2008). Structural Relationships among Organisation Service Orientation, Employee Service Performance, and Consumer Identification. *Service Industries Journal*, *28*(9), 1247–1263. doi:10.1080/02642060802230189

Yalch, R., & Spangenberg, E. (1990). Effects of Store Music on Shopping Behaviour. *Journal of Services Marketing*, *4*, 31–39.

Yalch, R., & Spangenberg, E. (1993). Using Store Music for Retail Zoning: A Field Experiment. *Advances in Consumer Research. Association for Consumer Research (U. S.)*, *20*, 632–636.

Yalch, R., & Spangenberg, E. (2000). The Effects of Music in a Retail Setting on Real and Perceived Shopping Times. *Journal of Business Research*, *49*(2), 139–147. doi:10.1016/S0148-2963(99)00003-X

Yamak R. ve Küçükkale Y. (2000). Kapasite kullanım oranı ve enflasyon. In *Ekonomi ve Yönetim Bilimleri Dergisi* (pp. 101-111).

Yamak ve Ceylan (2006). Kapasite kullanım oranı ve enflasyon ilişkisinde asimetri. *C.Ü. İktisadi ve İdari Bilimler Dergisi*, *7*(2),1-18.

Yang, D.-J., Chou, D.-H., & Liu, J. (2012). A Study of Key Success Factors when Applying E-commerce to the Travel Industry. *International Journal of Business and Social Science*, *3*(8), 114–119.

Yani-de-Soriano, M., & Slater, S. (2009). Revisiting Druckers theory: Has consumerism led to the overuse of marketing. *Journal of Management History*, *15*(4), 452–466. doi:10.1108/17511340910987347

Yin, R. K. (2003). *Case study research: Design and methods* (Vol. 5). Sage.

Yip, G. S. (1989). Global strategy. in a world of nations? *Sloan Management Review*, *31*, 29–41.

Yi, Y. (1990). A critical review of consumer satisfaction. In V. A. Zeithaml (Ed.), *Review of marketing Chicago* (pp. 68–123). American Marketing Association.

Yi, Y., & Gong, T. (2006). The Antecedents and Consequences of Service Customer Citizenship and Badness Behavior. *Seoul Journal of Business*, *12*(2), 145–176.

Yoo, C., Park, J., & MacInnis, D. J. (1998). Effects of Store Characteristics and In-Store Emotional Experiences on Store Attitude. *Journal of Business Research*, *42*(3), 253–263. doi:10.1016/S0148-2963(97)00122-7

Yoon, S.-J., Choi, D.-C., & Park, J.-W. (2007). Service Orientation: Its Impact on Business Performance in the Medical Service Industry. *Service Industries Journal*, *27*(4), 371–388. doi:10.1080/02642060701346375

Youngberg, Q. (2009). Mommys American Dream in Edward Albees The American Dream. *The Explicator*, *67*(2), 108–110. doi:10.3200/EXPL.67.2.108-110

Yüksel, U., & Mryteza, V. (2009). An evaluation of strategic responses to consumer boycotts. *Journal of Business Research*, *62*(2), 248–259. doi:10.1016/j.jbusres.2008.01.032

Yurcan, B. (2016, June 24). Banking on the internet of things: More than restocking fridges. American Banker. Retrieved from http://www.americanbanker.com/news/bank-technology/banking-on-the-internet-of-things-more-than-restocking-fridges-1081676-1.html

Zairi, M. (2000). Managing customer satisfaction: A best practice perspective. *The TQM Magazine*, *12*(6), 389–494. doi:10.1108/09544780010351670

Zavestoski, S. (2002). Guest Editorial: Anticonsumption Attitudes. *Psychology and Marketing*, *19*(2), 121–126. doi:10.1002/mar.10005

Zavestoski, S. (Ed.). (2002). *Anti-Consumption Attitudes: Psychology & Marketing, Special Issue*. New York: Wiley.

Zeeshan, M., & Hatem Obaid, M. (2015). Impact of Music on Consumer Behaviour: A Perspective on Retail Atmospheric. *Asian Journal of Business and Management Sciences*, *3*(2), 56–63.

Zeithaml, V. A., Berry, L. L., & Parasuraman, A. (1988). Communication and Control Processes in the Delivery of Service Quality. *Journal of Marketing*, *52*(2), 35–48. doi:10.2307/1251263

Zemke, R., & Anderson, K. (1990). Customers from Hell. *Training (New York, N.Y.)*, *27*(2), 25–33.

Zhang, X. (2011). *Essays on Social Influence in Shopper Marketing* [Unpublished PhD Thesis]. Indiana University Kelley School of Business.

Zhang, J., Farris, P. W., Irvin, J. W., Kushwaha, T., Steenburgh, T. J., & Weitz, B. A. (2010). Crafting integrated multi-channel retailing strategies. *Journal of Interactive Marketing*, *24*(2), 168–180. doi:10.1016/j.intmar.2010.02.002

Zohar, D. (1990). *The Quantum Self: Human Nature and Consciousness Defined by the New Physics*. New York: Quill.

About the Contributors

Hans Kaufmann is currently Professor in Marketing in the School of Business of the University of Nicosia after appointments as manager and Professor and course leader of company management at University of Applied Management Studies Mannheim, Germany, consultant and academic in 5 European countries. He was President of CIRCLE (2007-2009) and is currently Vice-President of EMBRI and was a founding member in both institutions. He is a board member of the American Marketing Association Global Marketing SIG. He is member of the editorial board of a variety of journals and an Associate Editor of the World Review of Entrepreneurship, Management and Sustainable Development. He published a large number of journal articles and is author/editor of 8 books (mainly in the field of Consumer Behaviour and Marketing) and 4 Electronic Books (Thompson Reuters accredited conference proceedings). He is Visiting Professor to the International Business School of Vilnius University and an Adjunct Professor of the University of Vitez.

Mohammad Fateh Ali Khan Panni is an Assistant Professor in the School of Business at City University, Bangladesh. He has an MPhil degree (by research) in the area of marketing from Multimedia University, Malaysia. He has published many research articles in the area of consumerism, CRM, CKM, brand loyalty, online shopping behavior, internet banking green consumer behavior index and educational marketing etc. in numerous international journals like JLERI, IJBEP, IJECRM, WJBAM, JIKM, IJTEM, Amfiteatru Economic. Currently, he is a research committee member of three different research interest committees such as marketing, ethics and social responsibility and green economy consortium of Euromed Research Business Institute (EMRBI). He is also regularly involved as a track chair of Annual Euromed Conferences. He regularly reviews paper for different international refereed journals and has already served as a reviewer in AJBM, AJAR, WREMSD, IJEBR, AJMM, JIKM etc. He has co-edited two edited reference books-one on customer centric marketing strategies and the other on consumerism (IGI Global Publication). He is an editorial team member of African Journal of Marketing Management (AJMM) (Academic Journal series) and a listed reviewer of Journal of Information and Knowledge Management (JIKM) (World Scientific Publication).

***

Emel Baydan is a graduate student and she is currently working on her Master's thesis.

Angelo Bonfanti, Ph.D., is an Associate Professor of Business Management at the Department of Business Administration, University of Verona (Italy). He received his Ph.D. from the "Parthenope" University of Naples (Italy) and is a member of the Editorial Review Team of Sinergie Italian Journal of Management. His current research interests include service management and marketing, retail management, higher education, and social entrepreneurship. His publications have appeared in Journal of Services Marketing, Corporate Communication: An International Journal, Management Decision, and The TQM Journal.

Elena Candelo is an Associate Professor of Strategic Management Elena Candelo, degree in Economics with 110 and Honorable mention – Faculty of Economics, Turin University and PhD in Business Management. She is Associate Professor in Strategic Management at University of Turin – Department of Management. Post graduate course: Marketing Management, Strategic management. Graduate course: Strategies in automotive industry, Multinational companies' strategies. Degree course: Strategic Management, Marketing. Member of the Research Board - Department of Management. Director and member of the Scientific Committee of several Masters. Recent publication about: branding, corporate social responsibility, marketing. Main Research Areas: strategic management, brand management, corporate social responsibility, management of tourist destinations, automotive industry.

Cecilia Casalegno is a Researcher and Lecturer at the Department of Management, University of Turin. She teaches in Marketing, Communication, Human resource management. She has several publications in marketing and communication. She is visiting professor at Universitat Autònoma de Barcelona and visiting researcher at Darden Business School (Virginia).

Sadullah Çelik is an associate professor in the Department of Economics (Eng.), Marmara University Faculty of Economics, Istanbul, Turkey. He received his BA and MA in Economics from Marmara University Faculty of Economics and Administrative Sciences, Istanbul, Turkey. He received his PhD in Economics from the University of Nebraska-Lincoln, USA. He has authored numerous articles about applied economics, international economics, behavioral economics and consumer sentiment in Turkish and English and co-authored a book about construction industry in Turkey in Turkish and authored two book chapters about consumer confidence. In addition, he has coordinated a project under the authority of Marmara University on day of the week effect in consumer confidence. Furthermore, he has organized the 73rd International Atlantic Economic Conference of the International Atlantic Economic Society. Besides, he has attended several international and national conferences presenting papers, serving as a discussant and chair and organizing invited sessions. Likewise, he has refereed numerous articles for international journals. Moreover, he has served three years as the LLP-Erasmus Coordinator for the Department of Economics, Marmara University Faculty of Economics and Administrative Sciences. He also supervised several MA theses and PhD dissertations of student from many universities such as Istanbul Bilgi University, Istanbul Commerce University and Marmara University. He has also lectured in many universities as visiting scholar such as Bahcesehir University, Dogus University, Halic University, Istanbul Bilgi University, Istanbul Commerce University and Maltepe University.

Chiara Civera is Research Fellow at the University of Turin, Department of Management and Ph.D. in Business and Management. She has been spending 2 years as visiting researcher at London South Bank University in London (UK) and a semester at Darden Business School, University of Virginia, United States. During the academic career, she has been worked also as business consultant for medium and large companies operating in various sectors, in the UK and in Italy, focusing mainly on business strategy, commercial development and marketing strategy. The main subjects of interest and current researches are: corporate social responsibility, stakeholder theory, marketing, branding, communication, non-profit sector management and fundraising strategies. She is currently lecturer of Marketing Management.

Ileana Georgiana Gheorghe holds the position of Associate Professor in the Department of Business Administration, Faculty of Economics, Petroleum-Gas University of Ploiesti Romania. She obtained a Ph.D. in Economics from Bucharest University of Economic Studies. She has published about 50 international papers in outstanding journals (h-index 8), 1 book chapter in an edited book and 2 authored books, being interested in Human Resources Management, Green Economics and Social Responsibility. She also participated in research projects in the field Human Resources Development.

Tomislav Gregur was born on 3rd of March in 1989 in Koprivnica, Croatia. After finishing gymnasium in Koprivnica in 2008, he went to Faculty of Economics & Business on University of Zagreb, Croatia. In 2014, he finished Master degree, majoring in Trade.

Alicia Izquierdo Yusta is an Associate Professor at the Department of Marketing of the University of Burgos (Spain). She has participated in different Conferences and Seminars worldwide and has written several articles in different high standing international journals in different international journals Total Quality Management and Business Excellence; Service Business; Innovar, European Journal of Marketing etc.). Her main research lines are e-commerce, Technologies adaptation, marketing communications, sales promotions and product and services innovation. Member of the following Associations European Marketing Academy (EMAC) and The European Association for Education and Research in Commercial Distribution (EAERCD).

Anne M. Lavack (Ph.D., University of British Columbia) is a retired Professor in the School of Business and Economics at Thompson Rivers University in Kamloops, Canada. She has previously published articles in a variety of journals including Journal of Advertising, Journal of Public Policy and Marketing, and Social Marketing Quarterly.

Sandra Maria Correia Loureiro is Professor of Marketing at the Instituto Universitário de Lisboa ISCTE-IUL and a researcher in the Business Research Unit (BRU/UNIDE) and SOCIUS Research Centers. Her current research interests include consumer-brand relationships, online purchase behaviors, tourism marketing, and corporate social responsibility issues. Her papers have been published in a variety of peer-reviewed journals that include International Journal of Hospitality Management, Journal of Travel and Tourism Marketing, journal of Service Management, Journal of Cleaner Production or Journal of Brand Management. Her work has also been presented at respected international conferences such as EMAC, ANZMAC, and KAMS-GMC. Sandra serves as a reviewer for several international journals and conferences and has participated in several research projects funded by the EU and FCT (Foundation for Science and Technology). She recently won the 2012 Best Paper Premier Award presented by the Global Marketing Conference (comprised of EMAC, ANZMAC, KSMS, and the Japanese Association of Marketing).

Maria Pilar Martinez Ruiz is an Associate Professor at the Department of Marketing of the University of Castilla-La Mancha (Spain). She has participated in different Conferences and Seminars worldwide and has written several articles in different high standing international journals (e.g., Journal of the Operational Research Society, European Journal of Marketing, The International Journal of Market Research, European Journal of Operational Research, etc.). Her main research lines are retailing, marketing communications, sales promotions and product and services innovation. Member of the following associations: Academy of Marketing Science (AMS), European Marketing Academy (EMAC) and The European Association for Education and Research in Commercial Distribution (EAERCD). She was co-track chair of the Pricing and Retailing Track at the 75 editions of the Summer´s Educators AMA Conference (celebrated in 2012 in Chicago).

Michael D. Myers is Professor of Information Systems and Head of the Department of Information Systems and Operations Management at the University of Auckland Business School. His research focuses on the relationship between IT and people in an organizational context, and how this context can be studied. He has published 24 articles in A* journals as ranked by the Australian Business Deans' Council. Michael won the Best Paper award (with Heinz Klein) for the most outstanding paper published in MIS Quarterly in 1999. This paper has been cited over 4000 times. He also won the Best Paper Award (with Lynda Harvey) for the best paper published in Information Technology & People in 1997 and the Emerald Literati Network Outstanding Paper Award 2012 (with Michelle Soakell) for the most outstanding paper published in VINE in 2011. He previously served as Senior Editor of MIS Quarterly from 2001-2005, as Senior Editor of Information Systems Research from 2008-2010, and currently serves as Senior Editor of Information & Organization and Pacific Asia Journal of the AIS. He also served as President of the Association for Information Systems (AIS) in 2006-2007 and as Chair of the International Federation of Information Processing (IFIP) Working Group 8.2 from 2006-2008. Michael is a Fellow of the Association for Information Systems.

Petra Nylund is an Assistant Professor at the University of Vic. She has a Ph.D. in Management from IESE and an M.Sc. in Engineering and Business Management from KTH, Stockholm. Her research and teaching focus on different aspects of innovation, knowledge, and strategy. She is currently enthusiastic about the development of innovation ecosystems. Prior to joining academia Dr. Nylund worked as a corporate development manager and business consultant in Africa, Latin America, and in Europe.

Ioanna Papasolomou is a Professor and the Head of the Department of Marketing, School of Business Administration, at the University of Nicosia in Cyprus. She has contributed papers to a number of international conferences and journals such as the Journal of Marketing Management, Marketing Intelligence and Planning, Journal of Brand Management, Journal of Product and Brand Management, and the Journal of Marketing Communications. She has also contributed chapters and case studies to several academic books. She is a reviewer for a number of academic journals such as the Journal of Marketing Communications, International Journal of Corporate Communications, the International Journal of Social Responsibility, and Euro Mediterranean Journal in Business.

Sanda Renko, PhD is a Full Professor at Trade Department at Faculty of Economics and Business, University of Zagreb, Croatia. She is the coordinator for several courses: retailing and wholesaling, Business logistics, Fashion retailing, services in retailing, benchmarking, category management, etc.

She has published chapters in book and scientific journals in the area of her interest, such as the British Food Journal, Journal of Food Products Marketing, Journal of Retailing and Consumer Services, Business Excellence, etc. She is the guest editor for the British Food Journal, Journal of Food Products Marketing, etc.

Asher Rospigliosi is a principal lecturer in digital marketing, e-business and management information systems. He currently conducts research into social media and graduate employability. He has a substantial and successful commercial track record in the development and management of online systems for commerce and education, including the PPAi award winning Gamespot UK. His areas of specialist interest include big data and the impact of CMC (particularly internet based communication) on society, business, organisations, planning, learning, employment and knowledge.

Irene Samanta is an Assistant Professor of International Marketing at Piraeus University of Applied Sciences. Dr. Samanta, after her basic studies in Business Administration, she continues her Post Graduate studies in University of Paisley (U.K.) where she obtains an M.Sc. in International Marketing. She has been completed her Academic studies with Ph.D. from University of the West of Scotland (U.K.). She is author of several research papers published in international journals. She is co-author of six books as well as editor of chapter books, a monograph and working papers.

Violeta Sima holds the position of Associate Professor in the Department of Business Administration, Faculty of Economics, Petroleum-Gas University of Ploiesti Romania. She obtained a Ph.D. in Economic Cybernetics and Statistics from Bucharest University of Economic Studies. She has published about 55 international papers in outstanding journals (h-index 10), four book chapters in edited books and 4 authored books. Her research and teaching interests encompass Customer Relationship Management, Marketing Research, Business to Business Marketing, Green Marketing and Social Responsibility. She has participated in research projects in the field of Marketing and Human Resources Development.

Özlem Taşseven is an Associate Professor of Quantitative Methods at Dogus University Department of Economics and Finance, Istanbul-Turkey. Dr. Ozlem has a BS in Statistics from Middle East University (1995), a Master degree in Economics from Middle East University (2000) and a PhD in Economics from Newcastle University in United Kingdom. Her research interests lie in econometric analyses including time series, panel data analyses, applied macroeconomics and finance, statistics. She has taught Statistics, economics, econometrics and research methods courses, among others, at both graduate and undergraduate levels. She is in the editorial board of Dogus University Journal, Banking and Finance Letters Journal.

Tuure Tuunanen is a professor in the Department of Computer Science and Information Systems at the University of Jyväskylä. He is also a global faculty fellow of the Center for Service Leadership at Arizona State University. He holds a DSc (Econ) from the Helsinki School of Economics. His research has been in the cross-sections of information systems, software engineering, and marketing science and is interested in multi-disciplinary research in the area of service innovation. His current research interests lie in the areas of information systems development methods and processes, service engineering, and IT enabled services. More about his research can be found at http://www.tuunanen.fi.

Eric Viardot is Director of the Global Innovation Management Centre and permanent professor of marketing and strategy at EADA Business School in Barcelona. He has a doctorate in management. He is a graduate of the HEC Business School, Paris, and the Institute of Political Sciences, Paris. He has been working in different marketing positions for Hewlett-Packard in France, Canada and the US Eric. He was then a financial director for a large international NGO in Asia and Central America. After that, he joined Bain and Company as a senior consultant and had numerous assignments in Europe including a large international retail company. Eric Viardot has published various books and articles on strategic management and marketing. He is currently the co-editor of the International Journal of Technology Marketing and a member of the editorial board of Technovation. Eric Viardot teaches regularly in executive programs in Europe. He is an active consultant and trainer and has worked with several major multinational corporations.

Lisa Watson (Ph.D., Bond University) is an Associate Professor in the Paul J. Hill School of Business at the University of Regina in Regina, Canada. She has previously published articles in a variety of journals including Social Marketing Quarterly, Canadian Public Policy, and European Journal of Marketing.

Dursun Yener had PhD degree in Marmara Univesity, Turkey on Production Management and Marketing. His research area is consumer behaviour and marketing theory. He has many research papers published in national and international journals. He works in Management Department at Istanbul Medeniyet University since 2015.

Ana Zarco is an Associate Professor of Innovation and Marketing. Economics and Business Department, Universitat Oberta de Catalunya (UOC). Part-time professor at ICADE. Pontificia of Comillas University PhD in Economics and Business Sciences from the University of Castilla-la Mancha, Spain. Post degree in Building Models in Ecology and Natural Resources Management from Politecnica University of Catalonia. Until 2002, She carried out her teaching and research activities in the Marketing Area of the University of Castilla la Mancha, and during short periods in East Anglia University, Brighton University (U.K) and Chapingo University (Mexico). From 2003 to 2006 she has been a codirector of the Master's Degree Programme in Marketing and Communication Management, and from 2006 to 2012 she was served as Programmme Director of the Bachelor's Degree in Business Administration at UOC. As a researcher, her main areas of research interest concern product innovation, brand image and identity and marketing/e-learning interface. She is author of several books and articles on these areas, and serve as a reviewer and associated editor of several international journals in the marketing area.

Index

F

G

H

I

L

M

N

O

P

R

S

T

U

W

Z

www.ingramcontent.com/pod-product-compliance
Lightning Source LLC
LaVergne TN
LVHW060359300926
849162LV00006B/1307